COOP 2014 - Proceedings
of the 11th International Conference
on the Design of Cooperative Systems,
27–30 May 2014, Nice (France)

Chiara Rossitto · Luigina Ciolfi
David Martin · Bernard Conein
Editors

COOP 2014 - Proceedings of the 11th International Conference on the Design of Cooperative Systems, 27–30 May 2014, Nice (France)

Springer

Editors
Chiara Rossitto
Computer and Systems Sciences
Stockholm University
Kista
Sweden

Luigina Ciolfi
Sheffield Hallam University C3RI
Sheffield
UK

David Martin
Xerox Research Centre Europe
Meylan
France

Bernard Conein
Sociology and Ethnology
Université de Nice-Sophia Antipolis
Nice
France

ISBN 978-3-319-38177-0   ISBN 978-3-319-06498-7   (eBook)
DOI 10.1007/978-3-319-06498-7
Springer Cham Heidelberg New York Dordrecht London

Printed on acid-free paper

Springer is part of Springer Science+Business Media (www.springer.com)

Preface

This volume presents the Proceedings of the 11th International Conference on the Design of Cooperative Systems (COOP 2014), held in Nice, France from 27 to 30 May 2014. The hosting venue was The Maison des Sciences de l'Homme et de la Société Sud-Est within the Université de Nice-Sophia Antipolis. The conference is a venue for multidisciplinary research contributing to the design, assessment, and analysis of cooperative systems and their integration in organizations, public venues, and everyday life. COOP emerged from the European tradition of Computer-Supported Cooperative Work (CSCW) and Cognitive Ergonomics as practiced in France.

COOP 2014 received 58 full paper submissions. After careful review, 28 papers were selected for presentation within a single track at the conference and they are collected together in these proceedings. They provide a good reflection of the variety of research activities in the field, where there is an increasing interest in investigating the use and design of information and communication technologies (ICT) in all aspects of everyday life and society, and not merely in the workplace, and certainly not the workplace conceived of narrowly as office work. The papers cover a diversity of research topics, from healthcare to sustainable mobility to disaster response, in settings from all over the world. They comprise case studies, design work and evaluation, and methodological and theoretical topics. For the first time, the proceedings include eight papers presented in an Early Career Researchers Track which was established to give young researchers the opportunity to discuss their work with an international community. We were particularly pleased with this strong showing from early career researchers. At the conference we also held a full, diverse program of workshops and had two high quality keynote speakers: Dr. Julia Tanney of the University of Kent and Dr. Jayne Wallace of the University of Dundee.

This collection of papers provides a picture of new developments and classic topics of research around cooperative systems, based on the principle that a deep knowledge of cooperative practices is a key to understanding technology impacts and producing quality designs. The articles presented here will appeal to researchers and practitioners alike, as they combine an understanding of the nature of work and social, organizational, and societal matters with the problems, practicalities, and possibilities offered by novel digital technologies.

Many people worked hard to ensure the success of this conference and we would like to thank them here: all the authors who submitted high quality papers; all those who contributed to the organization and the activities of the workshops; our keynote speakers; the 54 members of our global program committee, who dedicated their time and energy to reviewing; the workshop, doctoral colloquium, and early career research track chairs; all our local organizers; and finally, our student volunteers, for helping the smooth running of the conference.

March 2014   Chiara Rossitto
                                                                Luigina Ciolfi
                                                                David Martin
                                                                Bernard Conein

Conference Committee

- *Organizing Chair*: Bernard Conein (University of Nice-Sophia Antipolis)
- *Scientific Co-Chairs*: Luigina Ciolfi (Sheffield Hallam University, UK) and David Martin (Xerox Research Centre Europe, France)
- *Workshop and Masterclasses Co-Chairs*: Nina Boulus-Rødje (IT University of Copenhagen, Denmark) and Michael Prilla (Ruhr-Universität Bochum, Germany)
- *Early-Career Researchers Track Chair*: Barry Brown (Mobile Life Center, Sweden)
- *Doctoral Colloquium Co-Chairs*: Liam Bannon (University of Limerick, Ireland and University of Aarhus, Denmark) and Myriam Lewkowicz (Université de Technologie de Troyes, France)
- *Proceedings Chair*: Chiara Rossitto (University of Stockholm, Sweden)
- *Local arrangements*: Jean-Charles Briquet-Laugier (MSHS Sud-Est, France); Alain Giboin (INRIA, France)

Program Committee

- Carmelo Ardito, Italy
- Gabriela Avram, Ireland
- Mark Ackerman, USA
- Michael Baker, France
- Flore Barcellini, France
- Liam Bannon, Ireland
- Susanne Bødker, Denmark
- Jean-Francois Boujut, France
- Nina Boulus-Rødje, Denmark
- Barry Brown, Sweden
- Beatrice Cahour, France
- Peter Carstensen, Denmark
- Lars Rune Christensen, Denmark
- Luigina Ciolfi, UK

- Antonella De Angeli, Italy
- Giorgio De Michelis, Italy
- Boris De Ruyter, The Netherlands
- Cleidson De Souza, Brazil
- Monica Divitini, Norway
- Julie Dugdale, France
- Myriam Frejus, France
- Alain Giboin, France
- Tom Gross, Germany
- Richard Harper, UK
- Thomas Herrmann, Germany
- Giulio Jacucci, Finland
- Karine Lan Hing Ting, France
- Catherine Letondal, France
- Myriam Lewkowicz, France
- Christian Licoppe, France
- Jan Ljundberg, Sweden
- David Martin, France
- Anders Morch, Norway
- Claudia Müller, Germany
- Keiichi Nakata, Japan
- Bernhard Nett, Germany
- Laurence Nigay, France
- Maria Normark, Södertörn University
- Jacki O'Neill, France
- Volkmar Pipek, Germany
- Michael Prilla, Germany
- Wolfgang Prinz, Germany
- Dave Randall, UK
- Stuart Reeves, UK
- Marc Relieu, France
- Markus Rohde, Germany
- John Rooksby, UK
- Chiara Rossitto, Sweden
- Mark Rouncefield, UK
- Pascal Salembier, France
- Kjeld Schmidt, Denmark
- Carla Simone, Italy
- Hilda Tellioglu, Austria
- Volker Wulf, Germany

Contents

Contributors

Ignacio Aedo DEI—Interactive Systems Group, Universidad Carlos III de Madrid, Madrid, Spain

Khuloud Abou Amsha CNRS, Troyes University of Technology, Troyes, France

Nazareno Andrade Systems and Computing Department, Universidade Federal de Campina Grande, Campina Grande, Brazil

Mark Beecroft dot.rural Digital Economy Hub, University of Aberdeen, Aberdeen, UK

Olav W. Bertelsen Department of Computer Science, Center for Participatory-IT, Aarhus University, Aarhus N, Denmark

Nicola J. Bidwell Department of Informatics, University of Pretoria, Pretoria, South Africa; Digital Ethnography Group, Royal Melbourne Institute of Technology, Melbourne, Australia

Pernille Bjørn IT University of Copenhagen, Copenhagen, Denmark; University of California, Irvine, CA, USA

Susanne Bødker Department of Computer Science, Aarhus University, Aarhus, Denmark

Federico Cabitza Università degli Studi di Milano-Bicocca, Milano, Italy

Antonella Carassa Università della Svizzera italiana, Lugano, Switzerland

Stefania Castellani Xerox Research Centre Europe, Meylan, France

Alan Chamberlain Mixed Reality Lab, Computer Science, University of Nottingham, Nottingham, UK

Yunan Chen Department of Informatics, University of California, Irvine, USA

Lars Rune Christensen Aalborg University, Aalborg, Denmark

Tommaso Colombino Xerox Research Centre Europe, Meylan, France

David Corsar dot.rural Digital Economy Hub, University of Aberdeen, Aberdeen, UK

Aparecido Fabiano Pinatti de Carvalho Multidisciplinary Design Group, Institute of Design and Assessment of Technology, Vienna University of Technology, Vienna, Austria

Shloka Desai University of Arizona, Tucson, USA

Paloma Díaz DEI—Interactive Systems Group, Universidad Carlos III de Madrid, Madrid, Spain

David Díez DEI—Interactive Systems Group, Universidad Carlos III de Madrid, Madrid, Spain

Gunnar Ellingsen Telemedicine and E-Health Research Group, University of Tromsø, Tromsø, Norway

Joel E. Fischer The Mixed Reality Lab, University of Nottingham, Nottingham, UK

Angus Forbes University of Arizona, Tucson, USA

Thomas Fritz University of Zurich, Zurich, Switzerland

Rinku Gajera Xerox Research Centre India, Bangalore, India

Chris Greenhalgh The Mixed Reality Lab, University of Nottingham, Nottingham, UK

Benjamin Hanrahan Xerox Research Centre Europe, Meylan, France

Thomas Herrmann Department Information and Technology Management, University of Bochum, Bochum, Germany

Tobias Höllerer University of California, Santa Barbara, USA

Kululwa Jampo Department of Informatics, University of Pretoria, Pretoria, South Africa

Rasmus Eskild Jensen IT University of Copenhagen, Copenhagen, Denmark

Wenchao Jiang The Mixed Reality Lab, University of Nottingham, Nottingham, UK

Andruid Kerne Interface Ecology Lab, Texas A&M University, College Station, USA

Eli Larsen Telemedicine and E-Health Research Group, Norwegian Centre for Telemedicine, Tromsø, Norway

Myriam Lewkowicz Troyes University of Technology, Troyes, France

Grant McKenzie University of California, Santa Barbara, USAUniversity of Arizona, Tucson, USA; Universidad Nacional Autonoma de Mexico, Mexico City, Mexico

Johanna Meurer Information Systems and New Media, University of Siegen, Siegen, Germany

Marius Mikalsen Norwegian University of Technology and Science (NTNU) and SINTEF, Trondheim, Norway

Aline Morais Systems and Computing Department, Universidade Federal de Campina Grande, Campina Grande, Brazil

John Nelson dot.rural Digital Economy Hub, University of Aberdeen, Aberdeen, UK

Mika P. Nieminen Aalto University School of Science, Espoo, Finland

Alexander Nolte Department Information and Technology Management, University of Bochum, Bochum, Germany

Jacki O'Neill Microsoft Research India, Bangalore, India

Leysia Palen University of Colorado Boulder, Boulder, CO, USA

Nadia Pantidi The Mixed Reality Lab, University of Nottingham, Nottingham, UK

Konstantinos Papangelis dot.rural Digital Economy Hub, University of Aberdeen, Aberdeen, UK

Elena Parmiggiani Department of Computer and Information Science, NTNU, Trondheim, Norway

Kathleen Pine Intel Labs, Hillsboro, Oregon, USA

Anna Maria Polli Department of Computer Science, Aarhus University, Aarhus, Denmark

Michael Prilla Information and Technology Management, University of Bochum, Bochum, Germany

Sarvapali D. Ramchurn Agents, Interaction and Complexity Group, University of Southampton, Southampton, UK

Ilaria Redaelli Università della Svizzera italiana, Lugano, Switzerland

Steven Reece Pattern Analysis and Machine Learning, University of Oxford, Oxford, UK

Thomas Reitmaier Department of Computer Science, University of Cape Town, Cape Town, South Africa

Tom Rodden The Mixed Reality Lab, University of Nottingham, Nottingham, UK

Saiph Savage University of California, Santa Barbara, USA

Kjeld Schmidt Copenhagen Business School, Copenhagen, Denmark; University of Siegen, Siegen, Germany

David Shepherd ABB Corporate Research, Raleigh, NC, USA

Carla Simone Università degli Studi di Milano-Bicocca, Milano, Italy

Robert Soden University of Colorado Boulder, Boulder, CO, USA

Somayajulu Sripada dot.rural Digital Economy Hub, University of Aberdeen, Aberdeen, UK

Martin Stein Information Systems and New Media, University of Siegen, Siegen, Germany

Sara Tena DEI—Interactive Systems Group, Universidad Carlos III de Madrid, Madrid, Spain

Carlos Toxtli Universidad Nacional Autonoma de Mexico, Mexico City, Mexico

Mari Ilona Tyllinen Aalto University School of Science, Espoo, Finland

Nagendra Velaga Civil Engineering Department, Indian Institute of Technology (IIT), Bombay, India

Dhaval Vyas Queensland University of Technology, Brisbane, QLD, Australia

Volker Wulf Information Systems and New Media, University of Siegen, Siegen, Germany

People, Plans and Place: Understanding and Supporting Responses to Rural Public Transport Disruption

Konstantinos Papangelis, Alan Chamberlain, Nagendra Velaga, David Corsar, Somayajulu Sripada, John Nelson and Mark Beecroft

Abstract Public transport information provision in rural areas is often fragmented and of poor quality at best and non-existent at worst. This can have a significant impact on the everyday life of the inhabitants of rural areas, particularly in terms of limiting their travel choices and thereby their opportunities to access goods, service and social networks. Inadequate information provision also poses significant challenges during times of transport disruption. In this paper we examine the responses from a series of interviews (69) and focus groups (9) in which we explored the rural passengers' experience during disruption, their coping strategies, and their behavioural responses to disruption. We identify that each passenger experiences disruption uniquely, and that the behavioral adaptation of the passenger relates to the severity and impact of the disruption. Furthermore, we identify that the most prevalent ways of mitigating the impacts of disruption is through time buffering and the use of kinship networks. Based on these findings and six co-design sessions with rural passengers we were able co-design and develop a prototype passenger information system to support the passenger during disruption. The results of this work aim to advance understandings of the interplay of technology, information provision, and passenger experience under disruption.

K. Papangelis (✉) · D. Corsar · S. Sripada · J. Nelson · M. Beecroft
dot.rural Digital Economy Hub, University of Aberdeen, Aberdeen, UK
e-mail: k.papangelis@abdn.ac.uk; angelis@abdn.ac.uk

D. Corsar
e-mail: dcorsar@abdn.ac.uk

A. Chamberlain
Mixed Reality Lab, Computer Science, University of Nottingham, Nottingham, UK
e-mail: alan.chamberlain@nottingham.ac.uk

N. Velaga
Civil Engineering Department, Indian Institute of Technology (IIT), Bombay, India

C. Rossitto et al. (eds.), *COOP 2014 - Proceedings of the 11th International Conference on the Design of Cooperative Systems, 27–30 May 2014, Nice (France)*, DOI: 10.1007/978-3-319-06498-7_1, © Springer International Publishing Switzerland 2014

1 Introduction

Rural communities face a range of challenges associated with accessibility and connectivity [1]. Limitations in transport infrastructure, information and services can reduce travel possibilities in rural areas and hinder access to opportunities relating to employment, education and business [2].

Technology has long been heralded as offering the potential to mitigate some of these barriers, by providing alternative means of access and connectivity [3]. For example; transport telematics (a term which encompasses a range of advanced computer-based information and communication technologies, navigation/positioning systems, and digital technologies) has been shown to improve the efficiency and service quality of transport systems [4–6]. Though such transport technologies have been widely deployed in urban and suburban areas in the developed world, their application in rural and remote rural areas has been very limited [7]. Velaga et al. [8] has identified two main reasons for this:

(a) Fewer passengers; so therefore there is little incentive to operators to provide current transport information.
(b) Rural areas are sparsely populated making it difficult to collect travel/traffic information from the system.

The lack of real-time passenger information (RTPI) systems in rural areas has resulted in the provision of fragmented and inaccurate passenger information. This has been documented as a contributing factor to the low public usage of public transport [9].

The potential exists for these technologies to contribute to the alleviation of accessibility and problems for rural passengers, as evidence exists that they can influence travel behaviour, cultivate positive attitudes towards the service provider and create positive perceptions of efficiency and security [1, 10–12].

In this study we consider disruption as a chance for reflection and re-evaluation of travel, and aim through interviews and focus groups to explore the interplay between disruption, travel behaviour, and passenger decision-making. Furthermore, based on the research findings, we design a set of technologies that aim to improve the passenger experience during disruption.

2 Related Research

Related previous work falls into two main areas: Real-Time Passenger Information (RTPI) and disruption, and transit information systems.

2.1 Previous Work in Transport Research

High quality information is a key enabler of successful transport service provision [13]. RTPI provision during transport disruptions is a major concern particularly for public transport riders in rural areas [14].

Velaga et al. [8] identifies RTPI as especially important for public transport users in rural areas, because the impact that disruption has upon rural passengers compared to urban passengers is likely to be greater. This is because passengers in rural areas usually have more limited transport connectivity, and have fewer alternative routes for a given origin/destination.

Papangelis et al. [15] suggest that RTPI information during disruption should be focused upon passenger needs,—which can be described as being for Timely, Accurate and Personalized (TAP) information. The same study categorises the passenger recovery process during disruption in phases, demonstrating that the TAP RTPI requirements depend upon the phase of the passenger recovery process being experienced during a disruption. They identify that the most important phase for minimising trip abandonment and affecting the travel behaviour during disruption is the response phase—in which the individuals take preventive measures to mitigate the potential effects or lessen the effects of disruption for the current and subsequent journeys.

Papangelis et al. [15] identify that individuals mainly make choices during disruption based on:

(a) The information the individuals have available before and during disruption,
(b) The perceived quality of information at hand,
(c) The passenger's trust in information,
(d) The passenger's ability to use the information.

This paper also discusses how the aforementioned affect behaviour during disruption, relating them to information provision scenarios based on current RTPI systems. The findings from this study suggest that even though an increasing number of real-time passenger information (RTPI) systems are being developed (e.g. [16]) to provide transport information, the role of real-time information in supporting travellers during service disruption is poorly understood, particularly in rural areas.

2.2 Related Work in Transit Information Systems

In recent years, mobile devices have started to play a significant role in the provision of passenger information. The most prominent mobile applications are Roadify (www.roadify.com), Seeclickfix (www.speedclickfix.com) and Waze (www.waze.com). Roadify crowdsources information about parking and the state of the public transport systems in New York, USA. Currently, roadify covers parking spaces, bus locations, subway arrival times and status (e.g. line disruptions). Seeclickfix enables residents to identify 'non emergency' public transport problems, and also provides administrative tools for organizations in order to effectively use the crowd sourced data. Waze is a mobile phone based in-car GPS system that crowdsources information about traffic congestion and incidents from its users and provides the data back through various channels (e.g. SMS, mobile application, e-mail).

Besides the commercial mobile applications, there have several academic social computing transit/computing projects. The most prominent examples are the OneBusAway RTPI system, and Tiramisu [16, 17]. OneBusAway, provides real-time bus information from bus operators for the Seattle area, USA. Having built a larger user community they noted some change in the travel behaviour of the users, such as, improved perception of personal safety. Tiramissu advances this work by not only providing real-time information about the bus service, but by allowing passengers to share their GPS traces, generate their arrival time and submit problem reports.

It should be noted that all of these systems focus exclusively on densely populated urban areas. Rural areas arguably have more pressing need for such real-time information as a majority of the journey planning scenarios cannot be adequately completed due to the operator data not reflecting real world situations or being incomplete, missing or inaccurate [8, 18].

In this paper, we aim to investigate rural passenger experiences during disruption, their coping strategies, their behavioural responses to disruption, and their disruption recovery phase behaviour. This forms the basis of a research-based study that aims to understand, design and develop a rural RTPI system to improve the passenger experience.

3 Methodology

As part of the study a series of interviews, focus groups and co-design sessions were undertaken with rural inhabitants, utilising a variety of transport modes in various locations in both Scotland and England. The geographic location of the areas where the interviews and focus groups were conducted is shown in Fig. 1.

The interviews were conducted in the Scottish borders area (labeled as one in Fig. 1) along the A7 (highway) corridor, which is mainly served by the 95/X95 bus services. These services operate between Edinburgh and Carlisle via the town of Hawick, and cover a distance of approximately 100 miles, passing through areas ranging from urban to extreme-rural. The 95/X95 mainly serves two types of passenger, (a) travellers that use the route from Carlisle to Edinburgh as a cheap alternative to the train service, and (b) locals that don't usually have access to a car and use the service for short trips for a variety of purposes (commuting, shopping, entertainment etc.). The interviews explored the common experiences, the shared culture and the individual stories of a representative sample of these two groups with

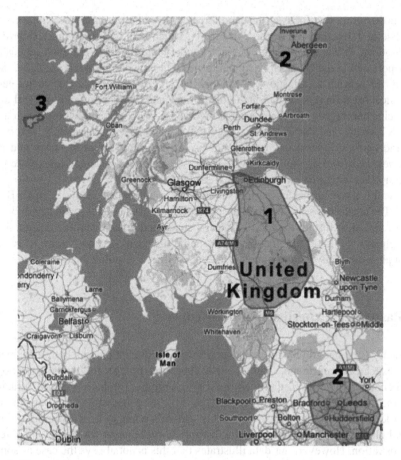

Fig. 1 The study area

regard to bus disruptions in order to elicit information regarding the effects of disruption in the everyday life of participants. The interviews took place during bus journeys when the passenger was in transit, and involved 69 participants (35 male, 34 female) with a mean age of 37.2 years. Each interview lasted approximately 18 min. It must be noted that the participants were recruited based on a pre-screening interview regarding their frequency of bus usage, rather than randomly selected.

In addition, four focus groups were conducted in the Universities of Aberdeen and Leeds in the UK (marked as two in Fig. 1). The participants were a mix of urban, rural bus, car users, and cyclists from the Aberdeen and West Yorkshire respectively. Each focus group was comprised of 8–11 participants with a mean age of 34 years, and lasted approximately 90 min. The participants were recruited through the use of email and flyers. The main discussion concentrated on the effects of disruption in everyday life, and the individuals' adaptation and decision-making processes during and after different types of transport-based disruptions.

Furthermore, five focus groups and three co-design sessions were conducted on the Isle of Tiree (marked as three in Fig. 1), which is based in the Inner Hebrides of Scotland. It has a population of eight hundred and the most common modes of transport within the island are demand responsive transportation, cars, and a twice a day air service to Glasgow, and a bi-weekly ferry to Oban. Due to its geographical location it is very prone to disruptions and there are often food, fuel and medicine shortages. The focus groups involved 5–7 participants with a mean age of 38.7 years, and lasted approximately 2 h. The discussion mainly revolved around two key issues: (a) the dependency of the islanders on the ferry and air services, and (b) the in-island travel. The co-design sessions aimed to explore the design space and create design exemplars.

Finally, three further co-design sessions were conducted in the Scottish Borders. The co-design sessions involved 5 participants each with a mean age of 34.2. These aimed to further explore the design space and consolidate the design. The participants of both the focus groups and co-design sessions were recruited through e-mails, flyers and announcements on the local notice boards.

4 Passenger Experience and Disruption

In each of the geographical areas that we studied, disruption was both a frequent and expected occurrence. This is well illustrated by the following quotations "Whenever I'm going further than my daily commute, I think it's always a factor for me", and "I just kind of accept that if I'm going anywhere outside the Aberdeen area there's going to be a delay—there's going to be a disruption in my travel plans". This expectation that a disruption might occur results in high levels of frustration. However, our data illustrates that this is not always the case as some disruptions are more acceptable than others. For example, man-made disruptions (e.g. strikes) are less tolerable than disruptions caused by nature (e.g. heavy rain or high winds). This may be ascertained by the following quote: "I would say that public transportation disruption is man-made and the other we can influence. So that's the main problem, for me. I was very upset when I was stuck somewhere on the beach, it was freezing cold and I couldn't get the bus because they were striking and I didn't know they were".

The aforementioned quote also supports our findings in regard to the experience of disruption as something that is experienced on a personal level. One person's perception of disruption may be perceived by another as an opportunity or inconvenience. The following two quotes illustrate this, "Some things, are just interruptions but it's when it affects what you've planned to do—you planned to have your breakfast on the train whilst doing your work because you are getting an early train, when you can't have your breakfast and you can't do your work then that's a disruption but if it's someone playing loud music then it's not really affecting your plans to sit on that train and get to a destination. For me, that would be the thing: whether it affects what my plans were for the journey", and " […] for example weather things, in my home country it's not an issue at all, so this I don't feel as a disruption. It makes it difficult but I don't feel it as a disruption."

Some individuals living in rural areas don't consider a disruption problematic if they can find ways to work around it. However, this mainly depends on the type of disruption and on the purpose of the journey. For example, individuals have reported that if they have to go to visit the doctor by train, and for some reason or other the service is disrupted, if there is a bus or flexible transport services instead of the train, they do not classify the disrupted service as a disruption, just as long as they arrive on time. This could suggest that some of the users of such services perceive the journey as being successful if they arrive on time. If they were to arrive late they may perceive the break in their journey as a disruption.

The study has also identified that certain groups of individuals are more vulnerable to disruptions than others. These can be summarised as:

- Families with young children,
- Individuals without family or friends,
- Those living in the outskirts of rural hubs or in hamlets,
- Individuals dependent on public transport,
- Individuals that don't have immediate access to private transport,
- Tourists or individuals that don't have knowledge of the locality.

These groups when questioned mention that disruption is becoming easier to cope with and to manage due to new technologies. They also mentioned said that they utilise a variety of formal and informal information channels (e.g. social media, websites, blogs, forums, etc.) in order to stay up to date, and exchange information [19]. Figure 2 illustrates an individual living in a hamlet in the Scottish borders informing her twitter followers that the A7 road works are causing delays longer than expected.

Nonetheless, individuals have stated that disruption can also have positive outcomes. These include: increased fitness from walking instead of taking the bus or driving, working from home, taking days off, and getting a break. The latter is illustrated through the following quotation: "Maybe it's not a positive thing for our climate, but you know if you work in a large office like I was in that incident, when something like that happens, because it's a break from the routine and there's a prospect that they might need to send people home, regardless of the fact they might need to spend five hours getting there, people do look at that as quite a positive experience, it's like that kind of—You get a buzz."

4.1 Coping Strategies

The most common coping strategy we have observed is 'time buffering'. Individuals assume that they will be late, or that something will go wrong and therefore in order to accommodate this they "build time on one end or the other"

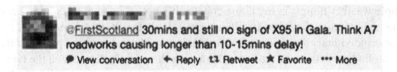

Fig. 2 Correcting and relaying official source information in twitter

of the journey in case this happens. This is further illustrated in the following two quotes: "By making that assumption I'm always building in time on one end or the other in which I can scramble for whatever I need. As far as my day-to-day commute is concerned I only rely on myself. So the only disruption is when I can't manage to do what I need to do.", and "I travel reasonably frequently down to West Wales and I travel at night because I know that the traffic disruption is going to be considerably less, it's just planning around it."

Access to information was deemed extremely important for shielding against disruption. During our initial interviews when we asked the participants 'how could you minimise disruption in your journey?' most of the interviewees answered that cars, mopeds and motorcycles are the best way to combat this, coupled with technological solutions that could provide real-time information about disruptions, and suggest ways to deal with them (technologies such as in-vehicle satellite-navigation systems). Focus group participants said that technologies and timely, accurate and personalised real-time information was the best way to guard against disruption. In addition, when asked to rank the reliability of public transport and cars in situations without real-time information, they ranked car higher as "it is more flexible". However, when presented with a mock-up of a technological solution that provided real-time information about all modes of public transport they ranked the reliability of the public transport and the car the same, "I will be more confident and when something goes wrong I will find a way around it."

We also identified that kinship networks were utilised as a way to protect against disruptions [15, 19]. Kinship networks are composed of weak and strong ties. The strong ties are individuals within the passenger kinship networks, which consist of family members, close friends, work colleagues, and school peers that are considered to be as close as familial links [20]. The weak ties are usually friends of people from their strong ties network, or other passengers, where they have a strong dependence on the connectivity to the individuals travel patterns. The information the passengers are seeking from these networks is usually to increase their situational awareness and information on how to mitigate the effects of disruptions. For example, during our passenger interviews, a participant mentioned that during the heavy snowfall in the Scottish Borders in 2010, she reached home safely, not because of information that the operator provided, but from information that the passenger received from a friend of a friend about a local man going through her village with his snow-plough. It was explained in our interview that the same individual, picked up other individuals that he did not know personally along the way only because they had shared common networks and ties.

4.2 Behavioural Responses to Disruption

Individuals living in rural areas have a wide array of behavioural responses to disruption, ranging from minor to major adaptations. Our study indicates that minor adaptations are more prevalent in regard to low impact disruptions, while major adaptations are more common in high impact disruptions as we will illustrate.

In low impact disruptions the journey is usually recovered and a change in travel behavior occurs in order to facilitate that particular journey, with little time being spent in the planning and on the decision making process. The individuals will usually base their actions on local knowledge, previous experience and momentary convenience. Examples of minor short term adaptations include: using local shops, staying overnight with friends, relying on family for lifts, switching mode, working from home, leaving early or late. However, if a low impact disruption becomes frequent it may lead to significant changes in the behaviour of an individual. During such disruptions the individuals spends more time in the planning and decision making process and bases their actions on long-term convenience. Examples include: keeping spare clothes at a friend's house, leaving earlier or later, avoiding social arrangements on the day of travel etc.

High impact disruptions lead to significant changes in the behaviour of the individual. The individual almost always plans a course of action, mainly based on previous experience and knowledge of the locality. A significant number of participants in both our interviews and focus groups mentioned that if a high impact disruption is infrequent they would only try to recover the journey if the purpose was important (e.g. commuting to work, visiting a doctor). The most common examples of behavioural adaptations to high impact infrequent disruptions are mode change, and route change. However, if a high impact disruption occurs often (even as often as once per month) it may result in life changing events, such as buying a car or relocating. The following quotes demonstrate this "I've moved—I use to live on Longtown but due to disruption I moved to Galashiels.", and "I used to commute with my bicycle every day. It's only about 8 miles but it's a really bad journey, and not in itself was a reason to buy a car, but I could not take it anymore!".

5 Co-designing a RTPI System to Support Rural Passengers During Disruption

As previously illustrated, during disruption individuals rarely have the knowledge or understanding to resolve the issues that emerge from a transport-based disruption. In order to resolve a disruptive situation the traveller usually requires more knowledge than a single person possesses and the required knowledge is often distributed among various individuals who have different perspectives and background knowledge. This illustrates a need for a system that recognizes the interaction between people and facilitates information exchange between users.

Based on this, we have conducted two rounds of three co-design sessions, with the purpose of designing such a system.

The first round of co-design sessions took place on the Isle of Tiree and aimed to identify a suitable design approach, recognise potential challenges and opportunities, and provide us with design exemplars.

In order achieve this we developed four conceptual models. Each model consisted of a description of a disruption scenario (that emerged during the interviews and the focus groups) and a proposed technological solution for that scenario. The scenarios illustrated various types of disruptions. These were: (a) an accident that caused an arterial road to close for a few days, (b) a bus service that constantly runs behind schedule, (c) heavy winds that cut the island of Tiree from the mainland for two weeks, (d) high congestion on an arterial road.

These were presented to the participants at the co-design sessions on the Isle of Tiree. During the sessions, the participants were asked to discuss the scenarios and the proposed solutions, and grade them depending on how strongly they recognised the problem as being a real problem that they faced, and how strongly they agreed that the proposed solution would help. Also, the participants were asked to discuss the conceptual models and provide feedback on what they liked, disliked and would improve about each solution. During all sessions the participants identified that all of the scenarios that were presented to them as ones they could relate to, and mentioned that systems are equally useful.

However, upon being queried on how they would use such a system, they stated that they would use it in combination with a variety of other information channels, such as social media, websites, blogs, forums, etc. One individual mentioned "having an app or being registered to an SMS service that provides you with real time information, delays, cancelations etc. is good but most of the times it simply does not work… and you end up checking multiple websites such as facebook and twitter to see if the information is recent." When we further started exploring this one individual mentioned "Wouldn't it be great if we could update the information or confirm it, if were there stuck on the bus?"

Upon further exploration of this, we started a discussion regarding an ecosystem of applications including Smartphone applications, SMS and e-mail services, websites, and community displays, where the user does not only act as consumer of information but as an information provider as well. Such a design could be based on a Smartphone application and an SMS service with the aim of helping individuals to understand and resolve the issues emerging from disruption by using the collective knowledge of various individuals that are in, or have been in the same situation by creating ad-hoc communities of users with similar needs and wants.

The SMS service the participants designed had two main functions (a) provision of bus location information and (b) creation of an ad-hoc chat where users in the same route can talk to each other. The SMS service aims to create a platform that will initiate dialogue and cooperation between passengers with the same issues and needs the Smartphone application the participants designed focused on the passenger experience during disruption. They did that by (a) enabling the user to validate, and update disruption information, (b) capture passenger experience

Fig. 3 Mock-ups of the Smartphone application that was designed during the co-design sessions

information about the bus service they are currently on, and (c) and by integrating the Smartphone. Figure 3 illustrates it.

The first round of co-design sessions illustrated the need for a technology that not only provides the opportunity and resources for social debate and discussion, but also fosters cultures of participation, and empowers the users to engage in informed participation.

A major component of such an approach is designing an initial technology (or set of technologies) that supports sharing of both an individual's and group's tacit knowledge, enables informed participation from people from all walks of life, and allows the contributors to modify it according to their needs, leading to 'living' information spaces. To make such a system a reality we adopted a modified meta-design approach that took into account the seeding, evolutionary growth, and reseeding (SER) model, and aimed to transition the users to meta-designers [21, 22]. This cyclical approach requires a strong initial core user base that actively contributes to the improvement of the solution throughout its lifecycle.

The prototype version of the system that we were planning to develop, aimed to satisfy the needs of the initial user base. We shortlisted a set of functions required during various stages of the journey (that emerged from the literature, our interviews and focus, groups) and through a card sorting exercise we identified that the most required functions are: (1) location-based information, (2) notification of disruptions and (3) metrics on information quality. Based on these, and the findings from the first round of co-design sessions, we co-designed a Smartphone app called GetThere[1] as part of a wider project known as the Informed Rural Passenger [23].

---

[1] http://www.gettherebus.com/

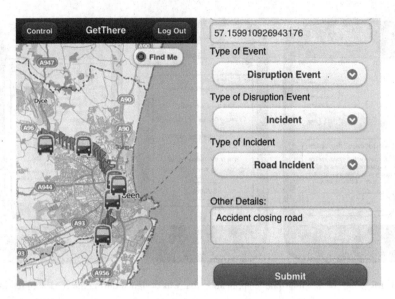

Fig. 4 Screenshots of the GetThere Smartphone application

GetThere crowdsources user location information, allowing a user to report disruption. It provides it to users, enables the users to validate, and update the disruption information. Figure 4 illustrates screenshots of the initially developed prototype version of GetThere.

We are also in the process of co-designing and developing an SMS service based on the findings of the first round of co-design sessions, and 3 further co-design sessions. These two technologies will form the initial version of our system.

The overall design of such an approach is characterised by three interrelated dimensions: (a) a social dimension for designing new practices and processes, (b) a cognitive dimension for understanding the interference between providing information and actively contributing to the development of the system, and (c) a technical dimension for creating new technologies that allow the participants to contribute new information without acquiring extensive technical skills. Our work so far has concentrated on the technical dimension. However, we plan on exploring the other dimensions in the immediate future.

Overall, our findings illustrate that multi-channel RTPI systems have the potential to bridge the gap between urban and rural passenger information provision, as they are more beneficial than traditional RTPI systems in rural areas. The key reasons for this is that they: (a) facilitate the capture of information at the right time and place; (b) provide non-invasive and cost effective methods for communicating personalised data that compares individual performance with relevant social group performance; (c) and social network sites running on the device facilitate communication of personalised data that relate to the participant's self-defined community.

6 Conclusion

In this paper we described our analysis results from 69 interviews and nine focus groups with rural dwellers in order to explore: (a) the passenger experience during disruption, (b) the behavioural responses to disruption, (c) and the coping strategies of the individuals. Furthermore, we conducted a series of co-design sessions, in which we designed a Smartphone application and an SMS-based service.

Our results from the interviews and focus groups indicate that disruption in rural areas is seen as an inherent characteristic of the transport system. Even though it usually leads to frustration, it is often not seen as a problem if there is a way around it. In addition, we have identified that infrequent disruptions lead more often than not, to micro adaptations in behaviour while frequent disruptions lead to major adaptations. Furthermore, our findings have illustrated that rural dwellers are more prepared to tackle disruption than their urban counterparts. However, this may depend on the individual, as certain groups (families with young children) are more vulnerable than others. Nevertheless, in the recent years information and new technologies are making these groups more resilient to disruption.

Based on these findings we have conducted two rounds of co-design sessions and we have designed a Smartphone application and an SMS service that aims to improve the passenger experience during disruption by providing the rural dwellers with real-time information. We are currently in the process of developing and deploying these solutions in the Scottish Borders.

These findings relate to and expand previous studies by providing an initial insight into the rural dweller's behavioural adaptation during disruption, and provide a step towards understanding the interplay between technology, passenger experience/behaviour, and disruption.

Acknowledgments The research described here is supported by the award made by the RCUK Digital Economy programme to the dot.rural Digital Economy Research Hub; award reference: EP/G066051/1. Further, we would like to acknowledge the RCUK research grant EP/J000604/2.

References

1. Chamberlain A, Crabtree A, Davies M, Greenhalgh C, Rodden T, Valchovska S, Glover K (2012) Fresh and local: the rural produce market as a site for co-design, ubiquitous technological intervention and digital-economic development. In: Proceedings of MUM 2012 11th international conference on mobile and ubiquitous multimedia. ACM, Essen, Germany
2. Chamberlain A, Crabtree A, Davies M (2013) Community engagement for research: contextual design in rural CSCW system development. In: Proceedings of the 6th international conference on communities and technology, C&T 2013. ACM, Munich, Germany
3. Chamberlain A, Crabtree A (2013) Innovation in the wild: ethnography, rurality and participation. In: 3rd participatory innovation conference, PIN-C. LUT Scientific and Expertise Publications, Lahti

4. Deeter D (2009) Real-time traveler information systems. NCHRP report 399, Transport Research Board, USA
5. Giannopoulos GA (2004) The application of information and communication technologies in transport. Eur J Oper Res 152:302–320
6. Sussman JM (2005) Perspectives on intelligent transportation systems. Springer, Berlin
7. Nalevanko AM, Henry A (2001) Advanced public transportation systems for rural areas: where do we start? How far should we go? TCRP Project B-17: final report
8. Velaga NR, Beecroft M, Nelson JD, Corsar D, Edwards P (2012) Transport poverty meets the digital divide: accessibility and connectivity in rural communities. J Transp Geogr 21:102–112
9. Scottish Executive Social Research (2006) How to plan and run flexible and demand responsive transport. A report by Derek Halden Consultancy. ISBN 0 7559 6061 0. At: http://www.scotland.gov.uk/Publications/2006/05/22101418/0. Accessed 12 March 2011
10. Wang X, Khattak AJ, Fan Y (2009) Role of dynamic information in supporting changes in travel behavior. Transp Res Rec 2138:85–93
11. Watkins KE, Ferris B, Borning A, Rutherford GS, Layton D (2011) Where is my bus? Impact of mobile real-time information on the perceived and actual wait time of transit riders. Transp Res Part A 45:839–848
12. Zhang F, Shen Q, Clifton K (2008) An examination of traveler responses to real-time bus arrival information using panel data. Transp Res Rec 2086:107–115
13. Ambrosino G, Nelson JD, Romanazzo M (eds) (2004) Demand responsive transport services: towards the flexible mobility agency. ENEA, Rome. ISBN 88-8286-043-4
14. Lu X, Gao S, Ben-Elia E (2011) Information impacts on route choice and learning behavior in a congested network: an experimental approach. In: 90th annual transportation research board meeting, Washington DC
15. Papangelis K, Velaga, NR, Sripada S, Beecroft M, Nelson JD, Anable, Farrington JH (2013a) Supporting rural public transport users during disruptions: the role of real time information. In: Proceedings of 92nd TRB annual meeting, Paper No. 13-2964
16. Ferris B, Watkins K, Borning A (2010) Onebusaway: results from providing real-time arrival information for public transit. In: Proceedings of CHI. ACM Press, pp 1807–1816
17. Ferris B, Watkins K, Borning A (2010) OneBusAway: location-aware tools for improving public transit usability. IEEE Pervasive Comput 9(1):13–19
18. Velaga NR, Nelson JD, Wright SD, Farrington JH (2012) The potential role of flexible transport services in filling gaps in rural public transport provision. J Publ Transp 15(1):33–53
19. Papangelis K, Corsar D, Sripada S, Beecroft M, Nelson JD, Edwards P, Velaga N, Anable J (2013) Examining the effects of disruption on travel behaviour in rural areas. In: Proceedings of 13th world conference in transport research
20. Ebaugh HR, Curry M (2000) Fictive kinship as social capital in new immigrant communities. Sociol Perspect 43(2):189–209
21. Fischer G, Gruding J, McCall R, Ostwald J, Redmiles D, Reeves B, Shipman F (2001) Seeding, evolutionary growth and reseeding: the incremental development of collaborative design environments. In: Coordination theory and collaboration technology. Lawrence Erlbaum Associates, Mahwah, pp 447–472
22. Fischer G (2011) Understanding, fostering and supporting cultures of participation. Interact Mag 42–53
23. Corsar D, Edwards P, Baillie C, Markovic M, Papangelis K, Nelson J (2013) GetThere: a rural passenger information system utilising linked data & citizen sensing. In: Proceedings of the ISWC 2013 posters & demonstrations track a track within the 12th international semantic web conference (ISWC 2013), vol 1035. CEUR Workshop Proceedings, Sydney, Australia, pp 85–88
24. Barley SR (1986) Technology as an occasion for structuring: evidence from observations of CT scanners and the social order of radiology departments. Adm Sci Q 31:78–108

25. Cairns S, Atkins S, Goodwin PG (2002) Disappearing traffic? The story so far. Proc Inst Civil Eng Municipal Eng 151(1):13–22
26. Caulfield B, Mahoney MO (2007) An examination of the public transport information requirements of users. IEEE Trans Intell Transp Syst 8(1):21–30
27. Granovetter MS (1973) The strength of weak ties. Am J Sociol 78(6):1
28. Heesen FH, Papangelis K, Velaga NR, Farrington JH (2013) Pathways to passenger resilience during rural transport disruption: a conceptual mode development. In: Proceedings of 45th annual university transport studies group (UTSG) conference
29. Maclean S, Dailey D (2001) MyBus: helping bus riders make informed decisions. IEEE Intell Syst 16(1):84–87
30. Politis I, Papaioannou P, Basbas S, Dimitriadis N (2010) Evaluation of a bus passenger information system from the users' point of view in the city of Thessaloniki, Greece. Res Transp Econ 29(1):249–255
31. Zhu S, Levinson DM (2010) A review of research on planned and unplanned disruptions to transportation networks. In: 89th annual transportation research board meeting, Washington DC

Visualizing Targeted Audiences

Saiph Savage, Angus Forbes, Carlos Toxtli, Grant McKenzie, Shloka Desai and Tobias Höllerer

Abstract Users of social networks can be passionate about sharing their political convictions, art projects, or business ventures. They often want to direct their social interactions to certain people in order to start collaborations or to raise awareness about issues they support. However, users generally have scattered, unstructured information about the characteristics of their audiences, making it difficult for them to deliver the right messages or interactions to the right people. Existing audience-targeting tools allow people to select potential candidates based on predefined lists, but the tools provide few insights about whether or not these people would be appropriate for a specific type of communication. We introduce an online tool, *Hax*, to explore instead the idea of using interactive data visualizations to help people dynamically identify audiences for their different sharing efforts. We provide the results of a preliminary empirical evaluation that shows the strength of the idea and points to areas for future research.

S. Savage (✉) · G. McKenzie · T. Höllerer
University of California, Santa Barbara, USA
e-mail: saiph@cs.ucsb.edu
URL: http://www.youtube.com/watch?v=vduSbDsAP30

G. McKenzie
e-mail: grant.mckenzie@geog.ucsb.edu

T. Höllerer
e-mail: holl@cs.ucsb.edu

S. Savage · C. Toxtli
Universidad Nacional Autonoma de Mexico, Mexico City, Mexico
e-mail: ctoxtli@fi-b.unam.mx

A. Forbes · S. Desai
University of Arizona, Tucson, USA
e-mail: angus.forbes@sista.arizona.edu

S. Desai
e-mail: shlokadesai@email.arizona.edu

C. Rossitto et al. (eds.), *COOP 2014 - Proceedings of the 11th International Conference on the Design of Cooperative Systems, 27–30 May 2014, Nice (France),* DOI: 10.1007/978-3-319-06498-7_2, © Springer International Publishing Switzerland 2014

Keywords Targeted audiences · Targeted sharing · Online audience · Selective sharing · Social networks · Online community · Facebook

1 Introduction

Healthy and successful collaborations are fostered through meaningful online interactions [6]. Users of social networks can create favorable collaborative environments by instigating new conversations, encouraging contributions, and advertising and promoting projects [7]. Participation and action can be encouraged via postings in an online community. For example, a user can create posts that invite other community members to view interesting shared content [22]. Perhaps counter intuitively, making posts to a large group does not necessarily increase the number of people that engaged with the posted content. Communication research has found that online users receive *fewer* replies when they share content with their entire network than they would if they share it instead with a small targeted audience [5, 17]. Sociological theory on disclosures also establishes that people are more likely to be responsive to a request when they feel as though they have been singled out based on an identification of their unique traits [18].

Many savvy users use different online sharing mechanisms to engage in *selective sharing*, directing content to specific predefined audiences [15]. These users first define collections of people with particular interests, and then post content contextualized so that it is relevant to the interests of the people in each of these collections. However maintaining up-to-date user collections can be difficult and time-consuming. This model is especially unsuitable for more dynamic collections, such as those based on the location, social affiliations, or popularity of the targeted users. For example, the administrators of an online group might want to target only the most influential users in the women's rights movement for promoting their group's cause, or the organizer of a social rally might only want to target those community members who are in town on a particular day. In these cases, predefined collections might be too coarse or include irrelevant users. Another technique involves selecting individuals to target on-the-fly and only sharing the content or message to them. This type of behavior allows for a more dynamic selective sharing experience that is context-driven. We will refer to this practice as *targeted sharing*.

Finding the right people at the right time is hard, especially in larger communities where it is difficult for a single user to keep track of every community member's specific interests and character traits. Previous work in social recommenders has explored the use of list-based interfaces in which a system recommends users with a certain expertise or skill set [14]. These systems do not allow people to easily explore and compare the different characteristics of the recommended individuals. However, these characteristics can play an important role when deciding whether or not they should be selected for a particular collaboration or interaction [28].

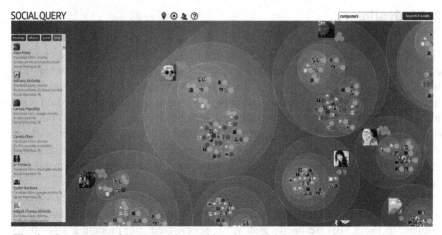

Fig. 1 Screen shots of *Hax's* social spread interface which lets users view the social groups of their potentially interested audiences

Interactive visualization tools can enable effective audience targeting by prompting a user to learn about their audience and to understand their different interests. To explore these ideas, we designed *Hax*.[1] Hax is a tool that provides a query interface and multiple visualizations to support users in dynamically choosing audiences for their targeted sharing tasks. We study how users engaged with this tool in the context of sharing and connecting with an audience in a Facebook *group*. Facebook designed groups to facilitate online community-building, and we can consider each group to be an online community of its own [1]. Figure 1 presents a screen shot of one of Hax's visualizations for targeting audiences within a Facebook group.

The contributions of this work are:

- A novel system for discovering and visualizing the shared interests of an online group or community;
- A novel system for visualizing the spatial-temporal constraints of people;
- A novel system for visualizing the social spread of people;
- A novel system for targeting audiences on-the-fly based on a thematic task or project;
- Providing a better understanding of the way in which data visualizations transform users' audience selection activities.

---

[1] *Hax* is the Mayan word for *exclusive*, referring to the idea that it is the unique characteristics of a person that are important when selecting him or her for a particular interaction or notification.

2 Motivation

One of the challenges in identifying community members to collaborate or share content with is the fact each person may have dynamic sharing and collaboration needs. For instance, a person might have just gotten a parking ticket and would like to discuss with legal experts ways of fighting the ticket; or a person could want to share a popular news piece she just read with others with like-minded political opinions. Changing events and needs affect who we want to interact with or exchange information with. As a result, social media tools need to offer dynamic mechanisms that let users easily find the people or audience that on-demand can cover their needs.

The data modeling techniques that work for content categorization and information retrieval can be adapted to mine people's interests and retrieve audiences relevant to users' diverse needs. But, while specialized data modeling algorithms exist that can correctly categorize data, they rarely fully capture the complex and ever-changing decision-making process for targeting an audience. We therefore opt to integrate data visualizations that incorporate a human-in-the-loop approach.

We designed different data visualizations that highlight specific traits, or *social signals*, of relevant community members in order to aid users in audience targeting tasks. Our exploration begins with the three social signals listed below. We briefly define the signal and the reasons for considering it. Note that other signals could have been contemplated, but we decided to begin with these as previous work has identified that they play an important role in targeting audiences [7, 29]:

1. **Shared interests**: This signal captures the personal thematic interests of each community member. Many researchers and practitioners view collaborations as a process that aggregates personal interests into collective choices through self-interested bargaining [29]. We believe this bargaining process can be facilitated by making users aware of the personal interests of others, and how they relate to the collaboration task they are promoting.
2. **Location**: This signal holds information about the countries, states, and cities where community members live. Collaborations supported by computers have traditionally provided users with the luxury of interacting with others without having to worry about their location [3]. However, location does play an important role when interacting and organizing events within the physical world [25] (e.g., a social rally) as others' spatial-temporal constraints can determine how much a person will engage in the activity [26].
3. **Social connectivity**: This signal holds information about the type of friends and social ties community members have. This signal is important because it can aid members in recognizing prospective newcomers who can help keep the community alive and active [7]. Additionally, the social connections of a member can also help in the spread of the community's messages and visions. Members could thus use this signal to identify the users whose social connectivity would help them the most in distributing certain content.

3 Background and Related Work

Editors have traditionally made decisions regarding the publishing and distributing of content [11], often relying on the expertise of marketing consultants for particular subjects or audiences. These consultants provided them with a clear picture of who their best audience was for a topic [11]. Via the Internet, anyone can now author, share, and distribute content. But, unlike editors, individual users typically don't have a clear image of their audience [4]. By understanding their audience and adequately targeting it, individuals could better engage their communities [21].

To overcome this lack of marketing knowledge, people rely on cues to estimate the traits of their online audiences. Unfortunately, only a few cues are available [4]. For example, a person might remember she friended her co-workers, and they are thus now in her audience. Without extensive investigation, it might be unclear exactly what these people care about [2, 8, 16]. In this work we explore how we can make audience cues more readily available for people. We study the impact these audience cues can have on a user's audience selection process.

Our tool, Hax, helps users of targeted sharing find a suitable audience for their content. This task is related to expert search in social networks in that the problem is finding a set of contacts that satisfy certain criteria with regard to their knowledge, traits, or social status. Perer et al. [23] present SaNDVis, a tool for visual social network analysis inside of an enterprise that also supports expertise location. In their usage study, they found that their tool helps users find authorities on certain topics, and moreover considers their location. Similarly, ContactMap [30] visualizes contacts along with their attributes and location. Work by Chen et al. [9] uses strong social links as a requirement for finding experts on a topic. Systems that support *social question asking* help users direct questions at people from their social network that are most likely to know an answer [10, 19, 21].

In summary, these works show interesting parallels to understanding and supporting targeted sharing. However, they focus either on user goals or audience characteristics that are distinctly different from those of targeted sharing.

3.1 Facebook Graph Search

Facebook's *Graph Search*[2] offers a natural language interface for searching one's social network; queries may consider several social variables. For instance, a typical query might be: *"TV shows liked by people who study computer science."* A query returns a ranked list of relevant Facebook users with some of their characteristics included, such as the city where they live, the music they like, how many friends they have on the site, among others. However, it is unclear if the design of Graph Search was influenced by the requirements of targeted sharing.

---

[2] https://www.facebook.com/about/graphsearch, accessed February 10, 2014.

The attributes and interactions modes it supports are limited. The task specificity and the richer interaction modes of the tool presented in this work aim to make it more useful and accessible for targeted sharing tasks.

3.2 Facebook Advertisement Targeting Options

Facebook offers advertisers options for ensuring that their ad will reach a targeted relevant audience.[3] Advertisers can target audiences based on users' location, age, zodiacal sign, interest, education, their friends, as well as whether they have liked their particular product in the past. Facebook's targeting options assume that the end-user has a clear image of who their desired audience is. While this design consideration can be effectively true for advertisers who have previously conducted market studies and identified the demographics of their clients, it is not necessarily valid for individual community members who engage in targeted sharing.

Bernstein et al. [4] identified that social media users consistently underestimate the audience size for their posts, guessing that their audience is just 27 % of its true size. It is therefore likely, that community members also will not have an exact idea regarding the characteristics and traits of their most relevant audience for a given post. The creation of online tools could be useful in helping end-users better visualize and understand potential audiences and their different characteristics.

4 Designing Hax

Hax is a web-based tool that supports targeted sharing on Facebook via a query that indicates the topic they are interested in posting content about. Hax includes a recommendation engine that accepts and processes such queries to produce a list of relevant community members based on their *likes*. For each returned member, the recommendation engine includes their signals (e.g., their *likes*, hometown, or number of friends) and a weighting. The visualization engine provides three different visual presentations emphasizing different aspects of the recommendations. Figure 2 presents an overview of the Hax components.

4.1 Recommendation Engine

The recommendation engine models the interests of community members based on their profile information. It then identifies those members whose interests are the

---

[3] https://www.facebook.com/help/www/131834970288134?rdrhc, accessed February 10, 2014.

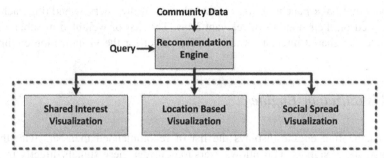

Fig. 2   The components of the *Hax* system

most relevant to a user's search query. We model the general interests of community members through their Facebook *likes*. A Facebook *like* typically has a name, a label, and a definition. For example, the *like* "*Everyday Feminism*" has the name "*Everyday Feminism*", the label "*Community Organization*", and the definition "*Everyday Feminism strives to stop the everyday violence, dominance, and silencing used against women*". We found that the curated labeling used by Facebook to categorize interests is very general, and does not enable an easy way to explore the data further. To counter this effect, we use topic models [24] to model the community's shared interests.

Given the nature of the data, we used a labeled Latent Dirichlet Allocation approach (labeled LDA) [24], similar to that proposed by Forbes et al. [13]. The discovered LDA topics correspond to the community's shared interests, and labels correspond to Facebook *likes*, and each document corresponds to a *like* with its definition. Specifically, we use a generative process to discover the interests shared by the community members. The process first detects the K number of unique labels associated to the community's *likes*. This sets the initial number of shared interests that will be considered. For each shared interest, a unique Like and its associated data is drawn with a Dirichlet distribution α. A multinomial mixture distribution θ^d over all K shared interests is drawn for each community member with a Dirichlet prior α_ϕ. Now, using information about the labels associated with the *likes* of the user, we restrict the definition of θ^d to be defined only to the shared interest associated with the labels present in their *likes*. After this step, each community member is represented as a mixture over shared interests. An end user's query is also modeled as a mixture over shared interests, except that, because it does not have any explicit labels, θ^d is not restricted. The community members who exhibit a shared interest mixture similar to that of the query are presented to the user via the interactive visualizations. We use the L_1 norm as our similarity metric. Our experimental experience, as well as related work in modeling micro blog conversations and users via topic models, suggest that using topic models to mine a community's shared interests is a feasible approach [20].

Given a search query, the recommendation engine first identifies the community's shared interest most relevant to the query. It then finds the community members that have Facebook *likes* most relevant to the query, weighting each of them based on their number of relevant *likes*. This list of weighted members and most relevant shared interests is then used as input for the visualization engine.

4.2 Visualization Engine

The visualization engine displays the list of recommended members with their weighted social signals. This allows users to consider these signals directly in her targeted sharing decision process. Hax provides three different interactive visualizations, each emphasizing different social signals. Following the visualization mantra [27], every visualization lets the user (a) obtain an overview of the community's social signals; (b) zoom into particular groups of members; and (c) obtain details of a desired user's social signals. This rich interaction is not possible with a list-based interface. List-based interfaces do not allow the user to easily obtain overviews and summaries of the data. Given that community users are often organizing things for the entire community, providing overviews of the members' interests can help users remain relevant. Tooltips could potentially be used for offering these data summaries. However, this is not sufficient as it does not allow users to zoom in and explore particular aspects of the data.

We provide a short description of each view below. Figure 3 presents the type of overviews each interface provides. Figure 4 shows example screenshots of the location-based, shared interest, and social spread interfaces.

4.2.1 Shared Interest Interface

Initially, the *shared interest interface* presents an overview of all of the discovered shared interests of the community (Fig. 3a). Shared interests are displayed as nodes on a grid. Each node has in its center the keyword most representative of the shared interest. Mousing over a shared interest displays in light green its most representative keywords, and in dark green its most representative Facebook labels. This view allows users to quickly identify the general interests of their community, as well as some of the most popular specific related interests.

When the user queries the system, a list of relevant members is displayed along with the community's shared interest topic most correlated to that query (Fig. 4, middle). Relevant members are visualized as a list of nodes on the right hand side of the interface. A large node in the center represents the most relevant shared interest topic; other shared interests are shown on the left for reference. Mousing over a member or a shared interest provides more information, e.g. the *likes* of a member that correlate to the query, the description of a *like*, or the Facebook labels associated with a shared interest.

The shared interest interface thus allows a user to quickly see the members that are likely to be interested or knowledgeable about a particular shared interest

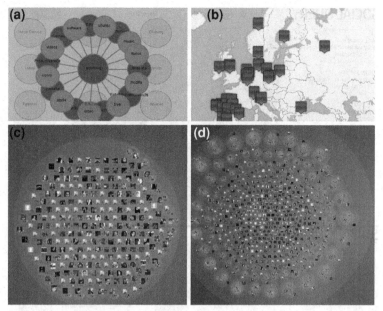

Fig. 3 Overviews given by each visualization **a** shared interest, **b** location-based interfaces, and **c, d** social spread interface

related to the query, and the user can easily investigate the connections between members, *likes*, labels, and shared interests.

4.2.2 Location-Based Interface

The *location-based interface* lets users visualize the geographical locations of the members relevant to their search query. This information can be important when targeting members for activities that take place in the physical world, such as meetings, events, or rallies. In addition, location also provides a sense of cultural context.

The interface shows recommended members on a geographic map, based on the city or place the member listed in their profile. At a first glance, the interface allows users to easily identify the geographical regions where the majority of the members interested in a particular topic reside (Fig. 3b). Users can also zoom in on any member, which will show a list of their relevant Likes, their profile photo, and a more detailed map of the area (Fig. 4, top). Since not every member lists their location, this interface only includes recommended members who have shared this information.

Facebook's targeting options for brands offers a filtering based on location. It is assumed that end-users have a good notion of the cities where their targeted audience live. However, given that users may share diverse and dynamic content

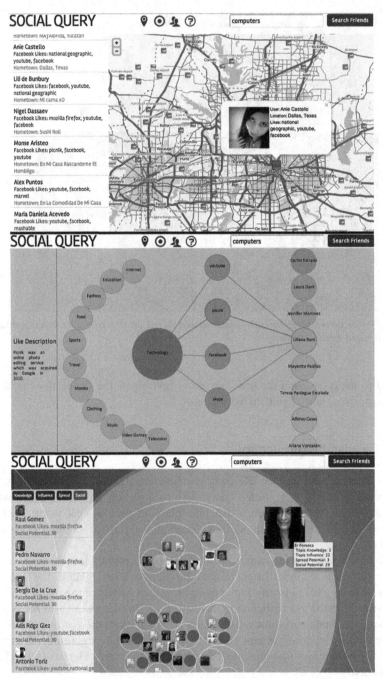

Fig. 4 Screen shots of a zoomed-in version of the different visualizations in *Hax* (*top* to *bottom*): location-based, shared interest, and social spread interfaces

with their group, it can be difficult for them to have a clear picture upfront of who their most relevant audience members are, or where they live.

We argue that location-based interfaces for targeting of audiences should allow users to obtain overviews of where their audiences are physically located, and then enable end-users to further explore the map on multiple levels. This enables users to consider community members' different physical affordances [26] in their decision process. Knowing others' physical affordances is important as it can influence their decisions for participating in an event [26].

4.2.3 Social Spread Interface

The *social spread interface* helps users identify the members with interests related to their query who at the same time have the most contacts or friends with relevant interests. This interface finds members that are not just potentially interested in certain content, but rather potentially interested members whose connections help them distribute or "spread" content to large audience. These are the people who bring value to the content, not necessarily by the comments they provide to the content, but rather though the links to their social contacts.

The social spread interface receives the list of recommended community members from the recommendation engine. For each member, the recommendation engine includes a list of her Facebook *likes* relevant to the user's query and a list of the member's Facebook friends who also have relevant Facebook *likes*. The visualization first structures the members based on their amount of relevant social connections. Members are structured in a spiral form (cf. Fig. 3d). The outer rings of the spiral present the members who have the most friends with the most interests related to the user's query. The center of the spiral contains the members who have the least friends with relevant interests. When all interested members exhibit approximately the same number of interested social contacts, members are arranged in a planar circle from left to right, top to bottom, based on their amount of relevant Likes (cf. Fig. 3c).

Each node in the spiral or circle represents a community member. Each member is presented with their relevant *likes*, photo, and relevant contacts. Each of these contacts is displayed with their own relevant *likes* and photo. Contacts are grouped and color-coded based on the *likes* they have in common with the community member and their relationship with the community itself. The more *likes* a community member has in common with a contact, the closer they both appear in the interface. Contacts with a light blue circle next to them are contacts that have no other connection with the community than their friendship to that particular member. Dark blue circles denote contacts that have one or more other friends who are also community members. Purple circles denote contacts that have friends who are friends with community members.

This view allows users to quickly identify the overall type of social connections that the community reveals for different topics. They can also zoom in and inspect particular members and their relevant social contacts. This enables end-users to easily adjust their messages (and who they mention) to content that can have a larger reach and impact. It also allows users to share content with members whose social contacts could be supportive to their cause.

The spiral structure of the visualization was inspired by the work of Katayoon et al. [12]. Their research found that complex visualizations of hierarchical data can become overcrowded and thus makes it difficult to see details about specific nodes. Their work thus proposed layouts focused on a node of interest that make use of phyllotactic patterns (spirals) via nested circles that are centered on the node of interest. This type of layout is designed to provide more space than traditional hierarchic visualizations. Space-saving designs become important given the overwhelming amount of possible members of an online community and the large amount of relevant contacts each member can have.

5 Usability Inspection of Hax

We conducted a survey study with users who utilized Hax as a tool to find relevant audiences for different content sharing tasks. We questioned participants about their experiences using Hax. We used qualitative coding to create a taxonomy of experiences that emerge from using data visualizations to target audiences. For our study, we worked closely with members of a specific Facebook group for which we were able to recruit participants.

5.1 Participants

Using the Facebook *group browser*,[4] we first identified groups with large number of members and then asked the group administrators whether their group would be interested in participating. We contacted the administrators from 10 different groups who we determined, based on information posted on their public Facebook profile, had a large percentage of members that were local to where we planned to carry out the study.

One group accepted the invitation: an activist group organizing social initiatives around the world. Its 2,000+ active members are distributed world-wide. The group covers a wide range of discussions and events, ranging from the philosophy of free software to the coordination of wildlife preservation rallies. We were granted access to the public Facebook profile of all its members. From this data, our system automatically discovered the groups' interests, and produced the three different data visualizations. 15 of the group members agreed to participate in our

---

[4] http://www.facebook.com/search.php?type=groups&q=%22keyword%22, accessed February 10, 2014.

evaluation: 2 female, 13 male, 4 long-term group members and 11 newcomers (less than one month in the group.) They ranged in age from 19 to 35. Participants came to our laboratory for the study, and received $10 USD for their time.

5.2 Procedure

Over the course of an hour session, each participant completed a series of targeted sharing tasks using Hax on a internet-connected laptop that we provided. We decided that participants would conduct tasks with Hax only, a not in comparison to Facebook's native interface, as Facebook is not particularly designed or tailored for the specific usage of finding relevant online audiences. However, participants were asked to reflect about the benefits and drawbacks of our data visualizations and traditional list-based interfaces. We used qualitative coding based on ground theory for our analysis.

In each task, participants were told to identify 10 candidates for targeted sharing. Each participant was given 15 different tasks that we statistically varied using a Latin square design. Each task came from 5 different scenarios that represented a few of the group's audience targeting needs. Group members not taking part in the evaluation helped edit the tasks and scenarios to reflect real needs. The five scenarios were: (1) Find audiences interested in a certain thematic post; (2) Find audiences to invite to a thematic event, and who are likely to attend; (3) Find audiences to help distribute a thematic article and get others to read it; (4) Find audiences who could help spread news about a thematic event and get others involved; (5) Find audiences who could start a discussion with the group on a certain topic.

As participants performed the tasks, they were observed by one of the researchers who took notes. After participants completed all tasks, they were asked to complete a questionnaire about their experience with Hax, strategies they adopted to complete the tasks, benefits and drawbacks they saw, and a comparison between Hax and list-based interfaces. The questionnaire is available online.[5] Two of the authors coded the responses by reading every questionnaire response and identifying key concepts about users' perspectives on using data visualizations to target audiences. Following grounded theory's coding criteria, we decided that a category would cover a general type of experience that emerges from using data visualizations to target audiences. A total of 4 main categories were identified by this process.

---

[5] http://www.surveymonkey.com/s/KND5CGF, accessed February 10, 2014.

5.3 Results

All participants were able to use Hax to complete all of the tasks assigned to them. Below we discuss each of the 4 categories that emerged from using data visualizations to target audiences. For some of the categories we provide quotes from the questionnaires to help illustrate the core of the category.

5.3.1 Serendipitous Discoveries

This experience is about feeling that data visualizations help one make discoveries about one's targeted audience. All participants reported that Hax prompted them to discover and learn new things about particular group members, and the group in general, something they felt was not facilitated with traditional list-based interfaces: "*...It was really neat to learn so easy and fast what everyone is into. I never experienced that with Facebook.*" Many participants mentioned out loud some of the new discoveries they made with Hax. Additionally, we observed that some started using Hax for their own personal explorations. Dynamic audience visualizations engage users and facilitate serendipitous discoveries of their social groups. This could help people share better content because they understand their audience more.

5.3.2 Visualizing Diffusion and Participation

This experience is about considering data visualizations to be helpful in finding large pools of people likely to take action in regard to a message, e.g., comment, or attend an invitation. 70 % of participants found Hax useful for distributing content to audiences who would be engaged with the content. Participants felt list-based targeting tools did not provide such perspective. Participants believed the location-based visualization facilitated finding audiences from big cities who could easily spread messages to large pools of actionable people, e.g., by making announcements on the streets about an event people could walk to. Participants also felt that by visualizing social connections and interests they could distribute content to mass audiences likely of participating in collaborative action afterwards, such as a discussion. Additionally, the location-based interface helped participants make a connection between the virtual event on Facebook and participation in the physical world, especially selecting an audience who could travel and attend: "*The map really made me think about the actual event, and like really including the person.*" It is interesting to observe how just having a map helped people integrate location in their audience decision process. Our results hint there is value in designing systems that enable users to visualize and explore others' spatial affordances. This signal could provide the perspective needed to make online interactions more realistic, especially compared to list-based interfaces that provide little spatial context.

Fig. 5 Hax at a university annual open exhibition which had hundreds of visitors

5.3.3 Audience Diversity

This experience is about feeling that data visualizations bring diversity to one's targeted audience selection process. Participants reported that the shared interest visualization helped them find relevant candidates who had different perspectives. Participants also mentioned that the location-based interface let them have more diverse selections: *"I tried to have diversity in who I selected. People who like the same things or are from the same town will have same interests and maybe not that much new to add."*

5.3.4 Audience Verification

This experience is about using data visualizations to verify the recommended audiences. 10 % of all participants reported this experience. Participants especially used the shared interest interface to figure out the meaning of the *likes* and to analyze whether it made sense to include certain candidates in their targeted audience: *"There were some brands [i.e., likes] that I didn't know, but the knowledge interface [i.e., shared interest visualization] helped me know what they were about."* Participants particularly enjoyed not having to leave the tool to comprehend the audience that our system recommended.

5.4 Open Deployment of Hax

Additionally, Hax has been installed on a large screen display for several hours in a well-attended university exhibition to further explore how average users experience this open-ended way of selecting audience candidates (cf. Fig. 5). Even without prior notice or instruction visitors to the exhibition were able to approach the display and begin interacting with Hax. During the deployment, approximately 150 visitors approached Hax: around 70 visitors interacted with Hax while the rest analyzed and studied Hax without interacting. Average interactions times were around 1 min.

6 Outlook and Discussion

Our results show that users can target their audiences through interactive data visualizations. Our data visualizations prompted users to learn more about their peers. They also helped people find diverse audiences for their different sharing tasks, something not facilitated by list based interfaces. This type of system design can help users to have more cultural sensitivity and to foster better social interactions and collaborations. Hax empowers users to consider not only others' interests, but also other traits, such as social, cultural, and spatial signals. This creates a more compelling sharing experience. We believe there is value in designing systems focused on the visualization of people's traits. Such systems could facilitate serendipitous discoveries and encourage diverse interactions. It is important to think about creating digital opportunities where strangers with different opinions can find each other and connect. Social media data mixed with data mining and visualization techniques provide a unique opportunity for giving users diversity. Our results encourage future studies that address audience understanding as a main visualization goal.

Acknowledgments This work was partially supported by a UC MEXUS-CONACYT fellowship, by the U.S. Army Research Laboratory under Cooperative Agreement No. W911NF-09-2-0053 and by NSF grant IIS-1058132. Special thanks to our participants and the anonymous reviewers whose thoughtful feedback helped improve the presentation of this work.

References

1. Askanase (2013) D Returning to facebook groups, May 2013. http://communityorganizer20.com/2012/05/31/returning-to-facebook-groups/
2. Barranco M, Noguera J, Castro J, Martnez L (2012) A context-aware mobile recommender system based on location and trajectory. In: Casillas J, Martnez-Lpez FJ, Corchado Rodrguez JM (eds) Management intelligent systems, vol. 171 of advances in intelligent systems and computing, Springer, Berlin, Heidelberg, pp 153–162
3. Bentley R, Hughes JA, Randall D, Rodden T, Sawyer P, Shapiro D, Sommerville I (1992) Ethnographically-informed systems design for air traffic control. In: Proceedings of the 1992 ACM conference on computer-supported cooperative work, CSCW '92, ACM, New York, pp 123–129
4. Bernstein MS, BakshyE, Burke M, Karrer B (2013) Quantifying the invisible audience in social networks. In: Proceedings of the SIGCHI conference on human factors in computing systems, CHI '13, ACM, New York, pp 21–30
5. Bernstein MS, Marcus A, Karger DR, Miller RC (2010) Enhancing directed content sharing on the web. In: Proceedings of the SIGCHI conference on human factors in computing systems, CHI '10, ACM, New York, pp 971–980
6. Brennan K, Monroy-Hernndez A, Resnick M (2010) Making projects, making friends: Online community as catalyst for interactive media creation. New Dir Youth Dev 2010(128):75–83
7. Butler B, Sproull L, Kiesler S, Kraut R (2001) Community effort in online groups: Who does the work and why? Leadership at a Distance: Research in Technologically-Supported Work

8. Chavez N, Savage R, NavaD, Savage S (2012) Enchantment under the sea: an intelligent environment for user friendly music mixing. In: Intelligent environments (IE), 2012 8th international conference on, pp 303–306, June 2012
9. Chen D, Tang J, Li J, Zhou L (2009) Discovering the staring people from social networks. In: Proceedings of the 18th international conference on the world wide web, ACM, New York, pp 1219–1220
10. Chen J, Geyer W, Dugan C, Muller M, Guy I (2009) Make new friends, but keep the old: recommending people on social networking sites. In: Proceedings of the SIGCHI conference on human factors in computing systems, CHI '09, ACM, New York, pp 201–210
11. Cheyne TL, Ritter FE (2001) Targeting audiences on the internet. Commun ACM 44(4):94–98
12. Etemad K, Carpendale S (2010) Symmetry and node focused visualization of large trees. In: GRAND NCE Annual Conference, GRAND
13. Forbes AG, Savage S, Höllerer T (2012) Visualizing and verifying directed social queries. In: IEEE workshop on interactive visual text analytics, IEEE
14. Gavalas D, Kasapakis V, Konstantopoulos C, Mastakas K, Pantziou GA (2013) survey on mobile tourism recommender systems. In: Communications and information technology (ICCIT), 2013 3rd international conference on (June 2013), pp 131–135
15. Kairam S, Brzozowski M, Huffaker D, Chi E (2012) Talking in circles: selective sharing in google + . In: Proceedings of the SIGCHI conference on human factors in computing systems, CHI '12, ACM, New York, pp 1065–1074
16. Lampinen A, Lehtinen V, Lehmuskallio A, Tamminen S (2011) We're in it together: interpersonal management of disclosure in social network services. In: Proceedings of the SIGCHI conference on human factors in computing systems, CHI '11, ACM, New York, pp 3217–3226
17. Latané B, Darley J (1968) Group inhibition of bystander intervention in emergencies. J Pers Soc Psychol 10(3):215–221
18. McCroskey JC, McCain TA (1974) The measurement of interpersonal attraction. Speech Monogr 41(3):261–266
19. McDonald DW, Ackerman MS (2000) Expertise recommender: a exible recommendation system and architecture. In: Proceedings of the 2000 ACM conference on computer-supported cooperative work, ACM, New York, pp 231–240
20. McKenzie G, Adams B, Janowicz K (2013) A thematic approach to user similarity built on geosocial check-ins. In: Association of geographic information laboratories in Europe. Springer, Heidelberg, pp 39–53
21. Nichols J, Zhou M, Yang H, Kang J-H, Sun XH (2013) Analyzing the quality of information solicited from targeted strangers on social media. In: Proceedings of the 2013 conference on computer-supported cooperative work, ACM, New York, pp 967–976
22. Otto P, Simon M (2008) Dynamic perspectives on social characteristics and sustainability in online community networks. Syst Dyn Rev 24(3):321–347
23. Perer AGuy I, Uziel E, Ronen I, Jacovi M (2011) Visual social network analytics for relationship discovery in the enterprise. In: 2011 IEEE conference on visual analytics science and technology (VAST), IEEE, New Jersey, pp 71–79
24. Ramage D, HallD, Nallapati R, Manning CD (2009) Labeled lda: a supervised topic model for credit attribution in multi-labeled corpora. In: Proceedings of the 2009 conference on empirical methods in natural language processing, vol 1 of EMNLP '09, Association for Computational Linguistics, pp 248–256
25. Raubal M, Miller H, Bridwell S (2004) User centered time geography for location-based services. Geografiska Annaler B 86(4):245–265
26. Savage NS, Baranski M, Chavez NE, Höllerer T (2012) I'm feeling loco: a location based context aware recommendation system. Advances in location-based services: 8th international symposium on location-based services, Vienna 2011 (2012), Springer, Heidelberg, pp 37

27. Shneiderman B (1996) The eyes have it: a task by data type taxonomy for information visualizations. In: Proceedings of the 1996 IEEE symposium on visual languages, VL '96, IEEE computer society (1996)
28. Singer L, Filho FMF, Cleary B, Treude C, Storey M-AD, Schneider K (2013) Mutual assessment in the social programmer ecosystem: an empirical investigation of developer profile aggregators. In: Proceedings of the 2013 conference on computer-supported cooperative work, ACM, New York, pp 103–116
29. Thomson AM, Perry JL (2006) Collaboration processes: Inside the black box. Public Adm Rev 66:20–32
30. Whittaker S, Jones Q, Nardi B, Creech M, Terveen L, Isaacs E, Hainsworth J (2004) Contactmap: organizing communication in a social desktop. ACM Trans Comput-Human Interact (TOCHI) 11(4):445–471

Reconsidering the Role of Plans and Planning in the Management of the Unexpected

Ilaria Redaelli and Antonella Carassa

Abstract Based on an in-depth field study of the planning practices of the Ramp Control tower of an Italian airport, this paper addresses the problem of the role of plans and planning in how organizations deal with contingencies. Research into organizations' management of the unexpected has thus far mostly opposed the ongoing comprehension of emerging factors in the role of plans and planning recognized as useful for the sole management of expected events or even as treating the organization's ability to detect the unexpected. Instead, our study of planning strategies shows that plans and planning play a key role in facing the unexpected and that the focus on the articulation work necessary for the plan set up and change contributes to our understanding of how plans might be designed so as to face uncertainty.

1 Introduction

The objective of this paper is twofold. On one hand it aims to show that existing organizational theories fail to recognize the variety of functions that plans play in the management of the organizational uncertainty due to their conceptualization of what the "unexpected" is. On the other hand, it shows that the understanding of the role of plans in the management of the unexpected might be significantly improved when focusing on the articulation work necessary to set them up.

In order to develop our argument we first present and comment on the theories that focus on the management of unexpected events in organizational settings and

I. Redaelli (✉) · A. Carassa
Università della Svizzera italiana, Lugano, Switzerland
e-mail: ilaria.redaelli@usi.ch

A. Carassa
e-mail: antonella.carassa@usi.ch

C. Rossitto et al. (eds.), *COOP 2014 - Proceedings of the 11th International Conference on the Design of Cooperative Systems, 27–30 May 2014, Nice (France)*, DOI: 10.1007/978-3-319-06498-7_3, © Springer International Publishing Switzerland 2014

we comment on them; we then present the ethnographic study that we used as a meaningful case. We conclude by commenting on our findings.

1.1 Organizations as Complex Adaptive Systems

This approach pursues the study of organizations as complex adaptive systems (CAS)—that is, characterized by nonlinear dynamics and emergent properties, by diverse agents interacting with each other, and by undergoing self-organizing [11, p. 4]. The study of organizations from this perspective implies that surprise is "inevitable because it is part of the natural order of things and cannot be avoided, eliminated or controlled." If surprise is the result of the fundamental unknowability of the world, the study of the unexpected could be carried out by approaching surprise as an opportunity instead of as an error, thereby allowing for the search of innovative approaches to situations (pp. 7–8).

1.2 Sense Making in Organizations

This approach developed by Weick [23] is strongly inspired by pragmatism[1] and focuses on the role of individual and organizational sense-making. It conceptualizes organizations as "impermanent"—that is, that they fabricate their permanence out of streaming of experience [25] thanks to retrospective sense-making [22], which is the active construction of sensible events out of discrepant events or surprise.[2] Weick's approach to the study of organizing has led to the development of research on the organizational capability of maintaining function and structure in the face of disruptions, or "organizational resilience" [24], and to the identification of "mindfulness" as a key factor for the maintenance of organizational reliability. In Weick and Sutcliffe's opinion, organizations are able to face the unexpected when they are able to counteract the tendency to seek confirmation of their expectations. Indeed, they assert that expectations of how the world operates provide a significant infrastructure for everyday life, but also bias people's perceptions of the world.

> People are more likely to search for confirming information and to ignore information that is inconsistent with their expectations [24].

---

[1] For ideas that have influenced Weick's theorizing of the study of organizations and organizing, see Weick [23].

[2] Weick asserts that the sense-making process has seven characteristics: it is grounded in identity construction; it is retrospective; it is enactive of sensible environments; it is social; it is ongoing; it is driven by plausibility more than by accuracy; and it is focused on and by extracted cues (see [22, p. 17]).

1.3 Resilient Engineering

This approach focuses on the resources that usually allow people to anticipate and adapt to the potential for surprise and failure [9, 10]. Such an approach takes for granted the organizations' awareness of the potential paths to failure and ability to act so as to forestall these possibilities. This is why engineering ergonomists are not so interested in defining a theory of "error," but instead in understanding how individuals and systems struggle to anticipate the path of failure and to increase and sustain failure-sensitive strategies in a world "fraught with gaps, hazards, trade-off." In this way, they can help the organizations' development of mechanisms to create foresight as well as anticipate and defend against the path of failure [30].

1.4 The Concept of "Situated Actions"

This approach developed by Suchman [19] highlights how actions depend in essential ways upon the material and social circumstances of their occurrence.

> The approach is to study how people use their circumstances to achieve intelligent action [19, p. 50].

Within such an approach—oriented to the understanding of how humans accomplish purposeful actions more than to the conceptualization of the organization's functioning—plans are recognized as resources for situated actions and as formulations of situated actions whose efficacy inevitably depends on their relationship with the circumstances in which actions occur.

> The significance of plans turns on their relation back to the unique circumstances and unarticulated practices of situated activity [19, p. 185].

1.5 The Features of Unexpected Events

The frames for the study of the how organizations deal with the unexpected, as previously described, have approached the problem of identifying the features of the unexpected events in different ways and they have developed a variety of conceptual tools that can be used as an aid in approaching organizational surprises.

Cunha et al. [6], inspired by the CAS theory, suggested a typology of unexpected events based on the combination of expected or unexpected issues with expected or unexpected processes, where identifiable issues are discrete entities while processes are the unfolding of some sequence whereby several non-identified causes interact to produce the unexpected outcome (Fig. 1).

	Expected processes	*Unexpected processes*
Expected issue	**Routines** Events that can be anticipated	**Creeping developments** Expected issues take unexpected shapes while unfolding
Unexpected issues	**Sudden events** Unexpected issues introduced impromptu lead to an expectable process and outcome	**Losses meaning** Novel, incomprehensible situations

Fig. 1 Adapted from [6]

Yet Weick and Sutcliffe [24] claimed that unexpected events are those events for which the organizations are not ready. In their opinion, unexpected events can take three different forms: events that were expected to happen but failed to occur; events that were not expected to happen but do happen; and events that were not thought about happening. Thus, organizations have two main problems for dealing with the unexpected: they need to increase their understanding of the third type of events—that is, imagine events that might occur—and they have to face the tendency of workers to normalize the unexpected—that is, treat unexpected events as if they were slight and innocuous deviations from the expected.

In the resilient engineering approach, as previously explained, there is not a particular interest in defining a theory of "error," but rather in understanding how individuals and systems struggle to anticipate the path of failure.

Similarly, Suchman is not interested in the development of a definition of the unexpected even though she sustains that every action occurs in circumstance that is not possible to fully anticipate and that are continuously changing around us. The unexpected is thus inevitably part of all purposeful action.

1.6 Plans and the Unexpected

Within these frames, plans—that is, organizational devices used to anticipate future events, and planning are recognized as playing a minor role in the management of the unexpected or even as treating the organization's capability to face the unexpected. Cunha et al. [6] asserted that plans and planning play a key role in the management of expected issues as standard operating procedures or organizational routines are usually formalized in the form of plans. Researchers within the resilient engineering approach, instead, showed the utility of plans in face of the pressure to increase efficiency [7] and demonstrated that the missed opportunities to re-plan in face of surprise constitute sources of failure [28], but a full comprehension of the role of plans in the management of the unexpected within this stream of research is still missing.

Suchman instead described plans as weak resources for the execution of actions in that they cannot represent all the changing circumstances of their occurrence, even though she recognized that their usefulness depends precisely on such a vagueness.

> By abstracting uniformities across situations, plans allow us to bring past experience and projected outcome to bear on our present actions [19, p. 185].

The concept of "situated action" and the characterization of plans as "weak resources" for their accomplishment strongly affected on the CSCW community and pushed several scholars to wonder about how plans are used in organizational settings. This stream of research showed that plans are multifariously used within organizations in that their relevance is occasioned in the circumstances of their use (see, among others: [1, 2, 4, 17, 18, 27]). Such a stream of research provided insightful advancement in the understanding how plans support cooperative work even though studies into how plans help face contingencies are still missing in such a community.

Weick [25] argued that plans are often used in organizations to preserve the illusion of permanence and keep surprise at minimum. In addition, Weick and Sutcliffe [24] claimed that plans play a key role in the normalization process of unexpected events that biases the possibility of organizations to recognize small events as signals that things are not developing as they would.

> People search for confirmation in other forms of expecting such as routines and plans ... Plans guide people to search narrowly for confirmation that plans are correct ... and plans lure you into overlooking a buildup of the unexpected (p. 26).

This is the reason why the sensitivity to action necessary for an organization to be mindful requires "less attention to plans and more attention to emergent outcomes that are set in motion by immediate actions" [26].

1.7 Building on the Conceptualizations of Plans for the Management of the Unexpected

It is our opinion that, within all these frames, plans and planning are not adequately investigated due to the conceptualization of the unexpected they provide. In particular, we contend that the approaches presented above fail to recognize the multifarious role of plans in the face of contingencies because they merge the concept of "unexpected" with that of "surprise," arguing that surprise cannot be managed by means of plans or underestimating that some changes in the circumstances of our acting might occur routinely and therefore might be managed by means of plans.[3]

---

[3] For a more detailed analysis on the relationship between "plans and situated actions," see Schmidt [18].

In other words, we contend that confusion exists about the conceptualization of the "unexpected" and that such confusion causes a systematic underestimation of the role of plans in the management of the unexpected. In our opinion, this confusion draws on two misunderstandings: to take what is unexpected as necessarily surprising and to consider what is extraordinary as necessarily requiring improvisation. Indeed, there might be unexpected events that are trivial contingencies or routine troubles and therefore not surprising at all—even if they disrupt the organizational functioning and plans might help deal with them, such as the client's last-minute request to transport a parcel received by a cargo company[4]; events that are extraordinary but still in the range of that for which one has ready-made contingency plans, such as the factory evacuation plan in case of fire; and extraordinary events for which one has to improvise solutions. In addition, we should consider that what is surprising for one person might not be so surprising for another as very often surprise emerges from a lack of attention. In fact, Weick and Sutcliffe's efforts aimed to understand the factors that deviate people's attention toward their actions in that this exposes them to the risk of being surprised by how things evolve and thus being overwhelmed by events.

In summary, we contend that, if the concept of unexpected is properly unpacked, then the study of the role of plans for its management might be enriched. In particular, once the concepts of surprise and unexpectedness are split up, it is possible to focus on how organizations deal with "routine unsurprising disruption"—that is, events that the organizational members consider likely to occur, but of which they do not know—for example the magnitude, frequency, and/or time of occurrence, which can threaten the organization's functioning.

This paper aims to contribute to such an effort by showing how plans and planning are used in the management of "routine disruption" in an Italian airport.

2 The Ethnographic Study

This paper was inspired by data collected in the course of an ethno-methodologically oriented ethnography [8, 14] designed to understand how planning—a widespread activity within organizations—is carried out for the successful accomplishment of work. Empirical materials were collected in the ramp control tower (RCT) of an Italian airport, which is the coordination center [20] for the handling activities on the ground.

The operators who work in such a service carry out two main activities. First, they inform all the personnel involved in aircraft fuelling, luggage loading and unloading, and passenger assistance during boarding and disembarkation procedures on the aircrafts' approach so that all these activities can be carried out with respect to the time limit defined by each airline company for their execution.

---

[4] We took this example from Weick and Sutcliffe [24].

Second, the RCT operators are responsible for the setup of the gate and stand allocation plans; that is, they have to plan the use of gates and parking areas for aircrafts to ensure that each plane finds its proper stand upon arrival, that the stand will be available for the duration of the plane's stop on the ground, and that a proper area will be available for the execution of the boarding procedures.

The RCT operators then have to match planes with stands and gates by considering the size of the aircrafts and the technical features of stands and gates. Some gates, in fact, allow only for boarding by bus, while other allow for boarding on foot. In addition, stands have different capacities, meaning that they can be used to park planes whose dimensions vary up to the stand maximum capacity; in addition, depending on planes' dimensions, adjacent stands cannot be used simultaneously to ensure that planes can maneuver when entering and leaving the stand. This means that possibilities and constraints in the stands' use emerge as a consequence of the planning itself.

The operators, who work in a 24-h service, ensure the continuity of planning over time by both planning in advance twice a day and "planning on the hoof" whenever necessary. Flight delays or arrivals ahead of time as well as flight cancellations or the addition of charter flights are the most frequent causes of changes to plans. Therefore, planning, which is carried out individually, and re-planning, which is accomplished by the operators on shift dialogically, intersect one another in the course of the day and planners and plan executors follow one another.

This research thus focused on how a team at work carries out distributed planning and changes the plan during its application as a consequence of occurrences that emerge in the execution of the planned activities.

The collection of empirical materials lasted eight months, during which the initial direct observation of the operators' activities was integrated with the audio-recordings of naturally occurring conversations and ethnographic interviews. The data collection was oriented to the study of the operators' deployment of their local knowledge [13]—that is, the corpus of knowledge (mostly informal) that is necessary for the orderly accomplishment of work and that emerges from what people have experienced and whose relevance depends on local circumstances of work (also see: [5]), during the plans set up and change. Thus, we focused on how they deploy their local knowledge in the accomplishment of articulation work—namely, the "activities necessary "to curb the distributed nature of complexly interdependent activities [16, p. 15].

3 Planning the Unexpected in the RCT

As previously explained, one of the RCT operators' main activities is the allocation of stands and gates to flights. The operators have to allocate stands and gates while respecting the flights' technical features and the safety and security requirements, but when planning they do more than this. The operators also plan to ensure the timely execution of handling activities as they know that the way they allocate stands and gates affects the possibility for the operators on the ramp to carry out the handling activities in a timely manner (see: [15]). However, the RCT operators also plan so as to be able to face the unexpected in that they plan and re-plan to create and maintain the plans' adaptive capacity. When planning, they define the buffering capacity of planning, its flexibility, and the margin using their local knowledge of the plans' tolerance—that is, their knowledge of the conditions that treat the usability of the plans and their knowledge of the capacity of their planning to compensate for such conditions. RCT operators define the kind of disruptions the plans can adsorb without the breakdown of the plans' structure, they actively plan to create and maintain the plans' ability to be restructured in response to external changes, and they plan and re-plan to control the plans' margins—namely, how precariously the plans are likely to operate relative to other performance boundaries.[5] In other words, RCT operators plan so they can re-plan and vice versa.

3.1 Defining the Buffering Capacity of Planning

When planning the RCT, operators do not try to face any kind of unexpected events; rather, they consider only events that they know are highly likely to occur and whose occurrence does not undermine the usefulness of the stand and gate allocation plans. Thus, for example, the operators do not plan to deal with a hijacking in that this is quite a rare event whose occurrence affects the functioning of the entire airport and, consequently, makes the stand and gate allocation plans useless or require substantial changes. Therefore, the operators plan and re-plan to be able to face changes in scheduled flights, such as flight delays or arrivals ahead of time and last-minute increases in the number of the incoming aircrafts. In fact, airline companies might add charter flights at any moment or flights might be diverted to the airport due to bad weather conditions that impede them from landing to the original location.

The selection of the unexpected events to plan for allows the operator to keep the complexity of planning under control and reduces the need for them to remake the plans entirely when the unexpected occurs. As the stand and gate allocation plan updates have to be carried out while executing other activities, it is preferable for the operators to develop plans that do not need to be continuously and entirely remade in order to avoid the increase of the workload that, in turn, might increase the risk of making mistakes.

---

[5] We identified such features of planning by drawing on Woods' work [29], but using his definition of buffering capacity, flexibility, margin, and tolerance in a substantially different way.

3.2 Creating and Maintaining Plans' Flexibility

The operators plan and re-plan to be able to face the unexpected by means of planning strategies that allow them to restructure the plans in response to external changes. In fact, they plan to create and maintain the availability of slack resources such as space and time and re-plan so as to be able to face contingencies while ensuring the availability of slack resources.

The operators ensure the availability of space that, for example, can be used to address the increase of the number of aircrafts to park, planning the allocation of stands in such a way that at least one is kept free. The RCT operators also develop plans to ensure the allowance of slack time between the boarding processes of flights assigned to the same gate and between the departure and arrival of flights allocated to the same stand as this enables them to address, for example, delays in flight arrivals or in the execution of boarding and/or turnaround activities. It is worth noting that the operators carry out such assessments of the duration of the slack time despite the organizational requirement, drawing on their knowledge of the amount of delay likely to occur and their knowledge of the time necessary for the execution of boarding by considering the number of passengers that must board.

The airport's protocols suggest maintaining 15 min of slack time between subsequent flights as a safety requirement, but the operators usually plan a longer slack time to compensate for potential changes in flights' arrivals or departures. In addition the operators change the amount of such slack time based on their knowledge of the circumstances that impact on changes in the scheduled times. Thus, for example, they keep the duration of the slack time longer in winter, when the probability of delays increases due to weather conditions, and they decrease it in other seasons.

> You have to consider that in winter aircrafts that move through airports in the north of Europe find snow and ice so it is likely that they arrive here with delays. We calculate at least 40 min in winter and 30 in the other seasons (Track 62 10/26/2011).[6]

3.3 Creating and Maintaining the Plans' Margins

The RCT operators' planning and re-planning to ensure the capability of facing unexpected needs to control the plans' margins—that is, keeping control of the precariousness of the plans. They do this mostly by developing plans to ensure the availability of the ramp personnel and equipment over time. The possibility of dealing with changes in the scheduled arrival and departure times and to assist

---

[6] This extract and the following one come from ethnographic interviews collected in the course of the study.

unexpected flights heavily depends on the availability of equipment and personnel necessary for assisting planes' movements on the ground and executing the handling activities. If, for example, unexpected planes arrive in the airport due to bad weather conditions, it is not enough to find a space to park them, but operators must also ensure that they will be handled and ready to reach their original destinations once cleared. In such cases it is not possible to rely the possibility of having extra personnel; even the airport equipment is a limited resource. Thus, RCT operators usually develop plans and re-plan so as to spare the personnel and the equipment at their disposal. The RCT operators succeed in doing this by minimizing the occasions that require the personnel's movement on the airside area as well as reduce the distances that they have to cross, such as by allocating as many planes as possible to the parking areas next to the terminal building.

In this way, the RCT operators prevent the ramp personnel's overload, which might affect the execution of the plans and favor their availability for the management of the unexpected. If the ramp personnel do not waste time in movement that can be avoided by planning, it is possible to use them to handle any unexpected planes as necessary, avoiding problems while assisting planes overall. This way of planning also reduces the need for ramp personnel to move the equipment, preserving it from damage and favoring its availability over time.

In addition, RCT operators spare resources planning so as to favor the intensive use of gates that allow for boarding on foot. In this way, they favor both the containment of the use of the airport resources, since boarding can be carried out without buses, and keep their use to the minimum necessary. As boarding on foot is quicker than boarding by bus, the intensive use of such gates allows for the use of airport resources sparingly and ensures their availability when the unexpected[7] occurs.

> OPERATOR The 6,553 has an estimated delay of 30 min. They estimate that it will depart after 30 min of delay because of a technical problem. It should arrive at 10 thereby overlapping with this plane.
> RESEARCHER But you have space so
> OPERATOR Yes, when I am sure about the delay I will move it. We will manage to find a gate with the boarding on foot (Track 69 11/02/2011).

In conclusion, it is worth noting that the airport's capacity to face unexpected changes in the time or number of flights depends on the adoption of all the planning strategies described thus far and that such planning strategies allow for compensating for changes in the scheduled times and the number of incoming planes quite interchangeably. If, in fact, the operators have to park one unexpected plane whose arrival and departure time is certain, they can manage to exploit the

---

[7] Such planning practices have been extensively described in Redaelli and Carassa [15] in order to show that the efficacy of the RCT operators' planning practices depends on their being suited for the management of space and time contemporaneously. This means that the RCT operators' planning strategies are multivalent in nature.

slack time between two subsequent flights; meanwhile, if it is not possible to compensate for the change of a scheduled flight using the slack time, the operators have the ability to use the slack space.

4 Discussion

Planning in the RCT contributes to the organization's capability to face disruptions in that it helps maintain the airport's functioning—namely, the maintenance of the organization's positive adjustments under challenging conditions, which organization studies address in terms of "resilience".[8] Organizational resilience is commonly recognized as relying upon a complex set of competences, processes, and structures that allow them to respond to change swiftly, among which we contend planning fully belongs. Planning in the RCT, in fact, helps prevent the exhaustion of the organization's capacity to adapt to disturbances; it is locally and globally adaptive and demonstrates the readiness to be updated when new challenges occur. In other words, it helps the organization escape the adaptive traps described by Woods and Branlat [31] that apply to individuals, groups, and organizations. If we apply Woods and Branlat's taxonomy to our data—that is, to plans and planning—we can readily see that plans in the RCT help prevent decompensation in that they are set up to exploit material and human resources with the precise purpose of increasing the system's capacity to compensate disturbances, such as changes in the number of flights and/or in their scheduled times. Planning is locally and globally adaptive in that the RCT operators do not plan simply to achieve their local goal of developing stand and gate allocation plans, but they also set up such plans with the precise purpose of supporting the achievement of the global organizational goal of preventing the depletion of the airport's resources on which its functioning depends in the long run. Last but not least, plans in the RCT are also set up in such a way to be revised when necessary, instead of forcing the RCT operators to stick to already-planned solutions.

The application of Woods and Branlat's taxonomy to our data helps understand that plans are not always brittle constructs that collapse in the face of unexpected events. Indeed, plans should be examined for their contribution to the maintenance of the organization's adaptation to changing conditions. Yet the application of such taxonomy does not help understand *how* plans support the organization's readiness to handle unexpected events. This is why we suggest looking at plans as artifacts in the service of imposing order—that is, as coordination artifacts—and then focusing on the coordinative practices deployed for their construction in order to determine how they maintain interdependencies among the stakeholders

---

[8] The term "resilience" is variously defined within organization studies (see: [21, 24, 29]), permitting the study of different aspects of resilient organizations, such as how they eliminate errors and unexpected events, learn from events and near events, and reflect on their own capability to adapt to unexpected circumstances.

involved in the successful and timely execution of flight execution, even when disturbances occur (see: [18]).

If the study of plans is oriented by the studies on coordination, it is possible to see that they help the management of disruptions when they support the integration of the solution of emergent problems with the solution of spatio-temporal regulation problems over time and that they succeed in this thanks to the articulation work deployed during both their set up and change. Plans and re-planning are carried out following the same principles that ensure the maintenance of their flexibility and margins over time and, with this, their capability to deal with the unexpected. Thus, the articulation work necessary for the plan setup is the element that can make the difference between the realization of a plan as a closed and stable plan and a tool that can adsorb uncertainty, even if up to a certain level.

This means that not only does articulation work help deal with the unexpected "on the spot," but that such articulation work can be crystallized in the form of artifacts, such as plans. Consequently, we cannot conceptualize re-planning as only a consequence of the failure of the plan, as some literature in organization studies does, but as articulation work necessary to make the plan changeable, thereby ensuring its use in the face of the unexpected.

This also means that, if we want to understand how plans maintain their capability to adapt to changing circumstances, we have to look at how they are designed and changed in situated circumstances. In addition, when we look at how the articulation work determines how resources are mobilized, we can understand that the organization's resilience cannot be seen as depending primarily on the level of the accumulated slack resources, as Vogus and Sutcliffe [21] suggested, but in terms of how they are made available.

In summary, instead of conceiving plans as subject to temporary disturbance, we should conceive them as tools that might reduce complexity and uncertainty.

5 Conclusions

Our data indicate that planning might significantly contribute to the maintenance of the organizational adaptive capacity to address changing demands, which happens when—thanks to precise planning strategies—plans are set up to compensate for unexpected events and to be changed when necessary.

Our data show how plans might be designed to adsorb variations and suggest studying how plans support the management of the unexpected trough the study of the articulation work necessary to set them up.

We know that our analysis helps explain how plans might contribute to the anticipation of the unexpected, rather than how they might contribute to the elimination of the unexpected (regarding the need to focus on both of these points, see: [21]). Nevertheless, we think that our work deserves attention for two main reasons. On one hand, it helps focus on how organizations deal with the unexpected they cannot eliminate but at least partially anticipate; on the other hand, it raises the need to focus on the role of artifacts and the processes for their production in the management of the unexpected, not only in terms of the role of individuals' and groups' behavior as—among others—Bechky and Okhuysen [3] indicated.

We think that the analysis of planning reported here contributes to the development of the theory of organizational resilience as Vogus and Sutcliffe [21] hoped for.[9] In particular, we think that the study of planning cannot be excluded from the debate on the role of slack resources or the deployment of existing resources, which is currently ongoing among scholars interested in the development of a theory of organizational resilience (see: [21]). Yet we also think that our study contributes to the understanding of the nature of plans that CSCW scholars are pursuing and we hope that others will follow our attempt as CSCW scholars have the theoretical and methodological tools necessary to do so.

Acknowledgments Thanks to reviewers and to Dave Randall with whom we discussed the role of plans in workplace settings.

References

1. Bardram JE (1997) Plans as situated action: an activity theory approach to workflow systems'. In: Proceedings of ECSCW'97: kluwer academic, Netherlands, pp 17–34
2. Bardram JE, Hansen, TR (2010) Why the plan doesn't hold- a study of situated planning, articulation and coordination work in a surgical ward. In: Quinn KI, Gutwin C, Tang JC (eds). In: Proceedings of the ACM conference on computer supported cooperative work, CSCW 2010, Savannah, Georgia, USA, February 6–10, ACM, pp 331–340
3. Bechky BA, Okhuysen GA (2011) Expecting the unexpected? How swat officers and film crews handle suprises. Acad Manage J 54(2):239–261
4. Bossen C, Markussen R (2010) Infrastructuring and ordering devices in health care: medication plans and practices on a hospital ward. Comput Support Coop Work 19(6):615–637
5. Carassa A (2000) La conoscenza entra in azione. In: Mantovani G (ed) Ergonomia. Il Mulino, Bologna, pp 123–150
6. Cunha MPe, Clegg SR, Kamoche K (2006) Surprise in management and organization: concept, sources and a typology. Br J Manage 17(4):317–329
7. Ferreira P, Wilson JR, Ryan B, Sharples S (2011) Measuring resilience in the planning of rail engineering work. In: Hollnagel E, Pariès J, Woods D, Wreathall J (eds) Resilience engineering in practice. Ashgate, Farnham, pp 145–156
8. Garfinkel H (1967) Studies in ethnomethodology. Prentice Hall, Englewood Cliffs (NJ)
9. Hollnagel E, Woods D, Leveson N (eds) (2006) Resilience engineering. Ashgate, Aldershot
10. Hollnagel E, Pariès J, Woods D, Wreathall J (eds) (2011) Resilience engineering in practice. Ashgate, Farnham
11. McDaniel RR, Driebe DJ (eds) (2005) Uncertainty and surprise in complex systems. Springer, Berlin

---

[9] It is our opinion that studies on wide-scale online interactions during emergency events conducted by Palen and Vieweg [12] should be considered in the study of how social networking might impact organizations' capability to face the unexpected.

12. Palen L, Vieweg S (2008) The emergence of online widescale interaction in unexpected events: assistance, alliance and retreat. In: Proceedings of the 2008 acm conference on computer supported cooperative work, CSCW 2008, San Diego, California, USA, Nov 8–12, 2008, ACM, pp 117–126
13. Randall D, O'Brien J, Rouncefield M, Hughes JA (1996) Organizational memory and CSCW: supporting the 'Mavis' phenomenon. In: Grundy J, Apperley M (eds) Proceedings of the Sixth Australian conference on HCI (OzCHI '96), IEEE, pp 26–35
14. Randall D, Harper R, Rouncefield M (2007) Fieldwork for design. Springer, London
15. Redaelli I, Carassa A (2013) Temporality in planning: the case of the allocation of parking areas for aircrafts. In: Proceedings of the 13th European conference on computer supported cooperative work, ECSCW 2013, 21–25 Sep 2013, Paphos, Cyprus, Springer, London, pp 45–62
16. Schmidt K, Simone C (1996) Coordination mechanisms: towards a conceptual foundation of CSCW systems design. Comput support coop work (CSCW): J Collaborative 5(2–3):155–200
17. Schmidt K (1999) Of maps and scripts: the status of formal constructs in cooperative work. Inf Softw Technol 41(6):319–329
18. Schmidt K (2011) Frail foundations. In: Schmidt K (ed) Cooperative work and coordinative practices. Springer, London, pp 359–389
19. Suchman LA (1987) Plans and situated actions: the problem of human-machine communication. Cambridge University Press, New York
20. Suchman LA (1997) Centres of coordination: a case and some themes. In: Resnick LB, Säljö R, Pontecorvo C, Burge B (eds) Discourse, tools, and reasoning: essays on situated cognition. Springer, Berlin, pp 41–62
21. Vogus TJ, Sutcliffe KM (2007) Organizational resilience: towards a theory and research agenda. In: IEEE international conference on systems, man and cybernetics, ISIC, pp 3418–3422
22. Weick KE (1995) Sensemaking in organizations. Sage, Thousand Oaks
23. Weick KE (2004) Vita contemplativa: mundane poetics: searching for wisdom in organization studies. Organ stud 25(4):653–668
24. Weick KE, Sutcliffe KM (2007) Managing the unexpected. Jossey-Bass, San Francisco
25. Weick KE (2009) Making sense of the organization: the impermanent organization, vol 2. Wiley, Chippenham
26. Weick KE, Putnam T (2009) Organizing for mindfulness. In: Weick KE (2009) Making sense of the organization: the impermanent organization, vol 2. Wiley, Chippenham
27. Whittaker S, Schwartz H (1999) Meetings of the board: the impact of scheduling medium on long term group coordination in software development. Comput Support Coop Work 8(3):175–205
28. Woods DD, Shattuck LG (2000) Distant supervision-local action given the potential for surprise. Cogn Technol Work 2:86–96
29. Woods D (2006) Essential characteristics of resilience. In: Hollnagel E, Woods D, Leveson N (eds) Resilience engineering. Ashgate, Aldershot, pp 21–34
30. Woods D, Hollnagel E (2006) Prologue: resilience engineering concepts. In: Hollnagel E, Woods D, Leveson N (eds) resilience engineering. Ashgate, Aldershot, pp 1–6
31. Woods D, Branlat M (2011) Basic patterns in how adptive systems fail. In: Hollnagel E, Pariès J, Woods D, Wreathall J (eds) Resilience engineering in practice. Ashgate, Farnham, pp 127–143

Supporting Team Coordination on the Ground: Requirements from a Mixed Reality Game

Joel E. Fischer, Wenchao Jiang, Andruid Kerne, Chris Greenhalgh,
Sarvapali D. Ramchurn, Steven Reece, Nadia Pantidi
and Tom Rodden

Abstract We generate requirements for time-critical distributed team support
relevant for domains such as disaster response. We present the Radiation Response
Game to investigate socio-technical issues regarding team coordination. Field
responders in this mixed-reality game use smartphones to coordinate, via text
messaging, GPS, and maps, with headquarters and each other. We conduct
interaction analysis to examine field observations and log data, revealing how
teams achieve local and remote coordination and maintain situational awareness.
We uncover requirements that highlight the role of local coordination, decision-
making resources, geospatial referencing and message handling.

J. E. Fischer (✉) · W. Jiang · C. Greenhalgh · N. Pantidi · T. Rodden
The Mixed Reality Lab, University of Nottingham, Nottingham NG8 1BB, UK
e-mail: jef@cs.nott.ac.uk

W. Jiang
e-mail: wxj@cs.nott.ac.uk

C. Greenhalgh
e-mail: cmg@cs.nott.ac.uk

N. Pantidi
e-mail: nxk@cs.nott.ac.uk

T. Rodden
e-mail: tdr@cs.nott.ac.uk

A. Kerne
Interface Ecology Lab, Texas A&M University, College Station, USA
e-mail: andruid@ecologylab.net

S. D. Ramchurn
Agents, Interaction and Complexity Group, University of Southampton, Southampton SO17
1BJ, UK
e-mail: sdr1@soton.ac.uk

S. Reece
Pattern Analysis and Machine Learning, University of Oxford, Oxford OX1 3PJ, UK
e-mail: reece@robots.ox.ac.uk

C. Rossitto et al. (eds.), *COOP 2014 - Proceedings of the 11th International
Conference on the Design of Cooperative Systems, 27–30 May 2014, Nice (France)*,
DOI: 10.1007/978-3-319-06498-7_4, © Springer International Publishing Switzerland 2014

1 Introduction

Highly coordinated, time-critical collaborative activities, such as disaster response (DR), have recently gained much attention of the collaborative systems community (e.g., [20]). Recent research initiatives at the boundary of Artificial Intelligence and Interactive Systems Design are proposing human-agent collectives (HACs) as a novel approach to designing systems to support such time-critical team coordination, where groups of humans and computational or embodied agents collaborate to achieve a common task.[1] Coordination is essential in such settings so that time critical interdependent activities such as search and rescue can be completed in a timely and satisfactory manner [4]. The critical nature of the DR domain makes it challenging to design and deploy HAC systems 'in the wild'. On the other hand, computational simulations of such scenarios are not only difficult to construct, but the veracity of results may be impossible to verify [26]. In turn, little is known about the design space for HAC systems to support time critical coordination settings such as DR, for example to help responders with spatial task prioritization [22].

What are the challenges and requirements in building systems to support team coordination in such settings? Before we introduce 'smart' agent systems, we need to understand how teams coordinate in time critical settings using communication and situation awareness tools. In order to explore this design space and to generate requirements for technologies to support team coordination, we developed the Radiation Response Game. We adopt a serious mixed-reality games approach to create a setting in which participants experience physical exertion and stress through bodily activity and time pressure, mirroring aspects of a real disaster setting [21]. We use game probes as a complementary approach to gathering system requirements for real-world settings, for example in addition to co-designing with users. Our game probe explores a socio-technical setting in which field responders receive guidance from a central command headquarters ('HQ'), inspired by the concept of the Sector Coordinator in USAR task forces [15]. Participants collaborate to save spatially distributed 'targets' in an area affected by a spreading 'radioactive cloud', both locally, with collocated 'field responders', as well as remotely, with HQ and with distant field responders. Based on interaction analysis of team coordination in the game we generate requirements for technologies to support team coordination in time critical settings.

2 Related Work

We review disaster simulations and games that underpin our mixed-reality games approach, and work on team coordination that underpins our methodology.

---

[1] http://www.orchid.ac.uk/

2.1 Disaster Simulations and Games

Computational simulations, particularly agent-based simulations of disasters, are the predominant approach in the computing literature to predict the consequences of "courses of action" [12], e.g., to model first responder information flow [23], or logistic distribution of emergency relief supplies (Lee et al. 2007).

Limitations of the veracity of computational simulations are manifold. For example, Simonovic highlights that simulations may rely on unrealistic geographical topography, and most importantly, may not account for "human psychosocial characteristics and individual movement, and (…) learning ability" [26]. The impact of emotional and physical responses likely in a disaster, such as stress, fear, exertion or panic [9] remains underaddressed in approaches that rely purely on computational simulation.

One of our work's main objectives is to study interaction and coordination situated in rich and 'messy' real-world socio-technical settings. As it is difficult to deploy technological prototypes in real disasters, game-like simulations have been adopted to study technology interaction in disaster scenarios, for example to prepare first responders for scenarios in which hazardous materials are involved [18]. Abbasi et al. [1] present a study in which locally distributed participants played the role of victims asking for help via social media in a simulated crisis, and participants that played the role of first responders used a coordination system to filter messages and mobilize the appropriate responder teams according to their assigned capabilities. Toups et al. [29] present the design and evaluation of the Team Coordination Game, which teaches participants effective cooperation and— in particular-communication, based on a *zero-fidelity simulation* of team coordination that focuses on distributed cognition in lieu of concrete details, yet draws directly from fire emergency response work practice.

We adopt a *serious-mixed reality games* approach [10] to create a *game probe* that enables studying team coordination, interaction and communication in a real-world disaster scenario whilst providing confidence in the efficacy of behavioural observations. Suspension of disbelief occurs frequently in the play of pervasive or mixed-reality games [27]. Mixed-reality games bridge the physical and the digital [2]. They serve as a vehicle to study distributed interactions across multiple devices and ubiquitous computing environments 'in the wild' [8].

2.2 Team Coordination

Malone and Crowston [19: 361] defines coordination as "the act of managing interdependencies between activities performed to achieve a goal".

In disaster response, team coordination is essential in order that groups of people can carry out interdependent activities together in a timely and satisfactory manner (cf. [4]). Disaster response experts report that "failures in team coordination are the most significant factor in critical emergency response" [29] that can cost human lives. Shared understanding, situation awareness, and alignment of cooperative action through on-going communication are key requirements to enable successful coordination. Convertino et al. [6] design and study a set of tools to support common ground and awareness in emergency management. For our game probe, we study how participants coordinate teams and perform spatially distributed, time critical tasks.

One important characteristic of large-scale disaster is the presence of multiple spatially distributed incidents [5]. To deal with multiple incidents, the disaster response team has to coordinate spatially distributed resources and personnel to carry out operations (e.g. search, rescue and evacuation).

Depending on the proliferation of incidents, response personnel may need to dispatch, deploy and redeploy limited resources. Coordination is required to efficiently allocate limited resources to multiple incidents with temporal and spatial constraints imposed by the nature of disasters.

Mixed-reality games (MRG) share a common set of characteristics with time critical settings, such as disaster response (DR):

- *Bridging the physical and the digital.* Both DR as well as MRGs routinely bridge the physical and the digital as part of their actors' coordination [2]. DR for example makes use of the twitterverse to inform real world response (e.g., [24]).
- *Orchestration.* DR and MRGs are both highly orchestrated activities. Authoring and orchestration tools 'behind the scenes' of an MRG, as well as player interfaces, provide managers, players and spectators with different temporal and spatial views of the game world in order to support the experience [7]. These settings are surprisingly comparable to the 'control room' of a disaster response operation, in their collections of sophisticated technological arrangements to communicate and coordinate real-time information streams, in order to create a holistic view amidst an immersive setting of interest.
- *On-the-ground and online.* In both DR, as well as in MRGs, people on the ground often work with people online to solve a common problem. Sarcevic et al. [24] show how understanding online content can foster understanding of medical coordination challenges in DR on the ground. MRGs often leverage the fact that people on the ground and online have different views of the world, which are turned into different abilities within the game [11].

These key characteristics illustrate the overlap between time-critical coordination in MRGs and DR. This perspective underlies our motivation to explore the approach of studying team coordination through a game probe.

To assess team coordination and performance, Borge et al. [3] analyse interaction, communication and tasks to identify primary team activities. Convertino et al. [6] analyse the turn-taking structure of communication and dialog acts (speech acts) to assess how participating teams use situational awareness tools.

We draw on interaction analysis [16] and message classification based on speech act theory [25] to assess participants' team coordination in the game probe. Methods are detailed further below.

3 The Radiation Response Game

We designed and implemented the Radiation Response Game in order to study team coordination through a location-based, mixed-reality game probe. In the following sections, we describe the game, including grounding the design rationale, game interfaces, iterative design process, and the system architecture.

3.1 Design Rationale

The Radiation Response Game is based on the fictitious scenario of radioactive explosions that create expanding and moving radioactive clouds, which pose a threat to responders on the ground (field responders), and (virtual) targets to be rescued from around the game area. We chose a radiation scenario because unlike disasters that cause physical devastation, radiation poses an 'invisible threat', which creates the need to monitor the environment closely with sensing devices, and to communicate frequently.

Field responders are supported by a centrally located 'headquarters' (HQ) control room, staffed by coordinators. Players exchange messages through an instant messaging style communication system. Messages are broadcast, which means they are visible to all players. While formal response teams tend to use radio to communicate (e.g., [29]), we chose text-based messages for its flexibility to support scenarios with many distributed field responders. Text messaging is a realistic option for increasing the throughput of coordinators severely constrained by time and workload.

We designed core game mechanics to provoke exploration of specific aspects of team coordination. The game mechanics are motivated by real world challenges of resource and task allocation for coordinating spatially distributed resources and personnel to carry out operations [5].

The game's two-tiered organisational structure is derived from real world disaster response organisation and from NIMS [14]. The game's HQ is loosely modelled on sector coordinators, whose role is to manage resources and communications between their assigned teams, and command and coordinate action within their sector [15]. Field responders are modelled on team leaders and members. We ignore this distinction to simplify roles, assignments, and game mechanics.

3.2 Responder Roles and Targets

Each field responder is assigned one of four roles:

 Medic   Firefighter   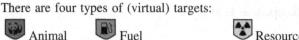 Soldier   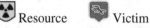 Transporter

There are four types of (virtual) targets:

Animal   Fuel   Resource   Victim

The objective of the field responders is to rescue as many targets as possible by 'carrying' them to a drop off zone. To pick up and carry one of the target objects, two responders with particular appropriate roles are required in immediate proximity to the object. For example, a soldier and a transporter are required to pick up and carry fuel, and a medic and a soldier are required to pick up an animal.

The role-target mapping mechanic requires players to engage in resource coordination. Field responders have to engage in 'agile teaming'—forming, disbanding, relocating and re-forming in teams over the course of the game in order to complete the game objective. This is an example of what Toups et al. [29] call, *information distribution*.

3.3 The Radioactive Cloud

The "cloud" is a danger zone that can incapacitate field responders. It imposes spatial and temporal constraints on task performance and health levels. The cloud is analogous to various spatial phenomena in disasters (e.g. spreading fires, diseases and floods). In order to incentivise communication between HQ and field responders, the spatial position and movement of the cloud is only known to HQ.

3.4 Command-and-Control Structure

The division of responsibility into HQ and field responders simulates a situation where volunteer responders are connected to a simple two level Command-and-control structure, similar to the real-time layer of the existing professional disaster response organizations (e.g., [5]).

3.5 Coordination Interfaces

Field responders are equipped with a 'Mobile Responder App' providing them with sensing and awareness capabilities (see Fig. 1). The app shows a measure of radioactivity (i.e., using a Geiger counter), their 'health level' based on radioactive

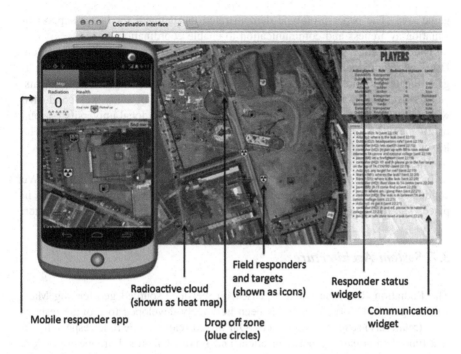

**Field responders
and targets
(shown as icons)**

**Radioactive cloud
(shown as heat map)**

**Responder status
widget**

Mobile responder app

**Drop off zone
(blue circles)**

**Communication
widget**

Fig. 1 Field responders and HQ coordinators have complimentary views of the game terrain (mobile responder app and HQ coordination interface)

exposure, and a GPS-enabled map of the game area with the targets to be collected and the drop off zones for the targets. Icons according to responder roles that additionally have their initials on them can be used to identify individuals. Another tab reveals the messaging widget to broadcast messages to the other field responders, and to headquarters.

HQ is operated by at least two coordinators. They access a browser-based 'coordination interface' that provides an overview of the game area, including real-time information of the players' locations (see Fig. 1). HQ can also broadcast messages to all field responders, and can review the responders' exposure and health levels. Importantly, only headquarters has a view of the radioactive cloud. 'Hotter' zones correspond to higher levels of radioactivity.

3.6 Iterative Design

We briefly describe three cycles of iterative game design and evaluation.

In the first iteration, we used a paper-based prototype to test and refine the core game mechanics. We recruited 12 participants, allocated one of four roles to them, and equipped them only with paper maps with locations of targets. They had to form different kinds of teams to retrieve the different kinds of boxes placed in the game area. The paper prototype demonstrated the demand for better support of situation awareness and communication to enable coordination.

The technology prototype was first tested with users in the second iteration. Users were equipped with the responder Smartphone app to communicate, navigate, locate and pick up targets in teams formed according to role requirements. HQ was staffed by members of the research team. A pilot study was conducted with members of the public that visited an Open Day at a local university. A total of 20 members of the public tested the game in four ad-hoc game trials. The lessons learned in the pilot study revealed problems with user interaction, networking, and game parameter tuning, which we subsequently addressed.

In the third iteration, we improved system stability and interface designs. We conducted a pilot study at the campus of another university, to test the system in place. The full-fledged study we report on here was conducted shortly thereafter.

3.7 System Architecture

The Radiation Response Game is based on the open-sourced geo-fencing Map-Attack[2] game platform, which has been iteratively developed to provide responsive, (relatively) scalable experiences. Our mixed-reality game relies especially on real-time data streaming between client and server. Client-side requests for less dynamic content use HTTP. Frequent events, such as location updates and radiation exposure, are streamed to clients to avoid the overhead of HTTP. In this way, field responders are kept informed in near real-time.

The platform is built using web technologies such as socket.io, node.js, Ruby Sinatra, and the Google Maps API. We built on the existing open source Map-Attack app for Android to develop the Mobile Responder App.

4 Study Design

To explore socio-technical issues around team coordination, we ran two Radiation Response Game sessions, with volunteers recruited from the local university. We describe participants, procedure, session configuration, and methods used to collect and analyse quantitative and qualitative data.

4.1 Participants

Study participants were recruited through posters and emails. A total of 18 participants were recruited (8 female); 7 participated in session A and 11 in session B.

---

[2] http://mapattack.org/

All participants were reimbursed with 15 pounds for 1.5 h of study. The majority of participants were students of the local university.

4.2 Procedure

Upon arrival in the HQ (set up in a meeting room at the local university), participants were briefed and asked to consent to participate. Roles were randomly assigned to all participants (HQ/field responders: firefighter, medic, transporter, soldier). Field responders were provided with a Smartphone; HQ coordinators with a laptop. Game rules and interfaces were introduced, and participants were assisted in setting up their phones and laptop clients. Field responders and HQ coordinators were given 5 min to discuss a common game strategy. All field responders were accompanied to the starting point within the designated game area, about 1 min walk from headquarters.

Once field responders were ready to start, HQ sent a "game start" message. Gameplay commenced for 30 min. A "Game over" message by HQ concluded the game. Field responders returned to HQ for the post-game session.

The post-game session consisted of a questionnaire aimed at collecting participants' feedback on (1) first impressions of the game; (2) usability of the system, and; (3) coordination issues in the game. A group interview was then conducted, before participants were debriefed and dismissed.

4.3 Game Configuration

The size of the game area on the local university campus was 400 by 400 m, without heavy traffic. The terrain of the game area includes grassland, a lake, buildings, roads, and footpaths and lawns. There are two drop off zones and 16 targets. The pilot study showed that this was a challenging, yet not too overwhelming number of targets to collect in a 30 min game session. There were four targets for each of the four target types. The pattern of cloud movement and expansion was the same for both game sessions.

4.4 Methods

We took a mixed methods approach to data collection and analysis. In addition to quantitative questionnaires, a semi-structured group interview was conducted aimed at eliciting important decision points, strategies and the overall decision-making process. Furthermore, five researchers with camcorders recorded the game play. One researcher recorded action in the HQ, and four other researchers each recorded a field responder team.

We developed a log file replay tool to help with data analysis of time stamped system logs that contain a complete record of the game play, including responders' GPS location, their health status and radioactive exposure, messages, cloud location, locations of target objects and task status.

4.4.1 Interaction Analysis of Local Coordination

We focus on the analysis of *local* field responders' interaction to unpack team coordination, including handling of messages sent by HQ. Video recordings of field action were catalogued to identify sequences (episodes) of interest (cf. [13]). Key decision points in teaming and task allocation served to index the episodes. Interesting distinct units of interaction were transcribed and triangulated with log files of relevant game activity for deeper analysis that we present in this paper.

4.4.2 Message Classification

How are remote messages used as a coordination resource? We used speech-act theory and the notion of adjacency pairs in linguistics to classify messages sent between and among responders and HQ.

According to speech act theory, utterances in dialogues can be considered as speech acts from three dimensions. We were primarily concerned with the illocutionary dimension of speech acts. Searle's classification of illocutionary acts [25] is used to categorize messages in the communication system.

5 Results

Here, we present findings from interaction analysis supported by message classification that reveal how team coordination was achieved. Overall, responders rescued 7 and 9 targets in session A and B respectively, out of 16 targets in total per session. Two players were incapacitated in session A, and 1 player was incapacitated in session B. 117 and 70 messages were sent in session A and B, respectively. We used Searle's classification of speech acts to categorize messages (see Table 1). We also add *requests* to the table to categorize all of the messages (Searle does not classify those as speech acts).

We present four episodes to illustrate team coordination. By example of the first episode, we unpack how field responders account for messages from HQ, in particular issues with how directives on task allocation and execution are addressed. An overview shows that directives from HQ are frequently not brought up locally. A further episode demonstrates how field responders instead draw on technological and embodied resources to achieve local coordination, without HQ involvement. Finally, two more examples illustrate how responders routinely employ messages as a resource to support situational awareness.

5.1 Responding to Directives from HQ

We examine how field responders deal with messages from HQ that attempt to allocate tasks and manage task execution (i.e., directives). Classification of messages showed that directives were exclusively sent by HQ, and that they were the most frequent kind of message (Table 1). Directives index (attempted) instances of remote coordination of field responders by HQ. The observed response to messages is critical to understanding relationships between local and remote coordination. The following episode depicts a team of three on their way to pick up fuel. Their path is blocked by radiation. Without a team, firefighter JH (on the left) has just joined soldier KY (on the right), and firefighter D2 who have just been allocated a task in a message by HQ.

KY: ((reading out message)) KY and D2, please walk fast to the junction and quickly return back ((laughs))
D2: Oh is that what we have to do? Ok so we have to run to (2.0) We need to work out where we have to run to first and then get (.) get it back. Which junction is that? If you run to the next (0.5) thing ((points)), and then come back (1.0) that would work (1.0) is it safer to go around?

[The team tries to go around the cloud but is stopped by radiation, realising their target is in the cloud. Meanwhile, D2 has left due to increased exposure.]

KY: So we have to run! [through the radiation]
JH: Do we have to run through the (.) through the radiation? ((looking at map))
KY: Yah this is what the headquarters told us to do ((looking at messages))
JH: I have a terrible feeling thats gonna kill us.
KY: But its gonna be meaningful ((laughs))
JH: We go around this corner, if it gets to half [referring to health] we should probably start running back.

[KY JH begin running into the cloud]

KY: ((yells)) OH OH! It's a hundred! [refers to radiation level]
JH: We are basically in the middle of it! We are basically in the middle of it!
KY: ((shouts)) I'm going back! Get the fuel first! Get the fuel first! Oh no!
JH: We are not prepared for that! I blame our HQ.

[They turn around and run back out of the cloud without the fuel.]

Table 1 Classification of messages (based on speech act theory)

Speech acts	Session A		Session B		Example	Total
	HQ	FR	HQ	FR		
Directives	57	0	32	0	JH pair up with BR to save animal in between TA centre and national college	89 (47 %)
Assertives	25	2	8	4	The leak around geospatial is bigger	39 (20 %)
Expressives	5	0	0	0	Good Job, JJ, TV and RL	5 (2 %)
Declarations	3	0	0	0	NOTICE-TEAM B: NS + TD	3 (1.6 %)
Commissives	0	4	0	4	Ok got it	8 (4 %)
Requests	8	6	1	19	Where's the leak?	34 (18 %)
Unclassified	7		2			9 (5 %)

This episode begins with a message by HQ attempting to help give directions to the target. D2's response to the message is hesitant (is that what we should do?). His following question (which junction is that?) suggests the referent in HQ's message is not understood. They attempt to go around the radiation. They realise their target is in the cloud. They refer back to the message to support their intent to go into the cloud to attempt to save the target (Yah this is what the headquarters told us to do). Having run into the cloud, they refer to the Geiger counter and realise the exposure is too high. Meanwhile, their health is decreasing rapidly. They abandon the task and flee to safety, whilst JH expresses his frustration (We are not prepared for that. I blame our HQ.).

First, the episode shows that geospatial referencing in messages can be problematic. It is unclear to the responders which junction HQ is referencing (and the responders do not ask for clarification), so they revise the route themselves. At the same time, they draw on the messages to justify their entering of the cloud. It does not occur to the responders that HQ allocated the task at an earlier time, before the cloud had covered the target. HQ does not update the responders on the increased danger, or revise their earlier task allocation. When the responder team fails to complete the task, they place blame instead of thinking self-critically.

5.2 Overview: How Field Responders Addressed Task Allocation Messages

Overall, out of the 43 task allocation directives HQ sent, the recipient field responders brought up only 15 messages in conversation in the team. The instances in which task allocation messages were addressed reveal the handling and value of HQ directives in the local coordination. Firstly, out of the 15 task allocation messages responders talked about, they decided to ignore the instructions only once. The responders ignored instructions because they were engaged in another task that they did not want to abandon. Secondly, four HQ instructions to rescue a certain target coincided with the same plan that had already been made locally by the responders. In 10 cases, field responders chose to follow the instructions. However, due to confusion and misunderstanding they failed to follow them correctly six times. In fact, only 2 instances of directives from the HQ led to task completion. For the remaining 14 saved targets, field responders had locally allocated the tasks without HQ.

5.3 Local Coordination Without HQ

As presented, field responders predominantly coordinated teaming and task allocation of targets that were saved without HQ involvement. The following episode illustrates how field responders achieve coordination of teaming and task allocation locally. We join the action as BR and another responder are waiting at the drop-off zone without a compatible teammate, as MF and his teammate join and drop-off their target.

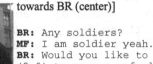

[MF (on the right) and teammate walking towards BR (center)]

BR: Any soldiers?
MF: I am soldier yeah.
BR: Would you like to pair with me?
(2.0) to rescue a fuel
MF: what are you after?
BR: I am a firefighter.
MF: Soldier and firefighter is fuel isn't it?
BR: yeah.
MF: What can we get? (2.0) ((looks at screen)) this one in the center? ((points at screen))
BR: ((glances MF's screen)) I think there are two people going for that. I think we should go for this one ((points at screen)).
MF: We are going to get killed ((both laugh)).

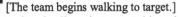

[The team begins walking to target.]

The episode shows how teaming and task allocation are achieved opportunistically between BR and MF, with BR already waiting at the drop-off zone. Field responders also confirmed their opportunistic behaviour in the interview:

Just save the closest target then just pair up and go to the other one [P2]
We just check, with that group, which target we can get. We see on the map to find the closet one we can get. [P4]

BR and MF can then be observed sharing the screen of his device and using the map to identify potential targets. They realise one of them is already being pursued by another team. They agree on another target to pursue. Note that messages do not play a role in this episode. It exemplifies how teaming and task allocation are achieved locally, without consulting HQ.

5.4 Messages as a Resource of Situational Awareness

In the Radiation Response Game, field responders need to be aware of what other responders are doing, where the 'danger zone' is (the cloud), and where it is likely to move. Awareness of each other's actions helps responders avoid conflicts in planning, while awareness of the danger zone is essential to survive. The following episode illustrates how responders use messages as a resource to gain situational awareness.

The episode takes place towards the end of game session B. The radioactive cloud has grown so much that navigation in the game area becomes increasingly difficult. MF is with a group of five responders, two of which are carrying an animal. The cloud is blocking their way towards the drop off zone; they stop.

MF: ((reads message from HQ out loud)) There is another leak around Geospatial. (1.0) Which is Ah: so there's a leak sprung up there. ((points)) Geospatial is like (.) that building right there. They say there is another leak. We should go all the way round (0.5) to the top left one, I think.

MF brings up HQ's message of the new leak, and suggests a route around the new cloud. The group ends up following MF's route suggestion as a result. News of the new cloud, provided by HQ, enables the group to change their route to avoid danger. We commonly observed responders sharing information that provides situational awareness through face-to-face conversation. In the previous example, MF shared the message with a group of responders he was with already. The following example takes place between D2 and his teammate, as they are approached by JH, who is currently without teammate.

JH: Where are you guys heading?
D2: To get the fuel.
JH: Okay. The closest one to you?
D2: I believe so.
JH: Ya okay cuz I think the leak is somewhere near the other one and the army. [referring to building]
D2: Oh (.) which one?
JH: They sent a message saying its between territorial army center.
D2: We are trying to get the one here ((points)).
JH: The closest one. Okay.

Making use of the map as he approaches them, JH asks the others to clarify which fuel they intend to pursue (the closest one to you?). He proceeds to inform the team that the "leak is somewhere near the other one". D2's response (Oh, which one?) suggests they did not know this. In turn, JH elaborates on the location of the cloud, using an anonymous "they" to refer to the source of his information. "They" is likely to refer to HQ as they previously sent a message with the information of the cloud's location. Conversational sharing of important information was a common resource responders employed to achieve and maintain situational awareness. However, requests for information were regularly not reciprocated with a response: out of 14 requests in session A, 8 were not responded upon; and in session B, 14 out of 20 requests were not responded upon.

6 Requirements for Team Coordination Support

We now discuss the requirements for team coordination that emerged from the game and relate them to broader concerns for the design of HAC systems that support team coordination.

The embodied game probe embedded responders in a challenging setting. They needed to communicate effectively to make time critical decisions on teaming and task allocation, both locally in the field as well as remotely through messaging. Field responders physically engage and navigate the environment to perform tasks while maintaining awareness of risk and danger. The data reveals multiple challenges for team coordination involving communication and decision-making.

6.1 Local Decision-making

The study showed that teaming and task allocation were predominantly organised locally among field responders, in an opportunistic, on-the-fly fashion. Despite the fact that headquarters attempted to coordinate task allocation remotely, few of these directives were brought to conversation locally. Only 2 out of 16 tasks that field responders completed were remotely allocated by HQ. Local decision-making needs to be supported by HAC systems that aim to support time-critical team coordination, and need to integrate capabilities to enable team-wide sharing of the local decisions.

6.2 Coordinate Resources

While field responders made decisions on teaming and task allocation in a seemingly ad hoc fashion, game data reveals how field responders draw on resources to achieve situational awareness in order to coordinate successfully.

A common understanding of the location and movement of the radiation cloud was achieved by sharing information from game messages verbally in a local group. Face-to-face talk was an essential resource for relaying information from the Mobile Responder App to teammates, such as radioactive exposure, others' whereabouts, task status, and other monitoring of the broadcast messages. Future HAC systems need to take into account that such *coordinate* resources are likely to be comprised of digital as well as embodied human resources.

6.3 Geospatial Referencing

The results show that geospatial referencing was problematic in various ways, particularly in directive messages sent to the field players. Participants had different levels of knowledge of the campus, which made understanding of landmark references uncertain. Some participants also struggled with making sense of north/south/east/west directions in relation to their current position and orientation. To deal with misunderstandings, players had to ask for clarification via messages or spend valuable time discussing the reference locally in order to understand it. Consistent with the findings of [28], designers need to think carefully about how the presentation layer of HAC systems may be augmented with information that facilitates geospatial referencing (e.g., grids, labelling etc.) to facilitate human in addition to machine readability.

6.4 Freshness of Messages

Problems arose from erroneous instructions or otherwise out-dated messages sent to field responders. In one case HQ sent a message in which two players with non-compatible roles were instructed to team up. This was particularly costly, as the players attempted to team up, and lost valuable time until they realised the game mechanics barred them from forming a team.

As demonstrated in one of the episodes, reading out-dated messages in a dynamically changing environment can contribute to responders taking dangerous actions that they believe to be safe, because they do not realise that the information is out-dated. However, in most cases, recipients managed to identify temporally irrelevant messages, and thus avoided following them.

To reduce confusion about message freshness, HAC systems should address these issues at the UI level, both for responders and for HQ. Develop functionality to flag messages as out-dated or retract incorrect messages. Up-to-date messages are particularly valuable. Thus, our findings support the use of fresh social media as a source of information for disaster response, despite problems that can arise with validation, because crowdsourced information will in many cases provide better coverage than official sources.

6.5 Acknowledgment of Messages

In most cases, field responders did not acknowledge or respond to messages sent by the HQ. This was particularly problematic for directives (task allocation), as task status and field responder compliance often had to be inferred by observing their location updates on the map. This consumed HQ attention, with negative impact on HQ's overall work on state assessment and task planning. Observations in the field suggest that the physical demands (e.g., co-located team movement through terrain at speed) and cognitive demands to maintain situational awareness (e.g., monitoring of radioactivity and messages) are likely factors that explain lack of acknowledgment.

As a result, user interfaces that enable and encourage field responders to quickly acknowledge HQ messages, with minimum cognitive load, should be considered for messaging in HAC systems in such high demand settings. For effective team coordination in disaster response, interface and workflow designs need to factor in cognitive load and task demands for effective information distribution.

7 Conclusions

The objective of the research presented here was to generate requirements for supporting time-critical team coordination. In particular, we focussed on a scenario in which responders coordinate role-based teaming and spatially distributed task allocation and execution using a real-time location and messaging system.

We presented the design and study of the Radiation Response Game as a mixed-reality game probe to investigate challenges for team coordination in a setting in which participants experience both physical strain through bodily activity, and cognitive challenge through time pressure and task complexity. We eschew high-fidelity simulations in favour of mixed-reality game probes as a platform for investigation of concomitant socio-technical issues: handling of mobile devices to communicate and maintain situational awareness (messaging, sensing, interaction, and display) intersect with face-to-face interaction, whilst the physio-cognitive challenges created through game mechanics and environment induce stress. We created a setting that allows exploring requirements to support team coordination of relevance to time-critical coordination domains such as real disaster response.

Findings from interaction analysis of field observations, triangulated with log files, reveal how field responders achieved coordination by drawing on local face-to-face conversation with fellow responders, and situational information provided by the interactive map, the Geiger counter, and the messages sent by HQ. Drawing on these findings, we generated requirements for supporting team coordination, emphasising the roles of local coordination, decision-making resources, geospatial referencing and message handling. These requirements inform future work on building human-centred HAC systems by emphasising the role of human interaction in team coordination in time-critical settings.

Acknowledgments We are grateful for the support by the EPSRC ORCHID project (EP/I011587/1). Thanks to the University of Nottingham's Horizon Digital Economy Research Institute for support provided by a sabbatical grant to the third author.

References

1. Abbasi M-A, Kumar S, Filho JAA, Liu H (2012) Lessons learned in using social media for disaster relief—ASU crisis response game. In: Proceedings of the 5th international conference on social comp, behavioral-cultural modeling and prediction. Springer, Berlin, pp 282–289
2. Benford S, Magerkurth C, Ljungstrand P (2005) Bridging the physical and digital in pervasive gaming. CACM 48(3):54–57
3. Borge M, Ganoe CH, Shih S-I, Carroll JM (2012) Patterns of team processes and breakdowns in information analysis tasks. In: Proceedings of CSCW'12. ACM Press
4. Bradshaw JM, Feltovich PJ, Johnson M (2011) Human-agent interaction. In: Boy GA (ed) The handbook of human-machine interaction: a human-centred design approach. Ashgate Publishing Company, Surrey, pp 283–299
5. Chen R, Sharman R, Rao HR, Upadhyaya SJ (2005) Design principles of coordinated multi-incident emergency response systems. Simulation 3495:177–202
6. Convertino G, Mentis HM, Slavkovic A, Rosson MB, Carroll JM (2011) Supporting common ground and awareness in emergency management planning. ToCHI 18(4):1–34
7. Crabtree A, Benford S, Rodden T, Greenhalgh C, Flintham M, Anastasi R, Drozd A, Adams M, Row-Farr J, Tandavanitj N, Steed A (2004) Orchestrating a mixed reality game 'on the ground'. In: Proceedings of CHI'04. ACM Press, pp 391–398
8. Crabtree A, Benford S, Greenhalgh C, Tennent P, Chalmers M, Brown B (2006) Supporting ethnographic studies of ubiquitous computing in the wild. In: Proceedings of DIS'06. ACM Press, pp 60–69
9. Drury J, Cocking C, Reicher S (2009) Everyone for themselves? A comparative study of crowd solidarity among emergency survivors. Brit J Soc Psychol Brit Psychol Soc 48(3):487–506
10. Fischer JE, Flintham M, Price D, Goulding J, Pantidi N, Rodden T (2012) Serious mixed reality games. In: Mixed reality games. Workshop at ACM CSCW 2012
11. Flintham M, Benford S, Anastasi R, Hemmings T, Crabtree A, Greenhalgh C, Tandavanitj N, Adams M, Row-Farr J (2003) Where on-line meets on the streets: experiences with mobile mixed reality games. In: Proceedings of CHI'03. ACM Press, pp 569–576
12. Hawe GI, Coates G, Wilson DT, Crouch RS (2012) Agent-based simulation for large-scale emergency response. ACM Comput Surv 45(1):1–51
13. Heath C, Hindmarsh J, Luff P (2010) Video in qualitative research. Sage, New York
14. Homeland Security (2008) National Incident Management System (NIMS)
15. INSARAG (International Search and Rescue Advisory Group) (2012) Assessment, search and coordination methodologies. INSARAG Technical Note, United Nations
16. Jordan B, Henderson A (1995) Interaction analysis: foundations and practice. J Learn Sci 4(1):39–103
17. Lee YM, Ghosh S, Ettl M (2009) Simulating distribution of emergency relief supplies for disaster response operations. In: Proceedings of winter simulation conference, pp 2797–2808
18. Losh E (2007) The birth of the virtual clinic. In: Proceedings of the 2007 ACM SIGGRAPH symposium on video games—Sandbox'07. ACM Press, pp 73–80
19. Malone TW, Crowston K (1990) What is coordination theory and how can it help design cooperative work systems? In: Proceedings of CSCW'90. ACM Press, pp 357–370
20. Mendonça D, Jefferson T, Harrald J (2007) Collaborative adhocracies and mix-and-match technologies in emergency management. Commun ACM 50(3):44–49

21. Pan American Health Organization (2001) Stresss management in disasters, Washington, DC
22. Ramchurn S, Polukarov M, Farinelli A (2010) Coalition formation with spatial and temporal constraints. In: Proceedings of AAMAS'10, IFAAMAS
23. Robinson CD, Brown DE (2005) First responder information flow simulation: a tool for technology assessment, pp 919–925
24. Sarcevic A, Palen L, White J, Starbird K, Bagdouri M, Anderson K (2012) "Beacons of hope" in decentralized coordination. In: Proceedings of CSCW'12. ACM Press, pp 47–56
25. Searle JR (1975) A taxonomy of illocutionary acts. In: Günderson K (ed) Language, mind, and knowledge. University of Minneapolis Press, Minneapolis, pp 344–369
26. Simonovic SP (2009) Systems approach to management of disasters: methods and applications. In: Disaster prevention and management, vol 20. Wiley, New York
27. Stenros J, Montola M, Waern A (2009) Pervasive game design strategies. Pervasive games: theories and design. Elsevier, New York
28. Toups ZO, Kerne A, Hamilton W (2009) Game design principles for engaging cooperative play: core mechanics and interfaces for non-mimetic simulation of fire emergency response. In: Proceedings of ACM SIGGRAPH games 2009. ACM Press, pp 71–78
29. Toups ZO, Kerne A, Hamilton WA (2011) The team coordination game. ACM Trans Comput-Hum Interact 18(4):1–37

Nothing Free About Free Market

Eli Larsen and Gunnar Ellingsen

Abstract This section sheds light on the effects of the different strategies that Norwegian authorities have adopted to enroll users and vendors in the task of establishing electronic prescriptions as a new national routine service. The case description highlights how stakeholders responded when the authorities needed integration between the new service and the information systems that physicians use in their daily work, namely the electronic patient record (EPR). The strategy that focused mainly on the vendors made it difficult to mobilize the users and the authorities staged themselves as the "real" customers of the project. An integration unit that the authorities developed was not embedded robustly with the existing infrastructure. The EPR is the most important information system that the health care institution uses and through the years this system has evolved to its improved current standard. In a country like Norway, with very few vendors, the EPR market is a very small and dedicated one. Any influence of this market from a powerful vendor, like the authorities, will affect the market in a significant way. The authorities that play a role in this market should not underestimate the negative effect that might result from a change in the EPRs' functionality, even if the intentions are solely positive for all stakeholders.

E. Larsen (✉)
Telemedicine and E-Health Research Group, Norwegian Centre for Telemedicine,
Tromsø, Norway
e-mail: eli.larsen@telemed.no

G. Ellingsen
Telemedicine and E-Health Research Group, University of Tromsø, Tromsø, Norway
e-mail: gunnar.Ellingsen@uit.no

C. Rossitto et al. (eds.), *COOP 2014 - Proceedings of the 11th International*
Conference on the Design of Cooperative Systems, 27–30 May 2014, Nice (France),
DOI: 10.1007/978-3-319-06498-7_5, © Springer International Publishing Switzerland 2014

1 Introduction

A highly functional health care information infrastructure is crucial for any Western government. The potential of information and communication technology (ICT) to improve quality and cut costs is particularly appealing as it offers a technological solution to the exponentially increasing public demands and limited funding that face most public sector health systems [11, 15, 17, 21]. Consequently, several countries have plans for, or are engaged in, developing national information infrastructures [16, 17, 23, 24].

However, the experiences so far suggest that it is a significant challenge to realize all the government-run programs [20]. Several studies have warned that many of these projects are a waste of funding and resources [2, 12] and may cause dissatisfaction among health professionals [1, 7]. Thus there are obvious reasons to believe that the scale and complexity of these projects tend to overlook organizational aspects and fail to deal with challenges emerging from local practices [4]. For instance, Greenhalgh et al. [7] report that in "failed" EPR projects, the designers typically missed the peculiarities of the local practices and produced artifacts that fitted poorly with the situated nature of clinical practice and the needs of the users.

The health authorities have basically two means to implement their policy: *funding* or *regulations*. Given the size of these projects, either of these might have significant impact on a carefully balanced health care market containing vendors and customers (private and public). To give one vendor preference in a development project (i.e., through funding) might disturb this delicate balance. Similarly, to implement heavy-handed regulative measures might have unexpected consequence for local practices.

Accordingly, we agree with Greenhalgh et al. [7] that we need to invest more research in the health care domain where we elaborate on how national ICT programs in healthcare are governed and how the key stakeholders are mobilized and integrated into these projects. Given that many national ICT programs span several years, it becomes necessary to also invest research of a longitudinal character that may better shed light on the nature of these projects, as per Pollock and Williams [19]. With this as our point of departure, we ask the following research questions: What useful strategies exist for the authorities to run national ICT projects in health care? How can the stakeholders be mobilized? And what is the effect of these strategies on the health care market and the targeted local practices?

For our theoretical base we draw on Information Infrastructure as it represents a powerful tool to analyze development of information systems that are interconnected in large coherent networks consisting of technical and non-technical elements.

Empirically, we conducted a longitudinal study of a national ICT project in Norway that aimed to establish electronic prescriptions as a routine service and replace the existing paper-based prescriptions. The project, ePrescription, was run by the Directorate of Health and depended on the involvement of many key stakeholders such as physicians, pharmacists, vendors, and public institutions.

The rest of the paper is organized as follows. First we elaborate on the theoretical foundation for the paper, followed by the description of the method. Then we present the case, which is subdivided into three time periods. In the discussion, we analyze how the project struggled to mobilize the healthcare users and their vendors and how the authorities ultimately positioned themselves as actors in the market. The conclusion rounds off this section.

2 Theoretical Framing

The broad scope of Western health care services and the high degree of specialization make healthcare a huge and complex sector that to a large extent is a national concern. Accordingly, using electronic services co-operatively between healthcare institutions has become a political issue [22]. Many countries develop their own specific strategies on how to deal with the challenges, however, many of the measures have so far lacked the hoped-for effects [1, 8]. It has been demonstrated that strong national governance with a large budget available is not synonymous with success. In fact, an example from England shows the opposite [8].

The recurring efforts to establish national ICT infrastructures in health care call for an analytical approach that can encompass the scale and complexity of these projects. In Greenhalgh's [8] analysis of the process in realizing the Summary Care Record (SCR), she underscores that:

> The most striking overall characteristic of the SCR and HealthSpace programmes was their scale and complexity. They can be thought of as emerging from a heterogeneous socio-technical network with multiple interlocking sub-networks.

In this regard, we find the concept of information infrastructure particularly promising. It is both a way to characterize empirically large-scale projects as well as a way to approach these phenomena analytically. An information infrastructure is typically stretched across space and time: it is shaped and used across many different locales and endures over long periods (decades rather than years). Hanseth and Lyytinen [10] define some of its key characteristics as:

1. Interconnectedness of numerous modules/systems like software applications, hardware items, and networks as well as e.g., regulations and strategies.
2. Dynamic portfolios of systems, which are not "designed" but evolve continually, as growth and innovation expand them.
3. Installed base of existing systems and work practices that is seldom created from scratch; rather, it grows from existing practices. The installed base exists both within organizations and within clusters of organizations.
4. Interdependencies of global measures and local work practices.

From an information infrastructure perspective, the local and the global constitute each other and interact continuously through a tensional relationship. This implies that local practices are enabled by large-scale or global technologies, which indicates that new electronic services have to adapt to the existing structure and will therefore face what Martin et al. [14] characterizes as the "design problem". The "design problem" becomes concerned not so much with the simple creation of new technical artefacts or the "computerization" and replacement of work practices, as with the effective integration of computer systems with existing and developing localized work practices. Creating services for health care will therefore most certainly imply a design that affects users in local practices as well as the existing infrastructural tools they are using: EPRs, laboratory systems, health networks, etc., i.e., the installed bases [18].

In the context of national healthcare information infrastructures, a particular challenge is related to the mobilization and coordination of multiple stakeholders in the design and implementation process. This was the focus of Aanestad and Jensen's [1] study of two Danish EPR projects, one initiated nationally and one initiated in local practice. The national project failed to realize an interoperable EPR while in comparison the small, local solution gradually scaled to become a nationwide solution for the sharing of EPR information. The national project followed an approach that required wide and long-term commitment from the stakeholders; however, it did not manage to achieve and maintain wide-enough stakeholder mobilization over a sufficiently long period of time.

Aanestad and Jensen [1] argue that the implementation strategy must deal with the multiple stakeholders involved and be able to mobilize and coordinate them and propose the notion of a modular implementation strategy. Such a strategy, made possible by appropriate modularity of the solution, allows the implementation to be organized in a way that does not require an initial widespread and long-term commitment from stakeholders. They suggest that solutions that provide immediate use value, by offering generic solutions to perceived practical problems, balance the stakeholders' costs and benefits, and solve a problem with minimal external dependencies. Such solutions can avoid some of the dilemmas often associated with large-scale information infrastructures. We can easily agree with Aanestad and Jensen [1]. However, in addition we also emphasize some characteristics of Western health care markets in smaller countries: here the market is relatively stable and limited. For instance, EPRs are technologies that customers seldom replace. In addition, the number of vendors tends also to be relatively small and each of them tends to address a well-defined market segment. This makes the vendors of EPRs gatekeepers in the development of electronic cooperation between healthcare systems [12], as well as other new functionalities. Any large-scale change that is to be implemented therefore requires a careful mobilization of these stakeholders.

No doubt this carefully balanced market situation will be transformed by the active role of governments. Callon [3] stressed that the market is a process in which calculative agencies oppose one another, without resorting to physical violence, to reach an acceptable compromise in the form of a contract and/or price.

The active role of governments implies that they also position themselves as actors in strategic, design, and implementation processes, which ultimately will affect the EPR market.

In addition, we should not forget that the ability to maneuver in this setting is shaped by a gradually evolving installed base [18]. Healthcare is a sector in which artefacts, information systems, work practices, and user's experience have over a number of decades created a tangled and complex web. This suggests that new technologies and organizational changes must pay careful attention to existing practices and technologies. From an information infrastructure perspective, then, it is crucial to build on and exploit the existing installed base rather than oppose it.

3 Method

The empirical data stem from a case study conducted in Norway where the authorities aimed to establish electronic prescriptions as a routine service.

An interpretative approach [25] was used to get a better understanding of the mechanisms influencing the development of electronic co-operation tools in the healthcare sector. The empirical material was gathered through a longitudinal process that started in 2004 and is ongoing in Norway. The following data input has been gathered:

- Strategic documents for ICT in Norwegian healthcare
- Project descriptions and evaluation reports
- 40 semi-structured interviews with key actors involved in governmental projects, representatives from the public authorities, and GPs
- 80 h of non-participant observation in weeks 1 and 3 of pilot testing

The interviews lasted between 15 and 160 min and with a few exceptions, took place in a location with which the interviewee was professionally affiliated. The information from all data, except interview data, has been plotted in a timetable in order to understand the background for the different events and how these have interfered with each other. The information from the interviews has been transcribed and sorted into themes. By combing all information elements through a hermeneutic circle process, it has been possible to understand the viewpoints of the different actors and how they affected the overall progress in the field.

The first author of the paper has in the period 2004–2009 been involved in a project adjoining the project under analysis. The projects coincided in such a way that significant information was detected concerning the author's own project. From 2009, the author has dedicated the scientific work to the national ICT project in Norwegian healthcare in general, and in particular to the ePrescription project.

4 Background

During the last decades some of the authorities' strategic work has resulted in the development of national information infrastructural services in Norwegian healthcare. The country's political parties have basically supported the chosen strategies and the theme has not been controversial. Different kinds of communication between hospitals, laboratories, general practitioners (GPs), and home care services have been at the center of this development.

In 1997, the North Norwegian Health Care Network (NNHN) was established as a project. The aim was to set up a dedicated ICT network for the exchange of information between health care institutions in the Northern Norwegian health region. The Health Directorate and Ministry of Health funded the project and decided that the other four health regions should do the same. In 2003, when the Norwegian Health Care network was established, the North Norwegian Health Care Network was merged into this organization. The Network offered secured connection to healthcare institutions and became a success.

In 2005, the Elin Project was established to contribute to developing user-friendly solutions for electronic health care-related communications for GPs. The project was partly financed by the authorities and has played a major role in the development of user requirements for ICT solutions supporting communication between GPs and other health care institutions, in such areas as exchange of admission and discharge letters, lab orders and reports, doctor's declarations, prescriptions, as well as communication with patients. The requirements have been implemented in solutions that have diffused to some extent, although a bit slower than expected. The Elin Project planned to develop electronic prescriptions, but experienced that the job was too complicated and expensive.

In 2005, the authorities tried to stimulate the sector by establishing a number of so-called Lighthouse Projects. A common factor for these projects was that they were led by local authorities and were supposed to establish electronic services between hospitals and community sectors. The Directorate of Health financed the public part of these projects, while the vendors that would develop the different services were not financed by the Lighthouse funds. These projects failed to deliver the intended results.

5 The Electronic Prescription Project

Along with the projects elaborated above, ePrescription was also a government-run project, which was started in 2005 and is still running.

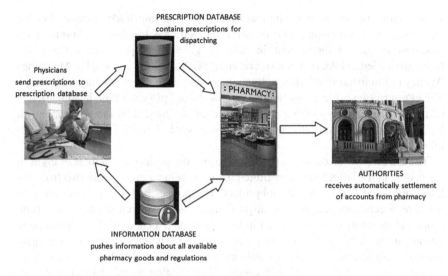

Fig. 1 The ePrescription service

5.1 "We Will Satisfy You All" (2005–2008)

The Norwegian Ministry of Health and Care Service initiated a project in 2005 to establish electronic prescriptions that would replace paper prescriptions. The most pressing argument was that the authorities needed a copy of all refundable prescriptions that were handled by the pharmacies. For this reason, the Office of the Auditor General encouraged the government to the triggering point for the ePrescription project, and funding for it was embedded in the state budget. However, the authorities play a limited role in the prescription value chain and were therefore dependent on main actors like the physicians, pharmacies, and vendors.

The ePrescription project was supposed to create a service that replaced paper prescriptions with electronic prescriptions and was expected to offer advantages to all the involved actors (see Fig. 1). The pharmacies would be able to handle the prescription faster and with less error to their customers and they could send electronic documentation to the National Insurance Administration. The GPs were expected to spend less time writing prescriptions and could therefore increase the quality of the prescription. The patient could have his or her prescription safely distributed to any pharmacy. Additionally, the authorities could distribute regulation changes more effectively.

It was intended for the electronic prescription service to be developed as an integrated part of the information system that already existed in the pharmacies and the GP offices. The development process of the ePrescription project started by establishing a project comprising four subprojects with representatives from all user groups affected by the new service. In addition to the project management by the Directorate of Health, the project included the main actors in the prescription value chain: the Norwegian Pharmaceutical Society (the trade organization for pharmacies in Norway and their owners), the National Insurance Administration (responsible for reimbursement in case of government-paid medication), the Norwegian Medical Association (representing GPs) and the Norwegian Medicines Agency (administering all information concerning available medicine in Norway). The ePrescription project represented a top-managed project within healthcare in a relatively small country with a sector that is mostly funded by the government. It had a budget of 30 million euro, which was several times larger than similar initiatives.

The Directorate hired several advisers to run the project and a total of eight to ten people in the Directorate constituted the management group, with two from the Directorate and two from each subproject. The project had, from an outside perspective, a generous budget at its disposal and was considered the most important project in its domain. It was rooted in the top management as well as the strategy documents in all the institutions that were involved. The high profile of the project caused considerable pressure to deliver results within deadlines. The project management focused on doing a good job in relation to the budget and time schedule.

The project group consisting of all main actors in the prescription value chain was created in a traditional spirit of democratic thinking: everybody that would use the system should influence the functionality. Specifications were stated as the result of a prolonged negotiation process between the user groups. This process was a round table negotiation discussing functionality on a principle level. Even though the representatives were familiar with the work practice in their respective domains, the specification was prepared without a close cooperation with users having day-to-day clinical experience in an iterative development process. The project planned to devise a service that would work across several organizational borders and was dependent on integration with existing information systems, similar to those in pharmacies, GPs, and hospitals. The vendors that would implement the service received a specification list with very few possibilities to cooperate with their users in order to create the service.

5.2 "Show Me the Money" (2005–2008)

The ePrescription project had a generous budget, but the money was for running the public part of the project. This became a serious problem for the subproject focusing on the physicians that would prescribe the medication, because they needed the ePrescription service to be integrated with the electronic patient record and were in this way dependent on cooperation with the EPR vendors. After some discussions between key stakeholders in the project and the project owner, some money was released that could be used to enroll the EPR vendors. In 2006, the six major vendors of EPRs were invited to participate in the project. However, government money and project plans from the Directorate of Health promising

benefits for all actors were not sufficient to mobilize the users, particularly physicians who could put pressure on their vendors. This lukewarm attitude among the
users made mobilization of the central stakeholders difficult.

The three vendors of the hospital-based EPRs demanded more precise
requirement specifications before they were willing to sign a contract, and the
development of electronic prescriptions in the hospital sector was put on hold. In
addition, the hospital sector was not willing to participate in the ePrescription
project. As a result, the Ministry of Health had to order National ICT, an institution
responsible for coordinating ICT-related initiatives in the hospital sector, to come
up with specifications from their domain.

> It is difficult to participate and come up with requirements because the medication is so
> tangled up in the rest of the activities in a hospital. Additionally, we understand that it will
> take years and years before this service is realized, and that is kind of demotivating.
> [Project participant from the hospital sector]

Two of the three vendors providing systems to GPs declined to participate
because they were in the process of developing a new EPR, and their development
teams were limited and therefore not able to cope with the amount of work that the
ePrescription functionality would require. Only the third vendor (with a market
share of about 75 % of the GP market) agreed to develop a pilot version. The
vendor was able to negotiate a payment that corresponded to 50 % of the stipu-
lated development costs.

5.3 A Living Hell (2008)

The biggest vendor within the GP sector did develop the ePrescription functionality. However, this vendor spent much more time than projected, partly because
the interface between the EPR and ePrescription was not defined in a sufficient
way. The ePrescription program was integrated with a completely new EPR that
the vendor developed, but unfortunately the vendor did not have time to test it
sufficiently in-house. The new EPR, including the ePrescription functionality, was
installed in May 2008 in a small municipality with only one medical office and one
pharmacy. The new EPR was very different from the one that the medical office
had used for years. Additionally, the new EPR had so many bugs that it was in no
way suited for professional use. These issues contributed to problems for the pilot
users, who received too much experimental software to test in a busy working
environment. The ePrescription pilot was characterized as a "living hell" by one
of the GPs that was part of the pilot and was frequently referred to as such in the
Norwegian media. Not surprisingly, the pilot was aborted after only three months.
The vendor had to discard most of the ePrescription work, because the ePrescription project had defined a new model for the service.

The authorities realized that they needed additional means (i.e., regulations) to
put the service into use. Since the beginning of the project, a parallel activity was

underway, namely changing the law so that establishment of a database with prescriptions could be carried out in a legal way. The new regulation became effective in April 2008, and thus was applicable even before the pilot took place. One of the paragraphs stated that it was mandatory for the physicians to use the ePrescription service when all the necessary technology was installed.

5.4 "Phoenix Rises from the Ashes" (2008–2009)

After the catastrophic pilot test of the ePrescription system in 2008, the project faced a situation in which the only vendor willing to provide integrated ePrescription functionality had failed. The project was about to come to a complete halt. In order to tempt the other two EPR vendors in the GP market, payment for integration was increased dramatically. In this way, the ePrescription project was able to mobilize a small but important part of the market:

> Only a few days after the termination of the pilot in Stor-Elvdal, we received a telephone call from the Directorate – this time with a payment that met our needs. We have never experienced a public project with an offer like that! We were able to hire two extra programmers and were able to carry out the integration within a relatively short while. [EPR vendor]

The vendors were forced to follow the framing defined by the project group. For instance, it was required that the physicians use smartcard every time they prescribe medication, and the possibilities for free text were kept to a minimum. The vendors were able to focus on developing the ePrescription client within a relatively short time. Good payment (unsurprisingly) sped up the integration process. The vendors received feedback during the development period by users who were invited to come and test the new function, and in May 2010, a new pilot test took place with a more positive result. However, the signing process was more bothersome than it had been previously and typically took longer to complete. Instead of signing a stack of paper prescriptions that the secretaries had prepared (prescriptions that were ordered via phone), the doctor had to sign one by one in the EPR. Each prescription demanded multiple tasks, requiring doctors to work an additional half-hour or more each day. The two EPR vendors were however able to fine-tune their functionality to a level that was acceptable to customers.

Then the electronic prescriptions were sent directly from the GPs' offices to the ePrescription database, and the patients did not pay anything for the receipts. This differed from the process that was established for the paper receipts, because the patients had had to pay for these in the GPs' offices. The patients who only renewed prescriptions by phone no longer needed to fetch the paper prescription and pay for it at the doctor's office. With the electronic prescription, they could buy their medications at the pharmacy without any charges connected to the prescription documentation. As a result, the workload for secretaries in the GPs' offices was greatly reduced.

Fig. 2 Prescription issues distribution according to sectors

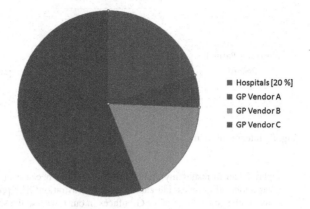

- Hospitals [20 %]
- GP Vendor A
- GP Vendor B
- GP Vendor C

5.5 *"Escaping Earth" (2010–2013)*

From the outset, the ePrescription project promised benefits for all the users of the ePrescription service, including the GPs. In order to fulfill this, integration between the EPR and the ePrescription service was essential. However, only the two smallest EPR vendors included the ePrescription functionality in their EPRs, which served a total of approximately 25 % of the EPR market among GPs (red and green sectors in Fig. 2). Considering that the hospital sector prescribes 20 % of prescriptions (blue sector in Fig. 2) and the largest GP vendor (violet sector in Fig. 2) had not provided a functional solution, the project was far from the goal of having all prescriptions processed electronically by 2010.

Due to the project's slow progress, there needed to be some speeding up of the process, and the strategy chosen was to develop a unit that could be implemented in the EPR, but at the same time lacking crucial integration with the hospitals' and the most sold GPs' EPR systems. A small international company got the job of developing the integration unit. This implied that the EPR vendors were "out of the loop" and were not expected to include ePrescription functionality in their EPRs. An integration unit was supposed to play along with the EPR with minimal effort by the EPR vendors. It was put out on an invitation to tender, and a foreign software company received the programming contract. The foreign company delivered according to the tender and the integration unit was offered to the EPR vendors. The vendor of the hospital EPRs was wary of using the free ePrescription module in combination with its EPRs and therefore decided to develop its own integration solution. However, the biggest EPR vendor for the GP practices decided to bundle the integration unit with its EPRs, and distributed the package to its customers according to a roll-out plan outlined by the Directorate of Health. The GPs who started using the EPR system with the integration unit experienced extensive problems. Not only was the prescription processing bothersome, but the entire EPR also became slow and unpredictable, as one GP recalled:

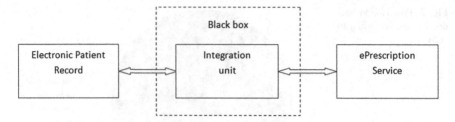

Fig. 3 Integration unit

> Today I had to restart my computer several times because my EPR crashed. Each reset takes about 10 minutes and causes a lot of frustration! The prescribing process is extremely cumbersome. Nine of 12 GP offices in our town use the same EPR system as we do, and they have all had similar experiences. Since we started to send electronic prescriptions, my workday has become longer, and I am not able to treat patients who drop in without an appointment, as I was able to earlier on. The EPR vendor support centre does not answer when we try to get in touch; I've heard that they have a latency of two hours. We have decided to hold back the annual fee until this problem has been solved. [GP]

Some GP offices experienced the changes in their workday to be so bothersome that they reported the situation as a risk for their patients.

The integration unit (see Fig. 3) had predefined input and output and appeared as a black box [13]. Due to this black box, the EPR vendor was not able to fine-tune the functionality between the EPR and the ePrescription service. Since an independent company had developed the unit, it did not have obligations to any adjustments of the software when the contract was completed. This implied that by delivering the integration unit bundled with the EPR, the EPR vendor became "responsible" for the total product portfolio. The EPR vendor experienced a lot of criticism and all objections were directed against the EPR system and the ePrescription service.

5.6 Benefits Are "in the Eye of the Beholder" (2012)

In November 2012, 90 % of all GP offices in Norway were technically able to send electronic prescriptions. This meant that they were connected to the Norwegian Health Network and had an EPR with ePrescription functionality. However, only 60 % actually used the ePrescription service, meaning that approximately half of the Norwegian GPs sent prescriptions electronically at that time. According to a Benefit Plan published in November 2012 by the Directorate of Health, the responsibility to achieve benefits and reduce the negative impact rests on each individual player.

Via the ePrescription project, the authorities have been able to receive an electronic copy of the required prescriptions, which are sent directly into the authorities' information system for further processing, in line with the preliminary goal. In comparison, the physicians did not receive more efficient handling, as the process of signing and sending electronic prescriptions took longer than the paper-based routines. For the GPs that used the free ePrescription integration unit, the working day became considerably longer. Some of the workload in the medical offices was shifted from the secretaries to the physicians due to the new pre-scription process. Some of the physicians express that the service was a huge step in the right direction, but overall, they were not particularly happy with the solution:

> I really can't see what the ePrescription has provided to me in a positive way. Functions, like for instance interaction check, were included in our EPR before we started to send the prescriptions electronically. The ones who are really happy about it are our patients because they get the prescription free without paying anything![GP]

6 Discussion

6.1 A Difficult Mobilization of Stakeholders

Creating a service to work across several institutional borders proved difficult, and ran into several design problems [14]. According to Hanseth and Lyytinen [10], the solution must persuade the initial users by itself, through targeting their needs and solving their problems in a way that does not assume a complete solution or a large user base, i.e., scalability, extension, and completeness of the solution should come later. However, such an approach is difficult when several heterogeneous user groups are supposed to interact simultaneously on the same service. Thus, the dilemma is to decide where to start development of a service involving multiple dependencies between several actors. For instance, a physician prescribing med-ication is dependent on a product catalog that shows which medication is available in the pharmacies and where the authorities pay some of the medication expenses. The physicians must also know the current regulations that state what kind of diseases give the patient the right to partial support. Similarly, the pharmacy needs to know whether the prescribing doctor has a license to prescribe the medication and must ensure that the patient has a legal right to partial support and is dependent on the reimbursement from the authorities because the patient only pays a certain part of the medication price. A service that would satisfy all these interdepen-dencies is difficult to design from a local practice, because it is dependent on development in a corresponding local practice in several other institutions, simultaneously. To overcome the "where to start" dilemma, the project chose to include all actors and develop the service from a top-down perspective. In order to mobilize, this was the least preferred strategy according to the information infrastructure literature.

The case shows that mobilizing the vendors was considered most important. While the project plan predicted benefits for all, no effort to mobilize the users was carried out. The first time the physicians were able to give the project any feedback was during the failed pilot. In this setting, the physicians were not able to sort out ePrescription functionality from the unfinished electronic patient records they struggled with. Thus, the pilot test in no way created any mobilization; rather, it accomplished the opposite.

If we were to follow the outlined strategy of Aanestad and Jensen [1], the project could have started with a module implementation strategy in order to create mobilization among the users. For instance, a starting point could be to distribute regulations to the physicians concerning reimbursement of medication expenses, followed by electronic applications and electronic answers to the applications. Distribution of the product range could also have been a separate module that is possible to develop separately. These modules might have created ideas that could have further identified added values for the users in the next phase. Such a strategy might have created a self-reinforcing/bootstrapping effect [9] that would achieve the necessary mobilization.

6.2 The "Real" Customer in the Market

The political philosophy that has been dominant in Western countries over the last decades is that the authorities shall ensure a free market that will be controlled by the customer, and by this principle, the product that is offered will be improved according to the customer's request [5, 6]. At the same time, the authorities have two ways of influencing the development of ICT in healthcare: through regulations and through funding [12], which will inevitably interact with a free market policy.

These philosophies pull in different directions. The free market philosophy leaves it up to the customers and vendors to steer the development, while regulations intend to push the sector in the directions that the authorities want, and the funding philosophy is somewhere in between. If the authorities in some way have interests in developing a service and pay the EPR vendors to do so, they clearly move away from the free market principle and become key players themselves [3].

The free market was the philosophy that influenced the ePrescription project from the outset, because the authorities founded only the project group itself and public actors (like the Norwegian Medicines Agency), but not the private vendors. The idea was that the customers would demand electronic prescriptions, and in this way push the vendors to deliver what was requested. EPR vendors sell and support a product that would be used by personnel in healthcare and serve as one of the most essential ICT systems in a contemporary healthcare institution. Developing new functionality in the EPR is a weighing of costs and benefits between the effort that must be made to develop the new functionality and the opportunities to defend the investment [12]. In practice, however, the EPR vendors did not experience this demand from their customers and were therefore not willing to develop any ePrescription functionality without payment from the authorities. Due to the lukewarm stance from the vendors, and indirectly from their customers, the authorities had to go even further by paying more money to the EPR vendors and paying for development of the integration unit offered to the EPR vendors that had not implemented the ePrescription functionality. By funding the EPR vendors to such an extent, the authorities staged themselves as the "real" customers of ePrescription.

6.3 Engaging with an Increasingly More Complex Installed Base

A key concept in the information infrastructure literature is that of the installed base and the necessity of cultivating it in an evolving process. In the following section, we analyze how this has not been taken into account in the ePrescription project. The development within Norwegian healthcare has during the last decades resulted in a complex installed base (see the background review). For instance, GPs are able to send electronic referrals to and receive discharge letters from the hospital; sick leaves and financial settlements are sent to the authorities; and laboratory orders and replies are communicated with laboratories. A new service has to find its place in this large-scale evolving information infrastructure.

Previously there was no way to interpret that the authorities had departed from the strategy of carefully cultivating the installed base. However, the decision to commission the integration unit implied a completely new strategy wherein the new technology was totally dismantled from the installed base. This proved to be fatal. The new unit was not embedded robustly with the existing infrastructure, the vendor or its policy of updating the software.

In information infrastructural terms, it was difficult for the users to see the various components apart from each other. Accordingly, when the GPs experienced the EPR becoming slow and difficult to work with, their dissatisfaction was directed against the EPR vendor, who found that their former popularity was replaced with frustration and mistrust. In this case, the integration had been kept on a strictly technical level—input signals and output signals were as prescribed. However, equally as important are all the socio-technical practices around a technology that has evolved over time.

7 Conclusions

The key analytical points of our study can be summarized as follows: First, a strategy that focused mainly on the vendors made it difficult to mobilize the users. The vendors' focus was dragged away from their customers' needs to the needs of the authorities, namely electronic copies of prescriptions for reimbursement purposes. Second, by funding the EPR vendors to the extent that they did in the ePrescription project, the authorities staged themselves as the "real" customers of the project. Hence, they acted opposite to the philosophy of user-driven development of information systems. Third, the integration unit that the authorities developed was not embedded robustly with the existing infrastructure, and here the authorities acted opposite to their former established strategies.

In sum, the EPR is the most important information system that the health care institution uses. These systems have been evolving through years of improvement. In a country like Norway, with very few vendors, the EPR market is a very small and dedicated one. Any influence of this market from a powerful customer, like the authorities, will affect the market in a significant way. The authorities that play a role in this market should not underestimate the negative effect that might be a result of a change in the EPRs' functionality, even if the intentions are solely positive for all stakeholders.

An early hands-on experience is crucial for realizing good and adapted functionality in the EPR. Users should be able at an early stage to see how the functionality plays along with their existing work practices, and they should also be able to give feedback during the development process in such a way that the new functionality can offer added value to the users. This is difficult to accomplish when it comes to inter-organizational services, for instance in the case of the ePrescription project. However, by breaking down a service into smaller modules, the effects are easier to see. The need for the project could have started with a module implementation strategy in order to create mobilization among the users.

References

1. Aanestad M, Jensen TB (2011) Building nation-wide information infrastructures in healthcare through modular implementation strategies. J Strateg Inf Syst 20(2):161–176
2. BBC News (2013) NHS IT system one of 'worst fiascos ever', say MPs. From http://www.bbc.co.uk/news/uk-politics-24130684
3. Callon M (1998) The laws of the markets. Sociological review monograph
4. Ellingsen G, Monteiro E (2005) The slight surprise of integration. Designing ubiquitous information environments: socio-technical issues and challenges. Springer, Berlin, pp 261–274
5. Friedman M, Friedman RD (2002) Capitalism and freedom. University of Chicago Press, Chicago
6. Gordon C (ed) (1991) Governmental rationality: an introduction. The foucault effect studies in governmentality. University of Chicago Press, Chicago
7. Greenhalgh T, Potts H, Wong G, Bark P, Swinglehurst D (2009) Tensions and paradoxes in electronic patient record research: a systematic literature review using the meta narrative method. Milbank Q 87(4):729–788
8. Greenhalgh T, Stramer K, Bratan T, Byrne E, Russell J, Potts HWW (2010) Adoption and non-adoption of a shared electronic summary record in England: a mixed-method case study. BMJ 341:c4564
9. Hanseth O, Aanestad M (2003) Design as bootstrapping. On the evolution of ICT networks in health care. Methods Inf Med 42(4):384–391

10. Hanseth O, Lyytinen K (2010) Design theory for dynamic complexity in information infrastructures: the case of building internet. J Inf Technol 25(1):1–19
11. Larsen E, Ellingsen G (2010) Facing the Lernaean Hydra: the nature of large-scale integration projects in healthcare. In: Scandinavian information systems research, pp 93–110
12. Larsen E, Mydske P (2013) Developing electronic cooperation tools: a case from Norwegian health care. Interactive J Med Res 2(1):e9–e9
13. Latour B (1987) Science in action: how to follow scientists and engineers through society. Harvard University Press, Cambridge
14. Martin D, Mariani J, Rouncefield M (2007) Managing integration work in an NHS electronic patient record (EPR) project. Health Inf J 13(1):47–56
15. Mundy D, Chadwick DW (2004) Electronic transmission of prescriptions: towards realising the dream. Int J Electron Healthc 1(1):112–125
16. NEHTA (2009) Strategic plan, Australia. From http://www.nehta.gov.au/about-us/strategy
17. Nictiz (2010) From https://www.nictiz.nl/
18. Pedersen R, Meum T, Ellingsen G (2012) Nursing terminologies as evolving large-scale information infrastructures. Scand J Inf Syst 24(1):55–82
19. Pollock N, Williams R (2010) E-infrastructures: How do we know and understand them? Strategic ethnography and the biography of artefacts. Comput Support Coop Work (CSCW) 19(6):521–556
20. Rodríguez C, Pozzebon M (2006) A paradoxical world: exploring the discursive construction of collaboration in a competitive institutional context. In: APROS 11: Asia-Pacific researchers in organization studies: 11th international colloquium, Melbourne, Australia, Asia-Pacific Researchers in Organisation Studies, 4–7 Dec 2005
21. Salmivalli L (2006) Governing the implementation of a complex information systems network:-the case of finnish electronic prescription. In: ACIS 2006 proceedings, p 55
22. Stroetmann KA, Artmann J, Stroetmann VN, Whitehousee D (2011) European countries on their journey towards national eHealth infrastructures. In: European commission DG information society and media ICT for health unit
23. Swedish Social Department (2010) Nationell eHelsa. From http://www.regeringen.se/sb/d/14914/a/148429
24. The Scottish Government (2010) The healthcare quality strategy for NHSScotland. From http://www.scotland.gov.uk/Resource/Doc/311667/0098354.pdf
25. Walsham G (1995) Interpretive case studies in IS research: nature and method. Eur J Inf Syst 4:74–81

Relation Work in Collocated and Distributed Collaboration

Lars Rune Christensen, Rasmus Eskild Jensen
and Pernille Bjørn

Abstract Creating social ties are important for collaborative work; however, in geographically distributed organizations e.g. global software development, making social ties requires extra work: Relation work. We find that characteristics of relation work as based upon shared history and experiences, emergent in personal and often humorous situations. Relation work is intertwined with other activities such as articulation work and it is rhythmic by following the work patterns of the participants. By comparing how relation work is conducted in collocated and geographically distributed settings we in this paper identify basic differences in relation work. Whereas collocated relation work is spontaneous, place-centric, and yet mobile, relation work in a distributed setting is semi-spontaneous, technology-mediated, and requires extra efforts.

1 Introduction

Social ties are important for the development of trust [18], commitment [23], and common ground [26] in collaboration. Nevertheless, several studies have demonstrated that creating trust [7] or mutual knowledge [12] in geographically

L. R. Christensen
Aalborg University, Aalborg, Denmark
e-mail: lrc@learning.aau.dk

R. E. Jensen · P. Bjørn (✉)
IT University of Copenhagen, Copenhagen, Denmark
e-mail: pbra@itu.dk

R. E. Jensen
e-mail: raej@itu.dk

P. Bjørn
University of California, Irvine, CA, USA

C. Rossitto et al. (eds.), *COOP 2014 - Proceedings of the 11th International
Conference on the Design of Cooperative Systems, 27–30 May 2014, Nice (France)*,
DOI: 10.1007/978-3-319-06498-7_6, © Springer International Publishing Switzerland 2014

distributed collaboration is difficult and dependent upon how people perceive their remote counterpart and act accordantly [10]. Creating and maintaining social ties is a significant challenge for globally distributed actors [20, 26], yet it is crucial for any kind of long-term collaboration in complex projects [27]. Social ties are positively associated with successful collaboration in globally distributed projects [21], where e.g. distributed actors in global software development, must create and maintain socio-technical connections across geographical, temporal, organizational, and cultural discontinuities [30]. Unfortunately, we know little about the work required to establish social ties within globally distributed organizations and much less about the role information technologies have in accomplishing such work.

Relation work is the work involved in creating and maintaining socio-technical relations within geographically distributed collaboration [4], and as such suggest a fruitful approach to understand the creation of social ties. In this paper, we examine how relation work is accomplished in practice by investigating the empirical data from an ethnographic study of global software development practices between IT developers in Denmark and the Philippines. We describe how relation work is conducted between participants located at the same geographical site, as well as how relation work is conducted between participants working at remote sites. Comparing ethnographically collocated and distributed settings is an useful approach to bring out the pertinent aspects of what makes collaboration function [25]. By comparing these two types of relation work as it is accomplished within the same global organization, we are able to identify more generic conceptualizations of relation work as well as distinguish between the two types of relation work as it is enacted in collocated and in distributed settings.

The paper is structured as follows. First, we present the theoretical framing of the paper, including the concept of relation work. Second, we describe the research setting and methods. Third, we present the comparative analysis of the collocated and distributed relation work, and fourth we discuss the general characteristics of relation work before finally offering our conclusion.

2 Relation Work

Global software development practice has been a long time interests for the field of CSCW [3, 11] and we know that knowledge management [1, 19], commitment and transparency [30], coordination [15], and trust [7] are important for such collaboration. Social relation matters within distributed work [13], and people, who voluntarily contribute their knowledge to others experiences an increase in their personal professional reputation [33]. It takes netWORK to engage in social ties across organizational communities [24], however while netWORK describe the work of creating social ties within communities, it is *not* concerned with the everyday practices of collaboration and the creation of social ties across collaborators in collocated and geographically distributed situations. Relation work is the work required to create technical and social connections that are critical for the everyday interaction within organizations [4]. The concept of relation work is based on observations of engineers working in a distributed setting who, as part of their practice, make an effort to make socio-technical connections across spatial, temporal, organizational, and societal discontinuities [2, p. 139]. *Our interest* in relation work is to zoom in and study how it unfolds in concrete work practices (not in terms of networks), which allows us to consider relation work in settings such as open office spaces, hallways, meeting rooms, at coffee machines, in parking lots, via email, telephone, videoconferences, instant messaging, Web 2.0, etc. Thus, this concept of relation work allows for a broader analysis of how relation work is performed in various contexts and settings, and with different tools.

The concept of relation work may be seen as a complement to the well-known concept of articulation work (see [31]); however, the distinctions between the two are significant. Collaboration entails work and extra activities of articulation work [29]. In this way, both articulation work and relation work constitute extra work. But whereas articulation work "refers to the specifics of putting together tasks, task sequences, tasks clusters—even aligning larger units such as lines of work and subprojects—in the service of work flow" [32, p. 164], relation work refers to the work required to enact social ties as well as technical infrastructure between participants. Strauss [32] posits the concept of articulation work as part of a theory of action that stresses the on-going efforts of actors to accomplish their tasks and goals in interaction with other actors. This is in opposition to a means-end view of action, where a linear process between start and end points is assumed. Strauss argues that the complexity within which action takes place, and the contingencies that most often arise, require an actor to continuously adjust and readjust his or her actions. Hence, action in its practice is a continuous readjustment of envisioned courses of action rather than a straight line from start to end. When we move to considering several cooperating actors in a distributed setting, the process of continuous readjustment is further complicated by the fact that actors may occupy different geographical settings, different time zones, and different organizational units. Making connections between cooperative actors under such circumstances *is an achievement* that we conceptualize as relation work. Relation work may be what forges the social and technical bonds between distributed actors that allow them to do other work, such as articulation work or software development.

The concept of relation work, as used in this study, is mainly concerned, then, with the achievement of connections between multiple distributed actors, and it can be seen as the relational aspect of a multi-site work trajectory. Relation work might be viewed as the relational aspect of articulation work, but we argue it is a complementary concept. In articulation work, communication is done to achieve agreement as to who does what, where, and when, whereas relation work is done to achieve socio-technical connections at a certain point in time for the purpose of facilitating multi-site cooperation.

3 Research Method

Investigating relation work as it is accomplished in global software development we examined the data we have collected from an ethnographic inquiry [8] within one organization in the period between December 2010 and Fall 2013. The data collection took form of a workplace study [28] of a particular organization, which was one out of five organizations studied as part of the larger NexGSD project (nexgsd.org). The empirical work reported upon here focuses on one case of global software development in the organization GlobalSoft. The setting for our fieldwork was a medium-sized software development company working with an offshoring model where the main activities were situated in Copenhagen, Denmark, and with an offshore software development department in Manila, Philippines.

Our empirical data sources comprise a mixture of interviews and observations. We investigated the organizational work practices in GlobalSoft applying a combination of interviews, observations, and workshops. In total, all three authors (initially we have one additional research assistant helping to collect data) together conducted 25 audio-recorded interviews (19 in Denmark, 9 in the Philippines) lasting 30–60 min and 4 workshops (2 in Denmark and 2 in the Philippines). Employees from all organizational levels took part, allowing us to compare perceptions of the corporate vice president with those of the junior developers. Observations were made in Manila for approximately 4 months in four periods (December 2010, July 2011, November 2011, and January 2012), and in Copenhagen over a period of 12 months (September 2011–October 2012). In addition, we also made screen capture of the distributed work over a period of one whole workday (counting both time zones) across several of the developers machines. All observations focused on cooperative work practices and technology use within the team.

4 Relation Work in Global Software Development

The reasons, which initially lead us to focus on relation work in the global software development case, was how the developers themselves pointed to how relation work was both significant and crucial for the success of the collaborative efforts. Our interview transcripts and fieldwork notes are full of the actors' own references to the significance of personal ties, bonds of friendship, camaraderie, solidarity, and team spirit. Several developers explained the need for creating social ties as a process of moving away from the dichotomy of "us" and "them", towards a common "we". The ideal situation as perceived from the practitioners' point of view is a situation where, for example, the project managers have such a close connection with the distributed participants that they are not afraid to let down their guards, show vulnerability, and ask for advice. As one project manager explained:

> The situations where the collaboration works well are when the project leaders are experienced and are not afraid of calling the Philippines to say for instance: 'I do not know everything yet, but what is your opinion?' I mean, include them [the Pilipino employees] in the project as if they where sitting right next to you, as a colleague. (Interview, project manager Copenhagen)

However, one thing is to state the need for social ties, another thing is to understand the work, which goes into creating social ties. In the following we dive into how relation work unfolds in various settings, collocated as well as distributed.

4.1 Collocated Relation Work

Water coolers and coffee machines are perhaps the archetypal locations for relation work in office buildings. There is even an informal expression—"water cooler chat"—that refers to the type of relaxed conversations *or* relation work that takes place among office workers in the communal area in which such a dispenser is located. A hot topic around the "water cooler" may be, for example, the company's outsourcing strategy, the latest iPhone, sports, politics, or reflections on the state of a particularly challenging global project and the exchange of experiences from such a project. In our fieldwork we observed informal conversations involving each of these topics in communal areas of the company, such as parking lots, staircases, lunchrooms, and hallways.

A common feature of such chat spurred by spontaneous encounters is that it is carried out in an off-the-record atmosphere in a personal and often confidential tone. It is, as with all relation work in the social sphere, directed toward the other actors as individuals, as human beings. Note that such spontaneous relation work in communal areas of an office building is mostly reserved for collocated actors, and one of the challenges of global project groups is precisely that they do not have such opportunities. Open office spaces were ubiquitous in the office environments in the company's locales in both Copenhagen and Manila. In such open office spaces it is possible to see and observe one another, and more to the point, it is possible to engage in relation work across the room. This organizational setup very much support relation work, as was noted in our observation notes:

> In Copenhagen the project team members are situated close to one another in an open office space. The desk that I have been allotted is placed there, too. From my seat I can see and hear conversations between project members going on at almost all the desks, and the volume level is fairly high. The external tester is having a chat with the new test manager about some new work assignments. The person next to me is talking about non-work related issues. (Observation, Denmark)

What is worth noting in this context is how the physical setting facilitates relation work, by access provided by the open office space and the colocation and close proximity it provides. In a setting such as an open office space, the collocated actors may walk to up to a fellow worker's desk or enter conversations and discussions that are audible in the room. It does not take a lot of analysis to see that relation work among distributed team members is not enabled in the same manner. Collocation matters.

Although the above example is from Copenhagen, the same type of seamless work and relation work was also observed at the company's Manila location, which also makes use of large open office spaces. In addition, there was another interesting way that relation work was conducted at the Manila location, namely via the use of instant messaging (IM). In contrast to the relation work based on walking around described above, in Manila the actors often remained seated at their desks and used instant messaging to communicate. In the Manila office instant messaging between collocated actors is used a lot and is viewed as the preferred interaction locally. When asked what IM is used for, the actors in Manila explained that IM is used to copy-paste strings of code for others to comment on or review; IM is used as an archive of old conversations that can be recaptured in order to solve present problems; IM is used to create awareness of new tasks assigned to specific developers; and IM is a social tool used for personal remarks, jokes and friendly banter. What is particularly pertinent here is that because IM is the preferred interaction, it also means that IM becomes the preferred interaction for conducting relation work, since relation work and work-related activities are intertwined. We note that this is a good example of the emergent nature and seamless integration of relation work with other work activities. The irony is that a tool that may be thought of as enabling communication between distributed actors is the preferred tool for communication, and with that, relation work, among actors collocated in an open office space, in this case, in Manila. The reason to why the developers in Manila tended to prefer IM as a medium for relation work could have something to do with the fact that the developers in Manila primarily was junior developers and as such was used to apply such technologies in everyday practice. The developers at the Danish location involved in the global setup were all senior developers with 13–14 years of experience and did not have the same perspective on IM as a tool for relation work. In general they prefer face-to-face interaction with their collocated colleagues.

Collocated relation work also takes place in connection to meetings. *Before* or *after* a meeting actors may walk the hallways to and from the meeting room and use this opportunity to exchange views and chat about the weather, family, or other small-talk topics. *During* meetings the actors may turn their attention away from the main conversations of the meeting, for example, away from the videoconference screen, and engage in sidebar conversations with colleagues seated near by. Such sidebar conversations are rarely possible among distributed actors in a videoconference meeting as the videoconferencing equipment would make the sidebar conversations audible to everyone—which goes against the very nature of sidebar conversations. Additionally, opportunities for relation work also occur during unexpected interruptions of the meeting in progress. Consider this example:

> The project manager in Copenhagen has scheduled an evaluation meeting with some of the key people on the project in Manila. The videoconferencing room was not the one they had originally scheduled, but the other one was occupied. The project leader makes the call, but he is unable to connect to the Manila office. The employees in Manila are waiting in a meeting room, but they cannot contact them. After 5 missed calls and still no connection, the project leader tries to make a call from his laptop, but that also fails. The meeting is now ten minutes late and there has still been no contact with the Manila office. The delay creates an opportunity for conversations among the people in the room, all sorts of topics, large and small, work related and non-work related, are discussed (field note).

This incident shows how technical infrastructure malfunctions can disturb a meeting; it also shows how delays may support local relation work. When technology fails to work it creates a break in the normal flow of work where collocated actors may engage in relation work. This is not to say that delays caused by technical malfunctions are only used for relation work—work-related talk also emerges. However, it was because of the disruption that the spontaneous opportunity for relation work occurred, and it is only a local opportunity—globally the relation work was impossible. Often we found that the official closure of meetings became very abrupt of the distributed setting (the technology is shut down), whereas the collocated meeting continues in small discussions—following up on work-related issues such as the economy, but also on non-work related matters. Note how the rhythm of relation work is choreographed with the patterns of the actors' practice (e.g., before, during, and after meetings) and how the physical setting plays an important part.

In sum, we may say that colocation in various forms provides ample opportunity for relation work, opportunities that are not provided as generously in the distributed arena. That is, many of the opportune settings for relation work are exclusive to collocated settings. Water coolers in communal areas, open office spaces, hallways, and meeting rooms are settings that are not easily reproduced remotely.

4.2 Distributed Relation Work

Although distributed actors are undersupplied with settings for relation work and the spontaneous opportunities for it that follow—and, as a consequence, are struggling with relation work—relation work do exist in the distributed arena. Lacking the opportunities for communication and interaction associated with physical proximity, distributed actors are reliant on a combination of information and communication technologies such as email, telephones, voice over IP (VoIP), social media, and IM. Common to all of these communication tools is that they are used for communication concerning work tasks as well as for relation work. It is fair to say that most communication involves a component of relation work. Consider the exchange via instant messaging between two software testers, one located in Copenhagen and the other situated in Manila (see Fig. 1).

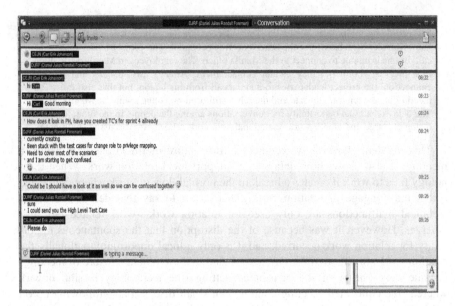

Fig. 1 Instant messaging exchange between two distributed actors (fictitious names are inserted for purposes of anonymity). It is important to notice that the developers in Manila tend to have American sounding names and as such our choice of fictitious names reflect this tendency

Note the empathy and solidarity expressed as Carl texts "could be I should have a look at it as well so we can be confused together;-)" as a reply to Daniel stating his confusion in connection to a complex set of test cases. It is quite evident from this and many examples like it that relation work is part of the communication about work tasks routinely carried out by the distributed actors on a daily basis. Some are also connected via social media such as Facebook and LinkedIn. However, there are limits to this kind of relation work; according to our data, the distributed actors often feel estranged from each other despite the abundance of communication tools at their disposal in the initial stages of our study. However, interestingly, towards the end of our study this had changed for particular participants. We believe that this change is associated with the development of the closely coupled collaboration over time (period between 2010–2013), which made the participants from both site to develop a shared history, and thus engage "spontaneous" communication through daily or weekly videoconference meetings. However initially, it was very difficult for the participants to engage in relation work.

Relation work among the distributed actors did occur during videoconference meetings. However, compared with collocated meetings, where it often manifests as sidebar discussions, relation work takes different form in videoconferences. The broadcast nature of contemporary videoconferencing equipment goes against or contradicts the personalized nature of relation work as it emerges in sidebar discussions. However, there are exceptions and cases where the broadcast nature of videoconference technology is exploited for the purposes of relation work. Consider the following example:

> In a videoconference with people in Copenhagen and Manila, they were discussing how the project had been executed. Suddenly, one of the IT-architects in Manila accidentally drops his pen, which he had been playing with during the meeting. He fumbles with the pen so it looks like he is throwing it toward the camera and at the people located in Copenhagen. The project manager in Copenhagen simulates the same sequence and throws his own pen toward the camera, and then he says, 'You can't hit us even when you are trying', and people laugh on both sides. (Observation, Denmark)

Thus, the videoconferencing technology supports a specific kind of relation work. With the exception of such creative (and rare) examples, relation work in videoconference meetings between distributed actors is curbed by the lack of technology support for the sort of sidebar conversations. The significant challenges associated with making a connection in a videoconference meeting may lead to awkward situations and the actors exhibiting a detached stance toward each other, unless if they have manage to create a routine practice through conducting frequent video meetings over time. In the end of our study it was clear that the key people in the project had developed more close bonds and routine practices in terms of how to execute meetings. This meant that the participants no longer had awkwardness of the distributed meetings, and especially during the testing phase in summer and Fall 2012 where agenda-less meetings were executed on a daily basis, the interaction across sites provide an opportunity for relation work. Interestingly, these daily meetings included spontaneous interaction and mentioning of smaller and larger aspects, which was going on at the different site, e.g. the mentioning if a developer was sick that day.

In sum, compared to collocated actors, it takes time to fully develop a work environment where distributed actors can perform relation work in a technology-mediated setting, since the participants needs to develop work practices across sites. Before such practices have developed opportunities for relation work is few.

5 Characteristics of Collocated and Distributed Relation Work

The results outlined above have implications for how we can characterize relation work as it is accomplished distributed and collocated. The main challenge is how to support relation work in a *distributed* setting, through organizational practices and technologies.

Seen from the practitioners' point of view, there are significant challenges associated with conducting relation work in a team where the individual team members are distributed, since the lack of proximity has a tendency to decouple the team members and presents a barrier to engaging in typical relation work activities such as small talk, spontaneous conversations, humor, and gossip. The barrier is partly a physical one, or more precisely, the lack of a physical space for relation work to unfold in makes it hard to perform these activities for the distributed team members. Typically, relation work is location-based; thus, without collocated places such as lunch tables, kitchens, hallways, and parking lots the physical collocation cannot structure relation work. As social beings, we behave differently in different places, and the physical proximity for relation work is simply missing for the distributed team members.

In the empirical data, we identified how relation work was conducted differently distributed and collocated. *Collocated relation work* tends to *spontaneously* emerge in situations, where the participants interact without pre-determined time and location. These situations are typically during coffee breaks, at the water cooler, or when meeting accidentally at the staircase or in hallways. In some cases, spontaneous relation work also happens when people move around, as in walk n' talk or in elevators. This type of local relation work situation has in prior work been labeled as water cooler talk [34], and it is not surprising that these situations are conducive to relation work. What is interesting is that this type of relation work is place-centric, since it happens in particular places, while being mobile, since people move around. As such, the combination of place and mobility becomes an interesting challenge if we are to think about creating organizational practices and technology supporting such work.

Now, if we turn to the *distributed execution of relation work*, the conditions for such work are very different. First, it is clear that people will not accidentally meet physically in the hallways or in the coffee room without technology mediation or particular prescribed organizational practices. In this way, relation work in distributed situations is more semi-spontaneous, since it does require particular initiative from an individual to be set in motion. However, when technologies such as IM are turned on, it does create the opportunity for remote participants to spontaneously ping the other party—but only if particular conditions are present, such as online communication tools and people's willingness to engage with their remote colleagues. In another study of distributed software development, we found that it was quite problematic that some of the participants at one of the locations refused to engage in IM conversations with the remote participants because it was disrupting the work [22]. In this way, awareness technologies [16] or social translucence technologies [15] could be said to support the distributed execution of relation work, since they will provide opportunities for making the work of remote participants visibly available for others to monitor and then guide people into situations where relation work can take place. For example, by knowing who is doing what and when at the remote location it becomes possible for participants to act accordantly, creating accountability [5].

However, because technologies will not automatically by themselves lead to relation work, it is critical that the organizational practices also stipulate support for relation work. For example, in GlobalSoft a so-called 'live-link' was created between the Danish and Philippines site such that an online image was projected from a Danish coffee machine into the Philippine kitchen at all times, and vice versa.

However, observing the interaction across sites over a long time period, it became clear that no spontaneous relation work or any other interaction occurred. This 'window of opportunity' for relation work did not make relation work happen remotely. For example, at most times the image in the Philippines projected an empty space with a coffee machine and maybe a cleaning person, due to the time difference across the sites. This observation suggests that the reliance on technology alone to facilitate relation work based upon the place-centric metaphor from the local setting does not work in a distributed setting. Thus, we need different conceptual foundations than place-based interaction [2, 17] for technology supporting relation work in the distributed setting. The question is; how do we make a window of opportunity for distributed relation work across geography as well as time zones?

Examining the empirical data on relation work in the distributed setting, it becomes clear that relation work is often intertwined with work-related communication (see the example from the IM conversation, from the screen capture session). These examples typically present very short exchanges, and they often emerge during scheduled collaborative activities, such as video meetings, where participants are already technologically connected. Without such technologies, the basic conditions for relation work to emerge are non-existent, since distributed relation is dependent upon technology. However, distributed relation work tends to end abruptly since the technology supporting it might suddenly shut down. Compared with local relation work, here relation work tends to fill out the sudden breakdowns and disruptions of technology by creating unplanned pauses in the ongoing collaboration, leaving participants a space for unstructured interaction. This observation would suggest that the organizational practice supporting relation work I remote setting is about creating open space for interaction supported by technology where participants can engage frequently in a less-structured manner, providing opportunities for small, unplanned encounters. This was what we saw e.g. in the daily agenda-less meetings, which emerged over time in our study. The transformation over time might be seen as a technology alignment process [6], where participants engaged in continuous iterative and reflective activities, which in the end emerged as a new technology-mediated situation where participants were able to collaborate, including engaging in relation work. We might say that what makes the opportunities for relation work in a distributed setting concerns the participants ability to create technology-in-use practices [9] and thus transform their engagement to foster closely-couple work despite the challenges of geographical distribution.

We have now shown the differences in relation work executed locally and globally; however, we also found similarities across the different types. These similarities are the more generic characteristics of relation work. In both situations, relation work is based on shared experiences and history. For example, in several incidents participants from the case referred to social events (dinners while travelling, pizza parties, gaming event, etc.) in their relation work. The reference to the shared history might be a small sentence within in a longer work-related discussion or a theme in itself during a disruption of a video meeting. The shared history served as a common ground [26] and made it possible for the participants to interact more smoothly, which also decreased participants' perception of distance [10]. A more general characteristic of relation work is that it is personal and often humorous. One example we noted was when the Philippine developer was playing with the pen during the video meeting and it looked like he was throwing it against that Danish participants. This incident became a humorous shared experience, which then could be brought up in new situations, creating stronger social ties among the participants. The humorous situations, such as referring during a client meeting to everyone sitting with their laptops as a LAN-party, or the 'Bar', are all part of the relation work created both locally and globally. Also, relation work has rhythmic patterns in the sense that it is executed in the situations depending on the work patterns of the participants. The organizational practices where the participants have daily short video meeting provide the space for relation work on top of the work-related interaction. Also, participants' coffee-drinking or the-drinking behaviors form a pattern for relation work at particular times, namely the breaks during the day. However, typically these will more support the collocated relation work.

To summarize, collocated relation work is spontaneous, place-centric, and yet mobile, while distributed relation work is semi-spontaneous, technology-mediated, and requires extra work in terms of creating the technical infrastructure making interaction possible. The general characteristics of relation concern a shared history and experiences and personal and often humorous content. Relation work is typically intertwined with other activities, such as articulation work, and it is rhythmic since participants' work patterns create particular opportunities for relation work.

Addressing the design challenge for what makes relation work technologies, which potentially may improve the relations and social ties among globally distributed actors, requires careful consideration of the differences between the collocated and the distributed, since relation work technologies should not necessarily be based on the notion that we want to resemble the collocated situations. Distributed work has different conditions, and we must design with these special conditions in mind yet still keep the basic characteristics of the work we want to support at the center of attention. In addition, we must include re-thinking the distributed organizational practices to support relation work, since technology alone cannot solve the issues.

We might ask ourselves why relation work is important for how we organize the work in distributed software development. What might we expect relation work in a distributed setting to accomplish that we could not do before? To answer this question we will return to one difficult challenge for globally distributed work, namely sub-group dynamics [13]. When people collaborate they have a tendency to create sub-groups, which in some situations is counterproductive for the collaboration. In particular, if the groups consist of participants who fall into several overlapping categories, the sub-groups have a tendency to be overemphasized negatively. For example, in the GlobalSoft case, an obvious category is that of nationality (Danish or Philippine). Another category that often emerges within the collaboration is junior versus senior developer, and since all Danes within this project are senior developers and most Philippine team members are junior developers, the overlap of these categories with the categories of nationality risk creating dichotomies such as 'we'/'them,' which was also explained to us by the participants. Now, by creating enabling conditions for engaging in distributed relation work, we would argue that the participants (Philippine as well as Danish) will experience their counterparts as individuals who do not fall into rigorously inescapable categories related to their nationality, but instead as culturally complex persons who share common interests, which can create a foundation for strong collaboration and innovation. We would argue that remotely well-executed relation work is critical for the organizational setup in offshoring situations, and information systems play an immensely important role for such situations.

6 Conclusion

Studying the collaborative work practices within distributed software development, we have focused on the work required by closely coupled teams to create and maintain social ties despite the geographical dispersion, making it possible for them to engage with complex interdependent work tasks: We have studied *relation work* in distributed software development. We found that relation work is conducted differently in the collocated and the distributed setting, and that it is accomplished differently in scheduled or emergent situations, and we propose a characterization of the differences and similarities in relation work.

We argue that by creating enabling opportunities for distributed relation work in terms of technology support as well as organizational practices, global companies can reduce the risk of unwanted sub-group dynamics across distributed sites. Reducing sub-group dynamics based on oversimplified categorizations (e.g., nationality) of people's behaviors, we will increase the opportunities for closely couple collaboration and create the possibility for innovative practices based on participants' different perspectives on the same issues. Our characterization of relation work can be used to inform managers how to create enabling conditions (for organizational practices and technology use) for relation work remotely as well as collocated.

Acknowledgements This research has been funded by the Danish Agency for Science, Technology and Innovation under the project "Next Generation Technology for Global Software Development", #10-092313.

References

1. Avram G, Bannon L, Bowers J, Sheehan A (2009) Bridging, patching and keeping the work flowing: defect resolution in distributed software development. Comput Support Coop Work Int J 18:477–507
2. Bjørn P (2011) Co-constructing globally collaborative spaces and places: an ethnographic study of how globally distributed engineers handle planning practice. In: Scandinavian conference information systems SCIS. Springer, Turku, Finland

3. Bjørn P, Bardram J, Avram G, Bannon L, Boden A, Redmiles D, Souza C, Wulf V (2014) Global software development in a CSCW perspective. Workshop paper in computer supported cooperative work and social computing (CSCW), ACM, Baltimore, USA

4. Bjørn P, Christensen LR (2011) Relation work: creating socio-technical connections in global engineering. In: European conference on computer supported cooperative work (ECSCW). Kluwer Academic, Aarhus, Denmark, pp 133–152

5. Bjørn P, Ngwenyama O (2009) Virtual team collaboration: building shared meaning, resolving breakdowns and creating translucence. Inf Syst J 19(3):227–253

6. Bjørn P, Ngwenyama O (2010) Technology alignment: a new area in virtual team research. IEEE Trans Prof Commun 53(4):382–400

7. Boden A, Nett B, Wulf V (2009) Trust and social capital: revisiting an offshoring failure story of a small German software company. In: European conference computer supported cooperative work (ECSCW'09), H.T. Ina Wagner, Ellen Balka, Carla Simone (ed.), Kluwer, Vienna, Austria

8. Blomberg J, Karasti H (2013) Reflections on 25 years of ethnography in CSCW. Comput Support Coop Work Int J 22:373–423

9. Boulus N, Bjørn P (2007) Constructing technology-in-use practices: EPR-adaption in Canada and Norway. In: 3rd International conference information technology in healthcare: socio-technical approaches. IOS Press, Sidney, Australia, pp 143–155

10. Bradner E, Mark G (2002) Why distance matters: effects on cooperation, persuasion and deception. In: CSCW, ACM, New Orleans, Louisiana, pp 226–235

11. Christensen L, Bjørn P (2014) Documentscape: intertextuality, sequentiality and autonomy at work. In: ACM CHI conference on human factors in computing systems, Toronto, ON, Canada

12. Cramton CD (2001) The mutual knowledge problem and its consequences for dispersed collaboration. Organ Sci 12(3):346–371

13. Cramton CD, Hinds P (2005) Subgroup dynamics in internationally distributed teams: Ethnocenterism or cross-national learning. Res Org Behav 26:233–265

14. Erickson T, Kellogg WA (2000) Social translucence: an approach to the designing systems that support social processes. ACM Trans Comput Hum Interact 7(1):59–83

15. Grinter R (2003) Recomposition: coordinating a web of software dependencies. Comput Support Coop Work Int J 12:297–327

16. Gutwin C, Penner R, Schneider K (2004) Group awareness in distributed software development. Comput Support Coop Work. ACM, New York, NY, USA

17. Harrison S, Tatar D (2008) Places: people, events, loci—the relations of semantic frames in the construction of place. Comput Support Coop Work Int J 17:97–133

18. Jarvenpaa SL, Leidner DE (1999) Communication and trust in global virtual teams. Org Sci 10(6):791–815

19. Jensen RE, Bjørn P (2012) Divergence and convergence in global software development: Cultural complextities as societal structures. In: COOP: design of cooperative systems. Springer, France, pp 123–136

20. Kiesler S, Cummings JN (2002) What Do we know about proximity and distance in work groups: a legacy of research. In: Hinds P, Kiesler S (eds) Distributed work. MIT Press, MAS, pp 57–83

21. Kotlarsky J, Oshri I (2005) Social ties, knowledge sharing and successful collaboration in globally distributed system development projects. Eur J Inf Syst 14(1):37–48

22. Matthiesen S, Bjørn P, Petersen L (2014) 'Figure out to code with the hands of others': recognizing cultural blind spots in global software development. Computer Supported Cooperative Work and Social Computing. ACM, Baltimore, USA, 2014

23. Nardi B (2005) Beyond bandwidth: dimensions of connections in interpersonal communication. Comput Support Coop Work Int J 14:91–130

24. Nardi B, Whittaker S, Schwarz H (2002) NetWORKers and their activity in intensional networks. Comput Support Coop Work Int J 11:205–242

25. O'Neill J, Martin D, Colobino T, Grasso A (2011) When a little knowledge isn't a dangerous thing. In: ACM CHI conference on human factors in computing systems, Vancouver, Canada
26. Olson GM, Olson JS (2000) Distance matters. Hum Comput Interact 15:139–178
27. Oshri I, Van Fenema P, Kotlarsky J (2008) Knowledge transfer in globally distributed teams: the role of transactive memory. Inf Syst J 18(6):593–616
28. Schmidt K (1998) The critical role of workplace studies in CSCW. In: Heath C, Hindmarsh J, Luff P (eds) Workplace studies, recovering work practices and informing design. Cambridge University Press, Cambridge
29. Schmidt K, Bannon L (1992) Taking CSCW seriously: supporting articulation work. Comput Support Coop Work Int J 1(1–2):7–40
30. Søderberg A-M, Krishna S, Bjørn P (2013) Global software development: commitment, trust and cultural sensitivity in strategic partnerships. J Int Manag 19(4):347–361
31. Strauss A (1985) Work and the division of labor. Sociol Q 26(1):1–19
32. Strauss A (1988) The articulation of project work: an organizational process. Sociol Q 29(2):163–178
33. Wasko M, Faraj S (2005) Why should I share? Examining social capital and knowledge contribution in electronic networks of practice. MIS Q 29(1):35–57
34. Wenger E (1998) Communities of practice: learning, meaning, and identity. Cambridge University Press

Of Corals and Web Portals: Towards a Digital Representation of Risk for the Cold-Water Corals in the Oil and Gas Sector

Elena Parmiggiani

Abstract Integrated Operations in the oil and gas industry depend on highly cooperative yet computer-mediated and distributed workflows across complex information infrastructures. In particular, offshore operations rely heavily on digital technologies to gain remote access to subsea oil or natural gas fields, and are at the same time subject to strict requirements by authorities to prevent pollution in the marine environment. Operators are consequently dependent on models and representations to assess and predict environmental risk. However, the heterogeneous disciplines operating a field cannot count on a shared perspective on environmental risk as their activities span across organizational and political boundaries. We present a case study from a Norwegian oil and gas company that is developing a set of tools and methodologies for providing heterogeneous users with awareness of the risk for the cold-water coral reefs off the coasts of Norway. In particular, we focus on the articulation work carried on to let representations and models compensate for the inevitable lack of shared awareness of environmental risk while at the same time fit the existing sociotechnical infrastructure. We discuss actors' strategies to foreground the infrastructure by: (1) *bootstrapping* the environmental data; (2) *mediating* with the existing corporate infrastructure; and (3) *enacting* the subsea context for operators.

Keywords Environmental risk · Awareness · Articulation work · Information infrastructure · Integrated operations

E. Parmiggiani (✉)
Department of Computer and Information Science, NTNU, Sem Sælands vei 7–9,
Trondheim, Norway
e-mail: parmiggi@idi.ntnu.no

C. Rossitto et al. (eds.), *COOP 2014 - Proceedings of the 11th International
Conference on the Design of Cooperative Systems, 27–30 May 2014, Nice (France)*,
DOI: 10.1007/978-3-319-06498-7_7, © Springer International Publishing Switzerland 2014

1 Introduction

The Norwegian continental shelf (NCS) is the Norwegian territory encompassing portions of the North Sea, the Norwegian Sea, the Barents Sea, and the Arctic Sea. Since oil was found in the late 1960s, as a result of technological innovation, the oil and natural gas industry has populated the NCS with a complex network of wells, subsea installations, pipelines, transportation vessels, fiber-optic cables for data transfer, and remotely operated vehicles. The NCS is also home for the world's largest population of a species of cold-water coral called *Lophelia pertusa*. Even though the intense activity of the fishery industry reportedly accounts for the damage of 30–50 % of *Lophelia* reefs [8], since the 1980s concern has been raised in connection with the distribution and the sociopolitical impact of offshore oil and gas operations. Despite the proliferation of laws and regulations to assess and prevent subsea environmental risk, no comprehensive regulatory framework is available today. As a consequence, companies are compelled to develop not only the technical devices but also the methodologies to establish and maintain an *awareness* of present and future risk and meet the legal requirements.

The Norwegian oil and gas industry association has labeled as *Integrated Operations* a new reality characterized by collaboration across organizational boundaries, the integration of people and technical tools, and the centralization of data repositories [22]. In particular, offshore operations are a highly cooperative effort that relies entirely on the collection of data from remote subsea locations by one company and its vendors and contractors thanks to hybrid networks of sensors and devices. All together they constitute large-scale sociotechnical systems—or *information infrastructures*—involving digital and non-digital artifacts and social practices that encompass heterogeneous professions. For example, drilling a new well requires, among others, drilling engineers in charge of monitoring the process, data engineers assessing the quality of the incoming data, geologists with knowledge of the reservoir, and the new emergent figure of the environmental coordinator monitoring the impact of operations on the subsea biological resources. The lack of shared awareness has deep reasons, mainly rooted in (1) the tendency towards a traditional organization structure; (2) the focus on educating domain specialists; (3) the specialized and silo-like nature of IT systems [11]. Cooperation therefore rests on a continuous balance that cannot provide for a shared awareness about the risk of the cold-water corals: each discipline looks at different kinds of object—the geologists at the reservoir, the drillers at the well and pipes, and so forth—and has different time constraints—drilling is a strictly real-time decision-making task, while the pollution on cold-water corals often becomes evident over the long term. However, the objects everyone is looking at have a common feature: they are not directly accessible by humans. The quest for risk awareness is therefore entirely dependent on digital artifacts like models, maps, and diagrams. In a word: representations. Reaching some level of awareness of subsea environmental risk in Integrated Operations must therefore on the one hand rely on technology-filtered information and, on the other hand, scaffold cooperation by providing a perspective that is meaningful for users that belong to heterogeneous professions.

CSCW has often focused on articulation work [30], intended as a collaborative set of interdependent yet distributed work activities that often exhibit sophisticated coordinative practices, even though strikingly few studies are set in the oil and gas industry, see e.g. [12, 28]. Moreover, the analysis of articulation practices has often been centered on the artifact [20]. We instead adopt an *infrastructural inversion* [4] to disclose a specific type of articulation work made of the coordinated practices that scaffold and adapt the information infrastructure as a whole.

In this paper, we want to investigate how tools and methodologies for cold-water coral risk prediction are developed to build and sustain risk awareness. We pose the following research question: *How is environmental risk awareness supported in the oil and gas information infrastructure?* In particular, we look at the articulation strategies to construct representations of risk for the inaccessible subsea reality in a research and development project (EnviroTime) in an international oil and gas company (NorthOil) in collaboration with industrial partners. EnviroTime is a highly cooperative project involving researchers with background in marine biology, environmental chemistry, anthropology, and computer science. We identify three articulation strategies used by NorthOil to compensate for the lack of shared environmental awareness: *bootstrapping* (to understand which environmental data should be available); *mediating* (to tie the new data to the existing infrastructure); and *enacting* (to let the subsea reality "live" for the diverse target users).

Thanks to a rich and multi-faceted case study, we contribute to CSCW by explicitly elaborating the notion of articulation work as a design strategy emerging in practice with reference to the large-scale settings of an information infrastructure. In so doing, we discuss the connection between articulation work and risk awareness through practices grounded on digital representations.

The remaining of this paper is organized as follows. In Sect. 2 we provide an overview of the theoretical framework guiding our analysis. In Sect. 3 we describe the empirical background and in Sect. 4 we outline the methodology adopted in our research. In Sect. 5 we present our findings that are further discussed in light of our theoretical lens in Sect. 6. Finally, in Sect. 7 we summarize our contribution and point at some future directions.

2 Theoretical Background

Awareness has been recognized to be a problematic concept in CSCW [6, 9, 10, 29]. Schmidt [29] provocatively remarks that the very first question we should ask is: *"awareness of what?"* (p. 288). Here we discuss awareness in the sense of the coordinative articulation practices [9] developed by actors to become aware of the environmental risk associated with their and others' activities in an offshore operational field. We take this as a point of departure by trying to understand how actors ask themselves the same question and what happens "behind the scenes" to leverage the relationship between computer-based representations and the reality they have to fit. The highly distributed yet interactive nature of oil and gas operations nevertheless requires us to look for explanatory concepts capable of taking aspects of distribution and technological mediation into account. The concept of information infrastructure is useful to delve into the large-scale and long-term nature of collaborative environments not only in the oil and gas business. Literature has also focused on how infrastructures support the temporal and spatial scale of environmental data curation and sharing, see e.g. [14]. The relevance of taking an information infrastructure perspective within CSCW is by now established [20, 26]. Inspired by research in the Information Systems (IS) and Science and Technology Studies, Ribes and Lee [26] point out that CSCW is well positioned to study infrastructures, but there is a need for a more detailed and systematic attention to this specific kind of computer-mediated collaborative work. The authors also argue how the themes unfolding from this perspective all account for the broader issue of technological delegation, as infrastructures cause a redistribution of labor between humans and technologies.

Both CSCW and IS have provided a vocabulary to analyze cooperative work in distributed settings, for instance with the notion of articulation work [30], as the invisible and often unrewarded work that is not formalized yet vital to keep an information infrastructure alive. Schmidt and Bannon [30] argue that CSCW should in particular treat articulation work as a design strategy, i.e. as an important input to requirement specifications for cooperative technologies. In general CSCW has studied articulation work as limited to particular settings and timeframes of technology design and implementation [20]. Our case represents in fact an effort to address the information infrastructure that unfolds "behind the scenes" of a situated reality. As a working definition, Monteiro et al. (ibid.) characterize information infrastructures as interconnected workplace information technologies that are open to number and types of users, embrace dynamically evolving portfolios of systems, and are constrained by an installed base of existing systems and practices. Infrastructures are also shaped and used across many different locales and endure over long periods (years or decades). Methodologically we adopt an *infrastructural inversion* [4] to shift the attention from the articulation work around one end artifact to the broader type of work required to let the infrastructure sustain the local implementations of technological artifacts. What we investigate in this paper is exactly the articulation, background work done as part of the EnviroTime project as a design strategy, aimed at both supporting and extending NorthOil's infrastructure. Articulation can for instance happen in practice by means of coordination mechanisms (CM), as described by Cabitza and Simone [6]. Among awareness-promotion CM, ordering systems (classification schemes, metadata structures) are used to articulate not actions directly, but rather the maintenance of specific structures that support the interconnection of actions (ibid.). Bringing to the fore this type of work is indeed core to analyze the political and social background an information infrastructure rests upon [5]. Common Information Spaces (CIS) have also been proposed as tools shared by cooperating actors to interpret and align their mutual work by building awareness of activities that are spatially and temporally asynchronous [2]. However, the concept of CIS has been criticized in literature, especially to understand what "information" really is and what should really be "common" [11, 28]. In our case study, the dilemmas the actors are facing are of the same nature: *What is environmental information in the oil and gas infrastructure? Should it be shared? How?*

3 Background Context and the EnviroTime Project

Today 78 oil or natural gas fields are in production on the NCS from the North Sea to the Barents Sea (source: www.npd.no). At the same time, a wide population of cold-water corals inhabits the NCS [8]. Coral reefs are in turn shelter to a fascinating range of marine fauna. While no harmful discharge was allowed in the 1980s by the Norwegian government in connection with human activities in the North Sea and the Norwegian Sea, today a much stricter constraint prevents any type of physical discharge outside northern Norway and on the Barents Sea [21]. In spite of this, as also acknowledged by our informants, authorities do not provide a detailed environmental regulatory framework [16]. Oil and gas companies carry on with an intense offshore activity on the NCS to search for, extract, and produce subsurface resources. One of the most delicate moments is represented by the drilling of a new well. Causes of pollution are for example the spreading of so-called drill cuttings (rock material removed from a borehole while drilling), drilling mud (material and fluids used to drill a borehole), or the occasional leakage of oil or natural gas from wells or pipelines. In order to be granted a license to operate in an area, companies must set up subsea monitoring programs to assess the present and future impact of oil and gas activities on the marine environment.

In this context, NorthOil (a pseudonym) is an oil and gas company headquartered in Norway with activities in more than 30 countries, but particularly concentrated on the NCS. The technological innovation in connection with the Integrated Operations regime enabled NorthOil to move its operations further offshore. Today numerous subsea installations are operated remotely, thanks for instance to intelligent sensors and devices and fiber-optics for real-time data transfer. Offshore activities therefore rely on highly computer-mediated work, where little contact point between humans and subsea life is possible. As part of the move towards Integrated Operations and to complement the lack of detailed environmental guidelines, NorthOil started the EnviroTime research and development project in 2011 to realize a new infrastructure for online environmental monitoring in collaboration with a number of industrial partners. Among them, Quality Certification Body (QCB, a pseudonym) was enrolled for its well-established methodology for predicting the environmental risk on cold-water corals based on offline data. Its target was now to merge it with NorthOil's technology and turn it into a thorough real-time framework. In particular, EnviroTime should provide NorthOil users with a web portal divided into two parts. The first part is based on a geographical information system (GIS) with updated predictions of risk for the coral reefs and mainly targeted at assisting the environmental coordinator, an emerging figure responsible for monitoring the impact of oil and gas activities on the natural resources. The displayed information would be the combination of data gathered from a number of sources (e.g. drilling and logging activities; reports from environmental surveyors and authorities). In turn, the environmental coordinator's decisions would impact on others' activities, e.g. if drilling has to be stopped or delayed in case of possible harm for the coral reefs. This GIS-based part of the portal thus provides an interface to a second part dedicated to the drilling engineers. Here, graphs and diagrams describe and log the tendency of key operational and environmental parameters (e.g., the drilling speed and how they relate to the particle sedimentation rate).

4 Research Method

Our research is grounded on the EnviroTime project as the main case study. We have conducted an extensive, ethnographically-informed fieldwork to follow actors in their daily articulation effort. The author has been granted access and a fixed desk in NorthOil research center. She has spent on average three days a week there from April 2012 until April 2014, conducting both participatory and unobtrusive observations in meetings, workshops, and teleconferences regarding EnviroTime. Several pages of field notes have been taken. In addition, she has conducted 24 semi-structured interviews (each lasting on average one hour) with participants in EnviroTime from NorthOil and QCB. The collection of internal documentation has been a further tool to acquire an overview of the company's policies and strategies.

The researcher applied a mix of an inductive and a deductive approach to data analysis. First, the data set (interview transcripts, field notes, documentation) was open coded. Keywords have then been iteratively clustered into broader categories of articulation strategies. The choice of the three final categories (*bootstrapping*; *mediating*; *enacting*) was inspired by the literature as discussed in Sect. 6. To increase validity, the categories were refined in collaboration with other members of the research group the researcher belongs to. The analysis process has been inspired by the interpretive tradition in Information Systems [32], grounded on the seven principles presented by Klein and Myers [15]. The principle of dialogical reasoning in particular accounts for how the case is presented to the reader. As data emerged, we decided to inject snapshots from the fieldwork into narratives (e.g. by quoting statements or short dialogues during meetings). The adoption of narratives for data analysis helps to reproduce an observed situation characterized by variable temporal embeddedness, eclectic data, and no clear boundaries [17].

Finally, we underline that NorthOil's research center did not equal our field site. Indeed, as indicated by Blomberg and Karasti [3], the site of a research inquiry is ultimately a construction by the researcher. The hermeneutic foundations of the interpretive approach provided a lens to understand EnviroTime as a process deeply entangled both with the sociotechnical context inside NorthOil, and with the sociopolitical context that NorthOil is part of. It is often physically impossible for the researcher to account for long-term phenomena spanning across vast communities. As described above, the EnviroTime project has all the features of a large-scale attempt in terms of organizations involved, end users, time span, and geographical distribution. Nonetheless, as underlined by Ribes [25], *"anytime there is a "large" endeavor you will find actors tasked with managing the problems associated with its scale"* (emphasis in original). Accordingly, we focused our attention on those actors in the field site that must develop articulation tools and techniques to discover and manage the scale of their infrastructure as part of their daily routine work.

5 Articulation Strategies for Environmental Risk Awareness

EnviroTime soon turned out to be much more than an issue of software development. In fact, two problems came to the surface related to environmental data management. First, the sensors that are traditionally used in oil and gas are not well suited to track slowly changing biological parameters. Second, marine biology is a highly fragmented discipline, so no standardized data management practices or metadata structures are available to guide oil and gas operators in a field that is not their domain of expertise. As a consequence, NorthOil decided to dedicate full-time resources to increase the knowledge about corals and other biological resources' reaction to the exposure to human activities. This element of novelty had then to be counter-balanced with the integration of new data management practices in the existing workflows. Environmental data have to be modeled and visualized in a format the end users are traditionally accustomed to. We identified three strategies that NorthOil and its project partners adopted in EnviroTime to overcome these issues. These strategies represent our formulation and thus not an explicit formalization by NorthOil. Moreover, they do not consist of three clear-cut moments in the history of the project; rather, they have been running in parallel and informed each other since the project's inception.

5.1 Bootstrapping: The Importance of the Real-Time Laboratory

Echoing Schmidt [29], the very first problem that EnviroTime had to face was: *When we talk about environmental risk, what should we be aware of in practice?* To collect data from an unmanned subsea environment, devices equipped with sensors have to be deployed. But which ones? And how? In this sense, the subsea environment needs to be "bootstrapped": meaningful parameters have to be obtained from a situated reality to be made part of the broader discourse of oil and gas. Before the official beginning of the EnviroTime project it was not really clear which type of environmental data have to be collected, how often, in what quantity, and from which locations. Also pressed by the need to apply for research funding, NorthOil opened two test settings, one (field A) in the Norwegian Sea, and the second (location Y) offshore north Norway where oil and gas operations are prohibited today.

5.1.1 Field A: Time is Business

In 2009 NorthOil elaborated a business case to demonstrate to authorities that the drill cuttings discharged during the drilling activity need not be taken onshore but could be left to sediment on the sea bed away from biological resources and the coral reefs in particular. Therefore the company developed a temporary real-time monitoring solution to track a number of parameters (e.g. water currents, pressure and temperature, particle sedimentation rate) to predict the possible dispersion of rock materials and sediments when drilling a new well. The chosen test location was an existing oil field (dubbed field A), where the company was seeking permission from authorities to open another well. As no fixed data transfer cables were available at field A, a surface buoy had been connected to the sensor rack on the seabed to send real-time data onshore through to a satellite link. Unfortunately, either due to the collision with a vessel or the bad weather, the buoy suddenly went lost after a few days. NorthOil had to plug in third-party software to model oceanic currents to infer the missing data and provide the authorities with a sufficient report. Time means money in the oil and gas industry. Despite the technical problem, the temporary real-time platform demonstrated that the discharged materials did not need to be taken onshore and could be deposited on the sea bed, away from the corals: "*If the drilling campaign is postponed of one month it can be much higher costs, so the time is very important to have a solution in the right time. Time is an important issue.*" (Environmental advisor, interview, December 2012).

5.1.2 Location Y: An Open Laboratory

A second test location was chosen at Y, an area rich of coral reefs where no technical infrastructure has ever been installed. Y is also a geographically strategic area. Here the NCS is at his narrowest, therefore constituting a relevant site to study biomass, fish migration and spawning, and water currents. It was therefore deemed a suitable laboratory, where NorthOil could monitor the baseline behavior of biological resources away from possible sources of stress due to human operations. As two NorthOil employees told us, attempts to deploy sensor racks and fiber-optic cables for real-time data transfer had begun in the early 2000s. However, technical failures and harsh weather conditions led to delays and unforeseen costs. At one point, data could be collected offline and stored in hard disks placed in the same support as the sensors and powered with a battery. Yet, as pointed above, time proved to be an important factor, so this approach did not demonstrate robust enough. In 2013 a fiber-optic cable was finally put in place, sending the sensor data straight from the sea floor to an onshore data center. As no legacy information was involved, NorthOil decided to implement an open web platform that the public could freely access. Historical and real-time data about water currents, presence of particles, salinity, and videos and images of the coral reefs became easy to visualize and download. The web platform proved a useful tool to attract the attention of research institutions in order to develop analytical tools and better sensors to investigate what is actually at stake "down there".

5.2 Mediating: Integrating Across Routines, Space, and Time

A system with the scope of EnviroTime could not, of course, be thought as disentangled from the existing and well-established infrastructure of oil and gas operations (its so-called installed base). Therefore, a second question the actors had to face was: *How to tie the process of awareness to the existing infrastructure?* NorthOil started to "cement" the foundation of the lessons learned from the A and Y test setting. A new stream in project was thus initiated, to extend and integrate the existing work processes with the new data governance practices learned in the A and Y test settings. We were directly involved in the regular meetings to discuss the data governance processes. Participants were enrolled among the project managers, the environmental advisors, and the IT leaders. This task soon proved a non-trivial one, as NorthOil has more than 30,000 formal work processes approved by the corporate management. One project manager explains the problem: *"Work processes for leveraging existing operational data like surveys, maps, production are already available. We must see where they integrate. We have to identify if there are gaps or non-gaps [in the list of] work processes to know if they need to be integrated or not. There is a whole group of side activities they do for every field every year for which there is no clear work process description today. Each department works in a slightly different way."* (Internal meeting, October 2013)

It stood clear how the problem of integrating the work processes was actually unfolding as a problem of integration at several levels. First of all, at that of the disciplines and their daily routines. One IT leader explains: *"When describing work processes we must focus on the interactions between environmental coordinators, GIS experts, etc. Today data are spread all over, in different formats, with no standard maintenance... the goal is to get control. Today we don't know what to do with the data we have, so we must describe routines"* (Internal meeting,

August 2013). Unfortunately the co-existence of environmental and technical information is not an obvious marriage. Two environmental advisors point out: *"Operational people do not understand the real-time relevance of tracking the fish status"… "But it could be something important to look at when drilling!"* (Internal meeting, August 2013)

Moreover, the problem of integration emerged at the level of handling incoming data across space, where spatiality can be that of the different data sources (e.g. databases, spreadsheets) but also that of the different vendors (e.g. for data analysis) or contractors (e.g. an external company logging drilling data in its proprietary format). The same IT advisor quoted above adds: *"It is important to have a description in the work processes about what to do with every different source and data. Every datum can come in different formats and timing and vendors. In this latter case there is a need for quality check. For example: what to do when a survey map comes from a vendor via mail?"* (Internal meeting, August 2013) Indeed, as new types of sensors and data analysis tools were adopted, new types of both raw and complex datasets became available, e.g. surveys, maps, which are often realized by vendors.

Nonetheless, data integration could also be read as a problem of integration across time: *"We must consider predictive simulations as historical data that lay in the future. For instance coral analysis provides a coral risk that is not observed (…). When data become historical then it is really important to have a data governance that handles these data contra predictions. It is not the real-time part that is difficult, but how to assemble and work with the static map layers. The real-time is much simpler to get to."* (IT advisor, internal meeting, August 2013)

The discussions in the meetings were thus soon directed towards what new information would constitute the master data in NorthOil infrastructure, i.e. the persistent and non-transactional data to be shared across multiple systems and processes in an organization. For example, maps resulting from the process of analyzing the risk factors for the coral reefs could be made available to drilling engineers. On the other hand, the EnviroTime project could benefit from the existing master data, e.g. about production activities, to understand the possible level of pollution on the biological resource (amount of discharges, possible chemicals adopted); or about the organization's employees to track the person responsible for a survey or for indicating a coral structure as safe.

5.3 Enacting: Representing the Subsea on the Desktop

Oil and gas operators are well-trained professionals with knowledge about their own subject matter. However, this knowledge is deeply intertwined with the technologies and information systems they commonly use to discover phenomena. As outlined above, cross-disciplinarity can face boundaries in terms of routines and spatial and timely constraints. As the EnviroTime portal had to speak to a rather heterogeneous group of end users, a further dilemma EnviroTime participants faced was: *How to represent subsea environmental risk in meaningful terms for the users*?

Before being enrolled in EnviroTime, Quality Certification Body (QCB) had developed an offline methodology to assess the risk for coral reefs in connection with human marine operations. This methodology had now to be incorporated in the machinery of EnviroTime. In practice, this means that it had to fit both the new real-time data flow and NorthOil infrastructure. A wide range of maps (or geographical objects) is available in NorthOil's installed base. Once a survey for biological resources has been completed, the responsible environmental coordinator for the area identifies the locations of the coral structures. Corals are thus positioned onto the existing maps and approximated as geometrical shapes, together with wells, pipelines, and other fixed technical infrastructure. The responsible environmental coordinator assigns a color to each coral based on the assessed health. Secondarily, GIS-based information is combined with the drilling plan and weather and ocean current forecasts into software modeling systems, to understand how the drilling discharges will spread and if they will sediment onto the coral structures. However, no software available to NorthOil puts together GIS and current models. QCB researchers therefore developed a script to resolve this lack of communication. As a result of this step, coral structures are mapped inside a "risk matrix". The matrix is used twice in EnviroTime. Once, to *portray* the conditions of corals before any drilling activities. In addition, EnviroTime participants initiated a discussion with NorthOil's GIS department to integrate the corporate maps with the new incoming real-time data. As a consequence, the risk matrix can be used a second time to *predict* the future impact during and after drilling. In general, the risk matrix is a well-known tool in risk assessment. The one realized by QCB researchers consists of an apparently simple 4 × 4 table, with the expected probability of pollution on the y-axis and its consequence on the x-axis. Each cell is filled with intuitive colors (red, green, yellow, orange) to signal the level of danger connected to each situation. Then the consequence for a given coral structure is mapped as a black dot for the calculated probable pollution. Such matrix is then included in the metadata structure with a set of attributes: corals are assigned an identity, a time, a space, a responsible person, and a condition (or health state).

6 Discussion: Articulation Work, Revisited

Monteiro et al. [20] state that researchers in CSCW should focus more on how order is produced and maintained for the large-scale and integrated working settings, or information infrastructures. The design and development of a cross-organizational system for real-time environmental risk prevention in Integrated Operations (as is the case for the EnviroTime project) requires that a level of order is indeed achieved across a distributed oil and gas organization (NorthOil). Order in EnviroTime rests upon an extensive digitalization, as the subsea reality can only be accessed through digital devices turning the natural environment into series of discrete data. These data have to be re-ordered as Lego blocks to re-construct a meaningful and relevant reality for the end users. We must thus delve into the design strategies to entangle a complex matter like environmental risk with the installed base of NorthOil.

This paper is not focused on providing specific design recommendations. The aim is to empirically investigate the evolving relationship between articulation work and awareness. We started with the story of a coral, *Lophelia*. But how do we build a digital representation of *Lophelia* in practice, so that it carries weight inside NorthOil? We adopted an information infrastructure perspective because we argue that, to be convincing, *Lophelia* has to be seen relationally, that is to say as an infrastructure. This is the motivation for the methodological choice of taking an infrastructural inversion [4] that allows us to look at the articulation strategies as moments of emergence of the infrastructure: "Understanding the nature of infra-structural work involves unfolding the political, ethical, and social choices that have been made throughout the development. Analytically (...) this is *shifting the emphasis from changes in infrastructural components to changes in infrastructural relations*" ([5], p. 99, emphasis added). In this sense articulation work is the lens to investigate the sense making process that goes about along the trajectory from subsea nature to maps displayed on a web browser. Thanks to an extensive eth-nographically informed fieldwork, we identified three interdependent articulation strategies to support awareness for subsea environmental risk and that the actors put in practice to define: (1) When are data *good enough*? (Bootstrapping); (2) When are data *compliant enough*? (Mediating); (3) When are data *relevant enough*? (Enacting)

As a first articulation strategy, we depicted the process of **bootstrapping** environmental data, in an attempt to get to know the unknown. We indeed borrow the term "bootstrapping" from Science and Technology Studies, in particular from Bowker [4] who describes the infrastructural work put in practice to conjure "global" parameters in highly contextualized and imperfect realities. As indicated by Schmidt and Bannon [30], in articulation work actors must often engage in activities that are extraneous to their daily tasks. Indeed we showed how Env-iroTime participants had to open the boxes of marine biology or corporate work processes that were previously alien to most of them. In the case of laboratory location Y, bootstrapping strategies emerge in practice as an ongoing effort of enforcing the trustworthiness of the early results. It is indeed important in an ethnographic study to attend the ongoing work to make systems trustworthy [13]. Location Y was chosen intentionally by NorthOil away from any existing human activity, to make sure that the environmental baseline obtained from the sensor-based measurements would not be believed as biased by human factors. In addi-tion, data were made freely accessible online. Therefore trustworthiness was also enforced by enrolling politically independent research institutions in the process. In the case of the tests run at field A, NorthOil realized how awareness should also be tied to the industrial production parameters that NorthOil must inevitably respond to. The tests were tailored in terms of a predefined business case that not only showed authorities that discharges can be handled in a safe way, but also showed the oil and gas sector that this approach led to saving time and money. We can read this effort as an instance of infrastructural inversion to discover the hidden referential structure that comes about in the politics of building and maintaining awareness.

Second, we labeled as **mediating** the phase where the EnviroTime project participants initiated a separate work package to understand how to adapt environmental data management to the installed base of NorthOil. Workflows in an oil and gas company must follow the approved work processes, which represent an institutional artifact all new information systems and practices should comply to. A well-calibrated integration of environmental data governance inside the legacy processes compensates for the fundamental lack of cross-discipline shared awareness. The infrastructure can include the invisible environmental work thanks to its reification into explicit representations [3]. We portrayed how this effort of mediating environmental information emerges as a problem of integrating data across *work processes* (the routines of each discipline); *time* (accumulated vs. future data); and *space* (different data sources, including different providers). On the one hand, the adaptation of work processes unfolds as a standardization cycle, where environmental data management practices are rendered compliant to the corporate-approved infrastructure. In latourian terms [18], a due process is granted to the unknown (nature) to gradually become a legitimate member of the known (the oil and gas business). On the other hand, space and time are tricky categories. Pollock and Williams [24] call for the need within CSCW to be more systematic in accounting for the multi-sited and longitudinal nature of corporate information infrastructure. Since the spatial and temporal scope of an infrastructure like EnviroTime might prove overwhelming for a single researcher, she operationalized Pollock and Williams's invitation by adopting the strategy of scaling ethnography [25] presented in Sect. 4. In so doing, the research could disclose how actors themselves deal with spatial (e.g. by defining work processes to handle third-party environmental surveys) and temporal (e.g. by defining routines to store new data to easily compare them with historical data) integration. However, mediation can prove difficult to achieve, due to the heterogeneous backgrounds of the professional communities involved and issues affecting the technologies adopted [23]. The solution might require pragmatic decisions to give a voice to those elements that should be the motivation for innovation (the corals, the environment) but that are often forgotten.

We finally identified a third articulation strategy as **enacting**. The term "enact" is inspired by Mol [19], who prefers it to "perform" to describe how objects become real when they are framed and played with when made part of a practice. In his review of the concept of awareness, Schmidt [29] argues that in order to understand the phenomenon of awareness in cooperative work, researchers should look at how the world in which cooperating actors act and interact is given to them as a meaningful world. Tradition in CSCW drawing for instance on actor-network theory has long acknowledged the relational co-evolution of work practices and technologies [1], in line with a conceptualization of information infrastructures as a sustained relation: "infrastructure... is part of the balance of action, tools, and the built environment, inseparable from them" ([31], p. 377). The maps and the graphs on the EnviroTime portal are necessarily imperfect technology-mediated representations aimed at portraying the far subsea reality for each professional group in their own terms inside their daily routines. For instance, integrating real-time environmental information with the known corporate map layers is a strategy to "construct" a meaningful picture of environmental risk. From a different angle, the strategies of enacting can be read as a matter of context awareness. EnviroTime embodies the process of reduction and objectification undergone by the environmental data that is due to the formal representational schemas of corporate technologies. It is not a question whether to reduce the environmental context, but how [7]. Tools to facilitate the rendering of contextual elements could be coordination mechanisms (CM) [6]. In our story, this might be the case of the integration script developed by QCB (see Sect. 5.3). Interestingly, the same code that QCB developers wrote embeds the phenomenon that EnviroTime is trying to portray, i.e. how human activities meet and overlap with the subsea natural environment. Also the risk matrix (Sect. 5.3) as a form of categorization for the coral structures is a CM, as an ordering system to govern the flow of work in assessing environmental risk. It is actually interesting to underline the convergence of these categorization tools towards the street categories (usage of green, red, and yellow colors from the semantics of the traffic light) to convey a straightforward message. The risk matrix is a commonly used tool in risk assessment in general. Here, we wanted to foreground how it is made to fit with the machinery of subsea environmental risk prediction.

7 Conclusions and Future Directions

Awarding the cold-water corals a primary role in the oil and gas offshore business is one of the keys towards the goal of Integrated Operations. Due to the distributed nature of traditional oil and gas disciplines, the development of cooperative systems cannot rely on the existence of a shared awareness of environmental risk, which must be based on representations of the unreachable reality of the seabed. In this paper, we portrayed the articulation work done as part of a large-scale research and development project in an oil and gas company to implement a system for real-time subsea environmental monitoring. By taking an information infrastructure perspective, we asked how articulation work can sustain the quest for risk awareness. We thus contributed by shifting the focus from the final digital artifacts that should enhance cooperation among actors, towards the infrastructure that supports them. We took an infrastructural inversion [4] to investigate the design strategies to adapt and extend the corporate infrastructure in a punctuated manner. For the sake of analysis we identified three of these strategies: bootstrapping, to become acquainted with the subsea reality; mediating, to adapt the biological data to the oil and gas corporate reality; and enacting, to let their representations become meaningful for operators. In so doing, we drew a connection between articulation work and the notion of awareness as a coordinative practice based on digital representations.

To conclude, we point at some future directions. EnviroTime is an ongoing project that has not reached a closure yet. Nevertheless, we invite future research to discover if EnviroTime could constitute a Common Information Space (CIS). Interestingly, the oil and gas associations promote a shift towards collaboration arenas to integrate personnel, a notion which was compared to that of CIS [11]. The notion of CIS was originally proposed by Bannon and Bødker [2] to describe a space actively constructed by the users who cooperate to shape and resolve meanings, at least temporarily. However, as pointed out by Rolland et al. [28] by grounding on Mol [19], the essential characteristic of CIS is the fact that they allow for a temporary resolution of meanings through representations by being *malleable* and *mutable*. It is too early to state whether the EnviroTime portal constitutes a CIS or if it will rather end up reproducing the same fragmentation it is meant to avoid. What we can say is that by foregrounding the infrastructure as it is being modified and extended by the actors, we can study how (digital) artifacts are made malleable offstage to reach for the necessary compatibility between the new requirement of risk awareness and the existing installed base.

A further aspect that future work should look at deals with the reconfiguration between human work and technological delegation in infrastructures entailed by initiatives like EnviroTime [26, 27]. The form of automation produced by artifacts like the integration script described above is only one example of the way technology can lead to a redistribution of work. This aspect has consequences also for the way ethnographically-informed studies in CSCW should account not just for how technical interventions are able to avoid human work, but also for *how* they substitute human work in *practice*. Thanks to EnviroTime, we saw how environmental experts became traceable, and thus accountable, for assessing the health status of coral structures. As pointed by Ribes et al. [27], technological delegation implies a redistribution of responsibilities for decision-making in organizations and reconfigures what becomes visible or invisible in the actors' work.

Acknowledgments This research is part of the "Digital Oil" project (www.doil.no) supported by the Verdikt program of the Norwegian Research Council (pr. nr. 213115) and is funded by the Center for Integrated Operations in the Petroleum Industry (www.iocenter.no). We are grateful to all of the professionals at NorthOil and QCB who agreed to participate in our research.

References

1. Aanestad M (2003) The camera as an actor design-in-use of telemedicine infrastructure in surgery. Comput Support Coop Work 12:1–20
2. Bannon L, Bødker S (1997) Constructing common information spaces. In: Proceedings of the 5th European conference on computer supported cooperative work. Springer, Netherlands, pp 81–96
3. Blomberg J, Karasti H (2013) Reflections on 25 years of ethnography in CSCW. Comput Support Coop Work 22:373–423
4. Bowker GC (1994) Science on the run information management and industrial geophysics at Schlumberger, 1920–1940. MIT Press, Cambridge

5. Bowker GC, Baker K, Millerand F, Ribes D (2010) Toward information infrastructure studies: ways of knowing in a networked environment. In: Hunsinger J, Klastrup L, Allen M (eds) International handbook of internet research. Springer, Netherlands, pp 97–117

6. Cabitza F, Simone C (2013) Computational coordination mechanisms: a tale of a struggle for flexibility. Comput Support Coop Work 22:475–529

7. Chalmers M (2004) A historical view of context. Comput Support Coop Work 13:223–247

8. Fosså JH, Mortensen PB, Furevik DM (2002) The deep-water coral *Lophelia pertusa* in Norwegian waters: distribution and fishery impact. Hydrobiologia 471:1–12

9. Gross T (2013) Supporting effortless coordination: 25 years of awareness research. Comput Support Coop Work 22:425–474

10. Heath C, Svensson MS, Hindmarsh J, Luff P, vom Lehn D (2002) Configuring awareness. Comput Support Coop Work 11:317–347

11. Hepsø V (2009) "Common" information spaces in knowledge intensive work: representation and negotiation of meaning in computer supported collaboration rooms. In: Handbook of research on knowledge—intensive organizations. Idea Group Publ, Hershey

12. Heyer C (2009) High-octane work: the oil and gas workplace. In: Wagner I, Tellioğlu H, Balka E, Simone C, Ciolfi L (eds) ECSCW 2009. Springer, London, pp 363–382

13. Jirotka M, Procter R, Hartswood M, Slack R, Simpson A, Coopmans C, Hinds C, Voss A (2005) Collaboration and trust in healthcare innovation: the eDiaMoND case study. Comput Support Coop Work 14:369–398

14. Karasti H, Baker KS, Halkola E (2006) Enriching the notion of data curation in e-science: data managing and information infrastructuring in the long term ecological research (LTER) network. Comput Support Coop Work 15:321–358

15. Klein HK, Myers MD (1999) A set of principles for conducting and evaluating interpretive studies in information systems. MIS Q 23:67–94

16. Knol M (2013) Making ecosystem-based management operational: integrated monitoring in Norway. Marit Stud 12:1–17

17. Langley A (1999) Strategies for theorizing from process data. Acad Manag Rev 24:691–710

18. Latour B (2004) The politics of nature. Harvard University Press, Cambridge

19. Mol A (2002) The body multiple: ontology in medical practice science and cultural theory. Duke University Press, Durham

20. Monteiro E, Pollock N, Hanseth O, Williams R (2013) From artefacts to infrastructures. Comput Support Coop Work 22:575–607

21. NME (2010) The royal norwegian ministry of the environment—report n. 10 to the Storting—first update to the integrated management of the marine environment of the Barents sea and the sea areas off the Lofoten Islands

22. Norsk olje og gass (2005) Integrated work processes: future work processes on the NCS

23. Parmiggiani E, Hepsø V (2013) Pragmatic information management for environmental monitoring in oil and gas. In: ECIS 2013 completed research, paper 65

24. Pollock N, Williams R (2010) e-Infrastructures: how do we know and understand them? Strategic ethnography and the biography of artefacts. Comput Support Coop Work 19:521–556

25. Ribes D (2014) Ethnography of scaling—or, how to fit a national research infrastructure in the room. Paper presented at the CSCW'14, Baltimore, MD, USA

26. Ribes D, Lee CP (2010) Sociotechnical studies of cyberinfrastructure and e-research: current themes and future trajectories. Comput Support Coop Work 19:231–244

27. Ribes D, Jackson S, Geiger S, Burton M, Finholt T (2013) Artifacts that organize: delegation in the distributed organization. Inf Organ 23:1–14

28. Rolland KH, Hepsø V, Monteiro E (2006) Conceptualizing common information spaces across heterogeneous contexts: mutable mobiles and side-effects of integration. In: Proceedings of the 20th anniversary conference on computer supported cooperative work, CSCW '06. ACM, New York, pp 493–500

29. Schmidt K (2002) The problem with 'awareness': introductory remarks on 'awareness in CSCW'. Comput Support Coop Work (CSCW) 11:285–298

30. Schmidt K, Bannon L (1992) Taking CSCW seriously: supporting articulation work. Comput Support Collaborative Work (CSCW) 1:1–70
31. Star SL (1999) The ethnography of infrastructure. Am Behav Sci 43:377–391
32. Walsham G (1995) Interpretive case studies in IS research: nature and method. Eur J Inf Syst 4:74–91

A Case Study of an Information Infrastructure Supporting Knowledge Work in Oil and Gas Exploration

Marius Mikalsen

Abstract It is well rehearsed in the fields of CSCW and IS that the relationship between the social and the material is bi-directional and shaped locally. But what happens when knowledge work is stretched across space and time, and the practice of today relies on actions and reflections done elsewhere and at different times? This paper presents an on-going case study of oil and gas exploration that takes steps to shed light on this emerging issue. I argue the relevance of framing the process of generating *interpretations* in oil and gas exploration in terms of *information infrastructures*. The case is representative for other cases where practitioners' reflections cannot immediately be confirmed by empirical observation. Through a discussion on the concepts of *coordination* and *accumulation* across the dimensions of space and time, I outline how an able information infrastructure in this domain must balance the dualism of the concepts of *naturalisation* and *historification*.

1 Introduction

In the beginning there were seeps, and oil and gas exploration was straightforward. Every major petroleum-bearing basin of the world has numerous oil seeps where oil seeps naturally to the surface. Explorers focused their search on areas near seepages, where oil bubbled up to the surface naturally [11]. Now however, the easy finds have been done. Given still increasing demand, and high prices, oil and gas companies must explore in areas that are difficult to reach, such as several

M. Mikalsen (✉)
Norwegian University of Technology and Science (NTNU) and SINTEF, 7491 Trondheim, Norway
e-mail: marius.mikalsen@sintef.no

C. Rossitto et al. (eds.), *COOP 2014 - Proceedings of the 11th International Conference on the Design of Cooperative Systems, 27–30 May 2014, Nice (France)*, DOI: 10.1007/978-3-319-06498-7_8, © Springer International Publishing Switzerland 2014

kilometres below the seabed. New discoveries are made possible by combinations of new exploration methods (human interpretations) and new technology. Still today however, drilling an exploration well is the only certain way to confirm the presence of hydrocarbons deep down in the earths crust. But drilling is difficult and expensive. The floating rigs are dipping on the surface, drifting kilometers, while trying to hit the reservoir 5 km below sea level, and perhaps 2 km to the side. The cost of running such a floating rig can be up to 500,000 USD per day (day rates for each rig type drawn from the RigLogix database, accessed 06/11/ 2013), and one exploration well can cost tens of millions of USD and upwards. This is in addition to the environmental risks involved in drilling. Drilling such a well therefore is a process O&G companies only will do when the probability is *high enough* that there is a presence of technically and economically recoverable reserves.

This paper brings forward a case of modern O&G exploration and shows how it is a sociomaterial [17] and highly information-centric process, involving a complex combination of information systems, large amounts of heterogeneous data (*the material*), and several teams cooperating across space and time (*the social*). This sociomaterial assembly can be seen as an *information infrastructure (II)*, a concept originating in science and technology studies. One of the early definitions [21] explains an II consisting of these "*dimensions*"; embedded (inside of other structures such as social arrangements and other technologies), transparent (supports tasks invisibly), reach and scope (across space and time), learned as part of membership (of a community of practice), links with conventions of practice (II shapes and is shaped by practice), embodies standards (plugs into other IIs and tools using standards), installed base (built organically, not revolutionary), becomes visible on breakdown (normally invisible, but very noticeable when it breaks down). The notion of II has evolved from Star and Ruhleder's focus on sharing learning within and across communities, through focus on how the II is shaped locally to a current focus on how there is a tension between the local and the global due to lack of global control, and is currently defined as "*a shared, open (and unbounded), heterogeneous and evolving socio-technical system (which we call installed base) consisting of a set of IT capabilities and their user, operations and design communities*" [10]. Mayernik et al. [14] explains how the same concept of II is also increasingly used in Computer Supported Cooperative Work (CSCW); "*Coordinating technology development and scientific research is a growing theme of Computer Supported Cooperative Work (CSCW) studies, with many open questions*", particularly in e-science, where "*large scale distributed computational, data and communication, infrastructures and middleware*" is applied to emerge new kinds of scientific practice.

This paper address the following research question: What are the characteristics of the social and the material parts of the II that cooperate and co-produce *interpretations* of the subsurface materiality across space and time?

In answering this research question, this paper serves three purposes. First, I take steps to "unearth", to use Mayernik et al.'s (ibid.) term, the II in oil and gas exploration. Understanding the nuances in as many particular cases as possible is crucial for the understanding of II as a phenomenon, because it is so interwoven with coordinative practices that *"are not generic but domain specific"* and *"in order to develop the conceptual foundation for such technologies, in-depth studies of professional work and the concomitant coordinative practices are critically important"* [20]. Taken together, ethnographic accounts can support generalisation [7] that can inform II design and evolution, see e.g. [10]. Second, I make an argument that there is a need to not only address capabilities, applications and platforms in situ, but also focus on accumulation of data across spatiotemporal dimensions of the II, and how this influence collaborative work and coordination. To do this, I will draw on literature from the domains of information systems (IS) and CSCW. I will discuss the O&G exploration process as an on-going naturalisation process of interpretations that is constructed collaboratively. I will show how interpretations are shaped and moulded over *"different contexts over extended periods of time"* [15], or to frame it otherwise, through *"asynchronous remote collaboration"* [5], involving several geoscientists and different geoscientific disciplines as *"competent actors reflecting"* [18] on historical interpretations, continuously refining them. An obvious challenge here is to locate relevant data in a vast amount of data, a process that is performed by people and multitude of search and database tools. Equally important however, but easier to overlook, is to *"make the invisible naturalisation visible"* [4], that is, to support the need of the reflective practitioners to, in a sense, interpret the interpretations done elsewhere and in the past. Third and finally, I will discuss these concepts towards contributions from the domain of healthcare. The reason for so doing is that exploration for new subsurface petroleum resources, similar to that of health, is a case where collaboratively built representations, residing in information systems, are the primary sources upon which practitioners must reflect and make decisions, effectively deprived of the possibility of immediate empirical verification of their reflections and interpretations.

The rest of the paper is organised as follows. In the following method Sect. 1 explain the context of this study, how data is generated, and how it is analysed. Section 3 analyses and frames oil and gas exploration case as an information infrastructure, shows what an interpretation is in this domain, the inscription devices used in the infrastructure and how they are used for accumulation and coordination. Section 4 discuss, compares and contrasts the notions of accumulation and coordination from CSCW healthcare works with this case and how the information infrastructure as a consequence need to balance the dualism between naturalisation and historificazion. Finally, in Sect. 5, I summarise and suggest some interesting vistas for continued work on this theme.

2 Method

2.1 Study Context

NorthOil (an acronym) is an international oil and gas company established in the 1970s and headquartered in Northern Europe, currently employing 30,000 people with activities in 35 countries.

The unit of study is exploration. Oil and gas exploration is the initial phase in petroleum operations that includes generation of a prospect and drilling of an exploration well. The key questions NorthOil wants answered are: (1) where are the hydrocarbons, (2) how much hydrocarbons are there? (3) Will it flow? (4) what is the best way to produce it (bordering to the disciplines of field assessment and production). Summarized the task at hand for exploration is to answer the ultimate question of: Can this reservoir (when identified) profitably produce hydrocarbons?

In NorthOil exploration, geoscientists like e.g. geologists and geophysicists (I will use "G&G personnel" or simply "**G&G**" as a collective term for this group, in fact, in NorthOil all geoscientist are collectively named G&G even if they are geochemists for example) are continuously interpreting the company's vast amount of subsurface data. Geologists know rocks and the formations they make in the earth crust. Geophysicists can look at physical characteristics, such as magnetics and gravitation to indicate rocks and formations exist below. Other geoscience disciplines are also supporting the interpretation process, such as geochemists, that study chemical elements in rocks and minerals and the movement of such elements into soil and water systems. Creating different kinds of interpretations is a multidisciplinary effort including different kind of geoscientific disciplines.

There are two thousand G&G in NorthOil. Two hundred **Project Data Managers (PDMs)** support the G&G with quality assuring, storing, and retrieving data. **Central Data Managers (CDM)** are responsible for maintaining the company datastores and keeping data synchronized across datastores. This is necessary to deal with the complexity of the II in terms of storing, accessing and managing all the geological and geophysical information that has accumulated over time.

G&G and PDMs are organized in units based on what geographical areas they are exploring. Currently these areas are North America, Norway, International west, and International East. The unit I am studying is Norway, and it is further divided into Licenses North Sea, Licenses North (Norwegian Sea and Barents Sea), and Access projects. The first two are more mature areas where there are already established commercial and technically viable fields and production. Access projects explore new fields and prepares for license rounds. The team I am following is working on North Sea licenses that are areas where NorthOil is presently partner in a license and need to find and assess the best places to extract hydrocarbons in the license. The team is located in an office building and sits in landscapes, where two to five people share offices. They have PCs (windows workstations), typically with more than one screen (which is handy when looking at subsurface models and geographic information systems—GIS).

Table 1 Data sources

Data source	Examples	Collection
Semi structured interviews	Interviews with exploration geologists, geophysicists and geochemists, exploration PDMs, CDMs	8 audio recorded
Participant observation	Group meetings, project meetings, informal meetings, chatting during lunch	20 pages of machine written notes
Document analysis	Official portal, internal documentation, email communication, plans, strategies, training material	Stored digitally

2.2 Data Collection and Analysis

This article draws on empirical data from an ongoing study of NorthOil exploration and reports on a 6 months field study.

I have so far been present there in 5 different periods for 14 days total (periods ranging from 1 to 4 days), combining data collection activities such as participatory observation, informal chats, and interviews. The case study is ongoing.

A summary of the data sources foreseen is given in (Table 1).

It is a large dataset and it is unstructured. Langley outline a number of different strategies for making sense of such process data [12].We need not to choose one, she explains, but we must be aware of the strengths and weaknesses of each strategy, and the potential they have to build theory that is *"accurate, parsimonious, general, and useful"* (ibid, p 691). In the analysis I work close to the empirical material, the texts that has been generated from notes, interviews, presentations and documents.

3 The Oil and Gas Exploration Information Infrastructure

The overall process of exploration has the following steps. First there is a global basin screening and ranking to determine what basins to work with. Following this, basin and prospect evaluation is done. Here the goal is to identify prospects for drilling. The prospects are quality controlled, approved and ranked. Exploration drilling is done and the discovery is evaluated. Finally, the feasibility of the prospect is appraised. The process can take several years from beginning to end, for instance it can take years from a successful prospect evaluation until exploration drilling is actually conducted, due to constantly changing priorities. This means also, that the fact check of the interpretations done in preparation of a prospect, will come in a final drill report, potentially several years after they were originally done.

In all of these phases different kinds of interpretations are done (the following section detail the notion of interpretations). All of these phases are highly data intensive. Typically the G&G will need an overview of all relevant data in an exploration area defined within quadrants and blocks. Quadrants are 1° by 1°, and blocks of 15 min of latitude by 20 min of longitude (12 blocks in a quadrant). A request for well data could be formulated as *"within quad 35, find me all wells which have total depth of more than 3000 m"* (from interview with access project geologist).

There is a lot of data available. In the corporate data store alone there is in excess of 110 TB (2,011 numbers). Data is brought to G&G primarily from two main sources, Diskos DB and the corporate data store. The Diskos DB is a national database where all oil and gas companies operating on the Norwegian continental shelf are required by law to store all of their seismic, well and production data. Searching for public data (such as production licenses, exploration wellbores, discoveries, fields, development wellbores and business areas) is available through a Public Data Portal.[1] The corporate data store holds NorthOil's proprietary interpreted data, such as seismic interpretations, well data, production logs, and maps. Business information such as license areas, infrastructure and business associates are also included. The database has thousands of tables and attributes.

Northoil's Exploration II involves a lot of different people, roles, processes and technology. There is an obvious need of NorthOil to define proper processes and work flows for this. Just considering the complexity of the systems alone, a PDM says when asked for an overview of the systems they operate: *"I will try to find a list, but it is a challenge we have, there are too many lists"* (from field notes). There are so many systems that it has resulted in too many list trying to give overview of the systems. A CDM confirms the concern of complexity *"I wonder how much complexity an organisation like NorthOil can handle"* (CDM informant, from field notes).

3.1 Interpretations

Geologists and the geophysicists work primarily on two categories of data, seismic data and well data respectively. From seismic data, a structural model is interpreted (mostly done by geophysicists). From the well data, the physical properties of the rocks are interpreted (mostly done by geologists). By combining the structural model with the physical properties, a higher order model is created, a more accurate interpretation if you will. The seismic data is rather coarse grained and covers large areas that cannot otherwise be measured in detail. Properties that can be found in seismic data are; horizons, faults, structure, salt and other bodies, amplitude anomalies, fluid presence, traps and rock properties. For the well data there are lots of precise measurements, but rather sparse areal coverage. From the well you can get several kinds of petrophysical and geo-mechanical data. This data is then interpreted geophysical and geological.

---

[1] Available here http://www.pdp.diskos.com (accessed 09/10/2013).

3.1.1 Geophysical Interpretations: Seismic Interpretation and Well Correlation

In geophysics, *seismic interpretation* is the analysis of seismic data to generate reasonable models and predictions about the properties and structures of the subsurface. Interpretation of such seismic data is the primary concern of geophysicists.

> *Well correlation* matches rock layers between wells "*When a well is drilled a record of the rock layers in the well is made on a well log. The rock layers between well logs are correlated to make a cross section. The correlation is started with a marker bed or key horizon. The marker bed is a distinctive rock layer that is easy to identify. Volcanic ash layers; thin beds of coal, limestone, or sandstone; and fossil zones are good marker beds. A key horizon is the top or bottom of a thick, distinctive rock layer. After correlating the marker bed or key horizon, the rock layers above and below the marker beds can then be correlated on physical similarity and their position in the sequence of layers.*" [11].

3.1.2 Geological Interpretations: Time-Depth Conversion, Picks and Gridding

Since seismic data are recorded in seconds (time domain), and well log is recorded in meters or feet (depth domain). This makes the vertical scales on each different and cannot be directly compared, which is what you want to do in the correlation as described above. If you know the seismic velocity through each layer, you can do a *time-depth conversion* on the seismic data to make it compatible with well-log data [11]. This process is iterative, in that it that begins with seismic processing (as described above), seismic velocity analysis and study of well data to refine the conversion. In order to improve the conversion, acoustic logs, check-shot surveys and vertical seismic profiles can improve correlation of well logs and drilling data with surface seismic data.

The typical seismic refers shows structure of the rocks and their characteristic layering, but it does not show individual sedimentary rock layers or the rock type [11]. To increase the value of the seismic record, G&G need to identify the individual sedimentary rock layers, so that potential reservoir rock (hydrocarbon producing) and seals (trap rock) can be found. This is done by running the seismic lines through wells that has been drilled, using well log and physical samples as basis for identifying subsurface rock layers in the seismic record.

The well log is in itself also interpreted by mapping the physical measurements and samples to rock formations found in different sources. *Picks* are done, which is the interpretation of data, such as creating seismic section based on marker beds or geologic picks, such as formation tops interpreted from well logs to improve interpretations.

Gridding is the process of determining values for grid elements on a map. The grid element values are chosen from nearby data points ("picks"). Gridding is usually applied to one characteristic per map, such as structure, thickness, porosity, permeability or saturation.

3.2 Inscription for Coordination and Accumulation in the II

Two applications are key in the information infrastructure are used by the G&G to create the interpretations we have seen in the above section. This is Petrel (from Schlumberger) and Openworks (from Landmark). These are so called *"interpretation tools"* that is, the tools where G&G access the data (loaded from the datastores by the PDMs), do their interpretations, and store them. There are historical and political reasons for why there are two different tools originating in a company merger some time ago. Petrel and Openworks are different in many regards, for instance Openworks runs on Linux and is accessed as a virtual machine on G&Gs PCs. Petrel runs native on the PC. A key difference is also that at the time of writing, Petrel (at least the version used in NorthOil) does not include its own database, while openworks runs on an Oracle database. This has interesting implications for the accumulation and coordination, as we will discuss in the next section.

Exploration begins by creating a new exploration project in Openworks by defining the geographical borders of the area to be explored (defining the *blocks* and *quadrants* to be included). Ideally, and in accordance with the defined workflow, a new project should be defined, but typically G&G will extend a bordering project, because they then know that they get all the data that is in that project and reduce the danger of missing some key information. The G&G collaborates with the PDMs that help them get the data they need. For instance they would like to have or "rock core permeability and porosity filtered by location, stratigraphic unit and depth" (source; G&G presentation), or; *"in quad 35, find me all wells which have total depth of more than 3000 m or a certain pressure of 200 bars or based on types of stratigraphic units or sand"* or *"find all wells in block X that took more than 30 days to drill, and had problems that resulted in blowouts"*. For seismic data, a request can be *"I want all the surveys in quadrant X, block Y, shot from 1990 by company Z"* (source: G&G informant).

Also, previous interpretations are interesting, and it is relevant to be able to find all interpretations done by a person in one area in one time period because you know that person and trust what he did in that period in that area. This can typically be data that has not been made "STAT" (meaning the official, quality controlled version) meaning it is not in the corporate data store, but rather in Openworks projects as "unofficial" versions. Interestingly, also the corporate data store did not earlier register whose interpretation that was the official "STAT" one. Now this has been changed and an official interpretation will always be linked to whom it was that did the interpretation, so that G&G always can see who did it.

The G&G ask the PDMs for all the seismic in an area, and one G&G report that the results are presented as A4 pages printouts of all the surveys (with outlines) found in the area that may be relevant, and they go through it together to determine what is to be loaded into the project. The process takes 2–3 days. Ideally, G&G would want to have all data that is found and relevant gridded up in a map, in their interpretation tool.

The corporate data store, the Diskos DB and other Openworks projects are searched to find data. The amount of information is the same regardless if you are working on access projects (exploring new areas) or mature fields already in production. This is because in access fields you are exploring larger geographical areas, making rougher more coarse grained interpretations, and therefore include for example 300 wells, while in the North Sea you could include 300 wells exploring a much smaller geographic area.

Some data that is of interest to the G&G are old enough to not having been digitalized, and need to be access in physical copies. Other information is so new, like really fresh drill reports or interpretations, that they are not in the official data stores yet. This information then is found e.g. in team sites. All content in the team sites are indexed and searchable, but access control regimes limits what you can access and not. This is considered a *"huge problem"* (source: PDM informant).

When the G&G has done an interpretation, e.g. interpreting a pick from a well log to determine a formation, they need to name it. There are standardized names and lists for picks, so that a G&G should choose from a "pick list" of formations in order to categorize their pick. This is not always done however, and one enters another name using free text ("formation Rogaland" instead of "Rogaland formation" for example). Using the same standardized category allows correlation between wells. One wish to follow standards (particularly that others do it), but it is often not done. One potential reason is that a lot of lithographic details are finer grained than the official categories allow.

As stated above a key difference between Petrel and Openworks is that Openworks includes its own database. Projects are created and stored in Openworks while many (if not most) work in Petrel. PDMs then need to keep an exact mirror of the data available in Petrel, and make sure to copy back to the Openworks database the interpretations that the G&G feels should me made available for others, that is not official (STAT) as in the corporate data store but rather, something that is good enough to share. This is a key difference from working in Openworks itself. While working in Openworks, everything stored directly in the DB, with the effect that it was available for searches by the PDM afterwards so that it can be retrieved, if needed for some reason or another, in some future exploration. Now, for the G&G working in Petrel, they have to make explicit decisions to upload data to the Openworks DB. This is often not done. One reason is the time constraints, one always needs to run off to the next area to explore, and there is no time to tidy up (uploading) the data. Second, to do a deliberate upload make the interpretation seem more "official" than the G&G feels it is, and they are therefore more hesitant. An unfortunate side effect is that potentially relevant interpretations done in Petrel, but not uploaded, are lost.

4 Spatiotemporal Accumulations and Coordination in Interpretation Work

The above empirical account shows how collaboration is achieved in a case that is clearly not restricted to the local, but rather where coordinating activities and shared understanding must be performed in an *"unbounded"* II [10], using data that is generated across space and time. In the discussion, I will draw on CSCW studies from the healthcare domain and point out some similarities but also some notable differences in the domain of O&G exploration.

Berg [2] argues that we need to seek empirical accounts of what it is "reading and writing artifacts" do within medical practice. Berg suggests giving a *"minimalist, empirical depiction of what it is information technologies can be occasioned to do without falling back on the essentialist, non-relational accounts we want to avoid?"* (ibid.). In his analysis he finds coordination and accumulation to be the two central capacities that reading and writing artifacts can be occasioned to perform in work practices. The reading and writing artifacts that Berg studies are arguably less complex than the II perspective on inscription devices that I have described above (Berg's order form and fluid balance sheet in one medical record application versus Openworks and Petrel that has many features, such as helping in construct interpretations, algorithms and tools for 3D modeling for instance). The key capacity is the same, however, and hence the unit of analysis here; the *accumulation* of data in the O&G exploration II and the *coordination* it entails.

4.1 Coordination

In a more recent work, Bansler et al. [1] explains how CSCW studies over the last decade has shown how the medical record is *"complex and variegated"* and that studies has focused on *"the coordinative practices of clinical staff with special emphasis on the role of the medical record in these practices"*, and the medical record is best viewed as *"an ecology of artifacts"* and a *"heterogeneous assembly of specialized representational and coordinative artifacts"*. These characteristics are similar to those of II. In their continued analysis, Bansler et al. narrows their focus down to one artifact, the progress notes and explains how it is *"is constructed in an ongoing process of aggregation and arrangement of test results and observations, of offering hypotheses and suggestions, of deduction and allusion, of explicit reference and tacit omission."* and that the notes coordinate; *"They function as a cognitive artifact that facilitates memory and recall and they enable collaborative sense-making and coordination of actions in a highly complex, distributed work practice."* (ibid.). On a similar note, Berg [2] explains how information technologies *"afford the increased distribution of work practices over a greater number of entities, and over more times and spaces"*. Fitzpatrick and Ellingsen also shows how CSCW over the last 25 years has evolved from artifact mediated healthcare work, through locating healthcare in space and time, to expanding contexts of healthcare work with *"large scale implementations - integration and standardization challenges"* [8]. This coordination over time and space in the domain of healthcare is similar to what we see in the empirical account above. Data is entered into the different data stores from many places and many sources, of many kinds and about many places. At certain times, for different reasons, the area becomes interesting, and the II is searched for all data belonging to that area. The G&G want an overview of all the data, for then to be able to select what data is relevant to them. To aid their work, and select what to use and not, they need to know meta-data, such as when is the data from, who made it, etc. They buy and trade data if the company does not already have what they need, a case where the metadata becomes even more relevant. The data, and data about the data (metadata) entered yesterday, guides in many ways the work performed today. The hasty performance when creating the yesteryears final drill report for example, constrains and shapes the work performed today, e.g. by forcing the G&G of today to investigate more to fill in the gaps that exist in the report. They question the report and fill in the gaps, making new interpretations. Questioning the interpretations of others is something the G&G do, and something that is key for the II to support, as we shall see when we discuss *accumulation* below.

4.2 Accumulation

Accumulation in reading and writing artifacts Berg [2] says; *"reorganizes individual inscriptions into aggregates – through its spatial layout, or through computational operations"*. The notion of inscriptions here draws on Latour's study of scientific laboratory work, where he finds that the production of scientific *"fact"* is a process of *"literary inscription"* in scientific papers. Latour [13] explains; *"A text or statement can thus be read as "containing" or "being about a fact" when readers are sufficiently convinced that there is no debate about it and the processes of literary inscription are forgotten"*. Latour points to how all the debate and all the "messy" process of generating the "fact" is at certain points forgotten, and it is accepted in the community as facts. Berg [2] explain from the medical domain; *"Rather than having to check all the individual entries, nurses and doctors can work from the aggregated fluid balance, or wait for the monitor to beep when e.g. a patient's blood pressure drops below a certain point"*. The fact that you "can" does of course not mean that you do, or should. In the exploration case described above, they certainly do not accept the accumulations, or layered inscriptions, simply as facts, but rather indications that needs to be questioned. Remember they want to have an overview of all the relevant (given some criteria) data in an area. From that, they select the data they want to work with to create their interpretation. So, different from scientists that sometimes accept things as facts by referring to e.g. a theory in a paper, a paper where the link from the data to the theory is absent, the G&G need to be able to always get to the data that supports the current interpretation. Accumulation therefore is not a tool for simplification, but rather tools for questioning and reflection.

Bansler et al. [1] attributing questioning practice also to scientists, draws similarities between the clinicians progress notes in the domain of health, to the practice of research: *"In a way that is similar to a scientific community's evolving repertoire of papers (apart from the imperative to act that is defining of clinical work), some entries serve to present bits of fact (similar to research notes), other entries serve to outline treatment plans or strategies (research problems and hypotheses), while other entries again serve to review what has been learned so far. Written over time by several clinicians, often from different specialisms, in a highly distributed process, the progress notes serve to reflect ongoing external developments, to select and counterpoise bits of data, to formulate hypotheses as to causation, to suggest lines of action, etc"*. The argument that data is "counterpoised", at certain points in the patient trajectory (or biography), resonates well with how the G&G gradually build interpretations from the historical archive.

4.3 The Information Infrastructure Should Naturalize and Historicize to Support Cooperation

Different kinds of interpretations (e.g. geological and geophysical picks, horizons) are generated at certain times at certain places, but becomes part of an installed base in the information infrastructure, resides there, prepared to enable generation of gradually new interpretations, in concurrent cycles. Gradually new and improved inscriptions (interpretations) are made on the inscription devices, inscription upon inscription. But when is the inscription finished? When is it a fact? When is a "stabilized representation" ready? The answer seems to be never. It is an ongoing naturalization process. Bowker and Leigh-Star [4] discuss how objects naturalize, objects being defines as *"stuff and things, tools, artifacts and techniques, and ideas, stories and memories—objects that are treated as consequential by community members"* and thereby also relevant to data such as in our case, explains: *"Naturalization means stripping away the contingencies of an object's creation and its situated nature. A naturalized object has lost its anthropological strangeness. It is in that narrow sense desituated—members have forgotten the local nature of the object's meaning or the actions that go into maintaining and recreating its meaning."*. But it is not fixed. Objects become naturalized in certain communities at certain times, along *"trajectories of naturalization"* and it is not known a priori whether an object will become naturalised, or how long it will be so (ibid.). An interpretation in the II will move in and out of naturalization trajectories throughout time and space, and an interpretation is constructed upon combinations of earlier and new interpretations, being stable and natural at certain points of time, (e.g. a prospect or a final well report), before being moved away from the focus, stored, becoming a part of the accumulated archive in the II. G&Gs insist on having flexibility in choosing their own naming schemes (categories in Bowker's terms), creating "unfinished" drill reports, and how concerned they are with the meta-data (who created the data, what equipment, when was it created). The II is consequently need to exercise flexibility—e.g. as when the PDMs accept jobs, how they clean the data, the data that need to migrate between Petrel and Openworks, being archived in different datastores and accessed in a variety of ways and forms. For Bowker studying biodiversity infrastructures [3], this is a key insight; the II must reflect the diversity of the work at hand, but equally important, keep a historical record of it. When working with the complex issues of describing nature (be that the case of a human and their disease as in the cases of Berg and Bansler et al., rock formations as in my case, or biodiversity as in Bowker's case), practitioners face two emerging issues. First, that the way we store information and categorize it is *performative*, in that it shapes how we view the world. If all we store is "Rogaland formation" although it is considered too broad a category, we, over time, construct a reality based on the "Rogaland formation". Second, as a consequence of the first, we will have irreversibility. If all we store is "Rogaland formation", we cannot go back (in a DBs consisting of 110 Tb and counting), to recreate the lost categories. We have lost the reasons why "formation Rogaland" was relevant.

It is interesting to note in the empirical account how the two inscription devices of openworks and Petrel affect the building of such historical accounts. In Openworks, with the DB structure, interpretations were saved behind the scenes, and fixed by the PDMs. In Petrel, the process is made more explicit, and a barrier is made towards saving. This creates a challenge. Bowker [3] would argue towards the Openworks approach as a strategy out of the "*irreversibility*" bind. You may not save everything, but you should aim for "*deep historicization of our datasets*" (*ibid.*). The goal is to categorize and formalize historical perceptions of data, so as to enable the practitioner in one location of today to understand the data generated by practitioners elsewhere, from the past. The same principle is found when discussing the importance of context and how the design of the system influence and constrain to what degree the context can be captured and shared; "*...any computer system that affords representation and awareness of human activity necessarily involves a degree of reduction and objectification, due to the formal representational schemes of programs and databases, and finite capacities for storage, communication and calculation.*" [6]. The II constrains and enables to what degree historificazion is feasible. The awareness of the history needs to be coupled to the work and tools practitioners use, not separated from them. To achieve this, we need "*to make coordination and collaborative functionalities an aspect of the collaborative artifact rather than of a collaborative application*" [5]. The empirical case here suggests that an II view would move the focus away from a single artifact of cooperation and seek more holistic explanations with potentially more power. How both the PDM plays a pivotal role in storing and accessing the correct data as well and the possibility of the datastores to support queries of contextualized historical data (who created the data? who was the interpreter? etc.). This is the sociomaterial working of an II. Schmidt, in explaining the fragmentation of CSCW, shows how the field have moved from computer mediated communication, through office automation, to CSCW where the key problem "...*is not "communication" or "resource sharing"*, but *"the cooperating actors' control of their interaction and, by implication, of the computational regulation of their interaction"* [19]. These issues of coordination are not restricted to the local either *"Indeed, coordinating interdependent activities across space is one of the problems faced by actors engaged in cooperative work "in the wild.""* (Ibid. p 237), and perhaps we could add, across time, implying asynchronous coordination, as noted by Cabitza and Simone: *"Too often the fact that actors actively monitor and proactively display awareness information is disregarded in favor of undifferentiated mechanisms of notification. In doing so, the fact that the proactive part of the phenomenon remains unsupported, especially in asynchronous remote collaboration, is weighted against the fact that the resulting technology might seem easier for the user to appropriate and surely simpler for the designer to construct."* [5].

5 Concluding Remarks and Future Work

In the discussion above I have discussed accounts from the CSCW healthcare literature with observations in oil and gas exploration, using an II approach. While both Berg and Bansler et al. consider specific artifacts to be coordinative, we see from the description above the sociomaterial components (social; G&G, PDMs; material; Openworks and Petrel) that go into an II to enable it to store, process, and retrieve historical data to support the reflection of today. I have started unearthing an II in exploration with the focus on data in the form of interpretations, and *what* is standardized *when* in the biography of the interpretations it is standardized and for *whom* it applies [15]. Williams and Pollock [22], although focusing on systems rather than data, also argue for the notion of studying IIs from a biography point of view based on a growing dissatisfaction with the *"single site implementation study"*. Systems and data need, in an II perspective, to be placed in broader perspective, to understand the "locales and actors" that play a role in shaping the performance of the II, to; *"develop better temporal understanding of ERP implementations that include not simply the immediate response by actors but also the multiple and often longer-term temporal conceptions that might surround deployment and appropriation"* (ibid.).

In this work I have taken the first steps of unearthing the II of oil and gas exploration in terms of coordination, accumulation, historificazion and naturalization. I have empirically shown the relevance of *"deep historicization"* of datasets in an II, giving practitioners the ability to properly reflect and make proper interpretations. This is inline with recent work from Haavik [9], who frames this sociomaterial process as *"sensework"* (as separated from sensemaking) being characterized as sociomaterial (different distributed teams in hi-tech environment), cognition and meaning is indistinguishable from work itself, there is no final right solution, nothing is final, only worked on, and sense connotes sensors (no direct empirical confirmation is possible). Future research here should provide insight into the data and models of an II that shape and are being shaped by spatiotemporal independent reflective practice. Finally, it is relevant in this setting, given the role of nature, to extend the notion of materiality in the sociomateriality debate from the interplay between the social organization and their information systems, towards also including additional levels, such as the physical materiality of nature and how it is dealt with [16]. In so doing, interesting challenges emerge, both for the CSCW and IS field, in how we methodologically and analytically address the bi-directional impact between the material nature, the materiality of the II representing nature, and the social organization.

References

1. Bansler J et al (2013) Physicians' progress notes. In: Bertelsen OW et al (eds) ECSCW 2013: proceedings of the 13th European conference on computer supported cooperative work, 21–25 Sept 2013, Paphos, Cyprus. Springer, London, pp 123–142. Available at http://link. springer.com/chapter/10.1007/978-1-4471-5346-7_7. Accessed 7 Nov 2013
2. Berg M (1999) Accumulating and coordinating: occasions for information technologies in medical work. Comput Support Coop Work (CSCW) 8(4):373–401
3. Bowker GC (2000) Biodiversity datadiversity. Soc Stud Sci 30(5):643–683
4. Bowker GC, Star SL (1999) Sorting things out: classification and its consequences. MIT Press, Cambridge
5. Cabitza F, Simone C (2013) Computational coordination mechanisms: a tale of a struggle for flexibility. Comput Support Coop Work (CSCW) 22(4–6):475–529
6. Chalmers M (2004) A historical view of context. Comput Support Coop Work 13(3–4):223–247
7. Crabtree A, Tolmie P, Rouncefield M (2013) How many bloody examples do you want? Fieldwork and generalisation. In: Bertelsen OW et al (eds) ECSCW 2013: proceedings of the 13th European conference on computer supported cooperative work, 21–25 Sept 2013, Paphos, Cyprus. Springer, London, pp 1–20. Available at http://dblp.l3s.de/d2r/page/publications/conf/ecscw/CrabtreeTR13. Accessed 7 Nov 2013
8. Fitzpatrick G, Ellingsen G (2013) A review of 25 years of CSCW research in healthcare: contributions, challenges and future agendas. Comput Support Coop Work (CSCW) 22(4–6):609–665
9. Haavik TK (2014) Sensework. Comput Support Coop Work (CSCW). Springer, The Netherlands, p 1–30. doi:10.1007/s10606-014-9199-9
10. Hanseth O, Lyytinen K (2010) Design theory for dynamic complexity in information infrastructures: the case of building internet. J Inf Technol 25(1):1–19
11. Hyne NJ (2001) Nontechnical guide to petroleum geology, exploration, drilling, and production. PennWell Books, Tulsa, Oklahoma
12. Langley A (1999) Strategies for theorizing from process data. Acad Manage Rev 24(4):691
13. Latour B, Woolgar S (1986) Laboratory life: the construction of scientific facts. Princeton University Press, Princeton
14. Mayernik MS, Wallis JC, Borgman CL (2013) Unearthing the infrastructure: humans and sensors in field-based scientific research. Comput Support Coop Work (CSCW) 22(1):65–101
15. Monteiro E et al (2012) From artefacts to infrastructures. Comput Support Coop Work (CSCW) 22(4–6):575–607

16. Østerlie T, Almklov PG, Hepsø V (2012) Dual materiality and knowing in petroleum production. Inf Organ 22(2):85–105
17. Parmiggiani E, Mikalsen M (2013) The facets of sociomateriality: a systematic mapping of emerging concepts and definitions. In: Aanestad M, Bratteteig T (eds.) Nordic contributions in IS research. Lecture notes in business information processing. Springer, Berlin, pp 87–103. Available at http://link.springer.com/chapter/10.1007/978-3-642-39832-2_6. Accessed 7 Nov 2013
18. Prilla M, Pammer V, Krogstie B (2013) Fostering collaborative redesign of work practice: challenges for tools supporting reflection at work. In: Bertelsen OW et al (eds) ECSCW 2013: proceedings of the 13th European conference on computer supported cooperative work, 21–25 Sept 2013, Paphos, Cyprus. Springer, London, pp 249–268. Available at http://link.springer.com/chapter/10.1007/978-1-4471-5346-7_13. Accessed 7 Nov 2013
19. Schmidt K (2009) Divided by a common acronym: on the fragmentation of CSCW. In: Wagner I et al (eds) ECSCW 2009. Springer, London, pp 223–242. Available at http://link.springer.com/chapter/10.1007/978-1-84882-854-4_14. Accessed 7 Nov 2013
20. Schmidt K (2011) The concept of 'work' in CSCW. Comput Support Coop Work 20(4–5):341–401
21. Star SL, Ruhleder K (1996) Steps toward an ecology of infrastructure: design and access for large information spaces. Inf Syst Res 7:111–134
22. Williams R, Pollock N (2012) Research commentary—moving beyond the single site implementation study: how (and why) we should study the biography of packaged enterprise solutions. Inf Syst Res 23(1):1–22

Between Initial Familiarity and Future Use: A Case of Collocated Collaborative Writing

Susanne Bødker and Anna Maria Polli

Abstract This paper reports on a design experiment in an art gallery, where we explored visitor practices of commenting on art, and how they were shaped in interaction with a newly designed collocated, collaborative writing technology. In particular we investigate what potentials previous practices carry with them that may affect early use and further development of use. We base our analyses on interviews in the art gallery and on socio-cultural theories of artefact-mediated learning and collaboration. The analyses help identify three forms of collaborative writing, which are placed in the space between future use possibilities and initial familiarity based on everyday practices. These forms met and at times collided in a space where the actual use was shaped. We furthermore look back on initial assumptions made in design regarding a productive collaborative writing style, and confront these with the three above forms of practice. The initial familiarity leads to two different early practices that get in the way of each other, and the collaborative writing idea. They point instead towards a discursive sharing of individual feelings, a different kind of past experiences than anticipated in design.

Keywords Collocated collaborative installation · Early use · Developmental process of use · Initial familiarity · Future use

1 Introduction

In this paper we take our starting point in an explorative use setting where a collocated collaborative writing platform was set up to support people in sharing their interpretations of art pieces in an art gallery. The ideas were

S. Bødker · A. M. Polli (✉)
Department of Computer Science, Aarhus University, Aarhus, Denmark
e-mail: ampo@cs.au.dk

S. Bødker
e-mail: bodker@cs.au.dk

C. Rossitto et al. (eds.), *COOP 2014 - Proceedings of the 11th International Conference on the Design of Cooperative Systems, 27–30 May 2014, Nice (France)*, DOI: 10.1007/978-3-319-06498-7_9, © Springer International Publishing Switzerland 2014

- to support contributions from people when they were in the art gallery
- to give access to a format of contributions that was open to be shaped by the audience/contributors without previous introduction
- to give access to the contributions of others so as to produce a shared text, inspired by the way Wikipedia gives access to sharing entries
- while also bridging the divide between the artist who produces the artwork, the curator who traditionally produces an authoritative curative text, and the audience who discuss among themselves, in particular in small groups that visit the art gallery together. This was somewhat pretentiously framed as 'democratic curation' even though it may be a direct replacement of a curational text.

There is a wide body of work related to the use of Wikipedia-like technologies in museums and art galleries, and we don't want to discuss neither museum technologies in general, nor the potential for using Wikipedia in such settings. Macdonald [13] gives an excellent overview of art institutions, the curatorial process, and the deployment of IT in museums in general. Thom-Santelli et al. [18] discuss the development of art expertise and the connected feeling of ownership in a museum gallery, where novices and experts together were collaboratively tagging the exhibition. Galani and Chalmers [11] evaluate a prototyping experiment where physically and virtually co-located visitors collaborate. Ciolfi et al. [9] discuss two technological installations where visitors were engaged in reflection, discussion and debate around the exhibits. The idea that a Wikipedia-like technology may move curation towards more openness and democracy is unfolded in the context of museums by Phillips [15].

In the current paper, we are interested in what happened when visitors got introduced to the new technological artifact, more than we are concerned with longer-term evaluation or wider issues of the usefulness of such technologies in art galleries, where temporary exhibitions are shown.

The paper introduces the study and the use situation further, introducing a socio-cultural theoretical framing and methods. It moves on from there to analyze the data and bring out findings. The socio-cultural framing fundamentally helps understand human practices, how they are shaped in interaction with artifact ecologies, and how they carry with them potentials for further development.

2 Set-up and Deployment

The research project (LAA–Local Area Artwork) was deployed at the art gallery Kunsthal Aarhus, a venue for contemporary art. We had in total three meetings with the artists and their curator to introduce the LAA idea, to test and discuss the prototype. Additionally we had four separate preparation meetings with the staff of the art gallery. After a discussion with the management and the staff from the gallery, an exhibition by the local artists Afgang 13, in May 2013 was selected. The exhibition, entitled New G, was a traditional exhibition including paintings,

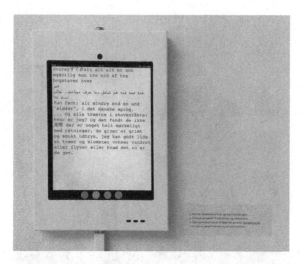

Fig. 1 One digital panel with a small label next to it providing connection instructions

sculptures and installations. This art gallery usually presents curated exhibitions, where artists have produced their art pieces and put them to show in the art gallery and together with the curator describe the artwork and its relation to the exhibition. The art gallery and the artists allowed us to experiment with the text often accompanying the artwork. The idea was to let people write a collaborative interpretation of the artwork on our digital panels (see Fig. 1), which were positioned next to the art piece. We studied the use of installation and how the audience would write a text together during the exhibition period (Fig. 2).

Our research instrument consisted of six iPads or, as we call them, panels, which were deployed in the three rooms of the exhibition. In this setting visitors, artists, curators and the staff were invited to engage with or through our panels. The artists, the curators and the staff were familiar with the project as we discussed them in length together. The visitors were briefed to the research project and the new technology when entering the art gallery. Visitors we offered to interact with the text on the panels through their own Smartphones, requiring no installation, since a web page was automatically launched when the user/Smartphone was in the vicinity of a panel. While standing in front of the artwork and the display, people could edit and write new text (Fig. 2). When connected to the Wi-Fi, and upon opening a web-browser, they were automatically redirected to the editable version of the digital panel. We assumed that there was very little learning needed, since a small label next to the panels provided connection instructions (Fig. 1).

At the start of the exhibition, the panels were deliberately left blank to provoke and not limit the audience in their writings/usages. Neither did the curators provide any initial texts or interpretations about the artworks.

We applied the notion of Wikipedia into our design, to seek Wikipedia-style collaboration and participation with the artworks. For this purpose, we created

Fig. 2 Visitors interacting with the panels through their personal devices to write comments

these panels as shared surfaces where collocated visitors and people coming after each other could write joint interpretations. To emphasize the collocated use, the text was live-updated on the digital panel, and dots at the bottom of the panel showed how many people were actively editing (Fig. 1). The newly written text would appear in these respective colors to create awareness of the same-time editing of several people. All the written text was limited to the visible area of the one-page display, and no scrolling was enabled on the panel. When the display was full, the users got a notification on their phone to delete or edit what previously had been written. For details in respect to the implementation of the installation see [7, 12, 16]. As we return to, we carried out a number of empirical investigations throughout this exhibition period.

3 Theoretical Framing

In analyzing the material, we draw from socio-cultural research. This approach fundamentally aims at understanding human practices, how they are shaped in interaction with artifacts, and how they carry with them potentials for further development.

With our analytical perspective human beings are situated in a web of activities and ecologies of technological artifacts (cf. [5]). Accordingly, we are concerned with the ecology of artifacts into which new technological designs, such as the LAA, get placed and how such a technological design changes the artifact ecology. In addition, we are concerned with the activities from which users draw their experiences. Bødker and Christiansen [3] seek inspiration in [17], who is talking about the space of experience and the horizon of expectation. Ricoeur sees expectations always in the light of experience, and experience always from particular expectations. Accordingly, we are looking back at the quite early experiences that people had with the panels, how they relate these experiences to other artifacts and to past practices; what expectations they have when it comes to the usefulness of the panels in art exhibitions, and what understandings they evoke in explaining this.

In understanding how people talk about relating past experiences to expectations of future use, we seek inspiration from Bakhtin, [4, 19, p. 54], who talk about language and how a word is first somebody else's and then, when being picked up, first is half someone else's half one's own. It becomes one's own only when populated with one's own intentions, one's "accent", when one appropriates it. In continuation of socio-cultural theory we focus on the use of a new artifact and the way the users talk about this develop together. We are interested in the problems of introducing the LAA panels in art curation and discussions, as well as what potentials it holds, in particular for the visitors.

Engeström [10] points out that change processes are not fully predictable: When a new artifact is brought into use, its use cannot be predicted. Neither is use static and unchangeable. Hence, we need to understand better the relationships between the future use, and part practices and artifacts (see also [6]). Bødker and Christiansen [4] describe appropriation through anticipation, initial familiarity, development of repertoires of routines and the development of new forms of use. This perspective allows us to understand development of human practices in the meeting with what is in one way or another different from what the learners already are capable of, or the concept of the zone of proximal development which has come to mean the possible future practices, or developmental potentials, spanned out in confronting existing practice with other ways of doing similar things [2]. Our understanding of the LAA panels are as springboards [10] for such a development because, when placed into the art gallery they confront **existing practices**, trigger among users an **initial familiarity** that is based on these former practices, while they point ahead to **future use** possibilities [1].

What is interesting for this paper is to understand what users identify as initially familiar, what existing practices they draw on, what explicit or implicit "help" (or hindrances) they get from the artifact in forming their initial use, and how existing practices and new uses can somehow constitute the core potential for future use. This happens on the background of the network of actors and activities surrounding the meeting of the user with the artifact (Fig. 3). Again we will use the socio-cultural understanding of networks of activities [5] as activities that are interconnected and mediated by artifacts, always carried out by people. Are there any kinds of understanding that helps people across from initial familiarity to a consolidated use? Do some of the different kinds of initial familiarity clash? And to what extent do they help or hinder users in getting towards their own conception of future use?

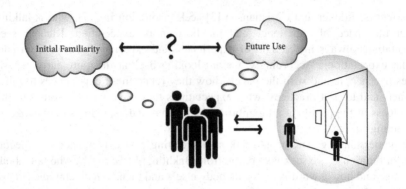

Fig. 3 The model: the relation between the exhibition visitors as we interview them, and the actual meeting with the technology in the exhibition, as well as the relation between the initial familiarity that they experience in the exhibition activating past practices, and the future use that they come to understand, or expect in the Ricoeurian sense. The analysis is focused on how the LAA mediates communication in the art gallery, and hence the space between initial familiarity and future use

4 Empirical Method

The project was deployed at the art gallery for over one month, a period of an exhibition, and accordingly our study was limited in time. Over this period we carried out several kinds of activity that we will not go into further here: we e.g. carried out panel discussions with artists, curators and staff from the art gallery and we asked visitors to fill out short questionnaires. In focus in this paper are 13 exit interviews on-site with 19 visitors and our log of different user activities where we recorded the history of written, edited and deleted text by participants over the whole exhibition period.

The semi-structured exit interviews were carried out with visitors, who were interviewed individually and in pairs (see Table 1). The interviews lasted from 20 to 45 min. A variety of people were invited to the interviews, both those who engaged with our installation and those who were with them, which included families, couples, and individuals. The interviewee's age was broad and ranged from around 15 to 65.

The 13 interviews were transcribed, and the transcripts were used as a basis for the bottom-up analysis, where the quotes were extracted and categorized. Since we worked with interview data, this analysis primarily helped us understand how people talk about their use, triggered by the actual use of the panels. We triangulated these analyses with the above theoretical understanding of learnable artifacts and with the log data of how people actually used the panels.

Since the exit interviews were made after brief visits in the exhibition, the data mainly allowed us to dig deeper into what initial familiarity the artifact seemed to activate in the visitors, and what future uses they imagined based on these very

Table 1 List of interviews

	Interviewee's description	Initials
Interview #1	A couple (woman and man) in their 20s	(1M) & (1C)
Interview #2	Woman in her mid 60s, visiting alone	(2)
Interview #3	Man in his early 40s, visiting alone	(3)
Interview #4	A couple (woman and man) in their end-20s	(4D) & (4L)
Interview #5	Woman, teenager, visiting with her parents	(5)
Interview #6	Man in his end 30s, visiting alone	(6)
Interview #7	Daughter (early 20s) and father (late 50s)	(7A) & (7P)
Interview #8	A couple (woman and man) in their early 30s	(8K) & (8E)
Interview #9	Man in his mid 50s, visiting with his family	(9)
Interview #10	Siblings (woman and man) in their mid 20s	(10V) & (10M)
Interview #11	Man in his early 50s, visiting with a friend	(11)
Interview #12	A couple (woman and man) in their mid 30s	(12M) & (12C)
Interview #13	Woman in her early 30s, visiting alone	(13)

early encounters with the LAA. In addition the interviews gave some indications as to the very early learning that happened in and outside use, and the conditions that people thought they encountered for activating former practices in possible future use.

5 Findings and Analyses

In the following section we present our findings and analysis. After setting the scene by describing the network of people and their activities as well as the challenges of formal and informal learning in LAA we turn to future uses. These are grouped under three headings, and emphasize the various kinds of use of our research instrument: In the interviews, participants were indicating diverse understandings of *future use* of the technology, and we are trying to identify the diversity of these. More than a handful of types of usages were talked about in the interviews, and we will further look into three of those to understand specifically the collaborative side of possible future uses. After introducing each of the usages, another important question will be answered: Where do these future uses come from? What influences the interviewees to develop these expectations of particular future uses? We use people's expression of *initial familiarity* to address how particular images of use have come into existence as expectation of future use for the users. We found in our analysis many ways in which interviewees talk about what in LAA they recognized (as what) and on which they immediately draw their initial use. In fact we find a long list of overlapping artifacts and practices. These practices are in several ways the starting point for the learning and we are interested to learn how they are brought into a new context and are made useful in the interaction with the LAA.

5.1 Network of Communities and Activities

An art exhibition is the home of an intrinsic network of activities many of which go into the shaping of the art experience for the visitors: Art pieces have been selected by curators with some kind of idea and sense of quality in mind. In an art gallery like Kunsthal Aarhus, the physical layout of the building plays an important role for how the exhibition can be brought together. The artists at the same time have produced the art pieces from some sort of idea. There may be a dialogue between the curators and the artists regarding the process and exhibition. Traditionally, the curator (and not e.g. the artist) gets to do an interpretation of the art piece that gets conveyed to the spectators in (roughly) an A4 size text. The curator or curators also arrange the exhibition. The audience, the spectators, willingly or unwillingly, gets to see the result, to walk the exhibition, to engage with the artwork, as well as with the curations (which may also include catalogs etc.). Some of the audience may know what the exhibition is about while others don't. Some people come in groups, while others come alone. Some of these people are indeed more knowledgeable than others, and some are quite happy to share this knowledge.

It is into this network that we brought LAA with the hypothesis that it could extend the engagement among visitors while getting rid of or lessening the authoritative voice of curator in the exhibition, much in the same way as Wikipedia can be seen as a platform for encyclopedia without appointed experts.

5.2 Getting Started with LAA

LAA is indeed based on the idea that very little learning or introduction is needed outside of actual use. As a matter of fact it has been based on three basic ideas, one being that people can interact with the panels on their own devices with zero install [7] and direct access on the phone/device to the text on the panels; that basically LAA offers mainly a blank sheet of paper where it is legitimate to write anything, and finally that a bit of very minimal instruction could be given by the art gallery staff at the entrance of the gallery (when purchasing tickets). The question to be asked is obviously whether this sufficed? In the following sections we discuss what kinds of assumptions people made regarding use and in those sections we return to how they then draw upon earlier experiences in use (and when they talk about it).

The question that we look into much further in the following is which elements of LAA that may or may not support the collaboration and learning among visitors in the art gallery?

5.3 *Future Use as* Sharing Reflections

In this section we will elaborate on the first future use possibility **Sharing Reflections**, which is talked about several times throughout the interviews. People talked about a kind of use, where they would share their experiences about the art works. *"I think it's positive just that people reflect on things they see"* (6). This was a novel experience for visitors in an art gallery, and triggered people to think ahead. They were talking about our installation as: *"a possibility to make a comment about it (artwork), and then people who come another day, or later today could read it, that you could actually give your own point of view and someone will read it"* (1M). Those participants also wrote with the purpose of making others reflect from a different perspective: *"it also gives like an experience to the audience coming later and you write and they read that and you can affect their look upon the art piece"* (8 R2). Others were strengthening this possible use in the making by indicating: *"someone is writing short messages and it gives you an association, it could be nice to comment to that"* (9) or *"it's also nice to read what other people write, because you look at the work of art and then you have an opinion and you read the comments and [...] you adjust your own view on the artwork because you know what some other people think"* (7 R1). People read others comments to confront and adjust their point of view on the art piece. Figure 4, illustrates (from the log files) how participants share their reflections about one artwork, after adjusting and relating their comments to the previous written ones.

These interviewees see people writing their comments or reflections about the art piece on the panels, on the one hand to contribute to this interpretation panel, on the other hand to stimulate others coming later to think differently about an artwork. This again inspires others that read those, and perhaps adjust their view on the artwork accordingly. This socially recursive process of sharing reflections was detected in the interviewees' responses throughout the deployment period of our installation. People described this phenomenon as: *"a communication"* (13).

The idea of sharing their reflections may be to engage other visitors to think about the art from different perspectives. People explained they: *"commented on each others comments"* (4L) as a kind of meta-reflection or a reflection actually happening at two levels: First as a way of engaging among visitors that are present at the same time in the exhibition. Second in an indirect way, a communication of unknown users, where previous users have left comments on the panels that later users pick up on. Even though people were not present at the same time, many of the interviewees embraced the idea of having such reflective dialogues with other visitors about an artwork through the panels. Interviewees embraced the idea of following up on other's comments, which not only changed their ways of thinking about the art piece, but also in particular motivated them, to respond to these comments. When the interviewer was asked about their use: *"so you followed up on the previous comment that was written there?"* (11), one participant responded: *"yeah, we did that. Hopefully in a good way, I just wrote a short comment to him"* (11).

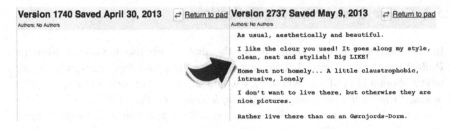

Version 1740 Saved April 30, 2013   ⇄ Return to pad   **Version 2737 Saved May 9, 2013**   ⇄ Return to pad

Authors: No Authors   Authors: No Authors

As usual, aesthetically and beautiful.

I like the clour you used! It goes along my style, clean, neat and stylish! Big LIKE!

Home but not homely... A little claustrophobic, intrusive, lonely

I don't want to live there, but otherwise they are nice pictures.

Rather live there than on an Gørnjords-Dorm.

Fig. 4 Screenshots from the transformation on the panels, from a blank screen to an active screen with several separate shared reflections (translated)

This quote illustrates the reflective cycle quite well: "*I interacted with him and he interacted with the sculpture and interacted with me too, at the same time*" *(11)*, or "*I thought about activating the audience instead of just the curator creates the direction and write something*" *(4D)*.

Sharing reflections is in consort with the idea of LAA that the curatorial writing switches from the hands of the curator to: "*every day people (who are) writing what they think about it.*" (1C). This indicates that this future use possibility points towards a social and more democratic interactivity, where various people are writing an interpretation and not just the curator. The traditional curatorial text is unchanged, but through involving visitors the text evolves over time within the exhibition period: "*you can also get, like a new piece of art out of it, because when people write what they feel when they see it, and you have to delete something, then it changes over time.*" (1C) This future use represents a further support to the design of LAA. As well as the matter of bringing people back to local places correlates to our idea of LAA. "*I would not mind, because I have a notion that art critics is going to flow away, since people have the opportunity to comment more through the net*" (11). This points out that people move away from traditional understandings of what happens in and around art galleries and towards something more interactive that seems to compare to various forms of commenting on the Internet.

Moving on to initial familiarity, we turn to four practices, which can be identified as previous understandings and actions that people brought into consideration for their initial use; or recognized as initial familiarity. These four, are indeed not the only ones that we identified, as we see below, but they are the four that most directly relate to **Sharing reflections** as future use.

1. Familiarity with curation texts

People know and compare the texts on the LAA panels with traditional art catalogues: "*a lot of time when you look at art, it's just like browsing through a catalogue*" (4A). They recognize that curators produce texts for art exhibitions, such as: "*there is someone who knows art, who describes this piece*" (1M).

2. Familiarity with getting involved and art interpretation

People interested in arts are familiar with: *"usually, when I go to an exhibition, I always interpret"* (3). Therefore people consider this practice as iterative cycle of communication: *"I interacted with him (the artist), he interacted with the sculpture and he interacted with me too, at the same time"* (11) or *"it's how to get a dialogue with an artist, that's the only way to talk to him to have a dialogue, for this it can be used"* (2).

3. Familiarity with off-line art discussions

"I have a friend who sent a text and sometimes he was going and passing by a shop in New York and then he was on the net and he wrote to us" (9). This indicates that people do not necessarily carry out art discussion in the local place, but also: *"it's like when you get used to it and use the internet, instead of reading a magazine and then you normally read the comments and when you then read it then in a printed magazine, you like the comments like that extra layer"* (1M).

4. Familiarity with the chat-room

"I like the idea of that like open chat-room thing, that sounds like a really good idea actually" (10M) or *"because more kind of a creative dialogue to have with strangers, so it's fun"* (4D). Or the following comment by (11): *"yeah I just stated: think about it, to the next person (...) that's all short, you don't have to write a long newspaper article, you just can make it short and then again you interact with people (interviewer: yes, and then you give the next guy to think about) (laughing) hopefully, that's interacting right?"*

People refer back to these four practices, when they are talking about the future use of sharing reflections, yet there is no direct way from these to the notion of sharing reflections: Classical curation texts (see Familiarity 1) are not about sharing reflections, yet people seem to recognize and even appreciate the input from somebody understanding art. Some of the people who are interested in art also share art discussions (Familiarity 3) and see themselves in a sort of hermeneutic loop with the artist and the art piece (Familiarity 2). In comparison with these three, the chat-room (Familiarity 4) comes out of a quite different space of experience, that has little to do with art specifically, yet is quite well reflected in the use of the panels in Fig. 4. The three first of these (Familiarity 1–3) are different in that (Familiarity 1) points to the role of the consumer of professional art texts whereas 2 and 3 are about sharing within the audience. Where the initial Familiarities 1–3 could just as well point to a future use that would be closer to a Wikipedia-style text production, it is no. 4 that helps understand that the kind of sharing of reflections that the visitors are after, is different from Wikipedia: *an actual dialogue between the visitors.*

This same structure will be now used to analyse two more future uses that were identified through the interviews, before we move on to address the bigger picture when these conceptions of future use meet.

Fig. 5 Screenshots indicating two characteristics of a guestbook, *left* greetings ("Hi Mom"), *right* initials of the author

5.4 Future Use as Guestbook

The second notion of future use relates to the guestbook metaphor. The design idea of the blank white screen of the panels evoked several ideas of what future uses may be like, such as applying the style of **writing like in a guestbook**, as when our participants were explaining about other visitors: *"they use it like a guest book"* (1C). Some people used the installation like a guestbook or Foursquare check-into say they were there. In Fig. 5 there are two evidences for writing as in a guestbook, on the left we have an indication of a greetings style and to the right we spotted initials from one of the authors, where we have the evidence that one of our interviewees stated: *"On the first one I wrote my name, on the others I didn't (laughing)"* (6).

When our interviewees talk about this style of possible future use it reflects a previous practice where people come to museums or other semi-public spaces and there is a guestbook available. Some people write comments in this about their visit and to state their presence.

5. Familiarity with tagging "I was here" and guest books

The analogy with guest books was drawn e.g. by an interviewee: *"I think it depends a lot on what people write, because if you use it just like a guestbook, just to write HI HI"* (1M), and several other interviewees also mention how the comments left by other audience is almost like tags: *"so it was not like a discussion, it was more like 'I was here, I liked it'"* (6).

The classical guestbook here meets both Foursquare check-ins and perhaps even more graffiti-like tagging in this future use. In this way, the practice of leaving a brief note to way "I was here" is understood and recognized by many visitors, through not without frustration, as we return to, as when (6) points out that it was not like a discussion. More straight forward the interviewees worry about clutter, and somehow the interviewees seem to worry about this guestbook style as a potential *waste of good writing space*.

We return to how this future use further collides with the other future uses in Sect. 5.7.

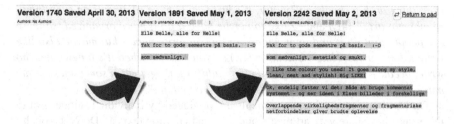

Fig. 6 Screenshots from a discussion about the artwork, where separate comments remind of a style of writing like on Facebook (note the mixed languages)

5.5 *Future Use as* Facebook wall

Some interviewees pointed towards another future use possibility, of **writing in the style as on the Facebook wall**, where they state it is: *"interesting that when there is a text, and then have a comment to the text and then like have a string, where there was a commented text"* (9). Another indication that people see a possible future use of Facebook originates from this comment: *"each piece of art that is on Facebook, then you could just have a wall, and then you know people write on the wall of the page and then you know, people comment on each other, then you can see the history start"* (12C). Further images of future use developed out of that openness, such as making **use of existing platforms**: *"it could be a great future, if you could take up the battle (of the discussion) on Twitter or on an online forum [...], because you have two opposing opinion of the artwork and could get into a nice discussion"* (4L). In Fig. 6 we illustrate the separately written interpretation of an artwork, where people write comments like on Facebook, separated with blank lines.

In this future use, the written text relates to the artwork, and the comments are meaningfully related to each other. While e.g. 4L indicates a future use that is wider than simply the well-known Facebook wall, this wall style is nonetheless quite directly appropriated by the visitors in writing on the LAA panels as can be seen in Fig. 6. They keep a strict distinction between the comments as they are familiar with from Facebook, and all in all this use shows a very direct link to the initial familiarity (6, below) of seeing the LAA panels as a version of the Facebook wall.

6. Familiarity with Facebook

Facebook often gets mentioned as an analogy from which people draw their experiences: *"then you could just have a wall, and then people write on the wall of the page and then you know, people comment on each other, then you can see the history start, something more, this was really like, this really looked like a white board, right?"* (13C) or *"yeah I mean, I post on Facebook, I write emails, I guess (...) I was writing on a website using my phone, so my phone was just my keyboard"* (12M). Further details are added e.g. by another interviewee: *"you post everything on Facebook, on Twitter, it's just people have comments on everything, so why not art?"* (4L) and *"I like to maybe have it a bit more organized, so there are people that do it and anonymous or you can write names but maybe also like write a time or just 'like' something (...) so you can see when it's a new one who write, because that kind of confused me, I didn't really get when sometimes people make like (...) a separation with the line or something"* (10V).

On Facebook (or Twitter) comments are produced by individuals alone, and in this sense they share with art pieces and classical curation texts a "Do-Not-Touch" atmosphere. As discussed in [7], people hesitate to delete the texts of others, which creates collisions with the one page format proposed in LAA. Hence, the acted out initial familiarity/future use in the gallery runs into problems when the screen fills up. This causes confusion, but apparently now enough for people to change their expectations for this kind of future use of LAA.

In the next section we look into how the early practices identified in the art gallery seem to be sustainable in the journey towards a future use.

5.6 The Sustainability of Early Practices

In the process of adopting a technology, people are dependent on technologies and practices that are well known to them, such as discussions on Facebook walls and discussions of art, as we have pointed to above. The questions that one may raise, however, given our theoretical framing is the extend to which these forms of initial familiarity also help users take the first steps towards more solid shared practices of collaborative use?

In the interviews, people themselves e.g. questioned the sustainability of the tagging or guestbook practices: *"People didn't really write so much, so it was not like a discussion, it was more like 'I was here, I liked it'"* (6) or, *"I think there is a problem, that a lot of the comments are not about the art, it is more like: Hi, hi I am using this. But I think it would be very nice, if it was like comments focusing on the piece of art"* (1M).

The Facebook practices seem more consistent in that they are already being used quite extensively in the art gallery (see Sect. 5.5). It seems that the early practices of e.g. texting or Facebook walls are more recognizable than that of e.g. shared editing such as in Wikipedia, which does not get mentioned in the interviews (despite the initial design idea), or than the practices of sharing reflections. Since people are familiar with these types of platforms or environments, such as Facebook or writing in a guestbook, they tend to draw upon these practices. People that applied the guestbook on the digital panel may have different daily practices, than the participants that were thinking of sharing their reflections on the panels. However, the above analysis indicates that sharing reflections in the long run may be limited by these writing styles, and hence that the limitations of guestbook and Facebook writing styles may in the longer perspective limit the possibilities of embracing this vision of future use.

Beyond the sustainability of initial practices we will look into this minefield of clashing uses in further detail in Sect. 5.7.

5.7 The Meeting of the Future Uses in the Art Gallery

We have identified three kinds of future uses, and six elements of initial familiarity that together were elements of shaping how people met the LAA panels and started one or more forms of collaboration mediated through the LAA panels. This space of mediation is, however, not just one where all forms of initial familiarity, and future use live equally smoothly alongside one another, it is more to the contrary.

First of all, the two future uses of sharing reflections and of guestbook tagging seemed ill at ease with each other: "*I could imagine if you can have a long discussion or something, if there is space enough? It could be fun and, I don't know, my impression was that it was rather…I didn't really read a lot, it was my impression that people didn't really write so much, so it was not like a discussion, it was more like 'I was here, I liked it'*" (6). This future use–"Hi, I liked it"–was sensed by some people as a hindrance, since it interfered with their expectations of more real communication.

Subsequently, some interviewees felt demotivated from noting down further thoughts about the artwork: "*I think it depends a lot on what people write, because if you use it just like a guest book, just to write 'HI HI', then you won't get so much out of it. [...] But I think that advantage comes when more people are more focused, on what they think of this piece of art, because that's what interesting for other people to read and to discuss more specific about each art piece*" (1M).

Others describe the same matter more specifically: "*there are different outcomes depending on how people use it, because if they use it like a guestbook, it is not that giving, and then, yeah, you can get like a new interpretation of the artwork, because it is every day people, writing what they think about it*" (1C). Subsequently the use of the guestbook writing style, illustrates a barrier that is preventive to sharing interpretations, and for the Facebook wall format discussions as well.

While perhaps more fragmented the Facebook future use seems more at ease with the sharing reflections, and it may actually be seen as one specific way of sharing reflections; a way where each statement is brief and left alone, even though it can be commented on.

In several ways the potential future uses and initially familiar kinds of use, are clashing with each other. Striking examples of contradicting uses exist across the Guestbook style, Facebook style and Sharing reflections use. And while one seems more obvious in the short term (Facebook wall) it does not necessary provide the shortest path, or even a path at all, to the vision of sharing reflections. The various kinds of initial familiarity confuse the participants and therefore eliminate each other and prohibit most likely a long lasting practice, turning the LAA into the battleground of various practices.

However, also confusion and disruptions were revealed, which are analogous to Bakhtin's resistance and the artefact talking back: *"well actually, I didn't understand exactly what it was, I thought because in summer I read some explanation about the art pieces (...) so maybe I thought it is just information about the art on those iPads, but then I saw like some other comments...."* (1M). These establishing uses are not just supportive for users to get started, they are confusing as well.

As discussed above, this may be preventive of developing reflections that are shared in a different sense than stating opinions that are being put in the open to be commented on. However, it is not clear from the interviews how far people imagine to be able to move when it comes to sharing reflections: Are they imagining a more genuine discussion, one-to-one or several visitors together?

Beyond the future uses that we identified from the interviews are the ones that we didn't see. Specifically, as we mentioned in the introduction, the design idea of a Wikipedia-like style of sharing an interpretation of the art piece is missing. It is missing both in what people actually did on the panels, and in how the interviewees talked about future practices and initial familiarity. Nobody mentions Wikipedia as an initial familiarity; a known object; a writing/editing style to depend on. LAA does not get picked up and used for actively editing and deleting others' comments so as to produce one coherent interpretation. Nobody mentions it as a future practice, and even though *sharing reflections* comes close it is still different: Where Wikipedia emphasizes a product or a shared object/outcome, the interviewees are more concerned with sharing their individual feelings and thoughts, so as to align those with the feelings and thoughts of others, and with the actual art piece.

6 Discussion

In this paper we have worked primarily with interview data, which have been connected also with log data from the panels. For this analysis, we got the most helpful data from the interviews, though we are going to continue working with the content of the log-files. There are a number of challenges with this approach some of which relate to making empirical studies of technologies in open and sporadic activities such as art galleries [8, 9]. When it comes to addressing future use possibilities, in particular and how people perceive of them based on very early use experiences, we find that interviews provide a better basis than e.g. observations of use. This is because neither the horizon of expectation nor the space of experience for that matter, are easily tapped into through observation, in particular when the actual interaction is brief and sporadic (Careful analysis of some amount of actual video data of use could give indications regarding initial familiarity and future use ideas). The two elements are largely linguistic, and we have treated them that way. The experiences, however are at the same time not as individual, retrospective or longitudinal as e.g. those considered by McCarthy and Wright [14]. For this reason, we find that there is room for better analytic methods in this space, and we see our work here as only the beginning.

In CSCW there has, in particular in the earlier years, been an extensive focus on collaborative writing. We have not spend much of our attention here on these writings, because there are many ways in which our work is quite far away from these many studies of focused co-writing in productive writing practices. As a matter of fact with our conclusion it seems to make more sense to compare our empirical material with other genres of (on-line) communication, be they email or chat-fora. A more systematic attempt at this, however, pertains to our future work.

The final comment goes to the design idea of the open design. Overall the assumption was that the blank editable sheet would lead some sort of shared something, perhaps even a productive co-production. Even though, designwise, we sat out to expect the unexpected, the analyses seem to point out that even this open format makes assumptions about future use, and that beyond this openness there is a next layer where it is quite difficult to make assumptions about which existing practices users may lend from when recognizing the design in initial familiarity, and when thinking about what this new design may be in future use.

7 Conclusion

We have identified three profound, yet contradictory, future uses and seen how they are mirrored in various forms of initial familiarity. Our users want to try to share reflections, but among them destroy this communication through scattered non-related guestbook comments. Two radically different ways of use get in the way of each other and seems to make the path towards a discursive sharing of individual feelings and thoughts less clear and perhaps impossible.

We designed an open installation, meaning there was little initial learning and introduction expected. Our analyses show that users nonetheless bring to the table, past experiences that strongly influence the possibilities of future use. This is inevitable and cannot as such be anticipated through better design, even though the theoretical framing and analytic method presented and applied in this helps drawing attention to the specific possibilities and hindrances in the specific context.

References

1. Bardram JE, Bertelsen OW (1995) Supporting the development of transparent interaction. In: Human-Computer interaction. Springer, Berlin, pp 79–90
2. Bertelsen OW, Bødker S (2003) Activity theory. HCI Models Theor Framew Multidiscip Sci 291–324
3. Bødker S, Christiansen E (1997) Scenarios as springboards in CSCW design. Soc. Sci. Tech. Syst. Coop. Work Gt. Divide Mahwah N. J. Lawrence Erlbaum Assoc., pp 217–234

4. Bødker S, Christiansen E (2012) Poetry in motion: appropriation of the world of apps. In: Proceedings of the 30th European conference on cognitive ergonomics, pp 78–84
5. Bødker S, Klokmose CN (2011) The human-artifact model: an activity theoretical approach to artifact ecologies. Human Comput Interact 26:315–371
6. Bødker S, Klokmose CN (2012) Dynamics in artifact ecologies. In: Proceedings of the 7th nordic conference on human-computer interaction: making sense through design, NordiCHI'12. ACM, New York, pp 448–457
7. Bødker S, Klokmose CN, Korn M, Polli AM (in Preparation) Participatory IT in semi-public spaces
8. Brown B, Reeves S, Sherwood S (2011) Into the wild: challenges and opportunities for field trial methods. In: Proceedings of the SIGCHI conference on human factors in computing systems, CHI'11. ACM, New York, pp 1657–1666
9. Ciolfi L, Bannon LJ, Fernström M (2008) Including visitor contributions in cultural heritage installations: designing for participation. Mus Manage Curatorship 23:353–365
10. Engeström Y (1987) Learning by expanding. an activity-theoretical approach to developmental research
11. Galani A, Chalmers M (2002) Can You See Me? Exploring co-visiting between physical and virtual visitors
12. Korn M, Klokmose CN (2012) Putting "Local" back into public Wifi hotspots. In: Proceedings of the 2012 ACM conference on ubiquitous computing, UbiComp'12. ACM, New York, pp 800–801
13. Macdonald S (2007) Interconnecting: museum visiting and exhibition design. CoDesign 3:149–162
14. McCarthy J, Wright P (2004) Technology as experience. Interactions 11:42–43
15. Phillips LB (2013) The temple and the bazaar: Wikipedia as a platform for open authority in museums. Curator Mus J 56:219–235
16. Polli AM, Korn M, Nylandsted Klokmose C (2013) Local area artworks: collaborative art interpretation on-site. In: Proceedings of the 2013 ACM conference on pervasive and ubiquitous computing adjunct publication, pp 79–82
17. Ricoeur P (1990) Time and narrative, vol 3. University of Chicago Press
18. Thom-Santelli J, Cosley D, Gay G (2010) What do you know? Experts, novices and territoriality in collaborative systems. In: Proceedings of the SIGCHI conference on human factors in computing systems, CHI'10. ACM, New York, pp 1685–1694
19. Wertsch JV (1998) Mind as action. Oxford University Press, New York

Suffering Beyond Negotiation: Towards a Biographic Perspective on Cooperative Design for Therapy

Olav W. Bertelsen

Abstract In this paper we argue that design in therapeutic domains (in a broad sense) depends on an understanding of the background for the engagement of the various users involved. It is specifically argued that an understanding of the life transforming process, or trajectory as opposed to design process and rational process of therapy has to be understood and that a possible cornerstone in such an understanding is a biographic concept inspired by Strauss' concepts of suffering. "Suffering" is discussed as a frame for enabling a subjective perspective to have a voice in design. That is to put a perspective center stage that is not based in the negotiation between rationalities. The paper draws examples from design based research projects over the last 5 years.

1 Introduction

The design of ICT based solutions and artifacts together with users, i.e. participatory design, is a cooperative process. Various actors are involved to collaboratively envision and build technologies for future practice. In workplace settings, the participatory design movement has emphasized the importance of involving workers to capture the various, often contradictory, interests, and to ensure that professional knowledge (including tacit knowledge) influences the design.

In recent years, ICT for the health care sector has been a growing arena for CSCW and participatory design. The health care sector presents a challenge with respect to how we understand collaboration and participation in relation to design. In many cases, the new ICT solution will influence and include patients at an active level. Not only in terms of quality of service, but also as more active

O. W. Bertelsen (✉)
Department of Computer Science, Center for Participatory-IT,
Aarhus University, Aabogade 34, 8200 Aarhus N, Denmark
e-mail: olavb@cs.au.dk

C. Rossitto et al. (eds.), *COOP 2014 - Proceedings of the 11th International Conference on the Design of Cooperative Systems, 27–30 May 2014, Nice (France)*, DOI: 10.1007/978-3-319-06498-7_10, © Springer International Publishing Switzerland 2014

participants in medical intervention. This is the case with telemedicine and similar approaches that aim to address the scarcity of medical personnel. Furthermore, this more active involvement of patients is a challenge to the traditional western medical paradigm that has mainly assumed that healthcare professionals and not patients should take an active role.

If patients are not to be understood as passive objects of medical intervention, it is a consequence of the basic ideas in participatory design to involve them as collaborators in the design process. This involvement is a challenge with respect to method, process and design activities. In a workplace setting, participants in design are part of a profession, and they act as voices of their profession in design. The heterogeneity faced by design can be, and has traditionally been, understood and managed in terms of mutual learning [8], negotiation [10], and similar concepts. Patients are not part of a profession, but more the central subject in a life changing process. Patients can be in denial, they can be very weak, they can be about to die, or in another "weak" state, in need for care. As objects of care it seems unlikely that they can cooperate in a traditionally staged participatory design process.

In this paper we aim to provide a new basis for understanding and staging cooperation among stakeholders in participatory design for therapeutic domains. We do so with inspiration from Strauss' and co-workers' concepts of trajectory and suffering. These are biographic concepts that provide a somehow operational understanding of the subjectivity of the patient. The claim we make is that such concepts are needed in order to see the patient as center.

2 Designing in Therapeutic Domains: Three Examples

To support the conceptual argument of the paper we introduce three design-led research projects in the therapeutic domains. Firstly, the adherence engineering project, aiming to develop means to ensure data quality in self-measurement in the unsupervised setting by collecting relevant context data [22]. Secondly, the neo-natal intensive care-project, aiming to design infrastructures enabling equality between stakeholders—parents, health care professionals etc.—around the pre-maturely born child [14]. Thirdly, we look into the mobile anxiety therapy project, aiming to design a mobile tool to support cognitive behavioral therapy [6].

2.1 Adherence Engineering: Patients as Object for Intervention and Control

The *adherence-engineering project* is introduced here as an example of engineering thinking, in relation to how patients cooperate in a health care situation.

Adherence is generally defined as the degree to which patients conform to the therapy, e.g. by taking their medication [24]. Measurement adherence is then defined as how the patient conforms to measurement guideline and instructions. Wagner et al. [22] address the challenge to support valid measurement of bio-medical data in the unsupervised setting. E.g., when patients are asked to measure their blood pressure at home.

Blood pressure is an important indicator in many conditions, such as compli-cated pregnancies, and hypertension is, by itself, a dangerous condition leading to strokes etc. At the same time it is complicated to measure. The measurement is technically fairly simple, but the blood pressure measured is quite sensitive to how the patient is positioned, when they have eaten, been drinking coffee or smoked recently, or if they are talking. Also, there is a white coat effect, which means that some patients have a higher blood pressure when getting it read in the clinic. A set of 13 guidelines exists, but all patients do not know them. Thus, while it makes much sense to let patients measure their own blood pressure (due to simplicity, economy, and white coat effect), it is hard for physicians to assess the quality of the data. In situations where blood pressure is an indication for intervention, e.g. medication for hypertension, the quality of data may be of less interest as long as the values are below the threshold. In many situations, however, more accuracy is needed. This leads to a wish for integrating measurement of the users adherence to measurement guidelines into blood pressure self-measurement devices.

Wagner et al. [22] formulated a conceptual framework for adherence engi-neering describing adherence verifiers, measuring the quality of data by assessing adherence to guidelines, and adherence aids, providing feedback and guidance for the patient. Subsequently, prototypes, testing various aspects, were built. The sensor chair detected if patients had their back rested and legs not crossed. The audio classifier analyzed the sound near the device to detect if the patient was talking. Both these approaches worked well. On top of this an integrating framework for collecting data sources and giving feedback to the patient was experimented with.

In the measurement adherence project a major challenge for design seemed to be to get a sufficiently nuanced understanding of the therapeutic domain and the users/patients perspective.

The question is, however, if it is possible to develop this strategy to a stage where adherence is controlled completely. The main challenge is that brute force engineering is expensive and complicated. It would be necessary to track every-thing patients were drinking, their movement, etc., and that seems unfeasible for the settings where self-measurement of blood pressure is administered today.

An alternative approach discussed in the adherence-engineering project was to find a feasible balance between measurements and reliance on patients' abilities to follow guidelines. It was speculated that some guidelines were more essential than others and if those were adhered to, the rest would also be. However, many studies [e.g. 15] show that patients have difficulties understanding the medical rationale behind treatment or measurement they are expected to adhere to, and that they some times deliberately tamper with data, conditions for measurement, etc. for reasons that can be hard to understand from the rational point of view of engi-neering and control. Thus, it may be difficult to decide which guidelines would be good indicators of complete adherence, partly because this could depend on the patients' subjective experience of the whole situation.

The discussion above could lead to a negated approach disregarding technical adherence engineering. An ordinary chair could be painted yellow and placed in the outpatient clinic, or in the home of the patient, and together with the patient a narrative about blood pressure measurement behavior on the yellow chair could be created. This kind of adherence engineering would be based in patients' subjectivity, and would acknowledge patients' active agency rather than aiming to take full control of the patient through technology.

The reported difficulties in the adherence-engineering project illustrate that even in fairly simple situations, like blood pressure self-measurement, it is difficult, if not impossible, to make useful design based on the ideal of the patient as an object for control.

2.2 Care Community: Patients as an Object of Care

The neonatal case, *care community*, is introduced here as an example of cooperative care, and how heterogeneity can be addressed through a joint structure for care.

Neonatal intensive care is administered when children are born so early that they will not be able to survive in a natural environment. The child is placed in an incubator and controlled constantly. Prematurely born children are not fully developed, and therefore most often require careful diagnosis and case-by-case intervention. In many cases the child suffers from malformations of vital organs, etc. At the same time, the parents will be in a process of coping with the premature birth. Furthermore, the child itself needs close contact with the mother in order to develop emotionally. In this complicated picture, nothing is relevant without the survival of the child as a biological entity.

In the Italian context, studied by Grönvall et al. [14], parents were only allowed to be in the ward, and thereby with their children, for very limited periods of time every day. This limitation was due to the immature baby's need for being in the controlled environment of the incubator, and partly a concern for the parents who have the chocking experience of expecting a healthy normal child and now becoming parents to an immature, ill, strangely looking creature instead.

In the design project, Grönvall et al. [14] developed a novel concept of care communities, embracing the heterogeneity of the situation around the prematurely born child, and they developed a vision and a number of prototypes of a system called Palpable time. This development was done in a cooperative design effort involving the researchers/designers, staff at the hospital and to some extent parents of prematurely born children. According to one of the participating pediatricians, the most revolutionary part of the project was the principle that parents, nurses and physicians could work together as a care community jointly aiming to save the child [14]. Thus, an important part of the project was about empowerment, in particular of the parents. An important aim was to change the power structures of the hospital, while not challenging the therapeutic regimen.

The Palpable time prototype was envisioned as an opportunity to create windows for cooperation between stakeholders in a system of configurable presence and absence. In these windows, everybody was thought to be on equal terms but in a way suiting each individual, profession or role. E.g. it was envisioned that the system could enable the mother at the same time to be intimately connected to the child through voice, heartbeat etc., and be absent enough not to be fully confronted with the clinical truth, that might be too unbearable.

The Palpable time prototype acknowledged the heterogeneity of perspectives on care. Parents coping with their new life situation and trying to stay in contact with their child, nurses ensuring the continuity of care, pediatricians administering the therapeutic regimen, etc.

However, it can be argued that the ideas of the care community and Palpable time result in a limiting understanding of the central "stakeholder", the child. Obviously, the child is unable to discuss the therapeutic regimen with the medical staff, but it may not mean that it should be understood merely as an *object* of care. While Grönvall et al. [14] carefully address the situation from the point of view of the parents within the therapeutic regimen, they do not address the subjective perspective of the child. The Italian medical perspective on neonatal intensive care is that the child should stay as much time as possible inside the "safe" environment of the incubator. In northern Europe the perspective is that the prematurely born should spend as much time in bodily contact with the parents, and parents are encouraged to spend as much time at the ward as possible. Which is better from a medical perspective is disputed. The interesting question is what would be best from the subjective standpoint of the child, at the specific point in time as well as in the lifespan of the child.

The care community project illustrated that design efforts focusing on the heterogeneity of a cooperative situation may be in danger of subsuming all perspectives under rational principles such as survival. Furthermore, it illustrates how the dominant perspective of care does not ensure an understanding of the *subjectivity* of the person being cared for, but rather reduces the person to an *object* of care. The child is center as an object, but not in center as a person.

2.3 Mobile Anxiety Therapy: Patients Subjective Incommensurability *with the Therapeutic Regimen*

The *mobile anxiety therapy* project is introduced here to illustrate the relation between therapeutic regimen, therapeutic practice and life transformation.

Anxiety disorder is a widespread problem in western societies, between 15 and 25 % of the Danish population will at some point in life develop an anxiety disorder [2]. Anxiety disorders can in some cases be invalidating, but good results have been obtained from using various forms of Cognitive Behavioral Therapy (CBT), with exposure as a central element [25]. However, the number of people suffering from an anxiety disorder means that many of the lighter cases never get treated, and some of the severe cases do not get treated due to the scarcity of therapist hours.

The mobile anxiety therapy project [6] was motivated by a wish to help people overcome anxiety in a more efficient manner. The aim was to develop a mobile tool that could support anxiety therapy. The researchers collaborated with therapists and patients[1] from a center for anxiety therapy providing a 3-month, full time program for young people. Typically, patients suffered from social phobia or agoraphobia. Early design ideas assumed that initial warning of the build-up of anxiety attacks provided by biosensors connected to the mobile device [4], would be a great help. Technically, that turned out not to be feasible, but fortunately it also turned out that anxiety is a condition that it is easy to learn to sense and measure. This lead to the design of a mobile application that was much more closely related to the existing practice in the anxiety therapy center.

Designers cooperated with therapist and patients to learn about anxiety and about the anxiety program. Together they developed ways to integrate therapeutic instruments into the mobile device. Central elements included a version of a CBT five column scheme for constructing alternative thoughts; an anxiety diary; plans for exposure exercises, including encouragements to do them; means of relaxation including music; and reassuring sentences. Most of the actual contents for these elements had been constructed by each of the patients as part of the therapeutic program. Thus, the application became a tool to bridge the gab between the clinical setting of the program, and the non-clinical situations outside in the world where anxiety attacks normally occur.

An important issue in the mobile anxiety therapy project was to make sure that patients were not hurt by the design activities, e.g. by being overly exposed to social situations during design workshops. The solution was to involve patients who were in the final stage of the program. In that way, design activities simultaneously became therapeutic activities in the sense that they exposed patients to new social situations and provided situations were they were forced to talk about anxiety with "strangers". Thus, cooperative design was subsumed under the therapeutic strategy. A further advantage of involving patients at the late stage was that they had developed an awareness of the process of change they were undergoing.

Two complementary or conflicting perspectives on the mobile application emerged in the project: as an addition to the therapist's arsenal of tools, or as an instrument for patients' to expand and relate therapy to their lives at large. The mobile application became a boundary object [19]. It turned out that these conflicting perspectives on the application were instances of a more general tension between therapy and life transformation. For the therapist, anxiety could be cured

---

[1] For the sake of consistency over the three examples the client, or students in the anxiety program are referred to as patients.

through the therapeutic program's strategy and practice. For the patients, life was in transformation, and therapy represented change and a challenge to the life they knew, as well as a safe place in life. An example of this tension was the various forms of safety behavior enabling patients to cope with daily life but somehow leaving or even enforcing anxiety, e.g. by avoiding certain situations or places. An important part of the therapeutic strategy was to help patients break out of safety behavior, and at the end of the program staying attached to the program and the center for anxiety was understood as a form of safety behavior by the therapeutic regimen. From the point of view of the patients, this contact was seen as an enhanced possibility to manage life. Thus, the design project uncovered a possibly deeper conflict between the perspective of life transformation held by the patients, and the perspective of the therapeutic regimen curing anxiety disorder in 3 month. Understanding this conflict is also key to the design of aids to keep doing the exposure exercises, leave the safe harbor of therapy, etc. To better understand this tension, a concept of patients' subjective life transformation, i.e. a biographical concept, is needed.

When patients enter the anxiety program, they have most often built an identity as someone suffering from anxiety. Through the program, they change that identity. The program, when successful, is a turning point in their lives, but the program is still just an intermezzo. Before and after, they depend on their own strategies for coping with the world as possibly anxiety provoking. They will need to integrate themselves and their new strategies as not suffering from anxiety into their world. This trajectory of patients' changed perspective points to how awareness of self changes from possibly non-anxious, through anxious, though the therapeutic program as someone working full time to recover from anxiety, to the after treatment situation of being (hopefully) a post anxiety recoverer.

Recovering from anxiety includes more than conforming to the therapeutic program. While the therapeutic regimen is based firmly in cognitive behavioral therapy, the trajectory of the recovering person across various contexts would be based more loosely in that regimen, and could also include, e.g. maintaining elements of safety behavior at a non-detrimental level. From the point of view of patients, it seemed as a possibility to transfer insights and new practice from the therapeutic program further into life outside therapy that was the most important aspect.

The mobile anxiety therapy project shows that fundamentally different processes overlap in therapy, and that in order to design it is important to understand both sides of the cooperative arrangement. As the concepts of therapy are very strong, equally strong concepts of subjectivity of patients are needed.

3 What Is the Problem and Why Do We Need a New Concept

The above three examples show, in different ways, how systems design is problematic if patients' subjective perspectives are not taken into account. Subjective perspective is in this context not only a matter of understanding the interests of patients and prioritizing what is best for them. The subjective perspective is how patients understand, feel and relate to therapeutic intervention and technology in the complex context of their own lives.

The adherence-engineering project provides an example of how the conceptually simple idea of technical control becomes impossible to realize if it is not paired with insights into the patients' perspective.

The care community project example provides an example of a rational perspective on care and survival that does not take the subjective life of neither child nor parents into account as primary concerns.

The mobile anxiety therapy project provides an example of the tension between therapeutic regimen and patients' life management, as it surfaced in the course of cooperative design.

3.1 Stakeholders

The three cases introduced above, illustrate several distinct types of stakeholders and processes. In the adherence engineering case, the patients are immediately affected by the introduction of a new device for blood pressure self measurement, and successful design is highly depending on a clear understanding of the patients' perception of the measurement situation. The possibility of getting more reliable measurements obviously makes the job easier for health care professionals also. Self-measurement can be a case of a well-known routine for some patients, but for others it can be part of a more critical sickness situation. It may be helpful to understand both.

The neonatal intensive care case presents another level of complexity. The prematurely born is affected and basic survival is the most important goal. For the parents having a prematurely born child in intensive care is a serious life-transforming crisis. For the healthcare professionals, however, working for a prematurely born to survive is a recurring standard task. Their quality of working life will be affected by changed technology and organizational concepts, and they go through a process of change across their experience of hundreds of cases.

In the anxiety therapy case, it is patients' process of recovering from anxiety that is primarily affected, though the working life of the therapists may change too. What makes the anxiety case different from the self-measurement case, is that anxiety therapy does not become routine. It is a life transforming process per se, and every step is a challenge for the patient. In order to design for this case, an understanding of the therapeutic regimen is important, but it is equally important to be able to address the relation between the therapeutic regimen and the actual change processes going on with the patients.

3.2 Processes

How can patients and relatives be involved in design, when they are undergoing critical life transformation? In such situations, involving users means that we will be involving them in a design process that addresses a process they are themselves in the midst of, and that design may intervene directly in the transformation of that users' life. The stakeholders in the three cases are involved in a multitude of processes that are overlapping and intertwined, but not necessarily comparable or commensurable. With respect to participation, participatory design has a concern for the active involvement of stakeholders, in particular end-users, in the process of design [3]. Furthermore, the three examples show that the active, co-determinate, engaged involvement of patients in the therapeutic intervention is also an important issue. It seems that the active involvement in therapy may be a precondition for involvement in design. From the above examples we can identify at least four types of process relevant for an understanding of the involvement of users.

The IT-design process is the change process organized by systems developers leading to the introduction of new IT-based artifacts. The process may involve actual users or it may be driven by an idea, or specification. The three examples illustrate that design is not going on in an otherwise frozen world, and that other processes are important to understand in order to do design. In some cases the design process occurring in practice can be contrasted to idealized ideas, e.g. in the form of methods, of how design should be undertaken.

The therapeutic intervention process is the actual process in which patients receive therapy and care in order to recover from, or get to manage their illness. The actual course of therapeutic intervention is the realization of a therapeutic regimen, but implemented by the actual therapist and including exceptions, method mix, etc. These processes of therapeutic intervention, in turn, evolve over time.

The therapeutic regimen is the principles and procedures of ideal therapeutic intervention. The historically evolving guidelines condensed from experience of the profession, and based in medical research. The CBT program for anxiety, or the 13 guidelines for blood pressure measurement are components of therapeutic regimens.

The life transforming process of illness and cure is the process patients undergo as whole human beings. The baby's struggle for survival, recovery from anxiety, etc. This is a subjective process.

While the relation between design on one hand and the dynamic relation between therapeutic regimen and therapeutic practice on the other is potentially complicated in the same sense work-oriented design always is, it is the relation between patients' life transformation, and the other processes that appears hard to address in the three examples. The deeper layers of patients' life transformation seem incommensurable with the other processes.

3.3 Cooperative Design

Cooperative or participatory design of IT focuses on the involvement of stakeholders in the process of design; in particular those stakeholders that are directly
affected by the new systems, and in particular those who are most often left out of
the process.

The early trade union projects realized that technology was not neutral, and that
workers therefore needed their own experts, to ensure that their perspectives were
brought to the table in the power struggle with management [3]. Thus, Ehn and
Sandberg [10] proposed a model for systems design as negotiation between
workers and management.

Subsequent projects, e.g. the UTOPIA project [3], learned that workers were
unable to make sense of the systems models provided by their own experts. Non-IT
professionals were unable to translate formal systems descriptions into an
understanding of how work would be in the prospective work arrangements.
Therefore, new types of design representations such as organizational games [9],
and Mock-ups [11] were invented to capture the heterogeneity of perspectives on
technology and to enable to participants to cooperate across professional
differences.

Mutual learning became a central concept in organizing cooperation across the
heterogeneous perspectives, knowledge and competencies of interested designers
and stakeholders [8].

Thus, participatory design envisioned and practiced design as a *rational discourse* among the interested parties. Not necessarily formalizable and rationalistic,
but happening in a room where perspectives are sharable through language and
design artifacts (prototypes, etc.). In the three examples, involving patients in the
(rational) discourse of participatory design was a challenge, as they were weak,
chocked, fragile etc.

3.4 Care, Rationality and Rationality of Care

In discussing cooperative design, [7] take up Noddings' [17] concept of care
rationality as a counter point to technical rationality. The concept is relational and
reciprocal, based on the caring persons own experience of being cared for, and it is
concrete, situational rather than formal and abstract. In the concept of this paper, it
is a limitation that Noddings' [17] argument is mostly based in philosophical ethics
that seems to remain quite abstract. A more concretely based alternative is provided by Wærness [21], who discusses rationality of care from a sociological
perspective in an effort to make visible the invisible work of care traditionally
done by women outside the realm of scientifically based, controlled procedures.
The rationality of care is understood as opposed to scientific rationality, and is
based more on intuition, experience and improvisation than on procedures and

formal education. In the context of the three examples, a focus on the rationality of care can provide new insights.

In the adherence-engineering project, it seemed to be a goal to avoid caring rationality. The project represents a scientification of a domain, the home etc. that was otherwise a domain of care. In the mind of the engineer, the various practices expressed by nurses, e.g. tugging the patient in with a blanket if the measurement is too high and then repeating it later, seemed like a kind of witchcraft that should be avoided.

In the neonatal intensive care project, the neonatal intensive care ward was a kingdom of scientific rationality. This was the background for one of the pediatricians stating that the most ambitious part of the project was not the incubators based on smart materials and non-existing sensor and actuator technology, but the very concept of a care community. Probably because he realized that care community implies an acknowledgement of the rationality of care.

In the mobile anxiety therapy, it was a clear dynamic between scientific and caring rationality in the way therapy was carried out. CBT itself is a paradigm relying on well-described procedures, but in the practice of the anxiety program a lot of improvisation, method mixing, individual adaptation etc. was seen.

However, the concepts of rationality of care (Wærness) and care rationality (Noddings) both tend to understand the cared for person as an object. The actions, knowledge, perspective, etc. of the caregiver is what is central to understand. While both authors emphasize reciprocity in care, and the caregiver's sense of the needs of the person cared for, this is still seen from the caregiver perspective. Thus, the person being cared for is kept in the position as *object of care*.

While the two concepts provide a more complete picture of therapeutic work and the relation between care and therapy on one side and the patient on the other, they at the same time indirectly reveal that the subjectivity of the patient becomes a residual category. Patients seem only to exist through their reflection through therapy and care. Thus, a set of concepts setting patients at the center, are needed.

4 Suffering: An Exemplary Biographic Concept

The concept trajectory was coined by Strauss and Glaser in 1968 in the context of the dying person [20]. It aims to describe the specifics of the total situation of the dying person; the biological process of bodily decay, and the unplanned process of becoming dead, the un-orderliness of the surrounding social context, the bewildered state of relatives, etc. Riemann and Schütze [18] argue that trajectories, in the Strauss sense, are about suffering, and the whole context of the suffering person. Obviously, the concept of trajectory is a specific grounded theory based on the studies of dying and of chronic illness [18]. Therefore, the specific models of e.g. the stages of chronic illness trajectories may not be found in e.g. the context of rehabilitation. However, it is as a biographic perspective centered with the suffering person, the concept trajectory brings a new understanding to IT-design. It is not just a matter of viewing the situation from the point of view of various stakeholders including the patient. It is a matter of realizing that the rationality of design and of work, including medical work, does not apply for the suffering person as such. Riemann and Schütze [18] argue that the concept of biographical trajectory can be somehow generalized from the sociological analysis of suffering.

In this section we introduce Anselm Strauss' and colleagues' concept of suffering and trajectory as a basis for a discussion of subjective and biographic perspectives in design [18, 20]. By aiming for a biographic approach, we want to emphasize the concrete subjectivity played out through actual events in the course of life. A biographic perspective on subjectivity emphasizes process and change as opposed to more static aspects such as identity or personality. That is not to say that personality and identity are not relevant aspects in understanding subjectivity, though. We mainly build this discussion on Riemann and Schütze's account.

> We believe it is necessary for an understanding of suffering to leave the paradigm of intentional social action, and to start conceptually from social processes of "being driven" and losing control over one's life circumstances. [18, p. 336]

Thus, the concept of suffering points to the fundamental incommensurability between the suffering person and healthcare professionals, designers and others. It is the subjective standpoint of the patient in the trajectory of illness. Suffering is constantly changing and cannot be rationalized. Compared to Noddings' [17] and Wærness' [21] perspectives on care, the biographic concept of suffering maintains a focus on the suffering person where Noddings proposes a universalized philosophical concept of a non-universal relationship, and Wærness is mostly occupied with a sociological analysis of the invisible work of the caring person. Suffering, in the case of the dying person, implies the dissolution of rationality and personality. Thus the concept of suffering provides an extreme biographic perspective. Thus, it can serve as a Leitmotif for the development of a biographic perspective as a basis for new ways of understanding the involvement of patients in cooperative design.

Studies in computer supported cooperative work have addressed therapeutic domains, often aiming for general domain sensitivity rather than narrow implications for design, and pointing to the un-orderliness in contrast to formalized structures in organizations. In particular the works of Strauss and colleagues have been influential. For example, Graham et al. [13] discuss how Strauss' concept of trajectory can be operational for a design-oriented understanding of the healthcare domain. However, they take a mostly organizational, objectified view in their analysis of ethnographic data, and seem to understand the concept of trajectory in a less empathetic and subjectivist way. For them it is mainly a correction to traditional bureaucratic models of the organization of human behavior, understood as a frame for describing visible behavior rather than a model for understanding various fundamentally different subjective backgrounds for action and participation.

In their book, "Technology as Experience", McCarthy and Wright [16] introduce the subjectivist concept of "an experience", in the broader conceptual context of "felt life". While their focus is on the singular events rather than on trajectories, their analysis of four threads of experience, six ways of sense making etc. provide specific handles for an understanding of concrete, felt life with technology or other arrangements that would complement the Strauss inspired, biographic concepts. Could be a useful complement to the concept of suffering and of trajectory in actual analysis and design. The work reported by Wallace et al. [23] provides an interesting example of biographic design, based in critical design (e.g. [12]) and aesthetic experience. They worked together with one couple, where the wife was suffering from dementia, to produce jewelry that could help maintain memory and sense of self for the wife.

4.1 Biographically Informed Design Alternatives in the Three Projects

Through a biographic perspective inspired by Strauss concept of suffering, a number of shortcomings in the three projects can be discussed and insights into alternatives can be obtained.

In the *adherence engineering* project patients were involved through studies of the settings for blood pressure self-measurements. The typical inaccuracy of measurements was studied through observations and interviews. However, it was not at all made clear through the framework developed in the project [22], how to create a balanced combination of technical adherence aids and verifiers and means of adherence not based in technology. An approach could be to study specific groups of patients at a much more detailed level. Aarhus and Ballegaard [1] report on a broad range of studies of how patients managed illness with technology in their own homes, and they point to difficulties in integrating these activities with other activities in the home. As one example they point to issues of visibility of the health technology. Aarhus and Ballegaard [1] further point to examples of how pregnant diabetics understood blood glucose measurement in terms of connectedness with their child, and not in terms of technical measurement. Thus, a next step in building an adherence-engineering framework could be to address bio-medical self-measurement in the context of specific patients' illness trajectories [20]. For example, for patients in the phase of denial, the technical adherence aids proposed by Wagner et al. [22] would not be effective. A consequence of such a biographic approach would be to understand bio-medical measurement as boundary objects with one meaning in the clinical domain and another meaning in the context of illness trajectory (Tactics 1, 2 and 5 below).

The *care community* project adopted a stronger care perspective. At the same time a strong focus was placed on smart materials for preventing pressure, etc. While the researchers in the project felt that contact between mother and child was valuable, the scientifically based therapeutic regimen of the hospital forced them to address that value through technical means. The scientific rationality of medicine and technology ruled. With a biographic concept like suffering it is possible to generate a version of the child's subjectivity and trajectory, and possibly do the same for the parents. While it is impossible to interview the child in neonatal intensive care, it is possible to observe them across their life span. It is indeed possible to get subjective accounts of how the time in intensive care affected the person later in life. While this may be rationalized in terms of attachment theory, the important point is that the biographic perspective of the suffering child and its trajectory into, and in, life would have helped the researchers in the care community project to become more insisting about ways to reunite what medical technology had separated. And it would have provided researchers with a critical stance towards their own technical solutions. This could have powered an insistence on moving the child back with the parents when at all possible, and then develop technology that could transfer the protection of the incubator out of it. (Tactics 1, 2, 4 and 5 below.)

In the *mobile anxiety therapy* project, patients were involved actively in design activities. The therapists had a very well defined vision of the therapeutic regimen that would realistically help patients into a normal life. The basic rationale of this regimen was that patients should obtain control of anxiety, and consequently of their own lives. It became clear, however, that the patients did not share that vision. The patients took off from their positive experience with specific therapeutic measures, and general ideas of what would be nice to have. In general they did not focus on how various elements in a tool would support the therapeutic regimen of CBT within the limited time of the therapeutic program. The researchers (who also designed the prototypes) feared that patients could be harmed by design activities. Therefore, they proposed that design activities should double as therapeutic activities. Design should be subsumed under therapy. While this was a safe strategy, it also limited the possibilities to think beyond the existing therapeutic regimen. Design adopted the limitations of CBT. The biographic perspective of suffering and patient trajectory would have been a useful counterbalance to the CBT perspective. With this as a central part of early analysis, pragmatically subsuming design activities under the therapeutic strategy would not have been a Trojan horse[2] for the delineation of therapy inherent in CBT. It would not only have been possible to reflect actual practice, as opposed to the idealized therapeutic regimen, in design, but it would have been possible to think beyond existing therapeutic practice, designing for patients trajectory (Tactics 1, 2, 3, 4 and 5, below).

4.2 Biographically Informed Design Tactics

Based on the discussion in the previous section we extract a number of possible tactics, informed by a biographic perspective, for the design of IT support in therapeutic domains.

---

[2] Bertelsen [5] analyses systems development methods and tools as Trojan horses for a worldview.

Tactic 1: Take a biographic perspective, inspired by the concept of suffering, on stakeholders in design. Use this perspective to help understanding patients as interested collaborators with a specific type of agency (of suffering) rather than objects of therapeutic intervention. Do not assume that patients share, and act according to the rationality of therapy—or any rationality at all.

Tactic 2: Consider trajectories of life and illness, including life before and after therapy, as the basic units of analysis. Rely on personal accounts from patients and former patients.

Tactic 3: Relate product design activities to the distinct processes of therapeutic regimen, therapeutic practice and patient's trajectory when organizing design activities.

Tactic 4: In the practical involvement of patients in cooperative design, it can be necessary to subsume design activities, such as idea generation or prototyping, under therapeutic activities, e.g. to avoid harming patients. In doing so it is important not to limit design by conceptually subsuming it under the therapeutic regimen.

Tactic 5: Acknowledge design that contradicts or transcends established therapy.

5 Discussion

Based on three projects, we realized a need for a stronger set of concepts that could promote the voice of patients in design. As an answer to this need, the idea of a biographical perspective inspired by Strauss and colleagues' concepts of illness trajectory and suffering was introduced. This perspective was supported through a critical discussion of rationality and care.

The idea of the biographical perspective was validated through the identification of shortcomings in the three reported projects and exemplification of alternatives based in this perspective.

The subjectivism and critique of rationality brought about by the biographic concepts, not only relate to participation in design, but it also points to engaged cooperation, by patients, in illness and therapy more generally. This attempt to place patients at the center of agency is needed in relation to design. There may, however, be limits to equality in therapy when issues such as accountability, responsibility and professional judgment are taken into account. In practice many situations may not call for more active engagement by patients. Thus, the aim of this paper has not been to eliminate the perspective of professional healthcare workers.

The argument of the present paper has been taking of from examples in health care, emphasizing patients' inability to participate in rational design discourse and negotiation. It may make sense, however, also to consider if cooperative design in general is facing the same kind of difficulties. Hopefully, the way the concepts of suffering and trajectory facilitates biographic or subjective perspectives in therapeutic domains could inspire the further development of perspectives on participation and cooperation in other areas such as civic engagement.

Future work could include experiments with a set of operational guidelines for biographically based design. Such guidelines may be tried out in the context of the continued adherence-engineering project.

Acknowledgments Great thanks to one anonymous reviewer of an earlier version of this paper. Thanks to Karl Bertelsen Robak for comments on language, to Erik Grönvall for comments on this paper, to Susanne Bødker for comments on very early versions of this work. Most importantly thanks to collaborators in the three cases: Raphael Dobers, Erik Grönvall, Ulla Høybye, Gunnar Kramp, Patrizia Marti, Alessandro Pollini, Alessia Rullo, Svend Thielsen, Thomas Toftegaard, and not least Stefan Wagner.

References

1. Aarhus R, Ballegaard SA (2010) Negotiating boundaries: managing disease at home. In: Proceedings of CHI 2010, pp 1223–1232
2. Angstforeningen (2012) Årsrapport. http://angstforeningen.dk/uploads/tryksager/aarsrapport/aarsrapport2012.pdf
3. Bansler JP (1989) Systems development research in Scandinavia: three theoretical schools. Scand J Inf Syst 1:3–20
4. Bering PF (2008) Reflections on user involvement of anxiety patients. In: Workshop on participatory design in therapeutic contexts, in conjunction with NordiCHI
5. Bertelsen O (2000) Design artefacts. Towards a design oriented epistemology. Scand J Inf Syst (12): 15–27
6. Bertelsen OW, Dobers R, Høybye U, Kramp G, Thielsen SR (2010) Participatory design of IT-support for anxiety therapy. In: Proceedings of therapeutic strategies, Workshop at NordiCHI 2010
7. Bødker S, Ehn P, Knudsen JL, Kyng M, Madsen KH (1988) Computer support for cooperative design. In: Proceedings of conference on computer supported cooperative work (CSCW'88), Portland, Sept 1988
8. Bratteteig T (1997) Mutual learning—enabling cooperation on systems design. In: Braa K, Monteiro E (eds) Proceedings of IRIS'20, Oslo
9. Ehn P, Sjögren D (1991) From system description to script for action. In: Greenbaum J, Kyng M (eds) Design at work: cooperative design of computer systems. LEA, Hillsdale, pp 241–268
10. Ehn P, Sandberg Å (1976) God utredning: om vad utredare kan göra för att främja demokratin i förvaltningens beslutsfattande. Arbejdslivscentrum, Stockholm
11. Ehn P, Kyng M (1991) Cardboard computers: mocking-it-up or hands-on the future. In: Greenbaum J, Kyng M (eds) Design at work: cooperative design of computer systems. LEA, Hillsdale, pp 169–198
12. Gaver W, Dunne T, Pacenti E (1999) Cultural probes. Interactions 6:21–29
13. Graham C, Cheverst K, Rouncefield M (2006) Technology for the humdrum: trajectories, interactional needs and a care setting. Australas J Inf Syst 13:2
14. Grönvall E, Marti P, Pollini A, Rullo A, Bertelsen OW (2005) Palpable time for heterogeneous care communities. In: Proceedings of the 4th decennial conference on critical computing: between sense and sensibility (CC '05) ACM, pp 149–152
15. Grönvall E, Verdezoto N (2013) Beyond self-monitoring: understanding non-functional aspects of home-based healthcare technology. In: The proceedings of UbiComp 2013: the

   2013 ACM international joint conference on pervasive and ubiquitous computing, Zurich, Switzerland, Sept 2013, pp 8–12
16. McCarthy J, Wright P (2004) Technology as experience. The MIT press, Cambridge
17. Noddings N (1984) Caring. A feminine approach to ethics & moral education. University of California Press, Berkeley
18. Riemann C, Schütze F (1991) Trajectory as a basic theoretical concept for analyzing suffering and disorderly social processes. In: Maines DR (ed) Social organization and social process: essays in honor of Anselm Strauss. Hawthorne, NY
19. Star SL (1989) The structure of ill-structured solutions: boundary objects and heterogeneous distributed problem solving. In: Gasser L, Huhns MN (eds) Distributed artificial intelligence, vol II. Pitman Publishers, London, pp 37–54
20. Strauss A, Fagerhaug S, Suczec B, Wiener C (1985) Social organization of medical work. The University of Chicago Press, Chicago
21. Wærness K (1984) The rationality of caring. Econ Ind Democracy 5:185
22. Wagner S, Toftegaard TS, Bertelsen OW (2012) Challenges in blood pressure self-measurement. Intl J Telemedicine Appl 2012, Article ID 437350
23. Wallace J, Wright PC, McCarthy J, Green DP, Thomas J, Olivier P (2013) A design-led inquiry into personhood in dementia. In: Proceedings of the SIGCHI conference on human factors in computing systems (CHI '13). ACM, New York, pp 2617–2626
24. World Health Organization (WHO) (2003) Defining adherence. Adherence to long term therapies: evidence for action. WHO Report, 2003, Geneva, pp 3–4
25. Sanders DJ, Wills F (2007) Cognitive therapy: an introduction. SAGE, Thousand Oaks

"Through the Glassy Box": Supporting Appropriation in User Communities

Federico Cabitza and Carla Simone

Abstract Communities present considerable challenges for the design and application of supportive information technology (IT), especially in loosely-integrated and informal contexts, as it is often the case of Communities of Practice (CoP). An approach that actively supports user communities in the process of IT appropriation can help alleviate the impossibility of their members to rely on continuous professional support, and even enable complex forms of cooperative tailoring of their artifacts. The paper discusses the property of the accountability of IT applications as one of the basic enabling conditions for the appropriation of the technologies by their end-users, and for its most mature and sustainable form, that is End-User Development (EUD). We illustrate a framework, called Logic of Bricolage (LOB), proposed to both end-users and interested designers to describe (and make accountable) their EUD environments and systems, and facilitate both local appropriation and the sharing of experiences of IT adoption in CoPs.

1 Introduction

According to a oft-cited definition, "appropriation" can be seen as "the process by which people adopt and adapt technologies, fitting them into their working practices" [14]. Appropriation is a complex process whose success depends on the extent to what users are able to manage how "practices and technologies evolve around each other" [13]. As such, appropriation involves both social and technical concerns. From the social perspective (being appropriation but a form of practice),

F. Cabitza (✉) · C. Simone
Universita degli Studi di Milano-Bicocca, Milano, Italy
e-mail: cabitza@disco.unimib.it

C. Simone
e-mail: simone@disco.unimib.it

C. Rossitto et al. (eds.), *COOP 2014 - Proceedings of the 11th International Conference on the Design of Cooperative Systems, 27–30 May 2014, Nice (France)*, DOI: 10.1007/978-3-319-06498-7_11, © Springer International Publishing Switzerland 2014

the notion of Communities of Practice (CoPs) [27] characterizes the most favourable kind of work setting for a successful appropriation, as the negotiation and sharing of practices are part of the processes that constitute this kind of communities. From the technical perspective, the opacity of the technology is one of the main factors hindering a successful appropriation, especially when adaptation is concerned. Technological opacity can be generated by either the inherent complexity or rigidity of the technology; or by the way in which the technology has been actually constructed. In the first case, appropriation is necessarily bound to some workaround [16]: it is often the case that end users flank the complex, rigid (and often also imposed) technology by the so-called *shadow tools* [18]; these are simpler office applications, like spreadsheets and word processor templates, that are completely under the control of users and often are built in order to align with their situated practice and host the bunches of information that later users will transfer into the official applications of the information system at hand, as if this fictitious and often frail interoperability represented a post hoc compliance with the organization policies [2]. Here we want to focus on the second case, which regards the development of cooperative applications in a community environment. Our paper then regards the opportunity to develop design strategies that, on one hand, could make opaque systems more transparent to their users; and, on the other hand, counteract the inevitability of the scenario where formal and informal tools coexist in the organizational domain, and hence the risk that they mutually undermine their function, especially in the long run.

1.1 Black and Glossy Boxes

In discussing the notion of context, Dourish [14] made the point that when we focus on how users appropriate their software applications we should consider that the context is not something external to the applications, but rather something where the technologies are embedded, and where appropriation actually occurs. This would lead to reconsider the value, influentially advocated by Simon within the design sciences [25], of having technologies act as "black boxes" in the context of the user experience. In fact, this would rather shed light on the need to have tools that are more manifest to the involved actors, and become an observable part of the context where they make their decisions in regard to their adaptation, configuration and fit to their practices: like transparent boxes with respect to their inner functioning. Indeed, Dourish suggests three ways to facilitate appropriation: making users aware of the activities and the resources that are involved during their use of the system; making the system's own structure and behaviors accessible to users; allowing them to define and negotiate the information structures, as well as their static organization and dynamic articulation. Since the first requirement would require reflection capabilities that hardly can be added to systems that are not purposely designed to host them, here we focus on the last two approaches, which advocate for more accountable systems, if not "self-accounting" ones.

Thus, in this paper we characterize a purposely general framework that we called "Logic of Bricolage" (LOB) and first presented in [6]. This framework is intended to support appropriation by users by giving them the "words" to make their systems more "accountable". We use this term in the ethnomethodological sense of "observable and *reportable*". Our point is that these two capabilities should not be decoupled: the appropriation of a car cannot be achieved only by making the car hood of transparent glass, as it is well known that showing low-level details of a computational system will not make it more accessible and comprehensible by end users, but probably just the opposite. The accountability we refer to is rather obtained by providing the concepts and words so that even users can denote "the system's own structure and behaviors", or at least cope with a representation of these that is suitable to be handled by lay users.

On the other hand, the LOB framework is also conceived for the developers, which in an EUD context can include also skilled end-users, as a conceptual model supporting the design of applications where structure and behaviors are clearly decoupled, and a clear separation of concerns is established between the process of "making the bricks" and the process of "assembling" them into walls and houses. This effort also should be paid for the better appropriation by end users, if not to make the system's architecture cleaner and maintenance easier.

The paper first outlines the LOB framework, and presents the jargon it proposes to make EUD systems more accountable and transparent. Then we apply the framework to three existing EUD systems of applications, as an example of the post hoc exercise in which existing systems are compared on a common conceptual ground. We then discuss the potential implications of adopting the LOB, or any equivalent, framework in EUD practice to foster negotiation (that is mainly a discursive practice) and appropriation in communities of users.

2 A Primer on the Logic of Bricolage

In [17] Halverson has aptly proposed to evaluate the utility of any conceptual proposal, or theory, in the design of cooperative applications considering its potential on different planes of *power* (or afforded capabilities). After this contribution, we propose the LOB framework as an approach that can: (1) Facilitate practitioners in making sense of and describing their and others' systems. This regards to the *descriptive power* of frameworks and it applies to both communities of end-users, who make a common sense of what it is supplied to their community, and to communities of designers, who are supposed to present and make their solutions understandable within their reference community of IT practitioners. Similarly, (2) help designers talk about their solutions by providing them with a common vocabulary, i.e., a very concise lexicon whose available terms cover few but essential aspects of recurring EUD conceptual structures and underlying models and are defined with some degree of unambiguous formalization. This regards the so-called *rhetorical power* of LOB, for which it is aimed at facilitating the sharing of lessons learned, best practices and effective solutions, also on a narrative level [22]. Lastly, (3) both inform and guide the design of EUD proposals that could meet the challenging requirement to let the members of an end-users community develop and maintain practices of technology local tailoring and adaptation to their emerging and ever-changing needs. This regards the *applicative power* and is by far the most difficult "power" to sustain although it is the most precious one in terms of impact on real life practice.

As the terminological dimension is important for the intended powers of the LOB framework, in the rest of the section we will characterize the terms and concepts that make it useful in accounting for technological EUD applications. The expression *Logic of Bricolage* itself is chosen after [19] to denote the articulated environment, or application context, where end-users are called to *co-define* and *use* tools, to, respectively, build computational structures and their behaviors (*editing environments*), and to have those behaviors be executed at run time (*execution environment*). It therefore refers to a context endowed with some order and logic, but where the main valuable activity is an "orderly patchworking" and assemblage of pieces. Since the framework has been already presented in [6] along with its formalization through a generative grammar, in what follows, we will just recall the main concepts and elements.

The elements characterizing the LOB framework can be arranged into a conceptual architecture, that we depict in Fig. 1 where LOB terms are in italics and for each layer, its name and what it offers to the higher layers are specified. From the topmost layer of this architecture, we see as end users are enabled to create and use community-specific *applications* by interacting with the *editing and working environments*: to this aim, these environments expose apt building blocks (called *constructs*) through *specific editors* that are supported by the underlying EUD *platform* in terms of *primitives*. These latter are domain-independent functionalities that are expressed in terms of lower level Application Programming Interfaces (API). The platform in its turn is enabled by a regular infrastructure (i.e., an application server and operating system).

According to the bottom-up approach advocated within the LOB framework, *constructs* have to be identified during the inception phase of the framework for a specific end-user community, as a result of the interaction between its members and the IT professionals: these are also in charge of construction of the above mentioned API and primitives. After this point, end-users should be able to construct, tailor and appropriate applications through incremental and actually never-ending task-artifact cycles [11] in which members of this community agree over time upon what constraints and functionalities must be enacted by their supporting technology.

Constructs are distinguished between *Operand Constructs* and *Operator Constructs*: operands are the most atomic data structures that make sense in a specific domain; operators are all the micro-functions that are deemed necessary to be performed over the operands in the application domain; operators can be either *functional* or *actional*, to modify the value of the operands or to produce some effect in the computational environment (like, triggering a communication),

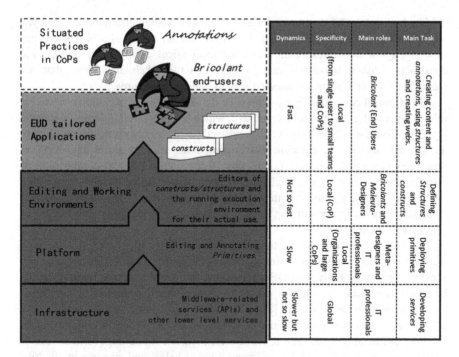

	Dynamics	Specificity	Main roles	Main Task
Situated Practices in CoPs / EUD tailored Applications	Fast	Local (from single user to small teams and CoPs)	Bricolant (End) Users	Creating content and annotations, using structures and creating webs.
Editing and Working Environments	Not so fast	Local (CoP)	Bricolants and Maieuta-Designers	Defining Structures and constructs
Platform	Slow	Local (Organizations and large CoPs)	Meta-Designers and IT professionals	Deploying primitives
Infrastructure	Slower but not so slow	Global	IT professionals	Developing services

(EUD tailored Applications: *structures*, *constructs*)

(Editing and Working Environments: Editors of *constructs/structures* and the running execution environment for their actual use.)

(Platform: Editing and Annotating *Primitives*.)

(Infrastructure: Middleware-related services (APIs) and other lower level services)

Fig. 1 A conceptual architecture for EUD environments supporting bricolage

respectively; in particular, (functional) Operator Constructs can be applied to operands to allow for the recursive construction of more complex operands from simpler ones.

End-users can arrange and compose together in a bottom-up fashion both kinds of *constructs* through two classes of editors, that define respectively, the rules of constructs composition to build the working spaces and artifacts, and their computational behaviors: these compositions are called *structures*, more precisely *Layout structures* and *Control structures*. In simple terms, *Control structures* specify the behaviors of *Layout structures*, i.e., how the artifact acts on the content inscribed therein, e.g., in response to events generated at interface level, and how this level interacts with users during the habitual use of the application.

Layout structures shape the "work spaces" that are recognized by end-users as constituted by the physically inscribed and computationally augmented artifacts where and by which they carry out their work. For example, in the domain of computer-aided design and collaborative drawing/editing, a Layout Structure is the working space where users arrange the docking bars of their preferred commands, symbol stencils and predefined configurations of elements that must be set up before the actual work begins. In document-based information systems, Layout Structures are the document templates of forms and charts that are used to both accumulate content and coordinate activities; such structures are endowed of both physical properties and symbolic properties, for instance, input controls (i.e., data fields), boilerplate text, iconic elements and any visual affordances conveyed through the graphical interface, which in LOB are all instances of Operand constructs. Layout structures result from the topological arrangement of Operand constructs. Layout structures can be aggregated in *Web Structures*, that are recursively defined as interconnected sets of Layout Structures.

Also Control Structures are recursively defined in terms of simpler rewriting rules, that is sort of "conditioned actions", which are expressed in terms of specific Operator Constructs. Conditions are expressed as functional constructs applied to the current state of computation that encompasses all application data. Control Structures can be of arbitrary complexity, from simple rules to composition of instructions in virtue of a special kind of operators (called *Connectors*). Control Structures are interpreted by the execution environment: by interpreting the Operator Constructs constituting them as more or less complex articulation of primitives (see Fig. 1).

The last feature offered by the LOB framework is the possibility to build *annotations*, that is any user-defined content that is created to be anchored to any another content. Notably, in LOB annotations can be nested, that is users should be able to *annotate annotations*, so as to allow for nested threads of comments and tags, as we described in [8]. Annotations are conceived as pieces of a collaborative and never-really-finished bricolage, which hosts informal communication and handover between practitioners, their silent and ungoverned work of meaning reconciliation, and the sedimentations of habits and customs in effective (yet still unsupported computationally) conventions of cooperative work [7]. Also Control Structures can be annotated to support their collaborative construction [5, p. 232].

3 LOB as a General Framework to Describe Existing Applications

In order to support our claim that the LOB can play as a general framework where to express environments supporting various kinds of EUD applications and make their structure more accountable, this section provides three examples of how the LOB terms and concepts can be used to describe different concrete environments. To make the above mentioned claim general enough, we consider three heterogeneous environments: first a document-based collaborative system designed to be highly tailorable according to the local work settings; then an environment that allows for the user defined integration of devices and software components supporting groups of cooperating actors; and lastly, an example of a multi-layered and flexible mashup composition environment that allows for the integration of data sources and functional components to produce enriched and personalized results. These three situations, that are bound together by the collaborative nature of the work that members of specific communities carry on, cover a significant amount of concrete cases where users express the requirement to be in full control of the development of their computational tools and make it a collective, incremental and often bottom up, spontaneous process.

3.1 WOAD: Constructing Webs of Active Documents

On the basis of field studies conducted in different work settings, especially in the healthcare domain, a document-based collaborative system, called Web of Active Documents (WOAD) has been proposed in [4]. The core concepts of WOAD can be summarized as follows in terms of: (1) the information structure is composed of hyperlinked active documents that can be annotated in every parts and sections and be associated with any other document, comment and computational behavior; (2) there is no rational and unified data model: users define their forms in a bottom up manner and, in so doing, the platform instantiates the underlying flat data structures that are necessary to store the content these forms will contain and to retrieve the full history of the process of filling in them; (3) the presentation layer is in full control of end users, who are called to both generate their own templates and specify how their appearance should change later in use under particular conditions by means mechanisms that are expressed in terms of if-then rules. Users can define local rules that act on the documents' content and, as hinted above, change how documents look like (i.e., their physical affordances), to make themselves aware of pertinent conditions according to some cooperative convention or business rule like, e.g., the need to revise the content of a form, or to consider it provisional, or to carefully consider some contextual condition. The LOB conceptual architecture offers a framework that incorporates the various WOAD's components in a coherent picture: in the following we associate the concrete items constituting WOAD with items of the LOB framework.

First, we specialize the constructs: remember that these are application domain dependent and therefore they have to be defined by the users in cooperation with designers and, when necessary, with IT professionals according to the needs of the specific application domain.

The **Operand constructs** in WOAD are called datoms (document atom): these are but any writable area with a unique name and a type (e.g., Integer, String). A datom can recursively be a composition of one or more datoms: e.g., the 'first name' datom (a string) and the 'family name' one (also a string) can be combined into a 'person name' datom that encompasses both. The **Operator constructs** are a selection of atomic functions: for example, as reported in [7] doctors from a medical setting required, besides the standard arithmetic and boolean operations, also a construct to perform the *average*, and another one checking the occurrence of a value in a given set (the *is-in* construct). A list of Actional Operator Constructs conceived to be applied to the Layout Structures or on their components has been derived from a series of field studies and it encompasses basic operations like *save*, *retrieve* and *store*; one of these constructs, namely *annotate*, can associate a didget (i.e., a document widget resulting from the instantiation of a datom) with an annotation. More complex operator constructs can be recursively defined by composing more elemental ones. **Web structures** are a graph of hyperlinked *templates*, i.e., WOAD **Layout Structures**; these latter are a set of didgets: a didget is a topological object, i.e., an Operand construct called datom (see above) that is put in some place, i.e., is coupled to a set of coordinates (that in WOAD are represented as Cartesian pairs with respect to the origin of the template). It is worthy of note the fact that the two datoms mentioned above (first name, family name) can be used to create a WOAD template (i.e., a Layout Structure), as well as a third datom, i.e., another Operand construct: in the former case the two-datom set is to be used in the execution environment in documents that are instances of the template encompassing it; in the latter case the set is intended to be used atomically as component itself of other templates (i.e., as a topological object) in the editing environment. In WOAD the **Control structures** are called *mechanisms*, i.e., if-then rules whose if-part is a Boolean expression that is recursively defined using the predefined datom names as variables, and the operators identified above, all together with the (obvious) constants of the basic types. The then-part is a sequence of actions that has to be performed on the template or on its inner components. Mechanisms are connected by the (implicit) OR connector. In WOAD, the **Primitives** that allow for the definition of both Layout and Control Structures are the following ones: *aggregate*, to build complex operands from simpler ones; *compose*, to build complex operators in terms of functional composition; *localize*, to associate a didget with a Cartesian coordinate with respect to the origin of a given template; *list*, to build sequences of if-then rules; Moreover, the *annotate* primitive associates a text with an operand construct.

As mentioned in the previous section, the Primitives are offered through an editing environment where Constructs and Structures can be defined. In WOAD this environment is constituted by two visual editors: one for the construction of mechanisms, and one for the construction of datoms and, by arranging these latter topologically in terms of didgets, templates.

3.2 CASMAS: Creating Hybrid Communities for Cooperation

Suppose that a set of applications and devices have to be integrated to support a set of actors that cooperate by means of them. According to the Community-Aware Multi Agent Systems (CASMAS) framework [20], both actors and their tools all are represented as *entities* and integration can be seen alike to becoming members of the same *community*: as such, they coordinate their behaviors through a shared information space that contains coordinative information, as well as the *behaviors* that are dynamically assigned to each entity to make it an active member of the community: in CASMAS communication is asynchronous but it is not message based. Instead, when an entity *posts* a request into the space, other entities will *react* to this request according to their current behaviors.

The CASMAS framework encompasses a language to specify entities and their behaviors. This language takes the declarative form of facts and rules (if-then patterns), which offers the possibility to express behaviors in a modular way, without the need to define complex and exhaustive control structures [21]. The rules constituting an entity's behavior express *what* the entity is expected to do *when* some conditions are satisfied: these conditions are matched against the facts contained in the community's space and in the entity's local memory; the action(s) that the entity should perform updates either the community space or the memory of the entity itself.

The integration of a software application/device is realized by inserting a fact in the memory of the entity representing it and by defining the behavior of this entity. The fact contains attribute-value pairs that specify the information the application/device makes available for sake of coordination with the other entities of the same community; the entity's behavior expresses conditions (among others) on the concrete application/device attributes (when) and invokes some of the functions the application/device exposes to the community (what): actually, the entity is a sort of wrapper that mediates between the concrete application/device and the integration environment (community).

As done for the WOAD framework, we associate each CASMAS feature with each item of the LOB framework.

In CASMAS, the **Operand constructs** are the facts that are contained in and exchanged across community space(s): CASMAS facts are expressed according to the syntax of the underlying rule-based language (currently, JBoss Drools[1]). The **Operator constructs** are the basic functions and predicates that are exposed by the underlying rule-based programming language; in particular the actional operator constructs (actions in CASMAS) support the asynchronous communication between entities as well as the storing and retrieval of information among the spaces and the local memories. In case of applications/devices' memories, the store/retrieve actions respectively put and get information to/from the data structures therein managed. The *spaces* that are implicitly connected through the entities that are members of more than one community are the LOB **Web structures**; each space is a **Layout structure** that contains the community's facts and the entities' ones; differently from WOAD, facts (i.e., operand constructs) are not geometrically localized within spaces, as CASMAS does not specify the coordinates of its topological objects (i.e. the facts within the spaces). The if-then rules connected through the OR connector and grouped according to the entities membership to the community are the CASMAS **Control structures**: their if-parts encompass sets of Operand and Operator constructs, as in WOAD; similarly, the then-part can either encompass the above mentioned *put* and *get* actional operator constructs, whenever the behavior regards applications/devices entities; or a *post*

---

[1] http://www.jboss.org/drools/

action, in the other cases. The CASMAS framework defines the same primitives seen for WOAD (except for the *localize* and *annotate* primitives), but it also encompasses the *put* and *get* primitives: the role of these primitives is to interact with the wrappers developed for each devices/application to be integrated and they are called in the actions having the same name.

3.3 DashMash: Flexible Configuration of EUD Mashups

Recently, an increasing number of environments where users can combine information flows from different data sources, the so-called mashups, has been proposed, also for commercial use (e.g., Yahoo Pipes). For sake of exemplification, we apply our exercise of LOB instantiation to the DashMash framework [10],[2] which we take as representative of a wide class of applications that allow for the collaborative user-driven aggregation of heterogeneous content. Indeed, *Dash-Mash* is a general-purpose EUD environment that adopts an approach in which the design-time and the use-time are strictly intertwined: end-users can autonomously define their own mashups and execute these latter "on the fly", to progressively check the result of their editing activities. Like most of the traditional approaches for the creation of mashups, also the DashMash approach is dataflow-oriented, i.e., end-users can only aggregate, filter and display data in the most meaningful way, e.g., a pie chart, a table or a map. On the other hand, the DashMash approach gives also the possibility to provide end-users with an environment that can be customized so as to meet their domain-specific requirements; essentially, this can be done in two ways: (1) through the development of domain-specific components that allow to interact with the functionalities provided by any kind of (local or remote) service; and (2) providing end-users with the access to data coming from private and domain-specific data sources, in addition to publicly accessible ones. Nevertheless, the approach used in DashMash provides end-users with an abstraction that makes them able to use the various mashup components (e.g., data sources, filters and data viewers) that are automatically composted on the basis of a pre-defined set of compatibility constraints, relieving end-users from the need to know any technical detail about the used components.

As for CASMAS, the DashMash **Control structures** are grouped to form the behavior of each *component*. These constructs allow for typical publish and subscribe patterns, like "if a new fact occurs, then publish an event" and "if a subscribed event occurs, then perform some operations". New facts or operations pertain to single components only. For example, if the component is the *Composition Handler*, then the new fact is any change in a component; the components influenced by this kind of event (i.e., the subscribers) activate the corresponding

---

[2] This task is less detailed than in the other two cases as the mentioned paper does not give all the necessary details.

Table 1 Synoptic table of LOB concepts applied to the frameworks analyzed

Framework	Primitives	Constructs	Structures	Annotations
WOAD	*aggregate, annotate, compose, list* and *localize*	*annotate, attach, average, cache, copy, correct, count, create, datom, delete, is-in, officialize, open/read, print, protect, retrieve, save, select, store, transmit* and *write*	*mechanisms* and *templates*	Yes
CASMAS	*aggregate, compose, get, list* and *put*	*get, post, put,* rule patterns and facts	*space* and *behaviors*	No
DashMash	data and events	*publish, subscribe,* and components, data and events	*workspaces* and sets of *workspaces*	No

operations: for example, if the change is about a Filter Component then all Data Components using this filter activate internal operations to send the data to the new Filter Component and at the end this later notifies that new-data are ready: this event is consumed by the Viewer Component subscribing this event for the specific data. In this view, the **Operand constructs** are the *data* and the *events*, while the main **Operators constructs** regard the publication of an event, and the subscription for a specific kind of event. In DashMash, the Web structure is the set of workspaces; each workspace is a **Layout structure** that is composed by two inner Layout structures: one contains the output of all the Viewer Components for what concerns the data (i.e., at the use level according to [1]); the second contains a standard description of the workspace *state* in terms of Components such as: Data Sources, Filters and Viewers (i.e., at the design level).

More traditional mashups that, differently from DashMash, are uniquely based on data flows can be described as graphs whose nodes are input-output transformations, and whose arcs express the kind of connection that hold between two nodes. In LOB terms, a mashup belonging to this class can be seen as a set of rewriting rules that transform inputs into outputs, where arcs are as connectors that express the appropriate structure of the data flow (e.g., either alternative or parallel flows).

Table 1 highlights how the LOB approach applies to the three frameworks characterized above. These three instantiations support our claim that the LOB architecture is at the same time general enough to formally describe different types of EUD application classes (e.g., information mashup, document-based systems, integration of applications), and yet detailed enough to define a concrete platform to apply recurring design patterns for EUD systems to be deployed in different application domains.

4 Discussion

In our aims, the previous section would show that, should the LOB framework fall short of demonstrating applicative power to the test of life, it can at least foster a scholarly debate, in virtue of its descriptive and rhetorical powers, on the need of having more frameworks with similar scope and aims. This should be true especially in the hybrid field where CoP-oriented and EUD-related concerns meet, and towards the dissemination of these concerns in multiple venues, research initiatives and digitization projects. Nowadays this need should be particularly felt especially by those researchers that espous the main tenet of the End User Development field (i.e., the idea that computational artifacts should be increasingly developed by end-users themselves), as to date this idea has not yet gained in popularity in IT production, let alone in regard to communities support. A seminal analysis of the reason for this gap between research and practice asserts that the approaches up to now "have not been developed to cover end users' entire scope of work" [26]: this work is primarily social and deeply grounded in communities of practice.

As stressed above, appropriation plays an important role in the perpetual evolution of these communities, as it regards patterns of technology *adoption* and *adaptation* that can only be learnt through situated practice and social participation, as well as through "the transformation of practice at a deeper level" than the mere customization [14]. Moreover, communities appropriate the technologies that mediate interactions among their members in complex and partly unanticipated ways [23]; this is because this process is intertwined with a great deal of invisible work, tacit knowledge, conventions, habits and mutual expectations, all essential elements in the constitution of communities of practice. As appropriation concretely relates also to specific ways to configure, adapt and tailor technologies, we share the wonder by Bodker [3], who observed how end-user tailoring is seldom taken in serious consideration when speaking of "design for communities". Here we are referring to tailoring not in terms of the individual adaptation of technology for personal use but rather to the "adaptation and further development [of computational technologies] through interaction and cooperation among people", which calls for specific methods and environments that enable end-users to create and maintain their own tools.

Thus, we observe a paradoxical phenomenon: on the one hand, designing technologies for CoPs is seldom articulated in terms of enabling their members to autonomously build and shape their own tools, that is the main concerns of EUD research [24]. On the other hand, EUD research seldom takes communities of users as a first class concept to fully account for the fact that end-users are most of the times members of complex social ensembles. The LOB framework aims to contribute to bridge this apparent gap by focusing on the need to improve both the accountability of the technologies, as well as of the methods and environments where these are built and appropriated.

To this regard, some differences and complementarities of LOB with respect to existing frameworks can be found and discussed. LOB shares some strong affinities with the concept of meta-design proposed in [15], and some affinities with the approach based on component design [28], and with the approach described in [12], which all acknowledge the substantial continuity between design and usage of software applications. Meta-design, in particular, is one of the most complete approaches to EUD, but it seems to formulate general principles that do not really consider the peculiarities of designing systems that must be appropriated in communities of practice. For instance meta-design does not consider the importance of annotations, which conversely LOB takes as the first kind of appropriation "at the surface" of the applications' interface. It does not consider the need of a formal language where items are defined in terms of others, that conversely LOB takes seriously as a way to mirror in computational structures how composite EUD applications can be composed of smaller building blocks. And lastly, meta-design to date does not articulate the two roles of EUD initiatives, i.e., users and designers with the fine-grained details of the LOB vocabulary that distinguishes between more passive end users (bricoleur), active end users (bricolant), more community-oriented designers (maieuta-designers) and designers more concerned with the technological platform (see Fig. 1 and [9] for more details on this comparison).

On the other hand, the LOB framework shares with Component design the focus on modularity, but differs from it with regard to the limits to end-user tailorability in the introduction of opaque components. The approach based on Software Shaping Workshops (SSWs) described in [12], unlike our proposal, is more aimed at the definition of an organization structure and of a methodology for EUD design, rather than at the definition of a conceptual framework and architecture supporting the description and shaping of each possible EUD environment; even more importantly, such an approach is strongly oriented at the shaping of the interaction of users with their tools (which are however constructed by IT professionals), rather than at informing the users' activity of autonomously defining their tools themselves. This is important especially in a community-oriented perspective since, although embedded in structured organizational settings, communities are sort of "autonomous" bodies (with respect to top–down ordering initiatives) within the scope of their constituting practices and artifact use.

5 Concluding Remarks

In this paper we have presented the LOB framework, as a design-oriented tool to distinguish and separate concerns in the conception and development of EUD-enabling platforms, associate these concerns with specific layers of a common reference architecture, and call objects pertaining to each layer with specific and evocative names, by following the precept to "keep it simple, but not simpler".

The reason why we presented such a framework is that we are convinced that in EUD "the best is yet to come". This claim is not to discard what has been done so far in this research field; on the contrary it is an invitation to recognize that the solutions that have been brought forth to allow end-users to create and maintain their computational tools autonomously have now reached a maturity level that *requires* a sort of backward reflection, as well as an effort to generalize local solutions and intuitions into general insights and concepts that could enable future reuse and discussion, especially for their application into real settings. We also believe that the key factor for this to happen is to "scale up" the experiences collected in the last ten years or so of research in EUD. In this regard, we see *appropriation* as the learning process by which each member of an end-user community understands what a technology can do for herself, and how it enables, constrains and shapes the community's practices, often well beyond the intentions of the technology designers. In this process, we have argued in this paper that the component-level accountability of the technology (in the ethnomethodological sense) is a basic requirement to pursue.

Unnecessary implementation details can (should!) be still made opaque to end-users, provided that they can *have the illusion* of being looking at the real "nuts and bolts" of their cars, and of being enabled to tweak and tune them up for the better functioning of their tools. This is what all EUD platforms ultimately aim to: to empower passive and "incompetent" users into "bricoleurs" that move and assemble what surround them in new forms of support. The creative potential of technological bricolage in organizations could also be seen as a thinking-out-of-the-box solution to cope with the current conundrum of having ever increasingly complicated information systems dealing with increasingly significant and complex portions of the socio-technical contexts in which they operate, thus increasing the risk of potentially serious and completely unintended consequences (as the risk of misalignment between the official information system and its shadow tools is just an example). Scattering functions and information nuggets in highly connected networks of processes and working spaces, respectively, with denser clusters that mirror responsibility and ownership boundaries of specific communities of end-users could be a direction to investigate further, instead of looking for forms of more or less disguised centralized control that still characterizes most of the current information systems.

This is the main direction we also aim to take in the further development of the Logic Of Bricolage that we presented in this paper as a contribution towards a feasibly ordered bricolage of partly persistent and partly transient structures that scaffold knowledge work and support cooperative work in real communities and organizations.

References

1. Ardito C, Buono P, Costabile MF, Lanzilotti R, Piccinno A (2012) End users as co-designers of their own tools and products. JVLC 23(2):78–90
2. Bowers J, Button G, Sharrock W (1995) Workflow from within and without: technology and cooperative work on the print industry shopfloor. In: ECSCW'95. Kluwer Academic Publishers, Dordrecht, pp 51–66

3. Bodker S (2006) When second wave HCI meets third wave challenges. ACM Press, New York, pp 1–8
4. Cabitza F, Simone C (2010) WOAD: a framework to enable the end-user development of coordination oriented functionalities. JOEUC 22(2):1–20 (IGI Global)
5. Cabitza F, Simone C (2012) Affording mechanisms: an integrated view of coordination and knowledge management. CSCW 21(2):227–260
6. Cabitza F, Simone C (2014) Building socially embedded technologies: implications on design. In: Designing socially embedded technologies. Springer (forthcoming)
7. Cabitza F, Simone C, Sarini M (2009) Leveraging coordinative conventions to promote collaboration awareness. CSCW 18(4):301–330
8. Cabitza F, Simone C, Locatelli MP (2012) Supporting artifact-mediated discourses through a recursive annotation tool. In GROUP '12: Proceedings of the 17th ACM international conference on Supporting group work. ACM, New York, NY, USA, pp 253–262
9. Cabitza F, Fogli D, Piccinno A (2014) "Each to his own": distinguishing activities, roles and artifacts in EUD practices. In: Empowering society through digital innovations, LNISO. Springer, Berlin
10. Cappiello C, Daniel F, Matera M, Picozzi M, Weiss M (2011) Enabling end user development through mashups: requirements, abstractions and innovation toolkits. LNCS, vol 6654, Springer, Berlin, pp 9–24
11. Carroll JM, Kellogg WA, Rosson MB (1991) The task-artifact cycle. In: Designing interaction: psychology at the human-computer interface. Cambridge University Press, Cambridge, pp 74–102
12. Costabile MF, Fogli D, Mussio P, Piccinno A (2007) Visual interactive systems for end-user development: a model-based design methodology. Trans Syst Man Cybern 37(6). IEEE
13. Dourish P (2001) Where the action is: the foundations of embodied interaction. MIT Press, Cambridge
14. Dourish P (2003) The appropriation of interactive technologies: some lessons from placeless documents. CSCW 12:465–490
15. Fischer G, Scharff E (2000) Meta-design: design for designers. In: DIS'00 ACM, New York, pp 396–405
16. Gasser L (1986) The integration of computing and routine work. ACM TOIS 4(3):205–225
17. Halverson C, Ackerman M, Erickson T, Kellogg WA (eds) (2008) Resources, co-evolution and artifacts: theory in CSCW. Springer, Berlin
18. Handel MJ, Poltrock S (2011) Working around official applications: experiences from a large engineering project. In: CSCW'11: ACM, pp 309–312
19. Lanzara G (1999) Between transient constructs and persistent structures: designing systems in action. J Strateg Inf Syst 8:331–349
20. Locatelli MP, Simone C (2012) End-users' integration of applications and devices: a cooperation based approach. In: From research to practice in the design of cooperative systems: results and open challenges. Springer, Berlin, pp 167–181
21. Myers BA, Pane JF, Ko A (2004) Natural programming languages and environments. Commun ACM 47(9):47–52
22. Orr J (1996) Talking about machines: an ethnography of a modern job. Cornell University Press, NY
23. Pipek V, Kahler H (2006) Supporting collaborative tailoring. In: End user development, vol 9. Springer, Berlin
24. Pipek V, Rosson MB, Stevens G, Wulf V (2009) Supporting the appropriation of ICT: end-user development in civil societies. In: Learning in communities. Springer, Berlin, pp 25–27
25. Simon HA (1996) The sciences of the artificial, 3rd edn. MIT Press, Cambridge
26. Syrjaenen AL, Kuutti K (2011) From technology to domain. ACM Press, New York, pp 244–251
27. Wenger E (1998) Communities of practice: learning, meaning, and identity. Cambridge University Press, Cambridge
28. Won M, Stiemerling O, Wulf V (2006) Component-based approaches to tailorable systems. In: End user development, vol 9. Springer, Berlin, pp 115–141

Bug Reproduction: A Collaborative Practice Within Software Maintenance Activities

Dhaval Vyas, Thomas Fritz and David Shepherd

Abstract Software development settings provide a great opportunity for CSCW researchers to study collaborative work. In this paper, we explore a specific work practice called *bug reproduction* that is a part of the software bug-fixing process. Bug reproduction is a highly collaborative process by which software developers attempt to locally replicate the 'environment' within which a bug was originally encountered. Customers, who encounter bugs in their everyday use of systems, play an important role in bug reproduction as they provide useful information to developers, in the form of steps for reproduction, software screenshots, trace logs, and other ways to describe a problem. Bug reproduction, however, poses major hurdles in software maintenance as it is often challenging to replicate the contextual aspects that are at play at the customers' end. To study the bug reproduction process from a human-centered perspective, we carried out an ethnographic study at a multinational engineering company. Using semi-structured interviews, a questionnaire and half-a-day observation of sixteen software developers working on different software maintenance projects, we studied bug reproduction. In this paper, we present a holistic view of bug reproduction practices from a real-world setting and discuss implications for designing tools to address the challenges developers face during bug reproduction.

D. Vyas (✉)
Queensland University of Technology, Brisbane, QLD, Australia
e-mail: d.vyas@qut.edu.au

T. Fritz
University of Zurich, Zurich, Switzerland
e-mail: fritz@ifi.uzh.ch

D. Shepherd
ABB Corporate Research, Raleigh, NC, USA
e-mail: david.shepherd@us.abb.com

C. Rossitto et al. (eds.), *COOP 2014 - Proceedings of the 11th International Conference on the Design of Cooperative Systems, 27–30 May 2014, Nice (France)*, DOI: 10.1007/978-3-319-06498-7_12, © Springer International Publishing Switzerland 2014

1 Introduction

Companies with a large software portfolio have in-house maintenance support. Their software maintenance divisions frequently get 'bugs' from customers as well as from testing and development teams who are continuously working towards adding new requirements and improving existing products. Maintenance divisions use bug tracking systems where all information related to bugs is stored: starting from when it was encountered to when it was implemented in a product.

Bug reproduction is a highly collaborative activity that starts at an early stage of bug-fixing process. When a bug is encountered, the bug reporter provides relevant information about the bug in a bug tracking system and describes how it can be recreated. Often detailed description of problems, software versions, screenshots, step-wise guidance or navigation is provided by attaching images, videos and textual information [4, 5, 11]. Using this information, developers locally re-create the scenario in which the bug was detected. When developers are able to successfully reproduce the bug on their own machines, they can answer several questions related to where a problem is located in the code and how it can be fixed. Previous studies have shown that bug reports often lack useful information that may be needed for bug reproduction [5]. Additionally, it is sometimes difficult for customers to know what type of information a software maintenance team will require in order to fix a bug. In cases where it may not be possible to reproduce a bug easily, developers ask for more details from customers. This causes delays and overheads in product development and maintenance.

In order to study the bug reproduction process in detail, to explore major hurdles and challenges developers face and to elicit ideas for developing tools to support bug reproduction, we carried out an ethnographic field study with sixteen developers in a software maintenance division of an engineering conglomerate. We studied their bug reproduction practices using semi-structured interviews, in situ observation sessions and a questionnaire. Our results provide a holistic view on the bug reproduction process, where we provide insights into what type of information is provided by customers, how bug reproduction is carried out and how that helps in fixing bugs. Our results show that insufficient information from customers, tedious logistical efforts for bug reproduction setups and the contextual issues of bugs are the three major challenges to bug reproduction. We also found that developers find 'steps for reproduction' and 'trace logs' to be the most important information for reproducing bugs. Surprisingly, our findings show that bug reproduction contributed towards improving developers' confidence for going about fixing bugs. Based on our findings, we provide several design implications such as the use of tracing and monitoring mechanisms at customers' site to allow quick access of useful information for developers, adding templates and annotations to bug tracking systems and connecting bug tracking systems with the work environments of relevant stakeholders involved in the bug reproduction cycle.

In the rest of this paper, we start by describing some related work in this field. We then describe our approach and methods used for this field study, followed by our findings. Finally, we provide implications for providing adequate support for bug reproduction activities.

1.1 Bug Reproduction and CSCW

The topic of bug reproduction has traditionally been studied in the software engineering and software maintenance communities. A study such as this can be relevant for the CSCW community for the following three reasons:

1. *Study Collaboration*: Bug reproduction presents an interesting case of collaborative practices between developers and bug reporters (customers or testers), where communication is rarely direct and often mediated through a bug tracking system or through other stakeholders such as product team managers and customer support professionals. The information communicated is often of a multi-modal nature (screen-shots, videos, texts) and is highly dependent on the context within which a bug is encountered.
2. *Empirical Value*: Unlike the methods used in the traditional software engineering research [4, 15, 16, 20, 26], we apply an ethnographic approach to gain access to the real-world practices of developers in their ongoing bug-fixing projects. This research will allow us to gain a holistic view of the bug reproduction process, where we can contribute towards an improved empirical foundation for understanding software bug-fixing practices.
3. *Design Ideas*: A user-centered approach such as ours would allow us to connect the empirical findings gained from ethnographic work to novel designs and tool ideas that can improve current practices of bug reproduction. This in fact is our main goal—to develop better tools to improve productivity and efficiency.

2 Related Work

In the following, we provide a short literature review on bug-fixing. We highlight the contributions from the CSCW community for studying software development activities and then move onto the traditional software engineering literature.

CSCW researchers have long been highlighting different collaborative aspects of software development practices. Empirical studies on groupware technologies have emphasized the role of group awareness [9], work dependencies [12], and aspects relating to collaborating work cultures [21]. Ethnographic methods are used to study specific practices related to, for example, the use of configuration management tools [8], workflow management activities [10] and software testing practices [18]. Within software development and maintenance teams, bug tracking systems serve as the medium through which not only developers and customer can coordinate their activities but other stakeholders such as product managers, testers, and customer support professionals can also interact and communicate. There are several studies on bug tracking systems done within the HCI/CSCW community [2, 8, 19, 22, 25]. Based on a qualitative study involving 15 developers, Bertram [3] highlighted that bug tracking systems were used as (1) a knowledge repository where activities from different stakeholders were getting stored, (2) a boundary object [24], to fulfill the needs of different stakeholders, and (3) a communication and coordination hub. Studies have shown that bug tracking system serves as a tool to negotiate specific details of bug-fixing activities [10].

Within the software engineering community, Zhang et al. [27] explored the most important factors that affect the bug-fixing process: type of bug, severity of bug, operating system, and description of bugs. The role of software users (or customers) in bug-fixing is also emphasized in several studies. Developers require different types of information from users in order to fix bugs. Bettenburg et al. [4] explored a set of information required in a bug report by collecting responses from 466 developers. Their study highlighted that bug reports often have a strong mismatch between what developers needed and what information was provided by users. Based on the analysis of 600 bug reports, Breu et al. [5] developed categories of questions that are asked by developers to the users who reported bugs. Frequently asked questions were related to missing information, clarifications, triaging, debugging, correction, status enquiry, resolution and process. Other similar studies included the use of card sorting methods [15] for exploring how bugs can be reported and resolved in the form of design recommendation for new bug tracking systems.

Several studies have explored the importance of different information required for bug reproduction, such as trace logs and steps to reproduce. For example, Schroter et al. [23] carried out an empirical study on the usage of stack traces by developers from the ECLIPSE project and found that bug reports with stack traces are fixed faster than bug reports without them. They also found that bugs are likely to be found in one of the top ten stack frames. Herbold et al. [11] developed a non-intrusive, easily to integrate GUI-based monitoring mechanism which would automatically collect usage logs of different user activities and allow replaying them for the purpose of reproducing bugs whenever they occur. It is also important to note that in some cases it might be embarrassing for companies when such privacy-centric data is reviled. To support this need, Casto et al. [6] developed a mechanism by which software developers are provided with new input values that can be as useful as the original input values that can be used in bug reproduction. This way less information is revealed to developers and companies' privacy is also protected.

3 Field Study

In our research, we aimed at gaining access to developers' natural practices to be able to learn about their software bug-fixing and in particular bug reproduction practices. We believed that an *in situ* account on developers may shed light on the social and situated nature of software bug-fixing activities.

3.1 Methods

Over a period of three months, we conducted an ethnographic field study of 16 software developers working in a software maintenance division of a multinational engineering conglomerate. These developers belonged to 8 different software product teams. We used the following three methods in our research.

1. **In situ Observations**: We video recorded developers' real-time software bug-fixing activities at their workspace. We started our observations from the beginning when a bug was reported and assigned to developers. These in situ observations in most cases lasted half-a-day; however, in some cases we prolonged our interactions with the developers to follow the complete bug-fixing process. At the end of our sessions, we collected all artefacts that were being used in their bug-fixing activities such as bug reports and related documents.
2. **Semi-structured Interviews**: Following the observations, we carried out semi-structured interview at developers' workspace, where we asked our participants questions related to their bug-fixing processes and practices. We aimed at getting insights into their use of different tools, their collaboration and communication practices, their use of bug tracking systems, and so on. Additionally, we asked participants to give an account of at least two bugs that they recently fixed. These interviews lasted for 45 min to 1 h per participant.
3. **Questionnaire**: At the completion of the observation and interview sessions, we sent out a questionnaire to all 16 participants. We developed this questionnaire using the inputs from observation and interview sessions. The questionnaire used five-point Likert scale and focused on understanding participants' preferences related to bug reproduction practices, e.g. what type of information is most useful, how bug reproduction helps in following bug-fixing activities.

3.2 Participants

In the facility where we were carrying out our research, there were more than 800 software developers working on a large variety of products from domains such as automation, power and robotics. Our selection of developers aimed at adding heterogeneity in our data sample and hence allowing generalizability in our findings. To recruit software developers for our study, we contacted division managers of these different product domains and using their help recruited developers from different software development teams. We also ensured that we selected no more than two developers from one team.

Table 1 provides participant details of our field study. In general, we involved developers who were working on SCADA (supervisory control and data

Table 1 Participant details

Product type	No. of developers	No. of bugs studied
SCADA products	5	6—Observation; 6—Interviews
Automation SW 1	3	2—Observation; 6—Interviews
Automation SW 2	4	3—Observation; 3—Interviews
Robotics SW	1	2—Interviews
Power product	3	3—Observation; 6—Interviews
Total	16	39

acquisition), automation, power and robotics products. From these 16 developers, we studied 39 bug-fixing cases taking into account the natural practices of these developers. From our field study, we collected a large amount of videos, field and interview notes, bug reports and bug-related artefacts. The results presented below were obtained through a qualitative analysis [7] of our collected data. We started by creating a large affinity wall [13] using post-its and used open-coding to derive larger concepts and categories.

4 Results

From our field study, we derived several interesting perspectives on bug reproduction and were able to identify important social dimensions to the bug reproduction process.

4.1 Social Process of Bug Reproduction

Software bug reproduction is an activity developers perform to locally recreate the situation in which a bug (or a defect) was originally observed at the site of a customer or a tester. It is a widely-used practice in software maintenance and typically starts at an early stage of big fixing activities. It is a highly social activity because it involves communication and collaboration between several actors, including developers, testers, customers, product managers, customer support professionals among others.

In our study, we attempted to capture a holistic view of bug reproduction. Figure 1 shows a high level view of the social side of the bug reproduction process, as reported by the developers who participated in our field study. This figure particularly focuses on the customer reported bugs. When a customer encounters a bug, he/she reports it to the customer support offered by the software company. Here, the customer provides all the basic information about the

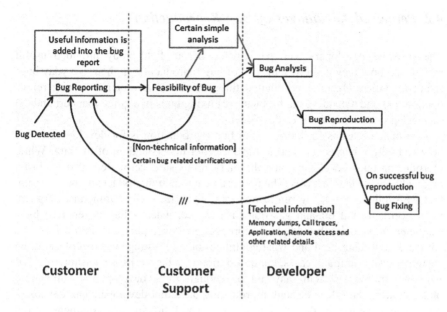

Fig. 1 The social process of bug reproduction

scenario within which the bug occurred. Using these details, the customer support professionals check the feasibility of the bug and check if all the software configurations are in place. At this stage, they would provide a fix, if the problem is simple such as a wrong configuration was used or date format mismatched. If they cannot fix the problem, they report it into the bug tracking system. Customer support professionals are not developers themselves; hence they cannot solve any technical problems. They work as a mediator between customers and developers. While the bug is reported into the bug tracker, the customer support team adds details such as software version and module, OS version, description of the problem and steps for reproduction into the bug tracker. If such information is not added the customer support professionals collaborates with the customer and adds this information. Once a bug is reported into a bug tracking system, it is assigned to a responsible product team manager based on the matching of appropriate software modules. The product team manager also does a feasibility check on the bug and assigns it to an adequate developer to fix this bug. As a part of an initial analysis of the bug, the developer starts the bug reproduction process utilizing the information that is provided in the bug tracker. If the developer needs more information regarding the bug, he contacts the customers using the help from customer support team. Developers rarely have direct contacts with the customer, but if needed they can also have direct phone calls or video chats with the customer.

4.2 Perceived Advantages of Bug Reproduction

The software developers who participated in our field study provided useful insights on how they perceived the use of bug reproduction in their everyday bug-fixing activities. Overall, we elicited three perceived advantages of bug reproduction: (1) understanding the problem; (2) fixing bugs in a quick manner; and (3) increasing confidence level of developers.

One of the reasons for carrying out bug reproduction is for developers to see how and why a bug occurs and to have a better understanding of the bug. While reproducing bugs developers gain the firsthand experience of steps that lead to a bug and how the bug behaves. The power and automation products of the company that we studied were being run in multiple industries such as minerals, pulp and paper, cement, and oil and gas domains. Hence, when a bug is reported by a customer, it is only through bug reproduction developers can know how the software was being used and what configuration and settings were in place at the customer's site. In many cases, the description of a bug or its screenshot provided in a bug tracking system may not be enough for a developer to sufficiently understand the bug. It is through reproducing bugs that developers can develop a better understanding of the problem at hand. The following is a comment from a developer, which indicates our finding:

> If there is a UI related or a printing related issue then bug reproduction may not be necessary. But if I get issue related to system crash or similar then I need to investigate how the software is configured on the site of the customer. We need to interact with them and get required information.

More importantly, a successful bug reproduction allows developers to fix bugs in a quicker manner. While debugging, a successful bug reproduction allows developers to better locate the precise area in the code where the problem is located. Bug reproduction saves a considerable amount of time as developers can focus on specific parts and flows of the code that need attention. A developer commented:

> There are thousands of lines of code in this software and it is impossible to know everything in it because some of the code is legacy. With bug reproduction we can limit our efforts. We need not find each and every flow inside the code. If we know that these are the steps to reproduce the bug then we can pinch on that particular flow in the code and target only that flow to solve the problem.

The third benefit of bug reproduction was that it increased the perceived confidence level of developers before actually fixing a bug. Successful bug reproduction meant that details provided by the bug reporter are enough and the developer can directly focus on the fix. This part will be elaborated in the later part of this paper.

5 A Holistic View of Bug Reproduction

5.1 When a Bug is Reported...

When a fault occurs during use, it is reported in a bug tracking system. A bug can be anything from a system crash or hang to any inconsistent behavior of a system. The bug initiator uses the bug tracking system to provide a description of the problem, details of the system configuration (e.g. product version, OS version), steps for recreating the bug, screenshots of the system interface and pointers to the location of the problem and other relevant information. Often this information is added to the bug report in the bug tracker; however, in some cases information is transferred via emails and file transfers. The bug tracking system serves as a common tool for multiple objectives for different stakeholders [1, 24].

Figure 2 is an excerpt from a bug report where the bug initiator has provided screenshots of a software that had a bug in it and pointed out certain fields in red color to indicate the problem. When a bug is reported by a tester or a developer, they tend to provide quite detailed, technical information in the bug report, where code patches, screenshots of a debugger and trace logs are attached. This way an effort is made by the bug initiator to provide detailed information about the bug.

Often, in the case of customer reported bugs, it was not easy for the customers to provide sufficient information in bug reports, as they themselves were not expert enough to provide such details. In such cases, developers would need to request details such as trace logs and memory dumps. There are two major challenges to this activity: (1) it may not be clear what information would be relevant to reproduce a bug, and (2) even when sufficient details are provided in the bug report a developer may not be able to reproduce the bug on his own machine. The following is a comment by a developer:

> Sometimes, customers miss to provide very basic information in their bug report and it takes us long time to reproduce the problem. One time, a customer missed to provide the correct time zone and we were not able to reproduce the problem for two weeks.

We observed the use of videos to provide information related to bugs. In particular, when it was important to convey some dynamic behaviors of bugs or some difficult to explain phenomenon videos were frequently used. The developers working on an embedded software for a power product portfolio dealt with hardware such as relays, breakers and transformers. In these cases, the use of videos to provide bug reproduction details was preferred by development teams. Here is a comment from of the developers from power products:

> Our partner team in Finland received this bug from a customer. When they could not fix it, they sent this bug to us. They also sent a video and trace-logs. This bug occurs once in may be 20 times. So, it is really hard for us find out the exact reasons. The video gives a dynamic view of the bug.

In the above case, the bug was reported by a customer. However the video was captured by a local development support team who had interacted with the

Fig. 2 An excerpt from a
bug report

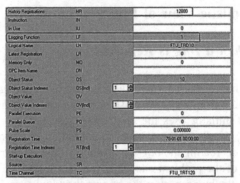

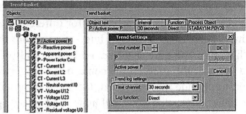

customer during the initial stages and attempted to fix the bug. The video had
captured the complete hardware setup so that the development team can have a
comprehensive knowledge of the system configuration.

There were several other cases, where bugs were reassigned to a different team
as it was not possible to reproduce it on the first try. This usually happened
between local and global development teams. In such cases, the development
teams interact with each other and usually the former development team provides
details related to their bug reproduction efforts. The following is a comment left on
a bug report by a development team to give details of their bug reproduction.

> There was no straight forward procedure to reproduce this error. I had done some random
> "monkey testing" for the WHMI. The WHMI was in timeout and after longer period of
> time I re-authenticated with Firefox browser (Event list was the page which was open
> before the timeout and SSL was enabled). After re-authentication the debugger stopped at
> the breakpoint (See attached image).

5.2 During Bug Reproduction…

After a bug goes through initial feasibility check, the responsible product team
manager assigns the bug to an appropriate developer of his team. Utilizing the
information provided by the bug initiator, the developer attempts to reproduce the
bug on his own machine.

In the case of a customer reported bug, timing becomes an important factor. Depending on the company's contract with customers, developers need to fix the bug and dispatch results in a week to 10 days. Hence, the reproduction needs to happen as soon as possible with minimal delays. For developers reproducing a bug require some effort in changing their current system configurations. Some development teams had access to a testing lab, where they can reproduce or test on specialized machines. However, the majority of developers were initially using their own machines for reproducing bugs and only when it was not possible to reproduce bugs, they went to the testing lab. The following is a comment made by a developer on how time consuming reproduction can be.

> Our team has a very dynamic bug-fixing process, although I do feel that it sometimes hampers our development process. When we get a bug, we have to remove our existing system settings and stop our ongoing development work, apply the customer's configurations, load all the software customer has been using. So, in all we end-up spending 1–2 days in only creating the right setup.

Developers rely heavily on the information supplied by customers; hence they tend to work with the data that is in bug trackers. Apart from the system configuration data, customers provide steps for reproducing, screenshots of the software's UI (e.g. Fig. 2), and a description of the problem referring to observed and expected behaviors. For customers, supplying this type of information is relatively easy as it is visible and observable. However, in case of a system crash or hang, the above mentioned information may not allow developers to successfully reproduce a bug and they often ask for more information from the customers. Often, customers themselves would not know or remember what exactly they did which caused the problem such as the system crash or hang. In such cases, developers try to extract trace logs and memory dumps from the customers' systems.

In cases, where it was not possible to reproduce a bug based on the given instructions, especially when bugs occur on the server, developers were able to remotely log into the customers' system and observe its behavior. Generally, customers allow remote log-in only when the system is not live. Additionally, developers use 'debug DLLs' to generate memory dumps from remotely debug customer's system. Here is a comment made by a developer:

> In a scenario where we cannot reproduce a bug on our own machine, we have the option of placing our debug DLLs in the customer's system and we can try to collect memory dumps this way. If we are able to reproduce then we use WinDBG debugger to debug the system.

There were also some challenges with the input that customers' were providing in bug trackers. In a small number of cases, developers reported that they received insufficient information from customers. There were examples where customers provided only a screenshot of their system or provided minimal description of the problem they were facing. In such cases, developers would randomly create use cases with certain interactions and try to reproduce bugs. The following is a comment made by one developer:

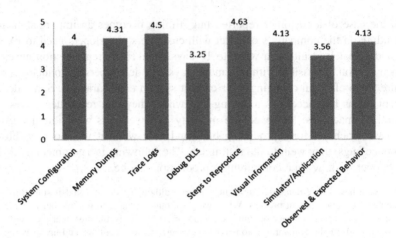

Fig. 3 Average rating of our participants' preference for different bug reproduction information (n = 16)

Recently, we had a bug which we have not been able to reproduce, till now. We have a Chinese version of our software and a customer reported a bug where Chinese fonts looked too small. All we had in the bug tracker was a screenshot of the system. No further information was provided. So we tried to reproduce this bug in different OSes. We tried Windows 7, 2008, Advanced Server R2, XP. We also changed the themes of the Windows, because themes also affect the font size. Our initial guess was Windows 7 as the title bars in the screenshot was matching it. When all these attempts failed, we asked the customer and he clarified that he was using Windows 2008 Advanced Server with the theme of Windows 7. Even then, we haven't been able to reproduce this bug in the customer's suggested environment.

Following the completion of our observation and interview sessions with all our participants, we sent out a questionnaire based on their qualitative feedback. A section of this questionnaire was about exploring developers' preference on 'what type of bug reproduction information they prefer from customers or testers'. We selected eight of the most frequently mentioned items from their feedback and asked them to rate these on a five-point Likert scale. Our main intention here was to validate the feedback of our participants and compare the importance of these individual items with one another. These eight items were: system configuration details (e.g. OS and product details, versions, hardware and software model); memory dumps, trace logs, debug DLLs, steps to reproduce, visual information (e.g. screenshots of software interface, videos); simulator or application used for testing; and observed and expected behaviors of the system. The result of this exercise is provided as a chart in Fig. 3. We found that 'steps to reproduce' ($\bar{x} = 4.63$) scored highest as the most preferred item for reproducing bugs, whereas the use of 'trace logs' ($\bar{x} = 4.5$) was also highly rated. 'Debug DLLs' ($\bar{x} = 3.25$) and 'simulator/application' ($\bar{x} = 3.56$) scored lower in our questionnaire, which suggests that these items served a niche requirement of our participants. These two items were by no means less important to the developers; in fact, these were used when other items turned out not to be helpful in reproducing a bug.

5.3 After a Bug is Reproduced...

Once developers are able to reproduce bugs, the fixing of bugs and further actions become clearer. Developers mentioned two main advantages of successful bug reproduction: (1) reducing the amount of fixing efforts and (2) giving confidence to developers in future actions on the bug.

When developers successfully reproduce bugs, using for example trace logs or memory dumps, they are actually able to locate specific lines of code where there is a problem. So, rather than looking and checking through a large amount of code—spread across different files, they reduce their efforts by going directly to the point where they need some fixing. Additionally, this also reduces their efforts for debugging, as the reproduction process indicates where a problem situated. The following are comments from two different developers:

> If I get steps to reproduce a bug, I will not have to look at other flows in the code. I just have to follow the flow that is described in the bug reproduction steps. For example, if there is a crash in a system, there could be more than one reason why it crashed. But it is important to know that during which activity it crashed, if we know these last two or three steps of the user then we are able to point out what exactly caused the crash.
>
> Bug reproduction helps in reaching functional level problems. It in fact gives a shortcut to reach to the problem, without having to go through the whole code.

In addition to reducing the overall efforts, bug reproduction also helps in supporting and informing further activities on bugs. Once a bug is reproduced, developers have to provide an analysis of the impact of the bug fix and provide details about what needs to be changed in the current system, what other features will be affected by the change, where else changes will be needed and provide test scenarios, among other things. As a testing team and a QA team will be part of the bug-fixing activity, they will provide their input on the proposed fix and analysis provided by the developer. The testing team will create their own test beds based on developers work and the QA team will verify the quality of the fix and provide their feedback on the bug tracker itself. The product manager and other senior level stake-holders would then take a call on how to proceed: whether to send this fix to the customer or add it to the next product release.

The questionnaire that we developed also had a question related to this part of the bug reproduction. Based on the observation sessions and interview feedback from our developers, we wanted to validate certain categories based on the question: 'how does bug reproduction help'. From their qualitative feedback, we selected six categories: understanding of bug patterns, limiting debugging efforts, locating fault in code areas, creating test cases, impact analysis and ensuring bug fix. On a five-point Likert scale, we asked all the 16 participants to rate these categories. As we described in the previous section, our main intention here was to validate the feedback of our participants and compare the importance of these individual items with one another. The result of this exercise is provided as a chart in Fig. 4. This figure shows that there is no strong difference among these categories. We found that 'understanding the bug pattern' ($\bar{x} = 4.29$) and 'ensuring

Fig. 4 Average rating of our
participants' perceived
advantages of bug
reproduction (n = 16)

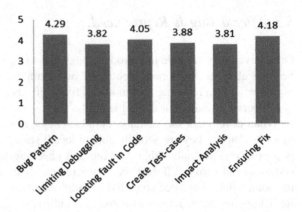

bug fix' ($\bar{x} = 4.18$) scored relatively higher. As such these two categories do not lead to any technical improvements for developers and other stake-holders. Rather, these two results point to the improved confidence level of developers. Understanding the bug pattern and getting an assurance of fixing a bug are the two subjective advantages a successful bug reproduction brings. Other categories such as impact analysis ($\bar{x} = 3.81$), creating test-cases ($\bar{x} = 3.88$) and locating fault in code areas ($\bar{x} = 4.05$) are the examples of technical improvements that bug reproduction supports.

6 Discussion

Studies [14, 17, 19] have shown that software developers spend a large amount of time on code evolution, bug-fixing and other maintenance related activities. From an HCI perspective, we have brought out the social side of software bug-fixing—in particular the practices related to bug reproduction. Unlike the studies done in the software engineering community [4, 15, 16, 20, 26], our study has focused on gaining access to the *in situ*, natural practices of developers working on real-world problems.

6.1 Challenges to Bug Reproduction

Our findings show that bug reproduction is a highly communication intensive activity. In our study, we found three major challenges to current bug reproduction practices: (1) lack of details from customers, (2) tedious logistical efforts, and (3) contextual issues of bugs.

Bug reproduction relies heavily on the inputs from customers. We found that developers often find insufficient information for reproducing bugs provided by customers. As a result they based their bug reproduction on previous experiences and hunches. This was shown in one of the examples where a developer who was provided with a screenshot of a bug, had to use his hunch to determine the OS of the customer's machine and had to try several different OS versions. Similarly, logistical efforts needed to reproduce a bug also posed a challenge. When a bug was reported, in order to reproduce it developers needed to configure their machine and apply the same setting in which the bug was reported at the customer's site. This would involve changing the OS of their local machine for the version on which the buggy software product runs. Importantly, when such an effort is required, developers had to interrupt their on-going work and carry out changes in their machines and get back to the original settings when a bug is reproduced and fixed. Thirdly, the contextual issues at a customer's site may not be easily predictable. In such cases, a customer may not be aware of the information that is required by the development team for solving a problem. For example, in the cases of a system crash or a system hang, it was not always possible for a customer to know the previous steps that led to the problem—which are typically required to reproduce such a bug.

6.2 Interaction with Customer

Developers rarely had direct interactions with customers for discussing bug reproduction related issues. The local and global support centers facilitate communication between both sides. In some cases, product managers of development teams get involved as mediators in this chain of communication. The local and global support professionals are not technically skilled to understand bugs in detail or to know if the information provided by customers is sufficient. Additionally, the language used by bug reporters may be very different from customer to customer. In many cases, customers would only be able to talk about the UI related interactions. Another issue when interacting with customers is that developers often face difficulty in accessing required information. At times, when developers would like to get access to trace-logs from a customer's machine they need to properly instruct their customers on how to install such patches that will yield trace-logs.

6.3 Practical and Subjective Sides of Bug Reproduction

Bug reproduction offered both practical and subjective advantages. On the practical side, bug reproduction helped developers locate the area where bugs were present in a quicker way, allowed them to carry out an impact analysis and helped them in creating use cases and scenarios for developing their fixes. Importantly, we also observed that there was a strong experiential side to bug reproduction activities. The main purpose of carrying out bug reproduction is for developers to be able to observe and experience how a bug occurs and how it behaves. This experience of being able to observe a bug is what adds to the confidence level of developers. Our results have shown the perceived advantages that a successful bug reproduction brings, such as increasing developers' confidence level by ensuring the bug fix and by providing indications about bug patterns. These aspects do not bring any technical advantages to developers, but they are perceptual and experiential in nature [19].

7 Implications

One of the most important aspects of bug reproduction is that it facilitates development teams not only to visualize a problem on their own machines, but in the process of reproducing a bug, it provides useful information about future activities related to bug-fixing. However, bug reproduction brings several challenges. A major problem that we observed was about communicating the *right* information, as in some cases customers provided insufficient information and in other cases customers did not know what information needs to be provided.

There are two important implications on the topic of supporting communication between customers (or bug reporters) and development teams. One implication is on developing tools that support customers in sufficiently understanding the encountered problems so that they can better provide appropriate and relevant information to the developer for fixing the bug. For example, tools may be developed to monitor activities of customers and on request or during a problem display records of these activities on an abstraction level that is adequate for the customer. This will empower customers to keep an account of their activities and provide relevant details at the time of reporting bugs. The second design implication is about supporting the automatic retrieval of 'relevant' information from a customer's local setup and making them available to the developers'. One of the ways this can be done is through the use of tracing mechanisms. Developers can build tracing mechanisms as a part of the software product that can be used to trace data related to the software usage in the field. This type of tracing could, for example, have different levels (mild, normal, extreme) which can be changed during runtime. Since tracing may increase the load on the software, the feature can be adapted based on the required level of detail. This way, whenever there is a bug reported in the system a responsible developer can easily extract the trace-log and can extract details about what led to such a bug. Privacy can be a major issue here as bugs reported by customers may have sensitive information. An approach similar to Castro et al. [6] could be explored to ensure that real values and data does not get misused. In addition to collecting the activity logs and trace logs, systems could also collect some contextual information related to the software setup (e.g. OS details) and configuration at place at the customer's site.

A bug tracking system is central in supporting communication and coordination between different parties involved in bug-fixing activities. Apart from some informal discussions on the phone, all important information is provided in the bug tracker. To deal with the issue of insufficient information provided by a customer, a template-based approach in bug trackers can be used. In this case, the bug tracker can have a dedicated section for bug reproduction where customers and support centers need to provide all the relevant information that may be required by a developer. Certain details can be made mandatory, for example, providing software product details, customers' system configurations, bug descriptions and other relevant details. Although, we did not generate any strong evidences in our research, developers tend to agree that certain information is required to deal with certain type of bugs. For example, in the cases of a software crash and hang, the use of trace-logs becomes very important. Similarly, a memory leak issue could also be a potential reason for software crash or hang, and in such cases memory dumps are also required by developers to study the bug. By making such details mandatory in a bug tracking system, a lot of time can be saved from a developers' point of view. Even better would be to dynamically adapt the template to the kind of bug reported and the system used, given that different systems might require different information for bug reproduction. We suggest that a detailed study can answer what kind of information is required by developers for specific bug types.

Our findings show that there are multiple people involved in the bug reproduction cycle, e.g. customer support professional, product managers, developers, testers and customers. Bug tracking systems should be appropriately integrated into the work environments of these different stakeholders, for example, a simple and natural language interface support for customers. Bug tracking systems can also add features for bug annotations or adding metadata so that better searching, filtering and sorting can be supported [3].

8 Conclusion

Bug reproduction is a social activity that involves participation from several stake holders besides developers and customers. Our findings show that the role of customers goes beyond merely reporting bugs. In fact, their interactions and inputs are needed at various stages of bug reproduction. From an ethnographic field study in an industrial setting, we examined current practices of bug reproduction and elicited challenges that developers face. Our results showed that developers find 'steps for reproduction' and 'trace logs' to be the most important information for reproducing bugs. At the same time, it showed that bug reproduction is as much a confidence building measure as a technical procedure that developers follow at the beginning of a bug-fixing activity. Based on our findings, we also provide several design recommendations such as the use of tracing and monitoring mechanisms, adding new features (templates and annotations) to bug tracking systems and appropriately integrating them into the work environments of different stakeholders.

References

1. Ackerman MS, Halverson C (1999) Considering an organization's memory. In: Proceedings of computer supported cooperative work, ACM, pp 39–48
2. Avram G, Bannon L, Bowers J, Sheehan A, Sullivan DK (2009) Bridging, patching and keeping the work flowing: defect resolution in distributed software development. Comput Support Coop Work 18(5–6):477–507
3. Bertram D, Voida A, Greenberg S, Walker R (2010) Communication, collaboration, and bugs: the social nature of issue tracking in small, collocated teams. In: Proceedings of the ACM conference on computer supported cooperative work, ACM, pp 291–300
4. Bettenburg N, Just S, Schröter A, Weiss C, Premraj R, Zimmermann T (2008) What makes a good bug report? In: Proceedings of the 16th ACM SIGSOFT international symposium on foundations of software engineering, pp 308–318
5. Breu S, Premraj R, Sillito J, Zimmermann T (2010) Information needs in bug reports: improving cooperation between developers and users. In: Proceedings of the 2010 ACM conference on computer supported cooperative work, ACM, pp 301–310
6. Castro M, Costa M, Martin JP (2008) Better bug reporting with better privacy. ACM SIGARCH Comput Archit News 36(1):319–328
7. Corbin J, Strauss A (eds) (2008) Basics of qualitative research: techniques and procedures
8. Grinter RE (1996) Supporting articulation work using software configuration management systems. Compute Support Coop Work (CSCW) 5(4):447–465
9. Gutwin C, Penner R, Schneider K (2004) Group awareness in distributed software development. In: Proceedings of the 2004 ACM conference on computer supported cooperative work, ACM, pp 72–81
10. Halverson CA, Ellis JB, Danis C, Kellogg WA (2006) Designing task visualizations to support the coordination of work in software development. In: Proceedings of the 2006 20th anniversary conference on computer supported cooperative work, ACM, pp 39–48
11. Herbold S, Grabowski J, Waack S, Bünting U (2011) Improved bug reporting and reproduction through non-intrusive GUI usage monitoring and automated replaying. In: IEEE 4th international conference on software testing, verification and validation workshops, pp 232–241
12. Herbsleb JD, Mockus A, Finholt TA, Grinter RE (2000) Distance, dependencies, and delay in a global collaboration. In: Proceedings of the 2000 ACM conference on computer supported cooperative work, ACM, pp 319–328
13. Holtzblatt K, Wendell JB, Wood S (2005) Rapid contextual design: a how-to guide to key techniques for user-centered design. Elsevier
14. Jones C (2013) The economics of software maintenance in the twenty first century. Unpublished manuscript. http://citeseerx.ist.psu.edu/viewdoc/summary?doi=10.1.1.88.7697. Accessed 22/11/2013)
15. Just S, Premraj R, Zimmermann T (2008) Towards the next generation of bug tracking systems. In: IEEE symposium on visual languages and human-centric computing, VL/HCC, IEEE, pp 82–85
16. Ko AJ, Myers BA, Coblenz MJ, Aung HH (2006) An exploratory study of how developers seek, relate, and collect relevant information during software maintenance tasks. IEEE Trans Softw Eng 32(12):971–987

17. LaToza TD, Venolia G, DeLine R (2006) Maintaining mental models: a study of developer work habits. In: Proceedings of the 28th international conference on software engineering, ACM, pp 492–501
18. Lientz BP, Swanson EB, Tompkins GE (1978) Characteristics of application software maintenance. Commun ACM 21(6):466–471
19. Martin D, Rooksby J, Rouncefield M, Sommerville I (2007) 'Good' organisational reasons for 'Bad' software testing: an ethnographic study of testing in a small software company. In: 29th international conference on software engineering, ICSE, IEEE
20. Müller S, Fritz T (2013) Stakeholders' information needs for artifacts and their dependencies in a real world context. International conference on software maintenance (ICSM), IEEE, pp 290–299
21. Ohira M, Hassan AE, Osawa N, Matsumoto KI (2012) The impact of bug management patterns on bug-fixing: a case study of eclipse projects. In: 28th international conference on software maintenance, IEEE, pp 264–273
22. Olson JS, Olson GM (2003) Culture surprises in remote software development teams. Queue 1(9):52
23. Schmidt K, Simone C (1996) Coordination mechanisms: towards a conceptual foundation of CSCW systems design. Compute Support Coop Work 5(2–3):155–200 (Kluwer Academic Press)
24. Schroter A, Bettenburg N, Premraj R (2010) Do stack traces help developers fix bugs? In: 7th IEEE working conference on mining software repositories, pp 118–121
25. Star SL, Griesemer JR (1989) Institutional ecology, 'translations' and boundary objects: amateurs and professionals in Berkeley's museum of vertebrate zoology, 1907–39. Soc Stud Sci 19(3):387–420
26. Tellioğlu H, Wagner I (1999) Software cultures. Commun ACM 42(12):71–77
27. Zhang F, Khomh F, Zou Y, Hassan AE (2012) An empirical study on factors impacting bug-fixing time. In: 19th working conference on reverse engineering (WCRE), IEEE, pp 225–234

Collaborative Work and Its Relationship to Technologically-Mediated Nomadicity

Aparecido Fabiano Pinatti de Carvalho

Abstract This paper explores the relationship between technologically-mediated nomadicity (Tm-N) and issues of computer supported collaborative work. It presents findings from a four-year research project, which set out to investigate issues of Tm-N in academic settings. The findings herein presented support the argument that Tm-N can be seen as a dynamic and emergent process, which unfolds through the enactment of an ecology of practices and permeates both the work and non-work dimension of the lives of those whose jobs allow or demand some flexibility as to *when* and *where* work assignments should be carried out. The main contributions of the paper are: (i) a holistic and in-depth frame to understanding technologically-mediated nomadicity, which provides a more fine-grained and nuanced account of assorted aspects of the notion, and (ii) an analysis on how collaborative activities and computer-mediated remote interactions are related to the spectrum of motivational forces that people draw on to engage in nomadicity.

1 Introduction

Over the past number of years increasing attention has been paid to technologically-mediated nomadic work practices, also known as technologically-mediated nomadicity (Tm-N) [5, 10], and to associated issues such as the development of computer technologies to support such practices and the understanding of background activities encompassed in their accomplishment, also called *mobilisation work* [22].

A. F. P. de Carvalho (✉)
Multidisciplinary Design Group, Institute of Design and Assessment of Technology,
Vienna University of Technology, Vienna, Austria
e-mail: Fabiano.Pinatti@tuwien.ac.at

C. Rossitto et al. (eds.), *COOP 2014 - Proceedings of the 11th International Conference on the Design of Cooperative Systems, 27–30 May 2014, Nice (France)*,
DOI: 10.1007/978-3-319-06498-7_13, © Springer International Publishing Switzerland 2014

Tm-N is herein defined as the process through which the workplace is mobilised to an assortment of locations with the help of computer technologies so that productive activities can be achieved from there. Studies like the ones presented by Kammas et al. [13], Cousins and Robey [6], Bean and Eisenberg [1], Rossitto and Eklund [24], Su and Mark [28], among others, explore some Tm-N related issues and investigate the challenges faced by people whose jobs allow or demand them to achieve their productive activities at different sites, who are henceforth referred to in this paper as T-Nomads (Tech-Nomads).

Notwithstanding the growing interest in the matter, relatively few researchers have directly addressed it in-depth. This article presents findings that advance the understanding of such a phenomenon, by introducing a new perspective on Tm-N and discussing in detail how collaborative activities and computer-mediated remote interactions are related to what I refer to as the *spectrum of Tm-N*: a view on Tm-N that sees it not as a fixed configuration of factors, but as a dynamic and emergent process that blurs the distinctions between the work and non-work dimensions of T-Nomads' lives.

On the one hand, practices around collaborative work and social interaction are crucial issues in the study of Tm-N as some studies on the subject have demonstrated before [3, 23, 28]. On the other hand, understanding issues of Tm-N is relevant for the design of effective technological solutions or work environments for those involved with it [24].

The findings herein presented are contextualised within a four-year research project, which investigated issues of Tm-N in academic settings [10]. Based on empirical evidence from qualitative data collected through extensive ethnographically-informed fieldwork, this paper discusses how different factors compose a spectrum of *motivational forces* that lead people to engage in Tm-N and elaborates on how collaborative activities and computer-mediated remote interactions have an influential role in it. The paper is contextualized in the CSCW (Computer Supported Cooperative Work) tradition of reporting on in-depth qualitative studies about work practices, technology mediation and the articulation of social relationships within work settings [26].

The remainder of this paper is organised as follows: Sects. 2 and 3 respectively introduce the context of the findings presented in the article and the methodology behind it. Section 4 elaborates on the new perspective on Tm-N introduced above. Section 5 goes on to present empirical data on the relationship between Tm-N and collaborative activities. Finally, Sect. 6 presents some concluding remarks.

2 Research Context

Despite the increasing number of studies on technologically-mediated nomadic practices, there remains a number of unexplored issues that are relevant for a better understanding of the matter [5].

Research on Tm-N has primarily focused on: (i) how people mobilise their work (e.g. [22]); (ii) where they engage in it (e.g. [24]); (iii) what impact can be imprinted upon organisations that decide to move towards a nomadic approach to business (i.e. having a nomadic workforce whose members would be allowed to work from wherever they would like to) (e.g. [3]); (iv) how technologies may support workers to get work done in and across several locations (e.g. [14, 23]); and (v) what aspects should be considered for their design (e.g. [15]).

However, these studies often take for granted how technologically-mediated nomadic practices are part of the T-Nomads' lives and neglect to some extent to explore the *reasons* why they engage in it. The impression gained from the literature on the matter is that there are some particular groups of people that are nomadic with the help of technologies, so it is possible to investigate how Tm-N unfolds by observing them. In order to clarify these issues, I have performed an in-depth ethnographic study of a group of T-Nomads: academics.

The focus of the study was on academics developing work in and across several locations as the flexibility of many of their work activities means that these can be performed at home, in the office, in cafés, restaurants, airports, airplanes, to name but a few locations. This *potential* "lack of a stable and fixed location" [24, p. 45] where work can be carried out characterises them as instances of T-Nomads.

The study featured sixteen academics of the University of Limerick, of which eight were men and eight were women. Participants fell into different age groups, ranging from the mid-thirties to late-fifties, working in different academic positions such as full/part time lecturers or research fellows and in different departments (Computing, Engineering, Sociology, Languages, Communication and Teaching and Learning). Thirteen of the participants were full time lecturers, two of them were part-time lecturers, and one of them was a research fellow with teaching and research responsibilities.

The *research questions* that led the investigation were to do with: (1) how Tm-N is evident in the work-life of academics; (2) in what ways computer technologies affect the process; and (3) what issues arise from engaging in it. As a study that aimed at contributing to human-centred computing fields of research, this investigation was particularly concerned with understanding people as they make use of computer technologies to deal with the nomadic aspect of their lives and with how technologies may impact the process.

In pursuing these research questions, it was possible to observe that Tm-N can be seen as a process that emerges from people's engagement with an *ecology of practices*, which involves a dialogue between human bodies and technologies as work gets accomplished in and across different sites, as will be further detailed in Sect. 4.

3 Methodology

In order to answer the aforementioned research questions, an ethnographically-informed approach was adopted, i.e. direct observation and in-depth interviews were used to collect data for the research. Using ethnographic approaches has become well-established within CSCW and HCI (Human–Computer Interaction) for the development of the necessary understanding to be applied to the design of new technologies [7].

Following the recommendations from the literature [9, 23, 28], multiple data collection instruments were used so that *triangulation* was possible.

At least one in-depth interview was conducted with each fieldwork participant. Most of them also participated in shadowing sessions, in which they were followed to the different locations where they accomplished work (e.g. office, lecture halls, university cafés, home, to name but a few). Some of the informants also participated in a follow-up interview that was performed some weeks after the shadowing session. A few participants also filled in and submitted diaries for analysis. The data collection process produced 16 in-depth interviews, 10 shadowing transcripts, 6 follow-up interviews and 6 diaries (see Table 1).

The study was situated within the qualitative paradigm, which offers methods that allow researchers to grasp, hear, catch and comprehend the meanings of actions and occurrences that are essential for good understanding to be achieved [8].

4 Tm-N as a Dynamic and Emergent Process

As previously mentioned, past and current research commonly starts from the premise that Tm-N is exclusively associated with inherently nomadic work, i.e. types of work that require people to move to different locations in order to accomplish their productive tasks. However, as this study progressed, it became evident that, whilst some types of work demand that people move to different locations in order to complete their work assignments (i.e. they are *inherently multilocated work*), certain types of work are not strictly nomadic but allow people to engage in work activities in different locations (i.e. they are *flexible work*). If people have/decide to move to different locations in order to work, Tm-N emerges from the way that they become involved in an ecology of practices to mobilise their workplace and accomplish work in and across multiple locations.

Therefore, the fieldwork findings suggest that Tm-N can be understood as a *dynamic* and *emergent* process associated with a *spectrum of motivational forces* and an *ecology of practices* for the *mobility of the workplace*[1]: *dynamic* because it is reconfigured according to the ways in which people think of their work-life, strategise about it and react in situations where tasks cannot be accomplished as planned; *emergent* because it has life cycles that reflect the accomplishment of work at assorted locations. As Wenger [29] notes, elements of emergent structures

---

[1] To bring resources such as printouts, laptops, mobile phones and other sorts of resources that may be used for setting up temporary workplaces and carrying out work.

Table 1 Overview of the data collection activities per participant

Participant[1]	Data collection activities			
	Interview	Shadowing[2]	Follow-up interview[3]	Diary[4]
Aoife	✔	½ working day	✔	–
Bridget	✔	–	–	–
Cathal	✔	–	–	–
Claus	✔	3 ½ working days	✔	1
Elaine	✔	½ working day	–	–
Gabriel	✔	–	–	–
James	✔	3 ½ working days	–	–
Jenny	✔	3 ½ working days	✔	1
Josh	✔	–	–	–
Kate	✔	½ working day	✔	1
Lucy	✔	3 working days	–	–
Maeve	✔	–	–	–
Marc	✔	–	–	–
Philip	✔	½ working day	✔	1
Shannon	✔	3 ½ working days	✔	2
Tom	✔	½ working day	–	–

[1] Fictional names are used to ensure confidentiality

[2] Total number of working days for which each participant was shadowed

[3] Follow-up interviews explored the themes emerging from the on-going data analysis being performed on the data collected during the first round of interviews, the shadowing sessions and the diaries. From the 16 participants, 6 agreed to participate in the last round of interviews

[4] Participants were asked to fill in a short diary recounting activities that they performed in a working day of their choice. A digital template, which could be printed out or filled in by using a word processor of choice, was provided to all participants. Five participants have returned their completed diaries; one of them filled in two diaries, reporting on two different working days

"come together, they develop, they evolve, they disperse, according to timing, the logic, the rhythms, and the social energy" (p. 96) of the process. Hence, as T-Nomads go on to engage in work in and across different locations, certain practices from their *Tm-N ecology* come together and once work is accomplished (or aborted) they fade away.

The notion of ecology has been used by several authors to refer to a mix of different elements that coexist and are related both to each other and to the context within which they exist [19, 27]. For instance, Nardi and Whittaker [19] define "information ecologies" as "local habitations of people, practices, technologies, and values" (p. 102).

The Tm-N ecology of practices was observed as people engaged in a series of different practices as they went on to accomplish work in multiple locations. Three elements were identified as key components of it: (1) *mobility*, which refers to the physical movements of people and resources; (2) *locations*, which refer to the geographical positions as well as the environment and infrastructure available in them; and (3) *workplace tokens*, which refer to all technological and/or informational resources that are necessary to set up temporary workplaces at the locations to where T-Nomads move. The diagrammatic illustration in Fig. 1, inspired by Eisenberg's representation of the identity process [11], attempts to depict the process and its nuances. The model corresponds to the main outcome of this research and was forged through a dialogue between a review of the literature and the analysis of the empirical data collected through fieldwork.

In summary, this new perspective on Tm-N describes the process at three different levels of abstraction, with the higher levels including elements of the lower ones. At the core of the process (level 1), which refers to the inner circle of Fig. 1, there is a spectrum of motivational forces that lead people to engage in Tm-N; in the "shell" of it (level 2), which concerns the outer circle in Fig. 1, lie the components of the ecology of practices employed by T-Nomads as Tm-N unfolds; finally, outside the process there are the work and non-work life contexts of which Tm-N is part (level 3). The focus of this paper is on the relationship between the core element of this new perspective, i.e. the Tm-N spectrum of motivational forces, and collaborative activities.

When it comes to the literature, it is possible to observe a dichotomy in the arguments associated with the reasons why people engage in Tm-N. Frequently, research studies point out the need to meet face-to-face or to use specific resources fixed in a given location as the solely reasons why people would engage in Tm-N. Thus, T-Nomads would *have to* move to those locations and take with them resources that would afford the accomplishment of their work [23, 24, 28]. In turn, a few studies stress the element of choice, describing how computer technologies allow T-Nomads to engage in work in locations where they can find comfort or in times that suit them best [1, 6, 25].

The fieldwork data collected in my study provided evidence that the factors leading to Tm-N are not as clear-cut as it was depicted in the literature. Choice and obligation emerged from the fieldwork data as two extremes of a spectrum of motivational forces that lead to Tm-N, as observable in the following vignette extracted from a diary provided by one of the fieldwork participants (Shannon, a full-time lecturer at the Department of Computer Science):

> Between Monday, May 9 and Wednesday May 18, I was in [my home country], attending to family business. On Sunday, May 15, I had more time for catching up with work [...] I chose to do work on that day. [...] I sat down in front of my laptop [...] and went through my UL email. There were a few emails I had seen before, but didn't have time to answer. One was from a secondary school student interested in our [undergraduate] programme. As I didn't know the answer to the question he was asking, I searched the Handbook of Academic Regulations that I downloaded from the UL website for that purpose. The answer was still not obvious, so I checked if my colleague Lucy was online on Skype and dared to bother her on a Sunday morning with a work question. Fortunately, she had the answer, so I was able to write the reply and send it. [...] Then, I was contacted via Yahoo Messenger by Luna [...] about a paper we were working on for [an Irish] conference. She shared the draft paper with me via Google Docs and asked for my opinion on the intro-duction. I made a few comments, then we discussed my contribution and made a plan about future work. As the weather was lovely, I decided to copy the [master programme] reports that I had to read and mark to my Kindle device and go out to do this. I found a nice café by the canal that's crossing [the city], sat at a table and ordered an ice coffee before starting to read. Initially I took out my paper notebook to make comments on the

Fig. 1 Tm-N as a dynamic
and emergent process

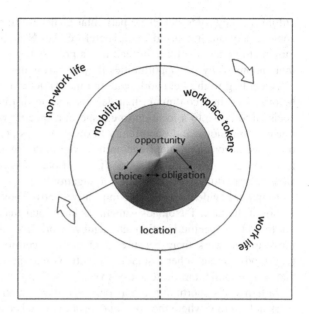

papers, but very soon I decided I'll try out the commenting facility on the Kindle [...] at times I was distracted by conversations taking place around me. I overheard a discussion about Facebook and hoaxes that drew my attention and I tried to Google the issue on my Android phone, using my mobile Orange connection. I made a note on my notebook (I haven't installed Delicious on the Android yet) to bookmark the issue and maybe use it in a lecture for [one of the modules I teach]... (Shannon's Diary 01).

The vignette above illustrates both the emergent and dynamic aspects of Tm-N. In regard to the former, the vignette depicts Shannon's engagement in different work activities during a trip to her country of origin to take care of family business. It recounts how she got some work done as she found herself at different locations for various reasons, and as necessary resources became available. It describes several practices that are part of Shannon's Tm-N ecology of practices: access to remote resources, integration with other people, the assemblage and mobilisation of information and technological resources, physical movements to assorted locations and the configuration of temporary workplaces.[2] As for the dynamic aspect of Tm-N, the vignette shows reconfigurations taking place in the nomadic process as work was being carried out. Above all, the excerpt supports the argument that Tm-N is not a process just to do with moving to a specific location because particular resources that are needed for accomplishing a given task will only be available there. Rather, Tm-N can be seen as a process that emerges from the way people deal with issues of their work and non-work lives: it sometimes happens to people as they are dealing with other aspects of their lives and it

---

[2] Some of the aforementioned practices have already been observed in Su and Mark's [28] study of T-Nomads.

unfolds as they try to achieve a particular goal, resulting in gradual change of the context they are immersed into. Therefore, Tm-N is not to do with a matter of moving to be a nomad, but instead it is a process triggered by people's needs and motivations or by the opportunities they are presented with.

According to the fieldwork data, the motivational forces leading to Tm-N can be organised in a continuum that depicts a scale of freedom associated with the decision to move to a location to engage in a specific work task. This continuum ranges from choice and opportunity to obligation, as portrayed in Fig. 2, which is organised according to the freedom involved in the decision to move to a specific location and accomplish work there (total freedom = choice; no decision[3] = opportunity; no freedom = obligation).[4]

Empirical evidence as the one introduced above showed that, depending on the nature of the task, T-Nomads sometimes have total freedom to decide whether or not to go to a specific location and achieve work from there. They may choose to move to and work there because it offers them comfort, inspiration, subsistence (e.g. food), among other resources. Situations like these are located at the choice end of the continuum presented above.

In terms of opportunity, it was observed that sometimes T-Nomads engage in work at locations where they do not expect to do so because some kind of resource was conveniently made available. Therefore, *they do not choose to move to the location in question* to work; however, once they are at a certain location *they may choose to opportunistically engage in work there* because time was available or another resource came into play. For this reason, it is suggested here that the freedom of choice associated with opportunity lies between choice and obligation. For instance, when someone is having lunch in a restaurant and a collaborator meets them unexpectedly, they may end up discussing and achieving some work on their collaborative project because of a looming deadline. On the other hand, if time is not an issue, they may choose to talk about everything but work.

Finally, some situations force T-Nomads to move to specific locations and to engage in work there, i.e. they do not have a choice but move to these locations. This usually happens when they have to use specific resources that are found only at those locations, or because they are required to be at that location due to company policies. For instance, in the case of the academics taking part in my

---

[3] 'no decision' means that the person did not decide to move to a location to engage in the work task in question. They move to the location due to some other reason, and then some resource becomes available and they opportunistically engage in the work task of reference.

[4] It is worth pointing out that the spectrum of motivational forces in Fig. 1 looks different because it is organised according to the possibility of one motivation to lead to another one. For instance, if someone chooses to move to a location and work on a determined assignment, one may engage in another work task as other resources are conveniently made available on site (e.g. inspiration, time or other people); hence, choice led to opportunity. Similarly, someone may choose to go to a location (like when they go and visit a relative) and an unexpected situation forces them to move to other location and engage in work from there (e.g. a call from the boss demanding that some action is taken with regard to something); in this case, choice was followed by obligation.

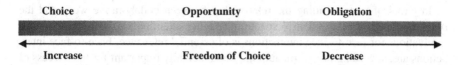

Fig. 2 Spectrum of nomadicity according to the *freedom of choice*

study, they are obliged to move to different lecture halls to deliver their lectures. Although they suggest that they can potentially[5] lecture from anywhere (e.g. in a square, in a pub, etc.), they are required to move and work in the rooms assigned to them because it is part of the university's scheduling system. Situations like these are placed at the opposite end of the spectrum of motivational forces that I identified in this paper.

To conclude, the new perspective on Tm-N herein detailed describe a holistic and in-depth frame to understand technologically-mediated nomadicity, in that it considers underlying motivations for T-Nomads to mobilise their workplace to and accomplish work in different locations as well as multiple configurations of the practices and of technological mediation that may occur as the process unfolds. Furthermore, it addresses the blurring of work and non-work dimensions of life, whose relevance has been acknowledged within CSCW field of research, but so far has not been sufficiently explored [4]. This holistic account is of special relevance to CSCW field of research, which is concerned with issues spanning over the use of computer technologies in context to support the accomplishment of work and to foster collaboration among different groups of people [26].

5 The Tm-N Spectrum and Issues of Collaborative Work

Collaborative activities have an influential role in Tm-N in that they may force people to move to different locations in order to meet collaborators and accomplish some work together, or they may provide opportunities from which Tm-N can emerge (e.g. when one unexpectedly meets a collaborator in a restaurant and accomplishes some work at that time and location). Therefore, it can be argued that collaborative work is intrinsically related to the *opportunity* and *obligation* regions of the Tm-N spectrum previously presented.

This section elaborates particularly on to what extent collaborative activities may influence people to move to different locations in order to meet face-to-face and how computer-mediated remote interactions can act both as an enabler and a disabler to Tm-N.

---

[5] They cannot do so when lecturing involves specific resources (particular equipment, for example) found only in some places.

In terms of understanding the relationship between collaborative work and the *obligation* region of the Tm-N spectrum, paying attention to the reasons and/or motivations for face-to-face interactions is of essential relevance. Face-to-face inter-actions are, according to several authors, fundamentally important for the success of some types of collaborative work [2, 19–21]. Researchers such as Olson and Olson [20] even present co-located interactions as something that will never be replaced or undermined, arguing that these types of interactions are crucial, especially at the beginning of collaborative efforts, for the establishment of the trust and common ground necessary for collaboration to succeed. Taking this into account, it is accept-able to think that collaborators would always have to move to a common place where they would engage in work and, therefore, Tm-N would be even more noticeable.

However, there is a portion of researchers who argue for the importance of mediated remote interactions for some types of collaborative work (e.g. [12, 19]). With regard to collaborative work performed by academics, the findings of this research point towards the direction of the argument defended by the latter group of researchers. Participants often associated co-located interactions with the social aspect of work and with the possibility of a more pleasant interaction, rather than a necessity for successfully accomplishing collaborative work, as emphasised by Tom, a full-time research fellow from the Department of Computer Science:

> [Face-to-face interactions] are not essential. It's possible now with all the computer communication and, shared workspace facilities that we have to effectively work col-laboratively without any face-to-face meetings. So, to me it's important for the social aspect. It's more fun or it can be. (Tom, Interview)

Furthermore, when it comes to productivity, participants frequently acknowl-edged that they could[6] achieve very positive results when they work over remote interactions, as Claus, a full time lecturer at the Department of Computer Science, states below:

> I think for research I have great results working on papers with people over the email only. When it's research work you can do that [...] With my supervisor here we had one of the best papers that we published was done completely on the email because he was in Australia, I was here. So after that he was shocked, 'we actually did this best paper when I wasn't in Ireland!' (laughs) (Claus, Interview).

---

[6] It is worth pointing out that productivity is not necessarily directly (or exclusively) related to remote interactions. The data analysis conducted for this research identified that both the distant and the co-located *modalities of collaboration* can effectively support productivity. Participants have pointed out that face-to-face interactions are inherently richer in terms of meaning, thus allowing the involved parts to reach a common understanding of and an agreement on underlying issues faster. Therefore, participants considered *immediacy* as one of the motivations for choosing face-to-face interactions when possible. On the other hand, participants recursively acknowl-edged that, when it comes to some modes of remote communication, e.g. email, on-line material can be easily shared and discussions can be easily recorded for future reference. In their views, such things favour productivity especially in the case of formal collaborative exchanges, which suggests that achieving productivity through a particular modality of collaboration is also related to the *nature of work*. Hence, one should keep in mind that issues of productivity are multifaceted and involves variables like type of collaboration, mode of interaction, nature of work, etc.

It could be argued that the successful episode reported by Claus is associated with the fact that the activity in question is a loosely coupled activity developed by two people who had already a well-established trust relationship, shared high common ground and were ready to collaborate and to use collaboration technologies; these are some aspects that Olson and Olson [20] and Olson et al. [21] claim as essential for remote collaborative work to have a chance to succeed.

Nonetheless, in contrast with the argument by Olson and Olson [20], who defend that co-located activities are the best way to achieve trust and common ground, the fieldwork data suggest that remote interactions are being increasingly used to do so. This becomes particularly noticeable when Kate, a full-time lecturer at the School of Languages, Literature, Culture and Communication, recounts how she started a collaborative project with people from a non-European country. She explains that the non-European group first contacted her research group by email and asked if they would be interested in collaborating in an international initiative. Later that year, after they had already agreed and started collaborating, they met at a conference "just to confirm" their relationship. For her, the fact that they do not meet face-to-face regularly is irrelevant:

> It's really irrelevant that we have only met maybe twice. We met in 2006 and we met again maybe in 2008 face-to-face, but it feels like we meet all the time because we have video conferences and things like that. It's only when I say it now, it doesn't feel like we've only met face-to-face twice because we're regularly in contact by email, video conferences, chat on the forums and so on. (Kate, Interview)

Aoife, a part-time lecturer in the Department of Sociology, explains that the way the first contact is established does not matter for a successful collaborative experience. For her, building trust and common ground depends much more on the person who is making the contact and the past achievements of that person, which in the academic world can be easily verified on the Internet nowadays:

> [...] it would depend on who the person was and what university they were coming from and what they were proposing. It would depend. The same criteria that if you met someone face-to-face I think would still apply, it doesn't really matter how someone approaches you necessarily if the rest of them is bona fide. It doesn't really matter if someone sends you an email or phones you, or if somebody approaches you at a conference or if somebody sends you a message. It depends really on what they're offering and who they are. (Aoife, Interview)

In Kate's experience, the constant contact via information and communication technologies even blurs the distinction between the physical and the remote. She mentions how they got so used to each other due to the constant contact via computer so that it seems that they meet personally more often than they do. This blurring of the distinctions between in-person and remote was noted by several other fieldwork participants as well. This is an relevant finding in that it suggests that trust and common ground can effectively be established over remote interaction, and show how collaboration may succeed even between people who have never met before, echoing findings by Nardi and Whittaker [19], who discusse how a mix of face-to-face and remote interactions might be particularly relevant and sometimes even more suitable to collaborative work than the single use of face-to-face interactions, as some authors would argue.[7]

This is a relevant finding because there are times when travelling to engage in face-to-face interactions is not feasible, as widely acknowledged in the literature (even in studies that cherish face-to-face interactions). One of the main constraints that the fieldwork informants indicated for face-to-face interactions was high costs both in terms of monetary and of time resources. Other reasons that participants indicated as motivations to opt for computer-mediated remote interactions were: increased facility for keeping track of discussions conducted via information and communication technologies; the avoidance of unpleasant collaborators[8]; and finally, preference.[9]

Reflecting on the possibilities for remote interactions and the motivations that would lead people to become involved in them is relevant to the understanding of Tm-N because remote interactions can potentially lead to a more stationary work style, meaning that Tm-N would be less common. As Makimoto and Manners [16] emphatically put it, computer technologies can afford the creation of both the "*ultimate nomad*" (p. 17), i.e. someone who is forever on the move, working in all different sorts of locations, and the "*ultimate 'couch potato'*" (ibid), which refers to workers who would never leave the living-room sofa and, making use of assorted computer technologies, would accomplish all their productive activities from there.

However, as discussed throughout Sect. 4, the findings of this research suggest that there are several other aspects driving Tm-N, which would lead people to keep engaging in it. Moreover, whilst remote interactions may limit Tm-N, they may favour it as well, as is explained by Philip, a full-time lecturer at the Department of Electronic and Computer Engineering:

> In terms of the distance learning I engage more and more now for example, in the last year or two, with Moodle and so as a consequence that nomadic lifestyle or that nomad dimension to my work has been reduced because of the access to virtual learning tools, or virtual learning resources. Yes. By the same token I now can grade efforts from my [...] students in a café. (Philip, Interview)

---

[7] That sheds some light on Olson and Olson's [20] questioning whether trust can be built over remote mediated interactions.

[8] Participants pointed out that, as a matter of fact, sometimes collaborators might not be the most sociable people that one has to deal with: they might be important collaborators, share the same ideas, add important expertise to the group, but they "*might not be the most enjoyable people*", in Tom's words.

[9] Some participants expressed that personal preference plays an important role in choosing between face-to-face and remote interactions. One particular participant expressed that, if she could, she would use mostly emails for communication: "*... not that I can't talk*", she says, "*I can talk forever, I just feel more comfortable in communicating that way and I feel I can think about what I have to say and I don't speak as fast and I've just better control maybe over my communication*" (Kate, Interview). In addition to deeper reflection, participants also appraised the support that email gives to asynchronous interaction: it facilitates collaboration between partners in different time zones, allows writing to be stopped and resumed as needed, etc.

Therefore, considering the improvements of computer technologies allowing people to engage in the most varied types of remote interactions in many different locations (in the past it would have been more difficult to engage in some types of remote interactions such as video conferences, which required expensive equipment available in specific rooms) and the different motivations people may have to move to different locations, there is actually a possibility that people will be increasingly nomadic.

Claus says that people like to have a rhythm in life and because of that they tend to engage in Tm-N. Staying in a single location may be very disruptive to life, according to him, so people will keep moving:

> You want to have some everyday routine. Work from home can be very, very, very boring life, can be very boring and lonely life. It sounds like an attractive idea: 'oh I can stay at home and work from home', but it actually disrupts the daily routine, the rhythm of life, some sort of rhythm that, [when] you wake up, you [want] go to work. (Claus, Interview)

In reality, the participants' views resonate with the views of different authors (e.g. [16, 18]). However, notwithstanding the benefits of remote mediated interactions, it is worth pointing out that face-to-face interactions are undoubtedly relevant to certain types of collaborative work, as widely explored in the literature and already noted in this paper. This is not disputed here. In fact, the fieldwork participants constantly mentioned varied attributes of face-to-face interactions, which would motivate them to opt for them when they have the possibility.

The data suggested that there is an increasing acceptance of collaboration started via remote interaction. However, participants like James, a full-time lecturer at the Department of Computer Science, drawn the attention to the fact that social media have empowered people in such a way that they have become *"complex social islands"* in the virtual space that sometimes do not correspond to the *"physical island"* they are on the real world, as some research on self-presentation in the online world has already suggested [17]. Some participants acknowledged that, although people may keep convincing profiles on the web, meeting face-to-face might help to identify whether something is not right. Therefore, if people do not feel totally secure about investing in collaborative activities that they are about to start with people that they have never met before, they can decide to meet in-person so trust can be built and goals can be set.

These findings shed light towards how collaborative work may influence people to move to specific locations in order to accomplish work, therefore intensifying the Tm-N process in the lives of those whose jobs allow them some flexibility in terms of where and when to engage in work. It also shows how remote mediated interactions can enable at the same time that they can disable Tm-N: they make it easy to T-Nomads to get connected to collaborators from wherever they are, thus creating opportunities for them to be working from several different locations at the same time that they allow them to stay put in a single location and work always from there.

6 Final Remarks

This paper advances the understanding of the notion of technologically-mediated nomadic practices by presenting empirical evidence supporting the argument that Tm-N can be seen as a dynamic and emergent process that is not to do exclusively with inherently nomadic work, but instead, to the way that people whose jobs involve or allow for flexible work arrangements approach the work and non-work dimensions of their lives.

As discussed in Sect. 4, Tm-N is directly associated with a spectrum of motivational forces that might result in work being brought into the non-work dimension of life as T-Nomads go on to work at locations that used to be traditionally devoted to non-work activities (e.g. private homes, cafés, etc.), and conversely, how family and personal matters are brought into the work dimension of life as workers deal with those matters at locations that used to be traditionally dedicated to work.

The findings herein presented, on the other hand, suggest that there is a spectrum of motivational forces that leads people to mobilise work resources and accomplish work in different locations. According to them, this spectrum ranges from choice, going through opportunity to obligation, i.e. it respectively encompasses situations in which people, with many possible combinations of them: (1) may choose to move to a new location in order to work; (2) take the opportunity to engage in work in the location they are as some resources such as time, inspiration, Internet connection or other people become conveniently available; and (3) must move to new locations to work because the resources they need can only be found there or because organisational policies require them to do so. This contrasts with the literature, which usually associates the reasons for people to engage in Tm-N either with choice or obligation. As discussed in Sect. 4, literature on the matter suggests that the main reason for people to get involved in Tm-N is to meet face-to-face due to collaborative activities or to use specific resources (e.g. pieces of equipment) that are available only at a given location.

In addition to the presentation of a more nuanced account of technologically-mediated nomadicity, the paper elaborates on the influential role that collaborative activities play in the Tm-N spectrum and discusses how remote interactions may enable and disable Tm-N at the same time. Whilst part of the findings presented in Sect. 5 confirms that face-to-face interactions are one of the important sources of motivations for people to move to assorted locations and accomplish work from there, hence intensifying the Tm-N process, another part of them shows that other reasons, e.g. costs, time availability, among others, may override the motivation for mobilising the workplace for a face-to-face meeting, especially due to technological developments that have made remote interactions more effective and acceptable. Nonetheless, although T-Nomads may decide not to move to meet face-to-face, they may choose to move to other places nearby due to other motivational factors and engage in computer-mediated remote collaborative work from there. In particular, the paper brings a significant contribution to the discussion about the appropriateness of remote interactions for establishing trust and common ground in collaborative projects that has been on for several years within the CSCW field of research. The findings herein presented support the argument that common ground and trust can be effectively built over remote mediated interactions.

Acknowledgments The author would like to thank Dr. Luigina Ciolfi and Dr. Breda Gray for the valuable feedback on the draft versions of this paper and to acknowledge that this research was part of the "Nomadic Work/Life" project at the University of Limerick (Ireland). The project was funded by the Irish Social Science Platform (ISSP) via the Institute for the Study of Knowledge in Society (ISKS) of the University of Limerick, Ireland.

References

1. Bean CJ, Eisenberg EM (2006) Employee sensemaking in the transition to nomadic work. J Organ Change Manage 19(2):210–222. doi:http://dx.doi.org/10.1108/09534810610648915
2. Bradner E, Mark G (2002) Why distance matters: effects on cooperation, persuasion and deception. In: Proceedings of the 2002 ACM conference on computer supported cooperative work, ACM, New Orleans, Louisiana, USA. doi:http://dx.doi.org/10.1145/587078.587110
3. Chen L, Nath R (2005) Nomadic culture: cultural support for working anytime, anywhere. Inf Syst Manage 22(4):56–64. doi:http://dx.doi.org/10.1201/1078.10580530/45520.22.4.20050901/90030.6
4. Ciolfi L (2013) Making place for work and life. In: ECSCW 2013 workshop "CSCW at the boundary of work and life", Paphos, Cyprus, 1–6
5. Ciolfi L, de Carvalho AFP (2014) Work practices, nomadicity and the mediational role of technology. J Comput Support Coop Work (CSCW) 23(2)
6. Cousins KC, Robey D (2005) Human agency in a wireless world: patterns of technology use in nomadic computing environments. Inf Organ 15(2):151–180. doi:http://dx.doi.org/10.1016/j.infoandorg.2005.02.008
7. Crabtree A, Rouncefield M, Tolmie P (2012) Doing design ethnography. Springer, London, p 205
8. Creswell JW (2007) Qualitative inquiry and research design: choosing among five approaches, 2nd edn. SAGE, Thousand Oaks, p 395
9. D'Andrea A, Ciolfi L, Gray B (2011) Methodological challenges and innovations in mobilities research. Mobilities 6(2):149–160. doi:http://dx.doi.org/10.1080/17450101.2011.552769
10. de Carvalho AFP (2013) Technologically-mediated nomadicity in academic settings: Tm-N as a dynamic and emergent process. PhD thesis, University of Limerick, Limerick, 359 pp
11. Gluesing JC (2008) Identity in a virtual world: the coevolution of technology, work, and lifecycle. In: Meerwarth TL, Gluesing JC, Jordan B (eds) Mobile work, mobile lives: cultural accounts of lived experiences, Blackwell Publishing Inc., Malden, pp 70–88. doi:http://dx.doi.org/10.1111/j.1556-4797.2008.00020.x
12. Hollan J, Stornetta S (1992) Beyond being there. In: Proceedings of the SIGCHI conference on human factors in computing systems, ACM, Monterey, California. doi:http://doi.acm.org/10.1145/142750.142769
13. Kammas S, Foley S, Rosenberg D (2003) Interface or interspace? Mediated communication for nomadic knowledge workers. In: Jacko J, Stephanidis C (eds) Human–computer interaction: theory and practice, part 2, 1 edn. CRC Press, Florida, pp 98–102

14. Kleinrock L (1996) Nomadicity: anytime, anywhere in a disconnected world. Mob Netw Appl 1(4):351–357
15. Lamming M, Eldridge M, Flynn M, Jones C, Pendlebury D (2000) Satchel: providing access to any document, any time, anywhere. ACM Trans Comput Human Interact (TOCHI) 7(3):322–352. doi:http://doi.acm.org/10.1145/355324.355326
16. Makimoto T, Manners D (1997) Digital nomad. Wiley, New York, p 256
17. Manago AM, Graham MB, Greenfield PM, Salimkhan G (2008) Self-presentation and gender on MySpace. J Appl Develop Psychol 29(6):446–458
18. Meerwarth TL, Gluesing JC, Jordan B (eds) (2008) Mobile work, mobile lives: cultural accounts of lived experiences. Blackwell Publishing Inc., Malden, 158 pp
19. Nardi BA, Whittaker S (2002) The place of face-to-face communication in distributed work. In: Hinds PJ, Kiesler S (eds) Distributed work. The MIT Press, Cambridge, pp 82–112
20. Olson GM, Olson JS (2000) Distance matters. Human-Comput Interact 15(2):139–178. doi:http://dx.doi.org/10.1207/S15327051HCI1523_4
21. Olson JR, Teasley S, Covi L, Olson GM (2002) The (currently) unique advantages of collocated work. In: Hinds PJ, Kiesler S (eds) Distributed work. The MIT Press, Cambridge, pp 113–136
22. Perry M, Brodie J (2006) Virtually connected, practically mobile. In: Andriessen JHE, Vartiainen M (eds) Mobile virtual work: a new paradigm? Springer, Berlin, pp 97–128. doi:http://dx.doi.org/10.1007/3-540-28365-X_2
23. Perry M, O'Hara K, Sellen A, Brown B, Harper R (2001) Dealing with mobility: understanding access anytime, anywhere. ACM Trans Comput Human Interact (TOCHI) 8(4):323–347. doi:http://doi.acm.org/10.1145/504704.504707
24. Rossitto C, Eklundh KS (2007) Managing work at several places: a case of project work in a nomadic group of students. In: Proceedings of the 14th European conference on cognitive ergonomics, ACM, New York, pp 45–51, 28–31 Aug 2007. doi:http://doi.acm.org/10.1145/1362550.1362562
25. Salazar C (2001) Building boundaries and negotiating work at home. In: Proceedings of the 2001 international ACM SIGGROUP conference on supporting group work, ACM, Boulder, Colorado, USA. doi:http://dx.doi.org/10.1145/500286.500311
26. Schmidt K, Bannon L (2013) Constructing CSCW: the first quarter century. J Comput Support Coop Work 22(4–6):345–372
27. Star SL, Ruhleder K (1994) Steps towards an ecology of infrastructure: complex problems in design and access for large-scale collaborative systems. In: Proceedings of the 1994 ACM conference on computer supported cooperative work, ACM, Chapel Hill, North Carolina, pp 253–264. doi:http://dx.doi.org/10.1145/192844.193021
28. Su NM, Mark G (2008) Designing for nomadic work. In: Proceedings of the 7th ACM conference on designing interactive systems, Cape Town, South Africa, 25–27 Feb 2008, ACM Press, New York, pp 305–314. doi:http://doi.acm.org/10.1145/1394445.1394478
29. Wenger E (1998) Communities of practice: learning, meaning, and identity. Cambridge University Press, Cambridge, p 318

Orality, Gender and Social Audio in Rural Africa

Nicola J. Bidwell, Thomas Reitmaier and Kululwa Jampo

Abstract We claim that digital platforms designed for people in low-income, low-literacy rural communities to share locally relevant, voice-based content did not widen dissemination because they were incompatible with the nuances of cooperation. We base this on a long-term study of interactions with prototypes to record, store and share voice files via a portable, communally owned display in South Africa. We discuss how men and women used, appropriated and interacted with the prototypes, and how the prototypes and use contexts supported different genres of orality and nonverbal elements of co-present interactions. Rhythm and mimicry of nonverbal elements participated in cooperation and, we argue, that engaging with such qualities enriches creativity in designing media sharing systems.

1 Introduction

Short-term studies show that digital platforms designed for people in low-income, low-literacy rural communities to share locally relevant, voice-based content did not widen dissemination. We argue that this is because design did not respond to the nuances of cooperation, and that engaging with co-present oral practices can enrich designing media sharing systems for use by different social groups in rural Africa.

N. J. Bidwell (✉) · K. Jampo
Department of Informatics, University of Pretoria, Pretoria, South Africa
e-mail: nic.bidwell@gmail.com

T. Reitmaier
Department of Computer Science, University of Cape Town, Cape Town, South Africa
e-mail: treitmaier@googlemail.com

N. J. Bidwell
Digital Ethnography Group, Royal Melbourne Institute of Technology, Melbourne, Australia

C. Rossitto et al. (eds.), *COOP 2014 - Proceedings of the 11th International Conference on the Design of Cooperative Systems, 27–30 May 2014, Nice (France),* DOI: 10.1007/978-3-319-06498-7_14, © Springer International Publishing Switzerland 2014

We support this claim with insights about relations between gender and interactions with voice-based prototypes in a long-term study in rural South Africa.

Efforts to design platforms for people in rural communities to create and share voice-based media intensified with increased access to phones in the "global South". Many efforts aim to mimic the benefits of exchanging livelihood-relevant information that local radio brought to technology-sparse settings. Some involve communal displays, such as to share audio-photo stories authored on camera-phones [16]. Most strategies for accessing voice-based information, however, focus on personal access to phones and distributed asynchronous interactions, such as Interactive Voice Forums (IVF) across lower-cost channels on phone networks. There are few prolonged studies, but some analyses show systems for personal access to digital information can amplify inequalities. For instance, few farmers in India conveyed what they learnt via an IVF to people researchers excluded [33]; and men participated more than women in IVFs in Tanzania [37] and India [29].

Focusing on personal access to digital information neglects the ways oral users in low-income communities share devices and media in co-present interactions. Some analyses in Africa relate sharing practices to collective ethics. In South Africa interactions with phones are affected by expectations about, and an ethos of, sharing and mutual support in low-income societies [2, 8, 42]; and, in Ghana, an illiterate woman's expectations of an intermediary's help to use a Talking Book links to social obligations and rights [18]. These practices reflect emphases on the communalist self in 75 % of African societies [19] and logics, described by key African philosophers, that a person "owes his existence to other people, including those of past generations and his contemporaries" [25: 141]. Some analyses suggest that sharing phones in Africa disadvantage women and that various dif-ferentiations participate in purchase, ownership, access and control e.g. [42]. In Uganda and Morocco moral orders and familial or gender hierarchies limit women's private access to phones, as well as cost and text-literacies [9, 13].

We often relate personal access to phones and digital content to democracy, independence and individual freedoms. Yet, bias towards individualist concepts of self often overlooks the effects of corporate power and neoliberal economics in embedding meanings in technology [3]. Further, while individual rights can benefit women, individualist concepts of self can also alienate people from their com-munities and disrupt the co-operation that enables their survival [41]. Obligations and conveniences intersect with experiences of pleasure in sharing [42] and wellness based in a sense of belonging; and, women often suffer most when communal practices collapse. In southern Africa, such issues may contribute to parents, authorities and religious groups' concerns about young people's use of social media [10] and, indeed, use of social media does seem to factor in altering social constructs [34]. Tensions arise between Western and African thought on emancipation. Postcolonial feminist critiques argue for addressing African social relations by starting in Africa [32]. Oyewumi [31, 32], for instance, claims that gender was not an organizing principle in Yoruba society prior Nigeria's coloni-zation [19, 31] and calls for attention to the process of gendering [32].

When considering gender and oral users we tend to ignore the gendering processes of producing, using and studying technology, and the way these processes also embed a certain writing culture. While authors note that complex language environments of phones are barriers to illiterate women's use [13], they do not discuss the deeper ways that technologies embed 'design languages' [26] and the logics of certain writing cultures [3, 7, 41]. For instance, formal schooling and gender affected people's ease with the speech styles required for voice input [11]. We often attribute multi-vocality and plurality to writing, but politics and economics privilege certain genres [28]. Gendering processes contribute to the way that men comprise 85 % of Wikipedia authors and dominate interactions in online forums, where women post and receive fewer messages [22]. Thus, since more technologists are men their preferences, such as for broadcast writing styles and displaying subject knowledge [21, 39], might limit designing to support women's styles, such to express emotions, seek or offer support and acknowledge their imagined audience [1, 21, 24, 38]. Indeed the logics of certain writing cultures in technology design might limit affordances for the diverse oral practices that contribute to communality in Africa [3, 15, 41]. For instance, reconstituting Somali verse in print embodies the individual subject more than orature [28]. Studies on oral users show links between social relations and orality; for instance, Botswanan users were at ease with voice-input to access football updates but favoured phone keypads to access information about HIV [30]; and, Indian women were uneasy using voice input in some circumstances [11]. Yet, design rarely responds to these links.

Deploying devices, such as phones, in new ways may improve access for oral users [13] but we propose that technologists can design systems more creatively by engaging with elements of co-present oral practices. We develop this claim by referring to men and women's use of systems to record, store and share voice files using a portable, communally-owned display in rural South Africa. Thus, next, we introduce the setting and how we engaged with inhabitants to gain insight about communication practices and deploy prototypes. Then we describe men and women's interactions with prototypes and reflect on how prototypes and use contexts supported different oral genres and nonverbal elements. We conclude that non-verbal qualities in remote and co-present interactions participate in cooperation and engaging with them can significantly enrich design.

2 Research Approach, Setting and Prototypes

Our research in Mankosi, in Eastern Cape's Wild Coast, was prompted by ethnography in an adjacent area [2, 5], and the difficulties that local Xhosa people have in communicating between villages. Mankosi consists of 580 households in twelve villages, spread over 30 km^2. Up to 15 adults and children live in each homestead, which comprise clusters of thatched, mud-brick rondavals, an occasional tin-roofed two-room dwelling, animal corrals and a garden for subsistence crops. Inhabitants do not have domestic electricity or water supplies so, over the day, they walk the very hilly terrain to communal resources. Inhabitants have many kin across villages but almost nobody has a car. There is only one bus a day that can take 2-h to traverse Mankosi and does not go to all villages. Households survive on around $150 per month, mostly in government grants and payments from family members who temporarily migrate for work.

We frame endeavors in Ethnographic Action Research (EAR), a methodology that links research to community-oriented in media/technology initiatives in real-world situations [38]. Central to our use of EAR is sustained local immersion and considering Mankosi's inhabitants as fellow researchers. Author-1 (A1), a woman in her 40s, lived in Mankosi for two years in total from 2010 to 2013 and Author-3 (A3) is in a team of five female and five male Local Researchers (LRs), aged 17–27 years at the time. LRs generate and interpret data, advise in design, trial prototypes and translate linguistically and culturally to mediate external understandings.

2.1 Generating Insights

We generated data on communication practices and needs using varied methods, including observation; contextual inquiry; interviews; diary studies; workshops; auto-ethnography; and, deploying earlier prototypes. Few local people speak English and in most activities A1 spoke in English, others spoke in isiXhosa and LRs translated. We recorded activities in handwritten notes, video or audio and sometimes photos. LRs verbally translated audiovisual records and we transcribed audio and/or annotated video. We used descriptive statistics to analyze responses to closed questions in interviews and thematically coded other responses and observations after activities. We cross-linked themes between activities and validated or revised interpretations of themes hermeneutically as new meanings emerged.

From the start, LRs and other inhabitants insisted we consult the Tribal Authority (TA) to gain approval to experiment with systems that might enable people to communicate between villages. We subsequently met the TA 40 times, often within community-wide meetings, to discuss ideas, plans and issues in trialing and sustaining systems. In Mankosi the TA consists of the Headman, a Subheadman in each village and messengers. TAs govern 36 % of South Africa's population and are independent of other political bodies, although Headmen receive a small state stipend. Headmen relate by clan to Chiefs and inherit their role patrilineally but they can re-place Subheadmen and women can assume TA roles.

After first meeting the TA we began to generate data that led to designing voice prototypes. LRs and other people video-recorded their own interviews, conversations, storytelling and presentations. They accumulated over 50 items featuring some 60 people, aged 14–80 years. We (A1, LRs) also began interviews about communication practices and phone use. We interviewed 141 people about phone ownership and use, and another 16 people about appropriating low-cost services [4]. Then, we generated data on the ways people manage mixtures of communication in their daily routines in diary studies across periods of 4–10 days. This involved individual or group interviews at the start and end, and 72 short individual interviews in between. We included six male and six female older owners of low-end phones, half of whom are illiterate and, ten younger, literate owners [8].

We deployed two Android tablets along with solar-powered, cell-phone Charging Stations in April 2011 [7]. Inhabitants chose two sites for the Stations that were 2.5 km, or 25-minutes walk, apart that are used for local administration and meetings: the homesteads of the Headman and a Subheadmen in Mankosi's poorest area, Ridge. We observed each Station site for over 80-h at different times of day and on different days of the week and times in the year, interviewed 40 people who left or collected phones and logged the distance between Stations and the homesteads of 40 users who charged phones each day. The tablets ran MXShare, a media sharing prototype developed in the UK that, we hoped, people would use when they came to charge their own phones [43]. We logged use of MXShare automatically and (A1, LRs) ran seven workshops to introduce MXShare to 24 inhabitants, including members of the TA and local Community Association, and six men and women in Ridge. We also ran two workshops to explore how tablets might support the popular, local soccer league and uploaded audio commentaries, video and photos from matches to promote tablet useage.

2.2 Communication Practices and Needs

Some 700 inhabitants charged phones at the Stations, many regularly, but few used MXShare. However, insights from deployments and other data on communication practices [3, 4, 6–8], informed the design of the voice prototype. In 2011, approximately 56 % of females and 76 % of males owned a cellphone, of which 25 % were feature-phones and none were smartphones. People under 35 years old are twice as likely to own a phone as older people, and younger males are more likely to own a phone than younger females. Older people often said they were not educated to use cheap text-based phone services and SMS comprised only 1.4 % of their use. In fact some 40 % of adults in Mankosi cannot read and write, although they often recognize some names or numbers. Inhabitants favour voice calls but keep these brief as they spend on average only ~$0.75 a week on airtime. Despite infrequent phone communication people have enduring social ties. Inhabitants are identified by their social relations, and many can trace their ancestry over 5 generations across Mankosi and adjacent areas. An everyday visibility within villages contributes to senses of belonging and security, and mutual familiarity and expectations of co-operation enable people to access phones via intermediaries. Such practices suggest that communality acutely shapes local concepts of self [7].

People exhibited preferences for recording voices in workshops and their own videos recorded or explained oral practices, such as telling poetry at ceremonies and folktales night, that related to gender, age, protocols and sense of identity. People also mentioned a need to record meetings. Meetings often entail walking for over 2-h and attending for 3-h, which limits turnout, so Subheadmen and Headman's messengers are the main conduits for information across villages. The TA's voluntary secretary does not disseminate the minutes and attendee's details, which he writes on paper during meetings, and Community Association members said that minutes did not always accurately report what was spoken. These practices fuel allegations about the TA's inertia, opacity and "forgetfulness". Yet, other inhabitants are not more likely to use phones to contact people farther than an hour's walk from their village and tend to split phone use between communicating with close contacts in their village and very far away for support. People's daily tasks often occur in places with poor network coverage and, with limited electricity access, they conserve charge by switching off phones; so, phone use is more planned than impromptu. People sustain close ties without frequent contact and do not judge the efficacy of information sharing according to Western time scales.

2.3 Prototypes

To respond to local preferences for voice and constraints on using cellphones we sought to use the tablets to trial systems to record, store, share and listen to voice recordings. A1 sent a technical specification to A2, in Cape Town, for Audio Repository (AR) [7], and then we (A1, A2) spoke, over the phone, about interactions on tablets that might support qualities of communication. An LR also visited Cape Town to discuss A2's provisional UIs, design constraints and opportunities and their respective experiences in designing, evaluating or trialing past prototypes [5]. Before we wrote the specifications for the next iteration, Our Voices, we (A1, A2) discussed ideas in Cape Town and during A2's first visit to Mankosi. After developing the most complex elements, A2 returned to Mankosi for two weeks and final UI and interaction design entwined with, and was inspired by, impromptu discussions with inhabitants and technical work at different sites where inhabitants were installing a wireless mesh network between villages [35].

Both AR and OV enable unregistered users to create and listen to public recordings and registered users to store audio files and send/receive files to/from other registered users on that tablet and their own phones over Bluetooth. OV also enables sharing files between tablets when they connect to the new Wi-Fi. We reluctantly opted for text-based registration, as speech recognition processing involves high quality recordings and electricity supplies that are unfeasible in Mankosi. Users register with names; a photo, taken using the tablet; and an alphabetic or numeric password on both AR and OV, and select their 'home' tablet for OV. AR enables creating 'Groups' of registered users, but OV enables users to alter the order of profiles on each tablet to cluster profiles by, say, social roles. To find their accounts users scroll vertically through profile photos for AR and OV.

For both AR and OV users press a button below a cassette tape icon to record (Fig. 1a). OV also enables users to attach, to the audio file, a verbal summary and/or a photo, taken with the tablet's camera. This aims to help users find their main audio files, but also offers a way to populate a voice-based help and feedback system.

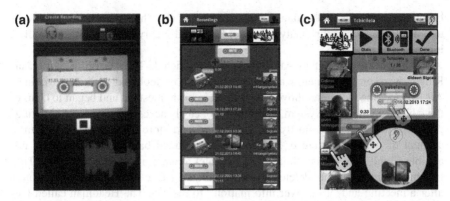

Fig. 1 AR/OV's interface to record (**a**); and OV's interfaces to find (**b**), tag and share (**c**) files

For both AR and OV, users scroll vertically to find a voice file, displayed alongside photos of those sharing it. Inhabitants did not always find a specific file easily in AR, partly because incorrect date stamps affected file ordering, after the tablet's battery drained. Thus, OV displays audio and/or photo tags; sorts files in the order they were recorded; highlights files that users have not yet played; and, plays the main file, or the short abstract about it, as users scroll (Fig 1b).

To share a file a user 'long-presses' on a tape icon and drags a small copy of the tape over a target user's photo or the 'public' icon, where it stays when the user lifts his/her finger to show that file is shared (Fig. 1c). AR enables users to share to 'Groups' of registered users, but OV enables re-sharing files and displays the provenance of sharing.

3 Use of and Interactions with Prototypes

Inhabitants used AR and OV for 10 and 9 months, respectively. Our account emphasises men's appropriation and use of AR and women's interactions with OV.

3.1 Audio Repository

We introduced AR in 7 workshops, lasting 2- to 4-h, in which LRs taught 50 women and men to use the prototype, in groups of 2–8. Illiterate and literate, old and young women and men readily learnt and taught each other to use AR, including the Headman who would not try MXShare. We interviewed 23 people in three groups, about their opinions of AR and sharing digital media. Inhabitants were enthusiastic and twice 30 women came to workshops when we expected six. They said they would use AR to leave messages for family members that might become mementoes and updates about events e.g. church, funerals. We observed use and after 9 months analyzed recordings and interviewed users and other inhabitants.

Despite wide interest in AR, access was restricted. The Charging Station at Ridge, overseen by women, was damaged and not re-deployed until after trialling AR [8]; and, the Headman moved the Station in his homestead and began to charge the tablet using another system, so AR was not easily accessible to people charging phones. Thus, AR was mostly used to record and store files in the Headman's account of which 35 were of meetings, 12 contained background chatter or no audible sound, one a chat about the tablet and another a song on the radio. The Headman said he had not deleted any files and used AR to remind himself of topics after a meeting and "to deliver information" to the TA. The Headman called the tablet his "witness". He listened with other TA members, rather than sharing to their accounts, Groups or to 'public', or logged-into his AR account for his secretary to listen alone in order to augment the minutes. This might relate to opinions, voiced by other inhabitants, that all recipients own shared files. The Headman recognized the topic or setting almost the instant he played a file and easily found a part of a recording of which 22 % were shorter than 10-min; 26 % of 10- to 20-min; 44 % of ½ to 1-h; and, 7 % exceeding 1-h, including one over 4-h.

Most recordings were made in community or TA meetings that address local issues, host councilors or municipal officers, resolve tribal law cases or involve a ceremony (Table 1). There were usually less than 5 recordings a month but in one month there were 17. The Headman decided that an issue warranted recording based on who spoke and "what they start to say". Only two files recorded a whole meeting and most files recorded one main topic from a meeting. Over half of files were recorded outdoors and wind, ambient music or children's chatter were audible in many. Most files contained only male voices and only two files contained exclusively female voices—at the opening of a pre-school (Table 1). Often 40 % of attendees at community meetings are women who, like young men, sit in groups on the ground; but men represent families. Indeed, the Headman asked us to delete temporary accounts made in workshops, of which 70 % were women, because other Headmen had reproached him for having too many female friends.

Various qualities of recordings indicated protocols of community meetings, where up to 100 people listen, without interrupting, and speak only after raising a hand, standing and removing their hats, if they are men. Speakers use different oral styles for testimony, argument and apology in cases; accounts of customs and experiences; and, notices and debate about communal resources. Older men speak boldly and gesture broadly to engage listeners and emphasise words (Fig. 2b, d); women and younger men are more discrete (Fig. 2c). The Headman, seated on chairs with other TA members and elder men, was usually silent until debate ended when he stated how an issue would proceed or be resolved (Fig. 2b, c). A young man carried the tablet between people as each stood to speak, thus many files included long pauses in speech and sounds of movements that connoted the relative orientation of recorder and speakers and distance between speakers (Fig. 2b–d).

Table 1 Number of recordings in community meetings grouped into broad genres, and the mean and standard deviation of different voices when we could distinguish them

Content of files	Number of files	Mean (St. Dev.) Male	Female
Communal resources: Land issues (2); Land and sand (2); Community Trust; Community Trust records (2).	7	7.3 (4.8)	0.4 (0.5)
Cases: Insult to TA; Insult related to circumcision; Pregnancy damages (2); Building without TA consent (2); Drunken fight; Fight at the soccer game; Fight within a family.	8	7.0 (4.1)	0.8 (0.42)
Narratives, notices, problem-solving: How royalty conferred a Subheadman his role; Subheadman's; dream about an ancestor (2); Circumcision and health; Insult at initiation school related to inter-community rivalry; Wage delays for community project workers; Wi-fi pilot; Charging Stations; White man's request to build.	9	6.0 (2.5)	0.3 (0.52)
Guest speakers and ceremony: Social support grant (2); Municipality (2); Welcome speeches at a pre-school opening.	5	2.0 (2.4)	4.2 (3.0)

The recorder's movement and the tablet's size also afforded visibility and twice in meetings men resisted recording as their permission had not been sought.

Many interactions with, and remarks about, AR articulated links between bodies and sociality. In workshops, women sat on grass mats huddled around tablets, which they held for each other, and men, sat on chairs, bent their bodies together to listen (Fig. 2a). The ways they physically shared the tablet resonated with the slow drag interaction for sharing files that was inspired by qualities of speaking and passing messages (Fig. 1c). In meetings men's movements responded to others' and in workshops men and women often made rhythmic hand gestures to depict interactions as they taught others to use AR. Younger people adapted their gestures to elders and protocol and the Headman related gestures and social roles to the display of profile photos in saying that a photo directly above his own implied disrespect as it depicted a young man using a rap-style gesture "over" his head.

3.2 Our Voices

The TA's control of AR, selectivity in recording and co-present sharing improved information reliability for those who have few ways to use phone services, but did not widen access. However our respect for local protocol and governance meant the

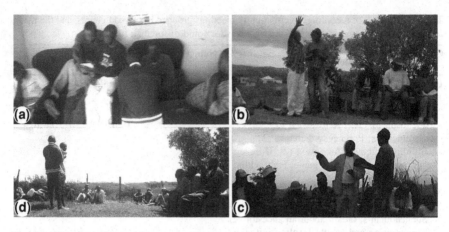

Fig. 2 a LRs teach TA members to use AR in workshops in the Headman's office. **b** In meetings the TA, seated on bench. **c, d** chose a young man to carry the tablet between speakers

TA supported our proposal to deploy OV on three tablets to be overseen by: the Headman; women in Ridge; and, male and female Community Association members, an hour's walk south of the Headman's. Seven men and 44 women participated in six workshops that introduced OV. Community Association members, aged 35–40 years, said they would use OV to record their meetings. Women in Ridge, aged 25–45 years, said they would record church to share with other women; children singing or saying funny things to share with close friends; and, TA members to share with the Headman; and, the radio. In the next 8 months the TA and Community Association used OV sporadically to record meetings but women in Ridge, who were proficient in use, rarely used their OV. The women said they had been too busy; yet they asked us to run more workshops, and showed us video filmed using the tablet. In the video women sang in harmony and tapped sticks as they walked in two close ranks to a syncretic church where they moved to pray and praise, which oriented us to qualities of their co-present interactions.

We adapted a phenomenological method to explore nonverbal elements [14] of co-present interactions. A2, the 28-year old, male designer in Cape Town, and A3, an 18-year old female LR, independently watched videos filmed during workshops that introduced OV 3 months before (Table 2). Videos varied in length and focus on interactions between people and with OV. First, A3 handwrote descriptions of the meanings of gestures she saw in 7 videos, then seven women who had attended earlier workshops, watched 4 videos on a laptop. A1, a women, and A3 then showed 10–20 second clips around the gestures A3 noted, with the sound off and in a different order than A3 had watched them, then longer sections to gain more insights. A3 translated and handwrote women's comments in English, which A1 emailed to A2 to compare with his own notes. A month later another group of seven women, who had also attended OV workshops, commented on video that interested A2, again with the sound off while A1 filmed. Finally, A1 and A2 watched video of the women's analysis sessions.

Table 2 Number of gestures that A2 and A3 analysed in a total of 17 clips of workshops with the TA and community association (CA) and three workshops with women in Ridge (R1, R2, R3)

Work-shop	People in video			Total length analysed hour:minutes:seconds		Total number of gestures	
	Men	Women	Including	by A3	by A2	A3	A2
TA	4–8	0	LR	00:12:52	–	6	–
CA	1	1		00:19:25	00:30:24	9	10
R1		9–10	LR, A1, A3	00:35:46	01:00:40	6	14
R2		1–8	A1, A3	01:49:28	02:29:20	29	15
R3		3	A3	00:43:19	–	3	–

A2 and A3 noted many different gestures and meanings about gestures (Table 3) and A2 noted more gestures than A3. Both noted women's symbolic gesture to pray at the start of a workshop and neither noted gestures of any children in video. Sometimes the same gesture was given different meanings; for instance, A2 noticed a woman laugh as she saw her photo on the tablet, but A3 noted that she was shy because she put her hands to her face. A2 and A3 noted 26 and 36 gestures, respectively, that directly related to OV. A2 noted details of fingers that pointed, poked, clicked, wiggled and swiped horizontally and vertically to learn, practice and gain proficiency in interactions, especially in close-up shots. In contrast, A3 often described gestures that explained an interaction or an abstract concept relating to OV but without directly touching the tablet. A3 also noted more full-body gestures, in fact A2 watched video focused on a proximal tablet three times before noticing a woman in the background who A3 had noted. A2 and A3 noted 3 and 17 gestures, respectively, in dialogues that did not directly relate to OV. Over half of the gestures that A3 noted enriched a vocal utterance and/or expressed a felt-experience and many that indexed people or objects.

The women and men usually sat close to each other, which A3 said 'Blacks' prefer. A2 noticed that people learnt that the tablet permits only one press at a time. For instance, at first three young women's interactions interfered with each other as they pressed the tablet but, within minutes, developed a rhythm in alternating touches and interacting with each other (Fig. 3f). One woman who had her arms wrapped around the shoulders of another, laying in front of her holding the tablet, pointed to an item on the screen, then a second woman pointed to the same item, as if to concur, and a third pressed it (Fig. 3f). When the women in this video watched it, they said their proximity and mutual dexterity was unsurprising but was not due to any special intimacy—they were not kin, close friends or members of the same churches and only spend time together when they walk to the forest to collect firewood every week. In contrast, co-ordination between a man and woman in the Community Association seemed unnatural (Fig. 3b). A2 noted that some participants, or an LR, held the finger of another to physically sculpt an interaction with the tablet, such as to drag a file. Women in sessions said that children learn by watching and that mothers rarely physically position a child's arm, hand or finger to sculpt fine body actions, such as to weave grass mats or grind corn.

Table 3 Examples from A2 and A3's notes on gestures in video of women, W, and men, M

Gestures to …	A2 and A3's descriptions
Talk in general	A3's hand is trying to make sure that everyone is clear about what she was saying; The W's hand is pointing side to side for explanation; W's hand is moving to show that she didn't know; Her hand is showing that something is easy; M moving his hands to try to explain his feeling
Index object, place, self or another person	The W is putting her hand to her cheek trying to show that she is talking about herself; LR's hand touches the person she is addressing; The old W is waving her hand to show that the other W must move far away; The old W is pointing her finger to the W next to her; A3's hand pointing to the tablet; The W is pointing to show that she needs something; LR's hand/finger is pointing to the tablet; All the W pointing their fingers to show us something; M pointing of fingers
Enhance teaching OV without touching the tablet	A3's hand is showing that something will follow; LR's hand shows that you must keep or save something; W's hands show that you must accept; A1 moving her hand side to side trying to say 'between you and I'; W's hand is trying to explain how to share the recording; W's hand is trying to explain to the W that after you press this something will appear; A1 pointing to show how to move; M gestures a sequence or recording amplitude timeline; The headman moving his hands to show the change; Moving his hands up and down the tablet but not pressing or touching the tablet, to explain a question; Twisting his hand to show a change; M scrolls back and forth and then questions through a gesture
Sculpt another's interaction with OV	A3 moving her finger forward and backward; A3's finger to the tablet to show the W; W showing her to press the tablet; A1 telling and showing the M to hold the tablet firmly
Co-ordinate touching the tablet between people	Helping each other swipe through the recordings; Scrolling slowly and deliberately with the backside of the finger, then accidentally logging on, neighbor presses cancel; One W points, then another at the same screen item, finally the third W presses; Swiping through the recordings one-by-one. Occasionally the other Ws poke at the tablet; W laying on floor is also pressing the tablet; W and M alternate their touches in a sort of unnatural way—only one person can press the tablet at a time

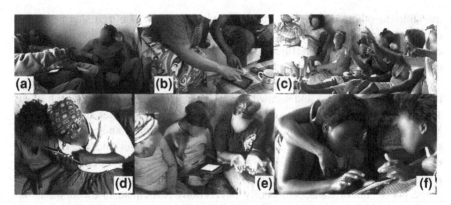

Fig. 3 In workshops a TA member **a** and women in Ridge **c** point in talking; and in learning to use OV Community Association members take turns **b**; women listen together **d**, to explain an accept button on the interface **e** and, co-ordinate their interactions **f**

Women finely coordinated gestures such as instantly pointing in unison in the same direction to confirm the location of a home they spoke about (Fig. 3c). They brought gesture and voice into correspondence when they analysed video, and complex conversations of entwined gestures and voice evolved. For instance, as one woman explained what A3's gesture in a video meant others chimed in and mimicked the gesture they saw. Their hands made vertical chopping motions with the same rhythm as they said, "this thing goes like this, this one like this". Women did not mimic video when they watched video without talking about it.

A2 and A3 observed movements that coordinated people spatially, such as leaning towards the tablet to listen, and noted 10 and 2 gestures, respectively, that physically moved tablets. Both also noted that people overtly give tablets and rarely take them from another's hand, and that gestures often indicated a bodily readiness for social prompts. In fact, A3 noted 11 instances when fingers or hands were "ready for action" in awaiting prompts or instructions to use OV or assist others. Gestures that indicated a bodily readiness also functioned symbolically, for instance one woman cupped her hands together as if to receive a tangible thing as she explained an "accept" button on the interface (Fig. 3e).

4 Interactions and Settings Supporting the Nuances of Co-operation

Women's engagement in analysis sessions, and appreciation of the relevance of non-verbal qualities of orality to OV, confirms the value of considering gestures and movements in co-present oral practices to design. Touch interfaces to shared tablets offer affordances for nonverbal communication and some of the interactions we designed reconciled with body movements in talking. AR and OV's interaction for sharing files resonated with flows of movements when people handed or carried the tablet to others or interacted together with it. We symbolized sharing with a palm-up open hand icon (Fig. 1b), which was similar to gestures women used to explain an "accept" button (Fig. 3e) and congruent with the phenomenon of taking only when given that we observed in different settings and social groups.

Women did not prioritize using OV but keenly joined in workshops, clustered in groups on grass mats, and seemed to enjoy camaraderie and helping each other. Their postures and movements differed from men who sat further apart on chairs. Men's gestures were larger and women's were more frequent and elaborate. These styles manifested in interactions with prototypes, the tablet and the content of recordings. This suggests different elements of orality contributed to accessing AR, along with the social patterns that privilege the Headman. Social relations shape bodily interactions, and bodily interactions participate in meanings about social roles; for instance, the Headman read meaning in the spatial arrangement of the photos of himself and a young man gesturing.

Distinct rhythms arose when men took turns to talk in meetings, without touching or looking at AR, and women coordinated to learn to use OV. The overall tempo is shaped by the richness of IsiXhosa—often three times longer in duration than its English translation. People's rhythms in speaking and/or interacting with the prototypes continuously adapted to each other, but coordination was more natural between women than between women and men. This is compatible with videos, LRs recorded, where inhabitants described former practices that encouraged conversation only between people of the same gender. Women in Ridge and men in the TA, respectively, have similar daily practices even though they do not spend time together every day. Each gender shares patterns of walking and talking and the macro rhythms of their daily practices shape their literacies in reading others' routines [8]. Our preliminary analysis, here, suggests that micro rhythms also tune co-operating.

A2 suggested that A1 adopted a rhythm in interacting with women that differs from talking with other researchers or with the TA, and that her inflections helped to guide him through the video. He also realized that he mimicked body movements in videos, especially those when people coordinated, such as to interact with or pass tablets. Thus, design discussions and conceptual translations were implicitly sensitized by the tempo of life in Mankosi, that A1 came to embody, and A2 experienced in mimicking body movements.

5 Conclusions

A3 often related gestures to felt-experiences, consistent with the way women are said to use "rapport talk" to set up intimacy [39] and share emotional content in speech [36]. A2 more often related gestures to the details of interactions, consistent with the way men use "report-talk" [39]. Women use gesture, body orientation, proximity, eye and bodily contact to establish immediacy and more adeptly send and discern nonverbal cues than men, who are more likely to misread nonverbal cues if not invested in conversation [27]. However, we apply these analytic categories cautiously, but not just because A2 and A3's languages, expertise and rural and urban locations differ. These differences are made [40] using a visual lens on data, and Oyewumi argues that Western visual logics are implicated in social division and hierarchy [31]. More important to our claim is that men and women *can* adapt to each other's cues to evolve common oral styles to increase communication efficiency, even remotely [25]. Convergence, from one conversational turn to the next, occurs for many elements including words, syntax [21], pauses, frequency, pitch and gesture [12]. Thus, while power asymmetries exist between men and women's oral practices, men, like A2, can adapt if they want.

In South Africa, 'ubuntu' refers to human's existential interdependence, and in Mankosi people sometimes refer to "acting as one". Their practice in speech, song, gesture and movement, however, is not merely symbolic but is a bodily becoming into a synchronized whole that performs in the cohesion enabling their resilience. Women often sing, and some dance, at the end of workshops and when they do A1 experiences a profound sense of togetherness. Diverse research from music to neuroscience, suggests that the rhythmic synchrony of bodies and voices is integral to sociality and enables being-together [17]. Self-synchrony supports inter-personal coordination by enabling us to adapt our speech to others and time syllables and pauses as we converse. Gill cites a study in which pairs of participants finely tuned their body movements to their own and the other's voice, while in isolated rooms using microphones [17]. Their rhythms aligned with the language they spoke but concurrent movement also arose without speech.

Jousse argues that gestes, or audible and visual movements in 3-D space, link thought, action, people and settings [23]. He relates gestes to *mimicry* and *rhythmicity* in our constant interaction with micro- and macro-settings. We suggest that men and women's daily practices and shared settings, respectively, contribute to tuning their bodies in co-present interactions and to meaning making. We also suggest that engaging designers' bodies in ways of knowing that are alive and lived [23], through mimicry and felt-experience, entangles their meaning-making within processes for synchrony [6] and, thus, entangles creativity in the rhythmicity and flow of the lives of the oral users for whom they design.

Intel's new smartphone, designed specifically for Africa, has a radio but no speaker for people to listen together; and, so-called, "multi-touch" interfaces to tablets are not designed for multiple people to interact. However, methods to engage designers' bodies in oral practices, through rhythm and mimicry can offer ways to balance the effects of bias towards individualising logics in technologies for creating and sharing digital media content in the global South. Our two iterations of modest voice prototypes enabled illiterate elders, with few ways to use low-cost phone services, to record and review community meetings and women to co-operate in and enjoy design activities. Engaging more fully in oral practices can also benefit design in the global North where users also share devices and files in co-present interactions [20], where nuances of communication can mean women can go unnoticed online [22], and where personal mobile devices increasingly seem to sever people from their proximal physical and social settings.

Acknowledgments Our research was funded by CSIR-Meraka, South Africa and partially by EPSRC grant (EP/H042857/1). We thank all inhabitants of Mankosi, especially LRs. We are grateful to Simon Robinson for MXShare; Matt Jones for tablets; Carlos Rey-Morano for WiFi; and Paula Kotze for support. We thank Gary Marsden for building the Charging Stations, and for his commitment, wisdom, confidence in us and friendship—we cherish our memories of him.

References

1. Argamon S, Koppel M, Fine J, Shimoni AR (2003) Gender, genre and writing style in formal written texts. Text 23(3)
2. Bidwell NJ (2009) Anchoring design to rural ways of doing and saying. In: Proceedings of INTERACT'09, IFIP, Springer, pp 686–699
3. Bidwell NJ (2014) Moving the centre to design social media with rural Africa. AI society: Knowledge, culture and communication, Forthcoming
4. Bidwell NJ, Lalmas M, Marsden G, Dlutu B et al (2011) Please call ME.N.U.4EVER: designing for 'Callback' in rural Africa. In: Proceedings of IWIPS'11, pp 117–138
5. Bidwell NJ, Reitmaier T, Marsden G, Hansen S (2010) Designing with mobile digital storytelling in rural Africa. In: Proceedings of CHI'10, ACM, pp 1593–1602
6. Bidwell NJ, Reitmaier T, Rey-Moreno C et al (2013) Timely relations in rural Africa. In: Proceedings of social implications of computers in developing countries, IFIP, pp 92–106
7. Bidwell NJ, Siya MJ (2013) Situating asynchronous voice in rural Africa. In: Proceedings of INTERACT'13, IFIP, Springer, pp 36–53
8. Bidwell NJ, Siya MJ, Marsden G et al (2013) Walking the social life of solar charging. Trans Comput Human Interact 20(4):1–33
9. Burrell J (2010) Evaluating shared access: social equality and the circulation of mobile phones in rural Uganda. J Comput Mediated Commun 15:230–250
10. Chigona W, Chigona A, Ngqokelela B, Mpofu S (2009) MXit: uses, perceptions and self-justifications. JIITO 4:1–16
11. Cuendet S, Medhi I, Bali K, Cuttrell E (2013) VideoKheti: making video content accessible to low-literate and novice users. In: CHI'13, ACM, pp 2633–2842
12. Danescu-Niculescu-Mizil C, Gamon M, Dumais S (2011) Mark my words! Linguistic style accommodation social media. WWW'11, pp 745–754
13. Dodson L, Sterling L, Bennett J (2013) Minding the gaps: cultural, technical and gender-based barriers to mobile use in oral-language berber communities. In: Proceedings of ICTD'13, ACM, pp 79–88
14. Donavon J, Brereton M, Bidwell NJ (2003) Understanding gestures at work. In: Proceedings of DIS'03, ACM
15. Finnegan R (2007) The oral and beyond: doing things with words in Africa. University of Chicago Press, Chicago
16. Frohlich DM, Rachovides D, Riga K et al (2009) StoryBank: mobile digital storytelling in a development context. In: Proceedings of CHI'09, ACM, pp 1761–1770
17. Gill SP (2012) Rhythmic synchrony and mediated interaction: towards a framework of rhythm in embodied interaction. AI Soc 27(1):111–127
18. Gorman T, Rose E, Yaaqoubi J et al (2011) Adapting usability testing for oral, rural users. In: Proceedings of CHI'11, ACM, pp 1437–1440
19. Hallen B (2009) A short history of African philosophy. Indiana University Press, Bloomington
20. Harper R, Regan T, Izadi S et al (2007) Trafficking: design for the viral exchange of TV content on mobile phones. In: Proceedings of Mobile HCI'07, ACM, pp 249–256
21. Hemphill L, Otterbacher J (2012) Learning the lingo? Gender, prestige and linguistic adaptation in review communities. In: Proceedings of CSCW'12, ACM, pp 305–314

22. Herring SC (2003) Gender and power in online communities. In: Holmes J, Meyeroff M (eds) The handbook of language and gender, Blackwell, Oxford, pp 202–228
23. Jousse M (2000) The anthropology of geste and rhythm. In: Sienaert E (ed), Sienaert E, Conolly J (trans). Mantis Publishing, Cape Town
24. Kivran-Swaine F, Brody S, Diakopoulos N, Naaman M (2012) Of joy and gender: emotional expression in online social networks. CSCW'12, ACM
25. Mbiti J (1990) African religions and philosophy, 2nd edn. Heinemann
26. Merritt S, Bardzell S (2011) Postcolonial language and culture theory for HCI4D. In: Proceedings of CHI EA' 11, ACM, pp 1675–1680
27. Miller R, Perlman D (2009) Intimate relationships. McGraw-Hill, New York, pp 143–176
28. Moolla FF (2012) When orature becomes literature. Comp Lit Stud 49(3):434–462
29. Mudliar P, Donner J, Thies W (2012) Emergent practices around CGNet Swara, voice forum for citizen journalism in rural India. In: Proceedings of ICTD'12, ACM, pp 159–168
30. Ndwe T, Barnard E, Mqhele E, Dlodlo E (2012) Effects of application type on the choice of interaction modality in IVR systems. In: Proceedings of SAICSIT'12, ACM, pp 236–242
31. Oyewumi O (1977) The invention of women making an african sense of western gender discourses. University of Minnesota Press, Minnesota
32. Oyewumi O (2010) Gender epistemologies in Africa: gendering traditions, spaces, social institutions, and identities. Palgrave Macmillan, UK
33. Patel N, Chittamuru D et al (2010) Avaaj Otalo: a field study of an interactive voice forum for small farmers in rural India. In: Proceedings of CHI'10, ACM, pp 733–742
34. Peters AN, Oren MA, Bidwell NJ (2013) Namibian and American cultural orientations toward facebook. In: Proceedings of CHI'EA'12, ACM, pp 2603–2608
35. Rey-Moreno C, Roro Z, Siya M, Tucker W (2013) Community-based solar power revenue alternative to improve sustainability of a rural wireless mesh network. In: Proceedings of ICTD13, ACM, pp 132–135
36. Snell WE, Miller R, Belk S (1998) Men's and women's emotional disclosures: the impact of disclosure recipient, culture and the masculine role. Sex Roles 21:467–486
37. Sullivan B (2012) Freedom to learn: blending interactive voice response and radio. Learning with community media, pp 131–135
38. Tacchi J, Slater D, Lewis P (2003) Evaluation community based media initiatives: an ethnographic action research approach. In: Proceedings of IT4D, UNESCO
39. Tannen D (1990) You just don't understand. HarperCollins Publication Inc., New York
40. Taylor, A. 2011. Out there. Proc. CHI'11, pp 685–694
41. Thiong'o N (1986) Decolonising the mind: the politics of language in African literature. James Currey Ltd and Heinemann. East African Publishers
42. Walton M, Haßreiter S et al (2012) Degrees of sharing: proximate media sharing and messaging by young people in Khayelitsha. In: Proceedings of Mobile HCI'12, ACM, pp 403–412
43. www.digitaleconomytoolkit.org

Observing the Work Practices of an Inter-professional Home Care Team: Supporting a Dynamic Approach for Quality Home Care Delivery

Khuloud Abou Amsha and Myriam Lewkowicz

Abstract We are reporting an observational study conducted as part of a French research project focusing on "domomedecine". The study explores collaborative activities in work practices of inter-professional teams aiming to deliver quality home care. The findings show the use of a variety of dynamic coordination mechanisms depending on patients' conditions. We suggest that future system design process considers the flexibility and the dynamicity of team-based care to support quality home care.

Keywords Home care · Team collaboration · Teamwork · Observational study

The PICADO project: research and development in the Fonds Unique Interministériel (FUI). It is also co-funded by the Champagne-Ardenne region, the Ile-de-France and the Municipality of Paris.

1 Introduction

This paper is about new collaborative practices currently implemented to accommodate the evolution of the care system in France. Healthcare professionals are adopting new practices to handle cost-containment policies and the need to take care of increasing numbers of patients and elderly people staying at home. In the health private sector, no standardization of these new collaborative practices is

K. Abou Amsha (✉) · M. Lewkowicz
Troyes University of Technology, ICD/Tech-CICO, UMR CNRS 6281, Troyes, France
e-mail: khuloud.abou_amsha@utt.fr

M. Lewkowicz
e-mail: myriam.lewkowicz@utt.fr

C. Rossitto et al. (eds.), *COOP 2014 - Proceedings of the 11th International Conference on the Design of Cooperative Systems, 27–30 May 2014, Nice (France)*, DOI: 10.1007/978-3-319-06498-7_15, © Springer International Publishing Switzerland 2014

suggested, and no computer-based system exists to support them. However, we can observe some local initiatives that are quoted as good examples, and some reflections at a national level to reform the care sector.

So we are at a turning point where it is important to understand the effective collaborative practices that are taking place in the local initiatives. This is vital if we are to be able to design more appropriate devices and services.

Therefore we have observed one inter-professional team which has adopted an integrated home care approach in the primary sector; this team is considered one of the few successful examples in France, as it manages to keep patients with complicated conditions at home and delivers high quality care. They consider patient' quality of life as a main objective. This self-created inter-professional team has collectively defined some coordinative mechanisms, but does not use any computer-based support.

This paper studies the new collaborative inter-professional practices taking place in this observed team and the coordination activities exhibited in these work practices. The aim is to provide useful insights to aid the design of future coordination technologies to support these emerging work practices.

In the following sections, we begin by explaining the context within the French health system that allows for further understanding of what makes changes in practice necessary. We then review the related work about focus shifting in healthcare studies and describe the setting and methodology in which we carried out our observations and report on our major findings. Finally, we discuss the implications for the design of technology supporting dynamic care teamwork in home care settings.

In this paper we refer to the teams adopting this approach of integrated home care as "inter-professional home care teams" or "home care teams" for short.

2 Context

2.1 Towards a More Integrated Care System

As in many developed countries, France has a growing number of elderly people with chronic conditions. This demographic shift goes with growing healthcare needs which challenge the re-organization of long-term care [19].

Until now, the French health system has performed very well in satisfying the expectations of the population, providing high-quality services, with freedom of choice and generally no waiting lists for treatment [20]. However, the health system faces socioeconomic disparities and geographic inequalities in the density of healthcare professionals. Furthermore, the rising expenditure and consequent deficits in statutory health insurance, together with a slowing of economic growth, and unemployment rising is of prime concern [7].

The French health system is amongst the most expensive in Europe. Cost-containment policies aiming at limiting supply and restricting coverage have been hindered by public discontent and ardent opposition by the medical professions which traditionally enjoy very liberal conditions of independent medical practice [10].

Facing these challenges, the French healthcare system is moving from a linkage-based model to a more integrated care system [22], a movement impaired by the current separation between health and social services; between institutional (hospital and long-term care) and community-based care services; between private, non-profit and public services; and between the various payment systems (public, insurances, fee-for-services) [9].

This aimed integrated approach of delivering care requires the French health workers to change their current autonomous practices and move toward a more collaborative approach.

2.2 The Rising of Home Care Delivery

Most of the patients now prefer to avoid hospitalization since a medical management and quality care can be offered to them at home with an equivalent level of safety.

Moreover, an increasing proportion of patients request to exercise more responsibility in making decisions about the care required for their conditions. This societal change is supported by the medical demonstration that the patient's active participation in the management of their illness seems to be a positive factor for their quality of life and, in some cases, survival. In addition, with an aging population, chronic diseases and disabilities are growing, if not dominant, in the health system. The development of ambulatory care is essential to provide appropriate medical and technological solutions that meet the economic requirements [12].

Indeed, ambulatory medicine favors a patient-centered approach instead of a disease-centered one. Thus, the implementation of ambulatory medicine requires adequate coordination of functions to ensure the realization of the patient care with quality comparable to those in hospital.

According to a report of the French Academy of Technologies in 2008, the emergence of these structures as an alternative to hospitalization, intended to answer the following: First, patients' demand of a medical care that minimizes rupture of family social or professional ties; second, a shortage of hospital beds and the objective to reduce hospital overload; finally, the need for savings in the care consumption [12]. This report introduced the "Domomédecine" concept that describes a health system that keeps the patient at home while allowing it to benefit from a set of medical and care acts comparable in number, and in quality, to those that could be done at the hospital. These medical and care acts can be complex, in that they exploit the most modern technologies available. Therefore, the best part of certain acts can be at home or during the socio-professional activities of the patient and the hospital becomes a contributor in this health system [12].

This study is part of a large French research project called PiCADO, which aims at designing, developing, testing, and evaluating the first operational system of "Domomédecine".

3 Related Work

Healthcare delivery is often an inherently collaborative effort. Due to the increasing specialization of modern medicine [23], providing care for a single patient requires the involvement of many different professionals [24].

This collaborative nature has motivated many studies exploring different aspects of collaborative behaviors in healthcare delivery practices. These include (1) temporal coordination, as we can see in Reddy and Dourish [18] study discussing the role of temporal patterns in providing individuals with the means to coordinate information and work, (2) mobility and spatiality reflected by the well-defined spatial specialization of healthcare services [3], which indicates the inherently distributed nature of healthcare work especially in a hospital setting, as noted by Bossen [5], and (3) formality of artifacts, as in Chen's work on the transitional artifact used to complete the gap between the formal documentation and the clinical work flow in an Emergency Department [6].

Another stream of studies focused on home care delivery, following the move of the developed world towards technology-enabled care in home and self-care. These studies explored different coordination and design challenges imposed by this move.

In these studies, many give special attention to the new role the patients and their family caregivers play especially in managing chronic diseases. For example Mamykina et al. [14] proposed an application empowering the patients to control their condition through the interaction with diabetes educators. Bardram et al. [4] explored the transformation in the patient-physician relationship based on the introduction of home-care monitoring equipment. Andersen et al. [1] explored telemonitoring practices and proposed a new socio-technical design approach, which transforms the role of patient in order to alleviate the problems of data interpretation, which are inherent in telemonitoring practices.

Other researchers explored home as a place for providing healthcare, and challenges and opportunities related to moving from healthcare settings to the patient's home. Palen and Aaløkke [15, p. 79] studied how the capacity of the patient to manage their medication can give healthcare workers indication on the patient status. Piras and Zanutto [17] described how patients keep their health information and use Personal Health Records at home. Balaam et al. [2] addressed problems that arise from sharing home with other family members; in their study, the use of TV as an interface for the rehabilitation at home raises for instance the issue of who could use the TV in the lounge room.

Recent studies related to home care are extending their focus and go beyond monitoring and data-transfer to include the support of a more holistic approach of collaboration between different actors in order to provide quality home care. This is expressed by Christensen and Grönvall [8] in their work that highlights the cooperative nature of home care work, and emphasizes on substantial articulation work needed among the actors, such as family members and care workers engaged in providing care.

Nevertheless, there has been little work done related to the specific issue of coordination between private health workers, professional caregivers and informal caregivers. This paper reports findings from a field study that addresses coordination activities among members of an inter-professional home care team.

In contrast to work done by Petrakou [16] where they studied coordination of actors across organizations in the domain of elderly home care, the case examined teams members that do not belong to any organization and thereby do not follow any predefined coordination protocol. In addition, the main objective of these teams is to enhance patient quality of life, and this affect the care delivery as they look at the patient as an actor of his own care plan.

The aim of this paper is to explore the work practices of home care teams and identify the used coordination mechanisms. In addition we propose some design implications suggested by the particularity of such collective work.

4 The Case Study

The "E-maison médicale" association is a group of different private health workers and professional caregivers, mainly located in several cities of the Troyes agglomeration (N–E of France). They aim at improving the quality of home care by creating inter-professional care teams.

We chose to situate our fieldwork in the city of Troyes because this city is facing the twin challenge of resource deficit and an increasing demand for care. Troyes is located in the Champagne-Ardenne region (one of the five regions in France) which has a growing aging population and suffers from an exodus of doctors [13]. In addition, this team-based initiative is one of the few successful examples of collaboration among different private health professionals for home care in France, where solo-based practices are more common between health workers [7].

4.1 History and Motivation

The association started in 2011, after a physician and a nurse being faced with the situation of one patient who wanted to spend his last moments at home. Despite his challenging situation, his family was determined to honor his choice.

The patient was terminally ill, he had been suffering from Alzheimer's disease, which is a progressive disease and can cause death. In addition, his status was aggravated by some pulmonary problems. This case required heavy medications and associated care.

To overcome the situation, the general practitioner and the nurse who were taking care of this patient had to question their way of providing care because they could not leave the patient and his family coping with this situation alone.

In order to deal with the situation, the doctor and nurse contacted and invited about ten of their private (freelance) colleagues working in the same geographic area, in order to discuss how they could set together a care plan. The solution was to create a team of freelance care professionals, who could deliver different treatments and care. This team helped the patient spend his last days at home, and comforted the main familial caregiver (his wife).

This success story was the spark that motivated the creation of an association to facilitate the establishment of relationships among local care professionals (freelance or employed), and to help set care plans that put together their different skills to fulfill the wishes of the patients and their families.

In 2012, the "E-maison médicale" association had about fifty members from different medical professions: professional caregivers, physiotherapists, biologists, physicians, pharmacists, nurses, and representatives of patients.

4.2 Status

This kind of pluridisciplinary team does not have any official status in the healthcare system, and they do not have any official shared responsibility of the patient. Each of the team members has a private work status, and has jumped into this team care approach as an opportunity to share experiences and to provide a better quality of care to their patients.

However, without any regulation to accompany this collaborative approach, working as a team is regarded as doing extra work for coordinating and communicating without having an appropriate reward. This is why few health workers have adopted this collaborative approach.

4.3 Functioning

The objective of this association is to enable the creation of links between health professionals in the local area. They are aiming at creating a multidisciplinary health team for each patient, organized as a network of professionals in order to allow the patient to receive care at home rather than being hospitalized (as long as they can benefit from a quality of care at least equal to the one delivered in the hospital).

Once enrolled through their doctor (or any other care professional who is a member of the association), patients and their families are recognized as part of a team that, depending on each patient's needs, may include nurses, dieticians, pharmacists, specialist physicians, mental health services and home care. All together, the members of the team participate in creating a "care plan" for each patient. This care plan, which captures the patient's personal goals, becomes a guide for all team members. The goal is to help the patient stay on top of their conditions, and to provide care that is continual, coordinated, and comprehensive.

If a patient or a family caregiver wishes to benefit from the system, but none of the health professionals around them are members of the association e-maison médicale, they can start benefitting from it if one of these professionals joins the association e-maison médicale.

The strategy of the association is to help all the patients to keep the same health partners and to motivate these partners to work as a team. They are aiming at creating a new way of working collaboratively, inspired by the way the hospital staff is working, but adapted to private workers in a city. In fact, each healthcare professional is very sensitive to their autonomy and individuality. The goal of the association is not then to standardize the work practices, but to combine different skills in order to improve the quality of home care delivery.

4.4 Illustration

Nicolas is suffering from Alzheimer's disease, which changed the lifestyle of his wife Jeannette. She did her best to adapt herself and to live with the disease, but the status of Nicolas is getting worse and the situation among them is becoming difficult to manage. On top of that, Nicolas is suffering from pulmonary problems that make it more difficult to keep him safe at home.

Jeanette is tired, so she started to search for help, but things became more complicated, as she realized that the solutions, which contacted organizations suggest are not necessarily compatible with her promise to not leave her husband alone, despite her exhaustion. Jeannette is not able anymore to provide all the necessary treatment and day care, a fact that raises the anxiety of the couple to be separated.

Jeannette's family doctor and the nurse who comes every week are part of the e-maison médicale association and they offered to set a network of care professionals to help in day care, and for the administration of the different treatments. Depending on the needs, the care professionals come several times a week or a day, the physician comes when this is necessary, the physiotherapist comes at home, and a homecare assistant comes when Jeannette needs to go out.

Jeannette is now able to count on the care professionals 24/7. In addition, as Nicolas now needs an oxygen tank, and other respiratory devices in case of emergency, the pharmacy delivered the necessary medical devices and medications.

To keep everybody informed about the status of the patient, the care professionals are using a "liaison notebook". This notebook is left at home and all care professionals as well as Jeannette put down their observations. The team is working with limited resources, but is succeeding in keeping Nicolas safe at home, and Jeannette did not need to spend her time calling for appointments.

5 Method and Setting

In order to investigate the collaborative practices of the home care teams we described above, we adopted multi-faceted ethnographic methods to gain meaningful insights of the nature and complexities of home care work practices:

- General observations of the activities performed by the members of the home care teams, and their use of artifacts;
- Interviews with team members.

We shadowed one team member (a registered nurse) in his tour during a period of three days (15 h total), and we observed his work in the homes of 12 different patients. The observer jotted down notes related to the provided care, the artifacts used, the information exchanged with other team members. During and after each visit, informal interviews were conducted with the different teams members.

In addition, in order to understand how health professionals manage the mix between their works on solo based-deal with this collective approach of care delivery, we interviewed three physicians who participate in team-based home care in the city of Troyes. Semi-structured interviews were conducted to understand the implication of this innovative approach on their daily practices.

The interview protocol focused on: (a) how do they participate in providing home care to their patients? (b) What sort of information do they share with other health professionals? (c) What sort of coordination tools do they use? (d) What is the role of the inter-professional team in providing quality home care?

Observation notes and interview transcripts were analyzed to explore working practices and to identify coordination mechanisms [21].

6 Findings

The members of the inter-professional care team are required to have a continuous arrangement and adjusting of their work practices, and the protocol/plan of care is negotiated with the patients and their families. Therefore, providing quality home care needs dynamic coordination mechanisms. Through our observation and data analysis we identified some coordination mechanisms [21], which support collaboration among the members of the home care teams.

After an overview of the work practices of the team members, through a case study, this section describes the coordinative artifacts in place and highlights the important factors contributing in a new vision of providing a high quality home care.

Unlike many organizational settings where collaboration occurs in fairly stable teams or places, inter-professional home care teams are dynamic and each team member may participate in multiple home care teams.

Team members are changed depending on the evolution of the patient's health and social situation, and on the patient's perception of their quality of life. Every change in the configuration of the team is negotiated collectively, together with the patient and their family caregivers. For instance, the team treated a paraplegic patient suffering from epilepsy at home, with his wife as the principle caregiver. This summer, the wife had to be absent for a month, which prompted the team to adapt the care plan. They decided to amend the frequency of their visits and to add a new home care helper to the team, to compensate the absence of the wife.

Patient and informal (mainly family) caregivers might be active in the care protocol, providing information and signaling problems, but this participation depends on the situation of the patient. We are going to illustrate this issue with the case of one diabetic patient and his management of his condition in collaboration with the home care team.

Bernard, like many people suffering from diabetes, is also suffering from heart disease and has a high blood pressure. Bernard's family doctor manages a lot of his care, but Bernard had to go three times to emergency during the last year because of problems that arose late at night, when his doctor's office is closed.

He and his family doctor have just enrolled in the e-maison médicale association. Being a member, the family doctor was able to contact other professionals in the area (the network provides an address book on its web site) and to offer Bernard the service of a nurse to control the observance of his treatment.

The small team made of the family doctor, the nurse and Bernard met in Bernard's home, and together they created a care plan that was suitable for Bernard's lifestyle.

The team set a liaison notebook (Fig. 1) to record information about Bernard's status, and Bernard was asked to record the results of his blood glucose tests and the meals he eats in different times of the day. In the beginning, the nurse was coming twice a day (morning and evening) to measure the tension and sugar level of the patient. Based on the test results and the type of food that Bernard ate or was planning to eat during the day, the nurse was able to decide the necessary insulin dose, and records all of that in the liaison notebook.

This communication between the nurse and the doctor about Bernard's status helped Bernard to avoid the evening emergencies.

After three months, thanks to the nurse's frequent tips, Bernard was able to manage his condition, and the team decided to reduce the number of visits to once a day only if Bernard would go on recording all necessary information for the rest of the day.

Fig. 1 Liaison notebook, in patient's home

6.1 Coordinative Artifacts for the Different Information Flows

By observing the collaborative practices of this association, we can identify two types of information flow and related artifacts:

1. Information on the patient's situation that has to be shared for the global care protocol to take place. This kind of information has to be recorded for other team members to get it, and might need collective reactions from all or some of the team members. For instance, a speech therapist is signaling the degradation in patient capacity of speaking due to dental problem which requires consulting a dentist.

The tool that is used for this objective of sharing information and making decision among the team members is the "liaison" notebook (Fig. 1), a simple notebook, which allows the different actors to add comments about the general status of the patient. It could be, for instance, measurements that have been requested by the physician (such as temperature, weight, blood pressure). In addition, the liaison notebook contains contact information (team members and family caregivers).

The information that is shared in the liaison notebook is considered as a shared secret; here we have to mention that the team members are aware that some of this information should not be shared officially because the law restricts communicating patient's medical information to non-health professionals. When the physician visits the patient, they review the notebooks and answer questions and requests made by other team members, for example if team member recommends nursing services or physiotherapy (for the patient to be reimbursed by social security services).

The freestyle liaison notebook is sometimes accompanied or replaced by more structured, specialized notebooks for certain diseases, like the "diabetic surveillance" notebook for diabetic patients (Fig. 2). Also, in the case of collaborating with more structured health settings, like hospitalization at home which is

Semaine du ---------------- au ----------------								
	Petit déjeuner			Déjeuner			Dîner		
	avant	*insuline*	*après*	*avant*	*insuline*	*après*	*avant*	*insuline*	*après*
	glycémie		*glycémie*	*glycémie*		*glycémie*	*glycémie*		*glycémie*
Lun									
notes									
Mar									
notes									
Merc									
notes									

Fig. 2 Notebook for diabetic patients

Fig. 3 Follow-up documents for hospitalization at home

provided when the patient needs heavier treatments, with more sophisticated medical devices, a folder containing patient's follow-up information is used (Fig. 3).

The use of these different communication logs ensure a smooth transfer of information about the care which is provided to the patient and the administrative tasks that have been done or have to be done for the patient to receive help and/or support. This is essential because the team members have few opportunities to meet face-to-face due to their private work status.

2. Medical or social information used by a team member to make a decision in the scope of their competence. For example, the result of blood glucose test for a diabetic patient in order to be able to make a decision about the dose of insulin to administer.

Fig. 4 Box of medications,
with notes on it

The member of the team keeps this kind of information in informal ways, like notes on the box of medications (Fig. 4). This information is the rationale behind their action and it might be communicated to other team members if necessary.

6.2 Collective Adjustments and Related Artifacts

Periodic meetings are arranged between the members of the home care team, the patient and the family caregivers. The frequency of these meetings depends on the evolution of the patient status (the frequency varies from every three months to every two years). The meeting is held at the patient's home to study the patient's situation, and modifies or not their treatment/care plan.

Meetings are also held in the case of social/medical emergency. Normally, these meetings do not include all the team members; the participation of a member depends on the relevance of the agenda to them (according to their roles in the team).

Delivering care in home environment involves a lot of negotiations, which are done mainly in the periodic meetings. For more daily or weekly-based adjustment, the team members use mobile phone and text messages to adjust their agenda. Team members need to adjust with the socio-professional activities of the patient and their family, for example if the patient is visiting relatives or will go out for dinner. It means that a lot of flexibility in organizing and adjusting appointments is needed. In addition, the unpredictable nature of the work practices of the team members makes it sometimes difficult to keep punctuality.

6.3 The Patient at the Center of the Approach

We have noticed the influence of shifting focus from providing healthcare to well-being. In this new innovative approach that we have observed, the will and preferences of the patient direct their care plans. Team members play an important role in continually training the patient to manage their condition and to be aware of the impact of their choices.

Also, this innovative approach fosters the team members to deal with the patient and their environment globally, and to go beyond the fee-based service, which is still the one in place in France.

7 Design Implications

Many studies focus on developing and deploying applications and devices to support long-term interaction between the patient, living with a chronic condition, and their clinician, e.g. [2, 11, 14].

However, the collaboration between the members of an inter-professional care team in home environment has been rarely studied. Challenges identified in the current study suggest that more robust technologies are needed to support coordination and activity awareness among the members of an inter-professional care team in the home care context. Specifically, the design of such technologies should encompass the concept of "dynamic team" where the team structure is always negotiated with the patient, their entourage, and other team members.

While designing future healthcare systems to support this kind of organization, one should consider also the double status of the team members: being at the same time a private worker and the member of a team.

This section presents two principles to follow when designing a system for supporting collaborative practices among the members of an inter-professional care team delivering home care.

7.1 Supporting Flexible Teams and Practices

The dynamic structure of the team depends on the evolution of the patient's care plan as well as their social and medical conditions. In addition, the private status of team members gives them the choice to stop working with a patient or to change their area of practice.

A system supporting dynamic home care teams needs to take into consideration this constant evolution of the team members. The difficulty resides in the non-standardization of the work practices. All the private health professionals may have different ways of administrating care and documenting it and it is then a challenge to propose a unified way of documenting and using information between team members. A support system has then to be able to create flexible ways of passing the information between current team members belonging to different professions and between old and new team members.

7.2 Supporting Different Levels of Information Flows

Our study showed that the information flows between the team members could be classified in two different levels: shared information and individual information supporting rationale tracking. A computer-based system may have a good potential to improve the situation by replacing and/or supplementing some existing ways of documenting and sharing information in a manner that ensures a better availability and more comprehensive information ensemble.

Understanding the nuanced relationship between the common shared information and the individual information can help the design preserving and managing the use and ownership of these two kinds of information.

As the shared information is created by a wide range of team members, it is for instance important to understand the roles the team members play in the common shared information flow, and the different artifacts they are using.

Similarly, we need to consider how individual information documentation (which may be shared with one or more members if necessary) can be supported with technology without requiring extra effort from users to duplicate the information.

In addition, we have observed that each team member creates and customizes some form of personal notes that serve as the primary coordinative artifact for facilitating tasks performance during daily visits. For example, they use a list with the interventions to do this day, information extracted from their agenda, they add information and remarks concerning the intervention in patient's home, and then reorganizes the information in the agenda (if they want to keep trace of that), or indicate any change on the liaison notebook. We then suggest that designing a system for supporting this teamwork should allow the team members to customize the presentation of the individual information they use to support their daily work practices.

8 Conclusion

This paper is reporting one of the observations and analyses made in a large French project funded by the "inter-ministries fund" which aims at defining a more integrated care system, for patients treated at home, and the computer-based system that could support this new integrated approach.

We think that a good understanding of effective collaborative practices taking place in local initiatives is a prerequisite to design the most appropriate devices and services. In this paper, we have investigated the coordination practices used by a network of local private care professionals in order to deliver a good quality of home care.

Our analysis of these work practices led us to identify different information flows and coordinative artifacts to support these flows. Following this analysis, we suggested two main principles for designing a collaborative system to support the work of inter-professional home care teams: Supporting flexible dynamic team collaboration and supporting different levels of information flows.

Further research is needed in: (1) the role of the patient in this care delivery approach. In contrast with more classical formal care settings, this integrated approach demands a greater participation of the patients and their caregivers. This implication might vary depending on the patient's health and social situation. (2) The necessary arrangements that are made when collaborating with more structured organizations, like hospitals.

Acknowledgments This work is supported by a grant from the Regional Council of Champagne Ardenne (convention n° E201207353). We would like to thank the team members of "e-maison medicale" association for their incredible support and cooperation.

References

1. Andersen T, Bjørn P, Kensing F, Moll J (2011) Designing for collaborative interpretation in telemonitoring: re-introducing patients as diagnostic agents. Int J Med Inform 80(8):e112–e126. doi:10.1016/j.ijmedinf.2010.09.010
2. Balaam M, Rennick Egglestone S, Fitzpatrick G, Rodden T, Hughes AM, Wilkinson A, Nind T et al (2011) Motivating mobility: designing for lived motivation in stroke rehabilitation. In: Proceedings of the SIGCHI conference on human factors in computing systems, CHI '11. ACM, New York, USA, pp 3073–3082. doi:10.1145/1978942.1979397, http://doi.acm.org/10.1145/1978942.1979397
3. Bardram JE, Bossen C (2005) Mobility work: the spatial dimension of collaboration at a hospital. Comput Support Coop Work 14(2):131–160. doi:10.1007/s10606-005-0989-y
4. Bardram JE, Bossen C, Thomsen A (2005) Designing for transformations in collaboration: a study of the deployment of homecare technology. In: International conference on supporting group work, pp 294–303. doi:10.1145/1099203.1099254
5. Bossen C (2002) The parameters of common information spaces: the heterogeneity of cooperative work at a hospital ward. In: Proceedings of the 2002 ACM conference on computer supported cooperative work, CSCW '02, pp 176–185. ACM, New York, USA. doi:10.1145/587078.587104, http://doi.acm.org/10.1145/587078.587104
6. Chen Y (2010) Documenting transitional information in EMR. In: Proceedings of the SIGCHI conference on human factors in computing systems, CHI '10, pp 1787–1796. ACM, New York, USA. doi:10.1145/1753326.1753594, http://doi.acm.org.proxy.utt.fr/10.1145/1753326.1753594
7. Chevreul K, Durand-Zaleski I, Bahrami S, Hernández-Quevedo C, Mladovsky P (2010) France: health system review. Health Syst Transit 12(6):1–291, xxi–xxii
8. Christensen LR, Grönvall E (2011) Challenges and opportunities for collaborative technologies for home care work. In: Bødker S, Bouvin NO, Wulf V, Ciolfi L, Lutters W (eds) ECSCW 2011: Proceedings of the 12th European conference on computer supported cooperative work, 24–28 Sep 2011, Aarhus Denmark, Springer London, pp 61–80. http://link.springer.com/chapter/10.1007/978-0-85729-913-0_4
9. Henrard J-C (2002) Le Système Français D'aide et de Soins Aux Personnes Âgées: Dossier «Vieillissement et Dépendance». Santé, Société et Solidarité 1(2):73–82. doi:10.3406/oss.2002.894
10. Imai Y, Jacobzone S, Lenain P (2000) The changing health system in France. OECD Economics Department Working Papers, Organisation for Economic Co-operation and Development, Paris. http://www.oecd-ilibrary.org/content/workingpaper/353501840323

11. Larsen SB, Bardram JE (2008) Competence articulation: alignment of competences and responsibilities in synchronous telemedical collaboration. In: Proceedings of the SIGCHI conference on human factors in computing systems, CHI '08. ACM, New York, USA, pp 553–562. doi:10.1145/1357054.1357144, http://doi.acm.org/10.1145/1357054.1357144

12. Lévi, Francis, and Christian Saguez (2008) Rapport de l'Academie Des Technologies - LE PATIENT, LES TECHNOLOGIES ET LA MÉDECINE AMBULATOIRE. http://www. academie-technologies.fr/fr/publication/rid/64/rtitle/rapports/lid//archive/1/ltitle//rid2/237/ r2title/commission-technologie-et-sante.html

13. Magniez C, Tonnellier F, Oswalt N, Lucas V, Castel Tallet M-A (2008) Quelles Zones «fragiles» Pour L'accès Aux Soins En Champagne-Ardenne? Revue d'Épidémiologie et de Santé Publique 56(6):S358

14. Mamykina L, Mynatt E, Davidson P, Greenblatt D (2008) MAHI: investigation of social scaffolding for reflective thinking in diabetes management. In: Proceedings of the SIGCHI conference on human factors in computing systems, CHI '08. ACM, New York, USA, pp 477–486. doi:10.1145/1357054.1357131, http://doi.acm.org/10.1145/1357054.1357131

15. Palen L, Aaløkke S (2006) Of pill boxes and piano benches: 'home-made' methods for managing medication. In: Proceedings of the 2006 20th anniversary conference on computer supported cooperative work, CSCW '06. ACM, New York, USA, 79–88. doi:10.1145/ 1180875.1180888, http://doi.acm.org/10.1145/1180875.1180888

16. Petrakou A (2007) Exploring cooperation through a binder: a context for IT tools in elderly care at home. In: Bannon LJ, Ina Wagner, Gutwin C, Richard HRH, Schmidt K ECSCW 2007. Springer, London, pp 271–90. http://link.springer.com/chapter/10.1007/ 978-1-84800-031-5_15

17. Piras EM, Zanutto A (2010) Prescriptions, X-rays and Grocery Lists. Designing a personal health record to support (the invisible work of) health information management in the household. Comput Support Coop Work (CSCW) 19(6):585–613. doi:10.1007/ s10606-010-9128-5

18. Reddy M, Dourish P (2002) A finger on the pulse: temporal rhythms and information seeking in medical work. In: Proceedings of the 2002 ACM conference on computer supported cooperative work, CSCW '02. ACM, New York, USA, pp 344–353. doi:10.1145/587078. 587126. http://doi.acm.org/10.1145/587078.587126

19. Robine J-M, Michel J-P (2004) Looking forward to a general theory on population aging. J Gerontol Ser A Biol Sci Med Sci 59(6):M590–597

20. Rodwin VG (2003) The health care system under French national health insurance: lessons for health reform in the United States. Am J Public Health 93(1):31–37

21. Schmidt K, Simone C (1996) Coordination mechanisms: towards a conceptual foundation of CSCW systems design. Comput Support Coop Work (CSCW) 5(2–3):155–200. doi:10.1007/ BF00133655

22. Somme D, de Stampa M (2011) Ten years of integrated care for the older in France. Int J Integr Care 11 (Special 10th Anniversary Edition). http://www.ncbi.nlm.nih.gov/pmc/ articles/PMC3284287/

23. Strauss AL (1997) Social organization of medical work. Transaction Publishers, New Brunswick, New Jersey

24. Tang C, Carpendale S (2007) An observational study on information flow during nurses' shift change. In: Proceedings of the SIGCHI conference on human factors in computing systems, CHI '07. ACM, New York, USA, pp 219–228. doi:10.1145/1240624.1240661, http://doi. acm.org.proxy.utt.fr/10.1145/1240624.1240661

Ethnography in Parallel

Rinku Gajera and Jacki O'Neill

Abstract Ethnography has been introduced into technology design lifecycles to help sensitise new technologies to the work practices of their intended users. This paper reports on how ethnography was used in parallel to technology prototyping in the design of a workflow system to improve accuracy and efficiency in banking in India. Unlike previously largely positive reports of how ethnography helps to shape design, the case study presented here highlights the difficulty of conducting ethnography in parallel to prototype development. The tight contingencies of the prototyping cycle meant that only some of the ethnographic findings were incorporated into the design—those that fitted easily with the envisaged prototype. However, the findings from the ethnography suggested more fundamental changes were required. In this case, there was no way to incorporate such changes. We discuss the impact of this on the solution and lessons drawn for future interventions.

Keywords Ethnography · Concurrent ethnography · Design · Prototyping · Banking · Workflow technology · Ethnomethodology · India

1 Setting the Scene

There has been much discussion of the role of ethnography in design in CSCW and HCI [1–3] since it first began to be used in the late eighties and early nineties to help designers to produce systems which take into account users actual work

R. Gajera (✉)
Xerox Research Centre India, Bangalore, India
e-mail: Rinku.Gajera@xerox.com

J. O'Neill
Microsoft Research India, Bangalore, India
e-mail: Jacki.Oneill@xerox.com

C. Rossitto et al. (eds.), *COOP 2014 - Proceedings of the 11th International Conference on the Design of Cooperative Systems, 27–30 May 2014, Nice (France)*, DOI: 10.1007/978-3-319-06498-7_16, © Springer International Publishing Switzerland 2014

practices. However, the most comprehensive discussions of how and when ethnography can be incorporated into industrial design lifecycles remains that from the Lancaster school in the 1990s [4–8]. Suggested processes for ethnography and systems design from the Lancaster school include quick and dirty ethnography [5, 6], concurrent ethnography [5, 6, 8], evaluative or sensitising ethnography [5, 6], the use of design probes [2] and perhaps the most ideal approach from the ethnographers perspective ethnography as the starting point for design [9]. We have had some success with this latter approach in industrial research, moving from an ethnographic understanding of a setting to technologies incorporated into products (see for e.g. [9, 10]). However, whilst it might be our ideal, it is not always possible and sometimes designers come to us ethnographers with technology ideas into which they would like somehow to infuse the users perspective. Since, like Hughes et al. [5, p. 6], we tend to believe that "...despite less than ideal circumstances [...] one can always learn something from ethnography" we are typically happy to oblige. In this paper, we report on an ethnographic study carried out in parallel to prototype development. This paper provides something of a cautionary tale however about how problems, both practical and conceptual, can prevent the full benefit of ethnography from being realized by taking such an approach. This is consequential for systems design, leading we will argue to a system which is likely to at worst fail or at best be worked around failing to bring its intended benefits [11]. We hope that this cautionary tale will help both systems designers and ethnographers from falling into the same trap. We briefly describe the technology project before reviewing the literature.

2 The Technology Prototype

The prototype, which we shall call BankFlow, aimed to reduce cost and improve efficiency in Indian banking. The Indian banking system faces particular challenges; growth in financial services is coupled with mandates to serve the rural unbanked, where footfall and income are lower yet branch costs remain fixed or more. Although banks are introducing Internet banking functionality, most processes will remain paper-based for considerable time. BankFlow was conceived of as a solution to help create branches with low capital and operational expense. It is a workflow solution which uses a Multi-Function (printing, scanning, email, etc.). Printer with document processing capabilities to redesign banking workflows. It includes workflows based around paper forms as well as electronic workflows. Promised benefits include removing costly and slow couriering of paper between branches and processing centres, reducing the amount of technology required to run a branch; enabling up front (partial) digitisation and improving efficiency and accuracy. It has been designed with the low bandwidth and intermittent connections of rural India in mind. It is near-term innovation to be quickly rolled out to address a current problem. BankFlow implements an account opening workflow, to demonstrate the capabilities of the technology.

3 Literature Review

Despite the transformational promises of technology, the annals of history are littered with systems which are only partially used or worked around, not really causing much damage but neither delivering the promised improvements [12–14]. There are a variety of reasons why systems do not produce the expected effects. There is a tendency to oversimplify the work to be supported and the skills and knowledge of the workers (e.g. [11, 14]), whilst at the same time overestimating the capabilities of the technology.

3.1 Ethnography and Technology Design

Ethnographic studies, in particular ethnomethodological ethnographies [15], have been used in the technology design lifecycle to try and address some of these issues. This is because they reveal the situated accomplishment of action and are used to make the social organisation of action visible and available to design reasoning [16]. A key role of ethnography in systems design is to reveal the complexities and contingencies of the workplace of which designers should at the very least be aware. The idea is to enhance design by enabling designers and ethnographers to explore "the practical implications for design of the incarnate social organisation of human action and how it may be supported, automated, or enhanced by a system" [1].

Ethnography—even in the form taken by the modern workplace study—is a lengthy process compared to typical requirements engineering techniques and this can mean it is difficult to fit into the design lifecycle [5, 6]. To address this various approaches have been suggested for incorporating ethnography into design:

- *'Quick and dirty' ethnography*, involving short focused studies (in a large domain) to get a general picture of the setting. The ethnographic findings feed into design through debrief meetings and a scoping document [5, 6]. In the example they give this did produce some useful findings, however in practice it wasn't as easy to be influential in design with this approach and "development work on the tool continued almost independently of the fieldwork" [5].
- *Concurrent ethnography*, where systems design takes place at the same time as ethnography, with iterations of ethnography and prototype development [5, 6]. Whilst in the ideal situation the initial ethnography precedes design, in practice, it is not clear how often this happens. Of the same project for example [8] describes the development of a generic highly configurable prototype going on at the same time as the initial ethnography. The findings of which are used to reconfigure future prototype iterations. The project they describe was successful, however it involved a small team with close communication doing research, so was not subject to the same constraints of an industrial development.

- *Evaluative ethnography* [5] involves an ethnographic study undertaken to provide a 'sanity check' [6] on an already formulated requirement proposal, with the findings being used to create a new more sensitized requirements specification. In their example, also successful, an ethnography of banking practice identified a fundamental mismatch between practice and the proposed technology, leading to the bank deciding not to buy. In this case certain crucial functionalities of the technology were fully worked out as this was a model the bank was buying in.
- What we call here *ethnography first* is the study of a domain of potential intervention with no preconceived design ideas, where design concepts come out of the observed setting itself [9]. When combined with an understanding of new advancements in technology this has proved to be a fruitful method for innovation [9, 10]. It is perhaps easiest carried out with a dedicated multi-disciplinary team set up to work in this way, but mainly it is a question of setting up the project in such a way that design does not start until analysis of ethnographic findings is completed.
- A final method comes from studying *technology probes*—where a lightweight technology is developed and put into the hands of users (e.g. [2]).

In this project the technology idea had already been conceived and ethnography and systems design were undertaken in parallel.

4 Methods and Field Site

We conducted a multi-sited ethnomethodological ethnographic study of a variety of different branches and processing centres located in southern India for one bank. Observations and open-ended interviews were conducted in nine bank branches and three document processing facilities. There are two types of document processing facilities serving the bank: (1) Back Office Processing Centres (BOPC), which carry out verification and processing work on the various documents (currently paper-based) they receive from the branches. The bank operates a hub and spoke model where one BOPC serves multiple branches, and (2) Digitization Centres in other locations which digitise the incoming scanned forms. Out of nine branches, three each were located in urban, semi-urban and rural areas. The document processing facilities were located in the large cities, for ease of access and the digitization centres in semi-urban areas, for lower costs. Overall the ethnographer spent around 60 h in the various branches, 23 h in two BOPCs and 12 h in one digitization centre in 2012. Since that the BankFlow prototype was to demonstrate an account opening workflow, the ethnographer followed the account opening process from start to finish to provide detailed insights with the aim of guiding prototype design. Account opening, a high-value process has considerable potential of improvement as it is somewhat error prone and involves costly and time consuming couriering of paper documents (which will increase as more rural branches open). Data was collected through detailed field notes, sketches and the collection of various arte-facts and paper forms used in the account opening process. Interviews and work-shops with the bank's management were undertaken. These investigated management's understanding of the pain points of account opening and their motivations for and satisfaction with the solutions they had thus far implemented. Their potential receptiveness to our technology prototype was also sought.

By understanding the detailed contingencies of the work and the orientations of the workers (and their customers), we hoped to be able to influence the design of the technology prototype. As mentioned in the introduction however, development of the technology prototype was going on in parallel to the ethnographic study. The schedule for the pilot imposed tight time constraints for the turnaround of the ethnographic findings. Furthermore, this parallel development had an impact on which ethnographic findings would influence design and the extent to which they could do so.

That is, the technology prototype was conceived when designers had only a high-level view of the work and was therefore based on a number of assumptions. Since prototype development had already begun before the study revealed the actual practices of account opening, many of these assumptions were built into the prototype and were not open to change. The result was that the ethnographic study only had a limited impact on prototype development. We will address this issue in the discussion. First, however, we report on the findings of the ethnographic study and the details of the prototype.

5 Ethnographic Study Findings

In the account opening workflow, we primarily studied bankers, analysts and data processors to understand how they actually carried out the work of account opening, what it means to follow the process and where (and why) their practices varied from the stated process. In this paper we focus on the work of bankers and analysts.

5.1 Overview of the Traditional Account Opening Process

Account opening is a largely paper based process. We describe first the 'ideal' process, i.e. how it is *meant* to work, before describing the *actual* practices undertaken.

Two different processes are in operation: (1) The Traditional Process (see Fig. 1) described in this section, used by 80 % of the branches and (2) The Scanning Process recently introduced in 20 % of branches where forms are scanned in the branch back office. This second process was introduced to improve efficiency and was still being rolled out. It is described in the section on Imple-mented Solutions.

Fig. 1 Traditional account opening process

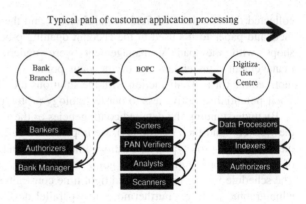

Typical path of customer application processing

To open an account, customers either come into a bank branch or are visited at home or work by a contract employee. In this paper we only discuss in-branch account opening. Customers and their banker fill out the necessary paper application forms, collect supporting documentation and provide an initial deposit. The banker verifies the provided information, using some software, signs and stamps the documents and creates a customer record on the bank's computerised file tracking system. An authoriser completes a second verification using the same software. Once the documents have been authorised, two copies of the authorisation are printed. One is given with the deposit to the bank teller. The second is attached to the application set (including application forms and up to 10 supporting documents such as ID, address proof etc.). These are couriered to the BOPC by end of each working day.

At the BOPC, the application sets are sorted by account type and passed to the PAN verification team. A PAN card is a photo ID card containing an individual's unique Permanent Account Number (similar to a US social security number). The PAN verification team checks that customer details on the application match those associated with the PAN using an online checking site. Each application set is then reviewed independently by two different analysts. Mistakes which are spotted at this stage are sent back to the bank branch. From here a reduced application set, containing just the double-sided application form and a copy of the ID and address proof, go to scanning. The sets are batch scanned and routed to the Digitisation Centre.

5.2 Problems with, and Solutions for, the Traditional Account Opening Process

The workshops with management highlighted some problems with the account opening process.

1. Couriering paper is expensive and slow.
2. Missing and inaccurate data is a major challenge. Incorrect forms are returned to the bank branch for correction. This to-and-froing of forms between branch and BOPC adds an undesired operational cost and further delays activation (up

to 10–15 days), leading to reduced customer satisfaction. The management therefore had a strong interest in avoiding what is known as First Time Not Right (FTNR) and branches were judged on the basis of this.

To address these problems, the management implemented various solutions:
(1) Paper checklist at BOPC (2) Verification Software (3) Branch level Scanning Process (4) Instant Accounts.

Paper checklist at BOPC. To improve the accuracy of the back office verification process two detailed 70–100 item paper checklists had been introduced to be used by Analysts. One generic and one specific to particular account types. For cost reasons, only a few personnel (who route and upload data) in the office have computers.

Verification software is a computerised version of the paper checklist introduced at branch level. The tool was envisioned as a proactive measure to reduce errors at the branch itself. Previously, verification was done by memory (relying on bankers' local knowledge and experience) this tool introduced a more formal verification process. Ideally, Bankers should go through each application set using the software to check rules whilst the **customer is present with them** and collect more information if required. The software is often updated with new policies.

Branch level Scanning Process. This solution involves a rearrangement of the physical infrastructure, with BOPC processes being introduced into a subset of branches (20 % at time of study). One or more analysts are based at branch level with computing and scanning resources to complete the back office processing steps in the branch. This solution has a different workflow to the Traditional Process described above: the aim is to introduce an instant workflow where each application is processed immediately. That is, once the bankers have processed and authorized *each* application, it is taken to the scanning room and signed off by the analysts. They prepare it for scanning, check the PAN number, then check the form using the Verification Software rather than paper checklists (as the analysts have the computing resources for the scanning process), then scan the form for data entry. The aim is to improve efficiency, by processing the applications more rapidly. This is an enabler for Instant Accounts.

Instant Accounts aim to enrol customers faster, by processing and activating customer accounts more rapidly (within 3 h). This process is based around a pack, including a bank card and cheque book, given to the customer when they enrol. When the account is activated the customer is notified by SMS and can complete transactions. Although the account opening deposit is not processed so rapidly, so the customer cannot, for example, withdraw on the basis of it.

5.3 Workers Orientations

Bankers in the branches, have a host of responsibilities besides assisting customers with their applications. However, their first priority is to assist as many in-coming customers as possible, taking the minimum time to do so during the customer opening hours. Administrative work is largely completed outside customer hours. Their primary orientation is to *customer throughput*. A second priority is to ensure that the data is correct and accurate. For this reason most work passes under multiple eyes, through different levels of verification with lots of signing, stamping and electronic authorisations. The concern here is to prevent fraud by customers and bank staff and the processes have been designed to maximise security and reduce risk. There is a tension between these checking and security focused features of the processes and the aim to provide efficient, friendly customer service. The orientations of the analysts in the BOPC are towards data accuracy, since their prime work is verification.

5.4 Actual Work Practices

The work practices observed differed in a number of ways from the ideal process, as workers attempted to get the work done in an efficient and effective way. The various solutions described above were often not used as intended.

During account opening, bankers are concerned with the twin priorities of customer throughput and data accuracy. Customers are often fitting in a visit to the bank at lunch time, on a Saturday or after work. Many customers observed doing account opening were visibly impatient and bankers have developed a number of practices to maximize customer throughput, including collaborative form filling, postponing the use of the verification software and chunking work. A number of different paper forms must be filled into open a bank account with many duplicating information. Officially the customer should complete the forms themselves, sign them and hand them to the bankers for checking. The bankers should then check the form using the verification software whilst the customer is present and collect any additional information. In reality the bankers filled in much of the information on the forms for the customer. Typically they would fill out the primary account opening application form *collaboratively with the customer* i.e. they would discuss the various fields with the customer, collect supporting documentation and so on. They would get the customer to sign any additional forms which the bankers themselves would fill in later after the customer has left, using information from the main application and supporting documents. They rarely used the verification software whilst the customer was present, however its use is required by process, so the forms are verified (almost mechanically) in batches at the end of the day with authorizations printed out. The bankers create the customer record on the file tracking system as and when they have time between customers. This work organization serves multiple purposes:

1. Customer throughput: it's both quicker for this customer and the following customers (reducing waiting).
2. It is more efficient as bankers can quickly identify which fields need to be filled and which not and it helps ensure the right information goes in the right field.

3. It helps ensure data accuracy as many customers are not well versed in English. In fact the bank provides local language versions of its forms as a reference only, which must still be completed in English but the instructions and field names in the native language is already helpful to customers. Variations in English spellings given supporting documents are common e.g. names but for the bank requires consistent spellings on all documentation.
4. It reduces the number of delays caused by illegible handwriting.
5. 'Filling-forms-for-my-customer' is considered good customer service.
6. Chunking similar work together, such as all verification work, is more efficient than undertaking the work as discreet tasks [7]. Whilst customer record creation is a quick task which can be fitted into free space throughout the day, verification is more time consuming and interruptions more costly, hence it is more productively done at the end of the day. Furthermore, verification requires bankers to re-enter some of the data on the verification software, taking more time.

After authorization, the application set and authorization document are sent for processing. What happens next depends on whether the branch has the Scanning Process or not. Where it doesn't, the forms are sent by courier to the BOPC. Whilst they take care of verification, the work is rather mechanical. Analysts spend around 10 min per application, going through the checklist. Where FTNR is detected the application is put on hold and the form couriered back to the bank for correction. The two main components of FTNR are data completeness (that is all the necessary fields are filled) and correctness (that is all the data entered is correct). It is this costly FTNR process that management is trying to reduce. Completed applications are scanned in batches of 15–20.

Where scanning is done in branch, the branch level analysts do all three BOPC processes: PAN checking, verification and scanning. Typically each branch has 2–6 analysts depending on branch size. In the official process, new account applications are meant to come to the analysts one at a time throughout the day as they are completed in the branch. However as mentioned above, they actually arrive after verification has taken place outside of customer hours. During the rest of the day the analysts are processing other documents which are done one at a time.

After second level authorisation in the branch the applications are dropped off at the scanning space, where the analyst stamps the forms to say they've been received. The analyst then does all the preparatory work before logging onto the scanning system. Preparatory work includes manually checking that all the required information is there. The analysts do this because once they log onto the system they have 2 h to complete everything, working in this way makes it easier to meet their targets. Bringing the scanning into the branch has had an interesting effect on FTNR. If the analyst spots an obvious mistake (e.g. salary not mentioned) before logging into the system she typically does not report it as FTNR, rather she returns the form to the branch to get it corrected. In the instances we saw this was considered as a favor to the branch staff (as it improves their FTNR rating) but it also works to the customers favor by reducing processing delays. However, the analysts complained that branch employees were becoming more relaxed about accuracy because errors weren't necessarily reported as FTNR. However, we have no evidence to say whether this is the case or not. Once all the preparatory work is completed, the analyst logs into the system and does the PAN checking, validation and scanning. Any mistakes spotted now are reported as FTNR. The scanning functionality on the scanning software remains the original batch scanning software, which further encourages scanning in batches, rather than the individual processing.

The only applications processed individually were those of selected customers, such as high net-worth customers. For the majority of the customers, Instant Accounts were not activated within 3 h, since the application forms were not processed until the end of the day.

5.5 Summary: Impact of Implemented Solutions

Underlying three of the solutions implemented by management to improve accuracy and efficiency—the verification software, branch scanning process and instant accounts—is the idea that work should be processed one application at a time as it is created. This idea of a one job at a time workflow has parallels to the print shop workflow described in [11]. As in that case, because this projected workflow does not fit with actual practice, the implemented technologies are not used as intended and thus do not give the expected benefits. In this case, there are a number of features of the work organization which work against this. Firstly, given the concern for customer throughput, extra time during the customer interaction is considered too great an overhead. Secondly, there is a strong preference for processing time consuming work in batches. Thirdly, the scanning technology is actually designed for batch scanning. Whilst taking a one at a time approach could potentially improve data accuracy, by identifying and resolving problems whilst the customer is present, it does not take account of the parallel need for customer throughput. Indeed whilst data accuracy is only a problem for less than 15 % of new account applications, undertaken the implemented measures to address this as designed would negatively impact on customer interaction time for all customers.

This does not mean the solutions have no value. The verification software is frequently updated with new policies, helping staff keep abreast with rule changes. The bankers reported that they valued this knowledge resource but as a verification tool considered it an 'additional workload' that they are obliged to use to fulfill management requirements. The branch scanning process still reduces courier cost and related processing delays. In effect then, rather than transforming work practices, the technologies were made at home in the existing workflow. This is not because the workers were somehow being contrary but because the solutions ignore one of the major priorities of the bankers—customer throughput—which impacts the whole workflow.

6 The BankFlow Prototype

Prototype development was going on in parallel to the ethnographic studies. Three successive iterations of the BankFlow prototype were developed to demonstrate different functionality and provide an exemplar of how the technology could positively impact on banking work. The prototypes all include at least one paper-based account opening workflow and the second and third prototypes also include an electronic account opening workflow. In this section we briefly describe the prototypes and where the ethnographic findings had influence on them. We then critically discuss the use of ethnography in this process.

BankFlow is a technology which can scan, process and help verify the forms before sending them directly to the back office. The overall aim of BankFlow was to save capital and operational expenditure for banks: BankFlow enables branches to be set up in remote locations with just one Multi-Function Printer (MFP) with an internet connection. Operational cost will be reduced as daily couriering of documents to the BOPC is no longer required and processing time is not dependent on couriering time.

The first iteration of BankFlow shows that it is possible to use this technology for sending forms between different locations whilst dealing with low bandwidth and intermittent internet connections. It incorporates (1) scanning of handwritten forms (2) image processing to separate form content from background (3) compression and (4) re-applying form background at the BOPC. This prototype was developed without any input from the fieldwork and at this stage there was no particular envisionment of how the technology would fit into the workflow. However, even though batch scanning was mentioned in the specifications it was not designed into the technology, the focus being on the more innovative and technologically challenging features of the process. The prototype's main advantage would be to reduce couriering costs and speed up processing time. A post hoc comment on this prototype came after visiting the BOPC: currently only a few analysts have access to computers. Either all would now need access if electronic forms are to be processed directly or the forms would need to be printed on arrival (introducing extra costs).

The second iteration of BankFlow included (1) support to help bankers verify the completeness of the forms they are submitting; (2) multilingual support—where customers can choose the language in which field names and instructions appear, whilst data entry remains in English; (3) a first version of an electronic workflow—where data is directly entered into the system and the completed forms printed out and signed by the customer (the bank has a hard requirement for signed paper copies). During the design of this iteration, the ethnographer had completed the first interviews in the BOPC and bank branches but had not yet undertaken the observational work. The early findings from these interviews fed into design in two ways: (1) the introduction of multilingual support, (2) completeness verification—the interviews of both branch staff and BOPC revealed that the two key components of FTNR are completeness and correctness. Since checking form completeness was deemed possible although not without technological challenges, the idea was incorporated into the prototype. However at this stage we had no details of what the actual situated work practices were around account opening as the observational study in the branches had not yet been undertaken. The developers therefore choose to focus on the technical challenges that the technology could solve rather than thinking at a system level, unfortunately their instantiation embodied assumptions about the process which turned out to be mistaken.

That BankFlow helps to check completeness is not in itself an issue, but it was how the workflow in which this would take place was envisaged that raises concerns *now that the observational study has been completed*. The envisaged paper form workflow consists of the following: The customer and banker fill out all the relevant paper forms for account opening and collect the supporting documentation. The paper form is then scanned using BankFlow, with the customer present. It automatically checks for completeness i.e. that all the required fields are filled in and for some fields that they contain the right alphanumeric entries. The system will provide details of any missing information, thus it should reduce the occurrence of FTNR, as the bankers can ask the customer for that information there and then. To correct this information the banker needs to add it to the original forms and rescan. The banker scans the relevant supporting documents and the system prompts the bankers to index key fields from the supporting documents. Since the customer is present and sharing the screen they can check the information is correct. Indexing involves entering 4–5 fields detailing the information on that particular supporting document. This reduces the amount of digitisation work that is required to take place in the digitisation centres and simultaneously creates the customer record. If this information is propagated to the various other banking systems, it can reduce duplicate data entry. All information is sent electronically to the back office for final verification and account activation.

We examine this envisaged workflow in the light of the ethnographic findings below but first we briefly describe the third iteration of BankFlow. The third prototype advances the electronic workflow with (1) web-based access so forms can be filled on larger PC screens, (2) prompting the banker as they enter information on contextually relevant new rules and changes in process (3) pre-filling various fields (branch location, employee code, account type) (4) propagating information between fields.

The prototypes above have been designed to offer some system level advantages such as (1) in an ideal case speeding up new account processing to 30 min (although this can only work where there is no queue and everything runs smoothly. It is likely to happen only with high-value account holders if at all.) (2) save courier time and cost (3) make bank branches in remote areas more cost effective (4) reduce the number of data processors in the digitisation centres.

6.1 Critical Evaluation of Bankflow

The completed ethnographic analysis leads us to have some concerns about how BankFlow will be used in practice in its current embodiment. Whilst the underlying technology idea would not seem to be problematic, the manner in which it has been implemented as a one-at-a-time workflow runs contrary to observed work practices. The paper-based and less sophisticated electronic workflow add time and effort up front in the branch whilst the customer is present with the aim of achieving efficiencies elsewhere. For example, all forms will need to be completed now whilst the customer is present, additionally they will need to be scanned and indexed. Furthermore, where a customer is not approved during verification, the time spent indexing up front is wasted. All this conflicts with the banker's orientation to customer throughput. Any benefit of efficiency in later parts of the process is likely to be outweighed by the delay during customer interaction. It is possible that in quiet rural branches this will not be so much of an issue, although it should be noted that the orientation to customer throughput is individual (keeping this customer interaction here as short as possible) as well as successive (processing successive customers rapidly or overlapping as currently paper allows ability to support any number of customers to reduce waiting). However, if used as intended it would have a greater disruptive impact in busier branches. If this is the case, it is likely to be worked around, just as the existing software verification technology is—relegated to the end of the day, negating some of the intended value in for example verification.

It is also not clear whether costs will be reduced by indexing up front. This idea of front loading is similar to that described in a study of another scanning solution, this time in a medical setting [17]. Both technologies were designed with the idea of making the entire workflow more efficient and reducing the amount of back office processing work. Vinckhuyzen and Plurkowski. [17] described the resulting shifting around of the work from clerks to (higher paid) medical professionals and how even so there was no reduction in workforce. Similarly here we need to ask whether this is really more efficient? Since indexing is only a small part of data entry, will that really reduce the digitization workforce and even if it does, given that the (higher paid) bankers will now have more work can that really be said to be more efficient[1]? A second question on efficiency in practice also relates to front-loading. The increased workload on every application aims to reduce FTNR from incomplete data. However, FTNR (including completeness and accuracy) runs at approximately 15 %. Thus every interaction time is increased as a way of detecting a small minority of problems.

This is not to say the system doesn't have value, it should significantly reduce couriering costs and it handles the problems of poor bandwidth in rural areas making banking more accessible. However it is unlikely to realize all the promised

---

[1] See [18] for a related discussion about whether getting rid of PA's is really beneficial when we dig below the easy-to-cost bottom line.

benefits at least in the paper-based workflow. The enhanced electronic workflow implemented in the third iteration could however offer benefits, *as long as it is quicker to complete upfront* with the customer than the current traditional practices. We have hope that it will be because it has a number of features to reduce the form filling burden, such as automatic completion of duplicate fields, contextual prompts etc.

However, as ethnographers it is disappointing that the most important findings from our study, that is the fundamental conflict between BankFlows envisaged workflow and the real work practices of bankers could not be incorporated into technology design. Rather only the more minor findings which were easy to implement and which fitted with the current technology conception were taken. The tight timeline and the parallel study and development cycle meant that full value was not made of the ethnographic study, leading to a better systemic solution.

7 Discussion

In this discussion we make some observations about the use of ethnography for design in parallel to the prototyping lifecycle in an industrial research setting. Whilst the BankFlow prototype has been created, it has not yet been piloted. Thus we don't know for certain what the outcomes of implementation will be. However, as Sacks [19] described technology doesn't change the underlying fundamentals of the work—bankers and customers will still be 'doing banking' whether in urban or rural branches, whether with or without our technology. The technology will have to be made at home with their existing practices. Unfortunately, in this case the workflow design conflicts with some of the fundamental work practices of bankers, instead it replicates the same mistakes as the previous solutions. It seems unlikely that WorkFlow will therefore be used as proposed and thus will not bring its full benefits.

7.1 Ethnography in Parallel

In this section we critically examine the place of ethnography in the systems design cycle as undertaken here and in comparison to some of the different processes described at the start of the paper. It should be clear that this is a post hoc analysis, undertaken because we wished to examine the reasons for the limited impact of the ethnographic study in this case in the hope to better impact the future iterations of the same prototype and that others can learn from our experience. Of the different ways of combining ethnography and design described at the start of this paper, the process followed here bears closest relation to the concurrent and evaluative ethnographies. In terms of concurrent ethnography, the timing was off—if the study and analysis could have been completed either prior to [6] or during the development of the first rather generic prototype [8] the ethnographic findings might have had a greater impact. The problem for us lay in the timing of the studies. The ethnographic analysis revealing how the social organization of the setting was achieved by the members was only completed after certain assumptions, which turned out to conflict with the workers orientations, had been 'hardwired' into the prototype and were thus considered too difficult to change. In terms of evaluative ethnography, could we not have provided a 'sanity check' of the design requirements in advance, rather than post-facto? Unfortunately, in our case as opposed to the banking project described in [5, 6] there was no pre-specified requirements documentation. Furthermore, in [5, 6] not only was the bank looking to buy an existing technology, they already had doubts about its fit, and so were ready to take on board the ethnographers findings. Whereas in our case, there was no single worked out requirements document up front, rather the requirements and design choices emerged over the iterations and unfortunately again the timing of the study was not favourable for influencing design at the point it was needed. The basic technology concept had already been created and at each stage of prototype iteration rather fundamental design decisions were made which were not open to amendment. Whilst they incorporated the findings which could easily be fitted into their existing conception, there was no space for going back to the drawing board or doing a major rethink when it became clear that the workflow design conflicted with the bankers work practices.

7.2 Scenic Features Versus Situated Action and the Role of Ethnography

So is it simply a question of timing? We do not believe so. Certainly timing is part of the issue—the practical problem we alluded to at the start of this paper. However we believe that this practical problem stemmed from a conceptual misunderstanding of what exactly ethnography was *for*. Originally studies were planned to start in advance of the prototype development, but they kept getting delayed because of problems of access. In part these problems were the normal sort of practical problems of access familiar to ethnographers everywhere (changing gatekeepers, negotiations with customers and so on). However, since this project started from an idea for a technology, it was naturally led by the engineers, not the ethnographers, and in hindsight we think that we and they had differing understandings of the role and outcomes of the ethnography. Although never fully formulated it appears that their expectations were that ethnography would help with the look and feel and detailing of the workflow of the interface and was therefore something that could be tacked on later.

In our experience of ethnomethodologically-informed ethnography for design, design is often influenced *both* by the scenic features [1] of a setting and by the deeper understanding of the situated nature of action [1, 3]. That is, compared to a formal process description which is typically divorced from the work itself, any information about the setting can prove useful in informing design. However, problems can arise when *only* the scenic features of the setting are incorporated. Unfortunately by their nature the scenic features are those which can typically be reported straight off, without the need for analysis and thus made immediately available for the designers. For example, in this case the provision of forms in local languages was an immediately reportable scenic feature of the setting, whereas the way in which account opening forms were processed to meet the situated contingencies of the work required an understanding of how the social orgnisation of the work was achieved. Furthermore, the designing in of completeness verification in prototype two might be seen as a cautionary tale against using incomplete first impressions and partial results rather than the detailed output of a completed and analysed ethnographic investigation. This is something that we imagine most ethnographers working in industry would have similar tales about. In this case however, the ethnographer had little choice but to provide these partial insights because of the constraints of the prototyping lifecycle.

This becomes even more problematic if systems designers start to believe that ethnography is about the description of scenic features, as this is likely to influence their understanding of what ethnography is *for*. That is, just as one can make a distinction between the scenic features of a setting and the analysis of *how* that setting comes to look as it does, one can find a parallel in how ethnography is used to influence systems design. That is it can be used to influence the 'surface' features of the system, such as the look and feel of the interface, but it can also speak to the fundamental principles on which that system is designed. This has been shown for example in the many ethnomethodological ethnographies which illustrate how technologies end up failing because they do not take account of the users work practices (e.g. [11, 20, 21]). What our paper offers is a cautionary tale of what can happen if ethnography is not well integrated with the design lifecycle. Ethnography as a starting point in any ideal design process is propagated by experts consistently [1, 3]. Also, challenges such as, time taken, vague and unsystematic methods and communicating broad results [6] are often discussed while integrating ethnography in design process, however not much has been discussed about the consequences a solution can have if ethnography is not preceding and given proportional time and space to fundamentally evolve the system design.

Whilst we still might believe that 'one can always learn something from ethnography' we would urge caution in ensuring at the start of the project that all parties in the collaboration are on the same page in their understanding of and expectations from ethnography. Since if the assumption that all ethnography is for is to influence surface features of the system is put into practice then one is likely to run into similar design problems as if one had not used ethnography at all.

References

1. Crabtree A (2003) Designing collaborative systems: a practical guide to ethnography. Springer, Heidelberg
2. Crabtree A, Chamberlain A, Davies M, Glover K, Reeves S, Rodden T, Tolmie P, Jones M (2013) Doing innovation in the wild. In: Proceedings of the biannual conference of the Italian chapter of SIGCHI. ACM
3. Randall D, Harper R, Rouncefield M (2007) Fieldwork for design: theory and practice. Springer, Heidelberg
4. Hughes JA, Randall D, Shapiro D (1992) From ethnographic record to system design. JCSCW 1(3):123–141
5. Hughes J, King V, Rodden T, Andersen H (1994) Moving out from the control room: ethnography in system design. In: Proceedings of CSCW. ACM, pp 429–439
6. Hughes J, O'Brien J, Rodden T, Rouncefield M, Sommerville I (1995) Presenting ethnography in the requirements process. In: Proceedings of the 2nd IEEE international symposium on requirements engineering, IEEE, pp 27–34
7. Rouncefield M, Hughes J, Rodden T, Viller S (1994) Working with "constant interruption". CSCW 94, ACM Press, New York
8. Sommerville I, Rodden T, Sawyer P, Bentley R (1992) Sociologists can be surprisingly useful in interactive systems design. In: Proceedings of HCI 92, CUP. People and computers, pp 341–341
9. O'Neill J, Castellani S, Roulland F, Hairon N, Juliano C, Dai L (2011) From ethnographic study to mixed reality, CSCW 2011
10. Castellani S, Grasso A, O'Neill J, Roulland F (2009) Designing technology as an embedded resource for troubleshooting. JCSCW 18(2–3):199–227
11. Bowers J, Button G, Sharrock W (1995) Workflow from within and without: technology and cooperative work on the print industry shopfloor. In: Proceedings of ECSCW'95
12. Hartswood M, Procter R, Rouncefield M, Slack R (2003) Making a case in medical work: implications for the electronic medical record. JCSCW 12(3):241–266
13. O'Neill J, Martin D, Colombino T, Roulland F, Willamowski J (2008) Colour management is a socio-technical problem. In: Proceedings of CSCW'08
14. Sachs P (1995) Transforming work: collaboration, learning and design. Commun ACM 38(9):36–44
15. Garfinkel H (1967) Studies in ethnomethodology. Prentice-Hall, Englewood Cliffs
16. Button G (2000) The ethnographic tradition and design. Des Stud 21:319–333
17. Vinckhuyzen E, Plurkowski L (2012) Implementing EMRs: learning from a video ethnography. In: Proceedings of EPIC 2012
18. Erickson T, Danis CM, Kellogg WA, Helander ME (2008) Assistance: the work practices of human administrative assistants and their implications for it and organizations. CSCW'08, pp 609–618
19. Sacks H (1972) Lectures on conversation. In: Jefferson G (ed) Lecture 3. Springer, Heidelberg (1972), pp 542–553. Blackwell, Oxford (1992)
20. Button G (1993) Technology in working order: studies of work, interaction, and technology. Routledge, London
21. Button G, Sharrock W (1997) The production of order and the order of production: possibilities for distributed organisations, work and technology in the print industry. In: Proceedings of the 5th European conference on computer supported cooperative work (pp 1–16). Springer Netherlands

Lessons Learnt Working with Performance Data in Call Centres

Tommaso Colombino, Benjamin Hanrahan and Stefania Castellani

Abstract This paper details the treatment of performance data in outsourced call centre operations, as encountered by a team of researchers throughout the course of a project. This project aimed at improving support for performance and motivation management in an outsourced customer care contact centre for a large telecommunications company. In particular, we focus on how the practices of capturing, aggregating, and presenting data reflect the operation's overall concern with "reporting upstream" and accountability. As well as, how the technological and organizational infrastructure of the call centre is shaped accordingly. We then discuss some emergent consequences of this organization of data management, which in particular take the form of some tensions between the emergent needs for data at certain levels of granularity and aggregation within the actual operations of the call centre, and its relative accuracy and availability.

Keywords Ethnography · Ethnomethodology · Call centre work · Performance data management

1 Introduction

Customer contact centres, or call centres, provide an interesting but challenging context for technological innovation. They are knowledge work environments built around a fairly strict productivity model and division of labour. They have

T. Colombino (✉) · B. Hanrahan · S. Castellani
Xerox Research Centre Europe, 6 chemin de Maupertuis, Meylan 38240, France
e-mail: Tommaso.colombino@xrce.xerox.com

B. Hanrahan
e-mail: Benjamin.hanrahan@xrce.xerox.com

S. Castellani
e-mail: Stefania.castellani@xrce.xerox.com

C. Rossitto et al. (eds.), *COOP 2014 - Proceedings of the 11th International Conference on the Design of Cooperative Systems, 27–30 May 2014, Nice (France)*, DOI: 10.1007/978-3-319-06498-7_17, © Springer International Publishing Switzerland 2014

complex data and information management systems that, particularly in outsour- ced operations, are subject to a tension between the need for standardization, efficiency, and replication of infrastructures with the particular requirements of multiple client organizations. Consequently, a lot of attention has been devoted to modeling call centre activities and for making simulations, what-if analysis, forecasting trends, to schedule work, and to organize appropriate trainings for call centre employees [1, 4–6]. Some attention has been devoted to the challenges of innovating certain aspects of customer contact work and remote assistance [7, 8] and to the collection of insights that could contribute to a successful implemen- tation of Customer Relationship Management system projects [9].

In our work we have focused less on the customer facing aspect in the work of individual agents (e.g. the aspect of problem solving over the phone) and more on the operational management of the call centre workforce as a whole, with par- ticular focus on the pervasive use of productivity metrics which are the direct product of the agents' call taking activities. In particular, this paper details the experiences of a group of researchers throughout the course of a project within an outsourced customer care contact centre for a large telecommunications company. The initial engagement with the call centre was through a series of ethnographic studies aimed at understanding performance management and compensation practices within the organization. In the course of the project we uncovered a number of emergent problems in the operations of the call centre. In particular, we focused on the lack of access to up-to-date information about performance and compensation for the agents of the call centre (the employees answering the phone and responding to customer queries) [3]. During our initial investigations we concluded that the primary causes for this lack of support were to be found in the lack of investment in innovation on the part of an organization built around a labour arbitrage business model, and a consequent lack of investment in the technological infrastructure of the call centre and the professionalization of its agents. To improve support for agents, we prototyped and deployed technologies designed to pull performance data from the call centres' existing technological infrastructure and provide near real-time feedback to agents and supervisors [2].

Through the process of integrating our technology prototypes with the infra- structure of the call centres, we discovered that the problem of data availability, accuracy, and relevancy (by which we mean aggregated and visualized to suit the purposes of a particular task at hand) was far more pervasive that we had initially assumed. This speaks to what Martin et al. [7] describe as a more general problem of implementation of procedure and practice through technology, particularly how this problem becomes vexing in a Business Process Outsourcing organization. Mostly because the organization designs its technological and organizational infrastructure around the imperatives of reducing cost to minimum terms and demonstrating value to the client organization through standardized productivity measures.

In this paper we want to focus on what we learnt about the practices of cap- turing, aggregating, and presenting data, and how they reflect the operation's overall concern with "reporting upstream." We then discuss some of the emergent consequences of this approach to data management, with a focus on the tensions that arise from the prioritising of different data needs within the call centre, in terms of granularity, aggregation, accuracy, and availability.

2 Work Structure and Infrastructure of Observed Outsourced Contact Centres

The type of call centres that we focused on in our ethnographic studies are outsourced customer contact centres for large telecommunications companies (the client organisations) who provide standard customer account management services (billing inquiries, adding or removing services from the contract, etc.) and often also some level of technical support (troubleshooting software and hardware problems). Incoming calls are managed through a phone switch that receives calls from one or more queues (which typically correspond to options selected by a customer through an Interactive Voice Response system) and distributes them to available agents.

Individual agents are logged into a phone switch that determines their "state" through a series of auxiliary codes (some of which the agents can select manually to put themselves in a particular state). An agent can therefore appear as "available" in the system and in a queue to receive incoming calls on a first-come first-serve basis, or "on a call," "on hold," "on a break," as having transferred a call to a different number, etc. Throughout any given shift in the call centre, all phone activity is logged, which means that there is a record of how much time any agent has spent in any given state and when.

This is one of the core mechanisms through which the call centre generates the data and the metrics, which are used to measure and report on its operational activities, and are generally referred to as Key Performance Indicators (KPIs). So, for example, the time the agent spends on the phone in conversation with a customer ("Talk Time") may be combined with the time the agent spends writing up the outcome of the phone call after it is finished ("After Call Work") and the time the agent keeps the customer on hold ("Hold Time") to create a metric that represents the overall time needed to handle that customer on that occasion ("Handle Time"). This metric can then be averaged over the time of a work shift, or week, or month of answered calls ("Average Handle Time").

The performance expectations of an outsourced call centre are typically defined by a Service Level Agreement (SLA), which is part of the service contract signed with the client organization. The call centre as a whole is expected to keep their aggregate average KPI values within the thresholds (or upper and lower threshold values) specified in the SLA—agents are therefore in turn expected to manage their phone calls so that their own average values fall within those thresholds as well. Typically, individual agents are grouped into teams of 10–15 workers to which supervisors are assigned from whom they receive periodic (weekly and monthly) feedback on their performance. Supervisors in turn report to Operations Managers, who are responsible for groups of 10–15 supervisors. This organizational hierarchy is designed to ensure control and supervision of a "floor" that may total 800–900 agents in some of the larger call centres.

Apart from the telephone switch data described above, the call centre also generates a large amount of "qualitative" data, which pertains more directly to the content of the interactions between agents and customers over the phone. The audio of all phone calls coming into the call centre is recorded. On top of that, a video screen capture of the agent's desktop is recorded for a subset of calls along with the audio. A sample of the total calls recorded for each agent is listened to— either by a supervisor, a quality assurance manager, or a member of the client organization—coded, and scored to produce a Quality Score. A small subset of the customers who call on any given day are also called back and asked to respond to a Customer Satisfaction Survey (CSAT). Like the phone switch data, Quality Scores and CSAT scores are initially associated to individual agents and then aggregated to produce overall performance metrics for the call centre as a whole.

To give an idea of the overall amount of data that is generated, we can say that in the type of call centres we observed, an agent may take up to 60–70 calls in an 8 or 10 h shift and that the number of agents for a single call centre (which may only be one of many operating on behalf of any given customer) is in the hundreds. And it is important to understand that while the core mission of a call centre is to provide assistance to customers, the logged data, that is the by-product of the interactions between customers and agents, is what is at the heart of the interaction between the client organization and the service provider, and having and presenting the right data is therefore a key operational concern.

3 How is Data Used in the Call Centre?

The actual technical infrastructure through which data is managed can vary slightly, but typically an outsourced services provider that manages customer contact centres will have a centralized Enterprise Data Warehouse. This warehouse collects all of the phone switch and qualitative data from various centres. The source of this data is a point that varies as well. For some functions within the call centre the data is pulled directly from the phone switch, and for others it is pulled from the data infrastructure of the client organization.

In the case of data coming from phone switches, it is important to note that the time logs of agent states or activities assigned to individual auxiliary codes are the raw data from which the Key Performance Indicators (KPIs) need to be calculated (as describe above in the case of Average Handle Time (AHT), which is the sum of a number of individual auxiliary codes divided by the number of calls over an interval of time). This means two things: (a) data as it is produced is not necessarily in itself "readable" or inherently meaningful; (b) given the sheer amount of data involved, producing readable data at any particular level of granularity or aggregation that might be relevant for a specific person or purpose at a specific point in time is not trivial in terms of time, computational cost, and infrastructure requirements.

In the point of view of the outsourced call centre provider, these and other factors lead to a fluid, non-homogeneous environment that is difficult to support with a general, technical solution for all customers. This results in the creation of many ad-hoc processes, e.g. reporting the current KPIs that agents need to focus on (these can change from month to month), checking the adherence of the agents' tracked status to their individual schedule (there are many exceptions that change from site to site), and upstream reporting. For all the flexibility that these ad-hoc processes provide, they lack scalability, reusability, and automation, often resulting in a fair amount of work to maintain and adapt to new needs.

The amount of work involved in these ad-hoc processes is tolerated (and often considered necessary) because periodic performance data is the key output for the service provider. This is how they communicate to the client organization how successfully they are in fulfilling the Service Level Agreement and often the basis for how the call centre is compensated for their work.

Based on our observations of call centre work and management, we can describe three fundamental uses of the data, each of which has its own criteria to meaningfully aggregate and represent or visualize the data:

- Real-time or near real-time monitoring of agent activity and overall operational status of inbound call activity;
- Agent performance management and feedback (including performance reviews, coaching, and calculation of compensation);
- Upstream reporting at various levels (agent team to call centre leadership, call centre to central operational management, service provider to client organization).

3.1 Real-Time Monitoring of Agent Activity and Metrics

The real-time or near real-time monitoring of phone switch and other types of data is done mostly to identify emergent and potentially problematic outlying situations. An example of this would be an agent who has been on a call for a very long period of time or not at their workstation when they should be.

In order to monitor for any of these situations, managers within the call centre typically have access to live or near real-time visualizations of switch data, in the form of tables that display the switch data for each agent and each auxiliary code that is being logged. With these tables managers can spot any obviously outlying situations. However, it should be noted that due to the large variation in what is a 'problematic' situation (in terms of both the values for a similar metric or even the metric itself), the support for locating these situations is minimal. Managers are required to do a visual scan of the table periodically. This ad-hoc approach to detecting 'problematic' situation is an example of a hidden inefficiency and creates new organizational issues. Most notably, there is a need to determine how much time should be devoted to the real-time monitoring of switch data and by whom. We observed several cases of agents who were on a particularly long and difficult phone call asking for assistance without waiting for someone to notice the abnormally long talk time on the switch monitor. Another aspect that should be noted is that this live switch data does not provide a longitudinal view or aggregate value in any way, and therefore is not useful in analysing performance trends.

Another example of near real-time monitoring can be found in the case of a metric that is generally referred to as "schedule adherence." Schedule adherence represents the adherence of the agents' tracked status, as detected through the phone switch, to their individual schedule. To give an example of how this works: an agent is scheduled to take his or her 10 min break at 11:00 am, but they are on a call with a customer until 11:02. At 11:02 they finish the call and put themselves in the auxiliary status for "break." They take their 10 min break and come back at 11:12. At this point they are 4 min out of adherence (2 min at either end of the 10 min break). This can be calculated automatically by matching the logs from the phone switch with the "expected" values as entered in a scheduling system. What cannot be detected automatically is whether any time "out of adherence" can be considered legitimate or not (the terms of which are usually defined in the SLA). In the case of the example above, being on a call with a customer may be considered a legitimate reason to deviate from schedule, and the 4 out of adherence minutes can be treated as an exception that will not be counted against the overall adherence metric.

An interesting feature of this is that in many of the call centres we observed there was no established or firmly enforced procedure for communicating exceptions, it was mostly or entirely done ad-hoc. They can be communicated by e-mail on a piecemeal basis, or collected on a paper roster by a supervisor who then e-mails a list of exceptions to workforce management, and keeping track of exceptions effectively depends on how prompt agents are in communicating them to their supervisors, assuming they remember to do so in the first place. One net result of this is that workforce analysts actually spend a considerable amount of time chasing down unreported exceptions. This requires a manual examination of adherence reports for individual agents, which display a time-stamped sequence log of agent auxiliary codes and whether each entry in the log is consistent with the schedule or not. Unreported inconsistencies between the log and the schedule can then be chased down with agents and supervisors to determine whether they fall under the terms of the SLA or not. This is a time consuming process which is difficult to automate because not all legitimate exceptions correspond to a specific auxiliary code—it is common practice, for example, to have generic auxiliary codes for a number of "unavailable" or "away from work-station" conditions which do not need to be differentiated for reporting purposes.

3.2 Agent Performance Management and Feedback

Agent performance management and feedback has two broad goals: to provide agents with the right level of "situational awareness", i.e. an understanding of their ongoing performance within the broader context of the operations of the call centre as a whole; and to provide the right motivation and performance related incentives to employees. Coaching sessions between agents and their direct supervisors typically take place every week, when supervisors review the ongoing performance of an agent (both with respect to the qualitative and quantitative metrics they are assessed on) and may provide specific goals and objectives for the agent to attain, as well as practical advice on how to get there.

Agents themselves generally have limited independent access to up-to-date and detailed data about their own performance, and we have addressed this issue and its consequences in some detail in a previous publication [3]. They do typically have access to a scorecard like the one shown in Fig. 1.

The scorecards give the agents an overview of their KPIs at a level of aggregation, which may or may not be relevant from the agents' point of view (for example, for the purpose of understanding how their compensation will be calculated or how far they are from achieving a performance based compensation target).

There are multiple reasons for the call centre to limit agent access to data, even if that data may very well be relevant to their everyday requirements. In the first instance there is a cost in terms of infrastructure and development that may be difficult to justify in a business model that is basically grounded in labour arbitrage and optimization of overhead costs. Part of that cost may actually be tied to licensing fees required to access and visualize switch data on individual workstations. On top of that, many call centres, rightly or wrongly, do not want to provide agents with easy access to data that may either distract them from their core activity of managing customers over the phone or indirectly encourage them to "work to the numbers"—i.e. leverage their understanding of the performance assessment and compensation mechanisms in order to hit the highest compensation rates without necessarily providing the best value to their organization [3]—if not outright game the system. In other instances the availability of performance data is controlled by the client organisation and the service provider can only pull the data at a predefined interval, e.g. once a day.

Whatever the reasons for limiting access to performance data within the call centre at the agent level (by which we mean both that the data is not directly accessible to the agents, and that where it is accessible it is not necessarily aggregated and visualized at the relevant level), the fact is that there are emergent needs for that data, and as we shall discuss in the following section, those needs are often addressed using data and systems that were put in place for different purposes.

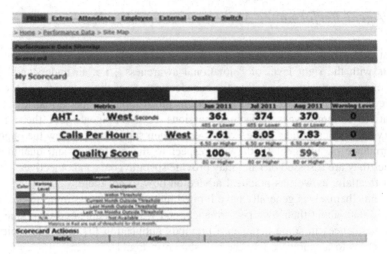

Fig. 1   Agent performance score card with KPI values displayed on a rolling 30 day average

3.3 Upstream Reporting

What should emerge quite clearly from the previous discussion of the organizational set-up of an outsourced call centre is that the measured performance of the call centre as a whole is quite literally the aggregate performance of all its agents. And given the number of levels in the organizational hierarchy (from agent, to team, to operations management, to call centre management, to multi-site client account management), it was no surprise to learn that there is quite a lot of reporting going on, and most of it upstream. Putting aside the agents themselves, who are at least spared the burden of having to create reports of their own performance by their supervisors (although as we have seen this also means they do not typically have access to data about their own performance), everybody else has to produce regular reports about their own area of responsibility.

This is the mechanism of performance management and accountability in the call centre—data is progressively aggregated and pushed upstream so that each level of the management chain can demonstrate that they are meeting their own performance targets to the managers above them, and hopefully performance issues that may have an impact on the call centre as a whole are caught and managed somewhere along the way.

It is a mechanism that also indirectly addresses a potentially costly problem for the call centre. In this paper we have discussed at length how telephone switch data is handled, because it is critical and because it is highly present in the call centre's everyday operations. But switch data is by no means the only kind of data—we have also talked about quality assessment data, customer survey data, scheduling and attendance data, payroll data, etc. All these different types of data are captured, stored and visualized through a number of different information systems, some perhaps proprietary to the client organization, some legacy, some off the shelf, some developed in-house by the outsourced service provider. Integrating these different sources of data at the infrastructure level is a cost that most outsourced service providers cannot afford. It is expensive as a development project in itself, and it would require costly and frequent adaptation and modification to provide everybody access to the requisite, integrated data.

Distributing the responsibility and the task of aggregating the data for particular purposes across the various levels of management means that the organization can get away with not having an integrated solution for handling all its data requirements. However, it also means that where data requirements emerge that had not been anticipated, or are not considered strategically important enough to devote an organizational process or information system to the task, people have to come up with their own solutions and workarounds.

In the following section, we will provide some examples of emergent data requirements, the sometimes less than ideal compromises used to meet those requirements, and ultimately the impact this problem had on our attempts to engage the business in research and innovation.

4 Practical Compromises in Data Management and Availability

In the previous section we outlined several of the ways in which data was designed to be used in the call centre. Within these designed uses, there were still aspects that were ad-hoc due to the fluidity of business requirements and non-homogeneity of the different call centres operated by the service provider. In this section we outline some of the emergent appropriations of these systems to solve new emergent problems within the call centre.

4.1 Detecting Agents Who Cheat

Live switch data can also help call centre management spot agents who are attempting to "game" the system to their advantage. An example of this was observed in call centres that pay their agents at hourly rates, regardless of the actual time spent on the phone with customers. The way agents would "game" the system was to continuously switch themselves in and out of available status to receive a phone call. Every time they did this, the phone switch would place them at the back of the queue to receive incoming phone calls. If used judiciously, this trick could effectively allow agents to go through an entire shift without taking any call whatsoever. The interesting feature of this example is that it would be relatively easy to detect it "indirectly" by looking at different representations of the data. An agent that takes no calls over a shift will have an average handle time that will not even compute for that shift, as it would have to divide by zero calls. However, an agent that takes one or two calls over a shift may have a relatively normal looking average handle time value for that shift, in which case the revealing metric would be the number of calls per hour or total calls taken over the shift.

This, while seemingly straightforward, reveals itself to be problematic in practice for a specific organizational reason, which has a direct consequence on the way the relevant data is routinely managed and made available: a call centre that pays agents through a flat rate as opposed to some productivity based mechanism is less likely to focus on metrics that directly relate to any individual agent's productivity, or if they do, they are unlikely to look at them at the right level of granularity. In other words, they will not routinely generate reports that show average values for talk time or calls per hour over a single shift (more likely they will for a period of a week, or on a rolling 30 day average), and may not have easy access (not to mention the time and willingness) to the tools to generate a daily report for the relevant metrics.

Since it is not easy to detect this behaviour, we observed call centre workforce management staff appropriating the switch monitor to detect agents "gaming" the system. This system is not designed for this use and does not provide a "record" of agents with revealing performance metrics, it does however provide the opportunity to observe agents switching themselves in and out of the available queue in real-time. As this emergent need had not been designed for, the call centre workers developed an ad-hoc solution. This introduces the identical practical problem as before, since this ad-hoc solution requires constant monitoring of the system by someone—the trade off between time and effort versus gain becomes very difficult to measure.

4.2 Providing Agents with Useful Performance Feedback

As already mentioned, supervisors in a call centre typically manage a team of 10–15 agents. While they may have different roles or responsibilities (i.e. specialize in dealing with specific queues or categories of problems), the key reason for dividing the workforce up into teams is to enforce an appropriate level of performance management. Supervisors therefore have two key responsibilities: coach, monitor, and report on the performance of their agents; and provide assistance in handling calls and customer issues when necessary.

As we discussed earlier in the paper, the level of access that the agents get to their own performance data varies greatly from place to place. In some call centres, Information Management Systems available to agents may provide access to live switch data, which allows them to see for how long they have been in any particular "state" (e.g. on a call, waiting for a call, unavailable, etc.). Because performance targets for agents (and for the call centre as a whole) are expressed as average values over some period of time (which typically corresponds to a pay period), live switch data does not give agents intelligible feedback about their ongoing performance with respect to their goals. The problem is that the reports or scorecards (see Fig. 1 for an example) with aggregated data the agents are typically provided with do not provide a very "dynamic" view of their own performance—they are updated irregularly, and always provide the same "view" of the data (for example, KPI values displayed on a thirty day rolling average).

Average KPI target values or thresholds for most agents do not change much from day to day, as they are written into the Service Level Agreement between the client organization and the outsourced service provider. However, there are two exceptions to this that create emergent data needs that agents and supervisors have to manage themselves.

The first exception arises from the optimization of agents' productivity, some agents work on more than one phone queue, each one of which corresponds to a different category or level of assistance (for example, providing support for both mobile phone and desktop computer products). These queues may have different target KPI values, and therefore the agents may have individual KPI targets that "shift" dynamically depending on how many calls they take of each type. This has the effect to render whatever tools are available to agents useless, as they were not designed with this in mind and can only show one set of target values (causing wildly inaccurate data to be displayed). This creates the need for supervisors to improvise solutions in order to communicate performance metrics to agents.

The second exception emerges from the fact that agents, irrespective of what the general target values for KPIs are within the call centre, are often given interim goals by their supervisors on a weekly basis. These interim goals are typically agreed to in coaching sessions with supervisors and designed to provide realistic and attainable goals in the short term, in particular for agents who are underperforming.

In practice this means that while agents are usually aware of what their individual targets are, it is harder for them to know where they are, in their own performance, with respect to those targets at any particular point in time. From the agents' point of view, this is not an issue that directly concerns their ability to provide assistance to customers over the phone. But because the organization is concerned with keeping its metrics within the parameters defined by the SLA, the agents do experience a certain level of direct (through their supervisors) and indirect (through compensation mechanisms that are at least in part performance-based) pressure to keep their KPIs within the expected values.

It falls upon the supervisors therefore to ensure that the agents have the right level of awareness of their ongoing performance. As mentioned earlier, there currently is no information system dedicated to providing agents with relevant performance data in a timely fashion [3] in call centres. Moreover, the subset of KPIs that might be relevant to a particular agent or team of agents is likely to be spread across a variety of different information systems that capture the data from a variety of sources.

Pulled from CCPM   Custom
                                                                                  formulas

	Specialist	ID	Calls(#)	Actual	Goal	Goal	Weight	GOAL +/-
5		1045213	740	424.25	537.56	126.71	100	113.31 Seconds
6		944804	590	429.02	540.39	125.96	100	111.37 Seconds
7		502799	520	486.75	532.88	109.48	100	46.13 Seconds
8		348131	969	497.59	536.63	107.85	100	39.04 Seconds
9		310447	1159	499.34	535.79	107.3	100	36.45 Seconds
10		947278	699	521.94	536	102.7	100	14.06 Seconds
11		1021181	771	527.64	535.85	101.56	100	8.21 Seconds
12		926146	219	542.29	529	97.55	67.74	-13.29 Seconds
13		1026372	479	599.42	529	88.25	100	-70.42 Seconds
14		989935	695	610.68	529	86.62	100	-81.68 Seconds
15		651397	845	624.41	536.27	85.88	100	-88.14 Seconds
16		973655	114	853.08	574.47	67.34	100.00 TOT_MET RC ACTL	-278.61 Seconds
17	Total	-	7800	6,616.42	6,452.85	97.53%	-	-163.57 Seconds
18			Total	# of Specialist	# of Green Specialist		% Team Green	0 Seconds
19				11.6774			7 59.94%	

Fig. 2   Custom pivot table showing agent average handle time values and percentage to goal

For example, in one call centre we observed that a supervisor needed to provide his agents with performance feedback for the following KPIs: value points (an arbitrary metric that assigns points that are used to calculate bonuses and provide a normalized ranking of agent performance); calls per hour (CPH); average handle time (AHT); customer satisfaction survey scores; and percentage of calls transferred. Of these metrics, three (value points, CPH, and AHT) could be pulled from a single information system the supervisor had ready access to, one (customer satisfaction survey scores) was available on a separate, client proprietary system, and the final one (calls transferred) was on a system the supervisor did not have access to at all, meaning he relied on his operations manager to forward the relevant data to him on a daily basis.

To make the data more relevant and accessible to the agents, the supervisor decided to create a series of custom pivot tables in Excel with custom formulas that cover each metric into a percent to goal value, colour coded red or green to provide immediate visual feedback on whether the values are within the thresholds or not. Figure 2 shows an example of the Custom Pivot Table.

The supervisor was then able to share the tables with his team, either by forwarding them through an internal chat client (if he felt it was urgent to bring the metrics to the attention of the agents), or by posting them on a shared team home page for the agents to access at their discretion.

While what was described above may seem like a relatively routine operation (and well within the expected responsibilities of a supervisor), it nevertheless is a less than ideal compromise from the supervisor's point of view. It leaves each agent at the mercy of their supervisor for information on their performance. More critically, the entirely manual operation of pulling data from various systems, pasting it into a spreadsheet and forwarding the information to the team, only creates a static snapshot of the data at a particular point in time, when the goal in fact is to provide agents with feedback about their *ongoing* performance. In other words, the entire operation needs to be repeated every time a supervisor wants to provide agents with an update on their ongoing performance.

4.3 Introducing Technological Innovation

These different observations about the data needs of the call center, particularly the deficit in communicating performance goals and progress between agents and their supervisors, led us to propose an intervention. The two goals for our system were to give better performance awareness mechanisms to agents and to give a more responsive channel of communication between agents and their supervisors.

Our initial effort was in providing the agents with a responsive, real-time visualization of their current performance with respect to their KPIs. This is detailed in a previous publication [3]. Our follow-up effort was to provide supervisors and their agents with a flexible infrastructure through which they could launch games and competitions that could be more responsive to both the needs of call centre and the more fluid needs of individuals [2].

One of the key objectives of our project was to provide much more responsive data to agents and supervisors. To realize this goal and deploy a tool to accomplish our goals required a significant amount of interaction with both the IT staff of various call centres as well as the developers for the service provider. This was necessary to understand how our tool would fit into the overall ecosystem and what capabilities needed to be developed by all interested parties. Trying to fit our tool within the existing infrastructure and obtaining the data with the required accuracy and timeliness that we required for our real time applications, turned out to be next to impossible. In some cases the infrastructure could not handle the load of providing real time reports of the data. In other cases the data was simply not made available by the client organizations in anything approaching real time. In the cases where our tool eventually was deployed the amount of effort required of the IT staff to provide near real time data was in the order of six to eight months.

Through these interactions with this arm of the organization and the detailed interrogation of the infrastructure through trying to deploy within it, we gained a much deeper insight into the reasons for the numerous improvised solutions that we encountered. We gained insight into how the data takes time to validate due to the imperfect and sometimes contradictory nature of the instruments used to capture the data. How the data's accuracy was negotiated and validated between the service provider and their client; which in turn impacted the rhythm that it was made available; and how changes to the different systems were prioritized. We often found that the IT staff and development staff were running at full capacity to keep up with the small set of emergent needs that arise for just communicating around the SLA with the client.

Through this process we learnt more about the call centre operation and policies than we did about the efficacy of our tool. The lessons that we learnt often represented limitations and barriers. Interestingly, and informatively, these are the same limitations that the call centre agents, supervisors, and managers also operate under. Ultimately, where our experiments and deployments were somewhat successfully completed, it was mostly because we found ways to improvise solutions to the barriers and limitations that we encountered, rather than by directly addressing the weakness in the technology or infrastructure.

5 Conclusion

In our initial investigations of call centres we observed many ad-hoc solutions to emergent performance data management problems in call centres. It was when we ourselves had to interrogate the infrastructure in which workers encountered, developed, and used these tools that we came to understand more about why they existed, and how addressing them was unlikely to be a simple matter of introducing technological innovations targeted at the problems revealed by the ethnographic studies. The way in which the emergent needs of workers and their supervisors are handled, sometimes in spite of the infrastructure, illuminates their problems and priorities. If an organisation believes that developing an ad-hoc solution, be it a tool or process, to a problem is merited and takes the time to build it, this is significant. The overall infrastructure that is provided gives insight into how management perceives the work of agents and supervisors and how they weigh these needs with their needs for upstream communication.

Thus, the infrastructure is a clear representation of the priorities of the organization as a whole. In our experience, it seems easy for management to forget that the lower priority items of workers must be given a degree of priority as time progresses or this functionality will suffer from starvation of resources. For these call centres the infrastructure that was developed shows a clear imbalance of functionality and support for upstream communication. This is understandable when situated within our other knowledge of call centre workings, as service providers have an important obligation to clearly provide upstream communication to the client organization.

Through this lens we can now provide answers to questions that vexed us at the beginning of the study. Data, that according to common sense should be captured, stored, and be made available in real time is not necessarily available in real life. This is because this capability is simply not important for the construction of reports for upstream reporting, nor is it critical to solving customer needs. It is however, critical information to provide to workers to understand their performance within the constraints given to them. Data is not often in the format one needs for your application or emergent need since they are logged according to the very specific needs of different applications.

Robust, reusable solutions to capturing data simply do not exist in this organization due to a business model based on labour arbitrage and low margins. Data is not always correct and sometimes even clearly wrong, but this is not visible or deemed important into an application or process that makes use of them. Applications that may be useful to some actors, may not be authorized by managers because that would provide those actors with access to data that the managers do not want those actors to have access to. Sometimes this is due to an aforementioned problem of data accuracy, if a new application is now displaying and using data at an earlier time in the process this creates problems by having to validate the data earlier, sometimes even at a lower granularity.

Throughout the course of our technology innovation project with the outsourced service provider, we acquired a rich understanding of the situated practices of the operational part of the organization through observation. Where the practical constraints of the research project did not allow us to observe the whole organization (and indeed assuming that the priorities, implicit or explicit, that apply to infrastructure and technology development and deployment would be directly observable in action at any other level of the organization), a hands on interrogation of their infrastructure through prototype development and integration provided an additional level of insight into the relationship between the business model, the organizational hierarchy, and the situated problems experienced by the call centre agents and managers we observed. This insight may turn out to be more valuable than the technology products that were ultimately developed and deployed, which essentially are more technologically sophisticated workarounds to the ones we originally described. That is, this value will be realised only if the organization itself gains awareness of the real impact of the strategic choices in technological infrastructure, research, and development. Defined and constrained as they may be by the business model and the routine work of its operations, they are also (perhaps unwittingly) constrained by the cost of those choices in terms of time lost, relative accuracy of its productivity measures, and ultimately quality of work experience for its employees.

References

1. Bourne J, Murray E, Iannone J, Keren S, McLean N, Bourke M, Fama J, Watson J, Nies JG, Lverly T (2008) Systems and methods for workforce optimization and integration, US published patent application 20080181389, July 2008
2. Castellani S, Hanrahan B, Colombino T, Grasso A (2013) Game mechanisms for production environments. In: CHI 2013 workshop on designing gamification: creating gameful and playful experiences, Paris, France, 27 April 2013
3. Colombino T, Castellani S, Grasso A, Willamowski J (2012) Agentville: supporting situational awareness and motivation in call centres. In: Proceedings of the 10th international conference on the design of cooperative systems, Marseille, France, May 29–June 1 2012
4. Cooper K (2008a) Performance motivation systems and methods for contact centers, US granted patent 7,412,402, August 2008

5. Ibrahim R, L'Ecuyer P, Regnard N, Shen H (2012) On the modeling and forecasting of call center arrivals. In: Laroque C, Himmelspach J, Pasupathy R, Rose O, Uhrmacher AM (eds) Proceedings of the 2012 winter simulation conference
6. Mehrotra V, Fama J (2003) Call center simulation modeling: methods, challenges, and opportunities. In: Chick S, Sanchez PJ, Ferrin D, Morrice DJ (eds) Proceedings of the 2003 winter simulation conference, pp 135–143
7. Martin D, O'Neill J, Randall D, Rouncefield M (2007) How can I help you? call centres, classification work and coordination. In: Computer supported cooperative work, vol 16. Springer, Heidelberg, pp 231–264
8. O'Neill J, Castellani S, Roulland R, Juliano C, Dai L, Hairon N (2011) From ethnographic study to mixed reality: a remote collaborative troubleshooting system. In: Proceedings of the 2011 ACM conference on computer supported cooperative work (CSCW), Hangzhou, China, 19–23 March 2011
9. Saeed KA, Grover V, Kettinger WJ, Guha S (2011) Organisational interventions and the successful implementation of customer relationship management (CRM) system projects. The database for advances in information systems, vol 42, no 2

User and Group Behavior in Computer Support for Collaborative Reflection in Practice: An Explorative Data Analysis

Michael Prilla

Abstract Although reflection in groups has been shown to be beneficial for many workplaces, there are little insights on how such collaborative reflection can be supported and how users apply the support in practice. This paper aims to diminish this lack by analyzing usage figures and qualitative information from four cases of using a tool supporting collaborative reflection. From the analysis, it derives means to describe individual user and group behavior as well as implications for the design and application of support for collaborative reflection in practice.

1 Introduction

Reflection is a common activity at work [1], e.g. when workers think about how to improve individual or common work, and when peers help each other to understand and change practice. Reflection can be understood as *going back to experiences, re-assessing them in the current context and learning from this for the future* [2], and has been described as a necessary *attitude* for nowadays' professional practice [3] or as a *mind-set* to be cultivated and spread in organizations [4]. As reflection depends on people's memories of experiences, which may be incomplete or blurred over time, and on the continuation of short-time reflection tools, can support reflection by providing data to reconstruct experiences and sustaining reflection outcomes between phases of reflection [5, 6].

It has been shown that groups reflecting together can create outcomes transcending individual reflection results by combining perspectives and implementing them on their own, which makes *collaborative reflection* attractive for change

M. Prilla (✉)
Information and Technology Management, University of Bochum, Bochum, Germany
e-mail: michael.prilla@rub.de

C. Rossitto et al. (eds.), *COOP 2014 - Proceedings of the 11th International Conference on the Design of Cooperative Systems, 27–30 May 2014, Nice (France)*, DOI: 10.1007/978-3-319-06498-7_18, © Springer International Publishing Switzerland 2014

processes in many workplaces [7–9]. Despite this potential of reflecting collaboratively, there are surprisingly little insights available supporting such collaborative reflection at work—existing work either focuses on individual reflection or on collaborative reflection in educational contexts. It needs to be understood that collaborative reflection differs from individual reflection: *People engaging in collaborative reflection have to make their experiences explicit, share and compare them with others and collaboratively create insights and ideas for future work* [6, 8, 10]. In contrast to individual reflection tools (e.g., [11]) this needs support for communication to exchange perspectives on experiences and discuss insights [12, 13]. However, there are little insights on how such support needs to be designed to support reflection groups. In addition, collaborative reflection on work differs from reflection in educational or research settings: In education and research, reflection can be understood and planned as an explicit part of learning or research processes, but in other work settings reflection neither follows directly from tasks conducted nor is a mandatory part of them, causing a shortage of time available for reflection. This means that although many workers recognize that reflection is helpful for them (e.g., [2, 3]), explicitly stepping back from the task and taking the time to reflect on it is not possible for them—the importance of other (primary) work tasks often leaves little time for explicit reflection. Reducing reflection to special settings like project debriefings [14] is no solution to this problem, as there are many other settings of collaborative reflection at work [6, 12], which cannot be covered by means like debriefings and solutions for them.

This paper aims to contribute to the few insights on tool support for collaborative reflection as described above by taking a closer look at the usage and resulting individual and group activities in a collaborative reflection tool. It analyses four case studies in different organizations with a total of 30 active users. From analysis of these studies, it describes insights on how people use tools for collaborative reflection and how groups work by using these tools. As a result, the paper describes means to characterize collaborative reflection tool usage and design.

2 Related Work: Collaborative Reflection and Tool Support

Besides *related work on collaborative reflection* in educational and research contexts research on collaborative reflection can also draw from existing work on collaborative work support such as sensemaking or group decision support. While overlaps with these concepts can be recognized easily, collaborative reflection differs from them in certain aspects. For example, work on *sensemaking* or *collective mind* [15, 16] emphasizes the need to collaboratively reach an understanding of past events, but sensemaking processes described in this work do not have a clear focus on deriving insights for future work, which is needed for reflection—otherwise reflection leads to common ground but not to change. Likewise, group decision support systems [17] are about exchanging perspectives and arriving at decisions in teams, but focus on the decision rather than other parts of collaboration such as reaching a common understanding [18]. Approaches of collaborative problem solving [19] use joint spaces to solve a problem, but have to deal with the problem that information known to all collaborators from the start tends to be followed more than information of individuals, resulting in a "shared information bias" [20]. Collaborative reflection, in contrast, needs exchange of experiences and critical discourse about members' perspectives to create a solution for the future.

Recent work takes up reflection as a topic for individual (e.g., [5, 21]) and group work (e.g., [6]), but does not analyze group behavior using such support. However, this work shows how supporting people to memorize and get back to experiences helps them learn about themselves [5, 6, 21] and that we need to differentiate reflection participants by interests in reflection activities (e.g. reporting experiences or commenting on them, [5]). On a methodological level, De Groot et al. [22], Fleck and Fitzpatrick [23] and Bjørn and Boulus [24] recently added analyses of collaborative reflection behavior among groups without technology support. This work shows that groups of reflection participants differ in their communication behavior in terms of being able to articulate problems and assumptions [24] and addressing each others' contributions in reflective communication [22]. It also shows how behavior and actions of individual reflection participants can influence the outcomes of reflection [23].

Concerning *tool support for reflection*, most tools proposed and evaluated in existing work primarily serve *individuals*, including learning diaries or portfolios [13, 25], tools to take pictures of events for later reminiscence or reflection [23] or capturing events with multimedia content and periodically reminding people of these events to foster reflection [5]. In line with our understanding of collaborative reflection as described above, by *collaborative reflection tool support* we mean tools that support activities such as reporting and sharing experiences, communicating about them and drawing conclusions together. However, among the few examples of such tools mentioned in literature are either generic tools such as shared whiteboards (e.g., [26]) or expert tools such as process model displays (e.g., [27]). To the knowledge of the authors, analyses of tools supporting collaborative reflection at work for different groups are not available. Given this lack and contrasting it with the potential of collaborative reflection at work, this paper aims to provide insights on the design and usage of collaborative reflection tools. It is aligned to research questions derived from the state of the art described above:

- How do people use tools supporting collaborative reflection at work?
- Which factors influence which types and situations of usage at work?
- How can we design tools supporting user groups in reflecting together at work?

3 Four Studies of Collaborative Reflection Support at Work

The Talk Reflection App was build to support workers in reflecting collaboratively on their communication and social interaction skills, which is a common and underrepresented learning problem [6]. The app is based on intensive research including ethnographic studies in different workplaces and participatory design workshops with potential users [6]. It was trialed in four different work settings.

3.1 The Talk Reflection App for Collaborative Reflection

Recognizing the lack of available tools to support such collaborative reflection, we built the Talk Reflection App as a prototype for tools of this kind. In our work, we found that workers recognize reflection as a valuable means to deal with stressful interactions, but that it was hard for them to find the time to reflect together, resulting in little improvements stemming from their reflection and in ideas from the few and brief collaborative reflection sessions not followed up on.

The Talk Reflection app supports the documentation of conversations and the articulation of individual and collaborative reflections on them by commenting on documented experiences. This, in line with related work [8, 10, 12, 13, 28], helps workers to explicate, share and reflect on experiences from conversations. The app supports multiple steps of collaborative reflection as described by [6]:

- **Creating experience reports**: The app supports users in documenting experiences by writing them down. This includes a description of the experience and personal reflections. Writing down experiences triggers individual reflection (e.g., [13]) and provides a basis to later remember the situation [6]. Figure 1 (left) shows a resulting report (no. 1) with a personal reflection annotated (2).
- **Sharing experience reports**: Experience reports remain private to users initially, but can be shared with others. Once they are shared, other users can find them as shown in Fig. 1 (right, no. 4). Sharing reports can be understood as asking others for comments on the experiences.
- **Reading shared experience reports**: Users can read shared experience reports as shown in Fig. 1 (left) and mark them for later reflection (no. 5). To make users aware of available reports, the app shows unread reports on its landing page and sends digests to users. Reading others' reports may be based on curiosity, but also on impression of interest and willingness to support others.
- **Commenting on experience reports**: To engage in reflection on shared experience reports users can create comments on shared reports as shown in Fig. 1 (left, 3). Comments may contain similar experiences of a user, suggestions for acting in the situation described or other reflective content. They may contain articulations of similar experiences, new perspectives or proposals for change.

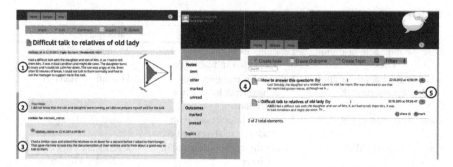

Fig. 1 The Talk Reflection App for collaborative reflection on social interactions

3.2 Four Cases of Support for Collaborative Reflection

The Talk Reflection App was used in four different cases to study the adoption and usage of tool support for collaborative reflection (see Table 1). In each of the cases, the focus of reflection was different, although all were closely related to social interaction and communication. The number of initial participants varied from 23 to 6 and the duration of studies varied from 32 to 63 days (see Table 2).

Cases 1 and 2 were conducted within the administration of two districts of a city in the UK, whose management wanted to support their employees in learning at work. **Case 1** included the interns working for the district for one year. Management wanted to support them in their new and oftentimes stressful experiences at work and to enable them to learn how to act in professional environments even after the internship. The interns knew each other from partly from introductory courses, but worked in different departments. **Case 2** featured participants from the same department in the two districts in order to enable workers to learn from each other beyond departmental boundaries, as they were doing similar work. Workers were located partly in the same buildings, and some knew each other. Thus, some of them had the opportunity to talk to each other frequently, but conversation opportunities across districts or with the overall manager were rare.

Case 3 was conducted with care staff in a UK care home dealing with residents suffering from dementia. In such homes medical aspects of care are covered by registered nurses, while staff doing the major part of care throughout the day is not highly educated. The manager wanted care staff to reflect on interactions with residents, relatives and other parties in order to increase service quality in the home.

Case 4 was conducted with physicians working in a German hospital. The participants worked on a neurological ward and dealt with emergency patients. Thus, they were highly educated and specialized in this work. The aim in Case 4 was to use reflection to support assistant physicians in learning about conversations with relatives, which is a stressful and important part of their work. In both cases, the participants worked together in the same unit and talked to each other every day.

Table 1 Cases of using the Talk Reflection App in practice

	Context	Objective(s)	Participants
Case 1	Public administration, UK	Learning about professional interaction in internships	22 Interns, 1 Manager
Case 2	Public administration department, UK	Support for merging two departments by practice reflection	11 Staff, 1 Manager
Case 3	Care home, UK	Improving interactions with residents, relatives and others	8 Staff, 1 Manager
Case 4	Hospital, GER	Improving conversations with relatives	4 Assistant Physicians, 2 Senior Physicians

Table 2 Usage figures for the cases, differentiated by items created by active users (first figure in cells) and items created by all users (second figure), including drop-outs after introduction

	Case 1	Case 2	Case 3	Case 4
Participants (active/all)	11/23	8/12	5/9	6/6
Duration (days)	32	32	63	49
Experience reports (active/all users)	15/26	45/51	12/15	19/21
Experience reports per user (active/all)	1.4/1.2	5.6/3.9	2.4/1.7	3.2/3
Experience reports per day (active/all)	0.5/0.8	1.4/1.6	0.2/0.2	0.4/0.4
Comments on experiences (active users)	35	53	18	28
Comments per experience documented	1.3	1	1.2	1.3
Comments per user (active users)	3.2	6.6	3.6	4
Comments per day (active users)	1.1	1.7	0.3	0.6

In all cases, at least one group member took responsibility for promoting and ensuring app usage. In Cases 1, 2 and 3 this was done by the respective managers and in Case 4 the two senior physicians took charge. It needs to be noted that there were differences in spatial proximity between the user groups: while in Cases 3 and 4 (and for some participants also in Case 2) the participants could talk to each other every day during work, in Case 1 (and for many participants also in Case 2) participants worked in different buildings and departments and thus communication was mainly possible via the tool.

3.3 Methodology, Tools and Data

For all of the four cases we used a similar scheme to run the studies. Before we introduced the app, we conducted a workshop with potential users of the tool to understand the needs of (collaborative) reflection in the respective organization and to create a frame for the study, including consulting on the possibilities to use the app in different work situations and to adapt it to the needs of the study partner. To introduce the app, we gathered the participants in a workshop and trained them to use it for collaborative reflection. For each case, we created a closed group in the app to enable them to share and discuss experiences only with participants of the test. During an introductory session the participants were asked to create accounts, to add experience reports to the app that described some of their recent experiences and to share the content. They were also asked to look at shared reports and create comments. Based on this, the additional features were walked through as well. Finalizing the training, we discussed with each group of participants questions on the usage and opportunities to use the app during work. Besides this introduction we did not impose any other constraint for using on the participants and left the way of using it to them and those responsible for the respective case.

To analyze the studies we used log files, content analysis and focus groups after the studies. Log files were used to analyze experience reports created, comments created and reports read according to their overall and average numbers. We complemented this usage analysis with qualitative information from two focus groups (Cases 2 and 4) and interviews in the other cases. To make sure to analyze only experience reports and comments containing reflective content, we used a coding scheme derived from [22, 23] to analyze whether content in the app was part of reflection and excluded non-reflective content. In particular, *documents* were excluded if we did not find traces of reflection in the document or comments on it (that is, if they did neither contain nor cause reflective content), while *comments* were judged per item. In addition, we found that some users had not used the app again after the introductory sessions without giving notice or reasons. We excluded the activities of these users and analyzed usage of the tools only for *active* users, who had *at least* created one document or comment after this session. Content of excluded users stayed in the data set, as others had commented on it. In the cleaned data set shown in Table 2, we only excluded a few content items but reduced the number of (active) users to 30 (as compared to 50 participants in total). Despite the loss in participants, this gives a better impression on how the app has been used for reflection. In addition, to cope with the different timespans in the cases (32 days in Cases 1 and 2 and 49 or 63 days in Cases 3 and 4 respectively), we calculated the average numbers of items created per day and the average number of items created per user in the table. We will mainly refer to the figures for active users unless mentioned differently.

3.4 Measuring (Collaborative) Reflection Activity in Tools

The lack of studies on tools to support collaborative reflection at work goes along with a *lack of measurements for analyzing collaborative reflection activity* in such tools. To cope with this lack, we combined means to analyze collaboration and insights from a literature analysis on collaborative reflection analysis in other contexts to create an own set of measurements for our analysis.

- **Adoption**: Collaborative reflection relies on participants well articulating experiences and sharing them with others [10, 13, 28, 29] as well as communicating about them, i.e. sharing their insights, perspectives and ideas to critically reflect on the experiences [6, 8, 30, 31]. Therefore, an initial measure of *adoption* of collaborative reflection tools can be found in the *number of experiences articulated* and shared as well as the *number of comments* made in the tool.

- **Activity**: For collaborative reflection to happen participants need to show interest in and give feedback on shared experiences articulated and shared with them [12, 22, 23, 32]. As a measure of such *collaborative activity* we therefore use the number of *experiences read by individuals* (measure of interest) and the *amount of shared experiences commented on* (measure of feedback given).
- **Quality**: In addition, *collaborative reflection quality* improves if participants engage in discussions rather than providing single comments (e.g., [22, 33]). The *average length of threads* created by comments in the Talk Reflection App was used to measure this quality (as also proposed by [34]), assuming that more items in a thread enable better discussions among participants.

These measures are related only to what happened in the tool, thus showing only digital reflection activity. We consider this view to be valuable as it shows the impact of the tool, especially for users who cannot talk to each other frequently or who cannot be present when others reflect face to face. Complementing this view with data on reflection outside tools on the same level of data quality would be valuable but creates an observer problem that we will tackle in further work.

4 Results: Usage of Reflection Support in the Cases

Concerning the **adoption and individual usage** of our app, Table 2 shows that most experiences were documented in Case 2, and that (despite a usage period twice as long) users in Case 3 produced least experience reports. Looking at the average figures shows that per user least reports were created in Case 1 (1.4), and that Cases 3 and 4 are in between (2.4 and 3.2 documents per user). Case 2 shows the highest daily productivity for experience reports (1.7 per day), Cases 1 and 4 (0.5 and 0.4) show about twice as much activity as Case 3 (0.2).

The figures for comments go along with the figures for documented experiences: Case 2 produced most comments (55 in total, 6.6 per user), while Case 3 created least comments (18). Case 2 was most active per day (1.7 comments), and in Case 1 users more frequently created comments (1.1 day) than in Cases 3 (0.3) and 4 (0.6). Looking at comments per report, however, we can see that Cases 1, 3 and 4 outperform Case 2, suggesting that overall there was more communication activity in these cases. It has to be mentioned that although the usage numbers look low (given the timespan) at first sight, one needs to understand that although stressful interactions create sustainable harm, they do not happen every day. The figures also suggest that Case 2 is a (positive) outlier[1] in terms of usage, and that the figures for the other cases represent average cases.

---

[1] It will be shown below that Case 2 is an outlier mainly because of massive activity of one user.

Table 3 Collaborative activity in the Talk Reflection App. To show the collaboration during the test, the table shows only data of *active users* in the cases

	Case 1	Case 2	Case 3	Case 4
Experience reports read	284	421	144	153
Experience reports read per active user	25.8	52.6	28.8	18.9
Experience reports read per day	12	14.3	2.4	3.1
Experiences commented on (percentage all)	21 (81 %)	23 (45 %)	11 (73 %)	18 (86 %)
Experience reports read per comment	8.1	7.8	8	4.7
Average length on threads	2.05	2.24	1,50	1,37
Threads including originator of experience	6 (29 %)	16 (70 %)	3 (27 %)	0 (0 %)

Table 2 also shows that between the groups there are differences in the frequency of experiences and comments created. We may therefore ask what caused these differences and whether they had an influence on collaborative reflection in the cases. Looking at such **collaborative reflection activity** (using measures as defined above, see Table 3) shows differences between the cases other than expected from the figures discussed above. *First*, while Case 2 is the most active case overall in terms of attention to experiences documented in the system (421 experience reports read in total) and an average length of communication threads of 2.24, the data also shows that Case 2 has low percentage of experiences being commented on (45 %): In Cases 1 and 4 the coverage of comments for documented experiences is twice as high (81 and 86 %). This suggests that in these cases there was a *different balance of interest* in content. In addition, it means that for Case 2 more than half of the documented experiences were not commented on, which may discourage users from sharing their experiences with others. *Second*, the cases differ in the average length of threads created by comments made on documented experiences. Cases 1 (2.05 comments per document commented on) and 2 (2.24) show longer threads than Cases 3 (1.5) and 4 (1.37). This indicates that reflective discussions were held more intensively in Cases 1 and 2. This may be explained by the spatial context of these cases: As described for the cases above, in Case 1 and (partly) Case 2 participants could not talk to each other face to face frequently, while this was possible for Cases 3 and 4. Therefore, users in Cases 1 and 2 may have seen more value in communicating via the tool. Participants of Case 4 approved this during the focus group by reporting that they had not created many comments but rather talked to each other directly. We can thus see that *spatial proximity of users* makes a difference in reflection tool usage.

We can state that the reflection group in Case 1 was *most active*, as it had a good coverage of documented experiences commented on and longer conversation threads. In contrast, the group in Case 2 also discussed intensively, but on a smaller percentage of experience reports. In Cases 3 and 4 users commented on many experiences, but discussions were shorter. In addition, for Cases 1–3 we see a similar number of read events per comment (about 8), while in Case 4 it took users to read more than three experiences less to create a comment (4.7). Differences in groups can therefore also be seen in the *responsiveness* to reports shared and in the *intensity of discussions*. They may affect the impact of collaborative reflection, as less communication lowers the chance to create insights together.

5 Analysis: Individual Roles and Group Characteristics

The discussions above show that our measures on experiences documented, comments created and shared experiences read help to describe and analyze reflection group behavior, but also that this does not fully explain group performance. Concerning **individual roles**, this raises the questions how the basic activities relate to each other in terms of groups using collaborative reflection tools. A Pearson correlation among all participants of the cases ($n = 30$) for these activities shows that there is a strong correlation ($r > 0.8$ for all pairs) between them (see Table 4).

The correlations suggest that for the average user the basic activities go along, meaning that the more one reads the more comments one makes etc. The diagrams of user activity in the cases (Fig. 2) shows good examples for this: for users such as U1.3, U2.1, U3.1 and U4.2 high figures for all activities can be found, while U1.4, U2.8 and U3.5 show how low figures for all activities.

Looking at individual behavior more closely reveals that there are other types of users, for whom the basic activities do not predict each other. Naturally, one would assume that users comment more than they document experiences, as there are more of opportunities to comment than difficult situations to write down, and that they read more experiences than they comment on, as usually not every read event will result in a comment (*#documented experiences* < *#comments* < < *#documents read*). As Fig. 2 shows, this shows for most users in the cases, but there are also users who created more content than they read (e.g., U4.1 and U4.6), who created more experience reports than comments (e.g., U2.1 and U3.1) or who showed high activity in creating content (documents for U4.1, comments for U4.6) despite little reading activity. The other way around, other users (e.g., U1.11, U3.4) show low activity in creating content but higher attention to shared content than others in their group. Looking at individual user behavior, we suggest four types of users for reflection support:

- **(Typical) Reflection participants**: For most users activity levels in creating experience reports, commenting and taking notice of shared reports (reading) go along. As a general pattern, increasing awareness for or activity in one of these activities is therefore likely to result in increase activity in general.
- **Documenters**: Some users mainly create experience reports, but create little or no comments (e.g., U4.1, U2.1 and U3.1—the latter created more documentations than comments). As one reason for this U4.1 told us that he had mainly wanted to share experiences that he found relevant for his colleagues, but did not see value in commenting on shared reports.

Table 4 Correlation of reflective activities in the studies (n = 30, all participants of all cases)

Pair	r	P
Experience reports created & comments created	0.919	<0.01
Experience reports created & experiences read	0.841	<0.01
Comments created and experiences read	0.815	<0.01

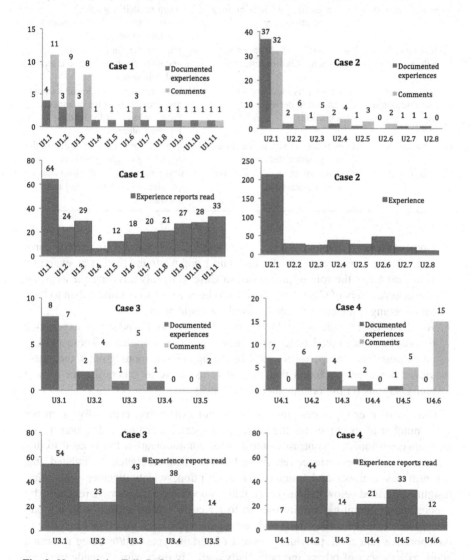

Fig. 2 Usage of the Talk Reflection App in the cases per active user and grouped by case. Documented experiences and comments created shown in the *upper* half of each quadrant, the number of documented experiences read is shown in the *lower* half of each quadrant

Table 5 Factors and interventions influencing group performance in reflection

Factor	Description	Intervention
Content creation and attention to shared content	Little content production, communication or attention to content harms performance	Motivating the creation of experience reports to motivate comments and read events
User type effects on group behavior	Specific roles may foster activity in a group, role division may reduce interaction	Foster activity of specific user types when needed (e.g., push documenters to also comment to push communication)
Critical mass for reflection	Users groups with little active users may fail in reflecting	Activate readers in groups by encouraging them to create reports and comments
Responsiveness and discussion activity	Low responsiveness and little discussion decrease impact of reflection	Make users aware of relevant content and prompt them for comments; create awareness for reading reports (interest)
Lead user push	Support for activity in the group, e.g. pushing discussions	Supporting dominant user effects in the beginning of group activity
Lead user flaws	Focusing attention too much on lead use activities	Limiting the focus on the lead user by pushing other content and users forward

- **Commenters**: Some users (e.g., U1.1, U2.3, U3.3 and U4.6) mainly commented on experience reports. In the focus group we found that, as an example, U4.6 had taken the role of an advisor in Case 4, mainly advising the assistant physicians. Users of Case 2 reported it had been easier to comment than to "get things going", meaning to get feedback on their reports.
- **Readers**: Users such as U1.11, U2.6, U3.4 and U4.4 read many experience reports but contributed little experience reports or comments. These participants thus form the periphery [35] in the app. From focus groups and interviews, however, we found that they were as active as others in face-to-face conversations on the documented experiences.

Our list of user types described above is not exhaustive, especially given the small number of examples for the latter three special user types. However, given that reflection tools (in contrast to most other communication tools) need to differentiate between experience reports and communication content articulated, this list provides a novel and unique user description, which together with other insights described below can help to provide support for collaborative reflection by supporting or inhibiting certain roles to foster collaborative reflection in a group (see Table 5). It also shows that inside or outside apps, each user type has a role in collaborative reflection, providing content of certain types and/or being informed about experiences of others and potentially active in discussions outside tools. In practice, of courses, roles are combined: we also found some users with aspects of two types, as described above.

Besides differences in user types, Fig. 2 also shows differences in the **group activity and performance**. Breaking discussion activity down to the participants in the groups, we can see from Fig. 2 that in Cases 2 and 4 more than half of the comments (U2.1, U4.6) and in Cases 2 and 3 more than two thirds of experience reports were created by one user (U2.1, U3.1). In the focus groups of Cases 2 and 4, this turned out to focus communication on these users: in Case 2 users told us it was hard to get feedback to own experiences, indicating communication was centered to reports created by U2.1; in Case 4 we were told that the presence of U4.6 had prevented some participants to create more comments. A participant from Case 3 reported that U3.1 had taken the role of being responsible for organizing reflection in the care home, which had resulted in her providing most of the content. These cases show how a *dominant user* may shape the structure of a group using collaborative reflection support tools, including positive (e.g., a push for activity) and negative (e.g., communication focus) consequences. The clarity of dominance in Case 2 (the activity of U2.1 is more than five times higher than other users' activity) explains the outlier position of Case 2 as discussed above—without counting in U2.1 the usage figures of Case 2 are similar to the other cases.

Concerning user types and homogeneity of the groups, we can see that in Cases 1 and 2 the group was more homogeneous (i.e. many users created documents and comments), while in Case 3 and especially in Case 4 user types were more heterogeneous, with a weight on creating comments in Case 3 (except U3.1) and a clear role division between commenting (U4.5, U4.6) and documenting experiences (U4.1, U4.3) as well as reading more (U4.2, U4.4, U4.5) or less (U4.1, U4.3, U4.6) in Case 4. Given these differences, we can identify three aspects describing participation in the technology-supported reflection groups in our cases:

- **Self-organized, broad reflection**: Case 1 shows the most homogeneous distribution of reflection activities among users. This can be interpreted as a self-organized reflection group without a clear leader, which discusses most experiences shared in the group intensively.
- **Lead user driven reflection**: Cases 2 and 4 show the strongest influences dominant users concerning documented experiences (Case 2) and comments (both cases). This creates a reflection group mainly focused on this user,
- **Reflection with separated roles**: Case 4 shows how participants of a reflection group can take different roles and thereby keep the group running with documenters 'feeding' commenters with content to comment on.

These differences in the groups' behaviors can also explain some differences in group performance. For example, the activity of the *dominant user* (U2.1) in Case 2 mainly caused the high percentage (70 %, see Table 3) of discussions in which the originator of an experience report was involved—U2.1 was involved as documenter *and* commenter in 13 of the 16 threads. However, the activity of U2.1 also resulted in a low percentage of experience reports created by other users commented on: among the 23 reports commented only three were not created by U2.1. This was also reported in the focus group of Case 2, in which people reported they felt others were less interested in their experiences due to a lack of comments as response to their reports. As a result, for successful usage of collaborative reflection support we need to *control dominance effects*. While the *role division* in Case 4 resulted in a high coverage of experience reports with comments, the figures also suggest that it has a negative effect on communication, as Case 4 has the lowest average length of threads. In a small groups with role division the originator of a report is often not part of the discussion group, resulting in a lack of a *critical mass of users* willing to discuss: In contrast to all other cases there was *no thread at all in Case 4 that involved the originator of an experience report* (see Table 3). This was also reported during the focus group, as users felt others were not willing to create comments.

6 Discussion: Implications for Socio-Technical Reflection Support

The analysis given above shows how groups using reflection tools differ from each other and which factors can explain these differences. These factors already consider environmental constraints: for example differences in spatial arrangement of participants in the cases most likely caused users in Cases 1 and 2 to communicate more in the app than users in Cases 3 and 4, who worked closely to each other and had many opportunities to talk to each other personally. Our insights—though preliminary—also allow an initial characterization of reflection groups and their participants to support such groups specifically:

- **Egalitarian reflection group**: Well-balanced group in terms of reports, comments and attention to shared content (main example Case 1, also Case 2 except lead user). Such groups show good collaborative reflection behavior, shortcomings can be found in the amount of reports created (as exemplified by Case 1).
- **Leader-based reflection group**: Seemingly very productive group driven by a dominant user (main example Case 2, but also Cases 3 and 4). Advantages are high amount of content and communication; the disadvantage is a focus on the dominant user and consequences for impact and motivation of others.
- **Polar reflection group**: A group with role division between commenters and documenters (main example Case 3). Advantages are higher certainties in reports and comments being created, resulting in higher coverage of reports with comments and better response rates. Disadvantages are low communication intensity and little overall impact on the group.
- **Underdeveloped reflection group**: In some groups, the reflection group characteristics may not be pronounced enough to support reflection (main example Case 3). This results in low communication and little acknowledgement of experience reports shared.

This differentiation overlaps with the three types of participation in collaborative reflection groups as described above. It explores these types deeper by discussing advantages, disadvantages and possible success of each model, including a fourth category describing a group setting in which reflection may not work.

As we illustrated, these different factors have positive and negative aspects on group performance—for example a dominant user may push activities in a reflection group, but may also reduce reflection quality. In addition, interventions concerning these factors may allow groups reflecting collaboratively to reduce disadvantages and benefit from certain advantages: For example, in underdeveloped groups it may be helpful to establish a leader to push reflection activity or in order to raise activity one might want to push polar groups more into egalitarian behavior by encouraging documenters to also comment. Table 5 shows an initial list of such factors as well as potentials for intervention.

Implementing collaborative reflection and applying the interventions as mentioned above is not only a matter of setting up reflection processes and supporting them by tools, but also of change in management (see also [33]). This means that in order to set reflection in practice there is a need to have one or more persons promoting reflection, being responsible for reflection in an organization and implementing it.

Besides these insights, our analysis showed that the activity we measured was not the only activity triggered by the use of the app—besides this, also a social practice of reflection among the group participants emerged where this was possible in terms of spatial arrangements. To understand collaborative reflection as it happens in practice also needs an understanding of these activities: Exploring them and combining them with the analysis of reflection in an app may give us a more comprehensive image of how reflection tools are used in practice and how we can design for socio-technical practices of collaborative reflection. Although difficult to achieve, as daily practice is hard to observe, this will be the next step of our work. Further work on understanding groups using collaborative reflection support may draw from our insights, characterization and interventions, but need to continue and adapt them. Such work needs further studies as presented here and may also benefit from qualitative analysis of the content created in apps.

Finally, besides an analysis as described in this paper, there is a need to analyze people not using tools supporting (collaborative) reflection. While this is more difficult in terms of accessing users, it may provide valuable insights for constraints to be met by such tools. Further work will need to take this into account.

References

1. Kolb DA (1984) Experiential learning: experience as the source of learning and development. Prentice-Hall Englewood Cliffs, New Jersey
2. Boud D (1985) Reflection: turning experience into learning. Kogan Page, London
3. Schön DA (1983) The reflective practitioner. Basic books New York

4. Reynolds M (1999) Critical reflection and management education: rehabilitating less hierarchical approaches. J Manage Educ 23(5):537–553
5. Isaacs E, Konrad A, Walendowski A, Lennig T, Hollis V, Whittaker S (2013) Echoes from the past: how technology mediated reflection improves well-being. In: Proceedings of the SIGCHI conference on human factors in computing systems, ACM, pp 1071–1080
6. Prilla M, Degeling M, Herrmann T (2012) Collaborative reflection at work: supporting informal learning at a healthcare workplace. In: Proceedings of the ACM international conference on supporting group work (GROUP 2012), pp 55–64
7. Dennis AR, George JF, Jessup LM, Nunamaker Jr JF, Vogel DR (1988) Information technology to support electronic meetings. MIS Q 12(4): 591–624
8. Hoyrup S (2004) Reflection as a core process in organisational learning. J Workplace Learn 16(8):442–454
9. Prilla M, Pammer V, Krogstie B (2013) Fostering collaborative redesign of work practice: challenges for tools supporting reflection at work. In: Proceedings of the European conference on computer supported cooperative work (ECSCW 2013)
10. Tigelaar D, Dolmans D, Meijer P, de Grave W, van der Vleuten C (2008) Teachers' interactions and their collaborative reflection processes during Peer meetings. Adv Health Sci Educ 13(3):289–308
11. Loo R, Thorpe K (2002) Using reflective learning journals to improve individual and team performance. Team Perform Manage 8(5):134
12. Daudelin MW (1996) Learning from experience through reflection. Org Dyn 24(3):36–48
13. Scott SG (2010) Enhancing reflection skills through learning portfolios: an empirical test. J Manage Educ 34(3):430–457
14. Kerth NL (2001) Project retrospectives. Dorset House, Shelburne
15. Crowston K, Kammerer EE (1998) Coordination and collective mind in software requirements development. IBM Syst J 37(2):227–245
16. Weick KE (1995) Sensemaking in organizations. Sage Publications Inc, Thousand Oaks
17. Dennis AR, George JF, Jessup LM, Nunamaker Jr JF, Vogel DR (1988) Information technology to support electronic meetings. MIS Q 591–624
18. Power DJ, Sharda R (2009) Decision support systems. Springer handbook of automation. Springer, Heidelberg, pp 1539–1548
19. Roschelle J, Teasley S (1995) The construction of shared knowledge in collaborative problem solving. Computer supported collaborative learning. Springer, Heidelberg, pp 69–97
20. Lockhorst D, Admiraal W, Pilot A, Veen W (2003) Analysis of electronic communication using 5 different perspectives. In: Proceedings Symposium conducted at the 30th Onderwijs Research Dagen (ORD), Kerkrade, Netherlands, 2003
21. Peesapati ST, Schwanda V, Schultz J, Lepage M, Jeong S, Cosley D (2010) Pensieve: supporting everyday reminiscence. In: Proceedings of the SIGCHI conference on human factors in computing systems, ACM, pp 2027–2036
22. De Groot E, Endedijk MD, Jaarsma ADC, Simons PR-J, van Beukelen P (2013) Critically reflective dialogues in learning communities of professionals. Stud Continuing Educ 0(0):1–23
23. Fleck R, Fitzpatrick G (2010) Reflecting on reflection: framing a design landscape. In: Proceedings of the 22nd conference of the computer-human interaction special interest group of Australia on computer-human interaction, ACM, pp 216–223
24. Bjørn P, Boulus N (2011) Dissenting in reflective conversations: critical components of doing action research. Action Res 9(3):282–302
25. Forneris SG, Peden-McAlpine C (2007) Evaluation of a reflective learning intervention to improve critical thinking in novice nurses. J Adv Nurs 57(4):410–421
26. Xiao L, Clark S, Rosson MB, Carroll JM (2008) Promoting reflective thinking in collaborative learning activities. In: Proceedings of the 2008 8th IEEE international conference on advanced learning technologies, IEEE Computer Society, pp 709–711
27. Lin X, Hmelo C, Kinzer CK, Secules TJ (1999) Designing technology to support reflection. Educ Tech Res Dev 47(3):43–62

28. White BY, Shimoda TA, Frederiksen JR (1999) Enabling students to construct theories of collaborative inquiry and reflective learning: computer support for metacognitive development. Int J Artif Intell Educ (IJAIED) 10:151–182
29. Järvinen A, Poikela E (2001) Modelling reflective and contextual learning at work. J Workplace Learn 13(7–8):282–290
30. Dyke M (2006) The role of the 'Other' in reflection, knowledge formation and action in a late modernity. Int J Lifelong Educ 25(2):105–123
31. Van Woerkom M, Croon M (2008) Operationalising critically reflective work behaviour. Pers Rev 37(3):317–331
32. Levina N (2005) Collaborating on multiparty information systems development projects: a collective reflection-in-action view. Inf Syst Res 16(2):109–130
33. Raelin JA (2002) I don't have time to think!" versus the art of reflective practice. Reflections 4(1):66–79
34. Lockhorst D, Admiraal W, Pilot A, Veen W (2003) Analysis of electronic communication using 5 different perspectives
35. Lave J, Wenger E (1991) Situated learning: legitimate peripheral participation. Cambridge University Press, Cambridge

From Crowdsourced Mapping
to Community Mapping: The
Post-earthquake Work
of OpenStreetMap Haiti

Robert Soden and Leysia Palen

Abstract The earthquake that struck Haiti on January 12, 2010 catalyzed a nascent set of efforts in then-emergent "volunteer technology communities." Among these was the response from OpenStreetMap, a volunteer-driven project that makes geospatial data free and openly available. Following the earthquake, remotely located volunteers rapidly mapped the affected areas to support the aid effort in a remarkable display of crowdsourced work. However, some within that effort believed that the impact and import of open and collaborative mapping techniques could provide much richer value to humanitarian aid work and the long-term development needs of the country. They launched an ambitious project that trialed methods for how to create sustainable and locally-owned community-mapping ecosystems in at-risk regions of the world. This paper describes how an organization that emerged out of the response—the Humanitarian OpenStreetMap Team—formalized their practices in relation to many different stakeholder needs with the aim for setting a model for how the potential of participatory, community mapping could be realized in Haiti and beyond.

1 Introduction

The paper describes events following the initial mapping response by the OpenStreetMap community to the January 12, 2010 Haiti earthquake. Over a 3-week period, 600 remotely located volunteer mappers built a base layer map for Haiti nearly from scratch. Though the initial crisis mapping activity by volunteer

R. Soden (✉) · L. Palen
University of Colorado Boulder, Boulder, CO, USA
e-mail: robert.soden@colorado.edu

L. Palen
e-mail: palen@colorado.edu

C. Rossitto et al. (eds.), *COOP 2014 - Proceedings of the 11th International Conference on the Design of Cooperative Systems, 27–30 May 2014, Nice (France)*, DOI: 10.1007/978-3-319-06498-7_19, © Springer International Publishing Switzerland 2014

mappers was remarkable and garnered a great deal of attention, the critical work of situating the map in Haiti, and of making the map useful and meaningful to humanitarian aid efforts, as well as to the people of Haiti themselves had just begun.

This paper places the map's creation by OpenStreetMap's large, distributed community in a larger context of humanitarian efforts that continued on the ground long after the earthquake struck. It reports on a project born out of the obligations its participants felt to maintain and localize the map in a country with highly limited resources—and whose mappable socio-physical features were undergoing rapid change due to infrastructure damage, movement of displaced persons, reconstruction efforts, and public health crises.

Specifically, we describe how an offshoot of the OpenStreetMap community, the Humanitarian OpenStreetMap Team (HOT), worked for 1.5 years after the earthquake to make the map useful to the international effort and the local Haitian community. This effort attempted to materialize a set of values, which included the idea that local ownership of the map's production was not only ethically appropriate, but also the best way to sustain local value and to maintain the map as a dynamic product with local knowledge. Before achieving that localization goal, however, the early international humanitarian response was challenged by heterogeneous, redundant mapping efforts that the fledgling HOT thought it could resolve. The concerted early attempt by HOT to resolve those problems was used to then mobilize their ultimate goal that the map be a locally owned and maintained resource, that could make the country more resilient in the face of future threats that would inevitably come its way.

Others have examined at a high level OSM's role in the immediate wave of the Haiti disaster response, describing the OSM map as an organizational-level boundary object [20] that served multiple social worlds. In this paper, we extend that depiction to describe in detail how OSM came to play such a role through a progression of sometimes contentious and always challenging work. We provide detailed narrative of how HOT actively sought to bring groups to OSM, and how they helped them articulate their relationship to a complex socio-technical artifact. We also investigate the creation of HOT, and how they combined ideals of participation [11] and open data with the opportunities of the social computing platform of OSM to yield an important form of social entrepreneurial work.

2 Method and Style of Reporting

We offer a synthesized interpretation of a sequence of events reported by people immersed in the Humanitarian OpenStreetMap Team organization (HOT). The first author is himself a former HOT board member and participated in some of the events described. The account therefore comes from direct participation with the OSM Haiti effort coupled with interviews and reviews of the account by the others who were involved in the Haiti response. This follows a similar style of auto-ethnographic reporting as conducted in Aoki's research of highly restricted combat information centers [1], where access would otherwise be difficult and/or brief. Our reporting has been supplemented with additional material, including academic publication, internal reports, white papers, and blogs generated during that time period.

3 Origins: The Rise of Crisis Mapping

The Haiti earthquake was a catalyzing event for many "volunteer technology communities" that provide humanitarian aid in emergency response. The year or so predating the earthquake—the 2008 and 2009 timeframe—was a period of great innovation and imagination around technology-abetted activism with respect to humanitarian work. Mobile computing and social media were becoming common, and activists and potential activists were beginning to envision what new possibilities existed for digital volunteerism focused on ideas of open data, open source software, and volunteered geographic information [15, 23, 27]—or what has become known as "crisis mapping."

Groups gathered in a variety of venues to brainstorm and commence work on their ideas. The earliest Crisis Camp events—whose concept was an elaboration of the "bar camp" idea—were held in May 2009 in Washington, DC, gathering many people from different backgrounds interested in "civic hacking" [47], joining together expertise in high tech and humanitarian work, and garnering the attention and support of the World Bank and civic action groups. The first International Crisis Mapper Conference took place in October 2009 from which an active community was launched. The Random Hacks of Kindness group sponsored by Google, Yahoo, and Microsoft hosted their first event in the San Francisco Bay Area in November 2009. The ideas and connections created during these events were supplemented by gathering interest from humanitarian GIS communities. In particular, a subset of the OpenStreetMap community was investigating ways in which open geospatial data created through crowdsourcing and other participatory methods could provide value to crisis response. OpenStreetMap, founded in 2004, was already well-established, but had not yet been applied in an organized fashion to large-scale humanitarian aid effort.

The January 12, 2010 Haiti earthquake, astonishing in the extent of its damage, came just as the early groundwork by these techno-humanitarian groups was being laid. People who connected through the events of 2009 drew in others alarmed by Haitian suffering, and mobilized—or converged [8, 10, 19]—as "technology volunteers," "digital volunteers" and "volunteer technologists." Crisis Camps proliferated throughout the US and Europe; Ushahidi responded to its first disaster arising from a natural hazard and conceptualized a reliable volunteer staff that eventually came to be known as the Standby Task Force; Humanity Road grew out of early "crisis tweeting" work; and the People Finder standard launched [4, 15, 16, 28, 35, 40, 41].

In what became one of the more immediately applicable solutions arising out of these efforts, the OpenStreetMap community mobilized around the extensive mapping needs of the response efforts in Haiti, giving impetus to the formalization of the Humanitarian OpenStreetMap Team.

4 OpenStreetMap

OpenStreetMap (OSM) was founded in 2004 at the University College London by Steve Coast, a computer science graduate student [6]. Coast and others were frustrated with the Ordnance Survey's restrictions on use of government-collected map data. They developed a simple database and web application and, using commercial GPS devices, began to map areas around London. The focus was on developing simple tools and ensuring the data were released under a license that would facilitate wide and varied use. Within 5 years, OSM had over 100,000 users and the project had spread to a number of countries [6]. Today it is a global project, with over 1.3 million registered users and active groups in at least 80 countries [31, 32] working towards a free and open map of the world.

OSM, which is sometimes called "the Wikipedia of maps," is a multi-faceted project that enables distributed work around a common product. It is a database that contains basic, or "framework" geographic data [9] for many parts of the world. It is also a website and set of software tools that allow users to contribute to, download, or otherwise interact with the database. In addition, OSM is a community that interacts through various channels including email lists, IRC channels, in-person conferences, meet ups and mapping parties, wiki pages and the OSM website. Finally it is a set of shared values and participant-enforced rules that guide how to should interact with the tools, data and community.

People active in OSM participate for a wide variety of reasons, but many focus on the ideology of and opportunities created by nonproprietary geospatial data [3]. Some come from private sector firms and want to deliver data or software applications to clients. Others enjoy mapping bicycle routes or historic areas; still others are enthusiasts who want to map their own neighborhoods alongside others in their communities. Research reveals that through these combined efforts in urban areas, the quality of maps, though varied, is generally high [13, 26].

Just before the Haiti earthquake, interest by the OSM community in humanitarian and development work was finding its footing, with a growing contingent who believed that the values of data openness and civic participation lent themselves well to these contexts. At the July 2009 State of the Map—the annual OSM conference—a number of "lightning talks" discussing application in developing countries indicated growing interest [29]. The first known use of OSM for humanitarian purposes was in the response to the October 2009 Tropical Storm Ondoy in the Philippines when OSM data were used by MapAction in situation reports and damage assessments [21, 24]. Several months later, the Haiti earthquake rapidly catalyzed and mobilized the prior but still fledging interest in humanitarian uses of OSM [15, 46].

5 The Crisis Mapping Response

5.1 Creation of the Map: January 2010–March 2010

Initial Mapping At the time of the earthquake, much of the available spatial data for the quake-affected area were in formats inaccessible to GIS users or were not detailed enough to guide response efforts. OSM itself had only a portion of the road network. Other major web-based maps had even less information. There was a clear and immediate demand for accurate and up-to-date maps to help guide logistics and support other elements of the response.

Facilitated by existing personal connections made through various open-source software projects, the International Crisis Mappers Conference and network, the Camp Roberts experiments [23], the Crisis Camps organized by The World Bank and others during 2009, the ecosystem of volunteer technologists began monitoring, collecting, collating and analyzing information from a range of sources across traditional and social media. Digital Globe, GeoEye and others made pre- and post-event high-resolution imagery available under permissive licenses [35]. Ideas that previously only been discussed in the hallways of barcamps and conferences were implemented post haste in hopes that they would support the array of actors responding to Haiti's earthquake.

OSM coordinated activities primarily through one of their existing listservs, and supplemented with IRC and the Haiti page on a wiki. The listserv of the International Conference of CrisisMappers was also used to coordinate OSM's activities along with other volunteer technology projects. Volunteer mappers took advantage of the imagery releases but also drew upon historic maps from the CIA and elsewhere [43, 44]. Roads and building footprints were among the primary types of information digitized, but mappers also attempted to identify damage to infrastructure and the impromptu camps set up by Haitians who had lost shelter [18]. In addition, the community provided rapid extracts of the database in formats that could be easily consumed by the traditional GIS tools used by responders; created new visualizations of the dataset; and developed a number of web services and products intended to facilitate the digitization of imagery or the use of OSM data [44].

Progress was rapid. A co-founder of HOT, Mikel Maron, blogged roughly 53 hours after the earthquake struck that over 400 unique editing sessions had taken place with significant improvements to the dataset were already visible [25]. An analysis of contributions to the OSM database for Haiti from January 12-February 12 found that there were close to 600 individual contributors during that period. Importantly, the same research also showed that the majority of individual contributors were from the pre-existing OSM Community, rather than new contributors [5], contrasting with other reports of disaster volunteerism [33, 47].

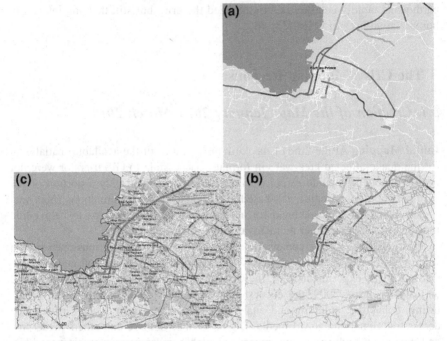

Fig. 1 Progression of the OSM dataset. Screenshots from January 10, January 12, and February 5, 2010, arranged clockwise (**a**, **b**, **c**). *Source* Mikel Maron and Shoaib Burq

Analysis by Haklay conducted in January 2010 found that in urban areas affected by the earthquake, OSM contained more detail than both the road dataset in common use at that time by the UN and Google Maps (2010b). However, as most of these data were created by digitizing satellite imagery, it was primarily composed of the geometry and location of major features only, and lacked significant attribute details such as road names and building uses at that time (Fig. 1).

Use on the Ground, Pre-Intervention by HOT Through the efforts of volunteers, OSM became the most detailed map of the quake-affected area available. Though use on the ground during the response is difficult to quantify, we know the following: many of the major GIS users involved in the Haiti response relied upon OSM, including OCHA and UNICEF [2]. Maps using OSM data were seen in many of the offices of the UN agencies operating at the UN Logistics Base ("LogBase"), a set of tents and trailers next to the international airport. The Fairfax County Virginia Urban Search and Rescue Team reported using OSM data on Garmins to assist with navigation [15]. Surveyors funded by the International Organization for Migration (IOM)—an organization that figures prominently over the next 18 months of HOT activity—added street names as early as February 2010 to assist with resettlement efforts [Fred Moine, personal communication]. The Executive Director of MapAction wrote that he "hesitate[d] to understate [OSM's] importance in our work in the field" [15]. The Mission 4636 and

Ushahidi projects used OSM both as a basemap and to assist the geotagging of incident reports coming in via SMS, Twitter and other sources [28].

5.2 Launch of the Humanitarian OpenStreetMap Team

The value of OSM for humanitarian work was first suggested in 2007 [22], based on the observation that the map was built on open data that could be readily changed by anyone with knowledge of a geographical area, and access. Future members of what would become the Humanitarian OpenStreet Map Team, or HOT, participated in many of the mobilizing 2009 events, which provided fertile opportunities to share ideas, strengthen personal connections, and develop and test tools including Walking Papers, a paper-based form of geospatial data recording during surveying that could be later digitized [23]. Some pre-Haiti humanitarian work including digitizing roads in Gaza; and making OSM data available in response to the October 2009 Tropical Storm Ondoy in the Philippines [24].

However, when the Haiti earthquake struck in January 2010, HOT was still an informal organization without defined roles or even a clear mission statement. HOT members met in mid-January 2010 to draft a further strategy for how to best support the relief effort [30], which included ideas for on-the-ground support. Subsequently, a World Bank-funded mission in February 2010 included OSM representatives who were able to document some of the uses of OSM by the response. Then, in late March with funding provided by MapAction, HOT launched its first mission to Haiti: a two-person effort spanning 3 weeks [37].

6 "Embedding" the Mapping Work in Haiti

Upon arrival, the team had no concrete plan of action or official host within the UN LogBase, the operations center near the Port au Prince airport where many international organizations were based. However, through personal connections to the International Office of Migration (IOM), HOT obtained a working space in the IOM tent and permission to camp at the edge of LogBase. The team used connections to gain the trust of other relevant GIS data users and producers there.

6.1 Building Trust and Identifying Needs

The team cast a wide net in their outreach. They arranged numerous meetings, gave presentations and launched a set of OSM training sessions, which attracted ultimately over 70 people during the three-week mission. These sessions—what the OSM community had historically called "Mapping Parties"—were facilitated by hardware kits purchased and assembled in the US and brought to Haiti. Locking pelican cases contained a laptop, GPS devices, printer/scanners, and USB drives preloaded with software and OSM data so that sessions could run without access to the internet.

This outreach served multiple purposes. The first was to further raise awareness of OSM among the GIS community active in Haiti. Many of the involved in the response had heard of or had already used OSM in some fashion; however, face-to-face meetings with these users helped build trust in the OSM dataset, allowed HOT to communicate the OSM vision, assist with technical questions, and better understand needs of users and their organizations.

Second, face-to-face interaction helped identify OSM champions within the response. Several of these champions later joined HOT as volunteers or paid employees. This early advocacy also led directly to a critical, funded partnership with IOM that allowed the OSM effort to persist in Haiti for a much longer duration, as we will explain.

A Vision for Collaborative Mapping in Haiti The face-to-face work of the mission also allowed for detailed technical discussions around the data collection priorities of the GIS community, which was important for the development of the HOT Humanitarian Data Model (HDM), a standardized way of collecting and sharing data that could be used as a way of facilitating collaborative approaches to mapping in Haiti. The teams could see that numerous heterogeneous field data collection and surveying activities were proliferating by the multiple organizations operating at LogBase, only sometimes in coordination with the Information Management Working Group. Multiple databases of schools, health facilities, and water and sanitation infrastructure were being designed, and scores of Haitians were being trained as surveyors by different groups. HOT felt that if the various efforts could be convinced to adopt common data models and to contribute the data they collected to OSM, this would benefit the whole of the response.

These promising collaborations, and the hope of facilitating further collaboration with others propelled HOT's ongoing work in Haiti. This vision also articulated the organization's goals eventually in at-risk developing regions beyond Haiti, seeding the idea that early, pre-disaster involvement led by local individuals and organizations could have better effect. HOT also recognized the importance of coordinating with the national government, which was suffering greatly from the earthquake. Between 20–40 % of Haiti's civil servants were injured or killed, and 28 of 29 ministry buildings were damaged or destroyed in the earthquake [17]. In the wake of these heavy losses, the government struggled to respond effectively and manage the influx of international organizations [7]. While neither the government or the responding agencies ever adopted OSM to the extent that HOT believed possible during its early work in Haiti, this vision was central to the ways in which the group conducted its work and outreach.

Fig. 2 First mapping party
in cite soleil. *Source* Authors

6.2 Partnerships and Localization

Haitian Civil Society In addition to outreach to international organizations, a key goal of HOT was to work with Haitian civilians to grow local ownership of OSM. Based on the prior success of the MapKibera slum-mapping project in Nairobi [12], with which several members of HOT were involved, the team worked to build connections with groups in Cite Soleil, one of Port au Prince's largest informal settlements. The first mapping party took place in Cite Soleil with about 15 people from the community on March 29, 2010 (Fig. 2).

Deepening the Relationship with IOM and Cite Soleil The second and third HOT missions to Haiti, supported by the World Bank, took place in May and June. By July 2010, members of HOT had spent a total of 52 days in-country and provided formal OSM trainings for around 300 Haitians and internationals, gave presentations and held meetings with numerous actors within the response effort and Haiti's government and civil society. Furthermore, residents from Cite Soleil who had attended the initial mapping party began to accompany HOT to deliver training in Haitian Kreyol, broadening the reach of the growing OSM community.

IOM sponsorship of the first three missions allowed HOT to spend significant time with IOM staff, facilitating social relationships between the organizations, and for HOT to come to understand IOM's work and priorities. HOT understood this to be an important relationship in the achievement of its goal to "embed" the map in Haiti for long-term use. Several IOM units began to express interest in how the OSM platform and the nascent OSM community in Haiti could support IOM's work. This lead to a contract between HOT and IOM—and transformed the nature of HOT's work in Haiti.

7 Expansion and Dispersion of OSM Work

7.1 Camp Mapping: Building the Team

In August 2010, HOT undertook its first IOM-funded mission to Port au Prince. This work was part of a broader effort of facilitating connections between IOM and the residents of the internally displaced persons (IDP) camps. HOT was responsible for designing and overseeing a process through which camp residents would participate in mapping critical camp infrastructure. The resulting maps would help IOM camp management efforts as well as be posted in public areas of the camps themselves. Significantly, IOM also agreed to hire 21 Haitian mappers full-time, the core of whom were the original HOT recruits from Cite Soleil. As a result of this investment by IOM, both HOT and the nascent Cite Soleil OSM community would organize themselves in new ways.

A Global Outlook, and the Incorporation of HOT Until this point, HOT was still an informal organization. A listserv had been set up in March 2010 where the Haiti work as well as volunteer support to new emergencies in Chile, Pakistan, and elsewhere was discussed. This facilitated some degree of broader coordination within the growing organization. However, ongoing work would need to be supported by funding in some form. Funding for the first three Haiti missions had all been channeled through third-party groups who were willing to adopt some risk by providing administrative support to the team. However, to move forward with IOM in Haiti, HOT needed to incorporate. In August, HOT incorporated as a US-based non-profit because many (though not all) of its board members resided there. The draft Articles of Incorporation were posted on the OSM wiki and discussed on the HOT listserv, furthering strengthening its identity among the distributed members. The initial board was comprised primarily of those who had travelled to Haiti on the missions, an influence that shows the significance of the Haiti event to shaping the future of HOT.

Community Localization, and the Incorporation of COSMHA The Cite Soleil residents hired by IOM served as both community mobilizers as well as surveyors. They trained and worked with residents in one of IOM-managed camps to map community assets. They had developed an identity and a working organizational structure of their own. A listserv for discussing the OSM in Haiti hosted conversations in French, English and Haitian Kreyol. A Facebook group further facilitated interaction and a sense of community. With the encouragement of HOT, the group decided to incorporate as a non-profit organization, COSMHA—the Comunite OpenStreetMap de Haiti.

7.2 The Cholera Outbreak: Proving the Model

The first reports of cholera in the central plain of Haiti came in October 2010. By the time of the fifth HOT mission arrived in November, there were serious concerns that cholera would spread through the country's poor water and sanitation infrastructure as well as its healthcare facilities to become a national epidemic. HOT, because of its relationship with IOM, was privy to many of the internal conversations relating to these concerns and began to advocate for refocusing the mapping team on the problem. This advocacy was driven both out of desire to contribute, but also as a strategic move to place OSM at the center of what appeared to be a significant new challenge facing the response effort.

The team had been making steady progress on the camp mapping activities but now their attention accordingly shifted toward locating cholera response infrastructure. Instead of working with camp residents to map their surroundings in predominantly urban areas, the mapping team now rode mini-buses and motorcycles to more rural areas. The IOM Mapping team, after just two months of operation, was charged with providing a weekly updated list of cholera response infrastructure to the UN Health Cluster, which coordinated the cholera epidemic response. These efforts, in the face of the new crisis, demonstrated the validity of HOT's belief that local actors, given proper technical assistance and sufficient resources, could take a leading role in crisis mapping activities in Haiti. Future pre-disaster work by HOT in Indonesia and elsewhere would be driven by similar conviction.

As a result of the increased visibility of the team due to the cholera project, HOT and its allies within IOM were able to push for an expansion of OSM activities. Beginning in January 2011, 1 year after the earthquake, IOM hired an additional 20 mappers from COSMHA, doubling the size of the team and providing funds to support the launch of satellite offices in Leogane, Jacmel, and Gonaives. As part of the plan, someone from HOT was then based in Haiti full-time to assist with project oversight, coordination, and training. This was HOT's first full-time employee.

7.3 Differentiation and Dispersion

This phase was a time of heightened OSM mapping activity in Haiti. Over 300 new volunteers participated in OSM training sessions between January and March 2011. Baseline surveying was completed for 31 communes during this period, a significant addition to the coverage and detail of the OSM dataset. In addition to the geographic and team expansion, increased effort was made to bring a number of other humanitarian organizations into the OSM Haiti community. Several of these hired full-time staff of their own to work on OSM.

However, the rapid growth in OSM activities in Haiti during this time presented new challenges. HOT and COSMHA struggled to simultaneously manage a geographically dispersed team while ensuring quality of the data being captured. Decline in general Haitian-relief funding as well as management changes in IOM as the reconstruction period came to an end strained relations between HOT and IOM. IOM was unhappy with the costs associated with the project, while HOT believed that further investments should be made to continue the development of

COSMHA's technical skills and status as an independent organization. Support for HOT and COSMHA within IOM began to decline in April and largely ended by June 2011, 1.5 years after the quake. By that time however, OSM was well established in Haiti. With the support of other donors and volunteers, both HOT and COSMHA are still active at of the time of this writing.

8 Discussion

HOT as an organization emerged by operating with a set of value-infused goals within a difficult and real-world context. It was through the creation of strategies to achieve those goals in response to uncertainties about a number of political, technical, social, financial, and geophysical issues in the environment that post-earthquake Haiti afforded that HOT came to define its vision for what it could do as a long-lived enterprise, and the approaches it would take to do so.

8.1 Instantiation of Ideals and Institutionalization of Practice

OSM in Haiti had distinct meanings for the different groups that engaged with it. Recalling Lin's positioning of OSM as a boundary object [20] that brought together "social worlds" [38, 39], we consider what our account reveals about the entities affected by and operating upon the map.

The existing, world-wide OSM community that remotely contributed much of the initial data through map tracing in the weeks following the earthquake saw the effort as a tangible means of contributing to the disaster response effort that had an additional consequence of demonstrating the value of the open data ideology. With some exception, the responders working in the field immediately after the quake were primarily consumers, rather than contributors, of the OSM data. They used it because it was freely available and contained more detail than alternatives. Some may have found the unorthodox method of its production either problematic or inspiring, but the decision to participate in OSM by using the data was largely driven by pragmatic concerns.

Many of the members of COSMHA saw the project as a means to participate in a response that had marginalized much of the Haitian population [36]. To some, the primary element certainly may have been financial: participation in OSM was a well-paying job with an international organization. However, much of the private conversation indicated more idealistic goals of helping their country and rebuilding their communities. It was not uncommon for the team to spend evenings and weekends voluntarily mapping their neighborhoods in addition to their full-time paid responsibilities.

Though Lin identifies government as one of the primary social worlds involved with OSM [20], HOT's on-the-ground experience was quite different. Even though the unique circumstances of post-quake Haiti might suggest more opportunities for OSM adoption, Haiti is not alone in this regard: Governments have struggled to articulate their relationship to volunteered geographic information projects [9].

HOT's work brought organizations and people to the map, and to the idea of community mapping. Its original values were clear, but how to materialize them were realized on the ground, in the face of both challenge and opportunity. HOT played a significant role in the articulation work necessary to create and maintain OSM as a boundary object across diverse groups involved in the response and reconstruction work in Haiti. HOT's commitment to shepherding the map and its social practices demonstrates that though crowdsourced projects (like the initial, remotely generated OSM Haiti map) can bring an effort quickly to a useful point, sustaining the effort requires careful management of relationships between entities, and between entities and their mutually produced artifact.

8.2 The Influence of Haiti on HOT and OSM

The extended Haiti effort helped transform HOT from an informal group to a registered non-profit organization with full-time staff, and is where HOT developed, tested and refined approaches and strategies that have since been deployed in other parts of the world. Several examples illustrate this influence. First, HOT worked during early missions with responding organizations to develop the Humanitarian Data Model (HDM) which guided what information to collect while surveying, and was based on the expressed needs of field-workers active in the country at the time. Efforts to simplify and finalize the HDM are ongoing, but the needs for such considerations are well-established [14]. Second, HOT went on to develop new software in response to lessons learned in Haiti: The HOT Tasking Manager supports the coordination of tracing efforts among multiple workers by allowing users to reserve particular sections of the map. The HOT Export Tool makes it easier to quickly extract particular portions of the overall OSM database, a common need expressed by many responders that HOT had to deal with in a patchwork approach during the Haiti response. These software now have wide use in HOT's subsequent projects in many parts of the world. Finally, there has been a shift in the overall conception of OSM by its more traditional community members to see it as now including humanitarian and development efforts.

8.3 Technology-Supported Social Entrepreneurship

We might consider the activities described here as a form of social entrepreneurship; that is, an entrepreneurial effort where the objectives are not for profit, but for social change. Such a view extends how people envision the increasingly popular ideas of micro-task based "human computation" to instead appreciate the broader commitments of digital contribution. It recognizes that a great deal of work must be done to make connections between on-line work and off-line humanitarian work in the field (see [45] for critique). Even in on-line efforts, the structures that sustain self-organizing groups are formalized by and around a smaller set of people who can propagate those structures over time [42].

As an entrepreneurial effort around new forms of data generation, it incorporates new ways of working that combine distributed work for critical parts of the effort, and localized work for differently critical other parts. It deeply integrates the materiality of technology and engages multiple social worlds. We think of this as *technology-supported social entrepreneurship* to call out this special intersection of social activism with technology that is itself self-consciously imbued with values of "how the world should work," as a HOT member explained.

It may be unnecessary in the future to call out the "technological" in social entrepreneurism, but for a time, we see value in drawing such attention because it enlightens how ideation of human organization unfolds around multiple facets of technological artifacts. At the core of this entrepreneurial effort reported here is the production, management and shared ownership of geospatial data, a valuable commodity to many industries, which is what makes OSM objectives both contentious and groundbreaking. When fiscally valuable data become available for humanitarian efforts, and certainly when concerted effort and funding go toward making such data accessible, editable and consumable by many, those actions themselves show a social entrepreneurial spirit that demonstrates new models for civic participation, innovation, and activism.

9 Conclusion

We see both the creation of HOT and its immediate work in Haiti as a serious attempt to secure OSM's role—and its ideology—in humanitarian self-help and external aid. The decisions during its first 1.5 years of existence are oriented toward making OSM useful and meaningful over a sustained amount of time and in a particular place. HOT's value-driven work sought to bring different social worlds together as a long-term sustainability strategy for OSM in Haiti. It is unlikely that the map's mere existence would have been enough to meaningfully sustain it within the country. The HOT effort in Haiti, and the subsequent creation of COSMHA, were concerted attempts to employ a workforce and set of partnerships to instantiate a domestic OSM effort in Haiti, and as model for what OSM and other volunteer technology communities could do, and have done since, in humanitarian efforts beyond Haiti.

References

1. Aoki P (2007) Back stage on the front lines: perspectives and performance in the combat information center. In: Proceedings of CHI, pp 717–726
2. Batty P (2010) OpenStreetMap in Haiti Part 1. Accessed Sept 2013 from http://www.youtube.com/watch?v=PyMTKABxaw4
3. Budhathoki NR, Haythornthwaite C (2013) Motivation for open collaboration crowd and community models & the case of OpenStreetMap. Am Behav Sci 57(5):548–575
4. Burns R, Shanley LA (2013) Connecting grassroots to government for disaster management: workshop summary, Wilson center manuscript
5. Chapman K (2010) OpenStreetMap in the first month after the Haiti quake http://web.archive.org/web/20101204051518/http://www.maploser.com/2010/09/06/openstreetmap-in-the-first-month-after-the-haiti-quake/
6. Chilton S (2009) Crowdsourcing is radically changing the geodata landscape: case study of openstreetmap. In: Proceedings of the 24th international cartographic conference
7. Dupuy A (2010) Disaster capitalism to the rescue: the international community and Haiti after the earthquake. NACLA Rep Am 43(4):14–19
8. Dynes R (1969) Organized Behavior in Disaster. Analysis and Conceptualization (No. DRC-Monograph Ser-3). Ohio State
9. Elwood S, Goodchild M, Sui D (2012) Researching volunteered geographic information: spatial data, geographic research, and new social practice. Ann Assoc Am Geogr 102(3):571–590
10. Fritz C, Mathewson J (1957) Convergence behavior in disasters: a problem in social control. Committee on disaster studies national academy of sciences NRC, Washington DC
11. Greenwood D, Levin M (2007) Introduction to action research: social research for social change. London, Sage Publications
12. Hagen E (2011) Mapping change: community information empowerment in Kibera. Innovations Technol Governance Globalization 6(1):69–94
13. Haklay M (2010) How good is volunteered geographical information? A comparative study of OpenStreetMap and ordnance survey datasets. Env Plann B: Plann Des 37(4):682
14. Haklay M (2010b). Haiti—further comparisons and the usability of geographic information in emergency situations. http://povesham.wordpress.com/2010/01/29/
15. Harvard Humanitarian Initiative (HHI) (2011) Disaster relief 2.0: the future of information sharing in humanitarian emergencies. Washington, D.C. and Berkshire, UK: UN Foundation & Vodafone Foundation Technology Partnership
16. Hughes, A, Palen, L, Sutton, J, Liu, S, & Vieweg, S. 2008. "Site-Seeing" in Disaster: An Examination of On-Line Social Convergence. In: Proceedings of ISCRAM
17. Human Rights Watch (HRW) (2011) World Report 2011. Seven Stories Press, New York
18. Keegan V (2010) Meet the Wikipedia of the mapping world. Guardian unlimited. http://www.guardian.co.uk/technology/2010/feb/04/mapping -open-source-victor-keegan
19. Kendra JM, Wachtendorf T (2003) Reconsidering convergence and converger: legitimacy in response to the world trade center disaster. Terrorism Disaster New Threats, New Ideas Res Soc Probl Pub Policy 11:97–122
20. Lin Yu-Wei (2011) A qualitative enquiry into OpenStreetMap making. New Rev Hypermedia Multimedia 17(1):53–71
21. MapAction. (2013) Map catalog: Philippines typhoons, Sept 2009 http://www.mapaction.org/deployments/maps.html?deployment_filter=187&start=10
22. Maron,M (2007). State of the map! http://brainoff.com/weblog/2007/07/16/1258
23. Maron M (2009a). OpenStreetMap at the camp roberts disaster response experiments. http://brainoff.com/weblog/2009/08/10/1410
24. Maron M (2009b). MapAction uses OpenStreetMap for Philippines response. http://brainoff.com/weblog/2009/10/08/1495

25. Maron M (2010). Haiti OpenStreetMap response. http://brainoff.com/weblog/2010/01/14/1518

26. Mashhadi A, Quattrone G, Capra L (2013) Putting ubiquitous crowd-sourcing into context. In: Proceedings of CSCW, pp 611–622

27. Meier P, Brodock K (2008) Crisis mapping Kenya's election violence: comparing mainstream news, citizen journalism and Ushahidi. Manuscript from the harvard humanitarian initiative

28. Munro R (2013) Crowdsourcing and the crisis-affected community. Info Retrieval 16(2):210–266

29. OpenStreetMap (2009) State of the map http://wiki.openstreetmap.org/wiki/State_Of_The_Map_2009

30. OpenStreetMap (2010) Hot Haiti strategy and proposal. Accessed Sept 2013 from http://wiki.openstreetmap.org/wiki/Humanitarian_OSM_Team/Haiti_Strategy_And_Proposal

31. OpenStreetMap (2013) Stats. http://wiki.openstreetmap.org/wiki/Stats#Users

32. OpenStreetMap (2013) Mailing lists. https://lists.openstreetmap.org/listinfo

33. Palen L, Liu S (2007) Citizen communications in crisis: anticipating a future of ICT-supported participation. In: Proceedings of CHI 2007, pp 727–736

34. Poorthuis A, Zook M (2013) Spaces of volunteered geographic information. In: Adams P, Craine J, Dittmer J (eds.) Ashgate research companion on geographies of media

35. Roche S, Propeck-Zimmermann E, Mericskay B (2013) GeoWeb and crisis management: Issues and perspectives of volunteered geographic information. GeoJournal 78(1):21–40

36. Sheller M (2013) The islanding effect: post-disaster mobility systems and humanitarian logistics in Haiti. Cult Geogr 20(2):185–204

37. Soden R (2010) Humanitarian OpenStreetMap team report from Haiti. http://developmentseed.org/blog/2010/mar/30/humanitarian-openstreetmap-team-report-haiti/

38. Star SL (2013) This is not a boundary object: reflections on the origin of a concept. Sci Technol Hum Values 35:601–617

39. Star SL, Griesemer J (1989) Institutional ecology, 'translations', and boundary objects: amateurs and professionals on Berkeley's museum of vertebrate zoology. Soc Stud Sci 19:387–420

40. Starbird K (2013) Delivering patients to sacré coeur: collective intelligence in digital volunteer communities. In: Proceedings of CHI, pp 801–810

41. Starbird, K., & Palen, L. 2011. "Voluntweeters:" Self-Organizing by Digital Volunteers in Times of Crisis. Proceedings of CHI, 1071-1080

42. Starbird K, Palen L (2013) Working and sustaining the virtual "disaster desk." In: Proceedings of CSCW, pp 491–502

43. Turner A, (2010) OpenStreetMap Haiti. http://opensource.com/osm

44. Wood H (2010) Haiti earthquake on OpenStreetMap. http://www.harrywood.co.uk/blog/2010/01/21/haiti-earthquake-on-openstreetmap/

45. Wulf V, Misaki K, Atam M, Randall D, Rohde M (2013) 'On the ground' in Sidi Bouzid: investigating social media use during the Tunisian revolution. In: Proceedings of CSCW, pp 1409–1418

46. Zook M, Graham M, Shelton T, Gorman S (2010) Volunteered geographic information and crowdsourcing disaster relief: a case study of the Haitian earthquake. World Health Med Policy 2:2

47. Zuckerman E (2010). Crisis Commons, and the challenges of distributed disaster response.http://web.archive.org/web/20101106141729/http://www.ethanzuckerman.com/blog/2010/09/02/crisis-commons-and-the-challenges-of-distributed-disaster-response

Memory Support Functionality in a Collaborative Space: Experiences from the Industry

Mari Ilona Tyllinen and Mika P. Nieminen

Abstract This chapter describes the results from industry pilots on a prototype of an interactive collaboration space DiWa, focusing on its memory support functionality i.e. meeting capture and retrieval. The data has been gathered with questionnaires, interviews, and observations. Our findings point out that even though these functionalities are mostly seen as useful by the participants their use was still very limited during the pilot period. This is in large part due to the novel and differing nature of these functionalities compared to prevalent practices of documenting meetings which are still very strong.

1 Introduction

In today's organizations collaboration and team work is a common activity in all fields of work. However, what is meant by collaboration may vary even within the same company. We have studied selected units from four Finnish organizations and their collaboration practices and developed an interactive space called Digital War room (DiWa) to support their work process. Special consideration has been put into supporting the working group's memory with functionalities that help in capturing and recalling the important events and issues that have been addressed during meetings. Currently these issues are mostly transcribed in personal note books and meeting minutes drafted by one of the meeting participants acting as a secretary.

M. I. Tyllinen (✉) · M. P. Nieminen
Aalto University School of Science, Espoo, Finland
e-mail: mari.tyllinen@aalto.fi

M. P. Nieminen
e-mail: mika.nieminen@aalto.fi

C. Rossitto et al. (eds.), *COOP 2014 - Proceedings of the 11th International Conference on the Design of Cooperative Systems, 27–30 May 2014, Nice (France)*, DOI: 10.1007/978-3-319-06498-7_20, © Springer International Publishing Switzerland 2014

The traditional meeting room and updating it with technological enhancements has received much attention in research since the 1990s. More recently, several multiple display environments have been developed such as iRoom [4], NiCE [7], SAGE [9], IMPROMPTU [3] and WeSpace [20]. Several projects have also concentrated on meeting capture and retrieval technologies, such as the AMI and AMIDA projects [16], IM2 [12] and integrated these functionalities into a meeting room, such as the meeting room at FXPAL [5] and MemTable [8]. Our interactive space, DiWa, is a loosely coupled multi-display environment (MDE) supporting group work with information and document sharing, enabling adaption of novel group work practices, and incorporating meeting capture and retrieval features.

Whittaker et al. [19] proposed in their review of previous work on meeting capture and retrieval systems that system adoption has been hindered by lack of a user-centered approach in the development. We have noticed that evaluation of interactive spaces has been done predominantly in laboratory settings using non-authentic meeting scenarios with recruited participants, which follows the traditional usability testing practice that emphasizes controlled laboratory studies. While these spaces have received positive results in such conditions, collaborative working environments are not solely about technology but very much about work practices and group dynamics. Thus, our approach has been to explore how such functionalities and technology would be received and used in real-life settings as part of everyday work. Since the DiWa environment has been designed so that it can be added on top of existing traditional meeting room facilities, there were possibilities for testing it in real surroundings with collaborating industrial partners. We acknowledge the uncertainties in running such pilots due to practical workplace constraints but appreciate the possibilities of getting access to real experiences, feedback, and suggestions. In this chapter we will discuss the results of industrial pilots both in Finland and in China and explore the implications for future development of such systems.

2 Related Research

Taking notes is a common activity during meetings. It has been found that this along with comprehending new information and participating actively in meetings is a cognitive challenge for the working memory (e.g. [15]). Kalnikaité et al. [11] have researched an ASR (automatic speech recognition) based tool, called Hotspots, for marking important events in a meeting by pressing a button. Their study shows that using the tool does not reduce contributing to meetings while supporting better recall of discussed contents than taking manual notes. In DiWa we wanted to explore this concept in real life, and have implemented a button to mark important events in the meeting.

The capturing and retrieval of meeting data has been studied in several projects. The IM2 project developed several meeting browser concepts with different types of interfaces [12] to access captured meetings. Whittaker et al. [19] have categorized meeting browsers to four categories based on their primary focus: audio, video, artefact and discourse browsers. The use cases for meeting retrieval systems have been both memory related (e.g. [8]) and related to understanding the meetings without being present (e.g. [13]). The meeting browsing functionality in DiWa resembles most closely that of artefact browsers, focusing on the artefacts that have been processed during the meeting and their later retrieval by the participants.

Accessing the information that is shared by a group of people working together is a common research problem. Berlin et al. [1] developed a file repository system for sharing items with a group of people working together and found that information saving strategies of individuals are not suitable when several persons work together. Cremers et al. [6] developed a project browser to support this information access for working teams by combining access to both multimedia meeting recordings and other project documents. MemTable [8] is an interactive tabletop system for collaboration that integrates meeting capture and retrieval functionalities such as transferring analog images to digital format, possibility to save audio embedded with other content and meeting retrieval with a timeline. The DiWa combines access to documents and other objects discussed and worked on during meetings with simple multimedia meeting recordings.

3 DiWa Collocated Collaboration Space

DiWa is an interactive collaborative environment for collocated small group work. The system is built using off-the-shelf hardware and software with an additional custom made windows client application and tailored database and web server. DiWa offers a technological environment for fluent sharing of both digital and analog artifacts, which are necessary aids for longitudinal project activities.

3.1 Design Process of the DiWa System

The DiWa system was developed using a user-centered design process based on Contextual Design [2]. Before the user study we performed a systematic literature review of related topics, which included 49 search terms that matched 13, 6 million articles of which 907 most relevant were selected, and ending with 168 article summaries in eight categories: Group Work, Work Practices, Space Design, System Design, Interaction, Requirements, System Possibilities and Video. Following the literary study we visited our four industrial partners to observe altogether 12 group work situations to learn about their current work places, work practices and the tools they use. We performed individual and group interviews for some of the employees in key roles according to a common set of themes. Based on the collected data, we constructed a detailed description and a flow model for each partner, as well as a consolidated physical model for the current collaborative work environments.

At a two-day analysis workshop we integrated the aforementioned materials to compile a specification of 82 requirements. These requirements were categorized into five groups: space and layout, work practices, ICT and technology, remote collaboration, and interaction. The project partners rated the requirements after which remote collaboration was considered out of scope. For more details on the requirements elicitation, please refer to Nieminen et al. [14].

Based on these requirements the DiWa system was developed in two phases. Between the two main versions of the system prototype we conducted light-weight trials with our partners at the university premises. This allowed us to gather their initial comments to justify necessary design decisions after the first prototype. The second prototype of our system was transferred to three of our partners in Finland and a separate DiWa space was constructed to a research facility in Beijing, China. Each industrial pilot lasted four to six weeks including some training and facilitation at each site. It should be noted that the system described in the next section and all collected data presented in this chapter refers to the final version of the second prototype in the condition it was following the spring 2013 pilots.

3.2 General System Description and User Interfaces

The most visible part of DiWa are the three 60 in. displays on movable stands, shown in Fig. 1. The screens are equipped with touch overlays and each is connected to a separate computer hidden behind a curtain. As a design feature the system components are color-coded to enable easy addressing of each screen and the displayed data therein. The desktop computers have orange, green, and purple curtains matching their respective desktop themes and identification labels on the keyboards and mice. These desktops are connected via a wireless router to a network-attached server (NAS) which acts as a backbone to the whole system running the database and a web server. The NAS works as a centralized repository for project files and history data, and it is accessible by all computers connected to the DiWa network. Additionally, the DiWa space includes a printer/scanner and a wirelessly connected digital camera to capture images from physical artifacts such as product mock-ups, audio recording equipment with two microphones and a separate audio mixer, and an IP camera for taking snapshots of the activities taking place in the facility. All the devices store their data to the central storage in the dedicated network. The messaging that interconnects the desktops is implemented using Pragmatic General Multicast (PGM) [17].

The client side of DiWa is implemented both as a windows client program DiWa Control Service (DiWaCS) and an HTML5 web portal DiWa Web Application (DiWaWA). DiWaCS is a small unobtrusive window positioned in the top of Windows desktop, shown in detail in Fig. 2 (also visible in Fig. 1). While it cannot be moved, the window can be minimized to the taskbar. It provides

Fig. 1 DiWa collaboration space with three large color-coded touch displays, movable furniture and additional meeting room equipment (*flip chart*)

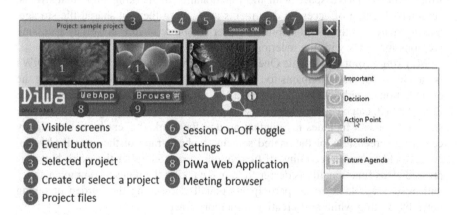

Fig. 2 DiWaCS user interface showing the contents of the event menu

rudimentary workspace and session management for the collaboration sessions, and implements the communication layer between all connected computers and the NAS. The client software can be installed on windows (laptop) computers so that they can connect to DiWa.

With DiWaCS users can drag-and-drop files and Uniform Resource Identifiers (URIs[1]) to be opened on any other computer running DiWaCS. Visible target screens representing the computers in DiWa display the desktop background images of the respective computers in the UI for easier recognition. By clicking on a target screen a user may also remote control that computer e.g. use her own

---

[1] Most common type of a URIs are the web addresses or URLs.

keyboard and mouse to type and point at the selected desktop (technically this is implemented by forwarding the human Interface Device events to the chosen computer using the multicast messaging layer), during a remote control the local screen is disabled. DiWaWa offers the same functionality in a web browser as DiWaCS, excluding remote controlling other computers.

3.3 Memory Support Functionality

Our previous work [18] identified based on the user study the current practices of saving and sharing records including their type and the systems used, the tools and ways of creating personal records and practices for returning to past records. The following categories of memory support functionality for an interactive space were identified: from personal to shared, from analog to digital, logging document handling, human-recorded timestamps, and snapshots. These aspects are constructed in the DiWa space with the functionality of marking important events, automatic logging of accessed documents and saving them in shared file storage, making shared editing responsibilities easier and more visible as well as accessing previous meetings with the meeting browser.

Marking important events One of the main memory support features of DiWa is the ability for all participants to timestamp any important events by pressing the event button on either DiWaCS or DiWaWA and selecting a type for the event (see Fig. 2) which can be chosen from a list of predefined tags or typing one's own. The snapshot concept includes the context around the marked event by automatically capturing screenshots of the shared screens, a photograph of the overall physical context and an audio recording of two minutes prior and after the event button is pressed. This functionality is designed to make taking the notes a common activity with results available to all participants equally, lessening the burden of taking notes by writing while still creating a memory trace.

Logging of accessed documents and saving them Supporting documentation (both analog and digital) is an important aspect of meetings. These documents form the contents of the meetings, while capturing and logging interactions with them provides the temporal or sequential context as a timeline. Both the created and discussed analog documents (transformed to digital form with the equipment in the space) as well as other digital documents opened, shared or created in the space are saved to the shared repository where all meeting participants have access to them during and after the meeting.

Shared editing The DiWa space facilitates creating digital content together. The provided remote control functions also allowed users to interact with the files they share with others, e.g. share a PowerPoint file to a common screen and then run the presentations from afar or several users can remote control the same desktop to collectively write documents.

Meeting Browser All the meeting information (documents and events) can be accessed on the DiWaWA via the Meeting Browser (see Fig. 3). The Meeting

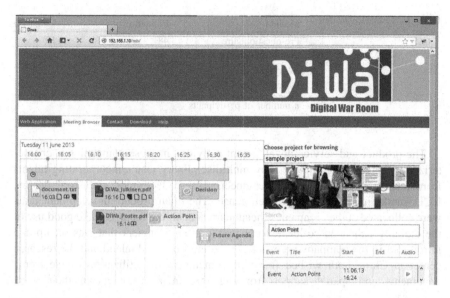

Fig. 3 DiWa Meeting browser showing the accessed documents, marked events. Action point event is selected showing a saved overall picture, captured screenshots and an audio recording

Browser has a timeline showing file interactions such as creation, modifying and opening times. These interactions are linked to files stored in the shared repository, thus allowing quick and simple access to them. On the timeline, events are shown with their respective event types.

Selecting an event (shown in Fig. 3) allows the users to see the snapshot images and to listen to the before-and-after audio recording.

4 Field Study

During spring 2013 the DiWa prototype was piloted in four organizations, three in Finland and one in China, for approximately one month at each site. The organizations involved were: two global product development companies, a public zoning unit of a local municipality and a Chinese research center co-designing community services. All of the participants involved special expertize from a wide variety of domains in fluent multi-disciplinary work. When reaching towards new international markets the companies had identified a growing need to collect more information about their customers and distributors and to understand their products' impact on their actual end-users. Much of this data is nowadays being gathered and reported in digital form: This forms a rich and versatile source of material to be used in product development.

Table 1 Methods and data

Method	Finland (n)	China (n)
Pre-questionnaire	48	10
Post-questionnaire	16	8
Interview	17	7
Observations	10 (situations)	–

n number of participants

The product and service development activities in these companies is characterized by intensive group work by multidisciplinary teams incorporating talents from mechanical and electrical engineering and electronics, industrial design, UCD, marketing and business intelligence. The main product development units were collocated at the companies' headquarters enabling them to make good use of the digitally enhanced co-located collaboration environment that was set up and introduced in the company premises. The zoning unit in Finland and the research center in China both wished for improvements in the utilization of electronic documents and spatial support for engaging their customers in their work processes.

Methods and Data The data was gathered with questionnaires, observations and interviews where the topic of this paper was one of the themes. The number of respondents for each method is shown in Table 1. The difference in the number of respondents between the pre- and post-questionnaire is due to the fact that the pre-questionnaire was given to everyone before their first meeting in DiWa while the post-questionnaires were opted to only those participants that had used DiWa two or more times during the piloting period (in Finland). All post-questionnaire respondents and organization's key contact persons were interviewed. The participants of our study in Finland were product development engineers, industrial designers, project managers and city planners. The participants of our study in China were service designers for elderly care services and the technical teams implementing the services.

Both questionnaires had both closed and open-ended questions. Of the 13 questions in the pre-questionnaire, 5 questions concerned the participants' reasons, tools and forms of personal note-taking as well as reasons and strategies for returning to past meetings. The post-questionnaire had 18 questions of which 4 questions were directly related to note taking practices during the meeting and returning to meetings while the other questions addressed topics related to the whole DiWa system, its functionalities and its use during the piloting period. In order to be able to compare the results with those of our peers, the categories used to evaluate the "frequency of use" (shown in Tables 2, 3 and 4) and the categories for "reasons to return to previous meeting" (shown in Table 5) are taken from the earlier study by Jaimes et al. [10]. Observations were made mostly on first use situations of a group in the space where the observer also acted as a technical facilitator, also one product development team was accompanied whenever they held meetings in DiWa. The interviews were conducted a few weeks after the

Table 2 Tools for taking personal notes

	Pen and paper		Computer		Smart phone		Digital camera	
	F	C	F	C	F	C	F	C
Always	21	0	8	10	4	0	0	0
Often	67	60	35.5	40	8	33	6	20
Sometimes	10	40	21	10	23	0	19	60
Rarely	2	0	25	30	40	45	50	10
Never	0	0	10.5	10	25	22	25	10

all values in percentages, F Finland (n = 48), C China (n = 10, except n = 9 for smartphone)

Table 3 Ways of taking personal notes

	Writing		Drawing		Taking photographs		Video recording		Audio recording	
	F	C	F	C	F	C	F	C	F	C
Always	37	20	2	0	0	0	0	0	0	0
Often	54	40	24	0	13	20	2	10	0	30
Sometimes	9	30	51	50	34	50	4	10	0	20
Rarely	0	0	21	20	36	20	45	40	32	30
Never	0	10	2	30	17	10	49	40	68	20

all values in percentages, F Finland (n = 47, except n = 46 for writing), C China (n = 10)

pilots at the organizations' premises. The interviews were based on the observations and the post-questionnaire and constructed as semi-structured addressing the experiences of holding a meeting in the DiWa interactive space.

The methods of the field study conducted in China were the same as in Finland. All materials were translated through English into Chinese by an official translation service. The interviews were carried out by a native Chinese speaker who was guided beforehand by one of the Finnish researchers. All gathered data was translated into English using translation services and delivered to Finland for analysis.

Data Analysis The data from the two pilot countries was analyzed separately. The closed-ended questions from the pre- and post-questionnaires were divided into categories of which three categories are relevant for this chapter: taking personal notes in meetings, used tools and ways for making notes and returning to past meetings. The open-ended questions from the post-questionnaires and the interviews were analyzed within the same analysis framework and coded by two researchers. The framework consisted of the following not mutually exclusive categories: current (practices, facilities and tools); expectations (for the system and team work); realization (of system and team work); memory support (DiWa functionalities, reasons for taking notes; reasons for returning to meetings); system evaluation; and work practices. Appropriate quotations were also coded to categories of positive, negative and problem. The data in the memory support category and its sub-categories were analyzed for this chapter.

Table 4 Ways of returning to past meetings

	Personal notes		Common notes		Distributed material		Asking others		Photos of white-board/flip chart		Photographs		Video recording		Audio recording	
	F	C	F	C	F	C	F	C	F	C	F	C	F	C	F	C
Always	30	0	8	0	4	0	2	0	0	0	0	0	0	0	0	0
Often	47	70	51	50	53	60	36	30	13	40	2	30	0	0	0	10
Sometimes	19	10	26	20	36	40	53	30	41	20	38	40	6	40	4	10
Rarely	4	20	13	30	7	0	9	40	39	40	43	30	51	30	34	80
Never	0	0	2	0	0	0	0	0	7	0	17	0	43	30	62	0

All values in percentages, F Finland (n = 47, except personal notes n = 46) and C China (n = 10)

Table 5 Importance of the reasons for returning to past meetings

Reason	Finland		China	
	Mode	Median	Mode	Median
To verify the truth when memory and descriptions are inconsistent	4	4	4	4
To listen to a portion of speech not heard	4	3.5	4.5	4
To recall an idea I had during a meeting	4	3	5	3.5
To listen to a portion of speech not understood	4	3	5	4.5
To keep in mind what customers or key-persons said	3	4	4	4
To reexamine other person's speech and its context to correctly understand meaning or intention	3.5	3.5	4	4
To know the results of discussions of ideas from earlier meetings with respect to current interest or problem	3	3	5	4
To obtain proof when someone denies having said something	–	2	2 4	3
To have accurate record of meetings	–	2	2 5	4.5
To check the consistency between present and earlier presentations	–	2	2 3	3

values on a scale of 1 (not important) to 5 (very important), *F* Finland, *C* China

5 Results

In this section we will present the results from our pilot studies with the space in Finland. The results are divided into four sections: taking notes, marking important events, accessing shared files and returning to previous meetings. This division is comparable to the memory support functionalities presented in Sect. 3.3, that is shared editing, marking important events, logging of accessed documents and saving them, and meeting browser. At the end of each section we will also present the differences in the Chinese pilot study results.

5.1 Taking Notes

Before DiWa In an open-ended question in the pre-questionnaire almost all of the respondents (N = 48) answered that they take personal notes at least when it is needed. The reasoning for taking notes seemed to fall into two most important categories: writing down decisions and other agreed upon items (19 respondents) and writing down own action points (17 respondents). Personal notes were also made quite frequently on generic issues or to support remembering (15 respondents). Only one respondent specified that he does not take general notes because a meeting memo is usually produced.

From Table 2 it can be seen that in Finland the most used tool to take notes was by far pen and paper, 88 % used it always or often. The least used tools of taking notes were smart phones, 65 % used it rarely or never, and digital cameras, 75 % used it rarely or never. The use of a computer was more diverse.

In Finland (Table 3) writing was the most used way of taking notes, 91 % used it always or often. Drawing was the second most used choice, however its use varied. Taking photographs was also used to some extent, however less popular. Video recording was used by very few, with only 2 % using it often. Audio recording was the least used way, with all respondents using it rarely or never.

During DiWa In the post-questionnaire 9 respondents (out of N = 16) reported that they did not take any personal notes while in DiWa. This is a clear transformation from the pre-DiWa situation where almost all respondents took personal notes. The reasons for not taking notes were that the group made common notes with the system or worked on some document together. However, 6 respondents reported using pen and paper for documenting, 5 respondents using their own computer, while smart phone, digital camera, common documents and the event marking functionality all received 2 responses, which makes 19 choices altogether. Those persons taking personal notes mostly used pen and paper for doing them and own computer was used mainly for documenting something for later use in the same meeting. It is also probable that smart phones were used for personal notes while the digital camera was that found in the DiWa-space for transferring analog documents to digital format into the DiWa system.

The interviews also clarified the above responses, making it clear that one of the common screens in DiWa was used frequently for writing common notes that everyone could contribute to. Also sometimes the participants felt that the work done in DiWa was captured in the documents that were edited together thus removing the need for notes. For the most part the way of documenting meetings in the space still followed a previously learned habit of writing memos.

In China The amount of personal notes and the reasons for taking them are quite similar than in Finland. As can be seen from the Tables 2 and 3 the clearest differences when comparing China to Finland are in the tools and ways of taking notes. There is a slight difference in using pen and paper, with 40 % using it only sometimes in China. Also the usage of smart phone and digital camera is different, they are used more in China than in Finland, with 33 and 20 % respectively using it often. Also the ways of taking notes differs from Finland, as can be seen from Table 3. Writing is used somewhat less than in Finland and drawing is used significantly less with 50 % using it rarely or never. However, photographs are taken somewhat more and audio recording is used significantly more with 30 % using it often.

Based on the post-questionnaire and interviews DiWa also had less impact in China on the practice of taking personal notes. In the post-questionnaire 5 respondents (out of N = 8) reported doing personal notes in the DiWa space. Also, 7 respondents used pen and paper, 6 respondents their own computer and 4 respondents a digital camera for taking the notes, while smart phone and event marking functionality were reportedly used by one respondent. Thus, surprisingly the use of pen and paper was significantly more common in DiWa than normally while the use of a smart phone less common. The reasons for this remain unclear.

5.2 Marking Important Events

These results are drawn from the post-questionnaire, interviews and observations. There was some event marking done during the pilot period, but mainly the event marking was not used at all. Participants identified several reasons for not using the event marking. Several of the reasons were related to the voice recording functionality specifically: it was felt that there simply would be too much information and data recorded and there would never be enough time to return to the recordings, some expressed the concern that other people would not like that they were being recorded or that the meetings would be too "outrageous" to listen afterwards.

Also, there was concern that using the event marking would lead to non-productive discussion, as things would then somehow, according to answers, be left undecided and a clear common understanding would not be reached. Writing a common memo together was seen as sufficient and thus the events were not seen as needed. Also the nature of the meetings (either "too short" or "traditional" according to answers) was seen as a reason for not needing them. However, the main reasons for not using the event marking were not as much related to not needing it as to its novelty as a practice. Even when participants felt marking events would be worth it, the unlikeness to prevalent practices made it difficult to remember during the meetings that such functionality even existed or realize at the time of the significant moments that it was a moment worth marking. It was also difficult to perceive those moments that would need to be returned to in the future.

However, the event marking was seen by many as useful and they had had moments during the piloting period where afterwards they wished they had realized to press the event button. These moments were especially related to being able to check something, mainly decisions, retrospectively. The participants were convinced that introducing the event marking functionality to real use would require an active approach with enough repetition over a longer time period.

In China The event functionality was not in effect used and the reasoning was that such functionality is not needed or not suitable because of not having access to DiWa afterwards. However, the request for using video recording instead of audio was stated in almost all the interviews whereas in Finland it was only seen as useful when designing physical objects. Also, the recording was hoped to comprise of everything that was done in the meetings.

5.3 Returning to Previous Meetings

Before using DiWa It can be seen from the pre-questionnaire responses that nearly all respondents return to past meetings often in some way, while just 3 respondents return only sometimes. The most used ways of returning to past meetings (see Table 4), which over 50 % of respondents used often or always, were personal notes, common notes and distributed material. Asking others was also somewhat frequent with 38 % of respondents doing it often or always. The least used ways, which over 90 % of respondents used rarely or never, were audio recording and video recording. The types of things respondents return for (N = 36) can be divided in the following most important categories: decisions and other agreed upon things (18 respondents), agreed tasks (15 respondents) and own tasks (10 respondents).

Returning to meetings held in DiWa When asked, what would be those things that they may need later from the meetings held in DiWa, the participants identified common memos and other documents that were worked on together as the most important, while decisions, hearing others comments again and personal notes were also mentioned. The meeting browser was used minimally during the pilot period. The main reason was seen to be the lack of sequential meetings over a longer time period, and as a result not many documents or events were generated into the project folder. Thus there was no need to return to earlier meetings and to know what was discussed in which meeting. The participants also expressed that they felt that the type of meetings held did not benefit from such functionality. However, they could not specify what type of meetings would benefit from it. Also, the calendar view of the meeting browser was seen as difficult, because it would be hard to remember when a meeting took place. One of the participants also expressed the view that the meeting browser was altogether useless, since there would never be enough time to return to all the information to analyze it.

Nevertheless, some participants viewed the meeting browsing functionality as very useful. They stated that they would especially benefit from it in two ways: one could return to the previous meeting in the beginning of the next and see what was agreed and continue work from there with the same documents; and it could help in recalling what was discussed overall and who were present in the meeting.

Possible reasons for returning When respondents were asked to imagine that they had access to a complete record of everything from meetings and rate reasons for using such a record, only few reasons were seen clearly as important (Table 5). These reasons were verifying the truth after inconsistent memory and descriptions and listening to unheard parts of speech. Some reasons were also rated clearly as not very important: having an accurate record of meetings, obtaining proof when something is denied having been said and checking consistency between presentations. All other reasons were seen as somewhat important.

In China In the ways of returning to previous meetings (pre-questionnaire) there were some differences. Personal notes were used somewhat less and asking others was used clearly less, while photographs (both of the whiteboard and other) were used clearly more as was both video and audio recording. The main reason for returning to previous meetings was for the main points and major discussions (10 responses), while also previous discussions related to present activities (4 responses) were identified as important. Own action points (2 responses), schedule (1 response) and next steps (1 response) were also indicated.

No differences were identified in the things that participants would need from the meetings held in DiWa. However, when asking about the possible reasons for returning to previous meetings, if participants had access to a full record of everything that happened, some significant differences between the answers could be identified. Overall, the ratings were higher as almost all reasons were seen as at least somewhat important. Having an accurate record of meetings and obtaining proof when someone denies having said something were significantly more important reasons for the Chinese respondents. Also knowing the results of discussions of ideas from earlier meetings with respect to current interests and listening to a part of speech that was not understood were clearly more important. There were slightly higher values also for these reasons: re-examining parts of speech and its context to correctly understand meaning or intention, recalling an own idea and checking the consistency between presentations.

6 Conclusions and Discussion

Our results on personal note taking before using DiWa correlate very well with the almost decade old findings of Jaimes et al. [10]. Both studies identify personal notes to self as the most common way to record meetings. Similarly the use of audio or video recordings are still rare, while the increased availability of (digital) cameras and camera phones has turned the tables on the use of pictures as memory aids. We conclude that availability of technology has only limited effect on the personal or collective habits of users.

However, in our study we found that note taking practices in meetings of the Finnish participants were affected by our interactive space. The use of personal notes was transformed into a common practice of writing the memos together or replaced by the act of creating something new together. It seems that DiWa with its functionalities was able to answer to the original need of facilitating creating a shared understanding of the meeting.

The use of event marking in our study was quite limited. It seems that because it was a completely novel concept it was hard to utilize and benefit from it in the short duration of the pilots. Trying the new tools and practices was seen to require significantly more time and an active attitude to grasp them fully. The novelty also made it difficult to see the benefits over existing practices. However, afterwards participants identified moments they would have wanted to mark and return to, thus not making the functionality obsolete.

When comparing the reasons to return to previous meetings our findings are dualistic. Chinese users rated the availability of an "accurate record of meetings" highest, perfect match with the previous study in Japan by Jaimes et al. [10], while our Finnish users rated the same reason as lowest. This indicates cultural differences between Nordic and Asian expectations for meeting memory support.

The main shortcoming of our study design appeared to be the too short duration of the pilot period which resulted in a lack of consecutive meetings and difficulty in forming new work practices. Also more ubiquitous and less-effort-demanding solutions need to be developed for decrease the need for traditional note taking and memo writing. Interesting possibilities emerge e.g. from context logging, speech and speaker recognition. Additional studies and experiments about future meeting practices in real-life settings appear important.

Acknowledgments The authors would like to thank Mikael Runonen for contributing to the data gathering, Nick Eriksson for technical implementation, Vikki du Preez for graphic design for DiWaCS/DiWaWa, Marko Nieminen for general leadership and Liu Jianbing and Pu Fan of Beijing Academy of Science and Technology for the pilots in China.

References

1. Berlin LM, Jeffries R, O'Day VL, Paepcke A, Wharton C (1993) Where did you put it? Issues in the design and use of a group memory. In: Proceedings of INTERACT 93 CHI 93 conference on human factors computing systems ACM, New York, pp 23–30
2. Beyer H, Holtzblatt K (1998) Contextual design: defining customer-centered systems. Morgan Kaufmann, San Francisco
3. Biehl JT, Baker WT, Bailey BP, Tan DS, Inkpen KM, Czerwinski M (2008) Impromptu: a new interaction framework for supporting collaboration in multiple display environments and its field evaluation for co-located software development. In: Proceeding of 26th annual SIGCHI conference on human factors computing systems ACM, Florence, pp 939–948
4. Borchers J, Ringel M, Tyler J, Fox A (2002) Stanford interactive workspaces: a framework for physical and graphical user interface prototyping. Wirel Commun IEEE 9:64–69
5. Chiu P, Kapuskar A, Reitmeier S, Wilcox L (2000) Room with a rear view. Meeting capture in a multimedia conference room. IEEE Multimed 7:48–54. doi:10.1109/93.895154
6. Cremers A, Kuijper I, Groenewegen P, Post W (2007) The project browser: supporting information access for a project team. In: Jacko J (ed) Human computer interaction HCI application service, Springer, Berlin, Heidelberg, pp 571–580
7. Haller M, Leitner J, Seifried T, Wallace JR, Scott SD, Richter C, Brandl P, Gokcezade A, Hunter S (2010) The nice discussion room: integrating paper and digital media to support co-located group meetings. In: Proceedings of 28th international conference on human factors computing systems ACM, Atlanta, pp 609–618
8. Hunter S, Maes P, Scott S, Kaufman H (2011) MemTable. In: Proceeding of 2011 annual conference on human factors computing systems—CHI 11, Vancouver, p 3305
9. Jagodic R, Renambot L, Johnson A, Leigh J, Deshpande S (2011) Enabling multi-user interaction in large high-resolution distributed environments. Future Gener Comput Syst 27:914–923. doi:10.1016/j.future.2010.11.018
10. Jaimes A, Omura K, Nagamine T, Hirata K (2004) Memory cues for meeting video retrieval. In: Proceedings of 1st ACM workshop continues archival retrieval of personal experiences, pp 74–85
11. Kalnikaitė V, Ehlen P, Whittaker S (2012) Markup as you talk: establishing effective memory cues while still contributing to a meeting. In: Proceedings of ACM 2012 conference on computing supported cooperative work ACM, New York, pp 349–358
12. Lalanne D, Ingold R, von Rotz D, Behera A, Mekhaldi D, Popescu-Belis A (2005) Using static documents as structured and thematic interfaces to multimedia meeting archives. In: Bengio S, Bourlard H (eds) Machine learning for multimodal interaction. Springer, Berlin, Heidelberg, pp 87–100
13. Lisowska A, Rajman M, Bui T (2005) ARCHIVUS: a system for accessing the content of recorded multimodal meetings. In: Bengio S, Bourlard H (eds) Machine learning for multimodal interaction. Springer, Berlin, Heidelberg, pp 291–304

14. Nieminen MP, Tyllinen M, Runonen M (2013) Digital war room for design: requirements for collocated group work spaces. In: Yamamoto S (ed) Human interface and the management of information. Information and interaction learning for learning, culture, collaboration and business. Springer, Berlin, Heidelberg, pp 352–361
15. Piolat A, Olive T, Kellogg RT (2005) Cognitive effort during note taking. Appl Cogn Psychol 19:291–312. doi:10.1002/acp.1086
16. Renals S, Hain T, Bourlard H (2007) Recognition and understanding of meetings the AMI and AMIDA projects. IEEE workshop automatic speech recognition and understanding 2007 ASRU, pp 238–247
17. Speakman T, Farinacci D, Lin S, Tweedly A, Bhaskar N, Edmonstone R, Johnson KM, Sumanasekera R, Vicisano L, Crowcroft J (2001) PGM reliable transport protocol specification. Req Comments RFC3208
18. Tyllinen M, Nieminen M (2013) Supporting Group and Personal Memory in an Interactive Space for Collaborative Work. In: Yamamoto S (ed) Hum. Interface Manag. Inf. Inf. Interact. Learn. Cult. Collab. Bus, Springer, Berlin Heidelberg, pp 381–390
19. Whittaker S, Tucker S, Swampillai K, Laban R (2008) Design and evaluation of systems to support interaction capture and retrieval. Pers Ubiquit Comput 12:197–221. doi:10.1007/s00779-007-0146-3
20. Wigdor D, Jiang H, Forlines C, Borkin M, Shen C (2009) WeSpace: the design development and deployment of a walk-up and share multi-surface visual collaboration system. In: Proceeding 27th international conference on human factors computing systems ACM, Boston, pp 1237–1246

Designing Cooperation for Sustainable Mobility: Mobile Methods in Ridesharing Contexts

Johanna Meurer, Martin Stein and Volker Wulf

Abstract Motivated by rising global energy demands and a growing awareness of the scarcity of natural resources sustainable mobility concepts are more in demand than ever before. One solution is offered by ridesharing concepts, realized with ICT-supported mobile interaction systems. However, current systems mainly address issues of comfort and efficiency and thus refer to mobility widely in functional terms of transport. We argue in this paper for a praxis-based exploration that refers to personal ridesharing experiences embedded in people's daily mobility and life world. We will show that a phenomenological inquiry provides added value in understanding practical challenges in a ridesharing context, and we will identify methods used to address practical challenges that can provide new starting points for design.

1 Introduction

Reacting to the discussion on global warming, the CSCW and HCI community has started to explore the design of tools to support alternative and sustainable mobility solutions. As private mobility causes 65 % of CO_2 pollution [10], an important part of this research focuses on car—and ridesharing solutions. Mostly such systems are dominated by a physical time-space understanding of mobility.

J. Meurer (✉) · M. Stein · V. Wulf
Information Systems and New Media, University of Siegen,
Hölderlinstr. 3, 57076 Siegen, Germany
e-mail: johanna.meurer@uni-siegen.de

M. Stein
e-mail: martin.stein@uni-siegen.de

V. Wulf
e-mail: volker.wulf@uni-siegen.de

C. Rossitto et al. (eds.), *COOP 2014 - Proceedings of the 11th International Conference on the Design of Cooperative Systems, 27–30 May 2014, Nice (France)*, DOI: 10.1007/978-3-319-06498-7_21, © Springer International Publishing Switzerland 2014

The essence of most systems builds formal input fields addressing the 'where' (in terms of starting point, distance and destination) and the 'when' (in terms of departure—and arrival time) of travelling, supporting most efficient and functional ridesharing. But mobility is more than a physical entity. Particularly, the famous mobility researcher John Urry [26] states that movement significantly affects the way the world appears to us: our relationship to each other, to space, time and place is mediated by movements through the material and the social world. Largely movement influences our relationships, and being on the move depends heavily on how we interpret the life-world. Thus ridesharing technology has to deal with complex socio-technical experiences of mobility.

This is why we replace the wide-spread rational transportation perspective and refer to the experience of daily mobility and ridesharing in particular as an appropriate starting point to facilitate ridesharing systems. In particular we aim to reconstruct methods used by people to organize their daily mobility to coordinate their mobility practices among each other. Using the analytical lens of a phenomenology perspective we will identify accounting practices, methods, people use to negotiate their ridesharing practices in cooperation.

2 Understanding Mobility in Current Ridesharing Systems

Ridesharing systems became popular in the 1970s to cope with the challenge of increasing environmental awareness, oil prices and transport collapse. People at that time joined together in ridesharing communities using slip-boxes in order to exchange offers and demands [10]. With this history in mind, it is not very surprising that the prevalent research focus lies over a long time on finding appropriate algorithms for matching rides of potential parties. The precondition for matching a driver with one or more passengers is that their mobility patterns are as congruent as possible, given travel time and route convergence [22, 24]. In this working tradition a physical understanding of mobility as movement through time and space is the benchmark, because rides can only be matched based on these characteristics. Meanwhile a flexible matching became a key concept for a successful ridesharing system. With the help of location aware Internet-enabled mobile phones short-term and even en-route notifications are possible. This constitutes the technical basis for more flexible and dynamic ridesharing systems [9, 10, 16]. Hence, these systems are still due to the same physical understanding of mobility. Mostly input boxes for departure and destination points allow only a wider range input possibilities.

Currently, ridesharing research in CSCW, and HCI literature undergoes a change in perspective, shifting from pure logistical concerns towards questions of social acceptance. Pioneer work has been done by Brereton et al. [1], or Ozenc et al. [17]. They argue that ridesharing systems can reach a wider mass of users, if social challenges concerning personal preferences of commuting choice and social interaction are solved. In this line of argumentation several new challenges for ridesharing systems came up like the inclusion of extended social networks [1, 9, 28], the improvement of communication processes [1, 27], or issues about trust, privacy and security [18, 28]. These works point out that it is necessary to understand that riding, meeting with people and participating at an event are related activities and that research is failing, if a broader view of the social situation in which people travel and meet is missing. However, mobility behavior is still considered as a derived demand. Still, systems mainly remain on an efficiency driven design approach focusing on 'hard facts' such as the point of departure, destination and timeframe. Issues like informal communication support, trust, security, or community building are mostly included as additional features, imposed to the systems. Hence, if we take the approach of [26] seriously, that means understanding the everyday experience of living is constituted by motilities and vice versa that mobility bound to our experience, we urgently need an appropriate methodical lens that is able to address ridesharing as a practice out of our live-worlds [15, 23].

3 A Phenomenological Perspective on Mobility Support Systems

Following this suggestion, we have to take a step back. Identifying the relevant aspects of mobility as a part of our life-world has an essential normative and meaningful character, and as such cannot be reduced to any physical concept like time or space [29]. Therefore, the focus of study should not be the materialized mobility as an entity of movement that can be measured, but rather, address mobility as a part of an intentional world, where it carries a meaning (e.g. is judged as enjoyable). Following the original meaning of mobility (lat mobilis = movable), addressing the individual needs of movement makes mobility to a question of perception, that is theoretically addressed in phenomenological theories [19]. However, among Dourish et al.'s argument, that

> 'the patterns and experience of movement are collective rather than individual experiences. Mobility is experienced through social and cultural lenses. We move individually but collectively we produce flows of people, capital, and activities that serve to structure and organize space' [6].

there exist a collective understanding of mobility. This is in accordance with the phenomenological tradition, too. Analyzing mobile experiences does not mean getting lost in a variety of individual sights, but that there are core principles people refer to in their own and mutual orientation in a mobile world. In this tradition we need an empirical phenomenology focusing on the revealing taken for granted, ordering principles used by people to constitute and make the ridesharing practice becoming accountable principles for mutual cooperation. Although phenomenological investigation aims to study the nature of the phenomena in question by analyzing from a first-person perspective, the constitutive structures of the consciousness experience, as a researcher, however, we have no direct access to someone else's first-person perspective. A fundamental claim of phenomenology is that something like direct experience does not exists. This is reflected in Garfinkel's expression that even if man is able to look into people's heads, one would not find much there, apart from brain mass: 'There is no reason to look under the skull science nothing of interest is to be found but brains' [7]. Garfinkel offered a methodical solution for this problem, because every sensation is always linguistically mediated, embedded in the mundane world of disclosure. The aim of empirical phenomenology studies is to recover the phenomenon from the various expressions and traces of social interaction left by people, so that the foreign perspective is made accountable [8]. Hence, empirically, we can only study ridesharing experiences the way people report on certain phenomenons. Approaching the socio-technical phenomenon of ridesharing means empirically to uncover the mundane configuration of the phenomenon as it manifests in peoples talk about it. Garfinkel used the term of ethno-methods to characterize the ordinary methods with which members of a certain practice constitute and make the orderly world accountable. His ideas were introduced in HCI and CSCW early by Ihde [11] and the concept of 'technomethodology', proposed by Button and Dourish [4] and further developed by Crabtree [5] or Büscher and Urry [2]. However, beside the famous work of Luff and Heath [13] there is still little work focusing on the nature of mobility practices. The chosen perspective is neither separated form meaning, nor individualistic, but as an ethnomethodological concept we assume that the significant values are expressed in ridesharing negotiation processes and in the detailed descriptions of the interviewees. We will show in the following that the chosen perspective on ridesharing allows new insights about the human-mobility relationship and new cues for technical innovation.

4 Investigating Mobile Methods

Addressing this question of 'what methods people apply for ridesharing coordination' we conducted an interview study. Interviews can provide detailed insights into the subjective life-worlds of individuals and therefore were chosen to investigate how subjective interpretations towards ridesharing were made accountable. We chose problem-centered interviews [30] for the data collection, because they aim at focusing on experiences, perceptions and reflections in relation to specified issues. On the basis of a question guide, therefore, we asked interviewees to reflect on and expand our themes in any way they chose. The semi-structured interviews were accompanied by a short questionnaire with the function to complement the study with additional biographical and socio-demographic background information about the interviewees. The questions asked were loosely structured around a topic list about the living arrangements within daily mobility routines and the way they dovetailed (or not) with available infrastructure like possessing a car, using public transport, or other forms of mobility like ridesharing. We were further interested in mobility choices, preferences and habits.

Table 1 Characteristics of interview participants (n = 21)

Category	Characteristics	Number of respondents
Sex	Male	5 (26 %)
	Female	16 (74 %)
Age	58–70 years	11 (53 %)
	70–80 years	10 (47 %)
	(Average: 69 years)	
Marital status	Married or living with a partner	12 (58 %)
	Widowed/Single/Separated	9 (42 %)
Housing tenure	Owned	13 (63 %)
	Rented	8 (37 %)
Self-rated technical competence	More good	6 (26 %)
	More bad	15 (74 %)
Population density	Low density	11 (53 %)
	High density	10 (47 %)
Travel modes[a]	Own car	17 (84 %)
	Public transportation	5 (21 %)
	Walking	8 (42 %)
	Regularly involved in Ridesharing	9 (47 %)

[a] Multiple answers are possible

Asking questions in a problem-centered interview provides some structure, but also provides for an open, iterative, and reflective response by both parties to the interview. Interviewers relied on reflective questioning and probing, prompting participants to provide additional detail, clarification and exemplification. Hence, we kept interviews as open as possible in order to gain individual insights in the issue of older adults' ridesharing experiences. The interviews were conducted in participants' homes by one of the researchers, audio-recorded and transcribed verbatim afterwards. The duration of interviews was driven by interviewees, and thus varies in length from 45 min to two and a half hours.

The initial contact with participants was made through various local senior organizations. We selected a heterogeneous group of seniors (N = 21) in relation to gender, age, local infrastructure, and in the transport systems typically used, in order to obtain a wider spectrum of ridesharing and mobility experiences. Table 1 provides an overview of the interviewees according to relevant categories. Pseudonyms are used to ensure participants' anonymity and confidentiality.

The region that participants come from has about 100,000 inhabitants in western Germany. One characteristic of this area is that it includes both urban and very rural areas. The only public transportation option available is bus, or train (mainly for inter-city travelling). The bus service is very limited, especially in rural areas. Additionally, the landscape is very hilly and diverse; meaning that travelling from one location to another can mean very indirect journeys. Thus, the focus in this study lies on an area with limited public transport system, that is close to the real life context of most older adults.

All interviewees were still mobile and take actively part in social events and life in general. They agreed to participate on a voluntary basis and no financial compensation was offered. Further, all of the interviewees committed to collaborating in a three-year project, commencing with these initial interviews. The overall project aim is to develop a mobility platform for older adults that follows a participatory design approach [31]. Participants from the outset were aware of the research aim of building a ridesharing platform customized for older adults needs and are overall positively positioned toward mobile ridesharing solutions.

In the analyzing process we used MAXQDA[1] software. First, interview transcripts were organized into different content parts to organize the data with the help of different code groups. Second, the data was analyzed under the leading question what are the strategies people describing to organize their ridesharing practice? In the following we will report on our findings on these issues.

5 Mobile Methods in Ridesharing Contexts

In the following section, we present the results of the outlined research agenda. We uncover phenomenological inquiries of ridesharing and of being mobile in general that provide results of coordination strategies in ridesharing settings. In the following chapter these findings derive as innovation seed for the design of technologies in supporting sustainable mobility practices.

5.1 Accounts of Mobility

One central aspect we found in our study was that people refer to concepts of activities when describing their daily mobility. During the interviews it became obvious that people talk about concrete, observable practices (such as 'shopping', 'going to the sports center', '—the cinema' or 'visiting a friend') in order to describe their daily mobility towards others. Referring to categories of (outdoor) activities functions as accounts of everyday mobility between the researcher and the interviewee, to describe plans or the way the people organize their mobility and was a very frequent observation in all of the interviews. This connection becomes explicit in in the following sequence:

> Interviewer: 'If you took a closer look at your everyday mobility, how would you describe it?' Mrs. Davis (57): 'What kind of mobility do you mean? Do you want to know what I am doing?'

---

[1] http://www.maxqda.com/ (last view: 01.01.2014).

This quote provides a good example of how difficult it is to operationalize mobility and refers to the circumstance that the concept of 'mobility' is not part of our every-day language for describing movements. Mobility is not a phenomenon or practice that can be observed like car driving, walking or waiting. Moreover, it is an abstract definition, primarily used in professional and/or scientific contexts. This makes it difficult for the interviewees to answer our question. In doing so, they used the mentioned activities concepts to make the organization of their every-day mobility accountable. Mrs. Davis proceed in the following way:

Ah well, when I'm mobile I go to the gym in the city, I go shopping, or go swimming with my neighbor (Mrs. Davis).

The example shows that mobility is equated with activities. In other words, we can say that activities are used to describe the organization of mobility. Hence, the sequence is an example of using activities to describe personal mobility as a method to communicate daily mobility practices. The accounting of activities, as illustrated in the case of Mrs. Davis, has fundamentally different implications than the reference to routes have. Routes, which build the basis of most ridesharing systems, can be identified by a street name, a famous place, or locations on a map. Activities like 'going to the cinema', or 'visiting a friend' do not refer to any concrete physical space, but rather have a social and cultural reference. Thus, in cooperative settings like ridesharing the concept of activities brings advantages in communication. When communicating in 'public', people need a common infor-mation basis so that strangers to ridesharing can follow shared rules. Referring to activities provides a *surplus* of information, which is excluded when only talking about routes. One example which demonstrates the benefit of activities providing points of orientation in ridesharing cooperation is illustrated in the following quote:

Yes, well, I'd prefer to go shopping with a friend and I wouldn't ask my neighbor if she could take me. You see, her lifestyle is different from mine, she is independent and—I'd be a burden if I was always calling round to ask her to drive to the supermarket or the doctor. (...) But it's different with our cinema group. It is nice to have this group and to drive together (Mrs. Anderson, 73).

Mrs. Anderson states that some activities are more likely to offer ridesharing opportunities than others. When sharing rides, in particular for short distances, people share not only the rides but also the activities, too. Hence describing activities such as 'going to the cinema' or 'going to the supermarket' includes different social information, which forms the basis for people to decide whether to join a ride or not. Mrs. Anderson's quote is not uncommon; we have a number of interview statements expressing the opinion that it is different with activities which render them suitable for ridesharing or not. Thus, referring to activities is used as a method for coordinating mutual ridesharing practices on a basal basis, that enable people to talk about their mobility and their future mobility plans.

5.2 Accounting for Social Uncertainty

Ridesharing entails a lot of uncertainties and communication work. Driver and passenger depend on each other in several respects, for instance when matching logistical concerns such as departure time, pick up points or organizing the return journey. Within the driving arrangements it became clear that activities provide first ordering methods people can refer to in ridesharing cooperation. As already shown in the previous section, some activities seem to lend themselves more to ridesharing than others. However, activities do not only provide information about the reason for movement, but about its 'framing', too. For example, going to the cinema is framed differently to a shopping trip. Both activities can be shared among two persons or a group of people, but are encountered in different ways: While going to the cinema has fixed spatial (the cinema is in a certain place) and temporal (movies start and end according to fixed time plans) limits, shopping trips are more openly framed. Shopping can be done according to different value stances; while one person might be in a rush to do the weekly shop, another person might want to stroll around, window shopping.

However, it has been stated that a fixed frame is advantageous and influences ridesharing positively, as the following quote illustrates:

> Well yes, they're fixed (arrangements)... well, there's a group of us who do things together... sometimes we drive to the cinema ... and erm yes, then you just ask 'do you want to go this evening or maybe tomorrow' and then one person says, 'yes, listen I'll drive' or [someone else says] 'I'll drive...That's what it's like (Mrs. Thomson, 64).

In this excerpt, Mrs. Thomson is talking about a ridesharing routine of regular cinema visits in a fixed group. However, not only is the group established, she also refers to a clear framework of the activity, which makes the cooperation process easy. She states that complex negotiation processes are unnecessary because of a fixed beginning and end. Further joint activities help to solve the organization of the return journey. Hence some activities are more suitable for ridesharing than others, because they are easier to deal with when cooperation is called for. Activities are not only means that enables people to talk about mobility as some kind of (social) places, but provide information about the wider context mobility is taking place, as well.

5.3 Accounting for Independence

All of the interviews were started with an open question about the personal meanings of mobility, in order to find out what is important for the interviewees within their daily mobility. It was interesting that every interviewee mentioned 'mobility independence' at least once during the interview. The following quote provides an insight into a typical answer given by interviewees to the question of what mobility means to them:

It (mobility) means being very independent and able to go to places. The bus services up here are really good and I'm really happy and that is important. You don't need anybody because the (bus) connections are excellent and you can get anywhere you like really quickly. That is very important for me. Yes, this is really very important to me (Mrs. Thomson, 76).

Mrs. Thomson who lives in a single-household in a suburban area without a car, regards her independence as an important element of her mobility. The mobility she mentions is concerned with individual capacities and actions as forms and expressions of her individual independence. Thus, by independence she means being able to manage her daily mobility by utilizing her own resources in accordance with her abilities and without depending on others. It is this understanding of independence as 'doing things alone' on the basis of one's own physical and cognitive abilities that turned out to be the dominant meaning of independence. Hence, our interviewees point out that it is not just about reaching the destination but 'managing to get there', re-affirming the own capacity to do so.

However, ridesharing entails by definition a degree of mutual dependency. Not only within coordinating logistical concerns about time of departure, pick up places and return. Further, people have to cooperate by negotiating some agreement about the 'intensity' of interaction—is one expected to talk? And how much? In particular Laurier showed that both parties have to find a way defining and negotiating their mutual relationship [12]. Further Sherlock compares both roles of passenger and driver with the roles of being a good 'host' and a good 'guest' [21]. Thus while guest and host are background 'politeness' categories to driver and passenger they are resources for moral assessment of each person's conduct during the journey. These kinds of relationship are, of course, not those found between family members or between longstanding, good friends. There, such issues are more or less settled as habitual. Hence, there appeared some asymmetry of decisional influence depending on both roles. The following sequence gives a good glimpse in typical statements about the guest and host role:

[Talking about sharing regular rides with her neighbor and going to a particular bar] Of course I depend on the driver. If the driver wants to go to '9 bar', drinking a coffee, I have to follow if I want or not. I don't like the '9 bar'. And in return when driving on Saturday to the market I would not go to 9 bar. Then people can decide whether they want to go to '9 bar' or drive back home with me (Mrs. White, 58).

There seems to be a mutual understanding that passengers as good guests have a duty to orient towards driver's habits. The same person explained further that she would expect to accommodate driver wishes in respect of start times for instance, and would not expect equal consideration from the driver. Hence, there is a mutual understanding that passengers should make few demands on drivers largely because there is a sense of having been 'invited'. Drivers, in short, are perceived as having more rights in negotiating the arrangements. This strong orientation along the driver is one expression of the dependence.

Interviewees reported about several methods to decrease dependence and establish a reciprocal relationship between both parties. This can be reached by integrating paying systems, alternating driver systems, or more informal, spending a coffee or chocolate.

5.4 Accounting for Flexibility

Beside the concept of 'mobility independence', 'decisional autonomy' is stated as an important personal issue. The concept refers to the way in which people seek to maintain and maximize their choices. Although it relates to the issue of independence, it is distinct from it. Quotes like following clearly express this position:

> Yes, a great deal [mobility means] everything. Everything... the decision too, just the thought of it even I CAN go, if I want... that is so important, you know? Even if I might not actually go anywhere but just... yes, just to know that if I wanted to go anywhere, I can just go to the garage, get in my car and drive off... and yes, I am scared of the day when that might not be the case any more (Mrs. Martinez, 77).

Mrs. Martinez who lives with her husband in a more rural area states the importance of the potential of mobility as a means of maintaining and enhancing travel opportunities, rather than the travelling itself. In this way mobility is seen as a means of being autonomous in and through the capacity to make decisions about where, when and how to travel on one's own. This issue of autonomous decision-making is in line with the findings of Sheller and Urry [20], or Urry [26] who argue that decisional and executional autonomy are key aspects of our perception of freedom and that mobility is widely considered as a symbol and facilitator of that freedom. In particular the bare existence of automobility produces desires for flexibility that so far only the car is able to satisfy. The seamlessness of the car journey makes other modes of travel inflexible and fragmented [25]. Thus, ride-sharing systems have to compete with personalized, subjective temporalities, as people live their lives in and through their cars. Several people stated that ride opportunities are not entirely predictable like the option of using the own car, with respect to time, route, etc., the potential passenger has to deal with a considerable amount of uncertainty. Relying on someone else means lining their activities up with the schedule of others, at least to some extent. The following sequence illustrates an issue that was stated by participants quite often and can be seen as a result of the passengers' loss of decisional autonomy:

> [With ridesharing] you've just got to follow suit, no matter how or when she's driving. I have to watch what anyone's doing, I can't look (when shopping) where I want and how long I want and what I want. Thus, I prefer to do it alone, you know [...] That's all those things, no, well it is (on my own) more independent (Mrs. Williams, 73).

The driver may have pragmatic reasons for the ride offer—saving money, company, etc., but in particular the passenger has to adjust to the driver without even knowing what exactly s/he is adjusting to. In summary the system of automobility coerces people to assemble contingent patterns of their mobility comparable to car usage. Thus, avoiding being inflexible people chose to share rides to activities that already have fixed borders and/or consists of a fixed group of people. Another instrument to avoid the feeling of being inflexible, can be reached trough awareness functions about mobility offers. Hence, 'flexible' and 'dynamic' ridesharing cannot be realized through formalized lists allowing a wider time span for meeting. Moreover, flexibility depends on socio-technically shaped practices, bounded to particular activities.

6 Discussion

There is a growing amount of research in CSCW and HCI stressing the need for an adequate supportive ridesharing system. While studies in controlled setups show benefits in using such ridesharing systems, there is still a lack of user confidence and marked acceptance (in particular for ridesharing in short distances), which might point to a failure of the existing design concepts [6, 14]. Although previous efforts provide a useful foundation for understanding and supporting ridesharing systems, they often miss the relevance of the embodied quality of mobility, and mainly argue on a technical level. Of course mobility has a physical substrate, as movement trough time and space, but mobility as a practice resides in the life-world of people. Thus, the design of support mobility systems has not necessarily to center around its physical character, confounded with a transportation under-standing of mobility. To meet these shortcomings a phenomenological inquiry to understand mobility activities as a practice that is embedded in the daily life of consumers turned out as helpful. The phenomenological perspective made applied methods visible, people use to address cooperation challenges, like the principles of activities, reciprocity, independence, or flexibility. Hence, these methods pro-vide not only answers to practical challenges, but further starting points to identify sensitizing inquiries for design, summarized in Table 2.

The identified challenges, methods and design ideas enrich the current state of the art in ridesharing systems. This becomes obvious in particular obvious within the concept of activities. Using activities as a baseline to organize ridesharing mobility is completely different form the current more or less formalized 'input fields' for the departure and destination that is part of the transportation per-spective. Further, using activities as basic concepts to organize people's mobility in ridesharing systems would allow dealing with issues like 'trust' or 'security' in new ways. For example one can imagine that particular people or certain groups can be invited to share specific activities. In this way the user can decide how to cope with sensitive activities and which kind of activities are appropriate for sharing. However, these two examples provide only glimpses in the benefits of the phenomenological approach. Beside the methods that we have identified, pro-viding a general orientation for the users in ridesharing practice, we have to examine how the users refer to them and how they are involved into practice. The

Table 2 Practical challenges, 'mobile methods' and design implications in ridesharing context

Challenges	Methods	Sensitizing for design
Talking about 'mobility' is challenging, because 'mobility' is neither praxis and nor phenomenon	When people talk about their motilities they refer to 'activities' (e.g. going to the cinema, or visiting friends)	The concept of activities can provide an alternative to formalized input fields for the departure and destination. People refer to activities in order to organize their mobility practices along each other
Cooperation in ridesharing situations means dealing with many uncertainties people have to solve	People developed several strategies for dealing with those social uncertainties in order to facilitate cooperation. Decreasing the uncertainties and cooperation effort, ridesharing is mainly based on routin basis and conducted within a fixed cycle of persons	Thus, support should be on hand so that those activities which are ore suitable for ridesharing can be identified more easily. Activities and related networks exert high influence on this issue and should be adaptable variables
Ridesharing is based on an informal economy, maintaining reciprocity between the 'host' and 'guest'. This balance has to be managed by the users	Users have developed several strategies for dealing with reciprocity. These depend on their relationships to each other and the kind of ridesharing established (e.g. whether it takes place on a regular basis, or has an alternating driver-system).	Flexible systems for paying can be adapted to the specific cooperation form between driver and passenger
In the age of automobility independent mobility is understood to have a very high value. As a practice dependent on cooperation, ridesharing poses difficulties.	Dealing with independence turned out to be a highly complex issue. People aim to minimize their dependence by the choosing the 'right' driver (preferably friends), or the 'right' event (like social events)	Autonomy can be secured in various ways, e.g. by making offers or maintaining a balanced ridesharing economy
Like independence, flexibility is very important in the age of automobility. This is also problematic in ridesharing situations because it is restricted to offers on ridesharing.	Because ridesharing harbors the risk of being highly inflexible, people tended to chose less flexible activities with fixed boundaries for sharing rides.	Dealing with these issues means allowing users to behave flexibly within activities and networks

concept of activities can help to identify those aims that are suitable for ridesharing and do not undermine independence or flexibility. Thus, there should be support to identify those activities that are more likely for ridesharing contexts. Further, it would be interesting to see in which way users would create ridesharing networks around particular activities and how they would use flexible paying systems, within particular activities and surrounding networks. Hence, the accounting methods identified provide general insights into the overall organization of cooperative ridesharing. They are however, interpreted individually, based on the own context that cause a need for considering the situatedness and subjective character of ridesharing.

7 Conclusion and Outlook

A key finding of our study is that the mobile methods identified are not only mechanisms used by people to make their own mobility practices accountable, but that they can function as an important source for technological innovation too. However these methods possess an indexical character, which means that they provide general means of mobility organization and refer to one's own mobility context at the same time because they are adopted individually. Thus the crux for further research on ridesharing cooperation is to allow users to contextualize these accounting practices along the following two approaches:

1. Providing contextualization for interpretation
   In order to provide a foundation for these indexical 'mobile methods', a turn in design is needed: it is not the intended use of an artifact which should be in the spotlight. Moreover, the primary aim of support technology should be to help people contextualize their mobility information by showing connections between mobility units and events in daily life. An approach towards bridging this gap lies in shifting the focus from providing solutions that refers to a time and space understanding of mobility transcribed in support technology. Systems should adapt technologies for capturing and tracking personal activities and integrate this information into the ridesharing data to foster learning. They should also reflect personal mobility practices. This interest is close to the concept of 'perceptual beta' [2], which means that technology is not a product but a process. The overall design may be changed or subtly 'tweaked' in response to emergent-user practices, recognizing the integral role of social innovation and providing communities mechanisms for inventing and negotiating acceptable new practices, meanings and sensitivities. The aim not the optimization itself, but to build a mirror for the users [3].
2. Making computational support adaptable
   Although we outlined some general methods of ridesharing practice, mobility is based on how individual experiences are conducted. One way to address the individual shaping of the methods is to make systems open to adaptation by

their users. Customization can be applied on several levels: for example, adaptability could make it possible to include individually defined users for certain activities or to define metrics and redefine comparable groups or classes of activities. The design challenge is not just about how people might use these individual devices, but also how they might create assemblies nomadically, to suit current mobility needs and circumstances.

Hence by changing the mode of experiences through the design of technical instruments, we as designers contribute to the constitution of people's life-world. A central implication is that the matter of design should not be an isolated artifact, but the co-evolution of the artifacts and the social practices in which they are embedded and allow cooperation. We believe that these connections will help people to reconcile their mobility practices with their intended lifestyle, creating an important opportunity for CSCW to contribute sustainable ridesharing solutions.

Acknowledgments We thank all interviewees for their participation, our student assistants for transcription work and discussions, our local partners for their support in addressing participants and University Heidelberg. Further we thank the BMBF for funding this project.

References

1. Brereton M, Roe P, Foth M, Bunker JM, Buys L (2009) Designing participation in agile ridesharing with mobile social software. In: Proceedings of the 21st annual conference of the Australian computer-human interaction special interest group: design: open 24/7, ACM, pp 257–260
2. Büscher M, Urry J (2009) Mobile methods and the empirical. Eur J Soc Theory 12(1):99–116
3. Büscher M, Urry J, Witchger K (2010) Mobile methods. Taylor & Francis
4. Button G, Dourish P (1996) Technomethodology: paradoxes and possibilities. In: Proceedings of the SIGCHI conference on human factors in computing systems, ACM, pp 19–26
5. Crabtree A (2004) Taking technomethodology seriously: hybrid change in the ethnomethodology—design relationship. Eur J Info Syst 13(3):195–209
6. Dourish P, Anderson K, Nafus D (2007) Cultural mobilities: diversity and agency in urban computing. In: Human-computer interaction–Interact 2007, Springer, pp 100–113
7. Garfinkel H (1963) A conception of and experiments with' trust as a condition of concerted stable actions. The production of reality: essays and readings on social interaction; pp 381–392
8. Garfinkel H (1967) Studies in ethnomethodology. Englewood Cliffs, NJ
9. Ghelawat S, Radke K, Brereton M (2010) Interaction, privacy and profiling considerations in local mobile social software: a prototype agile ride share system. In: Proceedings of the 22nd conference of the computer-human interaction special interest group of Australia on computer-human interaction, OZCHI '10. New York, NY, USA: ACM. pp 376–379
10. Handke V, Jonuschat H (2012) Flexible ridesharing: new opportunities and service concepts for sustainable mobility. Springer, Berlin
11. Ihde D (2002) Bodies in technology. U of Minnesota Press, Mineapolis (Bd. 5)
12. Laurier E, Lorimer H, Brown B, Jones O, Juhlin O, Noble A, Perry M et al (2008) Driving and 'passengering': notes on the ordinary organization of car travel. Mobilities 3(1):1–23

13. Luff P, Heath C (1998) Mobility in collaboration. In: Proceedings of the 1998 ACM conference on computer supported cooperative work, ACM pp 305–314
14. Massey D (1999) Space-Time, 'science' and the relationship between physical geography and human geography. Trans Inst Br Geogr 24(3):261–276
15. Meurer J, Stein M, Randall D, Rohde M, Wulf V (2014) Social dependency and mobile autonomy—supporting older adults mobility with ridesharing. In: Proceedings of the ICT 2014 ACM annual conference on human factors in computing systems CHI, Toronto
16. Mirisaee SH, Brereton M, Roe P (2011) Bridging the representation and interaction challenges of mobile context-aware computing: designing agile ridesharing. In: Proceedings of the 23rd Australian computer-human interaction conference, ACM, pp 221–224
17. Ozenc FK, Cranor LF, Morris JH (2011) Adapt-a-ride: understanding the dynamics of commuting preferences through an experience design framework. In: Proceedings of the 2011 conference on designing pleasurable products and interfaces, 61
18. Radke K, Brereton M, Mirisaee S, Ghelawat S, Boyd C, Nieto JG (2011) Tensions in developing a secure collective information practice-the case of agile ridesharing. In: Human-computer interaction–interact 2011, Springer, pp 524–532
19. Schütz A (1967) The phenomenology of the social world. Northwestern University Press, Evanston
20. Sheller M, Urry J (2003) Mobile transformations of 'public' and 'private' life. Theory, Cult Soc 20(3):107–125
21. Sherlock K (2001) Revisiting the concept of hosts and guests. Tourist Stud 1(3):271–295
22. Steger-Vonmetz DC (2005) Improving modal choice and transport efficiency with the virtual ridesharing agency. In: Proceedings of Intelligent transportation systems, 2005, IEEE, pp 994–999
23. Tamminen S, Oulasvirta A, Toiskallio K, Kankainen A (2004) Understanding mobile contexts. Pers Ubiquit Comput 8(2):135–143
24. Teodorović D, Dell'Orco M (2008) Mitigating traffic congestion: solving the ride-matching problem by bee colony optimization. Transp Plan Technol 31(2):135–152
25. Urry J (2004) The 'system' of automobility. Theory, Cult Soc 21(4–5):25–39
26. Urry J (2007) Mobilities. Cambridge, UK; Malden, MA: Polity
27. Wash R, Hemphill L, Resnick P (2005) Design decisions in the ridenow project. In: Proceedings of the 2005 international ACM siggroup conference on supporting group work, ACM pp 132–135
28. Wessels R, Pueboobpaphan R, Bie J, van Arem B (2011) Integrating online social networks with ridesharing systems: effects of detour and level of friend
29. Winch P (2002) The idea of a social science: and its relation to philosophy. Routledge
30. Witzel A, Reiter H (2012) The problem-centred interview. Sage
31. Wulf V, Rohde M, Pipek V, Stevens G (2011) Engaging with practices: design case studies as a research framework in CSCW. In: Proceedings of the ACM 2011 conference on computer supported cooperative work, ACM pp 505–512

Designing for Continuity: Assisting Emergency Planning Practice Through Computer-Supported Collaborative Technologies

Sara Tena, David Díez, Ignacio Aedo and Paloma Díaz

Abstract Emergency planning is an on-going process in which a group of experts collaborate for ensuring that a community has the necessary resources and procedures for facing an emergency situation. It is a sustaining pattern of analysis and decision, based on the unstable collaboration over time of heterogeneous groups of planners. With the purpose of understanding the challenges of supporting technologically a long-term collaborative activity such as the emergency planning, a two-year descriptive case study in a real work setting has been carried out. The analysis of its results has shown the necessity of providing a sense of continuity both in the reasoning of planners and the history of the practice. The final aim of the work is to identify a set of claims that addresses the design of such computer-based technologies that effectively assist emergency planning.

1 Introduction

The occurrence of an emergency situation can cause damages in people and properties. Hence, the organization of material and human resources to face emergency situations should not be left to improvisation. Emergency planning is concerned with ensuring that a community has the necessary people, equipment, and procedures to respond effectively to emergencies [1]. Though *"there is a tendency on the part of officials to see disaster planning as a product"* [2],

S. Tena (✉) · D. Díez · I. Aedo · P. Díaz
DEI—Interactive Systems Group, Universidad Carlos III de Madrid, Madrid, Spain
e-mail: stena@inf.uc3m.es

D. Díez
e-mail: ddiez@inf.uc3m.es

I. Aedo
e-mail: aedo@ia.uc3m.es

P. Díaz
e-mail: pdp@inf.uc3m.es

C. Rossitto et al. (eds.), *COOP 2014 - Proceedings of the 11th International Conference on the Design of Cooperative Systems, 27–30 May 2014, Nice (France)*, DOI: 10.1007/978-3-319-06498-7_22, © Springer International Publishing Switzerland 2014

emergency planning is more than the definition of written documentation. The written plan itself represents a snapshot at a specific point in time [3]; while emergency planning is actually an intellectual process which is concerned with deciding in advance what, when, why, how, and who shall do the work.

Emergency planning may be depicted as a long-time horizon activity in the sense that defining an optimal response requires the elaboration and implementation of succeeding plans. Moreover, emergency plans are not designed once and for all. During the elaboration of an emergency plan, the planning team usually meets several times in order to both exchange information and discuss about risks and resources assignments. This deliberation process is mainly based on the knowledge, experience, and lessons learned from previous plans. Similarly, emergency plans must evolve over time. An increase in population, the creation of a new road, or even the change of the flow of a river, could bring new threats and, consequently, the redesign of a plan. In this case, planners must joint their efforts to continuously analysis and review of previous emergency plans [4]. This process should be based on using the experience as a key to reflect about new threats and updates. Thus, defining an effective, flexible and timely response is based on creating a link during the definition of plans, on gathering a continuity that allows planners to bind past events and discussions with present situations and decisions.

So far, different authors have proved the feasibility and usefulness of applying computer-supported collaborative technologies so as to improve emergency planning [5, 6]. However, these authors have focused on supporting the collaboration in different spaces or among different backgrounds [5–8], leaving aside the implications of collaborating over time. In order to get a set of claims that address designing for continuity, this paper presents a descriptive case study carried out for 2 years. In keeping with the results of this case study, the achievement of continuity requires providing enough information to let planners to know what decisions were made, who made those decisions, and why they made them. Accordingly, designing computer-based collaborative technologies that effectively assist the emergency planning practice must be focused on capturing the rationale of the design as well as the underlying information that wrap decisions.

The structure of the remaining paper is as follows. Section 2 describes a two-year case study in the emergency-planning context. The results of such case study are presented in Sect. 3. These results show the necessity of creating a virtual link between planning periods during the definition of plans. The Sect. 4 presents a discussion of the necessity of designing for continuity, as well as a set of claims that guides the design of such computer-supported collaborative technologies that enrich emergency planning. Finally, conclusions and further work are presented.

2 A Descriptive Case Study

Emergency planning has been commonly recognized as a professional activity that can be improved through the use of collaborative technologies [5, 8]. With the purpose of understanding emergency planning and developing suitable collaborative technologies that assist such an activity, different empirical studies and fieldworks have been performed [5–8]. As an example, Carroll et al. [7] studied the support of tabletop exercises by using geospatial collaborative software. Similarly, Convertino [8–10] has been focused on assisting the development of common understanding through the use of annotated design tools. In succeeding works, thanks to the realization of a mid-term case study, Schafer et al. [5] have studied the community perspective of emergency planning, focusing on identifying the main collective tasks of the emergency-planning process and the way of supporting them. Despite their significance to understand the emergency planning practice, none of these works makes enough emphasis on studying the relevance of time to develop suitable emergency plans. In order to overcome this existing gap, a two-year descriptive case study was conducted.

This descriptive case study was divided into two main phases. The initial phase compiled exploratory efforts aimed at reaching a deep understanding of the emergency-planning activity. Second phase was focused on analyzing the implications of emergency planning as a long-term activity. In this second phase, the inquiry team conducted an empirical study in a real work setting. Following subsections are intended to explain the development of both phases.

2.1 Phase 1: Overview of the Emergency-Planning Activity

A knowledge base on emergency planning was initially obtained from the review of literature and the analysis of real emergency plans. Such review provided us knowledge about the main goals and tasks of the emergency-planning process, an overview of how emergency plans are designed, and understanding about which information is treated and documented during the process. With the aim of confirming these insights and deepening our knowledge about the emergency-planning activity, six interviews with emergency planning experts were conducted. Such experts work as emergency management coordinators in Spanish municipalities whose population is between 20,000 and 200,000 habitants—the Spanish legislation defines like a 'municipality' those neighborhoods whose population is within such a range. As emergency management coordinators of their respective municipalities, these experts are responsible of the definition of local plans that address the risks within the municipality.

The collection of information from the experts was based on the performance of semi-structured interviews. These interviews, with duration of approximately one hour per respondent, included a total of three closed questions and nine open questions. Closed questions were related to the background of the experts, while opened questions were focused on getting information about the performance of the activity: the number and profile of planning team members, the regular tasks carried out during the activity, the kind of resources used by the participants, or the type of communication channels that they utilize. Additionally, experts were questioned about the average time taken to define and develop an emergency plan.

2.1.1 Data Collection

As way of developing a mutual trust partnership with experts, the interviews were not digitally recorded. As an alternative, the researchers decided to handwrite notes during the interviews. Following the investigator triangulation technique [11], and in order to avoid sampling bias, the notes were taken by two researchers. These two researchers were focused on summarizing information, for which they quickly and consistently collect relevant aspects of the different issues of the interview. Additionally, key phrases and exact quotes were captured to highlight those aspects in which the responders make special emphasis. Once interviews were finished, all collected and registered data was transcribed for later analysis.

2.1.2 Data Analysis

Once the information was transcribed, the first task was to make sense of the collected information. To that end, it was necessary to use some encoding process that allowed developing a manageable classification or coding system [12]. This coding forced researchers to make judgments about the underlying sense of the interviews in order to determine which information was meaningful.

Initially, by the open coding process, the inquiry team developed a set of codes that included predefined and emergent codes. Predefined codes were categories and themes that they expected to see based on their prior knowledge about literature in emergency planning. Codes such as 'collaborative', 'multidisciplinary' or 'on-going' are included in this group. On the other hand, codes like 'experience' or 'long-term' came up as the data from the case study was reviewed. After that, the inquiry team closely reviewed and re-coded data creating a resulting coding scheme presented in Table 1. This coding scheme includes four macro-level codes, each comprising several micro-level codes.

The analysis of data showed a significant fact: during the interviews, experts made constant reference to the temporal aspects of the emergency planning activity. Most of the interviewees pointed out that the development of emergency plans is a long-term activity, usually distributed over weeks or months, rather than days. Moreover, they highlighted that emergency planning is not once and for all, but it is an ongoing process. An ongoing process based on the knowledge, experience, and lessons learned from previous plans. In this sense, effective emergency planning is a long-term activity extended over lengthy periods of time. The consequence should be the consideration of time as a key element in the structuring of the emergency planning activity.

Table 1 Coding scheme used to analysis the transcriptions of interviews

Code	Description
Practitioners	
Experience	Knowledge or skill acquired by such means over a period of time
Knowledge	Facts, information, and skills acquired by a person through experience or education
Background	A person's education, experience, and social circumstances
Process	
Collaborative	Produced or conducted by two or more parties working together
Multidisciplinary	Combining or involving several academic disciplines or professional specializations in an approach to a topic or problem
On-going	Still in progress
Long-term	Occurring over or relating to a long period of time
Interaction mode	
Co-located	Sharing a location or facility with someone
Distributed	Occur throughout different locations
Tasks	
Principal	Main tasks relevant in the emergency-planning process
Secondary	Less important task in the emergency-planning process

2.2 Phase 2: Identification of the Implications of the Long-Term

Once we became aware of the importance of temporal aspects to design plans, we decided to focus on examining the role of time in the performance of emergency planning. With this aim, a two-year case study was carried out in the local level. Local level, commonly referred as municipalities, is the base or reference level of emergency planning. Whilst state, national, or international levels are typically focused on coordination activities, planning activities lie in municipal governments [13, 14]. That means that the success of an emergency management operation will probably depend on the effectiveness of local emergency plans, including the quality of local resources and their deployment in emergency situations.

For conducting the study within the municipality, the emergency plan for winter (Winter Plan) was selected. The 'Winter Plan' is aimed to minimize the effects of snow and to restore the roads with the aim of not paralyzing the city and ensuring the restoration of local services as soon as possible. As consequence, this plan involves many local services and first responders such as police, civil protection service, civil guard, social service, environmental service, public construction service and a cleaning service company. In addition, the 'Winter Plan' was selected because of its validity period of four months. Every emergency plan has a validity period—the active lifespan for the plan. Once the validity period ends, emergency plans must be revised to accommodate existing changes in the legal framework, changes in the environment, and the lessons learnt from experience.

To give planners the opportunity of adapting plans during a two-year period, the validity period of the plan should not be longer than six months or be redesigned every year.

Once selected the emergency plan, the exploration was made through the use of the observation technique. This technique provided the opportunity to deepen in the understanding of who the practitioners are, how they work on a day-to-day basis, and how emergency planning is developed in the long-term. In keeping with methods triangulation technique [11], it was used a combination of direct and indirect observation. Direct observation was aimed to study the behavior of participants during planning meetings: their social relationships and group dynamics. Meanwhile, indirect observation allowed collecting data about the information exchanging between meetings, as well as the actions performed by planners to prepare such meetings.

2.2.1 Data Collection

The study of a complex activity such as emergency planning revealed us the need to combine different techniques of collecting data in order to achieve additional findings and to develop knowledge on the emergency-planning activity. Hence, based on the data triangulation idea [11] of using different data collection strategies to verify trends detected over a set of observations, information was collected through the use of field notes, video and audio records, and diaries. Field notes were used during the observations to compile key phrases, exact quotes with indications of emphasis and tone, sketches of the location, the history, steps, and context of any activity, and details that would be essential to study. Since capturing every moment and every word could be in some cases probably unneeded, the inquiry team focused on identifying patterns and phenomena within the activities [15]. Patterns are actions or ideas that keeps recurring—patterns of behavior, patterns in stories or patterns of responses to a question. For instance, a recurring action such as using drawings for expressing ideas could be considered a pattern of behavior. They could emerge during the case study when something is done repeatedly, but also during the analysis of data. Instead, phenomena are unusual behaviors—especially unusual methods of working—that could be interesting and whose consideration could benefit to people in their work. As an example, the unusual fact of comparing data during the meetings could be a phenomenon that provides a different perspective over data in meetings. With the aim of identifying patters and phenomena, field notes used to start recording the name of the person doing the research, the day, the time, and the place. Then, they include the facts and history of the activities using pseudonyms instead of real names to preserve the anonymity of the subjects. Similarly to the methodology used in the first phase, the notes were taken by two researchers [11]. As a complement, researchers video and audio recorded the meetings.

Additionally to field notes and video records taken by the inquiry team, we asked participants to make diaries [16] for recording events, items of behaviour, informal meetings as they occurred. With such an aim, participants recorded the date, the people involved, the goal of the meeting, and a description of how facts occurred. This information compiled all the facts, meetings, and discussions that took place between the meetings and in which researchers were unable to attend.

2.2.2 Data Analysis

One of the main challenges in case studies lies in the analysis phase, where ideas and findings emerge from fieldwork data. Raw data needs to be turned into a form that can be easily understood. To that end, two different data analysis techniques were used: affinity diagram and short vignettes. The former was focused on highlighting and categorizing information for identifying patterns, while the latter was focused on describing special issues identified during the observation.

Using affinity diagram for categorizing and organize data in groups to establish relationship among them [17], the first step followed by the inquiry team was to make things physical and visible. This would allow drawing connections across various pieces of data, adding them up to a conclusion, or creating something new that could came up by existing pieces of data [15]. With such a purpose, the inquiry team wrote data, quotes, and ideas on a post-it note and stuck them on a wall. Then, team members move and organize notes in groups, establishing relationships, and partnerships among different data. In this case, the team for constructing affinity diagrams consists of three people: the researchers that attend to the interviews and the meetings, and an external person. The external person, with experience in the design of emergency-management system, was included for providing a different perspective of the emergency-planning activity, during the categorization step.

In order to organize and compare data, this technique was applied after each year of planning, getting a total of two affinity diagrams. Figure 1 shows an example of the affinity diagrams obtained.

Since affinity diagram technique resulted very useful for identifying patterns, short vignettes [18] were used to depict phenomena. They consist on a brief description of a recurrent action or a special situation, and the consequences of them. In such descriptions, following the philosophy of other design artifacts such as persona, the names used in the short vignettes are not real. Examples of two short vignettes are presented below:

> During the definition of the routes, Pedro, the coordinator of civil protection realized that two routes was overlapped. The two routes were defined for cleaning the same zone of the city but with different snowplows. Therefore, they decided to change one of the routes and optimize the usage of the available resources
>
> While the planning team was discussing a task, civil protection members have to leave the meeting immediately for attending a fire emergency. Then, the rest of the members continue the meeting without being able to take into consideration the knowledge and experience of the civil protection members. It makes that, in the next meeting, civil protection members have to review what the planning team decided.

Fig. 1 Example of an
affinity diagram

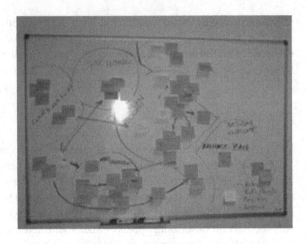

2.3 Results

Emergency planning is an activity distributed in time. Not only during the definition of the plan, based on meeting several times in a long period of time, but also throughout the life of the plan, due to the periodically performance of drilling and review meetings oriented to update and refine the plan. Following paragraphs explain different issues related to the long-term character of emergency planning.

2.3.1 Sustaining Pattern of Analysis and Decision

The first result to be established is the existence of a well-defined pattern of practice. Both years, the planning team follows a similar scheme: planners meet several times over a period of one month, starting approximately two months before the beginning of the winter session. The first of these meetings is oriented to finally establish the planning team, define a meeting schedule for the period, review internal plans and policies, and create a common understanding about previous winter sessions. Subsequently, the team meets several times to develop the plan. Once the development of the plan is finished, two team members—designed at the beginning of the process as annotators—write the emergency plan. This written document, considered as the main result of the emergency planning process, compiles all the information managed during meetings. Nevertheless, the emergency-planning process does not finish with the elaboration and delivery of the emergency plan. When the winter session ends, the planning team conduct a reviewing meeting, in which planners tracking down the implementation of the plan, identifying drawbacks and strong points. The second year of the study, due to the occurrence of a relevant snowstorm, the planning team conduct an additional reviewing meeting to analyse the performance during this emergency situation. In all cases, the result of the reviewing meeting is a written report that collects all relevant issues and problems discussed during the meeting.

2.3.2 Scattered Tasks

Emergency planning is a complex process that involves three main tasks: risk assessment, resources identification, and strategy definition [19]. Such description of the process can lead to think that emergency planning is a waterfall process. Nevertheless, the case study reveals that emergency planning is an iterative process in which planning tasks are scattered over time. As Fig. 2 shows, the risk assessment task is developed in meeting 1, 2, 3, and 4. Similarly, the resources identification task is carried out in meeting 2, 3, and 4. Therefore, planning tasks are not developed in just one meeting, but through several meetings scattered over time.

2.3.3 Emerging Constraints

Data analysis allowed identifying a pattern that is recurrent in emergency-planning practice. There are constraints that arise throughout the planning process and that have an influence in the development of the activity. As the below short vignette describes, during planning meetings some issues remain unresolved. This fact leads planners to resume tasks previously treated during the process.

> In reviewing the 'Winter Plan', after the response phase, they realized that some issues remain unresolved from the planning phase; they did not considered a risk derived from the locality characteristics. One of the streets has a slope too high that provokes cars sliding through the asphalt and crashing into walls when the street is snowy. Consequently, they need to analyse again and include some risks not previously considered for planning.

Therefore, emergency planning tasks are not performed successively, but in a non-linear way. After considering a task as completed, planners could return to it for including or refining things.

2.3.4 Temporal Gap

Aforementioned, the emergency planning process is developed into several meetings extended over time. The time between such meetings, in some cases, is only a few days or weeks, but in other cases the temporal gap is longer than four months. This fact makes that shared experiences, knowledge, and decisions from each meeting tend to be lost across the meetings and regenerated each time. During the observation of the planning process, the inquiry team have the opportunity of attending to a total of sixteen meetings distributed over time, in which participants lost useful information for the definition of the emergency plan.

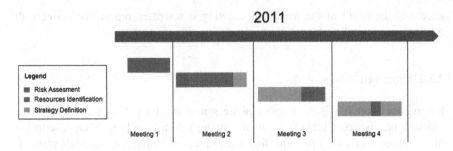

Fig. 2 Scattered tasks over time in the development of the emergency planning process

2.3.5 Unstable Participation

Emergency planning is an activity that takes place over long periods of time. Emergency plans are defined through different meetings extended over time. This causes that planning teams vary between such meetings, because of two different reasons: (1) their daily responsibilities. As professionals, team members have to meet their daily tasks and not always can attend to all the meetings. (2) the unpredictability of the context. Emergency planning is a critical context in which emergencies can arise anytime and, consequently, participants have to suddenly leave the meetings to assist them.

The variation of the participants directly impact on decisions during the definition of the emergency plans. Decisions are based on the background, knowledge, and experience of the participants. But, planning teams are not always composed by all the roles that should be involved in the definition of the plan and, therefore, the knowledge and experience is not the same through the whole process. As a result, the information shared, judgments, and decisions would depend not only on the role, but to the participant that is playing such role. Table 2 shows how the number of participants varies throughout the process, from initially 10 participants to 6 in the second meeting, 5 in the third meeting, and 8 in the fourth meeting.

2.3.6 Referring Backward

During the development of the plan, team members identify challenges and prioritize activities, analyse capabilities and hazards, exchange information about previous experience, and define procedures and strategies. This deliberation process is mainly based on the knowledge, experience, and lessons learned from previous plans. This makes them to continuously refer backward during meetings. They based on their on memory for recalling why they decide something and learn from their own decisions. For instance, during the second year of the study, participants recall to decisions made through the first year of planning:

Table 2 Meetings performed during 2011

Session	Date	No. Participants	Roles
1	05/09/2011	10	Security councilman (1), Civil protection (2), Civil guard (1), Social service (1), Environmental service (1), Police (2), Public construction Service (1), Cleaning service company (1)
2	12/09/2011	6	Civil protection (2), Environmental service (1) Police (1), Cleaning service company (1), Public construction service (1)
3	11/10/2011	5	Civil protection (2), Environmental service (1), Police (1), Cleaning service company (1)
4	07/11/2011	8	Security councilman (1), Civil protection (2), Environmental service (1), Police (2), Public construction service (1), Cleaning service company (1)

Last year we estimated 30 tonnes of melting products and it remained many kilos. This year we will try to save on melting products to avoid damaging the environment.

Tom: -Did you remember why we established a route through the 'Señora Sergia' street?

Anthony: -Yes, the last year we realized that the bus route needed to pass through this street for arriving to the school.

3 Discussion

Many activities in our society have a strong influence of time to achieve an optimal solution. Such long-term activities are characterized by the progressive refinement of the solution, covering a relatively long period of time. As our case study reveals, emergency planning may be regarded in this manner. Defining an effective, flexible and timely response to an emergency situation requires the continuous review, update and improvement of emergency plans. This ongoing process leads to the accumulation of reasoning, experiences, and knowledge; building a continuous understanding of planning that must be considered as foundations for further refinements.

Unfortunately, the limited capabilities of human beings as information processors hinder the maintenance of that understanding of planning. The unstable participation, the existence of long temporal gaps or the performance of scattered tasks disrupt the necessary continuity throughout the practice, hindering the reference to past experiences and the management of emergent constraints. As a consequence, the effectiveness of the activity is reduced. With the purpose of overcoming this limitation, emergency planners resort to create reports and dossiers than compile information about the emergency situation, the response, and the design process itself. Although these external artifacts are good enough to create a structured based of knowledge, not to support the reflection of planners, the referring backward, or the sustaining pattern of analysis and decision. As an alternative, computer-supported collaborative technologies could be a suitable mechanism to extend human limits and provide a necessary sense of continuity.

Time has been an important research issue in the Computer-Supported Collaborative Work (CSCW) community for more than two decades. And in the first conceptualizations of CSCW systems, time was considered as one of the basic dimensions that determine the way of collaborating, making a difference between synchronous and asynchronous collaboration [20]. This basic idea has been extended by several authors [21, 22], giving rise to the concept referred by Fischer et al. as "*long-term indirect collaboration*" [21]. By focusing on long-term, these authors explore technologies that support the intentions and actions of other who cannot be seen and contacted personally. In this way, supporting long-term indirect collaboration directly links up with the literature on design rationale [23–25] and group memory [26]. Computer-supported technologies that foster long-term collaboration must support not only the evolution of artifacts—in our case, emergency plans—but also the maintenance of the background context and rationale about the artifacts. Achieving continuity during the emergency planning practice is therefore based on providing enough information to let planner to know what decisions were made and why, who made those decisions, as well as what was the context in which the decisions were made. Taking this idea as a basis for designing for continuity, subsequent subsections present a set of claims that should address the design of those computer-based collaborative technologies that assist the emergency planning practice.

3.1 Capturing Collaborative Design Rationale

Empirical experiments have shown the benefits and improvements of collaboration in decision-making by documenting design decisions [27]. Design rationale helps to consider different perspectives, to detect conflicts between decisions, and to establish relationships between alternatives. In long-term processes such as emergency planning, where participants can change over time—team members may go away and new members arrive, capturing design rationale can help team members to maintain continuity in the reasoning. Being aware of what and why was decided would allow planners to understand the line of reasoning even if they could not attend to one or more meetings.

One of the main design challenges of capturing design rationale relies on overcoming the view of designers of design rationale as an "extra" step [22]. It would be difficult to encourage planners to capture their rationale if they felt such capture as additional work. As consequence, capturing rationale should be just made when it is strictly necessary. According to Schneider's approach [23], capturing rationale should be made for those specific tasks where rationale is expected to occur. Regarding the emergency-planning process, not all the planning tasks imply a design decision; instead reasoning is concentrated on the definition of response strategies in order to reduce risks. Similarly, efficiently capturing design decisions requires that the documentation of such reasoning must be embedded in the practice, without disrupting the planning process.

The use of digital knowledge representations—such as interactive maps or graphic representations—as exploratory design tools should be considered as a key mechanism to capturing the rationale of the design. On the one hand, this kind of tools will help planners to visualize the implications of choices and refine their ideas; on the other hand, they will allow automatically capturing strategies and alternatives. As an example, the definition of evacuation routes could be supported through an exploratory design tool that records requirements, alternatives routes, and even evacuation simulations. Automatic capturing techniques are essential mechanisms to capture rationale without interrupting the activity; however, these techniques usually record raw data what makes difficult the information retrieval process. The alternative will be a balance between user intervention and automatic capturing tools. Automatic-capturing techniques should be restricted to recording design decisions that can be supported through digital knowledge representations – e.g. evacuation routes, relocation points, elements of interest, location of resources, etc. This information should be additionally enriched with manual annotations provided by planners. The use of digital annotated designs will allow capturing the reasoning of planning in a semi-structured way [25], integrating the argumentation within the design artifact.

This reasoning of planning should be considered and treated as a collaborative effort; however, specific argumentations should be analyzed as individual contributions. The multidisciplinary of emergency planning implies that different planners, even representing the same service, can make different contributions depending on their responsibility, background, or involvement level. Hence, comments, opinions and judgments cannot be considered as anonymous, but personal identifiable. Logging user argumentation will allow further tracking of reasoning. Moreover, as a professional activity, emergency planning may be depicted as a procedural labor in the sense that many of the decisions are based on rules, legislation, and prescriptions. Divergent thinking, reflection and communication with artifacts are, of course, key elements to explore solutions; however, the reasoning resulting from this process is often based on declarative knowledge. In keeping with this idea, and in order to foster the capturing of rationale, it would be recommended the creation of rationale as a by-product [23] by attaching predefined rationale to a set of choices from which that the planners could choose.

3.2 Providing the History of the Practice

Being aware of the course of reasoning is an essential but not sufficient element for achieving continuity. The rationale of the design is commonly influenced and determined by the surrounding circumstances. Focusing on emergency planning, the definition of emergency plans is a collective effort distributed over time. As a collective activity, what a planning team defines is shaped by the composition of the group. Different participants exchange different experiences and judgments, providing a different understanding about situations. Hence, due to the unstable participation and the unpredictability of the context, the analysis of a previous decision requires knowing who was involved during the reasoning process. Moreover, emergency planning can be considered as a context-dependent activity that takes different forms in different areas or circumstances. As an example, law and legislation usually construct an implicit rationale that it is not specifically expressed by planners during meetings, but that determines their final decisions. In this case, using regular rationale-capturing techniques is not enough to be aware over time of this reasoning. Achieving continuity in emergency-planning practice therefore requires getting enough knowledge about the history in which the practice takes place. This history of the practice implies being aware not only of the reasoning of the design decisions, but also of the underlying information that wrap a decision.

As a way of providing relevant information of the history of the practice, approaches such as *group memory* go beyond capturing design rationale. Defined as *"the means by which knowledge from the past is brought to bear on present activities"* [26], group memory focus on providing not only the decisions made during the design process, but also the knowledge and experiences of the groups in the context of decision-making. However, this approach does no make emphasis either the context of the decisions, the people who made such decisions, or information related to the way in which the activity takes place over time. Consequently, our approach for providing the history of the practice relies in the distribution of essential information that allow planners to draw in their mind the big picture of how an emergency plan was designed. Drawing this big picture implies to get information related to *who* is the people involved in the process and *when* design takes place. *Who* refers to participants' background—regarding academic background and participants' experience. Regarding *when*, planning members should be aware of the context of design—current laws and regulations, environment, etc.- and the process history—meetings, tasks, steps, etc. Finally, information about the evolution of the plan must be recorded to provide the design history of the artifact.

4 Conclusions

Emergency planning is an activity distributed over time. Not only during the definition of the plan, based on meeting several times in a mid-term period, but also throughout the life of the plan, due to the performance of review meetings oriented to update and refine the plan. Thus, one of the main challenges of emergency planning should be the articulation of those activities distributed in time, creating a link between planning activities that allows planners to bind past events and discussions with present situations and decisions. Moreover, defining an optimum emergency plan is a long-time horizon issue that must be based on that accumulated knowledge acquired by planners during the practice. Effective emergency planning therefore requires continuity over time.

Maintaining continuity in planning makes it necessary for planners to be aware of the definition of the plan from the beginning of the process, so that there are not breakdowns or disruptions in the practice. It means that planning members should be aware not only of the evolution of the plan, but also of the previous decisions and their rationale, the planning context, the activities carried out to develop the plan, or the participants' background. Designing for continuity requires supporting which artifact has been defined, why the artifact was defined in that way, who was involved in such a definition, as well as when and where the definition took place.

Future work will be aimed at developing collaborative interactive systems that, based on the claims presented in this paper, assist the emergency planning practice. The development of these systems will allow us to evaluate the utility and effectiveness of providing continuity during the development of emergency plans.

Acknowledgments This work has been partly supported by the TIPEx project (TIN2010-19859-C03-01) funded by the Ministry of Science and Innovation (MICINN) of the Government of Spain.

References

1. Haynes SR, Wendy AS, Carroll JM (2007) Leveraging and limiting practical drift in emergency response planning. In: System sciences, 2007. HICSS 2007. 40th Hawaii international conference on system sciences, Hawaii, USA, 3–6 Jan 2007
2. Wenger DE, Charles CF, Thomas FJ (1980) Disaster beliefs and emergency planning. Irvington Publishers, New York
3. Perry RW, Lindell MK (2003) Preparedness for emergency response: guidelines for the emergency planning process. Disasters 27:336–350
4. Dynes RR, Drabek TE (1994) The structure of disaster research: its policy and disciplinary implications. Int J Mass Emergencies Disasters 12:5–23
5. Schafer WA, Carroll JM, Haynes SR, Abrams S (2008) Emergency management planning as collaborative community work. J Homel Secur Emerg Manage. doi:10.2202/1547-7355.1396
6. Schafer WA, Ganoe CH, Carroll JM (2007) Supporting community emergency management planning through a geocollaboration software architecture. Comput Support Coop Work (CSCW) 16(4–5):501–537
7. Carroll JM, Mentis M, Convertino G, Rosson MB, Ganoe C, Sinha H, Zhao D (2007) In: Prototyping collaborative geospatial emergency planning. Proceedings of ISCRAM, Delft, The Netherlands, 13–16 May 2007
8. Convertino G, Zhao D, Ganoe CH, Carroll JM, Rosson MB (2007) A role-based multiple view approach to distributed geo-collaboration. In: Human-Computer interaction. HCI applications and services, vol 4553. Springer, Heidelberg, pp 561–570
9. Convertino G, Neale DC, Hobby L, Carroll JM, Rosson MB (2004) A laboratory method for studying activity awareness. In: Proceedings of the third nordic conference on human-computer interaction, New York, USA, 23–27 Oct 2004

10. Convertino G, Wu A, Zhang XL, Ganoe CH, Hoffman B, Carroll JM (2008) Designing group annotations and process visualizations for role-based collaboration. Social computing, behavioral modeling, and prediction, Springer US, p 197–206
11. Blaikie NH (1991) A critique of the use of triangulation in social research. Qual Quant 25(2):115–136
12. Patton MQ (2005) Qualitative research. Wiley Online Library, Hoboken
13. Alexander D (2005) Towards the development of a standard in emergency planning. Disaster Prev Manage 14(2):158–175
14. Wolshon B, Urbina E, Wilmot C, Levitan M (2005) Review of policies and practices for hurricane evacuation. Transportation planning, preparedness, and response. Nat Hazards Rev 6(3):129–142
15. Saffer D (2010) Designing for interaction: creating innovative applications and devices. New Riders Publications
16. Wiseman V, Conteh L, Matovu F (2005) Using diaries to collect data in resource-poor settings: questions on design and implementation. Health Policy Plann 20(6):394–404
17. Beyer H, Holtzblatt K (1998) Contextual design: defining customer-centered systems. Morgan Kaufmann Publishers, Burlington
18. Yin RK (2003) Case study research: design and methods. Sage Publications, Thousand Oaks
19. Haddow G, Bullock J, Coppola DP (2010) Introduction to emergency management. Elsevier Science
20. Johansen R (1988) Groupware: computer support for business teams. The Free Press, New York
21. Fischer G (2004) Social creativity: turning barriers into opportunities for collaborative design. In: Proceedings of the eighth conference on participatory design: artful integration: interweaving media, materials and practices, vol 1. ACM, p 152–161
22. Conklin J, Burgess-Yakemovic K (1996) A process-oriented approach to design rationale. In: Moran T, Carroll J (eds) Design rationale concepts, techniques, and use, Lawrence Erlbaum Associates, 6(3):293–428
23. Schneider K (2006) Rationale as a by-product. In: Dutoit A, McCall R, Mistrik I, Paech B (eds) Rationale management in software engineering. Springer, Heidelberg, pp 91–109
24. Regli WC, Hu X, Atwood M, Sun W (2000) A survey of design rationale systems: approaches, representation, capture and retrieval. Eng Comput 16(3–4):209–235
25. Carroll JM, Moran TP (1991) Introduction to this special issue on design rationale. Hum–Comput Interact 6(3–4):197–200
26. Haseman WD, Nazareth DL, Paul S (2005) Implementation of group decision support system utilizing collective memory. Inf Manag 42(4):591–605
27. Falessi D, Cantone G, Becker M (2006) Documenting design decision rationale to improve individual and team design decision making: an experimental evaluation. In: Proceedings of the 2006 ACM/IEEE international symposium on empirical software engineering, ACM p 134–143

Combining Collaborative Modeling with Collaborative Creativity for Process Design

Thomas Herrmann and Alexander Nolte

Abstract This paper presents a solution of how systematic design within facilitated walkthrough workshops is combined with phases of non-linear ideation for the purpose of collaborative process modeling. In the context of socio-technically supported co-located meetings, three design cycles were run which led to an evolutionary improvement. The result is a set of features as part of a socio-technical solution allowing to seamlessly intertwine creative phases with walkthrough-oriented inspection and improvement of models. The set of features includes the possibility of simultaneous brainstorming on several topics, variation of prompts per brainstorming topic etc. Additional features are described to support the facilitator.

1 Introduction

Our objective is supporting co-located collaborative design of business processes or work processes. Since the basis of processes usually has a linear structure according to the underlying sequences, they can be inspected or designed step-by-step. We have developed such a step-by-step method—the socio-technical walkthrough—and applied it in several cases to make sure that the points of view of various stakeholders can be systematically included. The method usually is conducted in computer supported co-located meetings where each aspect of the process is inspected and discussed step-by-step [11]. We have realized that focusing on

T. Herrmann · A. Nolte (✉)
Department Information and Technology Management, Ruhr-University of Bochum,
Bochum, Germany
e-mail: nolte@iaw.rub.de

T. Herrmann
e-mail: herrmann@iaw.rub.de

C. Rossitto et al. (eds.), *COOP 2014 - Proceedings of the 11th International Conference on the Design of Cooperative Systems, 27–30 May 2014, Nice (France)*, DOI: 10.1007/978-3-319-06498-7_23, © Springer International Publishing Switzerland 2014

Fig. 1 Results of ideation
with loosely clustered
elements (*top*) and the final
process model after a series
of walkthroughs based on the
previous ideas (*bottom*)

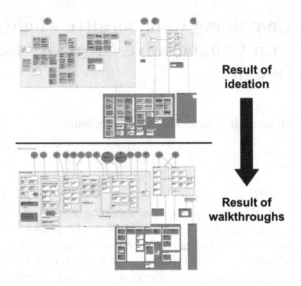

Result of
ideation

Result of
walkthroughs

such a systematical step-by-step procedure increases on the one hand the participation but neglects the available creativity of the participants [10]. Therefore we
decided to seamlessly integrate features for creativity support into tools for process
modeling as they are used in co-located meetings.

The relevant research is in the intersection of collaborative modeling [21] and
support for collaborative creativity [18]. Collaborative modeling can serve as a
methodological basis to include several stakeholders by combining methods of
facilitation and computer support. However, the methods for fostering creativity (e.g.
ThinkLets [2, 14]) are not seamlessly integrated into techniques for collaborative
modeling. In the field of business process modeling, it is only acknowledged, that
creativity is needed from time to time but is not systematically taken into account (cf.
the spare referencing to creativity e.g. in [8]). There are no elaborated concepts
available which describe how creative phases are supported in the course of the
analysis and improvement of modeled business processes. Consequently, the
available modeling tools do not seamlessly integrate features for creativity support
such as brainstorming. Even if brainstorming takes place it is conducted within
separated tools and the result has to be manually integrated into the process modeling
tool for further processing. This combination of different media is inefficient and can
disturb the creative flow [4]. To our knowledge we have developed and evaluated the
first tool for process modeling which seamlessly integrates brainstorming features.
Figure 1 illustrates how the results of applying the process modeling tool looked like
in a concrete project (see the sub-sections on the first and second design cycle); it
displays a transition which starts by collecting clustered ideas and leads to an
increased structuring, e.g. by re-arranging the elements and aligning them with arcs.

Apparently, current concepts for collaborative modeling fall short in flexibly
intertwining systematic modeling-walkthroughs with phases of non-linear ideation.

Thus our aim is to overcome this deficit by a set of features that are integrated into process modeling tools and support collaborative creativity in the context of facilitated meetings. In order to do so we propose a methodology and prototype and evaluate technical features in several design cycles with the first design cycle establishing a baseline of properties of our solution including requirements to be fulfilled.

The next section provides a review of the relevant literature upon collaboration and creativity. In the following methodological section, the methodological background, which is based on an action research approach [13], is outlined. The development and evaluation of the socio-technical solution is based on three design cycles, which lead to a set of features. The paper concludes with a summary of our findings and directions for future work.

2 Related Work

Process modeling is an established practice in most modern businesses, and it implicitly underlies many descriptions of how groupware can support collaborative work which usually integrates coordinative tasks as has been pointed out early by e.g. Malone and Crowston [17]. There is a variety of process modeling languages for the specific needs of e.g. software design [9]. Despite their obvious advantages, models often fail to cover real world phenomena as they force a once chosen level of detail to be carried out throughout the process (e.g. in [26]). This results in huge process descriptions that are hard to understand even for the modeling experts being involved in their creation. It has to be taken into account that many stakeholders in creative process design are domain experts with little knowledge about modeling methods. They need a modeling method which mainly supports communication between stakeholders and helps them to focus on the essential aspects. Therefore we mix formal with informal notational elements for modeling a process [11]. Other modeling notations such as the most recent incarnation of BPMN [19] also strive at becoming better understandable for non-expert modelers thus sacrificing rigor and the ability to directly compute code out of the resulting models. The developed features can at least partially be combined with this type of modeling notation.

While in some cases models are created by experts based upon upfront interviews or existing process descriptions, there are multiple concepts of integrating stakeholders into modeling. These range from stakeholders commenting on models in wikis [23] to a full scale integration into model manipulation [22]. The latter stream—called collaborative modeling [21]—stems from various different fields such as process management [22], system dynamics [24] and others [5]. The common goal is to to create a shared understanding about the problem domain among a group of people [1] thus resulting in a "*shared graphical representation of a system*" (derived from [21]). The underlying approaches are mostly based upon linear walkthroughs that are conducted during facilitated co-located workshops [11].

These walkthroughs are feasible e.g. when processes have to be visualized or analyzed based on current practice. By asking a number of predefined questions such as *"What comes next?"* or *"Who carries out that?"* the facilitator walks the participants through the process thus making sure that the participants don't miss out any important details [11].

While walkthroughs mainly are appropriate for reproducing, analyzing, refining and incrementally improving a piece of software, a dialogue structure of an interactive system [20]; a project documentation [27] or a process, their linearity hinders the creative design of processes or their parts. The integration of electronically supported creativity techniques into collaborative process modeling has not been considered systematically so far.

Research on supporting creativity techniques with groupware tries to reduce the variety of possible methods to a number of comprehensible principles, such as building analogies, provocation, or random based impulses [14]). The ThinkLet approach [2] describes an advanced set of computer based methods of ideation including creative idea finding. It is based on elaborated psychologically and empirically substantiated work [25] and tries to overcome typical shortcomings of brainstorming in groups like e.g. production blocking or free riding [7]. However, creativity techniques and ThinkLets do not describe the interaction with artifacts such as process models. So far, the main problem is that current strategies of electronic brainstorming—as pursued with ThinkLets—are mainly focused on participants' producing textual notes and sentences, which are usually too long to be directly transformed into elements of a process model. Therefore we suggest referring to brainstorming techniques [12] which produce short notes on cards as a basis.

Furthermore, our approach can benefit from principles and heuristics which have been studied throughout several years [10, 16] in the context of collaboratively drafting design artifacts: Smooth transition must be possible and controllable by the participants between work in solitude and collaborative interaction, between private and shared space, and between divergent ideation and convergent synthesizing.

3 Methodological Background

The empirical procedure took place as action research: We—the IMTM-research group at the University of Bochum—were involved as facilitators (three different persons)—in real projects or experimental settings where workshops were conducted to design or improve processes. Applying certain tools and methods to foster creative brainstorming can be considered as interventions. Afterwards, their effects have been exploratively investigated with the focus on identifying potentials of technical improvement [13]. The underlying objective was to fulfill criteria such as the quantity of ideas, the subjectively perceived intensity and continuity of ideation, the understandability of the contributions during discussion, and the

Fig. 2 The ModLab at the
University of Bochum

smoothness of integrating them into process models. The exploration was based on recordings of the session, on observations and on semi-structured interviews in order to gather as much diverse information as possible thus fostering the future development of the set of features. The resulting material was selectively evaluated by searching for needs and possibilities of improvement which served as input for the ongoing design of the tool as well as the underlying methodology. The most promising candidates were selected and implemented as new interventions to be tested in a next cycle.

The empirical investigation took place in a special collaboratory at the University of Bochum (ModLab) where an interactive large screen can be coupled with mobile devices through a wifi-network (c.f. Fig. 2). With the large screen, a whole process can be represented and the overall structure is comprehensible at a glance. Details can be studied by zooming or by standing directly in front of the screen. The model can be modified by directly interacting with the screen. Its development, including the brainstorming phases, was logged.

The screenshot which can be seen in Fig. 2 on the large screen is based on a specific process modeling tool—the SeeMe-Editor[1]—which was designed to draft process diagrams and to present them step-by-step to support the communication about the represented models. The ModLab provides audio and video equipment to record the interaction during meetings in real time including the displayed material on the large screen and the entire room from three different camera angles. To understand the influences and characteristics of tools which support or hinder the participants' collaboration and the facilitator's work, we had an experienced observer simultaneously taking notes. After each workshop we also conducted semi-structured interviews with the participants and with the facilitator.

In order to develop and improve the features for creativity support we went through three design cycles (c.f. Table 1). We started with an initial approach that contained no technological support for creativity itself but served as a predecessor

---

[1] See http://www.seeme-imtm.de for further details.

Table 1 Summary of design cycles

Task	Idea to assess
1 Identify suitable aspects of processes that are modeled afterwards	Brainstorming as a part of upfront planning for process design
2 Brainstorming as a part of process design with upfront planning of phases	Integration of brainstorming phases into process design
3 Brainstorming in process design with seamless switches between walk-through and ideation	Seamless switching between ideation and walkthrough oriented phases

for our tool design. Afterwards, we enhanced our modeling tool and evaluated the new version. With careful upfront planning we alternated phases of non-linear ideation with linear walkthrough oriented phases. The participants were scientist as well as people working in the area of services for elderly people. This study aimed at assessing the feasibility of the approach and testing the tool from the participants' as well as the facilitator's perspectives. The empirical investigation was a source for further requirements for the software as well as the setting. After integrating these findings into the tool, we continued with a third study. It was based on an artificial task as we wanted to assess to what extent seamless switching between linear and non-linear phases can affect the continuity of ideation. The participants were selected based upon their knowledge about the task which was the selection of applicants. Some of them had been in the situation of selecting applicants before while others were students that had taken part in selection processes.

4 Design Cycles

4.1 Baseline: Usage of Conventional Media

For preparing the design of processes or socio-technical solutions, we usually run brainstormings to collect first ideas about how the design should look like or which requirements have to be met. A typical example was identifying suitable services to support elderly people. The innovation was that these services should be ordered by using pen and paper technology. In order to identify appropriate aspects of the new services and their underlying processes, we used several of creativity techniques (c.f. [3] for a more elaborated description). Afterwards, the resulting ideas were assessed, merged and clustered during multiple phases. In between these phases the resulting material was digitalized for further refinement. While we found this alternating between different media to be useful for ideation as it sparked some more ideas [3], it also interrupted the workshop procedure multiple times. This observation supported the idea of integrating the results of brainstorming directly into the process modeling editor with which the ideas were transformed into the representation of a process-oriented socio-technical solution.

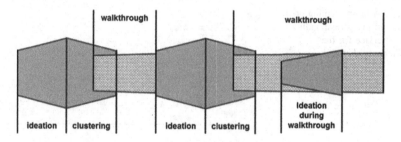

Fig. 3 Phases of linear walkthroughs combined with phases of ideation

From these first brainstorming studies we derived a set of requirements which should remain fulfilled as a baseline when employing electronic means for creativity support:

- Working with cards/short notes which can be separately positioned, sorted, clustered and arranged is an indispensable means to flexibly integrate ideas of several participants into a process model.
- People are encouraged to create short notes which are sufficiently explicit to indicate what they have meant.
- The number of ideas (about 5 per participant in 5 min) is an average productivity threshold which is achieved with pen and paper based methods and should be maintained if electronic support is employed.
- Simplicity matters: People get quickly adapted to the tools they use and must not be distracted by the employed technology.
- People have a phase during which they work in solitude and decide by themselves whether they want to receive additional sources for inspiration.
- Phases of ideation and convergent consolidation (such as clustering along categories, aligning or prioritizing elements in a walkthrough) are flexibly mixed (see Fig. 3).

4.2 First Improvement: Integrating Brainstorming into a Process Modeling Editor

We enhanced the process-modeling editor to allow for parallel contributions by multiple workshop participants. The enhancement consists of a simple web-interface (c.f. Fig. 4 bottom) that can be run by any browser capable device and be used by the workshop participants to contribute ideas. Typing in an idea into the text-input box of the interface results in a corresponding specially shaped (like a brainstorming card or post-it) element inside the model with the respective text as its label (c.f. Fig. 4 top). We deliberately chose to make the interface for the

Fig. 4 A brainstorming area (*top*) and the corresponding web-interface for the participants (*bottom*)

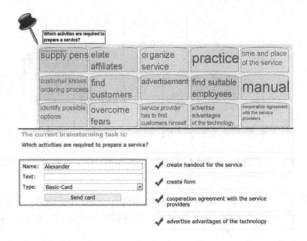

Table 2 Brainstorming facts with 7 participants

	Brainstorming 1	Brainstorming 2	Brainstorming 3
Task	Activities that are needed to prepare a service	Data that is required from the user	Activities that are needed to coordinate a service
Number of elements	39	46	44
Time	6 min	5 min	8 min
Duplicates	None	5	1

participants as simple as possible as we wanted them to stay focused on the task of ideation but not on a complicated interface.

Furthermore we enhanced the modeling tool so that the brainstorming cards can be dealt with in the same way like the other elements of the modeling notation. This allows facilitator to move items around, cluster them and create new items on demand. The facilitator can start a brainstorming session by creating an area—the braintable—that is represented with the process modeling tool and displays the brainstorming question, which is also shown on the participants' web interface, for example: "*Which activities are required to prepare a service?*". Afterwards the facilitator asked the participants to contribute to this topic (c.f. Table 2). When the facilitator felt that a sufficient number of ideas was delivered, he started clustering the contributions by asking the participants which contributions should be put together. He also asked them to order the resulting clusters with respect to the process to be drafted.

This tool was applied in several workshops with the same participants and the same topic: Developing a process that allows elderly persons to order services by filling in forms with a digital pen. During the process, the data is then transferred electronically to a service agency which coordinates the services. Because of the complexity of the new service process, different stakeholders had to be included like people working in the area of services for elderly people, persons having experience with technically supporting elderly people, researchers in the area of improving housing for elderly people etc. They contributed their ideas about the activities and data which will be needed in such a new service delivery and coordination process. Afterwards, these ideas were sorted and aligned to a process structure. Conducting a series of workshops in this context gave us the opportunity to eliminate minor bugs and make slight improvements and to observe the resulting effects.

Throughout the workshops an observer was present who kept track of the interaction of the participants with the tool. An additional modeler helped with operating the modeling tool or entered text if necessary. We also took snapshots of the resulting model after each phase and used the respective timestamps to analyze the number of contributions during each brainstorming phase, resulting in the numbers presented in Table 2. After the workshop we interviewed the facilitator to evaluate the interface.

Analysis and measure for improvements: In the first workshop we found that the interface worked considerably well—at least with respect to the productivity of the participants as they contributed 129 items in 19 min (c.f. Table 2), indicating that they had no problems when using the interface. We also observed idle phases where people did not contribute but rather seemed to wait for further inspiration or for the next task. This lead us to the idea that participants should be able to freely switch between multiple brainstorming tasks that are available at the same time, instead of working on one topic after another as it was the case with the tasks shown in Table 2. Figure 5 displays the solution which was employed in the third cycle. The snapshot shows that the participants works on the first question ("What happens within ...") while the second question ("How to select ...") is displayed at the bottom and can be activated whenever the participant wishes to switch to it. Furthermore, Fig. 5 shows that the participants can always see the history of their personal contributions which is another requirement which became apparent during our tests.

The baseline requirements from the first studies were met. The participants were not distracted by the new method and were mostly willing to deliver short notes although the entry field allowed them for longer contributions. However, sometimes participants made rather long contributions so that the resulting text was difficult to read from a distance. Therefore we decided to crop longer texts at a certain point adding the whole text as a comment to the element. These comments can be hidden or disclosed if needed (Fig. 6).

Most efficiency gains could be observed for the work of the facilitator. Time was saved since he had not to collect the cards and to pin them on a board (or to wait until the participants have done this). It was easy to cluster the items, to move them around, to create duplicates, to add comments, and to align the ideas to a process sequence. During the post-workshop interview, the facilitator reported that it was very difficult for him to deal with the brainstorming tables while keeping track of the communication in parallel. The resulting requirement is to allow the facilitator to prepare the brainstorming topics in advance and to activate or modify them during a workshop with a separated facilitator interface which is not visible for the participants. A further requirement was that the facilitator asked for an easy way to transform the symbol for the brainstorming cards into an element of the modeling notation like activities, events, roles or entities.

Brainstorming WebClient

⊰ **What happens within an innovative process of pre-selection?**   ⅋

| Prompt |

| Create Card |

Text: [   ]

Type: [Meta-BasicElement ▾]   **Send**

| History   ▣ |

2011-05-06 16:36:01:
use own networks   ✓

2011-05-06 16:35:54:
let applicants choose new media: video, presentation, etc.   ✓

2011-05-06 16:35:20:
create a profile from existing online data   ✓

2011-05-06 16:35:04:
internal facebook   ✓

⊰ **How to select applicants when they are onsite?**   »

Fig. 5 The enhanced brainstorming interface for the participants with multiple brainstorming questions

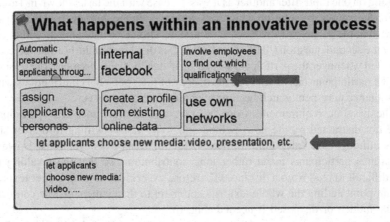

Fig. 6 Abbreviated contributions (marked with a *semicircle*) and a bubble displaying the complete contribution

4.3 Second Improvement: Fostering Continuous Ideation

After having adapted the tool with respect to the aforementioned requirements, we conducted a study with three workshops of 4–5 participants who were asked to go on with brainstorming ideas even after the facilitator has started to model a process on the basis of the received contributions. The underlying task was to design a process of selecting applicants for a place at university.

Each workshop itself was divided into four phases with an initial explanation of the setting, where we introduced the topics to the participants. One of the topics covered the process of pre-selecting applicants and the other one the process of selecting applicants onsite. The participants of the workshop were also told that they were allowed to contribute to each of the two brainstorming areas at any time throughout the whole study. After this explanation, we asked the participants to start contributing using iPads. This phase lasted for about 5–8 min. After this initial phase, the facilitator started clustering the contributed ideas with the help of the participants by asking the respective contributor to briefly explain her item and comment on its position in the process. The resulting clustering was done with respect to both the content of the contributions and their sequence in an innovative process of selecting applicants. Additionally, the facilitator challenged the participants to contribute additional ideas. After finishing the clustering, the participants had the final opportunity to provide further contributions in a brainstorming phase of about 5 min. The facilitators could use a control panel which allows them to determine whether the contributing of brainstorming ideas can go on during the phase of clustering or not.

In the interviews after each study, the participants told us that they mostly sought for inspiration by looking at the contributions of others. This led us to the conclusion that each participant works at her own speed and that in order to fully exploit their creative potential each participant has to be supported and prompted individually. Therefore, we decided to add the possibility of multiple prompts for each brainstorming question that can be distributed individually [25]. We developed an interface that can be used by the facilitator to prepare a number of additional prompts for each brainstorming area (Fig. 7 top). This can be done before or during the workshop e.g. while the participants have already started contributing. In order to distribute the prompts properly, the facilitator interface provides awareness by anonymous statistics about for how long each participant has been idle (c.f. *users idle in topic* in Fig. 7). The assigned prompts appear on the participants interface next to the corresponding brainstorming question (e.g. *Which roles are problem sources in similar processes?* in Fig. 7 bottom).

Another possible improvement became obvious by analyzing the clustering phase: Oftentimes the text of the contributions was not self-explanatory. So it became necessary to explain it and to add this explanation as a comment. During the study, the facilitator had to create these comments herself while keeping track of the ongoing discussion in parallel. This leads to the requirement that the participants should be able to comment on their own contributions.

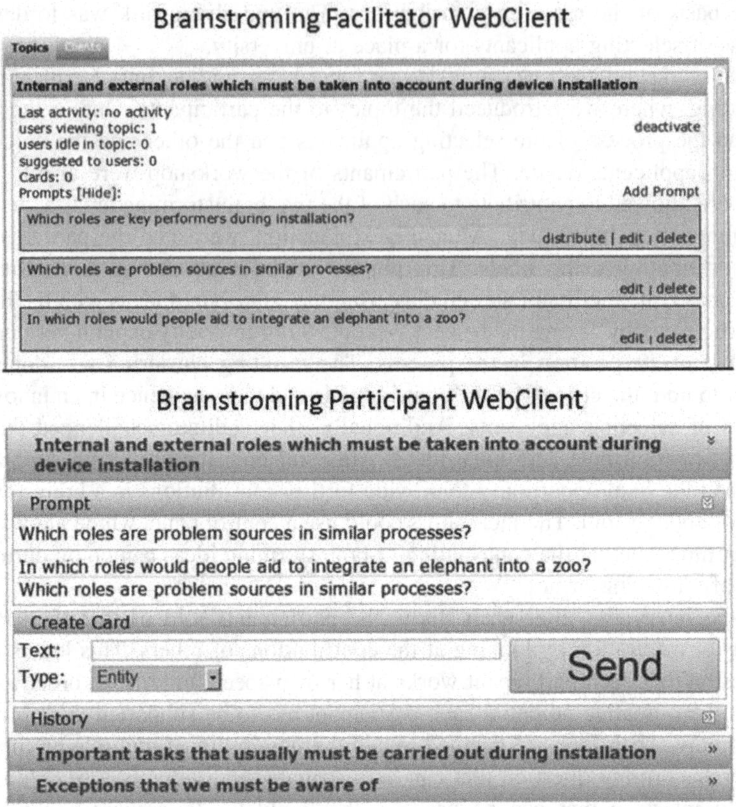

Brainstroming Facilitator WebClient

Brainstroming Participant WebClient

Fig. 7 The facilitator web-interface (*top*) and the interface of the participants (*bottom*)

5 Summary and Discussion of the Features of the Tool Support

5.1 The Process Modeling Tool

The ideation support within a process modeling tool proved of high relevance to allow for a smooth transition between phases of linear process design and more associative brainstorming (c.f. Fig. 3). For this integration, special areas for brainstorming (we call them braintables) can be created on demand anywhere within a process model. In addition, it is possible to transform every element within a process model into such a braintable in order to e.g. further dig into the details of this part of the process. All of these braintables have a suitable brainstorming question as a heading. It is possible to work on multiple parts (or perspectives) of the process at the same time by offering multiple braintables in parallel between which participants can freely choose. This possibility was explained at the beginning of the brainstorming. The participants have intuitively used this option without being repeatedly encouraged by the facilitator to do so.

While the participants can only see a list of their own contributions on their respective web interface, all contributions of the whole group have to be visible within the respective braintable in the context of the emerging process model. While the contributions are displayed in a format which is similar to paper cards by default (c.f. Fig. 6), the participants may also select that their contribution appears as a symbol of the process modeling notation. This option was not widely used; however the facilitators required that the neutral cards can be easily converted into process modeling symbols. These cards or symbols can be easily dragged and dropped and be embedded into other elements of the process model. We focus on a type of brainstorming where cards of fixed sizes are used since also the elements of most process modeling notations use symbols of limited size. Because of this limitation the length of the text entries is also limited so that the cards remain readable from a distance. However, if a participant's contribution exceeds the limit of length, the whole text has to be captured as well. This is done through a comment which is attached to the respective contribution and can be flexibly hidden or shown (c.f. Fig. 6). Furthermore, this kind of comments can also be added afterwards by the originator of a contribution to add further explanation.

5.1.1 Participants Web Interface

While the interactive wall and the canvas of the process modeling tool are the space of direct collaboration, the participants' web interface is their tool for work in solitude (see Fig. 7 bottom). Mostly they stayed focused on this tool after having checked if their first contribution is conveyed to the public screen. Afterwards a phase followed without glancing on the interactive wall. The interface allows them to enter text to make several contributions to a topic. Furthermore, it is possible for the participants to freely choose between multiple brainstorming topics if the facilitator has opted to provide them (e.g. *"Important tasks that usually must be carried out during installation"* and *"Exceptions that we must be aware of"* in Fig. 7 bottom. They may also select a symbol of the process modeling notation to determine how their contribution refers to the process model (c.f. *type* in Fig. 7 bottom).

In the context of a brainstorming question the participants can see various prompts which may foster their inspiration during the brainstorming. The need for prompts is described in the literature [25] and became obvious in the third design cycle when we tried to encourage the participants to continue with brainstorming. So far, we have not tested in a fourth cycle whether these prompts have a positive effect and do not violate the baseline requirements such as simplicity.

In order to keep track of their own ideas the participants can see a history of their own contributions for each brainstorming topic. After having sent a contribution, the respective participant may also add a comment to it. This is especially important during post-processing of the items as it is very likely that some contributions require further commenting due to their being very short. The participant's web interface is oriented on the role model of conventional brainstorming with cards: as soon as the idea is delivered to the public (i.e. conveyed to the modeling editor) it cannot be changed anymore—comments can only be added to the own contribution. This restriction was challenged by the participants who expected that the computer-based handling of cards should allow them to edit or delete their ideas afterwards. Meeting this expectation would allow the participants more flexibility but can also harm the consistency of the public presentation.

5.1.2 Facilitator Web Interface

The facilitator is responsible for integrating the brainstorming phases into the walkthrough oriented drafting of the process model. It proved insufficient to support this task exclusively with the integrated features of the enhanced process modeling tool. Therefore, additional support is provided with a separate web-interface that allows the facilitator to prepare brainstorming topics/questions and a number of prompts in advance. Furthermore it has to be possible to add or edit prompts and brainstorming topics on demand during the sessions.

Additional statistics—for example about idle times—allow the facilitator to understand the progression of the brainstorming. These statistics are anonymized: For instance, the facilitators can only see that one or more persons are inactive but not who they are. Based upon these statistics, the facilitator may influence the brainstorming procedure by deciding which brainstorming topics can be worked on, e.g. whether the participants should focus on one topic or whether they can freely choose between various brainstorming questions. Furthermore the facilitator may also flexibly assign prompts to all participants or to a selected group (e.g. those who stayed inactive for more than 5 min or those who limited their contributions to a single area while multiple areas are available). Finally the facilitator may also start and stop the brainstorming mode on demand if clustering or walkthrough oriented structuring has begun. This facilitator support has been derived from the third design circle but so far not been tested with respect to the complexity and effectiveness it causes during process modeling workshops.

5.2 Outlook

The presented solution helps to combine phases of non-linear ideation with systematic participatory design within facilitated, walkthrough-oriented workshops of process modeling. The collaboration support is focused on co-located meetings where various stakeholders are systematically included to discuss a new business or work process. One issue of innovation is that the support of collaborative creativity techniques is not separated from the actual design tool but is integrated into it. This is of general relevance for CSCW since the features which we have

developed can also be a role model for other areas such as collaborative archi-
tectural design, plant layout, requirements engineering etc. Furthermore, the
developed tool provides much more flexibility to the brainstorming participants
than traditional approaches. They do not have to wait until everybody's contributions are collected before they proceed with the next topic; they don't have to
deal with a topic which they are not interested in but can switch to other issues and
they can decide flexibly whether they want to read what others have contributed or
stay with their own ideas. This flexibility is so far hardly taken into account by
studies which explore the effects of electronic brainstorming (cf. [6, 15]). However, the possibilities for flexibility lead to the question whether some of the
remaining restrictions, such as being not able to delete or edit contributions which
have already been displayed to the public or to comment the ideas of others, should
be overcome. This consideration refers to a trade-off between flexibility and
consistency which requires further evaluation.

The features of the tool can be enhanced e.g. with respect to collaborative
clustering, sorting and filtering. It can be evaluated to what extent further features for
supporting convergence (sorting, prioritizing, comparing) can be integrated. The
ongoing evaluation may focus on whether the tool support for facilitators can be
easily handled during facilitating a meeting, or whether the support leads to dis-
tractive effects which restrict the facilitator's attention towards the ongoing communication. Furthermore, supporting the participants' imagination with prompts
could be enhanced: Instead of only using textual hints, multimedia support is helpful
to inspire them (e.g. with pictures, statistical data, music, stories etc.).

References

1. Barjis J et al (2009) Collaborative enterprise modeling. Advances in enterprise engineering
   II. Springer, New York, pp 50–62
2. Briggs R, de Vreede G-J (2009) ThinkLets: building blocks for concerted collaboration.
   Briggs and de Vreede, Nebraska
3. Carell A, Herrmann T (2010) Interaction and collaboration modes for integration inspiring
   information into technology-enhanced creativity workshops. In: Proceedings of the 43rd
   Hawaii international conference on system science (HICCS 43)
4. Csikszentmihalyi M (1997) Flow and the psychology of discovery and invention.
   HarperPerennial, New York
5. Dean DL et al (1994) Technological support for group process modeling. J Manage Inf Syst
   11(3):63
6. Dennis AR, Williams ML (2005) A meta-analysis of group side effects in electronic
   brainstorming: more heads are better than one. IJeC 1(1):24–42
7. Diehl M, Stroebe W (1987) Productivity loss in brainstorming groups: toward the solution of
   a riddle. J Pers Soc Psychol 53(3):497–509
8. Dumas M et al (2013) Fundamentals of business process management. Springer, New York
9. Fowler M (2004) UML distilled: a brief guide to the standard object modeling language.
   Addison-Wesley Professional
10. Herrmann T (2009) Design heuristics for computer supported collaborative creativity. In:
    42nd Hawaii international conference on system sciences. HICSS'09, pp 1–10

11. Herrmann T (2009) Systems Design with the Socio-Technical Walkthrough. In: Whitworth, B. and de Moore, A. (eds.) Handbook of Research on Socio-Technical Design and Social Networking Systems. Idea Group Publishing, Hershey, pp. 336–351
12. Higgins JM (1994) 101 creative problem solving techniques: the handbook of new ideas for business. New Management Publishing Company Florida
13. Hult M, Lennung S (1980) Towards a definition of action research: a note and bibliography. J Manage Stud 17(2):241–250
14. Knoll SW, Horton G (2010) Changing the perspective: improving generate thinkLets for ideation. In: Proceedings of the 2010 43rd Hawaii international conference on system sciences, pp 1–10
15. Kohn NW, Smith SM (2011) Collaborative fixation: effects of others' ideas on brainstorming. Appl Cogn Psychol 25(3):359–371
16. Lu IM, Mantei MM (1991) Idea management in a shared drawing tool. In: Bannon L et al (eds) Proceedings of the second European conference on computer-supported cooperative work. Springer, New York, pp 97–112
17. Malone TW, Crowston K (1994) The interdisciplinary study of coordination. ACM Comput Surv CSUR 26(1):87–119
18. Mamykina L et al (2002) Collaborative creativity. Commun ACM 45(10):96–99
19. (2006) OMG: business process modeling notation (BPMN) specification. Object Management Group
20. Polson PG et al (1992) Cognitive walkthroughs: a method for theory-based evaluation of user interfaces. Int J Man-Mach Stud 36(5):741–773
21. Renger M et al (2008) Challenges in collaborative modelling: a literature review and research agenda. Int J Simul Process Model 4(3):248–263
22. Rittgen P (2010) Collaborative modeling: roles, activities and team organization. Int J Inf Syst Model Des IJISMD 1(3):1–19
23. Rospocher M et al (2009) Moki: the modelling wiki. In: Lange C et al. (eds) Proceedings of the fourth workshop on semantic wikis (SemWiki 2009) at the 6th European semantic web conference, pp 113–127
24. Rouwette EAJA et al (2000) Group model building: a decision room approach. Simul Gaming 31(3):359–379
25. Santanen EL et al (2004) Causal relationships in creative problem solving: comparing facilitation interventions for ideation. J Manage Inf Syst 20(4):167–198
26. Scheer A-W, Cameron I (1992) Architecture of integrated information systems: foundations of enterprise modelling. Springer, New York
27. Yourdon E (1989) Structured walkthroughs. Yourdon Press Upper Saddle River, New Jersey, USA

The Relevance of Annotations Shared by Tourists and Residents on a Geo-Social Network During a Large-Scale Touristic Event: The Case of São João

Aline Morais and Nazareno Andrade

Abstract A common type of information in Geo-Social Networks (GSNs) is geolocated annotations with short personal comments about urban sites. Such annotations are deemed useful as tips and recommendations, and can help guide GSN users coming to these sites. During touristic events, GSNs typically acquire a large amount of annotations provided by a high number of tourists in collaboration with the city's residents. It is not clear, however, whether information shared by tourists and residents are equally relevant. Moreover, this relevance can be different both during and after the event, when the annotations are left as a legacy to residents. This work presents a case study about the relevance of GSN annotations shared by tourists and residents during a large-scale touristic event. The event in the case study is the São João, an event which yearly attracts 2 million people to the city of Campina Grande, Brazil. The analysis of content and quantitative measures of relevance shows that in this case study: (a) the relevance of GSN annotations varies significantly for annotations created by tourists and residents during the touristic event, as well as with primary audience of the venue where tip is shared and (b) the residents' annotations are found more relevant than those shared by tourists both during the touristic event and after the event is over. These results suggest that addressing differently tips created by residents in such events may increase the ability of the attendees of the event to find relevant information.

Keywords Large-scale event · Touristic event · Geo-social network · Relevance

A. Morais (✉) · N. Andrade
Systems and Computing Department, Universidade Federal de Campina Grande, Campina Grande, Brazil
e-mail: alinemm@lsd.ufcg.edu.br

N. Andrade
e-mail: nazareno@lsd.ufcg.edu.br

C. Rossitto et al. (eds.), *COOP 2014 - Proceedings of the 11th International Conference on the Design of Cooperative Systems, 27–30 May 2014, Nice (France)*, DOI: 10.1007/978-3-319-06498-7_24, © Springer International Publishing Switzerland 2014

1 Introduction

Geo-Social Networks (GSNs) are collaborative systems in which geolocated information is a central component. Among other uses, GSNs have been successfully applied for collectively annotating a city with peer-produced information. This success is most pronouncedly manifested through Foursquare, a network which at the time of writing has 40 millions of users, and annotations in cities spread in 56 countries.

Touristic events are large-scale urban celebrations that occur in a localized period of time and often attract a sizeable crowd to a host city, generating significant monetary flow, and possibly altering the urban routine. The crowd of attendees attracted to the host city, which may substantially increase its population, is made of *tourists*; such tourists attend the touristic event together with the city *residents*.

The dynamics of the touristic event likely impacts the functioning of GSNs used in the city. This impact can happen both due to a peak in the creation of annotations caused by the event attendees, and to the fact that there is a sudden increase in the diversity of backgrounds of the users creating annotations.

Consider the situation where during the touristic event tourists and residents annotate places in the GSN with opinions. If the annotations produced by tourists and residents are indeed different, the information produced during the touristic event may significantly influence decision-making based on the GSN. For example, suppose that residents do not find annotations created by tourists relevant, either during or after the event. If this is true, and residents are majorly exposed to this information by the GSN's mechanisms, residents may have their experience in the GSN significantly hampered. Conversely, it may be that tourists do not find the information produced by residents relevant, and are also impacted.

Possible reasons for this mismatch may result for instance from differences in interests, background, opinions and social norms. At the same time plurality increases diversity of opinions and has the potential of enriching the annotations created in a city, opinions may generate friction between groups with different viewpoints or needs.

This work investigates how tourists and residents produce and find relevance in annotations created during a massive touristic event. In this context, relevance represents how much a geolocated annotation is seen as useful to the users of the GSN. Our work investigates relevance creation through a case study focusing on the use of Foursquare during a Brazilian touristic event that annually attracts 2 million tourists to a city of 400,000 inhabitants. In this case study, we address the following research questions:

- Which factors affect the relevance of annotations created by tourists and residents during the touristic event?
- How relevant are annotations created by tourists and residents to all users of the GSN, and specifically to tourists or residents?
- How does the relevance of annotations produced by tourists and residents evolve after the touristic event?

Our results contribute for the understanding of how valuable information is created during the event, and how its relevance progresses overtime in the eyes of the different groups of stakeholders that participate in the GSN.

2 Touristic Events and Geo-Social Networks

Large-scale touristic events are a form of tourism that involves thousands of people simultaneously attending a same place for one or more common activities. Festivals, celebrations, holidays and sport matches or championships are common occurrences of such events [1].

During a touristic event, GSN users can be divided in two groups: tourists and residents. Although not crisp, categorizing GSN users this way highlights that typically residents are routinely immersed in the city, and as such possess deep contextual information about the city. Tourists, on the other hand, bring a diverse background and often a fresh view on venues, habits, and the city in general.

In large-scale touristic events, technology often plays a role in knowledge creation and as thus affects the experience of event attendees [2]. In particular, mobile technologies perform an increasingly important role for tourists, as they often demand contextualized and personalized services that improve their experience at previously unknown places [3]. Tourists can benefit from systems that eliminate uncertainty feelings in their visit on a new space [4]. Naturally, this demand is markedly present in touristic events, where hundreds or thousands of tourists come concurrently to a same city.

GSNs are location-based social networks, usually accessible through mobile technology. These networks can act as a proxy of real cities and provide better understanding of underlying structure and dynamics of human decision-making in urban contexts [5]. According with Lee and Sumiya [6], a touristic event in a city is reflected on GSNs used in the city with (a) a sudden increase in annotations related to an urban context, (b) an increase in the number of GSN's users for a short time period, and (c) movements of the local users unexpectedly becoming highly activated. This behavior is indeed observed in our data.

Previous research has started to explore the relation between a city, the GSNs used in it, and the role of tourists or events. Silva et al. [7] provide a method for creating a city image from the trail left by Foursquare users in it. This image can be used by tourists to explore the city and to perhaps decide whether to visit a city. On a different line of study, [8] explore how to use a GSN to match tourists interested in a site considering their complementarity skills. Munar and Jacobsen [9] present a qualitative study of tourist use of and trust in social media and other Internet-based travel information sources. Their results suggest that tourists have a high score of trustworthiness for GSN information during their learning process about an urban context.

Focusing on the information produced in a GSN, we see that multiple works in the literature propose ways of improving tourists' experience through GSNs. Salovaara and collaborators [10, 11] have explored how tourists can use a GSN to collectively create stories about large-scale events they have attended together, as well as to share media and comments during the event. Their research points to the viability of such approach in collective sense-making and to enable active sharing aspects of event spectatorship. Lee et al. [12], corroborate with their results that the analysis of information produced by GSN users improve the comprehension of other users about a city. The SPETA system aims at leveraging geolocated historical information to produce recommendations for tourists [13].

According to research of Salesses et al. [14], cities present different experiences to their visitors related to knowledgment about city and due to a set of urban features. This heterogenity among cities create the necessity to define metrics, based on GSN information, which measure the importance of information and the behaviours of urban contexts. These metrics can be: inequality among cities [14], mood of users [15], information entropy [16] or points of interest of users [17]. Based on that, there is other metric, called relevance, which defines whether the information is interesting or useful to users [18]. A study of [19], highlight the relevant information in commitment of users in GSN collaboration. Related to relevance of information, it was not found any research that used a calculation about this metric with GSNs, only theoretical descriptions.

In spite of several aspects having been investigated in the behavior of tourists in GSNs, there has been so far little attention given to quantitative comparisons of the relevance of information produced by this group and by residents, as well as to how the perception of such relevance varies for these two groups of users. Our study addresses this gap.

3 Case Study and Data Collection

The large-scale touristic event, GSN and city considered in our case study are, respectively, the Brazilian touristic event called São João, user activity in Foursquare during and after the event, and the city of Campina Grande. We now turn to describe the context and data collected and for this case study.

3.1 Brazilian Touristic Event

The touristic event chosen for our case study—São João in Campina Grande, Brazil—is a yearly popular celebration for the nativity of St. John the Baptist. The celebration was introduced in Brazil by the Portuguese in the period when Brazil was a colony (1500–1822). São João celebration happens nationwide, but is particularly popular in Northeastern Brazil [20].

Campina Grande's city hall advertises its São João as "the biggest São João in the world", and celebrates it promoting 30 days of festivities in month of June. During the celebrations, it is typical for a city to host concerts, typical dances and festivities both in open spaces, bars, and restaurants. Large crowds are also common in such festivities. The city has approximately 400,000 inhabitants, but during the 30 days of celebration, around 2 millions of tourists visit Campina Grande.

3.2 Foursquare

Foursquare describes itself as a mobile service that "gives you personalized recommendations and deals based on where you, your friends, and people with your tastes have been".[1] For that, Foursquare allows its users to share their location with their social network by "checking in" on a place [21]. Although places are often called venues, they can be any sort of urban site, from a home to a concert hall or bar.

Users can share their impressions about places in annotations. These annotations are known as *tips* in Foursquare lingo, and other users besides the tip's author can mark the annotation with *dones*, *to do*s and *like*s. *Done* marks are meant to inform a user has been in the venue of the tip and he or she has made use of the the opinion in the tip. *To do* marks are used by users who have never been in the venue of the tip, but would like to visit it motivated by the tip. Lastly, *like* marks are used to agree with the content of the tip [22].

We chose the Foursquare for our study due to its present popularity. At the time of writing, it is the GSN most used in the world, with 10 millions of users registered.[2] Moreover, the amount of users in Brazil increased 800 % between May 2011 and May 2012.[3]

3.3 Data Used

The methodology used for data collection is divided in two steps: the collection of check-ins during the touristic event and the collection of all past tips for the venues mentioned in sample of check-ins.

The first step in the collection was performed through the Twitter API, recording in real-time publicly available Foursquare check-ins made in Campina

---

[1] https://foursquare.com/about

[2] https://foursquare.com/infographics/10million

[3] http://www.telecompaper.com/news/foursquare-grows-800-percent-in-brazil-over-past-12-months–873993

Grande between June 7th 2013 to July 7th 2013. The data obtained for each check-in are date, author, venue, and home city of the check-in's author. Throughout our analysis, a user is considered as a tourist or resident based on his or her home city.

With the sample of check-ins, we construct a list of venues mentioned in the data. The second step in the data collection is recovering the full set of tips in each venue mentioned in the check-ins. This was done through the Foursquare API. For each tip, we obtain its content, and as metadata, its number of *to dos* and *dones*, as well as data about its author. The datasets about tips were created based on identical queries performed in July and August 2013. These represent the state of tips immediately after São João and 1 month afterwards. This second dataset will be used to investigate the decline in the relevance of tips over time.

3.4 Overview of Collected Data

We collected 2,823 check-ins, at 389 venues, shared during the event, of which 1,827 belong to tourists and 996 belong to residents. Moreover, we collected 699 tips, at 252 venues, created by GSN's users during São João, 123 belonging to tourists and 70 belonging to residents. Based on our sample, it is possible to infer (Wilcoxon test, p-value < 0.05) that during the event tourists shared significantly more tips than residents, while residents shared significantly more check-ins than tourists.

Although the quantity of tips are unlike between tourists and residents, the quantity of sharing related to tips' content is similar between tourists and residents during the touristic event, as showed on Fig. 1. Distribution of categories of tips shared by residents and tourists. Note that that because a tip can belong to multiple categories, the sum of proportions of tips in each category exceeds 100 %.

Related to venue visiting, residents tend to check-in and create tips mainly at eating venues, like restaurants, snack bars, candy shops, and pubs. When we observe the users groups, we realize that venues preferences are distinct during touristic event.

3.5 Content of Tips During Touristic Event

Initially, our study examined the textual content of tips to gain a general understanding of messages shared in the event. Manually inspecting the content of each tip in our dataset, we identified the following seven non-exclusive categories for tips:

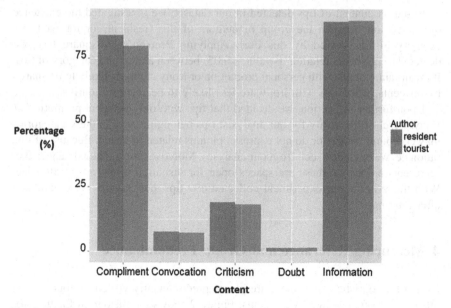

Fig. 1 Distribution of categories of tips shared by residents and tourists

- *Compliment*: express satisfaction with a venue. For example: *"It's an amazing place for having fun!"*[4];
- *Criticism*: express disappointment about a venue. For example: *"Don't come here, the food is awkward and the price is expensive"*;
- *Information*: communicate apparently useful information, such as Wi-Fi passwords, precise address, or schedule. For example: "18:30 p.m. *Best time to take a coffee here"*;
- *Doubt*: contain a question related to the venue. For example: *"Is the boarding tax R$1.50 or have I been robbed?"*;
- *Convocation*: call other users to visit a venue. For example: *"Let's go taste the best food in the region"*;
- *Irony*: express a message with opposite meaning of the obvious one. For example: *"the rush hour is the best time to wait a bus here #onlynot"*;
- *Personal Promotion*: messages containing personal information likely aiming at promoting a positive image for its author. For example: *"I'm at the gym, working out"*.

Two researchers were informed about the definitions of the categories and were convoked to evaluate 100 tips created during the event. A high degree of consensus between these experts emerged (inter-rater reliability > 95 %). This indicates a consistency in the classification we use.

---

[4] The content of all tip examples was translated from Portuguese by the authors.

Based on content of tips detected in our dataset, we investigated the existence of association between the group of authors of tips (residents or tourists) and category of tips shared by this user. Applying Pearson's chi-square test, we detected a significant relation (p-value <0.05) between author and category of tips. It means annotations with personal promotion or irony are more likely to be shared by residents, while tips with irony are less likely to be share by tourists.

Upon further inspection, we decided that tips with only personal promotion or irony present little utility for our analysis; tips belonging only to these categories may confound readers or do not express opinions related to venue. Because of this rationale, we excluded such from our analyses. Moreover, we excluded venues that represents homes, as these are spaces open for visitation to any event attendee. With this criteria, our experiment collected 699 tips, but 567 tips were validated after filtering.

4 Measuring Relevance and Group Predominance

During the touristic event, there are places predominantly visited by tourists and others most often visited by residents. Figure 2 shows the histogram for the proportion of check-ins made by tourists in each venue in our data. From it, it is possible to empirically define three groups of venues during the event. In our definition, predominantly resident venues are those with less than 40 % of check-ins made by tourists, predominantly tourist venues are those with more than 60 % of check-ins made by tourists, and the remainder venues are deemed neutral.

Naturally, some annotations are more relevant than others for a GSN's user. Foursquare provides two indicators of the relevance of a tip to users in general. The first is the quantity of users who were in a place and agreed publically with a tip through a *done* mark. The second is the sum of users who add the tip about urban place to a list in Foursquare through a *to do* mark. We leverage these two sources of information to quantitatively define the Relevance of an annotation for a group of GSN's users. In this work, the absolute relevance R of an annotation that was created during the event in Foursquare is defined as the sum of the numbers of *dones* (d) and *to dos* (o) for the annotation at a moment in time, divided by the length of time between the beginning of the touristic event and the measurement time (Δt), as showed Eq. 1.

$$R = \frac{d + o}{\Delta t} \tag{1}$$

To account for the fact that tips in more popular venues may attract more absolute relevance, throughout our analysis we consider relevance for tips as normalized considering other tips in the same venue. Our normalization is performed calculating the z-score of the absolute relevance of tips in each venue.

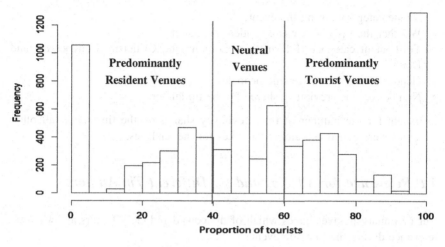

Fig. 2 Histogram about frequency of check-ins made by tourists at venues during the large-scale event

The dataset used to this research does not give enough information about the users who marked tips as to do or done. To solve this problem, we define the typical audience of a venue as a proxy about these GSN tips readers. For that, we first categorize venues in three types, according to the prevalence of residents or tourists in it. The Fig. 2 shows the distribution of venues, according to the proportion of tourists that checked in the venue during the event. It was identified three groups of venues: (a) predominantly resident venues, (b) neutral venues and (c) predominantly tourist venues.

We detected 15 venues mainly visited by residents and 72 venues predominantly visited by tourists, according to their check-ins.

5 Relevance of Tips Shared During Touristic Event

The first research question to which we direct our attention is: *which factors affect the relevance of tips created by tourists and residents during the touristic event?*

This analysis first examines the relevance of all tips created during the touristic event. After that, we separate tips according to whether their author is a resident or tourist, and finally we analyze the relevance of tips according to the type of venue (of tourists or of residents) which they annotate.

More formally, our study performs a regression analysis, and investigates the standardized coefficients obtained for the relation between the relevance of tips and factors related to the GSN. The list of factors considered as independent variables are as follows:

- Venue category during the event;
- Whether the tip's author is a resident or tourist;
- Tip content category (Information, Compliment, Criticism, Convocation and Doubt);
- Gender of the author (female or male);
- Number of tips previously shared by the tip author.

Except for the number of tips previously shared by the tip author, all other variables were coded as dummy variables for the analyses.

5.1 Relevance for All Tips and for Different Tip Authors

Our first analysis investigates which of the considered GSN factors affect the tip relevance during the touristic event.

The first step in this analysis is to perform a Kendall correlation test in order to eliminate multicolinearity among the GSN factors used as independent variables. We define the existence of correlation between two GSN factors when p-value < 0.05 and $-0.30 > \tau$ or $\tau > 0.30$. We used a non-parametric method because the grouping data based on type of authors was not homoscedastic and parametric.

Related to all tips created during the event, this method detected the multico-linearity among the following pairs of GSN factors: (a) type of author and category of venue ($\tau = 0.384$, p-value < 0.05) and (b) type of author and existence of compliment in a tip ($\tau = 0.319$, p-value < 0.05). Based on these results, we discard the existence of compliment and category of venue from our model.

Related to tourists' tips, it detected multicolinearity between category of venue and existence of convocation in a tip ($\tau = -0.342$, p-value < 0.05). It means that more touristic is the venue more tips with convocation it is. Based on results, the existence of convocation is out of model.

At last, the multicolinearity is present among the following pairs of residents' tips: (a) Gender of author and previous number of tips published by the author ($\tau = -0.523$, p-value <0.05); (b) Gender of author and existence of criticism in a tip ($\tau = -0.484$, p-value <0.05); (c) Type of venue and existence of criticism in a tip ($\tau = -0.553$, p-value <0.05); (d) Type of venue with existence of compliment on a tip ($\tau = 0.471$, p-value <0.05). Based on these results, the gender of authors and the category of venue were removed from the model of the relevance of residents' tips.

All our analyses apply negative binomial regression [23] in order to measure the effect of GSN factors on tips' relevance. This method was chosen due to the incidence of dummy variables in our data about GSN factors. After performing each regression, we calculate the standardized coefficient for each influential factor. The results for the three models (considering all tips, only those created by residents and only those created by tourists) are reported in Table 1.

Table 1 Factors that influence a tip relevance during a Brazilian touristic event

Tips created by	GSN factor	β	p-value
Residents + tourists (n = 148)	Is the author a tourist?	−0.268	<0.05
Residents (n = 54)	Is there convocation in tip?	−0.103	<0.05
	Previous tips of author	0.228	<0.05
Tourists (n = 94)	Is there compliment in tip?	−0.197	<0.05

According to our results, residents generally create tips more relevant that tourist's tips during the touristic event. Probably, it occurs due to the longer experience of residents with venues of their hometown. For example, some popular tips created by tourists during the event talked about their initial experience with venues during the touristic event:

> The best place of Campina Grande. Here you can have it all.

> Here they have Antarctica Original [a relatively uncommon beer brand], and it is really cold. Beans and fried quail are very good

> People spoke so much about the corned beef in butterfat that I tried it, and it is VERY GOOD!

> Don't come here if they have live music, impossible to chat, too loud music. Bar looks like a concert venue

On the other hand, the popular tips created by residents during the event express their apparently more experienced opinion, targeting unique aspects of venues:

> The caipirinha [a cocktail] here is worth every cent. If you ask them to make it strong, prepare yourself, as it is coming ready to get you drunk

> Deep fried cheese is tradition here. You can ask...

> If you are here, best just asking a full roast chicken, with vinaigrette and farofa.

> The shrimp cream in an Italian bread accompanied by a matte and peach ice tea is a wonder. On Tuesday, people go there to play chess.

Another finding based on the results is that the previous activity of tip author and the existence of convocation in tip influence the relevance of residents' tips. Participative residents have tips more relevant than tips of residents who interact little with GSN during touristic event. In an opposite direction, tips aiming to attract other GSN users to a venue tend to be less relevant than tips without convocation. Although tips with convocation promote the venues, they are of little relevance in our metric.

Moreover, tips created by tourists with compliments during the event tend to be less relevant than other tips created by these same authors. This may happen because a tourist compliment brings little besides easily accessible information. For example, there is a restaurant with many tips: the compliments made by residents are: *"Rather than say, the ambience and service are excellent. Worth checking out!"* and *"Good food, good assortment and excellent service"*. Furthermore, the compliments of tourists about this same place is a little bit less complex: *"Perfect Caipirinha* [a cocktail]*"* and *"So delicious"*.

We try to discover if the category of tip content determines different GSN factors that influence the tip's relevance. However, the models showed that tips with different contents have their relevance affected by same GSN factors (the type of tips' author) as the first model, which considered all tips.

In summary, the results from this section point that residents tend to create more relevant annotations in the GSN during the touristic event we study. Moreover, experienced residents create even more relevant tips. Among tourists, compliments seem to find little relevance for the general public, and the remaining considered factors have no significant influence on tip relevance.

5.2 Relevance for Different Venue Types

After confirming that residents tend to share tips more relevant than tourists, we investigate whether this happens due to the audience of tips' readers.

Using the venues' categorization, explained previously, we evaluate the relevance of tips created by residents/tourists to tourists/residents by evaluating the relevance of residents/tourists tips in predominantly tourist/resident venues. In doing so, we address to the following research question: *How relevant are annotations created by tourists and residents to other users of the GSN from their same group and from the other group?*

As the previous section, we use multicolinearity analysis among the GSN factors. At predominantly tourist venues, the multicolinearity is present between the existence of compliment in a tip and the type of author ($\tau = 0.30$, p-value <0.05). Based on this result, the existence of compliment is not used in the model of relevance in touristic venues.

For the predominantly resident venues, the multicolinearity is present between the author's gender and the existence of criticism in a tip ($\tau = -0.43$, p-value <0.05). Based on the result, the gender of tip author is not used in this model.

As in our previous analyses, the negative binomial regression is used. The results are showed in Table 2. According to the models, the only factor that has a substantial effect on the relevance of tips is the type of author. Notably, tourists' tips tend to be less relevant than residents' tips both in predominantly tourist venues and in predominantly resident venues.

These results point that residents provide more relevant tips for all audiences. Moreover, the relevance in their tips does not seem to come from an audience of friends, as the relevance of their tips tends to be higher even in predominantly tourist venues.

After detect the importance of residents' tips for all GSN venues, the next step is discover if the behavior of the Relevance of tip created during touristic event remains overtime.

Table 2 Factors that influence the tip relevance in different venues type during the event

Venues type	GSN factor	β	p-value
Predominantly tourist venues (n = 219)	Is the author a tourist?	−0.233	<0.05
Predominantly resident venues (n = 77)	Is the author a tourist?	−0.291	<0.05

6 The Relevance After Touristic Event

Our final research question is: *how does the relevance of annotations produced by tourists and residents evolve after the touristic event?* Answering such question, we aim to explore which kind of tips leave a more valuable legacy to GSN users after the event.

Recall that our data comprises measurements of the relevance of tips in two different moments after the touristic event: (a) in the month after the event (in July) and (b) 2 months after the event (in August).

Our analysis first examines whether the relevance of tips created by residents is still more relevant after the event. This test considers only tips with non-zero relevance until the end of the touristic event, July 7th. It also considers only the 252 venues of Campina Grande that remained open and functioning after the touristic event we study. Table 3 reports significant results in a non-parametric test of Wilcoxon comparing the means of tips' relevance in the two measurements. According our results, resident tips are consistent found more relevant after the event as well.

The relevance is a metric based on a temporal factor, so it is expected that it decreases over time. To evaluate how this decrease happens, we use as a second metric the decline speed in relevance between July and August for the tips studied. Similarly to before, we applied the Wilcoxon test (p-value <0.05) in order to evaluate the decline speed of tips belonging to residents and tourists (Table 4).

According to our results, the decline speed of relevance in residents' tips is the slowest in all venues. In other words, residents share tips, during the event, with longer validity than tourists' tips. Moreover, this behavior about tips' resident repeats at touristic venues and resident venues after event.

The legacy left by tips of residents can be seen by example of a tourist's and a resident's tip referring to same venue during the event. The tourist shares the following tip: *"This pub is the only one in Campina Grande that has a clean bathroom for ladies and the beer is always cold to drink"*. This opinion is useful indeed, but the description about venue does not suggest new experiences. On the other hand, the resident's tips express their experiences with more reliability: *"Try to drink the caipirinha here! It is the cheapest and the most delicious of region!"*. It seems the resident tried on many drinks and discovered that venue has the best one. Other example is about a very popular snack place in the city. The impressions of tourists are about the peculiar decoration about place, as *"Here I'm feel like in 50s"* or *"The atmosphere here is so ancient"*. However, the opinions of residents are about the personal experiences about same place, as *"The crunchy*

Table 3 Tips Relevance overtime (Wilcoxon test, p-value <0.05)

Dataset	Comparisons of tips' relevance at:		
	(a) all venues	(b) predominantly tourist venues	(c) predominantly resident venues
July measurement	Residents > tourists	Residents > tourists	Residents > tourists
August measurement	Residents > tourists	Residents > tourists	Residents > tourists

Table 4 Comparisons about decline speed per type of venues (Wilcoxon test, p-value <0.05)

Venues	Comparisons of decline speed
All venues	Decline speed of tourists > decline speed of residents
Predominantly resident venues	Decline speed of tourists > decline speed of residents
Predominantly tourist venues	Decline speed of tourists > decline speed of residents

passionfruit cake is delicious!" or *"Snacks and candies are good, but the service leaves a little to be desired".*

The results of this section showed that the contribution of tourists' tips created during the large-scale event left a short legacy to GSN users over time. One reason we speculate may cause this effect is related to absence of GSN mechanisms supporting users with different origins and participating models.

7 Conclusions

This work presents a case study in which tourists and residents create tips found to have significantly different levels of relevance in a GSN during a large-scale touristic event. Moreover, our analysis shows that the relevance of tips created by residents also decay significantly slower than those of tourists over time. Therefore, during and after the tourist event, residents' tips present more impact than tourists' tips to GSN's users. This suggests that tourists accept well residents' advices about the urban context, but the opposite does not occur.

Taken together, our results point first to the opportunity of better leveraging the origin of a tip creator during the event to increase overall relevance of information presented to users. Presently, GSNs treat users as homogeneous in terms of city experience Mechanisms sensitive to users origin and urban knowledge have the potential to positively affect the experience of GSN users during touristic events.

On a different perspective, our results also suggest that mechanisms that help tourists provide more relevant information have room to be applied. One possible avenue of work is to better leverage their diverse background, as long as this is done in a way perceived as relevant by residents and other tourists in the GSN. The results obtained in this work offer support to the improvement of recommendation techniques to GSN's users about places and decision making, friends to make, and tips according with their status as tourists or residents.

Finally, we observe that future work may benefit from exploring a more textured definition of how experienced users are in a city. Exemplifying with our context, Campina Grande has a significant population of students who reside in the city but were born in other cities. During a touristic event, such students may be considered in a point between a resident and tourist, which would then be extremes in a continuum. Future work may compare the behavior among attendees of the event with different levels of experience and knowledge of the city in order to further understand the effect of experience and expertness regarding the urban context in the GSN and in its use during large-scale events.

Acknowledgments Aline Morais thanks CAPES for financial support.

References

1. Poon A (1993) Tourism, technology and competitive strategies. CAB International
2. Stamboulis Y, Skayannis P (2002) Innovation strategies and technology for experience-based tourism. Ann Tourism Manage 24(2003):35–43
3. Egger R, Buhalis DE (2008) Tourism case studies, 1ᵃ edn. Elsevier Ltd, Oxford
4. Lu J, Sun GSL (2012) Location-based intelligent services of scenic areas. In: Proceedings in 2nd international conference on consumer electronics, communications and networks (CECNet)
5. Jiang B, Miao Y (2014) The evolution of natural cities from the perspective of location-based social media. arXiv preprint arXiv:1401.6756
6. Lee R, Sumiya K (2010) Measuring geographical regularities of crowd behaviors. In: Proceedings of the 2nd ACM SIGSPATIAL international workshop on location based social networks, pp 1–10
7. Silva T et al (2012) Visualizing the invisible image of cities. In: IEEE international conference on green computing and communications (GreenCom)
8. Gaete-Villegas J et al (2012) TraMSNET: a mobile social network application for tourism. In: ACM conference on ubiquitous computing, New York, USA
9. Munar AM, Jacobsen JKS (2013) Trust and involvement in tourism social media and web-based travel information sources. Scand J Hospitality Tourism 13(1):1–19
10. Salovaara A et al (2006) Collective creation and sense-making of mobile media. In: Proceedings of the SIGCHI conference on human factors in computing systems. ACM, pp 1211–1220
11. Jacucci G et al (2007) CoMedia: mobile group media for active spectatorship. In: Proceedings of the SIGCHI conference on human factors in computing systems. ACM, pp 1273–1282
12. Lee R et al (2013) Urban area characterization based on crowd behavioral lifelogs over Twitter. Personal and ubiquitous computing, pp 605–662
13. García-Crespo A et al (2009) SPETA: social pervasive e-tourism advisor. Telematics Inform 26:306–316
14. Salesses P, Schechtner K, Hidalgo CA (2013) The collaborative image of the city: mapping the inequality of urban perception. PLoS One 8(7):e68400
15. Evans L (2014) Being-towards the social: mood and orientation to location-based social media, computational things and applications. New Media & Society, 1461444813518183
16. Wang C, Huberman BA (2012) How random are online social interactions? vol 2. Scientific reports

17. Neis P, Zipf A (2012) Analyzing the contributor activity of a volunteered geographic information project—the case of openstreetmap. ISPRS Int J Geo-Inf 1(2):146–165
18. Lievrouw LA (2001) New media and the pluralization of life-worlds' a role for information in social differentiation. New Media Soc 3(1):7–28
19. Lai G, Wong O (2002) The tie effect on information dissemination: the spread of a commercial rumor in Hong Kong. Soc Netw 24(1):49–75
20. Cleary D, Jenkins D (2009) The rough guide to Brazil. Penguin, Harmondsworth, pp 338–339
21. Barkhuus L et al (2013) Representation and communication: challenges in interpreting large social media datasets. In: Computer supported cooperative work (CSCW), San Antonio, Texas, USA
22. Lindqvist J et al (2011) I'm the mayor of my house: examining why people use foursquare-a social-driven location sharing application. In: Conference on human factors in computing systems
23. Kaplan EL, Meier P (1958) Nonparametric estimation from incomplete observations, vol 282, 53 edn, American Statistical Association, Boston, pp 457–481

When Medical Expertise Meets Record Expertise: The Practices of Patient Accessible Medical Records in China

Yunan Chen and Kathleen Pine

Abstract Recent consumer, private sector, and governmental health informatics initiatives outline patient accessible medical records (PAMR) as key for engaging patients and supporting patient-clinician communication. However, many challenges have been encountered in designing usable digital systems for patients to access and use their medical records. Barriers to such systems include social, cultural, and policy constraints in addition to usability problems. In particular, questions of expertise, responsibility, and ownership surrounding medical records are often hotly contested between medical professionals and healthcare organizations. In broaching the design challenge of PAMR, much can be learned from examining existing practices for patient carried and accessible records in contexts where these practices are well established. We examine practices surrounding PAMR in a setting where medical records have long been managed by patients: the Chinese healthcare system. Through close examination of managing medical records and sharing medical health information, we find that these personal record practices in China enable a two-way medical records sharing practice between patients and their providers, which fundamentally reconfigures the patient role in healthcare process, facilitates development of 'record expertise' on the part of patients, and joint responsibility for health management. We use these findings to illuminate the potential benefits of PAMR, and to offer design considerations to optimize future systems design and deployment efforts in other contexts.

The two authors contributed equally to this work and are listed in alphabetical order.

Y. Chen
Department of Informatics, University of California, Irvine, USA
e-mail: yunanc@ics.uci.edu

K. Pine (✉)
Intel Labs, Hillsboro, Oregon, USA
e-mail: kathleen.pine@intel.com

C. Rossitto et al. (eds.), *COOP 2014 - Proceedings of the 11th International Conference on the Design of Cooperative Systems, 27–30 May 2014, Nice (France),*
DOI: 10.1007/978-3-319-06498-7_25, © Springer International Publishing Switzerland 2014

1 Introduction

Effective healthcare requires contributions from both healthcare providers and patients. However, patients' involvement has long been minimized in the health-care process. With limited health resources worldwide, the provider centric model is often less than optimal in treating patients. Thus, there is a call for innovative tools and methods to engage patients in their care, such as promoting patient awareness about their own health issues, educating them to have proper health knowledge, and supporting effective communication between patients and clinicians. In particular, it is believed that "in order for patients to be true partners in the health care encounter, they must have access to their own personal clinical health information" [1].

Recent consumer and policy initiatives promote the role of digital tools in achieving these aims, and prioritize the development of such tools as a key to digital health development across the globe [2–4]. Patient Accessible Medical Record (PAMS) Systems are increasingly designed and deployed to enhancing patients' involvement in their own care, such as Personal Health Records (PHR) [3]. Accessing clinician-generated information is critical to shift the provider-centered paradigm to one of patient-provider collaboration. As Piras and Zanutto [5] describe it, such patient-centered information exchange aims to redefine the patient as "...not 'the object described in documents exchanged among doctors,' but rather 'the actor most concerned with the flow of information through the carers' network" (p. 589).

The shift to digital health records systems has created a potential to re-think current health record practices and create new inclusive systems that give patients increased access to their medical records. However, despite the potential advantages, PHR systems have not been widely embraced, and a number of technical and policy barriers to adoption have been outlined [6]. For example, the high profile failure of GoogleHealth, a tool with a huge investment of human and financial resources, has been attributed to lack of consumer knowledge about e-health, lack of organization and provider involvement and willingness to transfer data, and privacy concerns [7]. The systems that have come into use are largely designed as an individual portal which allows patients to access their information online but that bears limited impact on the collaborative nature of patient care. It is clear that much work is needed to understand how to best design and deploy PAMR systems in practice. Further, little empirical research on cooperative work in healthcare examines information work of patients and information sharing and collaboration between patients and clinicians, home and healthcare organization.

The goal of this study is to explore the practices of PAMR in practice, and to draw design insights for future digital records systems that can encourage and engage patients' involvement in their own information and care. This study is timely and important as allowing patients to access their medical records, and promoting patient engagement in healthcare through digital systems has been a new trend in many western countries. However, the use of such systems relies not only on technological advancements, but also deep understandings about the records practices that patients engage in, which are inherently social and cultural. In this research we explore the design of PAMR systems through ethnographic research in a case where paper-based PAMR are in use. We conducted a field study in a large comprehensive hospital in China where patients are able to access, interact with, and manage their own paper-based medical records. In our study, the paper-based records resemble the concepts and goals that the digital systems, such as PHR, intend to achieve, and the potential such records practices afford for enhanced patient-provider collaborations.

This research makes multiple contributions to the ECSCW research tradition by examining medical record practices in a context in which little empirical research has been conducted (China), and through in-depth examination of collaborative information practices between clinicians and patients, thus bridging healthcare organizations and the domestic sphere of patient homes. Finally, this paper contributes by exploring patients' medical records management practices to inform future design and implementation of digital systems that support patient engagement and information sharing. Theoretically, we contribute an understanding of record expertise–a form of authoritative knowledge gained by patients through practices of managing records and collaboratively sharing medical information with clinicians.

2 Related Work

PAMR systems have been outlined as a major part of strategies to use health information technologies to improve the quality and efficiency of healthcare [8], and many initiatives in PAMR have been developed and led by industry and healthcare organizations. However, little research to date has been conducted on practices of using PAMR, such as PHR systems. Recent work in the Human-Computer Interaction and Computer Supported Cooperative Work areas has focused on developing methods to evaluate usability of PHR technology [9], the potential information needs and desires of intended PHR users [10], as well as the work of simply being a patient [11].

2.1 Benefits and Challenges of PAMR Systems

PAMR have long been in discussion in medical informatics and general medicine literatures worldwide. Multiple studies have found that access to one's medical record in either traditional paper format or electronically has the potential to enhance patients' understanding of their condition [12]; empower individuals to become active participants in their own care [13]; result in better medical management [14]; lead to more effective provider patient communication [12, 14];

improve electronic health record (EHR) accuracy and increasing compliance with health maintenance clinical guidelines [15]. Further, many studies demonstrate that access to one's health information using digital technologies is desired by majority of health care consumers.

On the other hand, although desirable by patients, there are multiple challenges to wide implementation and use of such systems. For instance, a national survey conducted with hospital CEOs in Canada indicates that patients experience low levels of accessibility to their medical records, with financial limitation to implement electronic records system and providers' unwillingness to provide access as two major barriers [16]. Similarly, research conducted in a hospital in Israel found 94 % of providers studied refused to give patients access to their records [4]. Physicians report worry about the negative impacts on sharing records to their own clinical practice and also cite fear of negative impacts on certain patients, for example, cancer patients, as reasons for refusing patient access to medical records [17]. Additionally, prior literature notes that health care consumers must understand and accept their roles and responsibilities related to their own health care [3, 18]. One previous study found that although patients were interested in enrolling in PHR when such a system was available to them, rarely had anyone requested a copy of their medical records previously [19]. Thus, motivating both clinicians and patients to accept and fully benefit from PAMR remains a significant topic in need of research. However, there is a lack of research on PAMR in general and particularly on how personal health information artifacts figure in relations between clinicians and patients.

2.2 Patient-Clinician Communication and Cooperative Work

Studying PAMR calls attention to the need to understand information sharing and collaboration between healthcare providers and consumers of healthcare, patients. Thus, PAMR provides an intriguing opportunity to examine cooperative work that extends between two different spheres, the organizational/institutional sphere of healthcare organizations and the domestic sphere of personal health [5]. Past research on cooperative work in healthcare focuses primarily on either the care coordination process among caregivers [20] or on the clinical collaboration process within healthcare settings [21, 22]. In the home setting, a rich body of research examines information sharing and collaboration between care supporters and care networks [20, 23]. However, little research to date examines the intersection of information practices of the home and healthcare organization, and fundamental tensions surrounding this intersection, such as knowledge, authority, and responsibility. Our research provides an initial attempt to address this gap through examining patient-provider communication and information sharing centered on medical record artifacts as a form of cooperative work.

Understanding opportunities and barriers for PAMR requires an understanding that designing such artifacts must take into account the inter-relation of these artifacts with practices of patient-clinician communication and information exchange that are inherently social, cultural, and material. Further, we argue that in understanding opportunities and barriers to PAMR, we must understand the questions that these artifacts-in-use raise for authority, expertise, and responsibility between patients and clinicians in cooperative work process. Medical anthropology research has previously taken a critical perspective of patient-clinician interactions, pointing out that power imbalances often pervade interactions between doctors and patients. Authoritative knowledge studies in particular point to the role of technological artifacts in perpetuating medical-scientific knowledge as the dominant form of knowledge in patient provider interactions [24]. Patients do not have access to this knowledge nor to the artifacts that produce or contain it, thus are unable to access authoritative knowledge about their bodies and the conditions of care.

More broadly, Practice theory [25–27] has previously been described in the design and CSCW domain in the work of scholars such as Schmidt [28]. A practice perspective shifts the researcher's view of "knowledge;" knowing is seen as relational, emergent, embodied, inscribed in artifacts, and only partly articulated in discourse [29]. A practice perspective emphasizes power, politics, and conflict as constitutive of experienced reality. Practices make certain ways of acting or feeling available to some participants and not others; these asymmetries are perpetuated in space and time in large part through objects such as information technologies.

Using ethnographic data consisting of observations and interviews, we examine how Chinese patients manage their medical records using a variety of artifacts accumulated and created over a lifetime of healthcare interactions. Further, we examine collaborative practices of sharing personal health information using personal record archives maintained by patients and how practices of patient management and patient-clinician sharing of records relate to social and cultural understandings of patient knowledge and responsibility in the Chinese context. Finally, we offer design insights for future digital PAMR.

3 Methodology

We conducted a qualitative study consisting of semi-structured interviews and non-participant observation examining the practices of patients' self-managed medical records at outpatient departments of a Chinese health organization. We chose to conduct this study in China because the outpatient medical records (paper-based) produced by health providers are given and thus managed by individual patients. This provided a unique setting to understand PAMR in use and how it can inform the design of digital systems that aim to function similarly. We obtained ethical approval from the university the researchers are affiliated with, and the approval of the scientific review board of the hospital being studied.

3.1 Participants

The hospital where this study was carried out is a nationally known comprehensive health organization. Patients of this hospital include both local residents having routine medical visits, to patients who traveled from other cities seeking treatment or second opinions for illnesses that they have been unable to obtain proper diagnosis or treatment for elsewhere. These two patient populations present an interesting case to study self-accessible patients record use since we are able to study a diverse set of the medical records practices engaged by patients.

Two participant populations were included: clinicians and patients. To gain an understanding of patient-clinician communication centered on PAMR, we recruited a total of four doctors, and 17 health consumers, including 13 patients and 4 family members from our field site. Family members were interviewed either when patients were younger than 18 years old or when family members served as the main information gatekeeper for the household. We focused on data collection from patients with chronic health conditions because we observed that this population engaged in record keeping practices to a greater extent than those who did not suffer from chronic conditions, thus provided an ideal sample in which we could examine these practices in depth given limited time for the study.

3.2 Data Collection and Analysis

To understand how patients' self-maintained medical records were used during the consultation process, we conducted observations of patient-clinician interactions surrounding patient medical records that occurred during medical visits. Observations were conducted in the medical consultation rooms located in each department. A total of 40 h of observations were performed in the consulting room, consisting of 76 patient consultations in total. Each observation session lasted for 4–5 h. During the observation, the researcher sat in an unobtrusive location within the consulting room. The research activities included jotting down brief observation notes, asking questions when patients/physicians were available, and tracking down critical incidents during the observations. Detailed observation notes were transcribed after each session. The researcher is a native speaker and previously majored in medicine. This ensured proper understandings of the patient-physician interactions in the consulting room.

In addition to exam-room observations, we also studied patients' records management practices through patient interviews. We did not observe patients' record-keeping behaviors at home since these activities may occur at any time private settings. Observing these activities was impractical from a data collection standpoint and also raised ethical questions surrounding patients' privacy in home settings. Instead, we used semi-structured interviews to explore patients' behaviors, attitudes, and practices around keeping, using, organizing records. In the study, we asked interviewees to show us the records they brought with them–this way we were able to see how records are organized and probed further to understand how patients prepared their records and managed their records at home. Interviews ranged from 25 to 60 min in length. 15 interviews were audio recorded and the rest were recorded with pen and paper [30]. Interview transcripts and observation notes were coded using an iterative open coding scheme to extract the medical records usage patterns in the consulting room.

4 Findings

In this section we describe two PARM practices. First, based on interviews with patients about their practices of managing records, we describe how they engaged in a series of record managing and organization activities outside of physician offices. Second, drawing on observations conducted in physician offices, we describe practices of exchanging patient carried records with health providers during medical visits. Through engaging in these two practices of managing and sharing records, patients were able to obtain familiarity with their own records and to provide necessary assistance to locate information for providers to use at the point of care.

4.1 Managing Records

Patients observed and interviewed in this study are able to fully access their outpatient medical records. The information patients can access includes medical history, diagnosis, prescriptions, lab results, radiology images and reports. At the study site, the chief complaint and medical history are handwritten on pocket-sized medical records book. Diagnosis and prescription information are entered into a hospital-wide information system first, then printed out and attached to the medical records book.

After the records are given to patients, they are responsible for taking care of their records on their own. Hence, the responsibility of keeping the medical records is shifted on to individual patients. It is the patients' responsibility to collect and maintain their records from different visits and manage them in a meaningful way for doctors to use. For instance, patients have to collect the test results from laboratory or radiology departments themselves and bring them back to physicians; patients also need to collect records they receive from different medical visits, or from different health organizations they choose to visit; eventually, patients are responsible to bring the records to their next medical visit for doctors to view their medical histories. This series of actions allows patients to be the owner and organizer of their own records. In the following, we describe a number of specific actions that are involved in the practice of managing records (Fig. 1).

First, patients store their records. It is not unusual to see patients bring in years of records during observation, or to learn they kept all their medical records carefully at home during interviews. In interviewing subjects, we found that most patients stored their records; there were no instances, in our study data, of patients not placing a high value on storing records and bringing records with them each time they came to a medical visit. The archive of personal records is extensive and lifelong, with most patients maintaining original records from when they were first diagnosed, along with all consequent visits for that particular disease. Each time a patient receives any type medical records, in the form of physician notes in a records book, x-rays, lab results, or other artifacts, the patient adds these records to their personal archive of medical information. Storage of records is very important to patients and this importance reflects the high degree of responsibility they feel for archiving and managing medical records for oneself and for one's family members. Most patients reported storing records in a single, valued location, either a series of bags kept together (sometimes hanging from a hook on the wall), or in a specified cabinet in the home. A husband of a 38-year-old tympanitis patient said: "*We put all the important records in the big plastic bag for each hospital visit and hang them on the wall in our bedroom.*" A mother of a congenital cataract patient described "*These [medical records] are the most important things for my child. I keep all the records for my child in a separate cabinet ever since he was born [the child is five years old now] and will track them'til he grows up, maybe for his whole life.*" Some patients even stored their records with other most important documents such as their ID and bank statements, indicating the importance of these medical records for patients.

Second, we found that most chronic care patients engaged in some amount of sorting of their personal records according to condition and importance. The growing body of medical records that patients archive over time leads to the development of sorting practices that allow people to keep their own and their family's records sorted in meaningful ways that facilitate usage. We found that patients suffering from chronic conditions that required ongoing care (or caring for household members with chronic conditions) tended to engage in more extensive sorting practices than patients who did not suffer from chronic conditions—this initial finding led us to conduct focused data collection with chronic disease patients. The high volume of medical records accumulated by those with chronic conditions made the need to sort records more pressing. Chronic sufferers were accustomed to frequent medical visits requiring well organized records, and dealing with the daily reality of chronic health problems made sorting records a high priority for these patients and their families.

Records were often separated and organized according to particular diseases and conditions and sometimes according to clinic. For chronic conditions, a separate subset of records was often created and maintained related solely to the trajectory of that condition. For example, one patient with diabetes (56 years old) described how she visits both a small clinic near her home for minor illnesses and the hospital where the study was carried out for diabetes care. Even though these two places use a unified record system where clinicians from different organizations can be unified in the same record book, she decided to have two books, one for each clinic, for the purposes of separating visits and more easily finding information. She said, *"Actually I could have had just one record book, but I am afraid that I cannot distinguish different medical visits…using two books is easier for me."* Later she said *"I put my medical card, record book, and medications for each clinic in a separate bag. This way I can just grab it on my way out and I have everything I need."* Similarly, another diabetes patient told us that she always pulls out blood test results and arranges them chronologically before going to the doctor, because this allows her to easily see and demonstrate how her diabetes is progressing over time. Patients arrange records both before storing them at home and in preparation for medical visits. Many patients interviewed reported reading through their records periodically at home as they arrange and re-arrange their archive of records, demonstrating that the patients in our sample actively engage with their medical information in the home and apart from interactions with clinicians.

Third, some of the patients in our study engaged in practices of annotating their records. This involves organizing their records in particular ways and marking, making notes, or creating new documents related to their records which are added to the patient's archive. For instance, one patient said, *"not only do I keep all my medical records and read them from time to time, I organize these [information] resources into a 'health information book' (Fig. 2)."* In showing the organized records to the researcher, he pointed out several sheets of lab results and said *"these red annotations indicate whether readings of lab results are increasing, or decreasing."* He proudly said: *"I developed this system all by myself."* Another common form of annotation reported by patients was creating their own typed record summary that synthesizes the lengthy health information into a brief summary. Typically, the summary lists records according to the dates of medical visits, and serves as an index page for patients to locate where the information for a particular visit was documented, and what was the key information generated in

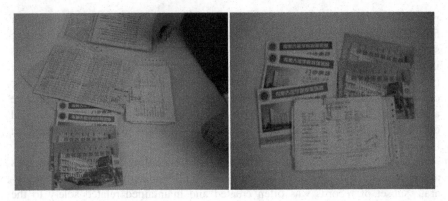

Fig. 2 Stored, sorted and annotated records by a chronic hyperthyroidism patient. *Left* sorted lab results. *Right* annotated summary page

each visit (Fig. 2). Again, intensive arranging and annotating of the personal record archive varied widely between patients and households, mostly following patients' and caregivers' own personal preferences and rules of using the records. Our interviews and observations revealed that the degree to which patients engaged in these practices varied such that that the more intense, long-term chronic disease sufferers had more elaborate systems for arranging and annotating that they had developed over time through managing archives and learning to organize records to facilitate communication with doctors through repeated visits.

4.2 Sharing Records

Demonstrating responsibility and involvement in one's own healthcare was the predominant reason patients reported for engaging in record management activities. The patients' self-managed records were brought back to medical visits and shared with clinicians, since patients felt that their own memory was inadequate in providing an accurate history to clinicians. Thus they believed that distributed, artifact-based memory of disease and treatment was crucial to receiving good care. Patient-clinician visits in our field site routinely involved detailed patient history based around the medical records that patients brought with them to visits.

Throughout the entire study, only a very few patients came back without their previous medical records. The shared medical information provided a basis for physicians to know the whole picture of patient's history and status so they could avoid possible overdose and drug interactions. In our sample of Chinese doctors, doing a thorough history was contingent on having access to patient-carried records. Clinicians felt that a verbal history was insufficient, as was a history based solely on their own clinic's records. Since patients are the owner and manager of their records in our field site, many of them were skilled at facilitating records sharing through bringing the records to the medical visits, and providing necessary help for doctors to read the information when they needed it. Observations of patient-clinician interactions revealed that patients who engaged in active sorting and annotating of their records were particularly skilled in engaging with clinicians in dialogue about their conditions. While some patients simply brought in piles of records from past visits, others brought carefully sorted, arranged, and annotated records, and these patients were able to more quickly find information requested by clinicians and converse with physicians about their condition and their care. The following two observations illustrate the process of records sharing between patients and clinicians during a medical visit.

Case one: a patient with 20-year history of diabetes

The patient came in with his wife, who was a vocal participant in interactions with the doctor.

The first thing that happened after the doctor greeted the patient was that the patient showed the doctor a self-written glucose log he had recorded for the past two weeks.

Doctor (pointing to one number): "why this one was so low?"

Wife: "we heard from others that Douzha (a special tofu product) can lower the blood sugar, so we tried it out, we didn't expect it to be this low in the first day."

Doctor, "what medication you are on now?"

Instead of answering the question verbally, the wife took out a stack of medical records she brought into the visit. Other than a few medical record books, she also brought a self-annotated "medical visit history" log summarizing his past medical issues. This table-like log contains doctor's name, the prescription, medication, dosages, lab test results, and his personal notes. Soon she handed a medical record book with a few pieces of lab test results. The doctor started reading them.

Patient: "I've been on insulin for a month."

Doctor: "oh, so how many units is he on? Is it 302 or 502?

Wife (points to the record in the doctor's hand): Actually I don't really know.

Doctor (sees number he needs and turns to patient for next question): "how's your kidney function?"

Wife: "the urine test reports are attached at the back of the record book."

Patient: "you know, I now exercise a lot. I walk almost 10 kilometers a day."

Doctor (nodding, and looking at the urine test reports) "yes that's really good for you."

Wife: "he has stroke 7 years ago that almost killed him....it is really difficult for us now. The insulin – he needs 8 shots, and also needs to test the blood sugar 4 to 5 times a day. We simply cannot travel anywhere in this situation now."

Doctor "why he is on insulin?"

Wife: "that was from last July or August, there was a few days he got really hungry during night, and had some cookies and milk." She describes how his glucose got out of control, and they went to the local clinic but it was too late. Since his glucose was out of control for a while, they had to start insulin treatment.

The doctor nodded, and advised the wife: "it is really important to have regular meals. You cannot eat too much, or adjust your insulin intake too frequently."

The doctor started reading the glucose log again. He pointed to another number and asked "what you had on that day?" The wife began describing what they ate on that day, the portion etc. The wife replies that they are doing better with diet, they used to buy wheat bread at the store, but her husband realized there is lots of sugar in it. Now we they bake it themselves.

Doctor (pointing to the log): see you have 5.2, then 9.2 then 5.2 again here...

Patient: the 9.2 one was because I ate snacks during the night.

Doctor, if that's the case, you can take a little bit insulin in the middle of the night to lower the sugar level.
Next the doctor renewed the prescription and ended the medical visit.

As demonstrated by the case above, patient-clinician interactions in our field site involved conversations about patient history and disease in which the patient's self-carried, and often personally arranged and annotated, medical records played a key role. Instead of being verbally reported to physicians, information requested by doctors is often communicated through sharing documents from the archive of medical records carried by the patient. Sharing records during medical visits consists of a series of cooperative actions performed jointly by patients and clinicians. These include reviewing, locating, and pointing out relevant information in the records, such as when the doctor above points to a glucose reading and asks why it is so low, the patient's wife locates the requested information in a particular record book, or when the patient's wife directs the doctor to look at the urinalysis results attached to the back of the record. In the process of reviewing, locating, and pointing out relevant information, the clinician is able to ascertain a patient history in dialogue with the patient (and the patient's family, as the case may be). The history is articulated through dialogue between clinician and patients, and is constructed using a number of documents from within the patient's personal archive of records, both self-created (such as the diabetes patient's summary sheet) and collected from different clinics over time (such as past urine test results).

When patients and clinicians review, locate, and point out key information through dialogue, clinicians typically ask a number of clarifying questions. For example, the doctor in out last example asks about an unusually low glucose level, in the process receiving a response about a change in diet, and then asks the patient and his wife directly about the patient's current treatment regime. This questioning is centered on review of records, and often results in patients producing nuanced details about symptoms, treatment, and relevant lifestyle factors. It is crucial to note that this conversation is not one-sided. Patients and family members also ask questions, direct the clinician to information they think is important, and voice opinions about the information in the records they are sharing. The vignette below, in which a gastritis patient discusses the severity of his illness with a doctor, offers a good example.

Case two: recently diagnosed gastritis patient seeking second opinion

The patient came in with two prior medical diagnoses at two other hospitals. He had never seen this doctor before, but had received a recommendation from a friend.
After introductions, the first thing the patient started to was describe his conditions. He tells the doctor he is on three medications right now. He reads the names of these medications from a small post-it held in his hand. He then pulled out his pathology, gastroscopy,colonoscopy and ultrasound reports from the previous visits. The patient tells the doctor that he has gut edema.
Doctor: "why did you think so?"
Patient (pointing to the lab result) "it's right there."
Doctor looks at the lab results and asks him what medications he is on right now. The patient shows the post-it note to the doctor.

The doctor takes the ultrasound images from the patient and starts checking the images. After looking at the lab results and the images, he explains to the patient that certain images look very serious, but the condition is in the process of recovering.

The patient says "I thought my edema is really severe, isn't it? You see this is the picture."

The doctor says "well, doing the test will cause some edema itself. But it's not as serious as you thought to be."

They go on the discuss medications, with the patient requesting a certain medication, and the doctor telling him that he may already be on too many medications. They discussed the treatment plan and the doctor entered the prescriptions in the computer system, wrote down the assessment in the medical record book, then printed out the prescriptions from the system, and gave them all to the patient.

In case two, the doctor directly asks the patient why he feels that he has a certain condition based on his symptoms, and the patient refers to test results that he has brought with him as part of his personal record archive. The doctor and patient then discussed the severity of the condition, with the doctor modulating concerns raised by the patient based on the images provided by the patient. It is important to note that the patient is actively enrolled in expressing his opinion about his condition, and he has access to his own test images, which he refers to when questioning the doctor about his condition. As in the first case, the history proceeds through a process of patient sharing records with the clinician as the clinician asks the patient about his condition. Through locating and sharing information, communication takes place through the information contained in the medical records, which are handed back and forth as they are discussed. Through the course of the dialogue, the patient offers his own interpretations of his condition. While the clinician does not always agree, the patient's opinion is heard and acknowledged by the clinician, who responds directly using the patient's own medical information to convey an expert opinion.

Our findings demonstrate that chronic care patients actively deploy the records expertise that they gain from managing their personal records, and use this expertise to question and discuss their conditions with clinicians. Clinicians are still the authoritative actors in the interaction, and often respond to patient comments and beliefs about their condition with different opinions based on medical expertise in interpreting medical information. However, it is notable that this conversation occurs through mutually constructed dialogue. Patients respond to questions, ask their own questions, offer additional information, and offer opinions as they locate information in their medical records for clinicians. We feel that there is a large connection between the practices of managing records one's records— which enables a patient to become familiar with the structure and content of the records—and in developing facility at sharing records with clinicians. Sharing records is not simply a matter of handing over records for the clinician to review, but of engaging in collaborative dialogue into understand the patient's history and condition. Our data reveal that some patients are more skilled in managing their records, usually due to increased engagement with their records necessitated by a chronic condition and frequent interaction with medical professionals.

In examining the role of record expertise in shaping patient-clinician interaction, our data show that the nature of the PAMR in our Chinese sample is a crucial in promoting different configurations of knowledge and responsibility. Patients are well versed in their own medical information, and are figured in the relationships as "experts" with knowledge of their own records. Clinicians, when seeking information, accept the records provided by patients as factual. While this could seemingly rise questions of professional hegemony, in the Chinese case clinicians retain professional expertise and authority in interpreting medical information. We observed multiple instances in which clinicians corrected patients' own self assessments, such as that above; in another case, we observed a diabetes who was very worried about her lymph cell counts. Her doctor told her that lymph counts were better left to a doctor's interpretation. While the practice of sharing records configures patients as experts of their own data, doctors retain authority in authoritative interpretation of this data. However, doctors in our sample expected patients to be active partners in a dialogue about a patient's history. Further, they viewed this artifact-centered dialogue as key to doing a "good" history, thus key to their own medical practice. No clinicians in our sample raised concerns about patients carrying their own medical records; this practice is "business as usual" in our context of study.

5 Discussion

Our findings explore how Chinese patients engage in a practice of managing their medical record at home and collaboratively sharing medical information with clinicians to develop a complete medical history and optimize care plans. Taking a practice approach to examine the relationship between social practices and information technologies calls attention to knowledge and power dynamics embedded in use [31]. Our study unveils aspects of knowledge and power dynamics that emerge through the interaction of social practices and personal health information artifacts that, we argue, can inform our understanding of collaborative information work between patients and clinicians and inform future design of digital PAMR.

First, through the practice of managing records, patients and patient family members engage in a series of activities to store, sort, organize, annotate, and arrange their medical records. Through these activities, patients become familiar and comfortable with the content and structure of medical information and medical record artifacts. A useful concept here is that of authoritative knowledge, drawn from Jordan [24]. Jordan argues that in any particular domain several knowledge systems exist, some of which carry more weight than others- often because they are associated with a stronger power base. Authoritative knowledge is constituted and re-constituted through an ongoing social process that builds on and reflects power relationships. In the medical domain, formal medical knowledge is 'authoritative knowledge,' Jordan argues that, in the ecology of practice in many healthcare organizations, access to information technologies systematically empowers clinicians and disempowers patients, who do not have access to technical systems and information that clinicians use in medical decision making. In many contexts, the medical record is inaccessible to patients and the information contained within it is impenetrable to patients; in contrast, Chinese patients gain both formal and tacit knowledge [32] of medical records through activities of engaging with their records over a lifetime. We refer to this knowledge as "record expertise" and see it as a different form of authoritative knowledge that patients obtained through practices of engaging with their medical records. In our definition, record expertise is an emergent quality of managing one's record over time that enables patients to move from passive receivers of information to active consumers and organizers of medical information.

Second, through gaining record expertise by managing records through the activities of storing, sorting, organizing, arranging and annotating, another key dynamic shifts, this time in the clinic at the site of care. Patients who are have record expertise engage in a practice of information sharing that leads to co-constructed plans and accounts of medical care. Take for the example the patient who insisted on showing the physician a key piece of information about past symptoms treated by a different physician. Knowledge structures provide the patient a key source of knowledge about their health and care, rather than a passive subject receiving treatment and information. In this way, the record expertise of the patient becomes an ongoing source of co-constructed knowledge. This results in more accurate information, particularly about medical history, while at the same time allowing potential for a more engaged patient in the care process.

Finally, the practice of sharing records reveals a sense of shared responsibility for medical care. Responsibility is shared between patients and clinicians, and between multiple clinicians who may see a patient over the course of a patient's lifetime, each contributing to the patient's archive of testing, diagnosis, and treatment records. It must be noted that an examination of malpractice and accountability for clinicians in the Chinese legal system is outside the scope of our study. Litigiousness is often cited as a reason for medical professional's concerns over sharing medical records with patients in other contexts. In our field site, it was apparent that there were no qualms with sharing records between clinics and clinicians- records are the property of the patient receiving care, not the clinic in which care is received. This places a large burden of responsibility on patients, but we found no patients who complained about the burden of managing records; on the contrary, patients in our sample put much time and energy into managing their record archive and that of their family members, in accordance with the importance they placed on these records as artifacts crucial to receiving good care.

In applying these insights to design of future digital PHR, some crucial considerations emerge. First, we find in the Chinese context that the practice of managing the record, through storing, sorting, arranging, and annotating their records. Technologies that allow patients to read their medical information will likely not engage patients to the same degree as a tool that promotes a practice of active record management in the home. Managing records promotes a sense of ownership over records, and facilitates patient-clinician cooperative work; in giving patients the ability to manage the presentation of their health to some degree, patients can become active partners with clinicians in cooperative medical records work. Second, it is essential that digital PHR tools facilitate practices of sharing information during the clinical encounter. When patients and clinicians are able to directly engage with record artifacts and exchange these artifacts in the clinic, information quality is improved, care plans are optimized, and the potential for collaborative decision making which casts patients as authoritative interaction partners emerges.

6 Conclusion

Despite high expectations and large expenditures on certain PAMR tools, many PAMR systems have not delivered on their promise. To date, few studies provide in depth ethnographic accounts of PHR tools in use, particularly outside of the U.S. and Europe. More studies of existing digital PHR and paper-based PAMR are needed. In this paper, we make strides toward filling this gap by presenting findings from an in-depth ethnographic study of PAMR in China. Chinese patients gain record expertise though a practice of managing medical record artifacts in the home, thus facilitating cooperative work between patients and clinicians and changing the tenor of the patient-clinician relationship from one that casts patients as passive recipients of information to active co-constructors of medical plans and accounts. In designing future digital PAMR tools, designers could benefit from applying insights from the Chinese case by designing records that promote practices of managing records in the home and sharing medical information during clinical encounters. Furthermore, we feel that studies of PAMR tools taking a practice perspective and occurring over the lifecycle of design and deployment, from case studies exploring existing PAMR practices through design, deployment, and use of digital PAMR technologies, will greatly facilitate the design of effective tools and ecologies of medical record practice.

References

1. Wiljer D, Urowitz S et al (2008) Patient accessible electronic health records: exploring recommendations for successful implementation strategies. J Med Internet Res 10(4):e34
2. (2004) Markle foundation. Working group on policies for electronic information sharing between doctors and patients: final report: connecting Americans to their healthcare
3. Tang PC, Ash JS, Bates DW, Overhage JM, Sands DZ (2006) Personal health records: definition, benefits, and strategies for overcoming barriers to adoption. JAMIA 13(2):121–126
4. Weiss M (1997) For doctors 'eyes only: medical records in two Israeli hospitals. Cult Med Psychiatry 21(3):283–302

5. Piras EM, Zanutto A (2010) Prescriptions, x-rays, and grocery lists: designing a personal health record to support (the invisible work of) health information management in the household. CSCW 19:585–613
6. Kahn J, Aulakh V, Bosworth A (2009) What it takes: characteristics of the ideal personal health record. Health Aff 28(2):369–376
7. (2011) InformationWeek. 5 reasons why GoogleHealth failed. Accessed online at http://www.informationweek.com/healthcare/electronic-health-records/5-reasons-why-google-health-failed/d/d-id/1098623? 29 Jun 2011
8. Tang PC (2003) Key capabilities of an electronic health record system. Institute of Medicine of the National Academies, Washington, D.C
9. Liu LS, Shih PC, Hayes GR (2011) Barriers to the adoption and use of personal health record systems. In: Proceedings of the 2011 iConference, pp 363–370
10. Leonard KJ, Casselman M, Wiljer D (2008) Who will demand access to their personal health record? A focus on users of health services and what they want. Healthc Q 11(1):92–96
11. Unruh KT, Pratt W (2007) Patients as actors: the patient's role in detecting, preventing, and recovering from medical errors. Int J Med Inf 76(S1):S236–S244
12. Cimino JJ, Patel VL et al (2002) The patient clinical information system (PatCIS): technical solutions for and experience with giving patients access to their electronic medical records. Int J Med Inf 68:113–127
13. Stein EJ, Furedy RL et al (1979) Patient access to medical records on a psychiatric inpatient unit. Am J Psychiartry 136:327–329
14. Earnest MA, Ross SE et al (2004) Use of a patient-accessible electronic medical record in a practice for congestive heart failure: patient and physician experiences. J Am Med Inf Assoc 11:410–417
15. Staroselsky M, Volk LA et al (2006) Improving electronic health record (EHR) accuracy and increasing compliance with health maintenance clinical guidelines through patient access and input. Int J Med Inf 75(10):693–700
16. Urowitz S, Wiljer D, Apatu E, Eysenbach G, Delenardo C, Harth T, Pai H, Leonard KJ (2008) Is Canada ready for patient accessible electronic health records? A national scan. BMC Med Inf Decis Mak 8(1):33
17. Ross AP (1986) The case against showing patients their records. Brit Med J (Clin Res Ed) 292(6520):578
18. Wald JS, Middleton B, Bloom A, Walmsley D, Gleason M, Nelson E, Li Q, Epstein M, Volk L, Bates DW (2004) A patient-controlled journal for an electronic medical record: issues and challenges. Stud Health Technol Inf 107(Pt 2):1166–1170
19. Ross SE et al (2003) The effects of promoting patient access to medical records: a review. J Am Med Inf Assoc JAMIA 10(2):129–138
20. Consolvo S, Roessler P, Shelton BE, LaMarca A, Schilit B, Bly S (2004) Technology for care networks of elders. IEEE Pervasive Comput 3(2):22–29
21. Lundberg N, Tellioğlu H (1999) Understanding complex coordination processes in health care. Scand J Inf Syst 1(2):157–181
22. Mejia DA, Morán AL, Favela J (2007) Supporting informal co-located collaboration in hospital work. In: Groupware: design, implementation, and use, pp 255–270
23. Chen Y, Ngo V, Park SY (2013) Caring for caregivers: designing for integrality. CSCW 2013:91–102
24. Jordan B (1993) Birth in four cultures: a cross cultural investigation of childbirth in Yucatan, Holland, Sweden, and the United States. Waveland Press, Prospect Heights, IL
25. Bourdieu P (1977) Outline of a theory of practice. Cambridge University Press, Cambridge
26. Garfinkel H (1967) Studies in ethnomethodology. Prentice-Hall, Englewood Cliffs
27. Giddens A (1986) The constitution of society. Polity Press, Cambridge
28. Schmidt K (2011) Cooperative work and coordinative practices. Springer, London, pp 3–27
29. Reckwitz A (2002) Toward a theory of social practices: a development in culturalist theorizing. Eur J Soc Theor 5(2):243–263

30. Emerson RM, Fretz RI, Shaw LL (2011) Writing ethnographic fieldnotes. University of Chicago Press, Chicago
31. Nicolini D (2012) Practice theory, work, and organization. Oxford University Press, Oxford
32. Polanyi M (1966) The tacit dimension. The University of Chicago Press, Chicago, IL

The Concept of 'Practice': What's the Point?

Kjeld Schmidt

Abstract The purpose of the present article is to argue that the point of using the concept of 'practice' in the context of CSCW and related research areas is to overcome the categorial separation of 'thinking' and 'acting' that is part and parcel of the received discourse about 'work' and thus to be able to focus sharply on and express the *unity* of the activities of work. The article shows that received concept of 'practice' has been developed in the course of centuries precisely as a way to focus on normatively regulated contingent activities.

In the course of the history of Computer-Supported Cooperative Work (CSCW), the concept of 'practice' has become a key concept and, indeed, arguably a concept defining of the field.[1] An indication of this development—albeit, admittedly, a very rough one—is that while the term 'practice' in the mid-1980s only occurred in about 25 % of papers in which the acronym CSCW also occurred, the frequency of use has increased steadily from year to year to the current level of about 75 %.[2] This indicator is of course crude but, still, the shift is significant enough: It has become common in CSCW to conceive of problems, observations, and findings in terms of 'practices' (cf., e.g., [25, 28, 43]). As Wulf et al. have argued recently: 'CSCW was the first research community in applied computer science which stressed the importance of an

---

[1] The article draws on arguments sketched and elaborated in different contexts in earlier publications [39, 40, 41, 42, 44] as well as in lectures delivered at the University of Oslo, Norway, 16 May 2013 and at the University of Siegen, Germany, 18 June 2013. The research has been supported by the Velux-Villum Foundations under the 'Computational Artifacts' project.
[2] The calculation is based searches of the co-occurrence of the terms 'CSCW' and 'practice' in documents on Google Scholar from 1983 to 2012 (5-year intervals).

K. Schmidt (✉)
Copenhagen Business School, Copenhagen, Denmark
e-mail: schmidt@cscw.dk

K. Schmidt
University of Siegen, Siegen, Germany

C. Rossitto et al. (eds.), *COOP 2014 - Proceedings of the 11th International*
Conference on the Design of Cooperative Systems, 27–30 May 2014, Nice (France),
DOI: 10.1007/978-3-319-06498-7_26, © Springer International Publishing Switzerland 2014

in-depth understanding of practices when designing ICT artefacts. From our point of view, this is the key achievement of the research field' [62, p. 505].

There are sound reasons for this shift. When in operation, coordination technologies intervene, in some cases radically, in the cooperative effort by interposing mechanical regulation of workers' interactions. The design of such interventionist technologies can not be based merely on a model of the application domain in the form of some idealized representation of prescribed or normal procedures; rather, the design must also account for the actual practice in which the system in question is to be integrated, its contingencies, variations, local circumstances. In the words of Suchman, 'some amount of appropriation into local circumstances will always be required. The question is not whether that work will need to be done, but with what ease or difficulty' [53, p. 139]. Indeed, in the case of coordination technologies, system rigidity may complicate coordination work unbearably and cause breakdowns. This insight is fundamental for CSCW. This then, in turn, raises the crucial question: How do we conceptualize the 'circumstances' into which the technology is to be integrated? Indeed, how do we compare 'circumstances'? That is, how do we compare findings from one setting with those from another or even from one day to the next? How do we determine which observed activities are instances of the same kind? In short, what is our *unit of analysis*? In response to this methodological conundrum, a prevalent approach—a version of the stark mentalism dominating social psychology—has been to introduce intractable constructs such as 'shared goal' as criteria of similarity. However, this move is obviously self-defeating, for it leads nowhere but to circular argumentation: How do we observe the presence of a 'shared goal' if not by observing that activities unfold in a coordinated manner? If so, does deficient coordination then indicate that lack of need of coordination? Does it even make sense to ascribe a shared goal to a collaborative effort characterized by division of labor? (cf., e.g., [41]).

The concept of 'practice' is being used in CSCW as a way out of such muddles. However, another muddle is threatening. In the course of recent decades, the concept of 'practice' has moved center-stage in social theory. The motivation for much of this orientation towards practice (or 'Practice Turn', the title of [37]) is that 'practice' is seen as a means for providing social theorizing with an 'ontological' (or transcendental) foundation, i.e., a foundation prior to building a framework bottom up from actual empirical studies. So far, without luck, for the concept of 'practice' is notoriously unfit for doing *that* kind of work. As a result, the term 'practice' is being used in confusing and confused ways: as another word for 'activity', 'culture', 'tradition', 'paradigm', 'embodied action', 'knowing how', and so forth. (For overviews of 'practice theory', cf. [32, 34]).

In CSCW the concept of 'practice' has moved center stage, not in an effort to build 'theories of practice that substitute magic and just-so stories for hard work' [49] but, rather, because researchers, in a distributed process of learning from experience, find that this concept, somehow, helps them express their research problems and empirical findings better than concepts such as 'shared goal', 'situation awareness', 'use situation', 'context', 'task', 'activity', 'work', 'tacit knowledge', 'actor network', 'articulation work', 'situated action', and so on.

However, the term 'practice' has so far been used quite informally in CSCW. But since it is now assuming the role of a cornerstone concept for CSCW, in that it is now increasingly deployed to define CSCW's research problem, our lack of conceptual clarity is not tenable. Worse, the general confusion about 'practice' in social theorizing is likely to seep through and cause havoc in CSCW as well. Since nothing is gained by substituting one muddle for another, a systematic discussion of the concept of 'practice', from a CSCW point of view, is surely called for. The question is, then, what is it that the concept of 'practice' does for us? What is the point of that concept for CSCW?

Now, concepts are institutions. In the words of the British philosopher John Austin, 'Our common stock of words embodies all the distinctions men have found worth drawing, and the connexions they have found worth marking, in the life-times of many generations' [8, p. 130]. The concept of 'practice' is no exception: it comes with a suite of connotations and references that we can only ignore at our peril, for if we do so we would not know what we are in fact saying. As Austin adduces, our conceptual scheme—what Gilbert Ryle called 'the logical geography of our concepts'—is the outcome of process of selection, typically evolutionary. Concepts, as institutions, have a history. Thus, in order to better grasp the concept of 'practice' it is helpful to realize that it evolved over several centuries and was sharpened precisely in order to be able to express the unity of the activities of work for the purpose of intervening in work practices and their organization.

The aim of the present article is to show just that.[3] The point of using the concept of 'practice' in the context of CSCW (but also partly in HCI, STS, Knowledge Management, Organization Theory, etc.) is to overcome the categorial separation of 'thinking' and 'acting' that is part and parcel of the received discourse about 'work'. That is, the point is that work, when conceived of as *a practice*, is not reduced to *mere activity*, more or less regular sequences of operation, but is taken to also encompass the ways in which workers competently handle contingencies and variations, ensure orderly alignment of their distributed activities, as well as sundry intellectual activities such as envisioning the outcome, devising methods and plans, identifying tasks, preparing and allocating tasks, etc.

1 The Original 'Practice Turn'

It is a remarkable paradox that the concept-pair 'theory' / 'practice' was originally formed by ancient Greeks philosophers as a way to express and justify the categorial *separation* of the two concepts. Both Plato and Aristotle made a distinction between *theoria* (contemplative activity), *poesis* (making, producing), and *praxis* (mere activity). Thus, in his *Nicomachean Ethics* Aristotle stated that the concepts

---

[3] I was originally inspired to investigate the history of the concept of 'practice' by an article by Alfred Schmidt [38].

of 'making [*poesis*] and acting [*praxis*] are different', pointing out that different kinds of reasoning are involved: 'the reasoned state of capacity to act is different from the reasoned state of capacity to make'. He was also careful to point out that '*praxis*' is not subsumed under '*poesis*'; they are of different kinds (*Nic. Ethics*, [7] 1140a). As for the reasoning involved in '*praxis*', Aristotle left nothing to guesswork: 'manual workers are like certain lifeless things which act indeed, but act without knowing what they do, as fire burns,—but while the lifeless things perform each of their functions by a natural tendency, the labourers perform them through habit' (*Metaphysics*, [6] 981a–b).

Aristotle thus conceived of the manual worker as an agency akin to a disciplined natural force: the worker accomplishes things, sure, but so does a fire; the point of the analogy being that workers, like fire, 'act without knowing what they do'. This is the crux of the aristocratic notion of '*praxis*' as conceived by Aristotle: 'The slave is the minister of practice' (*Politics*, [5] 1254a).

The contemporary concept of 'practice', as it is ordinarily used, is categorially distinct from that of the Ancients'; it is used *in contradiction to* the categorial separation we find in Aristotle; indeed, that is the point of it! It was developed in what could be seen as the original 'practice turn'—a movement that unfolded for centuries beginning with the early Modern Era (from the 15th century). We therefore call our ordinary concept of 'practice' the Modern concept.

The story is roughly like the following. With the early developments of a capitalist economy based on craft work ('mechanical arts') from about 1400, the classical notion of 'practice' as mindless activity was increasingly seen as problematic. As the historian Paolo Rossi puts it in his *Philosophy, Technology, and the Arts in the Early Modern Era* [36], between 1400 and 1700,

> A new view of labor, of the function of technical knowledge, and of the significance of artificial processes through which nature was altered and transformed clearly makes its way into the work of artists and experimentalists of the fifteenth century and into the treatises of engineers and technicians of the sixteenth century. [...] The men who toiled in the workshops, in the arsenals, and in the studios, or those who had dropped their disdain of practice, considered the operations conducted on these premises a form of cognition. [36, pp. ix f.]

Thus, the literature of the period is 'extraordinarily rich in treatises of a technical character, which at times were real manuals, and at times disconnected reflections on [the authors'] own work or procedures employed in the various arts.' (ibid., p. 15). In order to develop the emerging (eventually capitalist) economy, mastery of the theories of mathematics, physics, etc. was deemed quite insufficient; it became crucial for merchants, mechanists, and scholars to understand the actual role of practical reason and practical experience vis-à-vis the role of mathematics, physics, astronomy, etc. As Rossi puts it: 'The actual union between "discourse" and "practice," "speculation" and "manufacture," in reality presented serious problems' (ibid., p. 61). To exemplify this observation, Rossi quotes the Italian military engineer Bonaiuto Lorini who, in a treatise on fortifications [27], addressed the problem of the relation between the work of the 'purely speculative mathematician' and that of the 'practical mechanic':

The demonstrations and proportions found by the mathematician "between surface lines and imaginary bodies and separated from matter do not respond so perfectly when applied to material things", because the concepts with which the mathematician works "are not subject to those impediments which by nature are always conjoined to the matter that is worked on by the mechanic." The mechanic's judgment and ability consists in knowing how to foresee the difficulties deriving from the diversity of the materials with which he must work, and this is all the more difficult in that no such rules can be offered for "such accidental impediments". [36, pp. 61 f.]

Lorini continued:

Indeed, the material itself could present a very great impediment, as would be the case when material wheels have to be moved around their axes, which can be impeded by their own unequal weight, even more so when the wheels are sustained over such axes or poles that are not properly centered, all of which can tend to make motion difficult. The pure mathematician, however, imagines them as weightless and tied around invisible lines and points. ([27, Libro V], [36, p. 62])

In short, mathematical theory, for all its conceptual power, cannot encompass the multiplicity of the material world with which the mechanic has to cope. This is insight was revolutionary.

Over time, systematic studies of work practices of this kind developed into a great scientific research tradition, for which Agricola's study of work practices in the Bohemian metal trades [4] is exemplary. This tradition culminated in the large-scale project launched by the French Academy of Science in 1675, undertaken at the government's request and with the express purpose of producing systematic descriptions of the work practices and techniques of the about 200 crafts and trades ('*arts et métiers*') then in existence in France, from bakeries to pin manufactures: 'The king wished the Academy to work unceasingly upon a treatise on mechanics, in which theory and practice should be explained in clear manner that could be grasped by everyone' [2, p. 131]. As expressed in the Academy's own *mémoire* from 1699, it had undertaken the task of 'describing the crafts in their present condition', knowing full well that the task was 'dry, thorny, and not at all dazzling'. The eventual *Descriptions* were to 'penetrate to the ultimate details, although it would often prove very difficult to acquire them from artisans or to explain them', but as a result 'an infinity of practices, full of spirit and inventiveness, but generally unknown, will be drawn from their shadows'. The crafts would thereby be preserved for posterity, but in addition 'able men' who lacked the leisure to visit the artisans' workshops would be able to 'work on the perfection' of these practices, just as the Academy itself would not fail to remark if something might usefully be amended [1, pp. 117 f.].

With hundreds of 'arts and trades' to investigate and describe, the task undertaken by the Academy was of course enormous, as it involved extensive fieldwork in different lines of trade in different parts of the country. What is more, a systematic approach to the description of practices and representations of techniques (processes, implements, tools) was required and had to be developed. By 1757 only a few pieces of the accumulated analyses had been made publicly available. The reason for the obvious lack of visible progress—apart from the enormity of the task, of course—seems to have been dissatisfaction with the quality of the initial analytical work, which was seen as not sufficiently systematic and accurate. However, the Academy eventually succeeded in getting the publication process organized and from 1761 to 1788 altogether 81 treatises (about 100 volumes) were published under the title *Descriptions des arts et métiers*.[4]

The aim of all this, as stated in the Academy's preamble to the *Descriptions*, was not merely to 'examine and describe in turn all operations of the mechanical arts' but also and equally 'to contribute to their progress'. The Academy expected that 'new degrees of perfection of the arts' would be achieved when scholars undertake the effort of investigating and developing the 'often ingenious operations performed by the artisan in his workshop; when they see by themselves the needs of the art, its limitations, the difficulties that prevent it from going further, the assistance that one could transfer from one art to another and which the worker is rarely expected to know.' Subjecting work practices, which had slowly evolved from 'obscurity', to systematic study, rationalizing them, would show competent workers a way to 'overcome the obstacles that they have been unable to cross', a way to 'invent new tools', etc. The point was, as it was proudly put, *'éclairer la pratique'*—that is, to explain and enlighten practice [3, pp. xvi f.].

The 'dry, thorny, and not at all dazzling' effort had huge impact: 'there can be no doubt' that contemporaneously these scientific descriptions of arts and handicrafts 'exerted a potent influence in western Europe' [14, p. 1]. Furthermore, the *Descriptions* provided a model for scholars that received practices were accessible to scholarly analysis and might be much improved by application of the insights, methods, etc. of the physical, chemical, mechanical, etc. sciences.

Now, this great tradition of scholarly studies of mundane work practices and techniques ended at just this point. The 'practice turn' that was inaugurated in the 15th century fizzled out as the Industrial Revolution picked up speed (*circa* 1780–1830). But the reasons for the eclipse of practice studies are an important part of the history of the concept of 'practice': it sharpens its point.

2 Practice Studies Eclipsed

With the Industrial Revolution the drive to transform work practices continued unabated, but in a very different form. The focal interest of employers and engineers shifted to the seemingly infinite productivity potential of machine technology. New machine technologies and their incremental improvement were seen as decisive. Employers and their engineers could thus afford to conceive of the organization of work and work practices as trivial [21, 30, 31]. Machinery had the primacy and work practices were expected to somehow adapt. Work practices were not of concern to employers and even less so for academia. Thus, the great

---

[4] The *Descriptions* are available from http://gallica.bnf.fr

tradition of scholarly studies of mundane practices and techniques vanished from the agenda with the Industrial Revolution.

However, by the end of 19th century employers and their agents could no longer afford not to pay attention to the *organization of work*. Industrial workers had 'learned the game', as the historian Erik Hobsbawm puts it: they had experienced that the intensity of the working day was not determined by the traditional norms of 'a fair day's work' characteristic of pre-industrial society and had moreover realized that they, if organized, could influence the quantity of output significantly. Consequently, the issue of how to understand and deal with systematic output restriction became a primary concern of industrialists [21]. But the issue of understanding *work practices* for the purpose of their productive transformation remained off the agenda. Frederick W. Taylor's effort to transform the work of skilled machinists, for example, was not motivated by an interest in their practices with a view to the development of these but was rather an attempt to *eradicate* these practices—a utopian attempt to eliminate the sources of contingency and variation in the interest of managerial control. Thus, one will not find *any* description of the work practices of skilled machinists in Taylor's writings (e.g., [54–56]).

Similarly, one will have to look long and hard to find more than rudimentary descriptions of work practices in the entire literature of industrial sociology and sociology of work. The focus of interest of these disciplines was firmly centered on issues of social and managerial control (from 'industrial fatigue' to 'informal organization' to 'work climate' to 'wildcat strikes' to 'human resource management'). The difference with respect to Taylor's work is merely that where Taylor strove—in utopian rage—to eradicate practice, management doctrine and associated schools of industrial sociology, from the Hawthorne 'experiments' and on, interpreted and handled workers' organized control over the level of production as an expression of collective 'neuroses' and 'non-logical sentiments' and saw the 'informal organization' as a vehicle for those remnants from pre-industrial society [10, 29, 35]. Actual work practice was not an issue that could generate serious interest (cf. [18]).

Industrial and work sociology has of course for decades subjected the organization of work and changing demands on worker qualifications to systematic studies. This applies to, for example, studies of the relationship between the nature of production technology and the degree of workers' autonomy in their work, not only in the British 'socio-technical' tradition but also, and far more systematically, in the German tradition from Popitz and Bahrdt [33] to Kern and Schumann [24]. But these and similar traditions consistently conceive of work and the work situation as the resultant in an equation of multiple causal factors, primarily encompassing the technical systems of production. Machinery retained its conceptual primacy while practice was considered sociologically uninteresting.

Two centuries after the onslaught of Industrial Revolution, actual work practices remained managerially and academically uninteresting. Thus, in 1985, Anselm Strauss and his colleagues could observe that remarkably little writing in the sociology of work begins with work itself (except descriptively, not analytically) but rather focuses on the division of labor, on work roles, role relationships, careers, and the like [51, p. xi]. Not incidentally, of course, there are descriptions and analyses of work done by members of professions, occupations, and by organizational members, but intense focus on the work itself—its task sequences, its organization, its many variants and their conditions and consequences, its articulation, its evaluative processes—is far less usual. (ibid., p. 289). (For a similar assessment, cf. [48, pp. 85 f.])

What *did* survive the Industrial Revolution and its aftermath of ceaseless upheavals was the Modern concept of 'practice'. In fact, the perhaps most important outcome of the tradition of scholarly studies of work practices is the Modern concept of 'practice' itself. To explore the concept of 'practice' as we have received it and apply it more systematically, let us first revisit the original 'practice turn'.

3 The Heritage: The Modern Concept of 'Practice'

At an early stage in the course of the original 'practice turn', around 1600, Frances Bacon articulated the conceptual implication of this entire tradition of work and called for a reversal of the relationship between 'theory' and 'practice'. Bacon rejected the notion, received from 'the Ancients', that anything useful at all could be accomplished when men, in 'mad effort and useless combination of forces', 'endeavor by logic (which may be considered as a kind of athletic art) to strengthen the sinews of the understanding' ([9], Preface). Thus, in explicit contradiction of Plato and Aristotle, Bacon argued that theory and practice are *equals*, so to speak, and he was thereby able to even conceive of *theorizing proved wrong in practice*: 'sciences fair perhaps in theory, but in practice inefficient' (ibid., §. II: xlv):

> Although the roads to human power and to human knowledge lie close together and are nearly the same, nevertheless, on account of the pernicious and inveterate habit of dwelling on abstractions it is safer to begin and raise the sciences from those foundations which have relation to practice, and to let the active part itself be as the seal which prints and determines the contemplative counterpart. [9, § II: iv]

On this revolutionary view, ordinary working practices and practical knowledge were no longer categorially separated from and inferior to scientific knowledge and philosophy. It was conceivable to 'begin and raise the sciences from those foundations which have relation to practice'. However, Bacon's 'practice turn' was of course largely programmatic. Production at the time was craft-based and science immature: Galilei had just started his career when Bacon published his *Novum Organon* in 1620.

However, a century or so later, when Denis Diderot, together with Jean d'Alembert, edited the famous *Encyclopédie* (1751–1766), the original 'practice turn' was completed, and the new conception of science as grounded in practical experience that Bacon had vaguely sensed and promulgated could now become articulated most pointedly. Diderot thus wrote an article on 'Arts', i.e., the *practical* crafts, arts, techniques, and sciences, for the first volume of the *Encyclopédie* in which he, following Bacon, flatly observed that 'It is man's work [*l'industrie de l'homme*] applied to the products of nature', his effort to satisfy 'his needs', 'that has given birth to the sciences and the arts' [16, pp. 265 f.]. He then went on to describe the relation between 'theory' and 'practice' as a reciprocal one:

> every art has its speculation and its practice: the speculation is nothing but the idle knowledge of the rules of the art, the practical aspect is the habitual and unreflective application of the same rules. It is difficult, if not impossible, to develop the practice without speculation, and, reciprocally, to have a solid grasp of the speculation without the practice. There are in every art—with respect to the material, the instruments, and the operation—a multitude of circumstances which can only be learned in practice [*usage*]. It is for practice to present difficulties and pose phenomena, while it is for speculation to explain the phenomena and dissolve the difficulties; from which follows that hardly any but an artisan who masters reasoning that can talk well about his art. (ibid., p. 266, emphases deleted)

To illustrate his argument, Diderot discussed the relationship between academic geometry and the practical geometry as exercised in workshops:

> Everyone will readily agree that there are few artists who can dispense with the elements of mathematics. However, a paradox, the truth of which is not immediately obvious, is that, in many situations, these elements would actually harm them if the precepts were not corrected in practice by knowledge of a multitude of physical circumstances: knowledge of location, position, irregular forms, materials and their properties, elasticity, rigidity, friction, texture, durability, as well as the effects of air, water, cold, heat, dryness, etc. (ibid., p. 271)

For instance, Diderot argued, no levers exist 'for which one could calculate all conditions'. Among these conditions are a large number that are very important in practice:

> From this follows that a man who knows only intellectual [academic] geometry is usually rather incompetent and that an artist who knows only experimental geometry is very limited as a worker. But, in my opinion, experience shows us that it is easier for an artist to dispense with intellectual geometry than for any man to dispense with some experimental geometry. In spite of the calculus, the entire issue of friction has remained a matter for experimental and handicraft mathematics. [...] How many awful machines are not proposed daily by men who have deluded themselves that levers, wheels, pulleys, and cables perform in a machine as they do on paper and who have never taken part in manual work, and thus who never have known the difference in effect of one and the same machine in reality and as a plan?. (ibid.)

In other words, following Bacon, Diderot completely reversed the internal relationship of Aristotelian concept-pair '*theoria / praxis*'. When we talk of 'practice' we no longer conceive of it as mere regular activity devoid of 'reasoning' and 'deliberation'. The categorial separation of '*praxis*' and '*poesis*' has been dissolved, and both the 'capacity of make' and the 'capacity to act' have been united in the Modern concept of 'practice'—united but not conflated. The Modern concept of 'practice' expresses and is used for emphasizing the complex dialectics of general precepts and action.

A generation later, Immanuel Kant, with admirable precision, summarized the Modern concept of 'practice' as it had been developed in the course of four centuries:

One calls a conceptualization of rules, even of practical rules, a theory when these rules, as principles, are thought of in a certain generality and thus have been abstracted from a multitude of conditions that nonetheless necessarily influence their application. On the other hand, one does not call just any operation a praxis; rather, only such a purposive endeavor is considered a praxis that is taken to be attained by following certain generally accepted principles of procedure. [23, p. 127]

Let us unpack this, admittedly, rather compact proposition. The theory of, say, making bread, as expressed in cooking books and handed-down recipes, summarizes the experience of generations in the form of general rules and principles. But in formulating rules and principles, one abstracts from a plethora of more or less accidental conditions and circumstances such as, for instance, the quality and age of the flour, the humidity and temperature of the air, and so on, which are nevertheless to be taken into account by the baker in action. On the other hand, not everything the baker does can be ascribed to the practices of baking bread. That he perhaps drinks a cold beer while the dough is rising or surreptitiously kisses the maid while the bread is in the oven are not elements of this practice, however important they may be for his quality of life. The two concepts—'theory' and 'practice'—are mutually constitutive.

This concept of 'practice' is the Modern one. This concept is the same we find when, for instance, Ludwig Wittgenstein says that 'To establish a practice, rules are not enough; one also needs examples. Our rules leave back doors open, and the practice must speak for itself' ([61], § 139. My translation). It is the same we find in Winch [58], and in Bourdieu [12]. That is, in the Modern concept of 'practice', as summarized by Kant, we use the term 'practice' to designate activities that are governed by a 'theory', i.e., 'a conceptualization of rules' that have been 'abstracted from a multitude of conditions' and thus are 'applied' as 'general principles'. Now, and this is the important point, when applying these 'general principles' the 'circumstances', that were elided in abstracting the rules, again have to be faced and dealt with. In other words, the point of the Modern concept of 'practice' is to focus on the ways in which the competent actor in his or her action is taking the particular conditions into account while committed to and guided by the appropriate general principles ('theory', 'rules'). When studying a practice we are focusing on how the practitioners determine the nature of the situation, how they select effective and efficient techniques (materials, implements, bodily postures, methods, etc.), determine deviations from what has been assumed in the rule formulations, deal with routine troubles, recover from breakdowns, etc.

In applying the concept of 'practice' we are thus deviating drastically from conventional engineering and sociological approaches that assume that contingencies *can* be eliminated and hence that work *can* be reduced to mindless or mechanical execution of procedures, process descriptions, etc. that have been determined and choreographed in advance. This assumption—shared by Taylor as well as his later detractors (e.g., [13])—is closely related to Laplace's idea of an omniscient demon that by virtue of its knowledge of the state of the universe in its entirety at a given moment would be able to predict the future states of the universe with impeccable precision [26]. But however elaborate, sophisticated, and tested a plan, procedure, etc. might be, its realization in action is subjected to conditions, circumstances, variations, that may or may not have been anticipated. In the words of Holberg: 'For squinting at a seaman's chart / Is not the whole of steering' [22, act v, sc. 8]. This is what is referred to when we speak of 'practice'.

In sum, when conceived of as a practice, work is not reduced to *mere execution* of some given task (i.e., what Aristotle and his modern followers might consider mindless), but is taken to also encompass not only handling variations and contingencies but also what is done to envision outcome; devise methods and plan for probable contingencies; identify tasks to be performed; prepare operations; allocate or assume responsibility, as well as activities of coordinating, aligning, evaluating, instructing, learning, etc. The term 'practice' is in other words used to frame contingent activities as committed to criteria for correct conduct in the form for norms, rules, procedures, plans, etc. The noun 'practice' thus means *normatively regulated contingent activity*.

This much should be clear by now. But the concept of 'practice' can be tricky. Category mistakes abound. It is of course beyond the scope of this article to elaborate on the intricacies of this concept but a few brief remarks will suffice to indicate the issues.

1. A practice is constituted by the rules and principles adhered to by actors and by virtue of which they are accountable for their doings [59, §§ 143–242]. The rules and principles to which actors are committed in their contingent activities provide the criterion of similarity that enables them (and observers) to determine not only what is deemed correct conduct but also what is being deemed activities of the same kind. One practice differs from another in so far as the rules and principles differ.

2. That practices are normatively constituted tends to elude theorists. The snag is our distinction between 'mere regularity' and 'rule-following' ([19, 59, §§ 143–242]) or between 'natural regularity' and 'normative regularity' [57]. When we observe stable patterns or correlations, what we find is *mere regularity*. But when we observe that actors justify their actions and their justifications are accepted (or rejected), or give and receive instructions on how to conduct themselves in a certain line of activity, or correct themselves and accept corrections and sanctions with respect to their conduct, etc., then we are observing something *other* than natural regularity in behavior; we are finding instances of *normative regularity*.

3. 'Practice' belongs to the web of the *activity* concepts. A practice is something we perform or engage in; it has a temporal structure. However, 'practice' should not simply be conflated with the concept of 'activity'. An activity has 'genuine duration': it has a starting point and an end-point in time [60, §§ 71–83]. Our baker may begin preparing rolls Friday morning at 03:00, place the

hot rolls on the shelves in the shop at 05:00, and may then go to bed. At this point this particular sequence of activities ends, but not his practice nor the practice of baking bread. A lawyer does not cease to practice the law when she is fast asleep. When we refer to a specific practice, we are referring to a specific *category* of activity, namely, activities that are related by virtue of being committed to certain rules and principles.

4. To engage in a practice requires command of a repertoire of techniques (and perhaps technologies), the wielding of which requires concomitant qualifications or skills. But these concepts should not be assimilated. Practices and techniques are of different categories: Techniques are *means*, they are applied; practices are types of *activity*, they are performed. The concept of 'practice' is different from concepts of faculties such as 'skill' and 'technique' (or 'knowing-how', cf. [42]). The grammar of 'technique' runs parallel to that of 'qualification' ('competence', 'skill') but only for part of the journey: 'techniques' is a neutral expression of capacities (methods, tools) by means of which a task is doable. Techniques are typically also neutral in as much as one will often find the same technique used across different practices. The technique of, for instance, using a knife for cutting meat may be applied by a surgeon as well as by a butcher or an executioner; but they wield the knife for quite different purposes, with different concerns, by observing different criteria of priority. In short, 'skill' expresses *ability* but 'technique' *capacity*. All in all, the faculties are all acquired, possessed, and applied; they are not *performed*, as are practices.

5. When engaged in a practice, actors are confronted with the inexorability of action, in as much as avoidance or postponement of action may also have effects, perhaps unwanted. The practitioner does not have the privilege of an observer. He or she cannot afford the general skepticism demonstrated by Descartes when he in his *Philosophical Meditations* describes how he is sitting by the window overlooking a square somewhere in Northern Holland around 1640: 'if I look out of the window and see men crossing the square, which I just happen to have done, I normally say that I see the men themselves […]. Yet do I see more than hats and coats which could conceal automatons?' [15, p. 21]. But unless one is engaged in the alien practice of hunting down replicants, such as Rick Deckard in *Blade Runner,* it would not be sane to wonder whether the spectacle of bipedally locomoting shapes wearing coats and hats are indeed automatons and not humans. In our ordinary working practices, such skepticism is a luxury. In the course of action, the practitioner has to take for granted that things that look normal are in fact normal. Schütz [46] dubbed this stance 'the natural attitude'. The practitioner is faced with 'imposed relevances' that he or she has to cope with [11, 45]. Faced with the 'urgencies' of his or her work, the practitioner has to 'economize' any ambition that his effort be consistent, complete, etc. [12].

6. The concept of 'practice' is located in a rather troubled part of the 'geography of our conceptual scheme'. It is, for instance, adjacent to the concept of 'culture' but its grammar is distinctly different. 'Culture' is not an activity category. One *performs* a practice, but one does not *perform* a culture or a tradition; one belongs to it and one's behavior may exhibit traits typical of that

culture or tradition ('customs'). In addition, the term 'culture' is used in bewildering ways, encompassing prevalent patterns of everyday conduct (e.g., dietary preferences, table manners) as well as various 'ideological' phenomena (e.g., notions of virtue and duty, of what amounts to a 'good life'), and even cosmologies. By assimilating 'practice' with 'culture' or 'tradition', the point of the concept of 'practice' is elided, namely, the point that the 'theory' has a rationale in that it has been abstracted as a body of rules and principles *and* that one, in *applying* the 'theory', is again faced with the 'circumstances' from which the 'theory' has been abstracted. The unity of work is forfeited.

7. The methodological upshot of all this is that when we look at an activity as an instance of a practice, we identify it as constituted by a certain body of rules and principles, but *at the very same time* we look at the ways in which these rules and principles and associated skills and techniques (methods, tools) etc. are applied with respect to varying circumstances. A description of a practice will be incomplete if it does not account for the circumstances and their variation, for typical sources of variation, and for typical patterns of variation, just as it will be incomplete if it does not account for practitioners' strategies of handling these variations. Without accounting for the circumstances and the ways in which they are handled, our description would amount to nothing but yet another representation of the 'theory'.

8. It finally complicates the concept of 'practice' further that what Kant with some reservation refers to as 'theory' is itself a rather manifold phenomenon. There is, crudely put, on one hand official or codified 'theory' in the form of, say, mathematical theorems, 'natural laws', and otherwise established regularities; but the practitioners *also* apply rules and principles they have acquired through experience or emulation. They master a repertoire of strategies, procedures, routines, recipes, etc., just as they, through instruction and training, have developed professional perception [20], that is, the (visual, auditory, tactile) ability to distinguish objects, states, events that are known from experience to be of relevance for their effort (Schütz suggested the term 'typifications' for such distinctions, cf., e.g., [46, 47]). Where a novice or an observer perhaps merely notices that the dough now has swollen 'a lot' in the container, the baker may observe that it *now* is quite as it should be. That is, an adequate description of a given practice will also provide a reconstruction of the repertoire of rules and principles that practitioners employ routinely in their day's work, not only the official ('academic') ones, but also the not-yet canonized procedures and distinctions that are passed on through instruction, training, exercise, emulation, typically in an primarily oral culture. Accordingly, an analysis of a practice stands in a recursive relationship to that practice. When the not-yet canonized procedures and distinctions become described and their rationales accounted for, the analysis contributes—potentially—to increasing the validity and scope of the 'theory'. This should not come as a surprise, for the Modern concept of 'practice' was developed for exactly that purpose: as the conceptual underpinning of our intervening in our practices in order to rationalize them: *'éclairer la pratique'*—'explain' and 'enlighten practice' [3, pp. xvi f.].

4 The Point?

As demonstrated above, the Modern concept of 'practice' evolved over several centuries, as an intellectual accompaniment to the effort to understand and rationalize received craft practices that, 'born in obscurity', had to be transformed and appropriated into the emerging capitalist production. It was also argued, however, that with the emergence of machine technology employers and engineers lost interest in something as mundane as work practices. Industrial sociology accepted these mental blinders as demarcating its horizon.

Now, with the contemporary technological revolution, driven by computing technology and especially collaboration technology, the picture has changed completely, not just because of the radical transformations of work and organization afforded by these technologies, but also and especially because the very development of these technologies requires a deep understanding of work practices. This has been the case from the very beginning and is even more so today [39, Chap. 11]. Hence the renewed importance of the concept of 'practice'.

The development of conventional machine technology had been drastically constrained by the cost of building and modifying control mechanisms. And at the same time, even the most simple mechanical devices often had dramatic productivity effects. Against that background, the issue of adapting machine design to existing work practices could be and was largely, well, an non-issue. Workers rather had to adapt to the idiosyncrasies of the particular machine design. At the most, ergonomists were called in to take care of the design of 'human factors' aspects of the control interface (knobs, dials, and so forth). This was feasible because the design of the machine could be based on scientific theories and engineering models of the processes to be automated (such as those of cutting metal). The engineer could think of himself as possessing, within the confined and controlled domain in which the machine was to operate, powers akin to those of Laplace's demon. Understanding work practices was not considered an issue for engineering as a discipline.

With modern computing technology (i.e., the stored-program digital electronic computer in the form of the mass-produced microprocessor, supported by high-level programming languages, compilers, code libraries) the cost of building and modifying automatic control mechanisms, i.e., software, and hence machines has been reduced by orders of magnitude. And because of the drastically reduced cost of building control mechanisms in the form of software, computing technologies are penetrating work domains heretofore untouched by machine technology. Against that background, the issue of the integration of machinery into work practices has been turned upside-down. Understanding work practices as a basis for systems design has become a practical necessity. Technological research areas such as Human-Computer Interaction, Systems Development, Requirements Engineering, Participatory Design etc. arose to meet these challenges (in different ways).

For CSCW, the challenges are of course the same and yet, radically different. Coordination technologies are fundamentally new technologies in that they are designed and used for the purpose of computational regulation of human interaction.

That is, they are computational complements of coordinative practices. Design of such technologies cannot be predicated on an assumption that the designer can anticipate the behavior of the machine in anything approximating the foresight of Laplace's demon.

The point of the concept of 'practice' in the context of CSCW is exactly the same as the point of its original development in the Modern era: to focus on *the unity of action in work*. When we address activities as practices, we are looking at the ways in which the actor's commitment to the 'theory' is upheld in face of contingencies and in which the actor, in the 'fog of war', orients to the criteria provided by the general principles. Thus the concept of 'practice' does work similar to notions such as 'articulation work' [17, 50] or 'situated action' [52]. It is here noteworthy, however, that while Suchman does emphasize that 'plans are resources for situated actions' and thus insists on the unity of action in work, this insight is all but obliterated when it is stated that situated action is 'essentially ad hoc' (p. ix). In contrast, the Modern concept of 'practice' allows us to maintain a strict focus on the reciprocity of 'theory' and 'practice': *normatively regulated contingent activity*. And finally, by virtue of its focus on the reciprocity of 'theory' and 'practice', the concept of 'practice' provides a unit of analysis one does not find in, for example, the notion of 'articulation work' or in the notion of 'situated actions'. For when we talk about 'a practice' we are talking about an *identifiable category of activity* for which the criteria of similarity are the rules and principles to which actors are committed.

In sum, the concept of 'practice', as developed over four centuries in studies of ordinary work, does not lead to the mystifications inherent in notions like 'shared goal' or to the infinite regress of rule-skepticism as exemplified by, say, 'situated action'. Cooperative work practices are as observable as electromagnetic fields. We can observe and determine the normative make-up of a practice ('rules' and 'principles') when actors, for example, from time to time make excuses for particular actions ('Sorry, my mistake!'), justify their actions ('Well, I had to do it this way because that part there was defective'), sanction the actions of colleagues ('You were supposed to deliver this part at my workstation by lunch'), instruct novices ('Be careful with this!'), or ask for guidance ('Where do I put this draft when I'm done?'). It's a researchable program; it not only works in theory but also in practice.

References

1. Académie Royale des Sciences (1702) Histoire de l'Académie royale des sciences, M.DC.XCIX (1699), avec les mémoires de mathématique and de physique, tirez des registres de cette Académie, vol 1. Boudot, Gabriel Martin etc., Paris, 1732
2. Académie Royale des Sciences (1729–1734) Histoire de l'Académie royale des sciences depuis son etablissement en 1666 jusqu'en 1699, vols 1–13. Compagnie des libraires, Gabriel Martin, etc., Paris, 1732
3. Académie Royale des Sciences (1761) Avertisement de l'Academie des Sciences de Paris (1761). In Académie Royale des Sciences: Descriptions des arts et métiers, faites ou

approuvées par Messieurs de l'Académie royale des sciences de Paris. Société typographique, Neuchatel, 1771, vol 1, 2nd edn, pp xvi–xix

4. Agricola G (1556) De Re Metallica (Basel 1556). The Mining Magazine, London, 1912. Dover Publications, New York, 1950

5. Aristotle (c. 334-322 BCE-a) (1984) Politics. In: The complete works of Aristotle, vol 2, pp 1986–2129. Princeton University Press, Princeton

6. Aristotle (c. 334-322 BCE-b) (1984) Metaphysics. In: The complete works of Aristotle, vol 2, pp 1552–1728. Princeton University Press, Princeton

7. Aristotle (c. 334-322 BCE-c) (1984). Nicomachean Ethics. In: The complete works of Aristotle, vol 2, pp 1729–1867. Princeton University Press, Princeton

8. Austin JL (1961) Philosophical papers, 3rd edn. Oxford University Press, Oxford, 1979

9. Bacon F (1620) The new organon: or true directions concerning the interpretation of nature. In: The works. Taggard and Thompson, Boston, 1863

10. Barnard CI (1938) The functions of the executive. Harvard University Press, Cambridge, Mass

11. Bittner E (1973) Objectivity and realism in sociology. In: Psathas G (ed) Phenomenological sociology: issues and applications. Wiley, New York, pp 109–125

12. Bourdieu P (1980) Le sens pratique. Les Éditions de Minuit, Paris

13. Braverman H (1974) Labor and monopoly capital: the degradation of work in the twentieth century. Monthly Review Press, New York

14. Cole AH, Watts GB (1952) The handicrafts of France as recorded in the descriptions des Arts et Métiers, 1761–1788. Baker Library, Harvard Graduate School of Business Administration, Boston

15. Descartes R (1641) Meditations on first philosophy (Paris 1641). In: Descartes R (ed) The philosophical writings of descartes, vol 2. Cambridge University Press, Cambridge, 1984, pp 1–62

16. Diderot D (1751) Art (Encyclopédie, ou dictionnaire raisonné des sciences, des arts et des métiers, Paris, 1751). In: Œuvres, vol 1. Robert Laffont, Paris, 1994 (Philosophie), pp 265–276

17. Gerson EM, Star SL (1986) Analyzing due process in the workplace. ACM Trans Office Inf Syst 4(3):257–270

18. Gillespie R (1991) Manufacturing knowledge: a history of the Hawthorne experiments. Cambridge University Press, Cambridge (Paperback ed, 1993)

19. Hacker PMS (1988) Language, rules and pseudo-rules. Lang Commun 8(2) 159–172

20. Hanson NR (1958) Patterns of discovery: an inquiry into the conceptual foundations of science. Cambridge University Press, Cambridge

21. Hobsbawm EJ (1964) Laboring men: studies in the history of labour. Weidenfeld & Nicolson, London

22. Holberg L (1722) Den politiske Kandstøber: Comœdie. København. In: Comedies by Holberg (trans by Campbell OJ, Schenck F), New York, 1914

23. Kant I (1793) Über den Gemeinspruch: Das mag in der Theorie richtig sein, taugt aber nicht für die Praxis (Berlinische Monatsschrift, September 1793). In: Werke in zwölf Bänden. Frankfurt a. M.: Suhrkamp Verlag, 1964, vol XI, pp 125–172

24. Kern H, Schumann M (1970). Industriearbeit und Arbeiterbewußtsein: Eine empirische Untersuchung über den Einfluß der aktuellen technischen Entwicklung auf die industrielle Arbeit und das Arbeiterbewußtsein, vols 1–2. Frankfurt am Main: Europäische Verlagsanstalt

25. Kuutti K (2013) "Practice turn" and CSCW identity. In: Korn M et al (eds) ECSCW 2013 Adjunct proceedings: the 13th european conference on computer supported cooperative work, 21–25 Sept 2013, Paphos, Cyprus. Department of Computer Science, Aarhus University, Aarhus, Denmark, pp 39–44 (DAIMI PB—596)

26. Laplace P-S (1814) Essai philosophique sur les probabilités. Courcier, Paris

27. Lorini B (1596) Delle fortificationi di Buonaiuto Lorini, libri cinque: ne'quali si mostra con le piu facili regole la scienza con la pratica, di fortificare le città, & altri luoghi sopra diuersi siti […]. Gio, Venetia. Antonio Rampazetta

28. Luff P et al (eds) (2000) Workplace studies: recovering work practices and informing system design. Cambridge University Press, Cambridge
29. Mayo E (1933) The human problems of an industrial civilization. Macmillan, New York. Routledge, London, 2003
30. Montgomery D (1979) Workers' control in America: studies in the history of work, technology, and labor struggles. Cambridge University Press, Cambridge (Paperback ed 1980)
31. Nelson D (1995) Managers and workers: origins of the twentieth-century factory system in the United States, 1880–1920, 2nd edn. University of Wisconsin Press, Madison
32. Nicolini D (2012) Practice theory, work, and organization: an introduction. Oxford University Press, Oxford
33. Popitz H, Bahrdt HP (1957) Technik und Industriearbeit: Soziologische Untersuchungen in der Hüttenindustrie. J. C. B. Mohr, Tübingen
34. Reckwitz A (2002) Toward a theory of social practices: a development in culturalist theorizing. Eur J Soc Theory 5(2):243–263
35. Roethlisberger FJ, Dickson WJ (1939) Management and the worker: an account of a research program conducted by the Western Electric Company, Hawthorne Works, Chicago. Harvard University Press, Cambridge, Mass
36. Rossi P (1962) Philosophy, technology, and the arts in the early modern era (Trans. by Attanasio S (1962) I filosofi e le macchine, Feltrinelli Editiore, Milano). Harper & Row, New York, 1970
37. Schatzki TR et al (eds) (2001) The practice turn in contemporary theory. Routledge, London
38. Schmidt A (1974). Praxis. In: Backhaus H-G et al (eds) Gesellschaft: Beiträge zur Marxschen Theorie, vol 2. Frankfurt a. M.: Suhrkamp, pp 264–308
39. Schmidt K (2011) Cooperative work and coordinative practices: contributions to the conceptual foundations of computer-supported cooperative work (CSCW). Springer, London
40. Schmidt K (2011) The concept of "work" in CSCW. Comput Support Cooper Work (CSCW): J Collab Comput 20(4–5):341–401
41. Schmidt K (2012) Predicate or subject? Assorted notes on the metaphysical notion of "sharing". In Workshop: do we really need to share to cooperate? COOP 2012: 9th international conference on the design of cooperative system, Marseille, 29 May–1 June 2012
42. Schmidt K (2012) The trouble with "tacit knowledge". Comput Support Cooper Work (CSCW): J Collab Comput Work Pract 21(2–3):163–225
43. Schmidt K, Bannon LJ (2013) Constructing CSCW: the first quarter century. Comput Support Cooper Work (CSCW): J Collab Comput Work Pract 22(4–6):345–372
44. Schmidt K (2014) Praksisanalyse. In: Vikkelsø S, Kjær P (eds) Klassisk og moderne organisationsteori. Hans Reitzels Forlag, København, pp 157–180
45. Schütz A (A Schutz) (1947–1951) Reflections on the problem of relevance (Manuscript 1947–51). In: Collected papers, vol V. Phenomenology and the social sciences. Springer, Berlin, 2011
46. Schütz A (A Schutz) (1953) Common-sense and scientific interpretations of human action (Philosophy and phenomenological research, Sept 1953). In: Collected papers, vol I. The problem of social reality. Martinus Nijhoff, The Hague, 1962, pp 3–47
47. Schütz A (A Schutz) (1957) Equality and the meaning structure of the social world (1957). In: Collected papers, vol II. Studies in social theory. Martinus Nijhoff, The Hague, 1964, pp 226–273
48. Sharrock WW, Anderson RJ (1986) The ethnomethodologists. Ellis Horwood Publishers, Chichester
49. Stern DG (2003) The practical turn. In: Turner SP, Roth PA (eds) The Blackwell guide to the philosophy of the social sciences. Blackwell Publishing, Oxford, pp 185–206
50. Strauss AL (1985) Work and the division of labor. Sociol Q 26(1):1–19
51. Strauss AL et al (1985) Social organization of medical work. University of Chicago Press, Chicago

52. Suchman LA (1987) Plans and situated actions: the problem of human-machine communication. Cambridge University Press, Cambridge
53. Suchman LA (2002) Practice-based design of information systems: notes from the hyperdeveloped world. Inf Soc 18(2):139–144
54. Taylor FW (1903) Shop management. Harper & Brothers, New York, 1911
55. Taylor FW (1907) On the art of cutting metals: an address made at the opening of the annual meeting in New York. The American Society of Mechanical Engineers, New York, Dec 1906
56. Taylor FW (1911) The principles of scientific management. Harper & Brothers, W. W. Norton & Co., New York, 1967
57. Williams M (2010) Blind obedience: paradox and learning in the later Wittgenstein. Routledge, London
58. Winch P (1958) The idea of a social science and its relation to philosophy, 2nd edn. Routledge & Kegan Paul., London, 1990
59. Wittgenstein L (1945–1946) Philosophical investigations (Manuscript), revised 4th edn, 2009. Blackwell Publishers, Oxford
60. Wittgenstein L (1945–1948) Zettel (Manuscript), 2nd edn: 1st edn, 1967. Basil Blackwell Publishers. Oxford, 1981
61. Wittgenstein L (1949–1951). On certainty (Manuscript), 2nd edn: 1st edn, 1969. Basil Blackwell Publishers, Oxford, 1975
62. Wulf V et al (2011) Engaging with practices: design case studies as a research framework in CSCW. In: Hinds PJ et al (eds) CSCW'11: Proceedings of the ACM 2011 conference on computer supported cooperative work. ACM Press, New York, pp 505–512

Printed in the United States
By Bookmasters